A History of Russia
Volume I: To 1917

A History of Russia

Volume I: To 1917

Walter G. Moss

Department of History and Philosophy
Eastern Michigan University

The McGraw-Hill Companies, Inc.

New York St. Louis San Francisco Auckland Bogotá Caracas Lisbon
London Madrid Mexico City Milan Montreal New Delhi
San Juan Singapore Sydney Tokyo Toronto

McGraw-Hill

A Division of The McGraw·Hill Companies

A HISTORY OF RUSSIA
Volume I: To 1917

Acknowledgments

Chapter 3, page 35: *Thomas S. Noonan, "The Flourishing of Kiev's International and Domestic Trade, ca.
1100–ca. 1240." In I. S. Koropeckyj (ed.), Ukranian Economic History: Interpretive Essays (Cambridge,
Massachusetts: Harvard Ukranian Research Institute, 1991). © 1991, President and Fellows of Harvard
College. Reprinted by permission; Chapter 9, page 154: Jacques Margeret, The Russian Empire and
Grand Duchy of Muscovy: A 17th-Century French Account, trans. and ed. by Chester S. L. Dunning,
© 1983. Reprinted by permission of the University of Pittsburgh Press; Chapter 14, page 255: Christian
Hermann von Manstein, Contemporary Memoirs of Russia: From the Year 1727 to 1744, No. 7 in
Russia Through European Eyes. London: Frank Cass & Co. Ltd., 1968.*

This book is printed on acid-free paper.

1 2 3 4 5 6 7 8 9 0 DOC DOC 9 0 9 8 7 6

ISBN 0-07-043480-8

*This book was set in Palatino by Ruttle, Shaw & Wetherill, Inc.
The editors were Leslye Jackson and Ira C. Roberts;
the design manager was Charles A. Carson;
the production supervisor was Annette Mayeski.
The photo editor was Natalia Yamrom.
The cover was designed by Lisa Cicchetti.
Project Supervision was done by Ruttle, Shaw & Wetherill, Inc.
Maps by David Lindroth.
R. R. Donnelley & Sons Company was printer and binder.
Cover Photos: The Peter the Great Monument in Leningrad, courtesy Corbis-Bettmann; St. Basil's
Cathedral, Red Square, Moscow, courtesy UPI/Corbis-Bettmann; Russian Peasants Spending Their
Leisure Listening to the Balalaika, courtesy Corbis-Bettmann.*

Library of Congress Cataloging-in-Publication Data

Moss, Walter.
   A history of Russia / Walter G. Moss.
      p.   cm
   Includes bibliographical references and index.
   ISBN 0-07-043480-8 (v. 1: To 1917).—ISBN 0-07-043482-4 (v.
    2: Since 1855)
    1. Russia—History.   2. Soviet Union—History.   I. Title.
DK40.M67   1997
947—dc20   96-34845

htpp://www.mhcollege.com

About the Author

WALTER G. MOSS is a professor at Eastern Michigan University, where he has taught history since 1970. He was born in Cincinnati, where he attended Xavier University. After service as an officer in the U.S. Army, he enrolled at Georgetown University, where he earned his Ph.D. and wrote a dissertation on Vladimir Soloviev's polemics with Russian nationalists. He is the author of articles and numerous book reviews on Russian history, literature, and philosophy. He is also one of four authors of *The Twentieth Century: A Brief Global History*, now being prepared by McGraw-Hill for its 5th edition; co-author of *Growing Old* (Pocket Books, 1975); and the editor of *Humanistic Perspectives on Aging* (University of Michigan Institute of Gerontology, 1976). Between 1978 and 1995, he visited the former Soviet Union and Russia on ten occasions. Professor Moss has received grants from the National Endowment for the Humanities and served as a panelist for its Public Program Division. He can be reached at His_Moss@Online.emich.edu, or at WWW.mhcollege.com

To Nancy

Contents

Part I
THE RISE AND DISINTEGRATION
OF KIEVAN RUS

Part II
THE MONGOLS AND THE RISE OF MOSCOW TO 1533

Part III
MUSCOVY AND ITS EXPANSION, 1533–1689

Part IV
EARLY IMPERIAL RUSSIA, 1689–1855

Part V
LATE IMPERIAL RUSSIA, 1855–1917

List of Maps

Preface

The completion of this two-volume text has been made possible by the contributions of numerous people. My former professors at Georgetown University, especially Cyril Toumanoff, Olgerd Sherbowitz-Wetzor, Frank Fadner, and John Songster, helped prepare me to teach Russian history and contributed to my enthusiasm for it. For three decades my students have stimulated my desire to make it more intelligible to them. In numerous trips to the former Soviet Union, I learned much from the many Russians and other Soviet citizens with whom I spoke. My indebtedness to U.S. and other scholars is only hinted at by the many references to them or their works that are scattered throughout this text. More than most works of scholarship, a textbook depends on the primary research of hundreds of others. Among U.S. scholars, special thanks are due to the reviewers of this text, who provided many helpful suggestions and criticisms: Alan Ball, Marquette University; Charles E. Clark, University of Wisconsin-Stevens Point; Patricia Herlihy, Brown University; Hugh D. Hudson, Jr., Georgia State University; Robert E. Jones, University of Massachusetts, Amherst; Richard D. Lewis, St. Cloud State University; Gary Marker, State University of New York at Stony Brook; Thomas S. Noonan, University of Minnesota; and Ted Uldricks, University of North Carolina-Asheville.

At Eastern Michigan University, my colleague Leonas Sabaliunas has been kind enough to read and comment on many of my chapters, and his special concern with Lithuania has stimulated my own interest in nationalities that were once part of the Russian Empire or Soviet Union. Another colleague, James McDonald, has shared his knowledge of Russian geography with me, and David Geherin has furnished assistance on the correct use of the English language; Dick Goff and James Waltz were also helpful in various ways. Ira Wheatley and Margot Duley helped provide three semesters' release from teaching responsibilities so that I could complete this text, and Nancy Snyder and her secretarial staff constantly provided any secretarial assistance I requested. Brandon Laird and Charles Zwinak read many chapters and offered me the perspective of intelligent students of Russian history. Other students who assisted me with bibliographical and other help were Rick Czarnota, Judy Hannah, Andy Rowland, and Julie Thomas.

Among colleagues at other universities, I am grateful to Helen Graves and Paulis Lazda for their support. At McGraw-Hill, Chris Rogers first suggested that I write a Russian history text, and subsequently Niels Aaboe, David Follmer, Pamela Gordon, Leslye Jackson, and Amy Mack provided additional editorial support. David Lindroth produced the maps in the text. Nancy Dyer, Natalia Yamrom, and Elsa Peterson have provided assistance with illustrations and permissions, and Peg Markow and her assistants with copyediting and proofreading.

My greatest debt, I owe to my wife, Nancy. Not only has she shared many trips to Russia with me and put up with the many tribulations of having a spouse work on a text for seven years, but her own interest in Russian women and health care has helped broaden my knowledge of these subjects. Likewise, my understanding of law and architecture has been broadened by the interests of our daughter, Jenny, and our sons, Tom and Dan, in one or another of these subjects.

The spellings of Russian names used in this text are based on the Library of Congress system, though I have made a few alterations in the interest of making Russian names more accessible to U.S. students. I use "i" instead of "ii" for appropriate first name endings (thus Dmitri not Dmitrii), "y" instead of "ii" for appropriate last name endings (Kandinsky not Kandinskii), and "Yu" and "Ya" instead of "Iu" and "Ia" at the beginning of appropriate words (Yuri not Iuri). Familiar names such as Tchaikovsky and Yeltsin are rendered in keeping with the spellings to which we have become accustomed, and the names of émigré writers are generally spelled as they spell them in their Western publications (thus Aksyonov not Aksenov). The spelling of non-Russian individual names or geographical areas while subject to or within the boundaries of Kievan Rus, Muscovy, the Russian Empire, or the USSR are rendered according to their Russian spelling before the breakup of the USSR in 1991. Thus, Belorussia and Belorussians, not Belarus and Belarusians until after 1991. When dating internal Russian events that occurred before March 1917, I use the "Old Style" (O.S.) dates of the Julian calendar (by 1917, it was thirteen days behind the Gregorian calendar used in the West). International events, such as the diplomatic developments leading to World War I, are rendered according to the Gregorian calendar.

Walter G. Moss

A Note to Students

Over a century ago, the Russian socialist Alexander Herzen wrote that his father once picked up Karamzin's *History of the Russian State,* but then contemptuously put it down saying: "All these Iziaslaviches and Olgoviches, to whom can that be of interest?" To prevent a similar reaction and help you make some sense of all the "Iziaslaviches and Olgoviches," this text clusters many names around several main topics: (1) the struggle for and against political authority, including autocracy and dictatorship; (2) the expansion and contraction of Russia and its dealings with other nationalities and foreign powers; and (3) the life and culture of the Russian people.

While keeping these topics in the forefront, the text also reflects the realizatin of what Marc Raeff has referred to as the "messiness of history." Although we need generalizations to make sense of history, not all important historical facts fit into neat categories.

Archaeological and documentary evidence provide a sufficient enough foundation for us to begin our study of Russia in the late ninth century A.D. We begin, however, not with a Russia centered around Moscow, but with Kievan Rus, a unique state that was the common starting point for the history of all three of the East Slavic nations: Russia, Ukraine, and Belarus.

From the very beginnings of Kievan Rus, we will be dealing with a complex ethnic mosaic made up primarily of Slavs, Scandinavian Vikings (the Varangians), and Finno-Ugrians. Later on, after the Mongol invasion of the thirteenth century and the eventual rise of Moscow, we will see the expansion of a Russian state that at its height encompassed well over a hundred different nationalities. The story of that expansion—and later contraction—and Russia's dealings with these nationalities is an important part of Russian history. But this book's primary focus is on Russia; it barely touches on any distinct aspects of the social and cultural lives of Ukrainians, Georgians, Armenians, or other nationalities that were once a part of the Russian Empire or Soviet Union. Students desiring to know more about these nationalities and nations should turn to some of the excellent histories about them that are available. (See the section on nationalities and peoples in the General Bibliography at the end of this volume.)

The great Russian novelist Leo Tolstoy once criticized the historian Sergei Soloviev for concentrating too much on just the Russian government and neglecting those who "made the brocades, broadcloth, clothes, and damask cloth which the tsars and nobles flaunted, who trapped the black foxes and sables that were given to ambassadors, who mined the gold and iron, who raised the horses, cattle, and sheep, who constructed the houses, palaces, and churches, and who transported goods." In this history text, such everyday life is not ignored. Special attention is paid to the lives of women, children, and families; the material culture of the people (their food and drink, their health and housing); and their legal and illegal dealings with the state, including their crimes and the punishments they suffered.

A History of Russia
Volume I: To 1917

CHAPTER 1

Land and Peoples: From Ancient Times to the Present

As German troops discovered in late 1941, when fierce winter weather hindered them from taking Moscow, geography affects history. Although Russia's geography helped defeat the forces of Hitler, for centuries it had made life more difficult for Russians than for people located in less harsh lands.

Until the modern era, Rus and then Russians as well as other peoples were much more immediately affected than we are today, in our world of electricity and automobiles, by fields and rivers, crops and animals, heat and cold, rain and drought, and lightness and darkness. Thus, the physical world that surrounded them, their geography, was of utmost importance in determining their existence. Most Russians produced the majority of their own food and clothes. In their huts and log cabins, they had no more illumination than the weak light of a slowly burning wood splinter (*luchina*). Even the candlesticks and clay lamps of those who could afford them gave off little light. If people traveled, it was by foot, horse, or boat.

THE LAND: PHYSICAL FEATURES, CLIMATE, AND RESOURCES

The amount of territory controlled by Rus, Russian, and Soviet governments has varied considerably throughout Russia's long history (see Map 1.1), but the enormous size of Russia throughout most of its history has made centralized rule more difficult than in smaller countries. Prior to his death in 1015, the Rus prince Vladimir I ruled over about 800,000 square kilometers. In 1533, after substantial expansion but before moving into Siberia, the Russian government ruled over 2.8 million square kilometers. At the height of the Russian Empire, under the last Emperor, Nicholas II, the empire contained eight times as much territory (22.4 million square kilometers). Although the new Soviet government ruled over slightly less land in the period between the two world wars, victory in World War II enabled the U.S.S.R. to become as large as the

Growth of Russia 1533–1900

Russia (Muscovy) in 1533	Russian Empire in 1900

Union of Soviet Socialist Republics in 1930

Russian Empire in 1900	Soviet Union in 1930

MAP 1.1A,B

Union of Soviet Socialist Republics in 1950

Soviet Union in 1930	Soviet Union in 1950	Republic boundaries

Russia in 1993

Boundary of the Soviet Union in 1950   ◦ Capitals of U.S.S.R. successor states

MAP 1.1C,D

Russian Empire had once been. Following the collapse of the U.S.S.R. at the end of 1991, Russia was left with 17.1 million square kilometers, or 76 percent of the former Soviet Union.

Although smaller than the former U.S.S.R., Russia remains the largest country in the world and is about 1.8 times the size of the United States. From east to west, it extends about 10,000 kilometers (over 6,000 miles) and traverses eleven time zones. From north to south, it spans more than 4,000 kilometers (or about 2,500 miles). Alaska, which once belonged to Russia, and today is separated from Siberia only by the narrow Bering Straight, is closer to much of eastern Siberia than is Moscow.

Russia can be divided into European and Asiatic Russia, with the Ural Mountains being the dividing line. Although the Russian Empire and the U.S.S.R. contained additional Asiatic territories, Asiatic Russia today can be thought of as synonymous with Siberia (this definition of Siberia includes Russia's Far East, which is sometimes dealt with separately).

European Russia is primarily a large plain, as is western Siberia, which extends from the Urals to the Enisei River. The Urals are not very high, reaching only a little over 6,000 feet at their highest point. East of the Enisei River, the Siberian terrain becomes more hilly, and east of the Lena River stretching to the Pacific Ocean are various mountain ranges. Other mountain ranges exist in south-central and eastern Siberia, and the Caucasus Mountains are along Russia's southern border between the Black and Caspian seas.

Russia possesses many large rivers and lakes. The longest rivers are three Siberian ones, the Lena, the Irtysh and the Ob. The Enisei is fifth in size, behind the Volga River, European Russia's (and Europe's) largest river and almost as long as the American Mississippi. Most of the main Siberian rivers flow south to north and empty into the Arctic Ocean. The Irtysh flows through Kazakhstan before entering Siberia and empties into the Ob. The Amur River, which forms part of the Chinese-Russian border before turning northward and entering into the Pacific Ocean, is an exception and flows mainly west to east.

Although not as long as the greatest Siberian rivers, several of Russia's European rivers, such as the Dnieper and Volga, have played a greater historical role. In European Russia, most of the major rivers also flow northward, such as the Northern Dvina and Pechora, or southward, such as the Volga and Don. As in Siberia, many tributaries are located on an east-west axis. Several important rivers have their headwaters southeast of the city of Novgorod in the Valdai Hills. Here in heights of only about 1,000 feet above sea level, lakes and marshes give birth to the Volga, the Western Dvina, and the Dnieper. West of these Valdai Hills, some fifty to a hundred miles, are the Lovat and Volkhov rivers, divided by Lake Ilmen. Via connecting rivers, portages, and later in history, canals, the Lovat-Volkhov waterway and the three bigger rivers (the Volga, the Western Dvina, and the Dnieper) have provided water routes between the Baltic and the Black and Caspian seas.

Often, however, Russia was cut off from access to these seas. Its desire to obtain access, especially to the Baltic and Black seas, and then play a larger maritime role became significant in Russian foreign policy. Despite the breakup of the Soviet Union, Russia still has coastline on both seas, although not as much as earlier. The Western Dvina and Dnieper rivers, for example, now empty into sea waters outside Russian borders. Although its vast Arctic and Pacific ocean coastlines (the latter first reached in the seventeenth century) have been less significant in Russia's historical development, they have become more important in recent centuries.

Although lakes are especially numerous in the European northwestern part of the country, the greatest lake (in Russia or the world) in terms of water volume is Siberia's wondrous Lake Baikal. Despite being called a "sea," the Caspian, which Russia shares with several other former Soviet republics and Iran, is actually the world's largest lake if measured by surface area.

Russia's extreme northern location, comparable to Alaska's and Canada's, has combined with other factors to make Russia's climate harsh. Average January temperatures in some parts of northeastern Siberia are between –50°F and –60°F, although these areas can also experience very hot, but short, summers. Further south and west, temperatures are less extreme, but winters are still long and summers short. Average January temperatures in Novosibirsk hover around 0°F and in Moscow are about 14°F, only about 7° below Chicago's.

Russia's rainfall pattern is also less than ideal. Precipitation is heaviest in the northwest and diminishes as one moves southeast. In many parts of the country, including the Moscow area, rain tends to be less plentiful in the spring and early summer, when it would most help crops, and instead falls more heavily in the late summer. Taken together, Russia's northern location and unfavorable rainfall patterns have adversely affected Russian agriculture, which,

FIGURE 1.1. Lake Baikal and a small settlement on its western shore.

in turn, has affected many other aspects of Russian life from the people's diet to state revenues.

Not counting transitional areas, Russia can be divided into four main vegetation zones: From north to south, they are the tundra, taiga, mixed forest, and steppe (see Map 1.2). The tundra region is a treeless one where much of the ground beneath the surface remains permanently frozen year-round. Permafrost also extends south into much of the taiga forest zone. This is an area primarily of coniferous trees like the pine. Next comes the smaller mixed forest belt of both coniferous and leaf-bearing trees. This area is much more densely populated than the taiga and contains many of Russia's larger cities including Moscow. Taken together, Russia's two forest areas equal almost one-quarter of the world's total forest lands. South of the mixed forest is a steppe or prairie zone that originally contained few trees. A Central Asian desert zone that existed in the Soviet Union and the Russian Empire at its height is no longer under Russian control.

Russia's most fertile soils lie in a black-earth belt that can be found in the transitional area between the mixed forest and steppe and in the steppe itself. Because the transitional area receives more rain during appropriate times, it is the most productive agricultural area.

Further north, the soils of the mixed forest zone are not as favorable but have been farmed throughout much of Russian history. In early Russian history, peasants used the "slash-and-burn" technique of clearing lands by cutting trees and burning the stumps (the ashes making good fertilizer) before farming.

Literally from the cradle (made of wood) to the grave (in a wooden coffin), the forest and its products surrounded most Russians. The peasants often lived in pine or oak cabins amidst forest clearings. They and the town-dwellers used the wood of the forest not only for most houses, churches, and other buildings, but also for firewood, bast shoes, boats, icons, fortresses, city walls, plows, tools, and utensils. The forest provided furs and foods, such as meat, mushrooms, berries, and honey. Finally, it provided some protection, whether from steppe warriors in earlier times or from German invaders during World War II. But, as the great Russian historian Vasili Kliuchevsky (1841–1911) noted, the people's attitude toward the forest was ambivalent. With its darkness and denseness, its bears and brigands, it was like a harsh parent who both provided and punished.

The Rus and Russians had a different type of ambivalence toward the steppes, which were not only fertile, but also fearsome. Steppe plunderers often attacked Rus border regions, devastating towns and townspeople and carrying away slaves. Kievan Rus would finally come tumbling down when the last of the great steppe nomads, the Mongols, attacked not only borderlands, but also far into the interior of Kievan Rus.

If the people had ambivalent attitudes toward the forest and the steppes, Kliuchevsky thought that toward their rivers they had only unequivocal love, for these waterways provided fish and nourishing waters for humans and fields. Whether in summer or winter, the rivers were the best highways in the country and acted as the arteries of trade and contact with those beyond one's village or town.

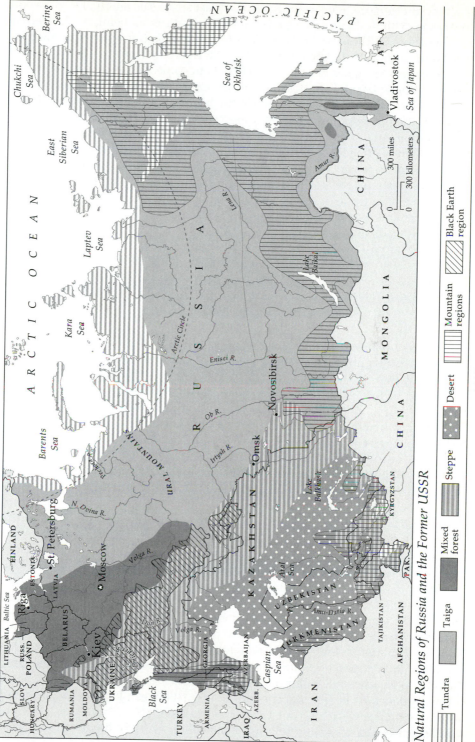

Natural Regions of Russia and the Former USSR

MAP 1.2

Tundra	Steppe	Black Earth region
Taiga	Desert	Mountain regions
Mixed forest		

Ancient folklore, however, suggests at least some Rus ambivalence toward the rivers. This folklore often perceived water spirits as being as dangerous and malicious as those of the forest. The female *rusalki* (nymphs), for example, lured and tickled young men to death in both river and forest.

Whereas nature has been harsh to Russia in some regards, it has been generous in others. Besides its great timber resources, Russia has possessed abundant wildlife, including many valuable fur-bearing animals. And it is a world leader in the possession of mineral resources, including mineral fuels. Among its abundant resources are coal, petroleum, natural gas, iron and iron alloys, copper, diamonds, gold, silver, lead, zinc, mercury, asbestos, potassium, magnesium, salt deposits, phosphate ores, sulfur, and limestone. Aluminum is about the only major mineral resource that Russia lacks. Of course, large quantities of many of these materials are in areas of Russia, especially Siberia, that have not always been part of the Russian state, and harsh climactic conditions have often made extraction costly and difficult.

GEOGRAPHY'S IMPACT ON COLONIZATION AND NATIONAL IDENTITY

Kliuchevsky believed that the history of his country was one of colonization, and there is little doubt that Russia's geographical conditions helped stimulate its colonization and expansion. Among other reasons, the Russians expanded to acquire better agricultural lands, Siberian furs, and access to warm-water ports.

This colonization was also encouraged by few natural barriers; an excellent artery of rivers; and fluid, poorly defined frontiers. Such porous frontiers, however, could be a danger and a source of contention as well as an opportunity. They contributed to the heavy emphasis on the military throughout most of Russian history. Russia today, like the U.S.S.R. before it, borders on more nations than any other country in the world.

Colonization led to the absorption of many non-Russian peoples and the creation of a multinational empire. Ruling over so many non-Russians affected both Russian domestic and foreign policies. In 1991, the difficulties of ruling over so many differing peoples helped lead to the collapse of the U.S.S.R.

The Eurasian location of Russia—part European, part Asian—was another geographical factor that had a significant impact on Russian history and culture. During the nineteenth century, Russian Slavophiles and Westernizers debated whether Russia was culturally part of Europe or not. Later on, the émigrés from the Russian Empire who founded "Eurasianism" in 1920 emphasized the importance of a Eurasian location. Just a few years earlier, the great Russian poet Alexander Blok had foreshadowed their doctrine in his poem "The Scythians." There he depicted Russians as between Europe and Asia, but also wrote: "Yes, we are Scythians! Yes, we are Asians."

Today, in the confusion following the collapse of the Soviet Union, Russians are once again vigorously debating their national identity and relationship to the West.

THE PEOPLES: FROM ANCIENT TIMES TO THE PRESENT

Long before there was any recorded history in Kievan Rus, a succession of nomadic warriors dominated the southern steppes of modern-day European Russia and Ukraine. This region was near the western end of a vast steppe area stretching almost uninterrupted from Manchuria to Hungary. From before 1000 B.C. to about 200 B.C., it was first the Cimmerians and then the Iranian-speaking Scythinas who controlled the high grassy area north of the Black Sea. Although historians know little of the first group, much more is known of the Scythians, thanks largely to ancient Greek sources and some fascinating archaeological finds displayed in museums such as St. Petersburg's Hermitage.

Around 200 B.C., another Iranian-speaking group, the Sarmatians, defeated the Scythians and then dominated the steppe until the Germanic Goths defeated them about 400 years later. In the 370s A.D., the Asiatic Huns displaced the Goths, who fled westward. Between Hun domination of the southern steppe and the beginnings of Kievan Rus in the late ninth century, other Asiatic groups, such as the Avars, Türks, Bulgars, and Khazars, succeeded each other in prominence in the region.

Both before and after the establishment of Kievan Rus, the nomadic peoples of the southern steppe tended to display similar characteristics. They generally were loose tribal federations. At first, they survived by breeding their horses and other animals on vast pastures, moving constantly to prevent overgrazing. Although the nomads could survive on their own, they almost always sought to enrich their lives through raiding or trading with more sedentary peoples. In both types of activities, their hardy horses were their most valuable asset, either as cavalry mounts or as trading commodities. More sedentary peoples needed to purchase the nomads' surplus horses for both domestic and military purposes—for more than 2,000 years (until the gunpowder revolution at the end of medieval times), horse-mounted warriors dominated warfare.

As time passed, at least some of the nomadic peoples became seminomadic, establishing permanent winter camps and becoming involved, at least for part of the year, in more sedentary occupations. Among both the Scythians and the Khazars, for example, the pure nomadic life became increasingly a privilege available to only elite elements within their tribal confederations.

Prior to the beginning of Kievan Rus, the Khazars were gathering tribute from many peoples, including some of the East Slavic tribes. They forged an important commercial state centered around the city of Itil, located on the lower Volga. From there they directed a tribute-gathering and trading empire ideally situated to do business with Byzantines, Arabs, Persians and other Asians, Volga Bulgars, Slavs, and Varangians (Scandinavian Vikings in the East Slavic lands). Although by the late ninth century many upper-class Khazars and their ruler had converted to Judaism, they were tolerant of other religions.

In the centuries that followed, the Rus, Russians, and other peoples of the forest traded, competed for steppe land, paid or collected tribute, warred, and sometimes allied with the peoples of the steppe (who included the Mongols). The impact of the steppe peoples on Russian history has been hotly debated, but most recent research indicates it was greater than the majority of past Russian and Soviet historians acknowledged.

No one knows for sure when the East Slavs first moved into the European lands they dominate today, primarily into the forest zone or the transitional belt between forest and steppe. The closeness of various Slavic languages has led some historians to suggest a common homeland for all Slavs—north of the Carpathian Mountains—and then a split, by the seventh century A.D., into southern, western, and eastern Slavic groups. From the first came the Slavs of Bulgaria and the Croats, Serbs, and Slovenes of what was once Yugoslavia. From the second came the Poles, Czechs, Slovaks, Moravians, and other smaller groups. From the last would eventually emerge the Russians, Ukrainians, and Belorussians.

In the Rus era, however, the three East Slavic nations were not yet distinct, and they and the state they formed, along with other peoples, became known simply as Rus. The Rus chronicles divide the East Slavs only by tribes—about a dozen of them at the dawn of Kievan Rus (see Map 2.1).

Prior to the extensive Slavic colonization of northern Rus, a process that continued throughout the Kievan Rus period, the area was settled primarily by many Finno-Ugric peoples. By the mid-ninth century, another group was present in future Rus territories—Scandinavian Vikings similar to those who burst upon other parts of Europe in this era. They already had sailed into the rivers and lakes leading from the Baltic to the Black and Caspian seas and begun to exploit the area—indeed the name "Rus" appears to have been first applied to these Vikings (or Varangians) before finally being used in its wider sense. Like many southern steppe peoples, these "nomads of the sea" were raiders and traders. They eventually played an important role in organizing the multiethnic trading and tribute-gathering elite that founded and furnished the political leadership for Kievan Rus. In the multiethnic lands that would become part of Kievan Rus, there were still other peoples, including descendants of those who had earlier inhabited the southern steppes.

By the time the Kievan Rus state collapsed in the thirteenth century, a Great Russian ethnic type was emerging from the East Slavic intermingling with the Finnish peoples of northern Russia. Some Finnish tribes, however, such as the Komi, the Mordvins, and the Mari, although subject to various pressures throughout Russian history, maintained their separate identities. (Komi, Mari El, and Mordovian Republics exist in present-day Russia, although the native peoples are outnumbered in each by Great Russians).

As the Russian state expanded in medieval and modern times, over one hundred other nationalities were brought under Russian control. Among them were the peoples of modern-day Ukraine and Belarus, Siberia, part of the Baltic area, the Caucasus, and Central Asia. In the Russian Empire's census of 1897 (which excluded Finland), those who listed their native language as Russian composed only 44.3 percent of the population. Using language as a rough

FIGURE 1.2. Peoples of the
Russian Empire from an
early nineteenth-century
engraving.
*(From Robert Wallace and
the Editors of Time-Life
Books,* Rise of Russia. *Time
Inc., New York, 1967, p.
132.)*

guide to ethnicity, Ukrainians made up 17.8 percent; Poles, 6.3 percent; and Belorussians, 4.7 percent. Among the non-Slavic population, the many Turkic
peoples, primarily in Central Asia and the Caucasus, together composed 10.8
percent. Jews were 4 percent, and other nationalities (such as Armenians,
Georgians, Latvians, Lithuanians, and Finnish peoples) each composed a
smaller percentage.

At the time of the breakup of the Soviet Union in December 1991, the Russians were just a bare majority in the U.S.S.R. In the new post-Soviet Russia,
however, the Great Russians in 1992 made up greater than 80 percent of the
total population of almost 150 million people. Although Tatars and Ukrainians
were the only other nationalities possessing more than 1 percent of the total,
more than one hundred national groups still existed within Russian borders.
Conversely, the 25 million Russians residing in other former Soviet republics
almost equaled the number of non-Russians still inside Russian borders.

SUGGESTED SOURCES

ADAMS, ARTHUR E., IAN M. MATLEY, and WILLIAM O. MCCAGG. *An Atlas of Russian and
    East European History.* New York, 1967.

ASCHERSON, NEAL. *Black Sea*. New York, 1995.

BATER, JAMES H. *The Soviet Scene: A Geographical Perspective*. London, 1989.

BATER, JAMES H., and R. A. FRENCH, eds. *Studies in Russian Historical Geography*. 2 vols. London, 1983.

CHEW, ALLEN F. *An Atlas of Russian History: Eleven Centuries of Changing Borders*. Rev. ed. New Haven, 1970.

COLE, J. P. *Geography of the Soviet Union*. London, 1984.

FORSYTH, JAMES. *A History of the Peoples of Siberia: Russia's North Asian Colony, 1581–1990*. Cambridge, Eng., 1992.

GILBERT, MARTIN. *Atlas of Russian History*. 2d ed. New York, 1993.

KAISER, ROBERT J. *The Geography of Nationalism in Russia and the USSR*. Princeton, 1994.

KATZ, ZEV, ROSEMARIE ROGERS, and FREDERIC T. HARNED, eds. *Handbook of Major Soviet Nationalities*. New York, 1975.

KERNER, ROBERT J. *The Urge to the Sea: The Course of Russian History*. Berkeley, 1942.

KLYUCHEVSKY (KLIUCHEVSKY), V. O. *The Course of Russian History*. Vols. 1 & 3. New York, 1960.

KOZLOV, VICKTOR. *The Peoples of the Soviet Union*. Bloomington, 1988.

LINCOLN, W. BRUCE. *The Conquest of a Continent: Siberia and the Russians*. New York, 1994.

LYDOLPH, PAUL E. *Geography of the USSR*. 5th ed. Elkhart Lake, Wis., 1990.

MONGAIT, A. L. *Archaeology in the U.S.S.R.* Baltimore, 1961.

NAHAYLO, BOHDAN, and VICTOR SWOBODA. *Soviet Disunion: A History of the Nationalities Problem in the USSR*. New York, 1990.

PARKER, W. H. *An Historical Geography of Russia*. Chicago, 1969.

PRITSAK, OMELJAN. *The Origin of Rus'*. Cambridge, Mass., 1981.

RH* 19, Nos. 1–4 (1992). This whole issue is devoted to "The Frontier in Russian History."

RIEBER, ALFRED J. "Persistent Factors in Russian Foreign Policy." In *Imperial Russian Foreign Policy*, ed. Hugh Ragsdale. Cambridge, Eng., 1993. This essay offers good insights on geography's impact on foreign policy.

RYWKIN, MICHAEL, ed. *Russian Colonial Expansion to 1917*. London, 1988.

SINOR, DENIS, ed. *The Cambridge History of Early Inner Asia*. Cambridge, Eng., 1990. This book contains excellent articles on early peoples of steppe and forest.

SMITH, GRAHAM, ed. *The Nationalities Question in the Soviet Union*. London, 1990.

STEPHAN, JOHN J. *The Russian Far East: A History*. Stanford, 1994.

SYMONS, LESLIE, ed. *The Soviet Union: A Systematic Geography*. London, 1990.

VERNADSKY, GEORGE. *Ancient Russia*. New Haven, 1964.

———. *The Origins of Russia*. Oxford, 1959.

WIECZYNSKI, JOSEPH L. *The Russian Frontier: The Impact of Borderlands Upon the Course of Early Russian History*. Charlottesville, 1976.

WIXMAN, RONALD. *The Peoples of the USSR: An Ethnographic Handbook*. Armonk, N.Y., 1984.

*See General Bibliography at the back of this text for a list of journal and anthology abbreviations.

PART ONE

The Rise and Disintegration of Kievan Rus

At the eastern end of Europe a new political entity arose by the end of the ninth century—Kievan Rus. Even though it continued in existence for almost four centuries, there is much that remains murky about it: Good primary sources are insufficient in number and reliability.

Kievan Rus was a multiethnic entity with most of its people being East Slavs, although Finno-Ugrians were plentiful in the north and northeast. Scandinavian Vikings called Varangians also played a key role in the new state and founded its political dynasty—the House of Riurik. These Varangians were part of the great Viking outburst of the ninth century, which propelled their excellent ships all over the seas and rivers of Europe and even far into the Atlantic.

Like some of the steppe peoples, the early Varangians were more than just plunderers, and they eventually turned to more systematic, less violent, methods of collecting wealth. They became more interested in trade and tribute-collecting. And they formed a Kievan Rus state, in which fines, taxes, and tribute (the latter two terms almost can be used interchangeably for this period) became more important than booty. The Varangians also intermarried with native peoples.

At first, the Riurikid leaders controlled little more than the country's chief waterways and the cities along them, but gradually their tribute-gathering arms extended into more remote areas. Yet, partly because of a complex and often challenged system of political succession, Riurikid leaders were never able to achieve the degree of political power later realized by grand princes and tsars in Muscovite Russia. In Kievan Rus, political authority was much more divided and fragmented.

In the course of several centuries, the Rus battled and made treaties with various states and peoples.

Among the most prominent were the Byzantine Empire, the Poles, the Bulgars of Bulgaria and the Volga, and several nomadic warrior peoples of the southern steppe or prairie. It was the Mongols, the last of the steppe peoples confronting Kievan Rus, who struck it a death blow between 1237 and 1241.

Just as the legally unlimited power of an autocrat did not exist in Kievan Rus, neither did another characteristic of late Muscovite Russia—serfdom. In ancient Rus, peasants were freer, not yet enserfed by noble masters. Yet as the period went on, princes rewarded more and more of their followers with lands, including some that peasant groups had formerly considered their own. Moreover, from the beginning of the tribute-collecting Riurikid dynasty, the Riurikids and the elite who supported them exploited the common people, thus beginning a long tradition of government and elite exploitation.

Partly as a result of the early princes' interest in trade, urban life was dynamic in Kievan Rus, and many towns existed. Yet, characteristic of medieval times, most of the population lived in the countryside and were peasants.

At the end of the tenth century, Kievan Rus's Prince Vladimir mandated Christianity for the Rus. It presented a means for unifying the beliefs of a diverse group of peoples and giving the Rus state greater cohesiveness. From the beginning, the princes, with the cooperation of early churchmen, made use of the new faith to underscore the sanctity of princely power. Although Christianity gained ground only slowly in the country-side, it quickly began to transform urban life and urban culture. The Christianization of Rus became the first of several attempts in Rus-Russian history whereby a governing urban elite attempted (always with mixed success) to impose major cultural changes on its mostly rural subjects. The buttressing of princely power by identifying princes (or later tsars) with Christ and Christian goals also continued long into the future.

Of course, Christianity was much more than just a political tool, and the reasons for its acceptance and its effects extended into personal, economic, social, and cultural spheres. For example, Christianity and the Byzantine and South Slavic influences that accompanied it stimulated the creation of a Rus high culture, which produced literary and artistic works of considerable merit.

Although leading churchmen attempted to further the Christian unity of Kievan Rus, certain political factors worked against them. During the twelfth and early thirteenth centuries, increasing centrifugal tendencies manifested themselves, as princes and principalities increasingly warred against each other. New centers arose to challenge Kiev's leadership. Three of these were the principalities of Vladimir-Suzdal in the northeast, Volhynia-Galicia in the southwest, and Novgorod in the north. At the same time, local princes were increasingly subdividing their principalities among their sons, who often engaged in fratricidal conflicts with one another and refused to unite against foreign foes. Thus, by late 1237, when the Mongols began their onslaught on Kievan Rus, its disintegration was already well underway.

CHAPTER 2

The Politics of Kievan Rus

The history of Kievan Rus's leading princes and an examination of its political structure revolve around five main domestic issues: (1) the role of the Varangians (Rus Vikings), (2) the tribute and trading emphasis of governing princes and their elite supporters, (3) the significance and impact of the acceptance of Christianity, (4) clan rule and succession questions, and (5) the complex and fragmented nature of political power. Some of these issues are also relevant to Kievan Rus's expansion and foreign policy, treated later in this chapter, and to economic, social, religious, and cultural questions, which are mainly dealt with in the next chapter.

THE PRINCES

Most of what we know of the Kievan Rus princes comes from chronicles of the time, especially from *The Primary Chronicle*. This important book was compiled and revised, primarily by monks, between about 1040 and 1118. Although it is an invaluable source, sometimes corroborated by other materials, it must be used cautiously. Its compilers were not as faithful to historical accuracy as are most modern historians and sometimes compromised it for other considerations, such as upholding Christianity, the ruling Riurikid dynasty, and the unity of Kievan Rus.

The problem of accuracy is almost immediately evident if we look at the entries for the years 860–862. First, Slavic and Finnish tribes refused to pay further tribute to the Varangians and drove them "back beyond the sea." But then almost immediately "tribe rose against tribe." Soon tired of such discord, the tribes got together and sent a delegation to ask a group of Varangians called Russes to "come to rule and reign" over them.[1] The leader of the group was Riurik, and he set himself up in Novgorod.

---

[1] Samuel Hazard Cross and Olgerd P. Sherbowitz-Wetzor, eds., *The Primary Chronicle* (Cambridge, Mass., 1953), p. 59.

Historians have debated the believability of the invitation, its date, and the connection of the name "Russes" to the term "Rus," which eventually became the name of the Kievan state and its people. Riurik himself remains a semi-legendary figure.

Many of these controversies are part of the "Normanist Controversy," which has been going on for two centuries. It revolves around the role of the Varangians (or Normans or Vikings) in founding and running Kievan Rus. Many native Russian and other East Slavic historians have been critical of the "Normanist theory" for overemphasizing the Norman role, and they have emphasized that Rus tribal society was already fairly complex and developed by the mid-ninth century. What is not open to doubt, however, is that the Varangians had been present on some East Slavic waterways and lands, primarily as warriors and traders, for many decades before the 860s and that the early Rus princes and most of their followers had Scandinavian names. Archaeological finds reveal a Scandinavian presence in Staraia Ladoga (just south of Lake Ladoga) from the mid-eighth century and at numerous other Rus sites during the ninth and tenth centuries. Besides this evidence, contemporary foreign observations mention the Varangians and reinforce the belief that Varangian princes and warriors played a key role in organizing and running the Kievan Rus government as a tribute-gathering and trade-pursuing entity.

From Oleg to Sviatoslav

According to the chronicle, Riurik on his deathbed entrusted his kinsman Oleg with both his realm and the guardianship of his young son, Igor. Oleg moved the Rus capital to Kiev and ruled there until 912. He also built stockaded towns along waterways and used them as bases from which to collect tribute from the surrounding Slavic and Finnish tribes. If we can believe the chronicle, his tribute-gathering arm reached all the way to Novgorod and Rostov, and he imposed a favorable trade treaty upon the Byzantine Empire.

Following the death of Oleg, Igor took over in Kiev. He ruled until 945, when he was killed by the Derevlians. This Slavic tribe residing northwest of Kiev does not fare well at the hands of the chronicle writers, who early on noted that they "existed in bestial fashion, and lived like cattle. They killed one another, ate every impure thing, and there was no marriage among them, but instead they seized upon maidens by capture."[2] Yet it was not their evil ways that led to Igor's death. The chronicle makes it clear that he tried to extract too much tribute from them.

Following his death, political power passed to his wife, Olga, who ruled as a regent for their young son Sviatoslav. She was the first woman ruler in Kiev and its first Christian ruler—after her conversion sometime in the middle of the century. In one of its most colorful, but no doubt embellished, stories, the chronicle relates how she began her reign by revenging her husband's death. By various stratagems, including getting some of the Derevlians drunk, she

[2] Ibid., p. 56.

buried alive, burned to death, and had her followers "cut down" varying numbers of them. After burning down one of their cities and giving some of them away as slaves, she imposed a heavy tribute on them. To prevent tribal rebellions in the future, she attempted—at least in the western principalities of Kievan Rus—to replace tribute-gathering expeditions with a regular system of tax collecting. After her death in 969, the chronicle states: "She was the first from Rus' to enter the kingdom of God."[3] She was later canonized a saint by the Russian church.

Olga's son Sviatoslav, ruler of Kievan Rus from 962 to 972, was one of Kiev's greatest warrior-princes and expansionists and the first with a Slavic name. In 971, he was described by a Byzantine source as broad-shouldered, with a gloomy and savage look, a long bushy mustache, a shaven head except for a lock of hair on one side, and a golden earring in one of his ears. On his various campaigns, this hardy warrior led by example, disdaining special comforts. Even though his mother had become a Christian, he did not follow her example. Nor did he wish, like her, to remain in Kiev. Several years after capturing Pereiaslavets on the Danube from the Bulgarians, he announced that he wished to reside there, at the center of his riches. After his mother's death, he appointed his three sons to rule in Kiev, Novgorod, and among the Derevlians, and he set off for Pereiaslavets. But a Byzantine-Bulgarian coalition defeated him and forced his retreat back to the land of Rus. Before he could reach Kiev, the nomadic Pechenegs attacked him and his men at the dangerous Dnieper cataracts in the steppe, a few hundred miles south of Kiev. They killed Sviatoslav and then took his skull—so the chronicle tells us—and made a drinking cup out of it.

The Kievan Heyday: Vladimir I and Yaroslav the Wise

In 980, after eight years of strife between the three sons of Sviatoslav, the youngest and lone survivor, Vladimir, emerged victorious. In 988, after earlier attempting to strengthen paganism, he took the most momentous step of his regime: He accepted Christianity and began imposing it on his subjects.

If only half the chronicle account of Vladimir is true, he was indeed a remarkable figure. He warred against Poles and Pechenegs, against Byzantines and Bulgars. No doubt exaggerating the contrast between his life before and after converting to Christianity, the chronicle notes that the pagan Vladimir was "insatiable in vice."[4] It credits him with 800 concubines and five wives, including the daughter of a defeated Polotsk prince, two Czech women, a Bulgarian woman, and his oldest brother's widow. The last was a former nun, brought back because of her beauty by Vladimir's father from one of his many campaigns. In the colorful and embellished chronicle account of Vladimir's survey of religious options for himself and his realm, he rejects Islam because "circumcision and abstinence from pork and wine were disagreeable to him.

[3] Ibid., p. 87.
[4] Ibid., p. 94.

FIGURE 2.1. The Dnieper River from a Kiev hill overlooking part of the Kievan Crypt (*Pecherskaia*) Monastery.

'Drinking,' said he, 'is the joy of the Russes. We cannot exist without that pleasure.' "[5]

The chronicle has Vladimir accepting Christianity after a careful examination of other options, including dispatching envoys to other countries to investigate their religions. Services in Constantinople's beautiful St. Sophia Cathedral especially moved Vladimir's men (see Chapter 3). Other advisers to Vladimir added that his wise grandmother Olga would not have chosen such a faith if it were evil. The chronicle also mentions another reason for the conversion: The Byzantine Emperor, Basil II, required it before he would allow the marriage of his sister Anna to Vladimir.

Of all the reasons stated in the chronicle, this last one seems most likely to have been true and significant. Basil II had requested, and subsequently received, Rus help in putting down rebellious subjects, and in exchange Vladimir wanted to marry Anna. His desire for such a wedding was not surprising. Among Rus's neighbors, the Byzantine Empire was the strongest political, trading, and cultural magnet. Accepting Christianity from the Byzantines offered many advantages. It was not just a religion, but, in present-day terms, an ideology.

In the Byzantine Empire, Christianity helped unite a multiethnic empire under an emperor, whom Byzantine churchmen taught was God's representa-

[5] Ibid., p. 97.

tive on earth. Although we can only guess what weight Vladimir and his advisers gave to various personal and political considerations, it is logical to conclude that Vladimir believed that Christianity would offer similar unifying advantages for Kievan Rus and himself. Christianizing Kievan Rus offered the promise of helping to overcome such divisions as that between the tribute-tax collectors (the princes and their followers) and those who paid, between different tribes and ethnic groups, and between political factions. Furthermore, nearby Bulgaria had already accepted Christianity a century earlier from the Byzantines. This meant that Slavic clergy and Christian materials and rituals in a Slavic language understandable to the Rus could quickly be imported.

Byzantine religious and cultural influences, many via Bulgaria, soon flooded Rus. After the great schism of 1054, between Orthodox Byzantium and Western Christendom, the Rus followed the Byzantine lead. They became part of an Eastern Orthodox sphere, different in many ways from Western Christendom, to which the Poles recently had adhered.

After Vladimir's conversion, he vigorously set out to destroy paganism and implant Christianity and a Christian culture among his people. Such efforts were not unusual for medieval monarchs. Although works about his life no doubt exaggerate his new saintliness, they do contain some truth. He apparently became more charitable to the poor and championed church building and education for the children of the elite. He warred less against fellow Christians and concentrated more on defeating the pagan Pechenegs.

But if Christian teachings were able to modify some princely behavior, they were unable to transform it completely. Many princes continued to struggle for larger shares of lands, tribute, and trade revenues. Just as Vladimir came to power only after a fratricidal struggle, so too some of his many sons battled against each other. For about a decade after his death in 1015, the strife continued.

At first, his oldest surviving son, Sviatopolk, seemed the victor. He took over in Kiev and became infamous in Russian history for killing several of his younger brothers, especially Boris and Gleb.

The murder of Boris and Gleb and the religious cult that developed around them and proclaimed them saints indicate better than any other evidence the extent of Christianity's influence on Rus political culture. On the one hand, the acceptance of Christianity did not prevent Sviatopolk or many other Kievan Rus princes from killing their brothers and other relatives; on the other hand, the cult that made Boris and Gleb the most honored saints in Kievan Rus revered the brothers because the stories about them insisted that they had refused to take up arms against their older brother and died like martyrs. Not only did the clergy hold up these two brothers as models for the Rus princes, but also many of the Rus princes themselves furthered the cult. The princes participated in services and ceremonies honoring the two saints and built numerous churches throughout Rus lands in their honor. The brotherly love attributed to Boris and Gleb became at least an ideal, if not often a reality.

The cult of Boris and Gleb was associated with a sanctification of princely power that extended beyond them to many other princes. The historian Michael Cherniavsky once calculated that one-third of about 180 Kievan Rus

FIGURE 2.2. Saints Boris and Gleb from an early fourteenth-century icon. (*Sovfoto.*)

saints were rulers. The writers and artists of the time, most of them churchmen and often dependent on princely good will, generally depicted Rus rulers as doing God's work by furthering Christianity in Rus lands and fighting against non-Christians. If killed in the course of performing such duties, the princes were often considered saintly martyrs.

Like many other systems of belief, Rus Christianity was furthered by an elite partly for self-serving reasons, but this did not prevent it from exercising some positive transforming influences.

Although Sviatopolk was successful in eliminating Boris, Gleb, and still another brother as potential rivals for the power and wealth he desired, he was not so fortunate in his dealings with a fourth brother, Yaroslav. At the time of Vladimir's death, Yaroslav was the prince of Novgorod and was expecting his father to attack him because Novgorod had refused to pay its tribute. Instead, he and the Novgorodians now warred against Sviatopolk and Kiev. Sviatopolk turned to Poles and nomad Pechenegs for help but was defeated by Yaroslav in 1019 and died in retreat.

Yaroslav, however, still had another brother to contend with—Mstislav. Only in 1024 did they fight their last battle and then divide the Rus land between them, with the Dnieper as a boundary: Yaroslav obtained Kiev and the area west of the river as well as the Novgorodian lands, and Mstislav ruled east of the Dnieper.

With the death of Mstislav without heirs in 1036, Yaroslav reunited most of the lands of Rus and ruled until 1054. It was during his reign that Kievan Rus reached its apex. For his intelligent leadership and love of wisdom, he became known as Yaroslav the Wise. Although he battled against foreign foes, his main achievements were domestic ones. He ordered the translation, production, and collection of many books, especially religious ones. He also oversaw the construction of the magnificent St. Sophia Cathedral in Kiev and furthered the development of the Russian church. Many historians believe that he mandated the compilation of the first written code of laws, *Russkaia Pravda* (Rus Justice). In a final testament to his five remaining sons, Yaroslav apportioned various cities to them and admonished them to love one another and to live in peace without quarreling.

The Last of the Great Kievan Princes: Vladimir Monomakh

Although the descendants of Yaroslav, and other Riurikid princes, alternated between peace and civil war, neither circumstance produced another prince worthy of note until Vladimir Monomakh became grand prince of Kiev in 1113. This occurred shortly after the death of his father and upon the request of Kievans, who earlier had broken out in revolt. Vladimir soon restored order and reduced the economic exploitation of the lower classes, which had helped lead to the uprising. Like his grandfather, Yaroslav the Wise, he left a testament to his sons, which gives us some idea of his character.

Following the death of Vladimir Monomakh in 1125, his son Mstislav ruled until his own death in 1132. Although Kievan Rus would continue for another century after 1132, it would become increasingly fragmented (see Chapter 4).

DOMESTIC POLITICS OF RUS

Although it is safe to say that in Kievan Rus autocracy (legally unlimited power exercised by a single ruler) never existed, it is more difficult to decipher exactly what did exist. Ingredients in the Kievan political pot included the relationship of Varangians to Slavs, of princes of different cities to one another, of political institutions within any one city to each other, and of chief cities with smaller towns and the surrounding countryside. Finally, political rebellions spiced up the pot's contents.

Vladimir Monomakh's Instructions To His Sons

In the material excerpted—from Leo Wiener, *Anthology of Russian Literature: From the Earliest Period to the Present Time* (New York, 1902) Vol. I, pp. 53–54—we see the type of prince that Vladimir desired each of his sons to be. John Fennell and Antony Stokes, *Early Russian Literature* (Berkeley, 1974), pp. 64–79, provide a good analysis of the whole testament and correctly warn us not to assume too much about Vladimir's own behavior from it. Nevertheless, the advice given here does at least tell us something of Vladimir's view of *ideal* princely behavior. Ellipses are mine.

When you are riding and have no engagement with anyone, and you know no other prayer, keep on repeating secretly: "Lord, have mercy upon me!" for it is better to say this prayer than to think idle things. Above all, forget not the destitute, but feed them according to your means, and give to the orphan, and protect the widow, and allow not the strong to oppress the people. Slay neither the righteous, nor the wrongdoer, nor order him to be slain who is guilty of death, and do not ruin a Christian soul.

Whenever you speak, whether it be a bad or a good word, swear not by the Lord, nor make the sign of the cross, for there is no need. If you have occasion to kiss the cross with your brothers or with anyone else, first inquire your heart whether you will keep the promise, then kiss it; and having kissed it,

see to it that you do not transgress, and your soul perish. As for the bishops, priests and abbots, receive their benediction in love, and do not keep away from them, but love them with all your might, and provide for them, that you may receive their prayers to God. Above all, have no pride in your hearts and minds, but say: "We are mortal, alive to-day, and to-morrow in the grave. All that Thou hast given us, is not ours, but Thine, and Thou hast entrusted it to us for but a few days." Put away no treasure in the earth, for that is a great sin.

Honour the elders as your father, and the younger ones as your brothers. . . . If you start out to a war, be not slack, depend not upon your generals, nor abandon yourselves to drinking and eating and sleeping. Put out the guards yourselves, and lie down to sleep only after you have placed the guards all around the army, and rise early. Do not take off your armour in haste, without examination, for many perishes suddenly through his negligence. Avoid lying and drunkenness and debauchery, for body and soul perish from them.

Whenever you travel over your lands, permit not the servants, neither your own, nor a stranger's, to do any damage in the villages, or in the fields, that they may not curse you. Wheresoever you go, and wherever you stay, give the destitute to eat and to drink. . . . Call on the sick, go to funerals, for we are all mortal, and pass not by a man without greeting him with kind words. Love your wives, but let them not rule you.

Varangians, Slavs, and Interprincely Relations

Even though some of the Slavic tribes rebelled against paying tribute to Varangian princes and their followers, Varangian-Slavic intermarriage soon diluted any possible ethnic shading to the resentment. Besides, today's concern with ethnicity and nationality was not part of the mentality of the time.

More significant is the question of interprincely relations. Were there any agreed-upon principles stipulating what the relationship should be? Apparently some feeling of clan solidarity existed among the Riurikid descendants of Prince Igor, and they seemed to view Kievan Rus as a large area to exploit collectively for their own gain. Prior to Yaroslav's death, the prince of Kiev was generally recognized as the senior or grand prince. He often appointed others, including his sons, to govern and exact tribute and taxes from other cities and surrounding territories. But how much power he really exercised over other city-states varied depending upon his strength and leadership and upon the willingness of other princes to cooperate with him. As we have seen, even the strong Vladimir was defied by his son Yaroslav in Novgorod, who refused to pass on to his father some of the tribute he had collected.

Another aspect of princely relations is the question of succession to the throne in Kiev. From the death of Igor until 1139, the general principle that seems to have operated was that the throne passed collaterally, that is from oldest brother to other brothers and even to cousins before moving on to the next generation. One exception to this principle was that it applied only to those whose father had sat on the Kievan throne. Because of this exception and because of the high death rate of Kievan princes, especially in battle and in fratricidal conflicts, the throne often passed from father to his oldest or only surviving son. But if collateral succession was recognized in principle—and even that is only a hypothesis—it was often challenged or its spirit violated. Vladimir and his son Yaroslav, for example, were both next in line to become princes of Kiev by succeeding an older brother on the throne, but neither waited for the natural death of the older brother but overthrew him.

The last testament of Yaroslav to his five sons attempted to prevent such conflicts. He bequeathed to each a large territory and admonished the four younger brothers to obey their oldest brother, Iziaslav, who was to be prince of Kiev and was to intercede for any brother wronged by one of the others.

Yaroslav no doubt wished his younger sons to maintain the ideal relations of lesser princes to the Kievan grand prince. Most specifically, these included answering the grand prince's call for military assistance against Rus foes—he, in turn, was to assist them if so threatened. Although Yaroslav did not spell all this out, he did tell his sons that if they loved one another and cooperated, they would vanquish their enemies. And if they did not, they would perish and bring destruction upon the Rus lands.

Yaroslav also seems to have bequeathed a more troubling legacy: the so-called rota system, by which he linked princely succession to certain territories. (It is also possible that some such method predated Yaroslav.) By the rota system, when the oldest brother ruling in Kiev died, he was to be succeeded by his next oldest brother, ruling in the next most important city, Chernigov. Then the next oldest brother would move up one slot to Chernigov and so on up the ladder.

Princely rights over various territories appear to have been extremely complex in Kievan Rus, with some lands being transferred from father to sons and others intended to be part of some sort of political ladder system. Even if some such system was recognized in theory, however, it did not work well in practice, for princely sons often wished to keep the lands ruled by their fathers and not see them pass to one of his brothers or cousins. The forty years following the death of Yaroslav in 1054 were full of princely strife.

In 1097, apparently recognizing that their recurring conflicts were more helpful to their pagan Polovtsy foe than to themselves, the grandsons of Yaroslav the Wise gathered for a conference at Liubech. At this Chernigov city they took a few steps back from any rota principle: They recognized each other's right to rule over the principalities Yaroslav had granted to their now deceased fathers.

If the Liubech conference weakened the princes' seniority rights, at least outside their fathers' principalities, it did little to sheathe their swords. Before the year was out, Yaroslav's descendants were once again conspiring and marching against one another. One of the victims was Vasilko, a great-grandson of Yaroslav, who also had received a small principality. A shepherd of his uncle Sviatopolk attacked him with a knife and put out both his eyes.

The Boyar Council and the Veche

In addition to princely power being limited by the appetites of competing princes, it was restricted in each principality by two other institutions of government: the boyar council and the *veche* (town assembly).

The composition and procedures of boyar councils were flexible and based on custom, rather than written law, and princes seem to have regularly consulted them about important decisions. The boyars included the prince's *druzhina* (a military retinue of perhaps several hundred men, originally living in or around his household) as well as other prominent citizens. Whereas normally a prince perhaps consulted only with a handful of his *druzhina*, he often called together a larger group of boyars when he felt more broad-based support was required. High-ranking clergymen also sometimes participated in these larger meetings.

Although the *veche* may have had its roots in older tribal practices, little mention of this more democratic institution is made in the chronicles until the eleventh century. The principal assemblies were in the capital cities of each principality. By ringing a special *veche* bell or using a town crier, a prince, official, or any other citizen could call together a meeting. All freemen were eligible to take part, but only male heads of household could vote.

Participants discussed and voted on local political issues and on major matters such as war or peace, especially if the prince wished to use the town militia to supplement his *druzhina*. Some assemblies even decided who should, or should not, be the ruler of a principality. The *veche* of Novgorod—often manipulated by powerful boyars—was especially notorious for showing an unwanted prince "the way out." Town meetings were often stormy affairs, and blows were sometimes exchanged before townsmen reached a consensus—decisions were supposed to be unanimous. Occasionally, Novgorod majorities even tossed unbending opponents off the Great Bridge, crossing the Volkhov, or expelled them from the city.

The legal system of Kievan Rus also makes it clear that princes' powers were limited, especially in Novgorod. If invited to rule by a *veche*, a prince might have to sign an agreement restricting the amount of money he could extract from the populace.

The relationship between the three main political institutions—the office of the prince, the boyar council, and the *veche*—varied considerably depending on time and place. Until the end of Yaroslav the Wise's reign (1054), the princes were dominant. But with the escalating princely conflict after his death, the town assemblies became more prominent in many areas. If in the latter Kievan period Novgorod was famous for its *veche*, Galicia was more notable for the undisguised strength of its boyars and Suzdal for its ruling princes.

Dominance of the Capital Cities and Rebellions

All three political institutions operated chiefly in each principality's capital city, which dominated the rest of the principality. In the eleventh century, for example, the prince of Polotsk ruled not only that city, but also over rural areas and other towns such as Minsk. By the early thirteenth century, the city of Novgorod presided over an empire that stretched east to the Ural Mountains and north to the White Sea.

The prince of a capital city usually appointed boyars or minor princes to administer and to collect taxes in outlying smaller cities and rural areas of his realm. Sometimes, like in the vast Novgorodian region, this involved a less direct rule over non-Slavic tribes and the occasional use of force to keep the taxes (or tribute) flowing. Under the jurisdiction of the prince's administrators, locally elected officials also participated in running local affairs. Although residents of smaller towns had the right to take part in meetings of the capital's *veche*, practical considerations prevented this from often occurring.

Some of the rebellions that occurred in Kievan Rus, such as that of the Derevlians against Prince Igor in 945, were due to the excessive financial demands of the Riurikid princes. *Veche*-princely strife and Christian-pagan conflicts were other leading causes of revolts.

A major uprising occurred in Kiev in 1068–69. It was precipitated by Prince Iziaslav's refusal of a *veche* request for arms and horses to continue a struggle against ravaging Polovtsy tribesmen. The anger of the townspeople led to the temporary flight of Iziaslav and the appointment of another prince. Several years later in the frequently rebellious city of Novgorod, a magician turned many of the people against their prince and Christianity before the prince "smote" him with an axe.[6]

Although there were other rebellions, just one more deserves consideration here: It occurred in Kiev in 1113. It began after the death of Prince Sviatopolk and after Vladimir Monomakh had refused a *veche* invitation to become the prince of Kiev. Mobs attacked the palace of a government official and the property of other government officials and some Jews. Upper-class elements now became alarmed and also implored Vladimir to take the throne, warning that if he did not, the property of boyars and the monasteries would

---

[6] Ibid., p. 154.

be attacked and plundered. The legislation that Vladimir enacted after heeding their call clarifies the situation that led to the revolt. Sviatopolk and some upper-class elements had been exploiting the lower classes, in both city and countryside, by such means as a salt monopoly and high interest rates.

The specific chronicle mention of mobs attacking and robbing Jews merits a pause to consider any possible antisemitism. The historian Vernadsky believes the rebellion was not antisemitic and suggests that Jewish financiers and wealthy merchants were attacked only because of their connection with Sviatopolk's financial policies. Even though it is true that modern racist views did not then exist in Kiev and the city usually displayed an admirable cosmopolitan spirit, it is difficult to rule out at least a tinge of anti-Jewish hostility in such circumstances. Christians in Kiev certainly believed their religion superior to Judaism, and violence had been perpetrated on Jews in other parts of Europe less than two decades earlier, at the time of the first Crusade. Kievan Christians might have been less prejudiced than some of their Western counterparts, but we cannot be sure.

Despite the likelihood that the chronicles of the times underreported and downplayed rebellions, it is clear that both the rural and the urban lower classes rebelled occasionally against what they considered excessive princely and upper-class financial demands. According to the clerical chroniclers, commoners, egged on by pagan magicians or soothsayers, also sometimes resisted the new Christian teachings.

SLAVIC-VARANGIAN EXPANSION AND FOREIGN POWERS

On the borders of Kievan Rus and beyond, the new state dealt with numerous non-East Slavic groups and powers. The frontiers were fluid, and attacks originated from both sides of the borders. This latter fact and the scant sources available make it unwise to pin labels like imperialist on combatants, whether they be Rus or Rus neighbors.

Usual reasons for Rus attacks included the desire to collect tribute and to facilitate and protect trade, communication, and frontier defenses. Kievan Rus's acceptance of Christianity and Vladimir I's marriage to the Byzantine princess Anna certainly upgraded Rus's international prestige and affected its dealings with other peoples and countries. Subsequently, Rus sources sometimes depicted attacks on pagan peoples like the Pechenegs and Polovtsy of the southern steppe regions as battles against "godless" or "infidel" foes. Yet during the Kievan Rus era, economic considerations rather than religious ones continued to be more significant in determining Rus relations with neighboring peoples.

The Rus were most successful in imposing tribute upon some of the pagan Baltic and Finnish tribes that extended from their northwestern to their northeastern boundaries. Starting in the northwest and moving along the periphery in a clockwise direction, let us now examine the situation more closely.

Kievan Rus, Slavic Tribes, and Neighboring Peoples, 900–1054

■ Controlled by Kievan Rus, c. 900

▨ Kievan Rus expansion to c. 1054

Slovenes Slavic tribes

KHAZARS Neighboring peoples

● Major cities

0   150   300 Miles

MAP 2.1

Tribes of the North

Vladimir I, Yaroslav the Wise, and Roman of Volhynia (d. 1205) all temporarily subjugated Lithuanian Yatvigians. Princes of Novgorod and Polotsk also dominated Baltic tribes, at least sporadically, such as the Estonian Chud. *The Primary Chronicle* mentions that the Varangians imposed tribute upon the Chud already in the middle of the ninth century, and Chud tribesmen often served on the side of Varangian princes such as Igor and Vladimir I. In 1030, Yaroslav the Wise conquered the Chud and founded the city of Yuriev, modern-day Tartu.

By the early thirteenth century, Novgorod and Polotsk were having trouble maintaining control over Baltic tribesmen south of the Gulf of Finland. This was due mainly to increasing competition from Germans, including crusading German knights, who moved eastward into the Baltic lands. The Novgorodian chronicle from 1190 to 1240 relates many battles against the Lithuanians and Chud, the latter especially being subjected to plunder, burnt villages, slaughtered cattle, and Novgorodian demands for tribute. After 1240, Novgorodians would be forced to contend directly with the more threatening Germanic knights, who dominated the Chud lands and Livonia (see Map 4.1).

On the northern shore of the Gulf of Finland, the Rus sporadically imposed tribute on the Finnish Yam. In the early thirteenth century, Novgorodian forces also subjugated Karelians to their east and, on orders from the Novgorodian prince, converted many of them to Christianity. Southeast of the Karelians, in the White Lake area, the Rus from the beginning collected tribute from the Finnish Ves and soon integrated them into the expanding Rus state.

From east of the Northern Dvina to the Urals, the Novgorodians attempted to gain tribute, especially furs, from three additional Finnish tribes: the Perm, Pechora, and Yugra. Although sometimes successful, they also faced rebellions. In 1193, for example, the Yugra cut down most of the troops sent to impose Novgorodian demands. Besides native rebellions, Novgorod faced twelfth- and thirteenth-century competition from Suzdalia (Vladimir-Suzdal), whose Rus princes also had their eyes on the lucrative furs.

Suzdalia was the chief Slavic antagonist of still another Finnish tribe, the Mordva, located to the east of Suzdalia. In 1221, the Suzdalian prince Yuri II began building the fortress town of Nizhnii Novgorod in Mordva territory at the Volga and Oka rivers junction. During the next decade and a half, he coordinated numerous campaigns against the Mordva, burning their lands; slaughtering their cattle; and killing, capturing, or scattering many of their people.

The Volga Bulgars and the Peoples of the Steppe

Before his successes against the Mordva, Yuri had first attacked the Volga Bulgars, who for generations had been collecting tribute from the Mordva. Competition for tribute and control of the furs in the forest lands of the Volga Finnish peoples had long been the chief source of contention between the Volga Bulgars and Rus.

The former had come to the Volga lands after the Khazars had defeated a Bulgar steppe confederation in the late seventh century—another Bulgar group moved westward into modern-day Bulgaria, where they subjugated the local Slavs. Originally Asiatic nomads, the Bulgars on the Volga, while continuing some nomadic grazing practices, gradually developed a more settled existence. They became major grain producers, Bulgar cities and crafts developed, and the Bulgars collected large quantities of furs from the northeastern Finnish peoples. They became adept traders; their location on the middle Volga put them at the center of north-south, east-west trade connecting Europe and Asia, Christian and Moslem civilizations. In 922, they converted to Islam.

The Rus both traded and fought numerous wars with them. Around 966, Sviatoslav attacked them. Vladimir I followed his father's example and assaulted them again in 985 and, after defeating them, made peace. According to *The Primary Chronicle*, the Bulgars stated: "May peace prevail between us till stone floats and straw sinks."[7]

Of course, peace did not last quite that long. Yet for the next 100 years, Rus-Bulgar relations were characterized much more by trade than by war.

In 1088, the Bulgars captured the Rus city of Murom (originally the home of the Finnic Murom people) and in succeeding decades became an increasing threat to the eastern borders of Murom-Riazan and Suzdalia. During the twelfth and early thirteenth centuries, however, Suzdalia became significantly stronger and gradually gained the upper hand over the Bulgars.

In 1220, Yuri II's large army captured and devastated much Bulgar territory. The vanquished sought and agreed to terms, including the loss of some territory, and peaceful relations were restored. Unbeknownst to either side, they were soon to encounter a much greater danger than each other—the Mongols.

Southwest of the Bulgar territory, the Rus faced successive Asiatic peoples who roamed the southern steppes north of the Black Sea and Caucasus. Three major groups followed each other in dominating the region: the Khazars, the Pechenegs, and the Polovtsy.

Dominant in the area after defeating the Bulgars in the late seventh century, the Khazars constructed a major empire centered on the lower Volga. In the beginning of the tenth century, this empire still included the Volga Bulgars and some Eastern Slavs among its tributaries. Most of Kievan Rus's early Asiatic trade passed through Khazar lands.

By the mid-tenth century, however, the Khazars had begun to weaken, and in the 960s the forces of the mighty Sviatoslav inflicted a shattering series of defeats on them. Their capital Itil and other Khazar strongholds were captured and plundered. In this same period, Sviatoslav subjugated the Slavic Viatichians, who resided along the Oka River and had been paying tribute to the Khazars. They now became his tributaries.

No doubt worried about Rus successes so close to its Black Sea possessions, the Byzantine Empire soon bribed Sviatoslav to divert his attention and forces westward against the Bulgars of Bulgaria. For this and other reasons, Rus influence on the lower Volga failed to develop; on the contrary, another Asiatic group now became dominant in the southern steppe area, the Pech-

---

[7] Ibid., p. 96.

enegs. The death of Sviatoslav at their hands, in 972, less than a decade after his great victory over the Khazars, was a foreshadowing of more conflict ahead with these formidable nomads.

Prior to the defeat of the Khazars, the Pechenegs had not been especially threatening to the Rus. In fact, Pecheneg mercenaries had assisted Igor in a campaign of 944 against the Byzantines. From 968 to 972, however, they allied with the Byzantines against Sviatoslav, who by then was threatening Byzantine interests in Bulgaria. From this period until Yaroslav the Wise drove them back from attacking Kiev around 1036, the Rus fought numerous battles with these nomads. This was especially true under Vladimir I, who fostered colonization along the Rus southern borderlands and built a series of forts there. Conflict over these border territories and the desire for booty and other economic gains—perhaps emanating from the Rus as well as the Pechenegs—seem to have been the main reasons for the warfare. Some historians have suggested that Vladimir was further motivated by a desire to unify Kievan Rus, and attacking the pagan Pechenegs was a means to this end.

As we have seen earlier, however, these conflicts did not prevent Sviatopolk, Vladimir's son, from using some Pecheneg mercenaries in his civil war against his brother Yaroslav. And if the entire history of Rus-Pecheneg relations is taken as a whole, it was characterized much more by mutually beneficial trading relations than by warfare.

In the 1060s, a new group of Turkish nomads, the Polovtsy (or Cumans) began dominating the southern steppe. Like Rus-Pecheneg relations, Rus-Polovtsy dealings included countless raids and wars. Vladimir Monomakh's claim that he signed nineteen peace treaties with the Polovtsy, either on his own or acting for his father, indicates how frequent the wars preceding the peaces must have been. A great classic of Rus literature, *The Tale of Igor's Campaign*, deals with a battle against the Polovtsy in 1185.

Yet Rus princes also traded with them, sometimes married their princesses, and often engaged bands of them to help fight against other Rus princes, especially in the early thirteenth century. At times Polovtsy even fought against each other in the service of contending Rus princes.

Although Rus's relations to the southeast were primarily with the Khazars, Pechenegs, and Polovtsy, the Kievan state also dealt with some of the many peoples of the Caucasus. This was especially true when Mstislav, the brother of Yaroslav the Wise, ruled over Tmutarakan on the Black Sea and over Ossetians and Circassians further inland—our knowledge of Rus rule over the remote Tmutarakan during the tenth and eleventh centuries is sketchy, but it certainly was an exception to the steppe peoples' general dominance of the zone north of the Black Sea.

Byzantium and Bulgaria

Mention of the Black Sea now brings us to one of Rus's most important neighbors, Byzantium. Although in decline from its earlier heyday, this empire, with its capital at Constantinople, was still a great center of civilization. It controlled most of the Balkan Peninsula. And it won not only the Rus, but also most of the Balkan Slavs over to Christianity, radiating its religious-cultural influence over their lands.

At first, the Rus chiefly sought favorable trade with the Byzantines. The Rus princes, warriors, and merchants—thanks largely to the tribute goods they collected—sailed down the Dnieper River to the Black Sea and Constantinople. There they traded furs, wax, honey, and slaves with the Byzantines, primarily for luxury goods. *The Primary Chronicle* relates how Prince Oleg furthered Rus trade by attacking Constantinople in 907 with 2,000 ships and land forces. After the Rus burned and destroyed palaces and churches on the outskirts of the city and tortured, beheaded, and flung various captives into the sea, the besieged government in the city agreed to Oleg's terms. The resulting agreement, as found in the chronicle, was indeed favorable to Oleg. The Byzantines agreed to a large monetary payment. They also agreed that future Rus trade would be tax-free and that the Byzantines would provide provisions for Rus merchants, both while in a suburb of Constantinople and for their journey homeward.

Although the chronicle account is somewhat suspect, the Rus undoubtedly won favorable trade concessions from Byzantium at about this time. Another treaty of 911 indicates that the Byzantine Empire was willing to trade on equal terms with the infant state of Kievan Rus.

Under subsequent Kievan princes, the Rus continued trading and occasionally warring with the Byzantines. *The Primary Chronicle* recounts numerous bloody details of campaigns against Byzantium. In 941, for example, Prince Igor's forces used some captives as targets for their arrows and drove iron nails through the heads of others. On this occasion, however, they were eventually bested and scattered by the Byzantines, who used "Greek fire," pipes through which they directed mysterious flames, on the Rus ships.

Despite such sporadic conflicts, Byzantium desired good relations with Kievan Rus. Winning the Rus over to Christianity could help achieve that goal. When Olga was baptized, it apparently occurred in Constantinople, with the Byzantine Emperor and Empress acting as her godparents. In the years after Vladimir's conversion in 988, Rus-Byzantine trade flourished, only occasionally marred by differences. Byzantine religious-cultural influences and church leaders began flowing into Rus. Other friendly contacts also increased. Following Vladimir I's example, some Rus princes and princesses married Byzantine royalty, and Rus princes and soldiers on occasion aided the Byzantine Emperor in military campaigns.

To the southeast of Rus stood Bulgaria, where the Asiatic Bulgars had played a role among native Slavic peoples analogous to that of the Varangians in Rus. Despite Bulgaria's adoption of Christianity and significant Byzantine Christian influences on it, the Bulgars often warred against the Byzantines. The Byzantines, however, had no desire to see Bulgaria fall under Sviatoslav's control. Following his successful campaigns against the Bulgars, the Byzantine Emperor sent troops to help defeat him. After Sviatoslav's departure, the Byzantines gradually subjugated Bulgaria to themselves, and Bulgarian-Rus relations were then mainly limited to the cultural-religious domain.

Hungary, Poland, and Other Western Contacts

North of Bulgaria and just across the Carpathian Mountains from the Rus principality of Galicia stood Hungary. Four Hungarian kings in this era had Rus wives. In the interprincely wars of the twelfth century, the Hungarians often allied with Rus Volhynia or Kiev against Galicia. In the late 1180s, the King of Hungary (Bela III) even succeeded in briefly placing his son Andrew on the Galician throne. In the three decades following the death of Prince Roman of Volhynia-Galicia in 1205, the Hungarians were almost constantly involved in Galician squabbles. But they were hardly alone. Other Rus principalities and Hungary's northern neighbor, Poland, also intervened in conflicts involving various Galician factions.

Despite such Polish interventions, the first reported major clash between the Poles and Rus was initiated by Vladimir I. According to *The Primary Chronicle* entry for 981, "he marched upon the Lyakhs [Poles] and took their cities: Peremÿshl', Cherven, and other towns"[8]—many Russian historians maintain, however, that they were more properly Rus towns and were primarily populated not by Poles, but by East Slavs. Following his conversion to Christianity, according to the chronicle, Vladimir lived in peace with Poland, also recently Christianized, albeit from Rome.

After the death of Vladimir, Poland temporarily regained the cities lost to Vladimir. In 1031, however, Yaroslav the Wise and his brother Mstislav marched into Poland with a large army and ravaged the countryside. They not only captured the disputed cities, but also many Poles, some of whom Yaroslav settled as colonists along the Pecheneg frontier.

During the next 200 years, trade and numerous Rus-Polish dynastic marriages coexisted with interventions in each other's affairs. This was especially true after both countries became more politically fragmented during the early twelfth century. In fact, sometimes the interventions were to help out an in-law—at least eighteen Rus princes or princesses in the Kievan period had Polish spouses. During the 1040s, for example, Yaroslav aided his brother-in-law Casimir the Restorer to put down the Polish Mazovians. Of course, princes from both countries also sought gains for themselves, such as disputed border territories.

Although Rus relations with border peoples and states were often punctuated with conflict, dealings with more distant European powers were more peaceful. The Rus traded with Scandinavians and Germans and sometimes married their royalty. A daughter of Vsevolod I of Kiev married the German Holy Roman Emperor Henry IV in 1089. Although Rus relations with France and England were not close, Anna, a daughter of Yaroslav the Wise, married Henry I, King of France; and Vladimir Monomakh married Gyda of England, daughter of King Harold II, who had been killed in the battle of Hastings by William the Conqueror.

---

[8] Ibid., p. 95.

As a result of such foreign marriages, the blood of many races ran through the veins of later Kievan princes. Vladimir Monomakh, for example, was the son of a Byzantine princess and the grandson of a Swedish princess. Thus, late Kievan princes and princesses, who continued such marriage practices, were walking symbols of a society still very much in touch with the larger world around them.

SUGGESTED SOURCES

CHADWICK, NORA. *The Beginnings of Russian History: An Enquiry Into Sources*. New York, 1946.

CHERNIAVSKY, MICHAEL. *Tsar and People: Studies in Russian Myths*. New Haven, 1961.

CROSS, SAMUEL HAZZARD, and OLGERD SHERBOWITZ-WETZOR, eds. *The Russian Primary Chronicle: Laurentian Text*. Cambridge, Mass., 1953.

DIMNIK, MARTIN. *The Dynasty of Chernigov, 1054–1146*. Toronto, 1994.

DUBOV, I. V. "The Ethnic History of Northeastern Rus', in the Ninth to Thirteenth Centuries." *RRH*, pp. 14–20.

ENNIS, MICHAEL. *Byzantium*. New York, 1989.

GOLDEN, PETER B. "Aspects of the Nomadic Factor in the Economic Development of Kievan Rus'." In *Ukrainian Economic History: Interpretive Essays*, ed. I. S. Koropeckyj. Cambridge, Mass., 1991.

GREKOV, BORIS. *Kiev Rus*. Moscow. 1959.

KOLLMANN, NANCY SHIELDS. "Collateral Succession in Kievan Rus'," *HUS* 14 (December 1990): 377–385.

LENHOFF, GAIL. *The Martyred Princes Boris and Gleb: A Socio-cultural Study of the Cult and the Texts*. Columbus, Ohio, 1989.

MARTIN, JANET. *Medieval Russia, 980–1584*. Cambridge, England, 1995. Chs. 1–2.

NOONAN, THOMAS S. "The Flourishing of Kiev's International and Domestic Trade, Ca. 1100–Ca. 1240." In *Ukrainian Economic History: Interpretive Essays*, ed. I. S. Koropeckyj. Cambridge, Mass., 1991.

———. "Kievan Rus." *MERSH* 16: 230–245.

NORWICH, JOHN JULIUS. *Byzantium*. 3 vols. London and New York, 1988–1996.

OBOLENSKY, DIMITRI. *The Byzantine Commonwealth: Eastern Europe, 500–1453*. London, 1971.

PALSSON, HERMANN, and PAUL EDWARDS, trans. *Vikings in Russia: Yngvar's Saga and Eymund's Saga*. Edinburgh, 1989.

PASZKIEWICZ, HENRYK. *The Making of the Russian Nation*. Chicago, 1963.

———. *The Origin of Russia*. New York, 1954.

POPPE, ANDRZEJ. "Christianity and Ideological Change in Kievan Rus': The First Hundred Years." *CASS* 25 (1991): 3–26.

———. "Once Again Concerning the Baptism of Olga, Archontissa of Rus'." *DOP* No. 46 (1992): 271–277.

PRITSAK, OMELJAN. *The Origin of Rus'*. Cambridge, Mass., 1981.

RH 19, Nos. 1–4 (1992). Contains several articles dealing with Rus frontiers.

RYBAKOV, BORIS. *Kievan Rus*. Moscow, 1989.

SAWYER, P. H. *The Age of the Vikings*. London, 1962.

———. *Kings and Vikings: Scandinavia and Europe, A.D. 700–1100*. London, 1982.

SOKOL, EDWARD D. "Veche." *MERSH* 41: 238–242.

VASILIEV, ALEXANDER A. *The Second Russian Attack on Constantinople*. Cambridge, Mass., 1951.

VERNADSKY, GEORGE. *Kievan Russia*. New Haven, 1948.

———. *The Origins of Russia*. Oxford, 1959.

VOLKOFF, VLADIMIR. *Vladimir: The Russian Viking*. London, 1984.

CHAPTER 3

Kievan Society, Religion, and Culture

Two phenomena that greatly affected political life also left a strong imprint on Rus's economy, society, and culture. The first was the tribute-and-trading emphasis of the Rus princes and their supporters, and the second was the Rus acceptance of Christianity. One leading Western scholar points to these developments in the Kievan principality in the following passage:

> Kiev's trade began in the tenth century but at that time it functioned as a mafioso extortion operation run by the princes. Kiev's true trade only started in the eleventh century and was sparked by the growing local demand for a variety of expensive and sophisticated goods by an increasingly sedentarized ruling class and a new ecclesiastical market. In this process, the Rus' conversion to Orthodoxy seems to have acted as a powerful catalyst in refining tastes, introducing new crafts and advanced methods, and creating markets.[1]

The relationship of the tribute extortioners (the princes and their followers) of the early Rus state with the ruling elite of late Kievan Rus is a complex question, but the latter certainly seem to have evolved primarily from the former. Payments extracted from the common people, whether in the form of tribute, taxes, customs duties, fines, or other means, continued to support the ruling elite throughout the Kievan Rus period. After the acceptance of Christianity, the church hierarchy became part of this elite, and it too received a share of the people's payments.

In exchange, however, the Rus elite provided some needed services, such as military protection from outside forces. And if Vladimir and the Rus elite supported the establishment of Christianity partly for their own interests, its spread in Rus still produced many positive consequences for the Rus people and their culture.

[1] Thomas S. Noonan, "The Flourishing of Kiev's International and Domestic Trade, ca. 1100–ca. 1240," in *Ukrainian Economic History: Interpretive Essays*, ed. I. S. Koropeckyj (Cambridge, Mass., 1991), p. 144.

THE TOWNS

It was in urban areas, where the elite mainly resided, that Rus Christianity developed first and only slowly spread into the countryside. The presence of the political, social, and religious elite in the towns, plus the towns' role as centers for tribute-gathering and trade, helped make urban life vigorous in Kievan Rus. By the end of the Kievan era, almost 300 towns existed. Although many contained fewer than 1,000 people, others were large. According to the historian Tikhomirov's estimates, Novgorod had between 10,000 and 15,000 people in the early eleventh century and between 20,000 and 30,000 during the early thirteenth century. In 1200, Kiev had about 40,000 to 50,000 inhabitants. Other fairly large towns included Chernigov, Galich, Pereiaslavl (in the south), Vladimir (in the northeast), Polotsk, and Smolensk. In comparison, Paris had about 60,000 inhabitants in the early thirteenth century and London about half of that.

Although some cities were founded by Varangian princes, others predated their arrival. Even before the establishment of the Kievan state, Slavs and other peoples had established fortresses. Usually overlooking a river, they often sat on high ground for defense purposes, and some of them eventually became pre-Kievan towns.

During the Kievan era, some old fortresses were enlarged or replaced with more secure citadels or kremlins. They were often surrounded by ditches or moats and ramparts made of the dug-up dirt. Topping the wooden fortress walls, there might be a platform surrounded by a wooden parapet with openings for archers to shoot at the enemy. The walls usually contained towers and at least one gate, sometimes made of stone. Although much bigger and stone-walled, Moscow's still-existing Kremlin gives some idea of Kievan Rus's citadels, as does the smaller one still standing in Novgorod (see Figure 6.1).

If the citadel symbolized a city's defense, its *posad* (suburb) embodied its trade. Only very small cities, such as frontier fortress towns, lacked a *posad*. Although no absolute segregation existed between those who lived in the citadel and those residing in the *posad*, elite elements were dominant in the citadel, which often sat up on a hill, and tradesmen and craftsmen generally settled and peddled their goods in the *posad*, which was frequently below the citadel and near a river. As a town's suburb grew, authorities also often fortified it but less extensively, for example, by putting earthen walls around it.

Most town buildings were wooden, partly for reasons of warmth. The chief exception was that of major churches. The most common wooden buildings resembled log cabins. Some houses were completely above ground; others, set up in hollowed-out pits, were partly subterranean. In larger cities, streets and walkways were made of logs. Although most students will never visit Kiev's Historical Museum to see its excellent scale model of ancient Kiev, many can more easily view Sergei Eisenstein's great film *Alexander Nevsky*, which transmits some idea of old Novgorod's look.

Craftsmen in Rus cities included the following: blacksmiths, bootmakers, bow-makers, carpenters, coppersmiths, glassmakers, goldsmiths, iconogra-

FIGURE 3.1. The Golden Gate of Kiev, a reconstruction of the main entrance to the city of Kiev, built during the reign of Yaroslav the Wise.

phers, jewelry-makers, locksmiths, potters, scribes, saddle-makers, shield-makers, shipbuilders, silversmiths, stonemasons, tanners, tinsmiths, and weavers. (This is only about half the number that could be listed.) In some large towns, craftsmen practicing a similar craft often resided near each other, and chronicles mentioned such areas as tanners' streets or carpenters' quarters.

In most towns, the busiest area was the *posad* marketplace. Here town criers often issued orders and made announcements. Here, besides urban craft products, people could buy grain, bread, salt, fish, meat, furs, honey, wax, flax, lard, and peasant-made artifacts. Prices fluctuated according to supply and demand.

FOREIGN AND DOMESTIC TRADE

Even before the beginnings of Kievan Rus, foreign and domestic trade was important in the future Rus lands. The city of Staraia Ladoga, for example, was a multiethnic international trading center already in the late eighth century. Archaeological findings here and elsewhere indicate an active Baltic-Volga trade that linked Europe with the Moslem world.

After the early Varangian princes gained control over trade routes and integrated their tribute gathering with international trade, the Dnieper route to Constantinople gradually gained more prominence. Rus trade with the Volga Bulgars and peoples of the steppe remained important throughout the Rus era. In the north, Novgorod gradually emerged as an important Baltic trading area, with foreign Baltic merchants residing in the city.

Chief Rus exports were furs, honey, wax, and especially in the early Kievan period, slaves. Other exports included flax, lard, hemp, hides, hops, sheepskin, walrus bones, and some handicraft items. Among the major imported goods were arms, fabrics, fruits and wine, glassware, expensive pottery, horses, amber and metal products, silver, silks, spices, and gems. The upper classes and the church were the primary buyers of such imports.

Demand for luxury items fostered their production, when possible, within Rus lands. Craftsmen in Kiev, for example, began producing increasing amounts of expensive jewelry. Some of it, along with other products such as religious wares and glass bracelets (which became commonplace), was sent to other cities, reflecting a growing intercity trade.

RURAL LIFE

Although town life was vigorous, at least four-fifths of the Rus population probably lived in the countryside, many of them clustered around towns. The rural inhabitants were primarily responsible for paying tribute or direct taxes—small cities paid lesser amounts, large cities were exempt, and the upper classes were exempt regardless of where they lived.

Most peasants eked out an existence for themselves by supplementing their farming yields with what the forests, lakes, and rivers offered. Land near lakes and rivers was more fertile and thus generally preferred. The type of farming practiced depended largely on geographical location and soils available. In the south, in the transitional forest-steppe and steppe lands, two-field and later three-field crop rotation were common. While such rotation, with variations, also existed in the northern forest zone, the "slash-and-burn" technique of clearing new forest lands remained popular. When these lands became exhausted, peasants often moved to new areas and slashed and burnt again. This contributed to the colonization of Rus lands and the dispersion of the Rus peasantry.

In the early Kievan era, peasants owned the overwhelming majority of rural lands—the St. Petersburg historian I. Froianov, among others, has argued that this was still true in the late Kievan era. Most peasants farmed in family or territorial communes, with the latter gradually becoming more common. Although little concrete evidence is available, peasants in territorial communes probably had private rights over segments of land and its produce, while sharing common pastures, forests, and streams.

During the eleventh century, princes, boyars, and the church became important landowners of country properties. Although many newly owned private lands might have been previously uninhabited, it seems likely that others were simply expropriated from the peasants farming them. The lands that princes gave to their boyar followers had no service strings attached. Thus, they were not like Western European fiefs, and feudalism in the sense that Western scholars use the word did not exist in Kievan Rus.

The peasants working on upper-class private landholdings were not serfs and thus were not permanently tied to the land of a private landowner. If they wished to farm land for their own use, they had to make payment (in money, produce, or labor) to the landowner. Some became indebted/indentured workers, not free to leave their master's service until they paid their debts. Others were simply hired hands.

If serfdom did not exist, however, slavery did, both in urban and rural areas. Some slaves worked on estates along with the peasants. People became slaves in a variety of ways, including capture in war, being born of slave parents, or running away before repaying a master his debt.

CLASS STRUCTURE AND THE MILITARY

The best evidence regarding the class structure of Kievan Rus comes from the era's law codes. Because we deal with the Christian clergy and the people under their jurisdiction later, here we are concerned only with the secular ladder. Beneath the princes and princesses at the top came the boyars and their families. By the late Kievan period, the boyars included both the prince's *druzhina*, whose members served the prince in various military and governmental capacities, and other prominent upper-class citizens. Beneath the boyars were several classes of free citizens, which included most merchants and urban workers. Next came the largest class, the peasants, including those working for private landowners.

At the bottom of the ladder came the indentured workers and urban and rural slaves. Frequent law code references to slaves make it clear that slaveholding by the upper classes in Kievan Rus was widespread. Some slaves were held only temporarily. Prisoners-of-war who were eventually ransomed fell into this category. Of course, permanent slaves had no rights and could even be killed by their owners, although this made little economic sense and therefore did not occur often.

The Kievan class structure was fairly fluid. The boyar class, for example, was open to newcomers who achieved prominence. The distinctions between classes were not as rigid as they might first seem. Despite being entrusted with important administrative and supervisory duties by their prince or boyar, some stewards were themselves slaves. (Partly because of the fluidity of Kievan social groupings, some historians have abandoned the use of the term "class" in describing the Kievan social structure, but used in a general sense it remains a useful term for this and later periods.)

For a prince and his *druzhina*, fighting was part of normal existence, as was death in battle. In his *Instruction to His Children*, Vladimir Monomakh stated that he had participated in eighty-three military campaigns. Standard equipment for a *druzhina* warrior included a helmet, body armor, a shield, a sword, and a spear. When not fighting, a prince and his *druzhina* enjoyed hunting. Vladimir Monomakh related that he hunted a hundred times a year, and, among other adventures, had been tossed by bison, gored by a stag and by an elk, had his sword torn from his thigh by a boar, and had his kneecap bitten by a bear.

For larger battles, the princes often used city militias and foreign mercenaries. If a prince called upon a militia, he generally provided some of its members with horses. He also provided some of their weapons. Mounted mercenaries from the steppe were especially skillful with bows and arrows and were an important supplement to a prince's own *druzhina* cavalry.

WOMEN

The position of women in Kievan Rus can be divided into two periods, the pre-Christian and Christian. Evidence for the first is murky, but it seems that among other deities, the native Slavs worshipped a Mother Earth fertility goddess and were in awe of other powerful female spirits such as the *rusalki* (water and tree nymphs). The early Rus also paid homage to fictional Amazon-like warrior heroines in some of their folk literature.

For this early period, *The Primary Chronicle* provides additional information. Although no doubt exaggerated in places, the accounts regarding women are generally believable. Although it states that the Polianian tribe respected peaceful marriage customs and monogamy, men in some other east Slavic tribes seized the women they wished by capture rather than by marrying properly, and they practiced polygamy. Princes such as Vladimir, before accepting Christianity, also took women against their will. The chronicle recounts that Princess Rogned refused to marry him, but that Vladimir attacked the forces of her father, the Prince of Polotsk, and, after killing her father and two brothers, took her for his bride. After speaking of his other wives and concubines, the chronicle later adds that he "seduced married women and violated young girls."[2]

In the chronicle account, Rogned's reply to her father's inquiry about marrying Vladimir is: "I will not draw off the boots of a slave's son."[3] Besides alluding to the lowly social position of Vladimir's mother (his grandmother's stewardess), the comment refers to the marriage ceremony custom of the bride removing her groom's boots as a sign of her submission. Another ritual was for the bride's father to hand over a whip to the groom. Both customs leave little doubt that the husband was the intended head of the household.

Yet, there are indications that the position of women in pre-Christian Rus

---

[2] Samuel Hazard Cross and Olgerd P. Sherbowitz-Wetzor, eds., *The Primary Chronicle* (Cambridge, Mass., 1953), p. 94.
[3] Ibid., p. 91.

was stronger than in some Western European countries. The story of Rogned tells us that at least in this one case a father did not force his daughter to marry against her will. The rule of the forceful Princess Olga and the chronicle's admiration for her are also notable, as is the presence of a few envoys for Russian princesses among a large Rus peace delegation to Constantinople in 945.

With the coming of Christianity, the position of women changed—no doubt gradually because pagan practices died out slowly in rural areas. In some ways, the church view of women was positive; at least it was of pious women. Mary, the mother of Jesus, was greatly revered and in the popular mind took on some attributes of Mother Earth. *The Primary Chronicle* (written and compiled by monks) quoted Solomon in the Bible when he elaborated on how a good woman was more precious than jewels. The church encouraged the proper treatment of widows. It opposed such customs as bride capture and polygamy and encouraged parents not to force their daughters into unwanted marriages. Church legal jurisdiction over matters such as divorce, adultery, rape, and property disputes between husband and wife probably helped women more than it hurt them, but divorce laws reflect more concern with a wife's guilt than a husband's, and church laws sometimes allowed a husband to punish his wife, for example, for stealing from him.

Furthermore, the church displayed a fear of women's sexuality and power. The advice of Vladimir Monomakh to his sons—"Love your wives, but let them not rule you"[4]—reflects well his church's ambivalence toward women. He also warned his sons against conversing with shameless women.

The monastic authors of *The Primary Chronicle* exhibit other examples of wariness about women. After writing of Vladimir I's licentious behavior, they add: "The charm of woman is an evil thing." They go on to quote Solomon: "Listen not to an evil woman. Honey flows from the lips of a licentious woman. . . . They who cleave to her shall die in hell."[5] Later in the account of Vladimir's conversion, a Byzantine scholar tells Vladimir: "the human race first sinned through women,"[6] and recounts the Biblical story of Adam and Eve.

Further church attitudes toward women are indicated by the prohibition on women from attending church services during their menstrual periods or for forty days after the birth of a child.

The status of women was reflected in civil as well as church laws. By the end of the Kievan era, an upper-class woman had the right to inherit and own moveable property, including the dowry she brought into her marriage. She could run the estate of a deceased husband, and her children could not dispose of her portion of her husband's will. Peasant and lower-class urban women's rights, however, were much more limited and generally ignored in legal documents.

[4] Leo Wiener, *Anthology of Russian Literature: From the Earliest Period to the Present Time* (New York, 1902), Vol. I, p. 54.
[5] Cross and Sherbowitz-Wetzor, p. 94.
[6] Ibid., p. 109.

Even upper-class women remained far from equal. Men had many economic and political rights women did not, especially regarding landed property and voting—only men could vote at *veche* meetings.

Although little is known about the economic roles of Rus urban women outside the household, there are legal references to handicraftswomen. One craft they were especially adept at was weaving. Out of hemp and flax yarn, they made both male and female garments.

SECULAR AND CHURCH LAW

There were primarily three sources of Kievan law: the community, the prince, and the church. In the early Kievan period, the judicial functions of a person's community were still of great importance. But with the passage of time and the coming of Christianity, they decreased in comparison to the powers of the princely and church courts.

The first written law code, Yaroslav's *Russkaia Pravda*, was based primarily on the customary law of Rus communities. It detailed which relatives were allowed to avenge a murder and how much compensation had to be paid for various crimes. Cutting off another's arm, leg, mustache, or beard necessitated payment, as did the theft of various articles. Following the death of Yaroslav, his sons and later princes made additions and revisions to the original code. The final revision, completed by the early thirteenth century, is commonly known as the Expanded *Pravda*.

The total effect of the law codes was to replace much blood vengeance with monetary fines. In addition, the revisions added a new class of payments that went to the prince for such crimes as killing his estate workers or stealing from him. The codes reflected both an attempt to change certain types of customary behavior and to enrich princely coffers.

Where possible, restitution for an offense was arranged outside of court. In the courts, the presiding official was often a trusted servitor, sometimes a slave, of the ruling prince. He acted primarily as a referee between a plaintiff and a defendant. While he accepted such proof as eyewitness accounts and written deeds, he often made decisions based upon less reliable evidence.

In a society of few written documents, the presiding official often had to rely on the fallible memories of community members. As a last and frequent resort, he could appeal to Divine intervention to help him reach a decision. Such appeals to God included oaths and ordeals by water or iron. The logic behind oaths was that individuals would not risk Divine displeasure by lying under oath; therefore it was likely that they were telling the truth. The hot iron ordeal, in which Divine intervention would supposedly keep an innocent person from being burnt, was apparently more common than the water ordeal. In the latter, an individual was thrown into the water with a rope attached, and probably with a hand bound to each foot. If the person bobbed back up, he or she was guilty—the pure water rejecting such an "unclean" person. If the individual sank, he or she was innocent—the attached rope presumably enabling the sinking person to be pulled out before drowning.

Although fines were the usual punishment, the Expanded *Pravda* also provided for harsher penalties, such as confiscation of property. Unprovoked murderers, horse thieves, arsonists, and repeat offenders were all liable to such punishment—and perhaps (the code's wording is unclear) to banishment. Imprisonment was uncommon, and the law did not provide for capital punishment, although it allowed the killing of a thief while caught in the act. This did not mean, however, that princes always refrained from killing other Rus they considered enemies.

An interesting aspect of Kievan law was the collective responsibility for certain crimes. For example, according to late Kievan law, a community was responsible collectively for paying a fine if it did not search for and turn over the murderer of one of the prince's men or dependents.

Regarding church legal rights, there is some dispute over the proper dating of statutes granting them. Yet it seems safe to assume that by the end of the Kievan era the church possessed such authority as outlined in statutes ascribed to Vladimir I and Yaroslav the Wise, at least in some parts of Rus.

By these statutes, the Orthodox bishops exercised legal jurisdiction over not only priests, nuns, and monks, but also over such church people as choir singers; wards of the church; and those who worked in church-run institutions, such as hospitals and asylums. Church courts had general jurisdiction not only over divorce, adultery, rape, and property disputes between husband and wife, but also over such matters as witchcraft, sorcery, soothsaying, kidnapping a girl, calling someone a whore or heretic, or beating one's mother or father. Finally, ecclesiastical courts dealt with various offenses against church property. One code prohibited leading cattle, fowl, or dogs into a church except during an emergency.

As unusual as many practices of Kievan law might seem to modern students, many of them, including ordeals, were also once common to other societies. If Rus law in many ways was "behind" Western law, it was largely due to the late arrival of statehood and Christianity. Even during the late Kievan period, government and church law still contended with tribal customary law. Perhaps partly because the government's judicial role was not yet as strong as in Byzantium or in many Western European countries, Rus governmental justice seems less harsh in many ways. Both capital and corporal punishment and the use of torture to obtain confessions were more common in the West and in Byzantium than in Kievan Rus.

RELIGION AND CULTURE

In both religion and culture, Kievan Rus was strongly influenced by the Byzantine Empire. These Byzantine influences, along with lesser foreign ones, mixed with native Slavic traditions to create a unique religious-cultural blend in the Rus lands.

Paganism and the Acceptance of Christianity

Prior to accepting Christianity, the Rus worshipped deities and spirits. Some had long been present among the Slavs, and others were brought by the Varangians. Much Rus worship was like that of other tribal religions around the world, yet it was especially characterized by a strong worship of earth and ancestor deities and spirits. Among those of the earth were the already mentioned Mother Earth and the *rusalki* (water and tree nymphs). Of the ancestral forces, Rod and Rozhanitsy were the most important. They were male and female fertility deities representing the reproductive power of a person's clan—the word *rod* meaning clan. Veneration of the *domovoi* (house spirit), thought to be the founder of the *rod*, also reflected the ancestor cult. Although less "sky"-oriented than some pagans, the early Rus revered several deities of the heavens, most notably Perun, the god of thunder.

Although Vladimir had earlier constructed a pantheon dedicated to pagan gods, *The Primary Chronicle* tells us that after accepting Christianity, he ordered the pagan idols destroyed. Sources indicate, however, continued pagan manifestations and resistance, especially in rural areas. Moreover, vestiges of Rus paganism continued up to modern times in folklore and certain folk customs. For many generations of Rus descendants, a strong love and regard for their ancestors and for mother earth was especially characteristic. The East Slavic nations were among only a small number of European peoples who continued using patronymic names—for example, Ivanovich or Ivanovna, indicating a son or daughter of Ivan. And the awareness of being part of a larger clan continued to affect Rus descendants' attitudes about community and personal destiny.

As in other countries, with the coming of Christianity certain elements of pagan feasts and rituals lived on in new, but subordinate, guises. For example, painting eggs at Easter had been earlier associated with pagan rituals welcoming the coming of spring. And Christian saints sometimes took over roles of pagan deities. The prophet Elijah for instance was ascribed the thunder-making powers of Perun. Church leaders tolerated some minor mingling of pagan vestiges with Christianity, but they severely criticized the continuing influence of sorcerers, whom many Rus continued to value for their magical and healing powers.

For a long time, scholars have written of *dvoeverie* (double-faith) to characterize Rus and Russian folk religion, which they believed remained basically pagan underneath its Christian surface. More recently, however, this approach has been criticized for failing to recognize that premodern believers of all social strata approached the world far differently than most modern Christians. Medieval Christianity and paganism shared many qualities that in today's more rationalized world are thought characteristic only of pagan beliefs. Scholars using the *dvoeverie* concept frequently drew too sharp a line between a Christian elite and pagan folk and failed to acknowledge that beliefs of commoners influenced the Christian elite and vice-versa.

Vladimir Christianizes Rus

The following account is an excerpt from Leo Wiener, *Anthology of Russian Literature: From the Earliest Period to the Present Time* (New York, 1902) Vol. I, pp. 67, 70. It is a translation from *The Primary Chronicle* for the years 987–988. This story of the conversion is shrouded in myths but reflects two important truths: The Rus greatly valued the beauty of Byzantine liturgy and church art and architecture, and Vladimir imposed Christianity and attacked Rus paganism. Bracketed material and ellipses are mine.

Said Vladimir: "The men we have sent away have come back. Let us hear what has happened!" And he said: "Speak before the druzhina!" and they spoke: . . . "We went to Greece [Byzantium], and they took us where they worship their God, and we do not know whether we were in heaven or upon earth, for there is not upon earth such sight or beauty. We were perplexed, but this much

we know that there God lives among men, and their service is better than in any other country. We cannot forget that beauty, for every man that has partaken of sweetness will not afterwards accept bitterness, and thus we can no longer remain in our former condition". . . .

Upon his return [from the Crimean city of Kherson, where the chronicle says Vladimir was baptized], he ordered the idols to be cast down, and some to be cut to pieces, and others to be consumed by fire; but Perun he had tied to the tail of a horse, and dragged down the hill over the Borichev to the brook. . . . As he was dragged along the brook to the Dnieper, the unbelievers wept over him, for they had not yet received the holy baptism, and he was cast into the Dnieper. . . .

After that Vladimir proclaimed throughout the whole city: "Whosoever will not appear to-morrow at the river, whether he be rich or poor, or a beggar, or a workingman, will be in my disfavour."

Following the events described above, the chronicle reports that a great multitude went into the Dnieper the next day to be baptized. Vladimir also forced children from leading families to be instructed in the new faith. In other cities, the chronicle says that he began "to invite"[7] the people to accept baptism, but undoubtedly Rus authorities—like those in many countries under similar circumstances—applied more pressure than that. Freedom of religion was not a characteristic of medieval life.

Church Organization and Byzantine Influences

The Rus church was under the jurisdiction of the patriarch of Constantinople, who normally selected its head, the metropolitan of Kiev. The metropolitan, in turn, at least in theory, appointed the Rus bishops. Local princes also had a say, as, to a lesser extent, did the populace, especially in Novgorod. Partly as a result of the wishes of princes in lesser towns, the number of Rus bishops increased from about three or four under Vladimir I to fifteen by 1237. Many of

[7] Ibid., p. 117.

the bishops during this more than 200 years came from Byzantium, as did all but two metropolitans.

Underneath the bishops were parish priests and deacons (white clergy), monks (black clergy), and nuns. As in Byzantium, only married men could become parish priests, whereas monks were not married, and only they could be ordained bishops. During the Kievan Rus period, the number of clergy, churches, and monasteries greatly increased. From 988 to 1240, records reveal the construction of 450 churches and monasteries, but Fennell is undoubtedly correct in assuming that these *known* constructions were only a small percentage of the total, especially of churches. The most famous monastery was the Kievan Crypt Monastery, founded in the middle of the eleventh century. Like some of the other monasteries, but even more so, it served as a center of writing and learning.

The year 1054 marked not only an important political milestone—the death of Yaroslav the Wise—but also a religious event of momentous consequences for the Rus people and their descendants. A legate from the pope in Rome excommunicated the patriarch of Constantinople. Because earlier tensions had existed between the two offices and it was by no means clear in 1054 that an irreconcilable schism had occurred, contemporaries did not then realize how significant that year's split would become.

The main cause for it was a dispute over papal authority, but doctrinal differences over certain aspects of the Holy Trinity—the famous *filioque* clause—also played an important part. Whether the Holy Spirit descended from just the Father (as Constantinople maintained) or from the Father *and* the Son (as Rome insisted) was a matter of utmost importance to many Christians of the time. This was especially true in Constantinople, where such religious issues were passionately discussed in the streets.

Although the effect on the Rus church was gradual, and animosity toward Rome was not strong during the Kievan era, from 1054 Rus Christianity was part of the Orthodox world. Eventually, this would contribute to animosity toward the West.

The influence of Byzantium on the new Rus church was great. More than 100 years before Vladimir's conversion, two Byzantine missionaries, Cyril and Methodius, had gone to Moravia (most of which today is in the Czech Republic) to convert the Moravians. The missionaries brought with them a Slavic alphabet and a written language based on a spoken Slavic dialect. This written language was almost immediately used for liturgical purposes. In the following generation, the successors of the two famous missionaries brought the new language to the Slavs of Bulgaria. Thus, by the end of the tenth century when the Rus converted, numerous Byzantine theological works had already been translated into a written language close to that spoken by the Rus.

This written language, modified slightly in the course of a century, was known as Old Church Slavonic. It became the language used in Rus church services and in many of their written works.

Numerous translations from Byzantine religious works flowed into Rus and supplemented the presence of the Byzantine-sent metropolitans and bishops. Thus, Kievan Christianity naturally took on many characteristics of Byzantine Christianity.

Additional Characteristics of Rus Christianity

Despite Byzantium's overwhelming influence, Rus's pre-Christian past and its own unique developments gave the new faith a special Rus coloring. It is revealed in Rus Christianity's religious ideals and emphases, which do not necessarily reflect the behavior of most Rus Christians.

A good place to begin is with the veneration of Boris and Gleb, already mentioned in connection with Rus's political culture. Rus Christians believed that by not resisting their brother's plot against them, the two princes humbly imitated the suffering and death of Christ. The historian Fedotov and others have emphasized how important this imitation of Christ's humility and willingness to suffer for others became to the Rus and Russian religious mind. Other prominent Rus saints, such as Abbot Theodosius of the Kievan Crypt Monastery, also displayed these characteristics.

Rus Christianity was colored by other tints that highlighted the spiritual transformation of all life and nature, the beauty of Christian liturgy and art, and the significance of the historical and eschatological. The eleventh-century "Sermon On Law and Grace" is a good example of the historical emphasis. In it, Ilarion, one of the two native Rus metropolitans, contrasts the faith of the Jews before Christ with that of Christians, and he concludes by considering Vladimir's contribution within this historical context. The historical perspective introduced along with Christianity helped differentiate the Rus mentality from that of most nomadic cultures, which were less concerned with historical continuity. The Rus also concerned themselves with the traditional eschatological subjects of the end of time, the Apocalypse, and the Last Judgment.

Despite the emphasis on suffering for Christ's sake and eschatology, the Rus were not morbid or pessimistic. Their asceticism was moderate, and many of their religious works were full of Christian optimism. Again Ilarion's "Sermon On Law and Grace" illustrates the point. In it, he calls upon the dead Vladimir I to:

> See also your city beaming in its grandeur! See your blossoming churches, see the growing Christianity, see the city gleaming in its adornment of saintly images, and fragrant with thyme, and re-echoing with hymns and divine, sacred songs! And seeing all this, rejoice and be glad, and praise the good God, the creator of all this.[8]

Finally, there was the Rus ethical hue. If the "Life of St. Theodosius" by the monk Nestor, we read not only of the saint's humility, meekness, and asceticism, but also of his love and charity. He cared for the poor and sick, sent bread to prisoners, and interceded with judges for those treated unfairly. He was not afraid to extend his strong ethical awareness into the realm of politics. After Sviatoslav II (son of Yaroslav the Wise) usurped the Kievan throne from his

---

[8] Wiener, Vol. I, p. 50.

brother Iziaslav, Theodosius openly criticized him and refused to recognize his right to it. He also attempted to keep peace between warring princes.

Peacekeeping and mediation efforts were the most common types of religious intervention into the secular political arena. The church's attitude toward political authority was generally to support the existing legal order and to emphasize that political power came from God. Church leaders encouraged princes not only to avoid fratricidal wars, but also to rule justly and with love for their subjects (especially the poor, orphans, and widows) and to protect and strengthen Kievan Rus against her enemies who were not Christian or, by the end of the Kievan period, not Orthodox. Works such as Vladimir Monomakh's "Instructions" (see Chapter 2) indicate that religious teachings strongly influenced at least some princes' views of ideal princely behavior.

As compared with Western religious thinkers, Rus churchmen devoted little effort to reconciling religion and reason. For various reasons, including the use of old Church Slavonic, there was less familiarity in Kievan Rus than in the West with ancient pre-Christian rational thinking. In the medieval West, the discovery and translation into Latin of various works of the Greek philosopher Aristotle especially helped to stimulate a turn to rational, philosophical, and semiscientific thought. This thrust left an important mark on both Western religious thought and on the culture as a whole. In Kievan theology and culture, however, we see no such imprint.

Christianity and Society

Although some historians have emphasized the church hierarchy's support for the Kievan princes and a social structure dominated by elite men, other historians have stressed the church role in humanizing social and cultural life. Marxism, the celebration (in 1988) of the millennium of Rus's Christianization, the collapse of Communist power in Russia, and feminist historical criticism of Christianity's male bias have all influenced the debate.

All sides have made some valid points. The church did receive part of the prince's tribute and increasingly became a major landowner. While not condemning slavery, however, it encouraged humane treatment of slaves and others from the lower classes; engaged in some charitable and philanthropic activities; and furthered education, literacy, literature, and art. Estimates about literacy and formal schooling vary widely for the Kievan Rus period. But a variety of sources, including birch-bark letters and graffiti, indicate considerable male and female urban literacy. Following the example of Vladimir I, princes and others founded various schools, many of them on church property. In this spread of literacy and learning, the clergy played a major part, as it did in promoting literature and art.

Literature and Art

Church influence on literature and art is intricately connected with Byzantium, which was the chief foreign influence on Kievan Rus culture. South Slavic literature (which also owed a strong debt to Byzantine Christianity) and Scandinavian literature were other sources of inspiration. The South Slavic liturgical language, Church Slavonic, became the basis of a Kievan Rus literary language. Again, as with religion, however, native Rus traditions and creativity intermingled with Byzantine and other lesser foreign influences to create a literature of some originality.

Of the different types of literature, the chronicles and religious writings were the most important. The chronicles were far more than just historical records. The monks and others who compiled them in different regions of the country often incorporated such diverse materials as folktales and didactic writings—for example, the "Instructions of Vladimir Monomakh." Some short tales, especially those embellishing the lives of princes and princesses, reflect Scandinavian influence. More plentiful than the chronicles were the religious writings, especially translations from Greek (sometimes arriving via Orthodox Bulgaria). Of native Rus religious works, several sermons and accounts of saints' lives (Boris and Gleb, Theodosius) are the most impressive.

A third prominent type of literature was more secular and poetic and included both oral and written works. Among the oral literature, the *byliny* hold first place. These epic poems were repeated for generations until finally written down many centuries after their first appearance. They deal with such legendary fictitious characters as the incredibly brave and strong Ilia of Murom, one of the brave *bogatyri* (knightly heroes) who served Prince Vladimir. Al-

FIGURE 3.2. Cathedral of St. Sophia, Novgorod, 1045–1050.

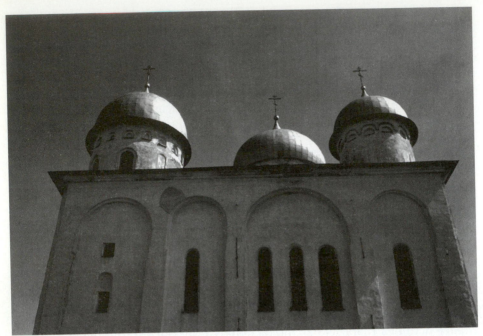

FIGURE 3.3. Cathedral of St. George at the Yuriev Monastery, Novgorod, 1119.

though of considerable literary merit, it is difficult to know which elements of these *byliny* set in Kievan times originated back then and which were added later.

With a secular written work such as *The Tale of Igor's Campaign* we are on surer footing—despite some doubters who contend that the work is an eighteenth-century forgery. It deals with an unsuccessful campaign of Prince Igor and other minor princes against the pagan Polovtsy in 1185. The unknown author praises the courage and bravery of the Rus princes but also laments the princely disunity that characterizes the times and benefits their enemies.

Like some other Kievan writings, it is not easy to classify. It contains neither a regular meter nor stanzas, and yet it is full of poetic devices and images. Omens and nature symbolism abound. For example, a solar eclipse occurs before the princes race into the steppe like "grey wolves," and Igor's wife laments like a cuckoo for her captured husband and calls upon the Dnieper to bring him back to her. The writer obviously felt at home in the world of nature, and the tale reflects an almost pagan veneration and respect for it. Because of its many artistic qualities, most critics consider it the greatest Kievan piece of literature that has survived.

In contrast to areas of the West or Asia (especially Persia) at that time, in Kievan Rus there was no love poetry. The lament of Igor's wife is about as close as we get. Nor was there any writing comparable to the Western goliardic

FIGURE 3.4. Church of the Intercession of the Virgin on the Nerl, Bogoliubovo, 1165.

verse or fabliaux stories, both of which were often satiric in tone and sexual in content.

In art and architecture, Byzantium influence and native Rus traditions are again blended, especially in the vital religious sphere. Church architecture was of two types, wooden and stone, with the first being more numerous. But fire and time have destroyed all the wooden churches of the era, whereas about two dozen stone churches have survived.

The most famous is St. Sophia (meaning Holy Wisdom) in Kiev, begun under the direction of Yaroslav the Wise. Originally it had thirteen cupolas, representing Christ and his twelve apostles, but over time, especially in the eighteenth century, more cupolas were added and its exterior modified. The interior of the church, however, is today more faithful to its original appearance, even if time has dimmed the beauty of its once vivid mosaics and frescoes. Mosaics such as that of Christ the Pantocrator (All-Ruler), in the main dome, and the Blessed Virgin Orans, in the altar apse, are works of high quality. Altogether, mosaicists used more than 100 different shades of glass cubes in the church's mosaics.

In Novgorod, two other famous churches still stand: another eleventh-century St. Sophia and the twelfth-century Cathedral of St. George at the Yuriev

FIGURE 3.5. The Cathedral of St. Demetrius, Vladimir, 1194–1197.

Monastery. Both are marked by their simple austerity. Their narrow windows and more elongated domes—as compared to the flatter domes favored by the Byzantines or even the original ones of Kiev's St. Sophia—reflect the needs of a harsher, more northern Novgorod climate. Reminiscent of warriors' helmets, the domes prevent the type of snow buildup flatter ones would allow. In the twelfth century, the stone exterior of Novgorod's St. Sophia was whitewashed, a practice that was often imitated in other parts of the country.

Three other impressive and still-standing twelfth-century churches are in the Suzdalian area, two in Vladimir and the third in nearby Bogoliubovo. The first to be constructed (1158–1160) was the Cathedral of the Assumption (or Dormition), but it soon suffered extensive damage and was rebuilt in the late 1180s (see Figure 5.1). It would later become a model for the church of the same name in Moscow's Kremlin.

Prince Andrei Bogoliubsky was responsible for the original Assumption cathedral, and in the mid-1160s he also had a few churches built at his Bogoli-

FIGURE 3.6. The Cathedral of St. Demetrius, Vladimir, decorative detail of exterior wall.

ubovo headquarters. The most beautiful was the Church of the Intercession of the Virgin on the Nerl (River)—some art historians consider it the finest of all medieval Rus and Russian churches.

In the mid-1190s, Vsevolod III had another impressive church constructed, this time back in Vladimir near the reconstructed Assumption Cathedral. It was named after a military saint-warrior, St. Demetrius of Salonika. The Cathedral of St. Demetrius (or Dmitri) resembled in several ways the Church of the Intercession of the Virgin on the Nerl. In contrast to the great churches of Kiev and Novgorod, the outside walls of these two Suzdalian churches were richly decorated with human, animal, and plant carvings, which served both a decorative and a symbolic purpose. The domestic and foreign inspirations for these carvings are disputed. Especially prominent on both churches, however, were the carvings of the warrior and wise ruler of Biblical times, King David. No doubt princes Andrei and Vsevolod both wished to present themselves as similar warrior-rulers.

In addition to frescoes and mosaics, icons were also present in the Rus churches. Although the great age of icon painting would come later, painters in Kievan Rus were already practicing this art inherited from the Byzantines. These religious pictures painted on wood were intended to instruct, both those who were literate and illiterate, and to be a promise of the eventual glory of a redeemed, transfigured world. Icons depicting Christ, the Virgin Mary, and Archangel Michael were popular, as were those of warrior saints like St. George and St. Demetrius. Individuals as well as churches possessed various sized icons, sometimes of their patron saints or special protectors—warriors, merchants, and other groups all had special saints. The belief that icons and other religious artifacts such as crosses protected Christians, either individually or collectively, was widespread.

Although Kievan Rus would become increasingly politically fragmented during the twelfth and early thirteenth centuries, its Christian literature and art would help maintain a consciousness of its religious and cultural oneness. It would prove to be an important legacy in the future.

SUGGESTED SOURCES*

BRUMFIELD, WILLIAM C. *A History of Russian Architecture*. Cambridge, England, 1993. Chs. 1–3.

BRUMFIELD, WILLIAM C., and MILOS M. VELIMIROVICH, eds. *Christianity and the Arts in Russia*. Cambridge, Eng., 1991. Pts. I & II.

CASS 25 (1991). The whole issue is devoted to Rus/Russian religion and religious culture, mainly in Kievan Rus.

FEDOTOV, G. P. *The Russian Religious Mind: Kievan Christianity, the Tenth to the Thirteenth Century*. New York, 1960.

———, ed. *A Treasury of Russian Spirituality*. New York, 1948.

FENNELL, JOHN. *A History of the Russian Church to 1448*. London, 1995. Pt. I.

FRANKLIN, SIMON. "Greek in Kievan Rus'." *DOP* No. 46 (1992): 69–81.

FRANKLIN, SIMON, trans. *Sermons and Rhetoric of Kievan Rus'*. Cambridge, Mass., 1991.

GASPAROV, BORIS, and OLGA RAEVSY-HUGHES, eds. *Slavic Cultures in the Middle Ages*. Berkeley, 1993.

GREKOV, B. D. *The Culture of Kiev Rus*. Moscow, 1947.

HAMANT, YVES. *The Christianization of Ancient Russia: A Millennium, 988–1988*. Paris, 1992.

HEPPELL, MURIEL, trans. *The Paterik of the Kievan Caves Monastery*. Cambridge, Mass., 1989.

HOLLINGSWORTH, PAUL, trans. *The Hagiography of Kievan Rus'*. Cambridge, Mass., 1992.

HUBBS, JOANNA. *Mother Russia: The Feminine Myth in Russian Culture*. Bloomington, 1988.

KAISER, DANIEL H. "The Economy of Kievan Rus': Evidence from the Pravda Russkaia." In *Ukrainian Economic History: Interpretive Essays*, ed. I. S. Koropeckyj. Cambridge, Mass., 1991.

———. *The Growth of the Law in Medieval Russia*. Princeton, 1980.

———, ed. *The Laws of Rus': Tenth to Fifteenth Centuries*. Salt Lake City, 1992.

LEVIN, EVE. "Dvoeverie and Popular Religion," In *Seeking God: The Recovery of Religious Identity in Orthodox Russia, Ukraine, and Georgia*, ed. Stephen K. Batalen. DeKalb, Ill., 1993.

MANN, ROBERT. *Lances Sing: A Study of the Igor Tale*. Columbus, Ohio, 1990.

*See also works cited in footnotes and general works on literature cited in the General Bibliography at the back of this volume.

MARTIN, JANET. *Medieval Russia, 980–1584*. Cambridge, England, 1995. Ch. 3.

MEZENTSEV, VOLODYMYR I. "The Territorial and Demographic Development of Medieval Kiev and Other Major Cities of Rus': A Comparative Analysis Based on Recent Archaeological Research." *RR* 48 (April 1989): 145–170.

MRECT, Pt. I. Contains *The Tale of Igor's Campaign*.

POPPE, ANDRZEJ. *The Rise of Christian Russia*. London, 1982.

PUSHKAREVA, N. L., and E. LEVIN, "Women in Medieval Novgorod from the Eleventh to the Fifteenth Centuries." *SSH* 23 (Spring 1985): 71–87.

RAPPOPORT, PAVEL A. *Building the Churches of Kievan Russia*. Brookfield, Vt., 1995.

RH 7, Pt. 3 (1980). The whole issue deals with the history of Kievan Rus.

SHCHAPOV, IA. N. *State and Church in Early Russia, 10th–13th Centuries*. New Rochelle, N.Y., 1993.

SSH 24 (Spring 1986). This issue is devoted to essays by I. Ia. Froianov on the history of Kievan Rus.

SUBTELNY, OREST. *Ukraine: A History*. 2d ed. Toronto, 1994. Ch. 2.

TIKHOMIROV, M. *The Towns of Ancient Rus*. Moscow, 1959.

VEDER, WILLIAM R., trans. *The Edificatory Prose of Kievan Rus'*. Cambridge, Mass. 1994.

VERNADSKY, GEORGE, ed. *Medieval Russian Laws*. New York, 1947.

ZGUTA, RUSSELL. "The Ordeal by Water (Swimming of Witches) in the East Slavic World." *SR* 36 (June 1977): 220–230.

CHAPTER 4

The Fragmentation of Kievan Rus and the Rise of New Centers

In the late Kievan era (1132–1237), political fragmentation proceeded rapidly. This was primarily due to internal tensions between the Riurikid princes. As the Riurikid clan increased, it found cooperation more difficult, and the collateral system of determining Kiev's grand prince became less operative than ever. Although control over Kiev remained a prize worth struggling for, princes increasingly concentrated on their own hereditary principalities. Both within Kievan Rus and among the Riurikids, centrifugal tendencies gained the upper hand, and new clans were formed among the descendants of the early princes. Kiev no longer produced its occasional strong, unifying ruler, and other political centers assumed increasing importance, partly as a result of growing economies that enabled them to challenge Kiev's former predominance. Three became especially significant: Vladimir-Suzdal (Suzdalia) in the Northeast, Galicia-Volhynia in the southwest, and the city-state of Novgorod in the north.

Of the three, Suzdalia, with its strong princes, became the most authoritarian. Conversely, Galicia's forceful boyars helped make Galicia-Volhynia less authoritarian but also less stable. In Novgorod, where the *veche* was fairly strong, the prince's powers became increasingly circumscribed. Yet Novgorod's practice of selecting outside princes provided pretexts for other principalities to interfere in its affairs. Its city politics was extremely fractious, and the city's wealthy boyars were too factionalized and self-serving to provide consistent enlightened leadership to the city-state.

RUS FRAGMENTATION AND THE POLITICAL DECLINE OF KIEV

For a century after 1132 and the death of Mstislav, son of Vladimir Monomakh, about a dozen separate Rus principalities contended with each other (see Map 4.1). It is even difficult to speak of Rus as a country, although it remained a

Rus Principalities and Territories
in the Early 13th Century

0   150   300 Miles

MAP 4.1

loose confederation. Only its common Riurikid ancestors, its remembrance of more unified days, and especially its shared religion and culture preserved a tenuous unity.

The Kievan principality especially was afflicted with political instability. Two reasons why were the breakdown of the collateral principle of princely succession and the gluttonous appetites of surrounding princes. Flux was greatest in three periods: (1) about the middle third of the twelfth century, when Kiev averaged one ruler every two years; (2) the first dozen years of the thirteenth century; and (3) the last five years (1235–1240) before the Mongols captured Kiev.

In 1169, toward the end of the first period of great flux, the forces of Suzdalia's Andrei Bogoliubsky sacked Kiev. Prince Andrei's father was the most famous of the younger sons of Monomakh; he was Yuri Dolgoruki (Yuri the Long-armed), prince of Suzdal and, more briefly, of Kiev. Allied with Bogoliubsky's men were others including Poles and Polovtsy. After besieging the city for weeks, this combined army took it and plundered it mercilessly, including the churches and some of their icons and other valued possessions.

Around 1200, during the second period of great flux, Prince Roman of Galicia-Volhynia captured Kiev and set up a lesser prince to rule there. A few years later, the ruling princely houses of Smolensk and Chernigov managed to put aside their usual rivalry temporarily and sent a combined force to capture and sack Kiev. This sacking seems to have been even worse than that of 1169. The attackers burnt parts of the city, looted the churches and monasteries, killed many people, and allowed Polovtsy auxiliary troops to take captives back with them to the steppe.

Within a few years, the princes of Smolensk and Chernigov once again were battling each other. Kiev bounced back and forth between the two princely houses until 1212, after which the Smolensk princes held the reigns of power for the next twenty-three years.

During the third and last cycle of flux, from 1235 to 1240, Kiev again bounced back and forth (seven times) and once again primarily between the ruling houses of Smolensk and Chernigov. Finally, in 1240, the Mongols abruptly halted the Rus conflict over Kiev by capturing the city, as they had many others in the previous few years.

Besides all the political instability, and in part because of it, Kiev's earlier dynamic growth began to slacken. By 1200, its territory was smaller than that of Novgorod, Vladimir-Suzdal, Smolensk, Polotsk, Galicia-Volhynia, or Chernigov. In addition to the political flux, Polovtsy raids and economic decline have often been listed as reasons for Kiev's increasing problems. More recent evidence and interpretations suggest, however, that these last two factors were not as significant as once thought. It was primarily Riurikid infighting, and not outside threats or economic decline, that contributed to Kiev's political weakening in the late Rus period.

Certainly one reason Kiev was so fought over by various princes was that it was such a great prize. The city itself remained among the two largest in Rus lands, the home of the Rus Orthodox metropolitan—a most important consideration—and a chief center of foreign trade.

RISE OF SUZDALIA

During the twelfth century, the northeastern area of Kievan Rus, between the Oka and Volga rivers, became increasingly important. By 1200, Vsevolod III, prince of Vladimir-Suzdal, was the strongest prince in all the Rus lands. He called himself "grand prince," and many other Kievan princes recognized him as the senior prince among the many descendants of Vladimir Monomakh. In that year, he sent his two-year-old son to be prince of Novgorod and appointed his ten-year-old son as prince of Pereiaslavl, a principality to the east of Kiev. To the south of Suzdalia, Vsevolod had dominated the princes of Murom-Riazan throughout the quarter century he had been in power.

What was the secret of his success? There were several, starting with geography. The principality he ruled was blessed with many rivers, including most of the upper Volga. Because some of these same rivers flowed out of or into neighboring territories, Suzdalia was in a good position to act as a middleman in east-west, north-south trade. During the late twelfth century, Vladimir became an especially important center for east-west trade that flowed westward from the Volga Bulgars through to Smolensk and beyond. Suzdalia was also ideally situated to interfere with Novgorodian trade that depended on the Volga and with Novgorodian tribute-gathering in the southeast portion of its territory.

In addition to its rivers, Suzdalia contained rich soil—the cities of Suzdal and Vladimir both lay within the fertile Vladimir Opole region. Furthermore, Suzdalia was not as harassed by foreign enemies as were the people of Kiev or Novgorod. By the end of the twelfth century, Suzdalia had its chief foreign foe, the Volga Bulgars, on the defensive.

Many historians have maintained that large numbers of Slavs migrated to Suzdalia mainly because of its more secure position during the late Kievan era, especially from the less secure and stable south. Certainly many new cities sprang up in the Suzdalian region, and by 1200 it was one of the most populated Rus principalities.

While geography provided Suzdalia the opportunity for increasing its power, four princes actualized this potential. The first was Yuri, who picked up the appellation Dolgoruki because of his interference or long reach into other principalities. In 1125 (the year his father, Vladimir Monomakh, died), he moved his northeast capital from the ancient city of Rostov to Suzdal. Until his death by poison in Kiev in 1157, he pursued a multifaceted policy that his two strong successors would imitate. It involved developing and colonizing Suzdalia—then still lightly populated by Finno-Ugrians and Slavs—and establishing control, or at least increased influence, in other important territories. These included the principalities of Kiev, where he became grand prince in 1155, Novgorod, Murom-Riazan, Chernigov, and the Volga Bulgar area.

The second important prince of Suzdalia was Andrei Bogoliubsky, Yuri's son by a Polovtsy princess. Although his father spent his last few years in Kiev, Andrei thought it unnecessary to go there to exercise whatever authority a grand prince could by then apply. Instead, after his forces sacked Kiev in 1169, he remained in Vladimir, which he had made the new capital of his northeast principality. Earlier, in an unsuccessful attempt to weaken Kiev and strengthen his capital, he even tried to persuade the Orthodox patriarch of Constantinople to appoint a separate metropolitan in Vladimir. Like his father, his life ended violently: In 1174 some of his boyars assassinated him. And like his father's death, his own prompted additional violence. When Yuri had died, the people of Kiev had sacked and pillaged his palace and estate and killed some of his Suzdalian followers. Now following Andrei's death in Bogoliubovo—the site of his princely palace near Vladimir and meaning the place "loved by God"—

FIGURE 4.1. Golden Gate of Vladimir. This main entrance to the city was built in 1164 and later altered.

some inhabitants sacked and pillaged his palace and the property of some of his officials.

After several years of conflict, Andrei's brother Vsevolod III assumed control and held it for thirty-six years until his death (of natural causes) in 1212. We have already examined his power in 1200. Like his father and brother, he strengthened Suzdalia, especially at the expense of Novgorod and the Volga Bulgars. Only toward the end of his reign did he suffer some serious setbacks. In the south in 1206, his son Yaroslav was kicked out of Pereiaslavl by the prince of Chernigov, who shortly before had succeeded in taking Kiev. A few years later, another son was forced out of Novgorod.

After the death of Vsevolod III in 1212, his sons spent the next six years either warring against each other or licking their wounds and waiting for another chance. Finally in 1218, Vsevolod's son Yuri took over undisputed control of Suzdalia and remained in power until 1238, when he died in battle at the hands of the Mongols.

This fourth strong prince of Suzdalia fought successful campaigns against the Volga Bulgars and the Finnish Mordva. Yet he remained primarily at peace with other Rus principalities and never exercised the influence over some of them that his father had. His rule enabled Suzdalia to be the most stable of the Rus principalities in the final decades before the Mongol invasion.

SIGNIFICANCE OF SUZDALIA

Besides its prominence in the late Kievan era, Suzdalia is significant for the historical controversy it has aroused. The dispute centers on the continuity of the region (including Moscow) with earlier Kievan Rus.

Early Russian historians such as Karamzin and Pogodin had few doubts that a strong continuity existed. While still recognizing considerable continuity, later nineteenth-century historians such as S. Soloviev and Kliuchevsky noticed some strong differences between Kiev and Suzdalia. Kliuchevsky, for example, believed that before the twelfth century, Suzdalia was a frontier area of primarily Finnish peoples. Then its strong colonizing princes and a great influx of Slavic peoples from the less secure south changed the region. The intermarrying of Slavs and Finns created a new ethnic type, the Russian or Great Russian. Overseeing colonization, the Suzdalian princes became more powerful than those in more developed Rus areas, where the boyars and veches (*vechi*) were more entrenched.

Furthermore, Kliuchevsky argued, the attitude of these strong northeastern princes toward the land they ruled was more proprietary than in other areas of Kievan Rus. They thought of it as their own private property, to rule or dispose of as they wished. The American historian Richard Pipes has developed these ideas even further and argued that this proprietary attitude is the key to understanding the Russian "patrimonial regime" that gradually

evolved. Such a regime, according to Pipes, failed to distinguish between political rule over a territory and private ownership of one's lands. This resulted in
the Russian princes attempting to rule their lands as they would their own private estates and households.

The Ukrainian historian Mykhailo Hruchevsky also saw differences between Suzdalia and Kiev but took the debate in a new direction. He argued
that it was primarily the southern principalities of Galicia and Volhynia (in
modern-day Ukraine), and not Suzdalia and then Moscow, that best carried on
the traditions and culture of Kievan Rus. He thought the claim of Russian historians to Kievan Rus was false and that Russian history began only with the
emergence of Vladimir-Suzdal. Rus history then belonged most properly to
Ukrainian history.

During the Soviet period, most twentieth-century émigré Ukrainian historians followed Hruchevsky's example. Opposing this view, many Russian historians reiterated what Moscow apologists desirous of gaining former Rus
lands had stated as early as the fifteenth century: that Moscow had the greatest
claim to the Kievan legacy.

A middle position—one taken here and by many historians—is to leave
aside who has the greatest claim and simply recognize Kievan Rus as a legitimate part of the history of all three East Slavic nationalities: the Russians,
Ukrainians, and Belorussians.

GALICIA AND VOLHYNIA

Galicia and Volhynia became distinct entities only in the eleventh century, but
by 1200 they had combined to become another important new area. Both principalities included disputed territories along the Rus-Polish border. Galicia
was the smaller of the two and the most western-reaching Rus territory. It
shared a border with not only Poland, but also Hungary and extended north-
eastward from the foothills of the Carpathian Mountains. Its capital, Galich,
was one of the fastest-growing cities in Rus before the Mongol invasion. Volhynia was to Galicia's north and shared its northern border with Lithuanian
tribes.

The geography of these two principalities helped decide their fate. Their
lands were fertile and well populated; Galicia contained valuable salt deposits;
and both territories possessed important rivers and cities that linked them
with north-south and east-west trade. Although less threatened by steppe nomads than the southeastern Rus lands, both sometimes struggled with Poland,
and Galicia contended with Hungary. These conflicts blended with internal
political instability to prevent the southwestern area from becoming a more
dominant force in late Rus politics. Hungary, for example, often supported Volhynia against Galicia or intervened in battles between Galician princes and
boyars.

The boyars of Galicia were the strongest in all Rus. Their fertile lands and
trading activities, especially the salt trade, provided a strong economic base,

and they were not afraid to challenge their prince. They even forced the strong Yaroslav Osmomysl (eight-minded), who reigned from 1153 to 1187, to discard his second wife, Anastasia, and later had her burnt at the stake. They ousted his son Vladimir, who had committed bigamy by marrying a priest's wife, until he returned with the support of foreign troops. In 1213, they took the unprecedented step of crowning one of their own as prince of Galicia—the only known case of a non-Riurikid prince on a Rus throne.

In Volhynia, the boyars were not so strong, and stronger princes were able to emerge there. A good example is Roman, who ruled from 1173 until 1205. In 1199, he brought Galicia under his control and at the beginning of the new century occupied Kiev and placed a minor Volhynian prince on its throne. He thus became the chief authority in most of the territory of modern-day Ukraine. Moreover, he fought successfully against the Lithuanians and Poles. According to legend, he even used Lithuanian captives in place of oxen to pull the plows on his estate. Although perhaps not literally true, the legend tells us something about this prince who liked to say: "You can't enjoy the honey without killing the bees."[1]

Even before Roman's death, however, Vsevolod III of Suzdalia had taken steps to limit his growing influence. After his death in 1205, the Galician boyars forced his widow and two young sons out of Galicia. Decades of Galician princely-boyar conflict and foreign intervention followed. Only in 1238 did Roman's oldest son, Daniel, retake part of Galicia. The following year he took Kiev, but to little avail; for in 1240 the Mongols vanquished it. Early the following year, they swept through Galicia and Volhynia, beginning a new chapter in the history of the region.

NOVGOROD

Although its growth in the late Kievan period was not as impressive as Suzdalia's, the region of Novgorod (or Lord Novgorod the Great, as it sometimes was called) was still on the rise. Despite certain disadvantages—poor agricultural conditions, the growing danger of formidable foreign enemies, and the interference of other regions in its princely selection process—Novgorod's population and economy continued to expand. Its prosperity rested upon its trade, handicrafts, and tribute-collecting.

Located on both sides of the Volkhov River, the city itself was connected by rivers, lakes, and portages to three great water trade routes: the Baltic Sea and the Volga and Dnieper rivers. Novgorodian merchants and ships traveled abroad, especially in the Baltic, and foreign merchants, primarily from Scandinavian and German lands, resided in Novgorod. To the southwest, near the territory's western border, lay the city of Pskov, which possessed political institutions similar to those of the larger Novgorod. To the east of Novgorod, addi-

[1] Quoted in Orest Subtelny, *Ukraine: A History*, 2d ed. (Toronto, 1994), p. 60.

FIGURE 4.2. Church of St. Paraskeva Piatnitsa on the Marketplace, Novgorod, 1207, later modified and partly reconstructed. The church was built by merchants, who venerated Paraskeva; later on, many women adopted her as a special patroness of women.

tional rivers furthered Novgorod's tribute-collecting in its vast hinterlands stretching to the Ural Mountains and the White Sea.

Besides being prosperous and large, Novgorod became increasingly tough on its princes. Earlier the oldest son of the grand prince of Kiev often ruled there—both Vladimir I and Yaroslav the Wise had been princes in Novgorod before becoming grand princes in Kiev. Although always guarding their rights vis-à-vis their prince, the people of Novgorod became increasingly insistent on them as Kiev weakened. In 1136, the Novgorodians arrested their prince, Vsevolod, son of Mstislav of Kiev, who had died four years earlier. They held him, his wife, children, and mother-in-law under guard until they selected a new prince from Chernigov. Then they expelled Vsevolod and his family.

The chief cause of the Novgorodians' displeasure with Vsevolod was a crushing defeat they had just suffered in a battle against Suzdalia, but there were other reasons too. They accused him of not caring for the common people, of desiring to become prince of another area, and of cowardly behavior in battle.

Prompted by their anger with Vsevolod, the Novgorodian *veche*, dominated by powerful boyars, took steps to weaken the powers of the princely office further. The Novgorodians began selecting their prince from a variety of other principalities, especially those of Suzdalia, Smolensk, and Chernigov. When they got tired of their prince, they increasingly "showed him the open road." They also restricted the prince's landowning rights in the city and confined him more to his headquarters out of town—the fortress of Gorodishche, which sat on the Volkhov, south of the city. As the century continued, the town's citizens further limited the prince's administrative and judicial duties. The one vital role he continued to perform was commanding Novgorod's military forces.

To see how Novgorod dealt with its princes in the late Rus era, we need only look at the city's chronicle, where the Novgorodians are continually chasing their prince out and obtaining a new one. Between 1154 and 1159, for example, they averaged better than a prince a year and ended the decade by arresting their prince, Sviatoslav Rostislavich, and his wife. Townspeople also sacked their possessions before sending envoys to Andrei Bogoliubsky in Suzdalia asking him to send a new prince. After he sent his nephew, a year later the Novgorodians dismissed him.

Sometimes, sensing danger ahead from dissatisfied citizens, the Novgorodian princes took it upon themselves to flee. One young prince in the early 1220s, Vsevolod, son of Yuri of Suzdalia, twice came in to replace another prince and twice fled, all in less than five years.

One cause of the frequent changing of princes was the lack of consensus among boyar families, who struggled with each other to influence the princely selection process.

As the powers of the prince declined, those of other officials, increasingly elected by the *veche*, grew stronger. The boyar *posadnik* became the chief city-state executive officer and even exercised some judicial powers. Another official was the *tysiatskii*, originally a commander of a 1,000-man city militia. During the twelfth century, his powers were broadened to include jurisdiction over various commercial dealings. Finally, the bishop (archbishop after 1165) of Novgorod, in whose selection the people of the city played a major role from 1156, also exercised increasing influence.

Yet Novgorodians kept a wary eye on these officials, especially their *posadnik*. Occasionally the wrath of the people would turn on him, and they would expel him or, less frequently, even plunder his property or kill him. They also jealously guarded certain autonomous rights in separate city districts or "ends" (numbering five by the end of the thirteenth century).

At the end of the Kievan era, Novgorod was facing increasing pressures from Lithuanians, Germans, and Swedes. Its need for a strong warrior prince increased; it found one in Alexander Nevsky. Even this future hero of Novgorod, however, would have such serious differences with the Novgorodians

Novgorodians Versus Their Prince

The following selection is from Robert Michell and Nevill Forbes, eds., *The Chronicle of Novgorod, 1016–1471* (London, Royal Historical Society, 1914), p. 25. Bracketed material and ellipsis are mine. This excerpt illustrates well not only the often stormy relations between Novgorod and its princes—and other officials—but also how other principalities often became involved in such conflicts.

The same year [1167] *Knyaz* [Prince] Svyatoslav went out of Novgorod to [the city of] Luki, and sent to Novgorod, saying thus to them, that: "I do not want to be *Knyaz* among you, it pleases me not." And the men of Novgorod having kissed the picture of the Holy Mother of God, said to themselves that: "We do not want him," and went to drive him away from Luki; and he, having heard that they are coming against him, went to Toropets, and the men of Novgorod sent to Russia [i.e., Kiev] to Mstislav for his son. And Svyatoslav went to the Volga, and Andrei [Bogoliubsky] gave him help, and he burned Novi-torg [Torzhok], and the men of Novi-torg retired to Novgorod; and he did much damage to their houses, and laid waste their villages. . . . Andrei combined with the men of Smolensk and Polotsk against Novgorod, and they occupied the roads, and seized the Novgorod emissaries everywhere, not letting Mstislav in Kiev know; imposing Svyatoslav on the town by force, and saying this word: "There is no other *Knyaz* for you than Svyatoslav." The men of Novgorod, however, heeded this not, and killed Zakhari the *Posadnik*, and Nerevin, and the herald Nesda, because they thought they gave information to Svyatoslav.

in late 1240 that he quit being their prince until, frightened by the advance of the Germanic knights, they persuaded him to return in 1241 (see Chapter 5).

CONCLUSION

Much of what is known of the late Kievan era comes from chronicles of the times. Reading them makes it difficult to disagree with the nationalist Russian historian Karamzin (1766–1820), who wrote of "internecine wars of faint-hearted princes, who, oblivious to the glory, good of the fatherland, slaughtered each other and ravaged the people."[2]

A judgment later applied to this period, to quote Karamzin again, was that "Russia . . . perished from the division of authority." But he added that afterward it "was saved by wise autocracy."[3] The autocracy he referred to was that of later Moscow princes such as Ivan III.

Thus, the legacy of the late Kievan period was more than just a weakening of Rus that made it more prone to collapse when the Mongols appeared. The

[2] Richard Pipes, ed. *Karamzin's Memoir on Ancient and Modern Russia* (New York, 1966), p. 105.
[3] Ibid., p. 110.

era also served later apologists for autocracy as a concrete example of the dangers of divided political authority.

Of course, this does not exhaust the late-Rus legacy. Some Russians and other East Slavs later chose to emphasize other aspects of Kievan Rus, for example, Novgorod's curtailment of princely power; Rus's continuing economic and urban vigor; its extensive contacts with other nations and peoples; or its rich, and increasingly Christian, culture.

*SUGGESTED SOURCES**

BIRNBAUM, HENRIK. *Lord Novgorod the Great: Essays in the History and Culture of a Medieval City-State.* Columbus, Ohio, 1981.

DIMNIK, MARTIN. *Mikhail, Prince of Chernigov and Grand Prince of Kiev, 1224–1246.* Toronto, 1981.

FENNELL, JOHN. *The Crisis of Medieval Russia, 1200–1304.* London, 1983. Chs. 1–3.

GOLDFRANK, DAVID M. "Andrei Bogoliubski." *MERSH* 1: 218–221.

HELLIE, RICHARD. "Yurii Dolgorukii." *MERSH* 45: 73–76.

HORAK, STEPHAN M. "Periodization and Terminology of the History of Eastern Slavs: Observation and Analyses." *SR* 31 (Summer 1972): 853–862.

HURWITZ, ELLEN S. *Prince Andrej Bogolubskij: The Man and the Myth.* Florence, 1980.

KLYUCHEVSKY (KLIUCHEVSKY), V. O. *The Course of Russian History.* Vol. 1. New York, 1960.

MARTIN, JANET. *Medieval Russia, 980–1584.* Cambridge, England, 1995. Ch. 4.

MICHELL, ROBERT, and NEVILL FORBES, eds. *The Chronicle of Novgorod, 1016–1471.* London, 1914 (Reprint, New York, 1970).

MILLER, DAVID B. "The Kievan Principality on the Eve of the Mongol Invasion: An Inquiry into Current Historical Research and Interpretation." *HUS* 10 (1986): 215–240.

PASZKIEWICZ, HENRYK. *The Rise of Moscow's Power.* Boulder, 1983.

PERFECKY, GEORGE, ed. *The Galician-Volynian Chronicle.* Munich, 1973.

PIPES, RICHARD. *Russia under the Old Regime.* New York, 1974. Ch. 2.

PRESNIAKOV, ALEXANDER E. *The Formation of the Great Russian State: A Study of Russian History in the Thirteenth to Fifteenth Centuries.* Chicago, 1970.

SSH 23 (Spring 85). The whole issue is devoted to medieval Novgorod.

ZENKOVSKY, SERGE A., ed. *The Nikonian Chronicle.* Vol. 2. Princeton, 1984.

*See also works cited in footnotes.

PART TWO

The Mongols and the Rise of Moscow to 1533

Mongols, Moscow, and the Russian Orthodox Church were the main forces influencing Russia from about 1240 to 1533. The Mongol invasion of 1237–1241 marked the collapse of Kievan Rus. For more than a century, the Mongols remained overlords over most of the old Rus territories. Yet within decades after the Mongols' sweeping victories, the Lithuanians began chipping away at their westernmost Rus conquests and adding them to their own. By 1380, Lithuania and Poland had already annexed most of the Belorussian and Ukrainian parts of old Rus. In that same year, the Muscovite prince Dmitri Donskoi won an important victory over the Mongols. Although Mongol control (or the "Tatar yoke," as Russian historians liked to call it) was not completely overthrown for another century, Dmitri's victory symbolized both the beginning of the erosion on Mongol subjugation and the rise of Moscow and the Russians (Great Russians).

Before the Muscovite state could completely throw off Mongol control and form a united and independent Russia, it had to overcome the divisive legacy of princely conflicts and defeat such rivals as Tver and the Republic of Novgorod. Princely discord stemmed in part from the problems of political succession. Both before and after the Mongol conquest, princely holdings had been getting smaller, as princes divided up their lands among their sons. With time and smaller landholdings, distinctions between being a private landholder and a public ruler began to disappear. So prominent did this tendency become that some historians have called the period from the late Kievan era to the late fifteenth–early sixteenth century "the appanage period"—an appanage designating one of these many princely landholdings.

Yet by the ascension of the infant Ivan IV in 1533, Moscow had already overcome most of the Russian divisiveness fostered by the princes' subdividing of their lands. Even by 1450, the grand prince of Moscow ruled over some 430,000 square kilometers; and by 1533 (after annexing Tver and the vast Novgorodian lands), Moscow controlled 2.8 million square kilometers, or about five times the size of modern France. Not only had the Muscovite princes united the Russians by 1533, but also they had begun to snip away at Polish-Lithuanian holdings in Ukraine and Belorussia. The *rise* of Moscow had occurred. Ivan IV's reign would mark the beginnings of the tsardom of Muscovy.

As Moscow by 1533 symbolized a new political center, so also it exemplified a new Russian civilization. Although Moscow's ruling elite remained just as concerned with economic gain as the Rus elite had been—perhaps even more so—Muscovy was more rural, more authoritarian, more centralized, and more hierarchical than Kievan Rus had been. Its peasants and townspeople were less free. Part of this was the price Muscovy had to pay to possess a military strong enough to deal with its enemies and expand rapidly. Its culture was primarily shaped by Orthodox beliefs, which now permeated deeper into the Russian countryside and soul. By holding itself up as the guardian of these beliefs, the Muscovite government strengthened its own control over the country.

CHAPTER 5

The Mongol Conquest
and Subjugation

The Mongols who conquered much of Asia and defeated and subjugated the Rus in 1237–1241 were actually a mixed group of mostly Mongol leaders and Turkic soldiers. Later Russian sources preferred the term "Tatar," itself of disputed origin, to designate these fierce peoples. For simplicity's sake, "Mongol" hereafter refers to all these conquering troops and officials.

For the remainder of the thirteenth century, the Mongols of the Golden Horde (or Kipchak) Khanate ruled over almost all the former Rus principalities, the southern steppes, the Volga valley, and much of western Siberia. Over the former Rus lands, they ruled indirectly, relying on cooperating Rus princes. Mongol administrators and armies ensured that the will of the khan was carried out, especially that tribute taxes were brought to him. As one scholar has noted, however, it was not the khan who decided what proportion of tribute would be paid by whom; rather "it was the Russian elite who made the tribute regressive, forcing the poor to pay the most."[1]

The conflict between princes, which had so characterized the late Kievan period, continued under the Mongols. In fact, it was heightened by the khan's practice of granting power to princes who pleased him, which increased princely competition and further eroded respect for seniority rights. Just as Kieven-era princes had often used Polovtsy nomads against their relatives, so now princes sometimes used troops furnished by the khan in their battles against their kinsmen.

Historians have long debated the effects of Mongol rule, which in the northeast would continue in varying degrees to 1480. The greatest impact was on economics and finance, administrative techniques, and military organization and tactics. Least affected were social and cultural life.

---

[1] Charles J. Halperin, *Russia and the Golden Horde: The Mongol Impact on Medieval Russian History* (Bloomington, 1985), p. 78.

THE MONGOL EMPIRE AND THE INVASION OF RUS

By 1222, a large Mongol empire had already come into existence. From Mongolia it spread southeastward into northern China, including Peking, and westward over many peoples, especially Turkic, throughout most of Central Asia, Iran, and Afghanistan. In 1222, Mongol armies swept through the Caucasus and defeated the Ossetians and Polovtsy.

The reasons for Mongol successes were many, beginning with Chinghis Khan. He united the various Mongol tribes in 1206, and he directed the Mongol conquests until his death in 1227. He combined military and political skills with a belief that he was fulfilling the divine will of Heaven. Yet it was his fierce nomadic horsemen, incredibly skilled with their bows and arrows, and his many siege weapons for capturing cities that most terrified his enemies. Other reasons for the spread of the Mongols' empire included its sociopolitical and military system. As new territories and peoples came under their control and their military expanded, the Mongols skillfully built upon and adapted their basic clan-tribal structure. This adaptation was furthered by a religious tolerance that was noted by practitioners of the major religions of the day, including Buddhism, Christianity, and Islam.

Like many nomads before them, including the Varangian "nomads of the sea," the Mongols were primarily interested in economic gain, not warfare for its own sake or the spreading of any type of belief system. After completing the creation of their empire, the Mongols desired peace. It was necessary to stimulate trade and their own profits, which they did by such steps as the creation of custom-free trading zones.

Despite the success of the Mongols, there is no evidence that the Rus heard of their victories until 1222 or 1223. At that time, the Polovtsy father-in-law of Prince Mstislav of Galicia came to him requesting armed assistance against the Mongols. To win over his son-in-law, Khan Kotian dispensed gifts of horses, camels, buffaloes, and girls. Won over by these gifts and the belief that further Polovtsy defeats would make the Mongols an even more formidable foe, Mstislav agreed to help. He managed to convince the princes of Kiev and Chernigov that they should all mount a joint Rus-Polovtsy campaign against these fierce intruders.

Because forces from Smolensk, Turov, and Volhynia also joined in, it appeared that the Rus were mounting a rare unified campaign. But Novgorod and Suzdalia did not participate, and the *Galician-Volhynian Chronicle* wrote that princely discord at the beginning of the battle contributed to the Rus defeat.

After more than a week's ride into the steppes, the main battle took place on the Kalka River near the Sea of Azov.[2] The Mongols routed the Rus and Polovtsy forces, killing nine Rus princes. Three of them, according to the *Nov-*

---

[2] Leo de Hartog in his *Russia and the Mongol Yoke: The History of the Russian Principalities and the Golden Horde, 1221–1502* (London, 1996), p. 25, suggests that the attack probably took place in 1222, not 1223 as generally stated.

gorod Chronicle, were suffocated under boards sat upon by dining Mongols. After pursuing the remaining Rus forces, perhaps half the original contingent, back to the Dnieper, the Mongols soon turned back eastward beyond the Volga (see Map 5.1). The Rus hoped they had seen the last of them.

After first subjugating the Volga Bulgars and other peoples to the east of the Rus in 1236 and 1237, however, the Mongols came back. Under Batu, grandson of Chinghis Khan, they sent envoys to Riazan demanding one-tenth of everything from men to horses. They probably also demanded capitulation. The princes of Riazan and Murom rejected such a tithe and, according to some accounts, also sent a delegation seeking help from Prince Yuri of Vladimir-Suzdal. Once again, however, Rus unity was lacking and Yuri furnished no immediate assistance. Meanwhile in December 1237, the Mongols assailed Riazan. Only then did Yuri send a small force. After five days, the Mongols captured the city—or rather its body-strewn and smoking ruins.

A few months later, after taking the small town of Moscow, the Mongols quickly conquered Vladimir, the capital of Suzdalia. They did so with weapons and equipment they often used to break the resistance of walled-in urban dwellers: catapults, battering rams, and scaling ladders. These supplemented their more traditional weapons of bows and arrows, swords, lances, and battle-axes.

The Mongols had learned of city-siege weapons from their enemies. The catapults were especially varied and effective and hurled all sorts of materials, including stones, clay pots with burning naphtha, and iron projectiles. In storming Vladimir, they hurled primarily stones. Some chronicle accounts wrote of stones falling like rain within the city.

Following the capture of Vladimir, Mongol armies won other battles in Suzdalia and took Torzhok in southern Novgorod. Then, after coming within seventy miles of the city of Novgorod, they inexplicably turned south. After a long siege of the northern Chernigov city of Kozelsk—seven weeks according to the *Galician-Volhynian Chronicle*—the Mongols took it.

For a time beginning in the summer of 1238, the Rus were spared further devastation. Instead, the Mongols strengthened their control of lands to the south and east. In 1239 or 1240, however, they returned and took the major southern towns of Pereiaslavl and Chernigov. On December 6, 1240, the feast of St. Nicholas, patron saint of the Rus, the Mongols captured Kiev. The chief cities of Galicia-Volhynia fell early the following year.

The Mongols' treatment of those within the walled cities was merciless. Yet chronicle accounts, as John Fennell has pointed out, should not be taken too literally. True, the Mongols often used terroristic methods to help spread panic among their enemies, but acts such as slaying *all* of the people within a city, or raping nuns, or killing children still at their mothers' breasts, probably did not occur as often as chronicle writers stated.

The victories of the Mongols were due to many causes. Weapons, tactics, the skill and hardiness of their troops, their information-gathering techniques, and their effective use of captives and conscripts from among earlier enemies all played a part. Their troops in Rus lands—perhaps some 130,000 in 1237—

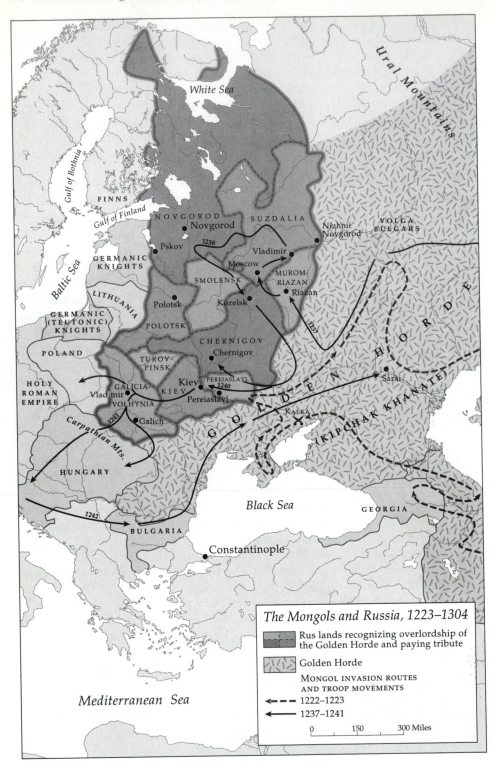

The Mongols and Russia, 1223–1304

- Rus lands recognizing overlordship of the Golden Horde and paying tribute
- Golden Horde

MONGOL INVASION ROUTES AND TROOP MOVEMENTS

- - - - 1222–1223
——— 1237–1241

0   150   300 Miles

MAP 5.1

FIGURE 5.1. Domes of the Cathedral of the Assumption, Vladimir. In 1238, after many townspeople had crowded into it seeking shelter, the Mongols cut them down or burned them to death.

also greatly outnumbered those available at any one time to the divided Rus. Although even a more united confederation probably would not have withstood the Mongol onslaught, there is little doubt that a woeful lack of cooperation among the various principalities made the Mongol's conquest easier than it might have been.

MONGOL RULE IN THE THIRTEENTH CENTURY

Following the conquest of Rus lands, the Mongols continued moving westward until they reached the Adriatic in 1242. Along the way, they defeated Poles, Czechs, Germanic Knights, Hungarians, and others. Countries further west in Europe feared they would be next. Then Batu received word of the death of Great Khan Ugedei, the son and successor of Chinghis Khan. Probably to participate in determining the next great khan, Batu ceased his advance and returned eastward. Soon afterward he established his headquarters at Sarai, near the Volga, some sixty-five miles north of Astrakhan.

Sarai soon became the capital of the Golden Horde, one of several Mongol khanates. We know from a Western envoy, Friar William Rubruck, that already by 1253 Batu's capital was an enormous tent city of about ten miles. Batu's

A Bishop's Sermon on the Mongol Invasion and Other Misfortunes

This selection, from Leon Wiener, *Anthology of Russian Literature: From the Earliest Period to the Present Time* (New York, 1902) Vol. I, pp. 105–106, is an excerpt from "A Sermon on Omens," by Serapion, Bishop of Vladimir (d. 1275). It gives the most common explanation for why God allowed such misfortunes as earthquakes and the Mongol devastation to be inflicted on the Christian Rus. This sermon also illustrates the point of Charles Halperin that Russian writers, while writing of the devastation of Mongol campaigns, preferred vagueness to an open recognition that Russia remained subject to Mongol political control. Bracketed material and ellipses are mine.

We did not obey the gospel, did not obey the apostles, nor the prophets, nor the great luminaries. . . . It is for this that God is punishing us with signs and earthquakes. He does not speak with His lips, but chastises with deeds. God has punished us with everything, but has not dispelled our evil habits: now He shakes the earth and makes it tremble: He wants to shake off our lawlessness and sins from the earth like leaves from a tree. If any should say that there have been earthquakes before, I shall not deny it. But what happened to us afterwards? Did we not have famine, and plague, and many wars? But we did not repent, until finally there came upon us a ruthless nation [the Mongols], at the instigation of God, and laid waste our land, and took into captivity whole cities, destroyed our holy churches, slew our fathers and brothers, violated our mothers and sisters. Now, my brothers, having experienced that, let us pray to our Lord, and make confession, lest we incur a greater wrath of the Lord, and bring down upon us a greater punishment than the first.

Much is still waiting for our repentance and for our conversion. If we turn away from corrupt and ruthless judgments, if we do away with bloody usury and all rapacity, thefts, robbery, blasphemy, lies, calumny, oaths, and denunciations, and other satanic deeds,—if we do away with all that, I know well that good things will come to us in this life and in the future life. . . . When will we, at last, turn away from our sins? Let us spare ourselves and our children! At what time have we seen so many sudden deaths? Many were taken away before they could care for their houses; many lay down well in the evening and never arose again. Have fear, I pray you, of this sudden parting! If we wander in the will of the Lord, God will comfort us with many a comfort, will cherish us as His sons, will take away from us earthly sorrow, will give us a peaceful exit into the future life, where we shall enjoy gladness, and endless happiness with those who do the will of the Lord.

own large tents sat in the middle of it. In one of them he held court, sitting up on a big gilded seat with one of his wives. Friar William's account states that Batu's face was then covered with red spots and that he was "about the height of my lord John de Beaumont"—as the historian Karamzin said: "It's a pity we have not had the honor of knowing Monsieur de Beaumont!"

To administer the former Rus lands, the Mongols relied heavily on cooperating Riurikid princes, overseen by Mongol officials. The latter were responsible specifically for census taking, the collection of tribute or taxes, the conscription of local men for Mongol military service, and the suppression of any opposition to Mongol rule. At first, many of them resided among the conquered peoples. Later in the century, more remote Golden Horde officials and special envoys to the princes oversaw the compliance of the princes and populace. Either way, Mongol military forces from the steppes were always available, if all else failed, to act as enforcers.

Usually before a prince was allowed to rule a district he had to receive a *yarlyk* or charter from the khan at Sarai or even from the great khan in the Mongolian capital of Karakorum (about 200 miles west-southwest of modern-day Ulan Bator). Fennell estimates that from 1242 to 1252, Suzdalian princes went to Batu or his son at least nineteen times and on four of these occasions were dispatched further to Karakorum. In Sarai, the princes had to endure humiliating rituals reminding them of their subservience to the khan. The khan also expected presents, and contenders for a princely charter no doubt realized that the worthier the gift, the better they might fare.

During the first sixty years after the Mongol conquest, the differences between former southern Rus principalities and those in the north greatly increased. Being closer to the Golden Horde and more directly under its rule, southern areas like Kiev quickly lost their lingering significance.

Being further to the west, and therefore further from Sarai, Daniel of Galicia-Volhynia was the south's strongest prince. But even he had to go to Sarai in 1246 and recognize the overlordship of Batu, although soon afterwards he attempted to throw off Batu's shackles. Although Daniel was unsuccessful in obtaining papal help for an anti-Mongol crusade, in 1253 Pope Innocent IV, via one of his representatives, did bestow a royal crown upon him. In 1259–1260, a Mongol army moved into Galicia-Volhynia and plundered some areas before retreating. Even though Daniel remained prince of the region until his death in 1264, he became a more obliging, if still resentful, Mongol vassal.

Other princes were even more unfortunate. For example, in Sarai, Batu executed Mikhail of Chernigov in 1246, probably for being too rebellious rather than—as chronicle accounts state—because he refused to worship Batu's idols.

MONGOL RULE AND RUSSIAN PRINCES: SUZDALIA AND NOVGOROD

Having briefly seen the early impact of the Mongols on the Rus in general, we now focus more specifically on Mongol dealings with the north, that is, with the Russians (Great Russians).

Alexander Nevsky

The first significant Russian prince to rule under the Mongols was Alexander Nevsky. When the Mongols conquered Rus, he was prince of Novgorod, and he soon led it to two important victories. For his first victory, against Sweden on the Neva River in 1240, he received (two centuries later) the appellation "Nevsky." His second victory, against the Germanic Knights on Lake Chud in 1242, brought him even more glory.

The Germanic Knights by this time represented a merger of two Catholic groups, the Livonian Order of Swordbearers and the Teutonic Knights. The first had existed for about forty years and had helped the Bishop of Riga subjugate many of the pagan people of Livonia (primarily modern-day Latvia). The second order, although founded in Palestine in the late twelfth century, had been active in the Baltic area for only a little over a decade (see Map 4.1).

A few years after the merger of the two orders in 1237, these Germanic Knights began threatening Novgorod. With the aid of some southern Estonians and the prince of Pskov, who was obviously at odds with his townspeople, the Germanic Knights captured Pskov in 1240. By 1241, they were within about twenty miles of Novgorod. It was at this point that the Novgorodians sent a delegation to Alexander—who recently had abdicated—pleading with him to return as their prince. He did so, recaptured Pskov, and pursued the foreigners into German-held Estonian territory. There at the battle on the ice of Lake Chud he defeated them.

Regarding this clash and the life of Alexander generally, it is necessary to

FIGURE 5.2. Saint Alexander Nevsky, a portrait of unknown artist. *(Sovfoto.)*

weed out the myths from the facts. Russian historians have often lavished praise on this hero, as has Eisenstein's great film *Alexander Nevsky*. The Orthodox Church eventually canonized him a saint. The English historian John Fennell has taken a different approach: He has been especially diligent attempting to debunk the myths that surround Nevsky's life.

Fennell has made at least four important points. First, several sources recounting the life of Alexander contain falsehoods. Second, the proportions of Alexander's two important victories have been greatly overblown. Fennell thinks it likely, for example, that a thirteenth-century Livonian chronicle is close to the truth when it writes of the losses of the German Knights at Lake Chud—twenty killed and six taken prisoner, excluding any Estonian losses. Third, the threat of the Catholic Germanic Knights to Orthodox Russia has been exaggerated; no unified Western scheme of aggression against Russia existed. Fourth, Alexander betrayed his brothers and appeased the Mongols.

Although the first three points can be granted, the fourth requires further exploration. After the death of Alexander's father, Yaroslav, in 1246, Alexander's uncle Sviatoslav succeeded him as grand prince of Vladimir, followed in 1248 by Alexander's younger brother Andrei. In 1252, Alexander went to Sarai. While he was there, the Mongols sent out an army against Andrei, who chafed at continued subservience to the Mongols. Andrei was defeated and fled the country. The Mongols then made Alexander grand prince of Vladimir in place of Andrei.

Alexander remained as grand prince until 1263. He continued his policy of battling in the west (Lithuanians, Swedes, and Germanic Knights were his chief enemies) and cooperating with the Mongols. When Novgorodians rebelled against Mongol census takers and tax collectors, as they did on several occasions, Alexander enforced the Mongols' will. The *Novgorod Chronicle* entry for 1257 even has Alexander cutting off noses and plucking out eyes of some of the leading rebels.

Yet Fennell's use of the word "appeasement," with all its World War II connotations, implies more than just cooperating with the Mongols. It suggests unheroic behavior. Many Russian historians, however, maintain that Alexander was just being wise, that cooperation with the Mongols seemed the only sensible policy and helped avert greater tragedy. After townspeople in major towns of Suzdalia drove out tax collectors (in 1262), Alexander apparently pleaded with the khan in Sarai for clemency. On the way back in 1263, he died.

The Brothers and Sons of Alexander Nevsky

The next forty years were ones of increasing dissension and division among the Russian princes and increasing Mongol military expeditions to support one or another of the contentious princes. Even during Alexander's reign as grand prince of Vladimir, he did not exercise nearly the control or influence over other Rus princes that his grandfather Vsevolod III had. Outside of Suzdalia, only Novgorod was under his control—usually indirectly and sometimes tenuously. Moreover, in Suzdalia itself, princes of many smaller districts considered themselves heads of their own realms. As grand prince of Vladimir, Alexander's relationship to them was analogous to what the grand prince of Kiev's once had been to lesser Rus princes.

Of course, all the Russian princes were now under the authority of the Golden Horde, which attempted to prevent any one Russian prince from becoming too strong: thus, the Mongol practice of granting many minor princes each a patent (*yarlyk*), which allowed them the right to rule within smaller districts of the former principality of Suzdalia. When Grand Prince Alexander called upon lesser princes to come to his aid against a foreign enemy, a traditional right of grand princes, he did so only under the directions of the khan at Sarai. Such, for example, was the case when he mustered Russian forces for a campaign against the Teutonic Knights in 1269.

From Alexander's death until the death of his son Andrei in 1304, four grand princes of Vladimir attempted to maintain some semblance of Alexander's already limited authority. The first two (up to 1277) were his brothers Yaroslav and Vasili, the last two his sons, Dmitri and Andrei. On two occasions, with the aid of Mongol troops, Andrei seized the grand princely title from the older Dmitri.

All four of Nevsky's successors, with mixed successes, tried to exercise authority over obstreperous Novgorod and usually also acted as prince of that city. Their authority was after all an important key to their financial well-being, both because of Novgorod's payments to the ruling prince and because of its good trading location. Yet more often than not, it was the citizens of Novgorod who came out on top, further restricting the princes' property-holding and judicial rights. Not even the princes' occasional attacks on Novgorod with the help of Mongol troops could reverse the erosion of princely powers.

While the powers of the prince eroded in Novgorod, those of the boyar elite increased. It is during this period that a boyar Council of Lords is first mentioned, and it became increasingly stronger. It consisted of past and present important officials and boyar representatives from each of the city's five districts. It was headed by the city's archbishop, and from this period on the *posadnik* was chosen annually only from among its members.

After seizing the grand princely crown from his brother for a second time in 1293, Nevsky's son Andrei continued in power for another decade, but his influence over other Suzdalian princes weakened. By 1300, there were over a dozen smaller principalities within the Suzdalian lands, and their princes were reluctant to cede any of their powers. Two of them, the princes of Moscow and Tver, increasingly competed with him and blocked his attempts to gain more lands. He died in 1304 a frustrated prince.

MONGOLS AND RUSSIAN HISTORIOGRAPHY

Although we examine subsequent Mongol control along with the rise of Moscow, it is here appropriate to analyze the overall Mongol impact on Russia. Although Russian historians such as Sergei Soloviev and Sergei Platonov

(1860–1933) have downplayed Mongol influence on Russian life, others such as George Vernadsky have emphasized its far-reaching and sometimes positive effects. Most Russian historians of its Communist period emphasized only the negative impact of the "Tatar yoke." Statements such as the following were common:

> The Tatar-Mongol rule was a terrible calamity for the Russian people. . . . The invasion and foreign yoke were the main causes of the subsequent economic, political and cultural backwardness of Russia.
>
> It took centuries for economic and cultural life to be restored in Russia to the level of the first quarter of the 13th century.[3]

Some Soviet historians stressed that by absorbing the Mongol's blows, Russia saved Western Europe from a terrible invasion. But as we have seen, the savior of Europe was more the death of Great Khan Ugedei.

Most recent Western scholarship, for example, that of Charles Halperin, provided a corrective to the Soviet historians' tendency to blame the Mongols for many of Russia's subsequent problems. It downplayed any long-lasting Mongol impact on Russia's social structure or culture. Although the Mongols had some influence on the development of Russian autocracy, its evolution owed more to internal factors than to outside influences, whether Mongol or, more significantly, Byzantine.

In other areas, however, the Mongol impact was considerable, although sometimes more positive than Soviet historians were willing to acknowledge. While the immediate economic consequences of the Mongol invasion were devastating and the Mongols for centuries continued to siphon off silver tribute, their rule also offered some lesser economic advantages. By the fourteenth century, their international trading network contributed to Russian economic growth. Some regions and classes benefited more than others, but the economic hardships suffered by commoners were due as much to Russian princes as to the Mongols.

For their own benefit, these princes, especially in Moscow, adopted some Mongol financial and tax-collecting practices as well as Mongol administrative methods and organization. Other Mongol spheres influencing Russian practices were its postal system, military organization and tactics, and diplomatic rituals.

The Mongol effect on Russia's treatment of criminals remains uncertain. Vernadsky believed that the introduction of capital and more widespread corporal punishment under Moscow rulers was largely due to Mongol influence. He admitted, however, that harsh Western influences might have been more significant in western areas of Russia. Again, however, internal developments were probably more important than either outside influence. One final impact of the Mongols, however, needs to be treated—their role in Moscow's rise to power. This is discussed in Chapter 6.

---

[3] S. Schmidt, K. Tarnovsky, I. Berkhin, *A Short History of the USSR* (Moscow, 1984), pp. 29–30.

SUGGESTED SOURCES*

Alexander Nevsky. A 1938 film directed by Sergei Eisenstein. Available on videocassette.

ALLSEN, THOMAS T. *Mongol Imperialism: The Policies of the Grand Qan Mongke in China, Russia, and the Islamic Lands, 1251–1259*. Berkeley, 1987.

DAWSON, CHRISTOPHER, ed. *The Mongol Mission: Narratives and Letters of the Franciscan Missionaries in Mongolia and China in the Thirteenth and Fourteenth Centuries*. London, 1955.

FEDOROV-DAVYDOV, G. A. *The Culture of the Golden Horde Cities*. Oxford, 1984.

FENNELL, JOHN. *The Crisis of Medieval Russia, 1200–1304*. London, 1983. Chs. 4–7.

HALPERIN, CHARLES J. "George Vernadsky, Eurasianism, the Mongols, and Russia." *SR* 41 (Fall 1982): 477–493.

———. "Soviet Historiography on Russia and the Mongols." *RR* 41 (July 1982): 306–322.

———. *The Tatar Yoke*. Columbus, Ohio, 1986.

MICHELL, ROBERT, and NEVILL FORBES, eds. *The Chronicle of Novgorod, 1016–1471*. London, 1914 (Reprint, New York, 1970).

MORGAN, DAVID. *The Mongols*. Oxford, 1986.

PASZKIEWICZ, HENRYK. *The Rise of Moscow's Power*. Boulder, 1983.

PERFECKY, GEORGE, ed. *The Galician-Volynian Chronicle*. Munich, 1973.

PRAWDIN, MICHAEL. *The Mongol Empire*. 2d ed. New York, 1967.

PRESNIAKOV, ALEXANDER E. *The Formation of the Great Russian State: A Study of Russian History in the Thirteenth to Fifteenth Centuries*. Chicago, 1970.

SOKOL, EDWARD D. "Batu Khan." *MERSH* 3: 163–165.

SPULER, BERTOLD. *The Mongols in History*. New York, 1971.

VERNADSKY, GEORGE. *The Mongols and Russia*. New Haven, 1953.

ZENKOVSKY, SERGE A., ed. *The Nikonian Chronicle*. Vol. 3. Princeton, 1985.

*See also works cited in footnotes.

CHAPTER 6

Moscow and Its Rivals, 1304–1533

Between 1304 and 1533, the successive princes of Moscow gradually emerged as the leaders of a new Russian state. They did so by first becoming the Mongols' most trusted viceroys and then by demonstrating their strength against increasingly divisive Mongols and other enemies. The support the Moscow princes generally received from the Orthodox hierarchy also helped them. Sometime before 1300, the metropolitan had moved from Kiev to Vladimir and in 1325 began residing in Moscow.

By the time of his death in 1505, Ivan III had brought most of Russia under his control, including powerful Novgorod and Moscow's chief Russian rival for so many years, Tver. Furthermore, he won from Lithuania other lands, primarily Ukrainian, which it had long dominated. He also started referring to himself as tsar and as autocrat. The collapse of the Byzantine Empire in 1453 and Ivan III's marriage to the niece of the last Byzantine Emperor helped to inflate his claims. So did a Mongol retreat from his armies in 1480. His son, Vasili III, continued his father's work. By Vasili's death in 1533, Moscow had expanded from a small principality to a Muscovite state (Russia) some sixty times larger than in 1300.

This remarkable expansion was driven primarily by the desires of Moscow princes and their followers for economic gain. Trade, tribute, and taxes remained as important to Muscovite princes as they had been to Kievan ones.

EMERGENCE OF MOSCOW, 1304–1389

Moscow's first chronicle mention was in 1147, and Prince Yuri Dolgoruki soon strengthened this small settlement by putting wooden walls around it. It sat above the Moscow river, on the western portion of the modern-day Kremlin. Only after Alexander Nevsky gave the area to his youngest son, Daniel, however, did it begin to be a major force in northeastern politics. By 1304, Daniel and his son Yuri, who succeeded him in 1303, had almost tripled the size of the

Moscow principality by taking over the districts of Kolomna, Mozhaisk, and Pereiaslavl-Zalesskii (see Map 6.1).

When the death of Andrei in 1304 created a vacancy for the position of grand prince of Vladimir, Yuri of Moscow (his nephew) and Mikhail of Tver (Andrei's cousin) vied with each other for the khan's patent. This began a period of intense rivalry between the princes of Tver and Moscow for the khan's favor.[1] For the next quarter century, the khan, pursuing a policy of playing the two princely houses against each other, favored first one then the other with the coveted title of grand prince of Vladimir. Finally in 1327, townspeople in Tver revolted against Mongol troops who had been sent there, and the Mongol khan in Sarai retaliated by sending troops to devastate Tver and other towns in that principality. Among those who led the troops was Prince Ivan of Moscow (later called Kalita or moneybag), the brother of Yuri, who had earlier been killed by a Tver prince.

Besides Tver's revolt, its growing closeness to Lithuania, a new rival of the Mongol Golden Horde, seems to have persuaded Khan Uzbeg to rely more now on Moscow's prince as his chief Russian vassal. After a brief interlude, the khan bestowed grand princely powers upon Ivan Kalita, probably in 1331. While enriching himself, Ivan proved a faithful vassal up to his death in 1341. He collected Mongols' taxes efficiently and made numerous trips to Sarai. For the Daniilovich dynasty (the descendants of Daniel, son of Alexander Nevsky), his two major accomplishments were gaining Orthodox Church backing for the dynasty[2] and the khan's support of his oldest son, Simeon, as his successor as grand prince.

The reigns of Simeon and his younger and only surviving brother, Ivan II (1353–1359), are bracketed between the more notable reigns of their father and of Ivan II's son, Dmitri Donskoi (1359–1389). In general, Ivan I's two sons continued the policies of their father. For most Russians, the most significant happening of the brothers' two decades of rule was the Black Death, which killed many Russians including Simeon and his two remaining sons (see Chapter 7).

When his father died in 1359, Prince Dmitri was only nine. Ever since Metropolitan Peter had come to reside in Moscow in 1325, the metropolitans generally had supported Moscow as opposed to Tver. Upon the death of Metropolitan Peter's successor in 1353, Moscow's Prince Simeon was able to obtain the appointment of Bishop Alexei of Vladimir as the new metropolitan. In 1362, Metropolitan Alexei helped the young Prince Dmitri obtain the great

---

[1] Janet Martin argues in *Medieval Russia, 980–1584* (Cambridge, England, 1995), pp. 174–75, 178–79, 375–79, that a succession system similar to the collateral system mentioned in Chapter 2 continued to be respected by most Rus princes after the Mongol conquest, and by that system Moscow's princes had no legitimate claim to the grand princely throne. She further asserts that this deficiency made Moscow more dependent on the Mongols and on "fashioning new bases of legitimacy."

[2] Martin, pp. 192–98, 391–93, 398, has pointed out that this backing was not absolute or without exceptions, and she emphasizes Orthodoxy's role in assisting the rise of Moscow less than I do. My position follows more those of Robert O. Crummey, *The Formation of Muscovy, 1304–1613* (London, 1987) and John Fennell, *A History of the Russian Church to 1448* (London, 1995).

Moscow and Its Competitors, 1304–1533

Muscovite boundaries in:
- 1304
- 1389
- 1462
- 1533

Lithuanian boundaries in:
- 1304
- 1377
- 1462

15th C. successor states of the Golden Horde

0   150   300 Miles

ARCTIC   OCEAN

White Sea

Archangel

N. Dvina R.

Ural Mountains

Yugra

Perm

Ustiug

Viatka

Gulf of Bothnia

Viborg

Beloozero

Galich

Gulf of Finland

Narva

Yam

Novgorod

Yaroslavl

Rostov

Kostroma

Nizhnii Novgorod

Kama R.

Kazan

Pskov

Vladimir

KHANATE OF KAZAN (from c. 1437)

NOGAI HORDE

Baltic Sea

GERMANIC KNIGHTS

W. Dvina R.

Tver

PEREIASLAVL-ZALESKII

Tushino

Moscow R.

Mozhaisk

Moscow

KOLOMNA

Oka R.

Samara

Neman R.

Polotsk

Kaluga

Tula

Kasimov

Riazan

Pronsk

Ural R.

GERMANIC KNIGHTS

Smolensk

Minsk

Briansk

Saratov

Kromy

Voronezh

Novgorod-Seversk

Chernigov

Putivl

Don R.

Sarai

Volga R.

Kiev

Dnieper R.

Donets R.

KHANATE OF ASTRAKHAN (from c. 1466)

HUNGARY

KHANATE OF CRIMEA (from c. 1427)

Black Sea

Caspian Sea

MAP 6.1

princely patent. And along with leading boyars, Alexei helped direct state affairs while Dmitri was still a boy.

Although Dmitri obtained the khan's patent, his reign (1359–1389) marked a new chapter in Mongol-Russian relations. Internal conflict weakened the Golden Horde—in the first two decades of Dmitri's reign, coups helped insure an average of one new khan per year—and gave Dmitri the opportunity to adopt a less subservient, more aggressive position to the reigning khan.

Dmitri made gains in three principal ways. First, he greatly strengthened Moscow's prestige and claim to the grand princely title; he was the first, for example, to dare bequeath the grand principality of Vladimir in his will. Second, by adding territories, primarily to the north and east of Moscow, he more than doubled Muscovy's size. Third, by defeating Mongol troops in two battles of 1378 and 1380, he significantly changed Russian attitudes toward the formerly invincible Mongols.

None of these gains was made easily. Princes of some of the other northeastern principalities challenged his leadership. This was especially true of Tver, which once again appeared strong for six or seven years until finally defeated by Dmitri in 1375. At different times it even had Lithuanian and some Mongol help. At times, Dmitri and competing Russian princes sought the grand princely patent from competing khan claimants. Despite some temporary setbacks, however, Dmitri generally maintained Mongol recognition of his grand princely rights. Ironically, however, the chief fame of this Mongol-supported prince rightly rests on his victories over the Mongols, especially at Kulikovo in 1380.

Conflict had been simmering between Dmitri and Mamai, the leader of one of the two major competing Golden Horde forces, ever since Mamai had supported Mikhail II of Tver's claim to the grand princely title in 1370. Then the princes of Nizhnii Novgorod, with Dmitri's encouragement, improved their region's defenses. Taking this as a hostile action, Mamai dispatched Mongol troops in 1374 to their capital, the city of Nizhnii Novgorod. The townspeople soon reacted to this reaction by rising up and killing many Mongols. Mamai then retaliated by twice ordering the ravaging of this Volga city, once in 1377 and again in 1378. Following these attacks, he sent an army directly against Dmitri's own territories. Dmitri's forces met it on the Vozha River and routed it.

Two years later, after arranging for Lithuanian help, Mamai himself led a large army up the Don River. The Russian prince of Riazan also agreed to support him. Receiving word of Mamai's preparation, Dmitri gathered a large Russian force from various districts. It seems, however, that Novgorod, Nizhnii Novgorod, and Tver failed to respond to his call.

The Russian troops—numbering perhaps 70,000—rendezvoused at Kolomna, southeast of Moscow, and headed for the Don. Shortly after crossing it, they engaged the Mongol forces at Kulikovo Field. Unfortunately for Mamai, neither the Lithuanians nor Riazan forces arrived in time. He was defeated and forced to flee south.

The Mongol hold over Russia was not yet ended. Two years after Kulikovo, a rival Mongol leader named Tokhtamysh, after defeating Mamai in

The Battle of Kulikovo

In this excerpt from the military tale *Zadonshchina*, we see a poetic, not completely factual, rendition of the famous 1380 battle. Yet most later Russians saw the conflict in the same general way: as a Moscow-led Christian Russian holy war against Moslem Tatar oppression (Islam had become the official religion of the Golden Horde early in the fourteenth century). The author of the tale was Sofoni of Riazan; the excerpt is from Leo Wiener, *Anthology of Russian Literature: From the Earliest Period to the Present Time* (New York, 1902) Vol. I, pp. 108–111. Bracketed material and ellipses are mine except for the ellipsis in the third paragraph, where they appear in Wiener's translation.

All the Russian princes came to the aid of Grand Prince Dmitri Ivanovich, and they spoke as follows: "Lord Grand Prince! Already do the pagan Tartars encroach upon our fields, and take away our patrimony. They stand between the Don and Dnieper, on the river Mecha. But we, Lord, will go beyond the swift river Don, will gain glory in all the lands, will be an object of conver-

sation for the old men, and a memory for the young." . . .

. . . the Russian princes have attacked the Tartar might, and they strike with their steel lances against the Tartar armour; the tempered swords thunder against the Tartar helmets on the field of Kulikovo, on the river Nepryadva. Black is the earth under the hoofs, but they had sowed the field with Tartar bones, and the earth was watered with their blood. . . . and they vanquished the Tartar horde on the field of Kulikovo, on the river Nepryadva. . . .

All over the Russian land there spread joy and merriment: the Russian glory was borne through the land, but shame and destruction came on the pagan Tartars, evil Mussulmans. . . . The Grand Prince by his own bravery and with his druzhina vanquished pagan Mamay for the sake of the Russian land and the Christian faith. The pagans deposited their own arms under the Russian swords, and the trumpets were not sounded, their voices were silent. Mamay galloped away from his druzhina, howled like a grey wolf, and ran away to the city of Khafest [Kaffa in the Crimea].

1381, ravaged Moscow. Dmitri once again became a loyal tax-collector for this new khan and brought troops into Novgorodian territory in 1386 to enforce payment of a special assessment to him.

Tokhtamysh's successful 1382 campaign also weakened Dmitri's influence among Russian princes. A few had even helped Tokhtamysh defeat Dmitri. His leverage over the Orthodox Church also lessened during the last years of his life—his mentor Metropolitan Alexei had died in 1378. But these setbacks were only temporary. The strengthening of Moscow, both in relation to other parts of Russia and to the Mongols, would continue after Dmitri's death in 1389. He had shown dramatically that the Mongols could be defeated in battle.

THE LITHUANIAN CHALLENGE

One of Moscow's chief enemies and rivals was Lithuania. Partly in reaction to the pressure of the Germanic Knights, Prince Mendovg (Mindaugas) united the Lithuanian tribes in the middle of the thirteenth century. Before his death in 1263, he expanded Lithuanian control into a portion of the former Rus principality of Polotsk.

For the remainder of the century, Lithuanian gains over former Rus lands were minimal. Lithuania was more concerned with its own internal political order and the expansive Germanic Knights on its western and northeastern borders. Its expansion began to accelerate again under Gedymin (Gedyminas), who ruled from 1316 to 1341. Through a shrewd combination of warfare, dynastic marriages, and diplomacy, he spread Lithuanian control over the rest of Belorussia and began penetrating southward into Ukraine. He also exercised strong influence on Novgorod and Pskov, both of which welcomed a counterweight to play off against Muscovite interference, and he established good relations with the princely house of Tver, even marrying one of his daughters to Prince Dmitri of Tver (1322–1325).

Gedymin's two sons Olgerd (Algirdas) and Keistut (Kestutis), who ruled jointly after him, continued Lithuanian expansion to the south and east. Olgerd was especially successful. Defeating Mongol forces, he established his authority over the lands of Kiev, Chernigov, much of Smolensk, and the rest of Volhynia. In 1368 and again in 1370, he attacked Moscow in support of his ally Mikhail II of Tver, although on neither occasion was their combined force able to capture the city. Before Olgerd's death in 1377, the Grand Principality of Lithuania was the largest state in Europe. It controlled about half of old Kievan Rus, and about 70 percent of its people were descendants of the Rus and were Orthodox.

The leaders of Lithuania had created a large political federation more by co-option than by conquest. Many East Slavs welcomed them as preferable to Mongol overlords. Once brought into the new federation, these East Slavs made up the bulk of Lithuania's armies in the south, which battled mainly with the Mongols and their supporters.

A political, social, and cultural merging also took place. While Lithuanian princes were given control over large principalities, such as Volhynia and Kiev, many Slavic princes and nobles maintained their positions and estates. Numerous Lithuanian princes and nobles intermarried with their Slavic counterparts and accepted many of their customs and even Orthodoxy. The Slavic language spoken by most of the Slavs in the new state became its official government language. Olgerd consciously thought of himself as a gatherer of the Rus lands, and many Ukrainian historians, following the example of Hrushevsky, have maintained that the Grand Principality of Lithuania continued the traditions of Kievan Rus more faithfully than did Moscow.

Both Gedymin and Olgerd realized the political importance of Orthodoxy. Olgerd himself possibly accepted Orthodoxy—his sons certainly did, although some later changed to Catholicism. Gedymin and Olgerd only occasionally were able to persuade the patriarch in Constantinople to appoint a separate Orthodox metropolitan for their country. Otherwise, the Moscow metropolitan had jurisdiction over the Lithuanian Orthodox. Olgerd, however, complained of the favoritism Metropolitan Alexei showered upon Moscow.

There was some justification to Olgerd's charge. There were also more Orthodox believers in the Lithuanian territories than in those under Moscow's control. Thus, Patriarch Philotheus in Constantinople responded by appointing in 1375 a Bulgarian named Cyprian to a separate metropolitanate in Lithuania. The patriarch intended for it to exist only temporarily—until the death of old Metropolitan Alexei of Moscow, at which time the conciliatory Cyprian was to become metropolitan over the Orthodox in both Russia and Lithuania.

Olgerd died in 1377 and Metropolitan Alexei in 1378, but Dmitri Donskoi still had more than another decade to live, and he supported his own metropolitan claimant. Only after Dmitri's death in 1389 did Cyprian assume full control over a single united metropolitanate, once again headquartered in Moscow.

By then, however, a more momentous event had occurred in the struggle for Orthodox hearts and the Kievan Rus legacy. Threatened by the Germanic Knights and some internal challenges to his authority, Olgerd's son Jagiello (Jogailo) had allied with Poland. In the Treaty of Krewo (1385), he promised to marry the Polish queen, Jadwiga, and, along with his nobles, convert to Catholicism. Although the treaty marked the beginning of four centuries of dynastic and later (1569) constitutional union with Poland and brought many advantages to the Lithuanians, in the long run it weakened their hold over former Kievan Rus lands. As the Catholic religion and Polish culture increasingly influenced the Lithuanian elite, the gap widened between Catholic Lithuanians and the Orthodox Slavs they ruled over in Belorussian and Ukrainian lands.

MOSCOW'S STRUGGLES AND SUCCESSES, 1389–1462

During the long reigns of Vasili I (1389–1425) and Vasili II (1425–1462), son and grandson of Dmitri Donskoi, Moscow's ruling dynasty became stronger. But Moscow's rise was a ragged one with many rises and plunges. Before the dynasty could emerge strengthened, it had to overcome Lithuanian and Mongol challenges, differences with the Orthodox patriarchs in Constantinople (who pursued their own religious-political agenda), and civil wars within Muscovy. Moscow's ultimate successes were due less to the political skills of the first two Vasilis than to the increasing handicaps hampering its enemies and rivals.

Lithuania, the Mongols, and Moscow

At first, the acceptance of Catholicism by Jagiello in 1385 did not noticeably hinder Lithuania in its struggle with Moscow. Jagiello's marriage and conversion seemed to create an awesome new Polish-Lithuanian union.

Jagiello's championing of Catholicism and unleashing of Polish influence in his grand principality, however, soon awakened opposition, especially among Orthodox Slavs but also among some Lithuanians. Apparently with some encouragement from Moscow, a forceful challenger to Jagiello rose to lead them, his cousin Vitovt (Vytautas). In 1392, Jagiello was forced to recognize his de facto control over Lithuania, although Jagiello himself kept the title King of Poland-Lithuania. This rivalry, however, did not seem to hamper Lithuania in its policy of eastward expansion.

By his death in 1430, Vitovt appeared to have strengthened Lithuania's dominance in the old Rus lands. He gained additional territory in the Smolensk area and was recognized as the protector of Tver as well as of the upper Oka River princes south of Moscow. Furthermore, the princes of Riazan and Pronsk signed a treaty shortly before his death, acknowledging him as their sovereign. In Pskov and Novgorod, he wielded considerable influence, forcing both to pay indemnities for ceasing campaigns against them (in 1426 and 1428, respectively).

Surprisingly enough, he accomplished all this while generally maintaining good relations with Moscow. In 1391, he married his daughter Sophia to Vasili I. Thereafter, he exercised some influence on his son-in-law, and after Vasili I's death, Vitovt supported Vasili II (his own grandson) in his battle against other claimants to the Moscow throne.

Further south, despite losing a major battle to the Golden Horde in 1399, Vitovt took advantage of the Horde's gradual disintegration to extend Lithuanian dominance to the Black Sea.

In the religious sphere, however, Vitovt was less successful. When Metropolitan Cyprian died in 1406, Vitovt nominated one successor and Vasili I another. The patriarch chose Vasili's candidate, Photius, and Vitovt ultimately had little choice but to recognize him as the spiritual head of Lithuania's Orthodox subjects.

The next important episode in this ongoing spiritual saga centered around Photius's successor, Isidore. He was previously a Byzantine abbot sympathetic to reunion between Catholics and Orthodox. Like his patriarch, he hoped reunion would bring Western help against the Moslem Ottoman Turks, then slicing away at the Byzantine Empire. In 1437, Isidore left Moscow in charge of a delegation to an ecumenical council in Italy. At this Ferrara-Florence council, he played an important role in reestablishing Orthodox-Catholic union.

After returning to Moscow in 1441, following stopovers in east-central Europe and Kiev, Isidore proclaimed the new church unity at the Kremlin's main cathedral, the Assumption. Upon witnessing such ecumenical fervor, Vasili II arrested Isidore and confined him in the Chudov Monastery. Vasili then met with a council of Russian bishops, which was already alarmed at what it had heard from earlier returning members of Isidore's delegation.

To Vasili II and the bishops' council the terms accepted at the Council of Ferrara-Florence were unacceptable. They believed too much had been forsaken, especially the Orthodox belief regarding the Holy Spirit's procession from God the Father alone and Orthodox opposition to papal supremacy. They now rejected both Isidore and his message of reunion.

At the end of 1448, after Isidore had long since left Russian territory, another council of Russian bishops met and selected, on their own, a new metropolitan, Bishop Iona of Riazan. The break with the Byzantine patriarch, now realigned with Rome, was complete. When in 1453, Constantinople finally fell to the Turks, many Russian Orthodox leaders saw it as God's punishment for Byzantium's apostasy.

The effect of all these Russian-Byzantine church dealings was to solidify just what the Lithuanian leaders had always feared: too close a relationship between Moscow and the metropolitan. Even after the first Turkish-appointed patriarch returned to Orthodoxy, the Russian Orthodox Church continued to act independently.

A Lithuanian response soon followed. The Catholic King Casimir IV had by this time firmly brought all Poland-Lithuania under his control, and in 1458 he accomplished what his predecessors had failed to do: he established a permanent Orthodox metropolitanate in Kiev. Thereafter the Catholic Polish-Lithuanian lay leaders controlled Orthodox religious appointments in their realm. Although an apparent victory for Casimir, the separate metropolitanate just further isolated Moscow's metropolitan, making him more dependent than ever on the Orthodox Moscow grand prince.

From all these slowly evolving Orthodox religious developments in the lands of old Rus, Ivan III of Moscow would soon begin collecting more tangible gains. If these gains were still largely in the future, Moscow's dividends from growing Mongol disunity were already being cashed in. First, there was the conflict between the Golden Horde's Khan Tokhtamysh and the infamous conqueror and empire-builder Tamerlane, who by 1370 had become the real power in the Mongol Chagatai khanate. In the early 1390s, Vasili I took advantage of Tokhtamysh's troubles to annex parts of the Nizhnii Novgorod area. After Tokhtamysh fled to Lithuania, allied with Vitovt, and continued his fight against Tamerlane's victorious Golden Horde ally Edigei (d. 1419), Vasili noted the challenge to Edigei and suspended tribute payments to him.

Although racked with internal divisiveness, the Golden Horde did not expire without some last attacks on Moscow. In 1408, for example, Khan Edigei raided Moscow, pillaged areas around the city, and left only after Moscow agreed to pay him 3,000 rubles.

During the reign of Vasili II, the Golden Horde finally split apart. Out of it emerged three main khanates: those of Kazan, the Crimea, and Sarai (later Astrakhan). The division did not mean an end to Mongol demands or raids upon Russia, but it greatly reduced their effectiveness. Vasili II and his successors now could play off various Mongol factions against each other. In the second half of his reign, Vasili even recruited sons of one of the rival khans, along with their followers. The most prominent of them, Kasim, formed a Russian puppet khanate on the Oka River, southeast of Moscow. This khanate of Kasimov, as it was called after its founder, became a vital defensive outpost against Mongol attacks.

Princely Conflict over Moscow

When Vasili II came to the throne in 1425, he was only ten, and the first decades of his reign were punctuated with challenges to his authority and with civil war. The chief challengers were Vasili's uncle Yuri of the northern region of Galich, who died in 1434, and then his sons Vasili and Dmitri (Shemiaka). Moscow's Daniilovich dynasty had been fortunate to this point in that births and deaths within it had made it easy to determine successors, but uncle Yuri insisted on the old collateral principle—succession passing first from brother to brother, rather than father to son. In 1433, Yuri marched on Moscow and briefly grabbed power; in 1446, after Vasili had returned from four months as a Mongol prisoner, Dmitri did the same. Following both these brief interludes, Vasili II regained his throne, although on the second occasion not before being blinded on Dmitri's orders. This blinding was a reciprocal act for the earlier blinding of Dmitri's brother Vasili on orders from Vasili II.

Aided by his own internal victories and Mongol divisiveness, Vasili now strengthened both Moscow's standing and his own authority. In 1448, he made his eight-year-old son, Ivan, co-ruler and heir to his throne, and he did it without seeking Mongol approval. The next year he signed a treaty with Casimir IV of Poland-Lithuania, allowing both rulers to concentrate more on other matters than their disputed mutual borders. Among other provisions, the treaty recognized Moscow's predominance in Novgorod and Pskov. In 1456, while Casimir was fighting a war with the Germanic Knights, the blind Vasili and his army attacked and defeated Novgorod, which had earlier given final support to his rival Dmitri. Finally, Vasili increased his control over junior appanage princes who ruled over small Daniilovich territories (like Mozhaisk and Serpukhov).

Although he had begun his reign as a ten-year-old boy sitting shakily on his throne and subsequently suffered many ups and downs, when Vasili died in 1462 he left a much stronger Muscovy to his son. Both Moscow and the office of grand prince now held unchallenged supremacy, if not yet complete control, over other Great Russian areas and princes. The Golden Horde was no more, and Muscovy was stronger than any of its remnants. Although still mighty under Casimir IV, Poland-Lithuania was preoccupied with other matters at home and abroad, and its dominant Catholicism left it vulnerable in its Orthodox border territories.

THE END OF NOVGORODIAN INDEPENDENCE AND THE TRIUMPH OF MOSCOW, 1462–1533

Ivan III (1462–1505) and his son, Vasili III (1505–1533), completed Moscow's quest to dominate Great Russia. Of the two rulers, Ivan III (the Great) accomplished the most, and Russian historians have called him "the gatherer of the Russian lands."

Ivan III and Vasili III: The Men and Their Goals

The only physical description left to us of Ivan III was by the Italian Ambrogio Contarini—one of a growing number of foreign observers who now appear in Russia. Contarini said Ivan was tall, thin, and handsome. Ivan's youthful experiences—observing the plots against his father, being named co-ruler at eight, married at twelve, a father at eighteen, leading a campaign against a Mongol army at eighteen or nineteen—must have helped mature him early. After coming to the throne at twenty-two, his words and deeds reveal a skillful politician: active but cautious; cold-blooded, but not blood-thirsty; opportunistic, yet possessing an ultimate goal. His goal was to expand Muscovite territory and to create a strong, centralized government to run the expanded state.

Although also strong and clever, Vasili III's character is a bit harder to discern. He was the son of a Byzantine princess (Ivan's second wife) and, like his father, had some military and government experience before assuming the throne at twenty-six. He also had undergone some trying times before succeeding his father. Ivan had first designated as his heir a grandson, the son of a deceased son from his first marriage. Only about five years later, in 1502, did he reverse himself and name Vasili as heir.

Like his father, Vasili also had two wives. He sent the first one to a convent to become a nun (she had produced no children) and then married a Lithuanian immigrant princess, Elena Glinskaia. Apparently to please his young bride, he shaved off his beard, a highly unusual act for a Russian ruler.

As with earlier Muscovite princes, economic considerations remained important to these two rulers. It affected their dealings with Novgorod and other Russian and foreign lands and many of their internal policies.[3]

Moscow's Conquest of Novgorod and Other Russian Lands

When Ivan III became grand prince of Moscow in 1462, four other independent Great Russian principalities still existed—Yaroslavl, Riazan, Rostov, and Tver—plus the independent city states of Novgorod, Pskov, and Viatka. The first areas Ivan III annexed (by 1474) were the small ones of Yaroslavl and Rostov, both already under Moscow's dominance. He also solidified Moscow's influence over Riazan by marrying his sister to Riazan's Prince Vasili. But his largest conquest was Novgorod. In 1471, he defeated it in battle and in 1478 annexed it.

By the beginning of Ivan III's reign, Novgorod had experienced some decline from its heyday. It had always depended on fur tribute, especially from Finnic tribes, and on exporting fur as an essential part of its extensive foreign trade. During the fourteenth and early fifteenth centuries, Novgorod's government and upper classes had developed an extensive network for gathering and trading grey squirrel skins, a type of fur that had become fashionable in Europe. The chief buyers of these skins were German merchants, some of them part of the Hanseatic League, a powerful Germanic trading association with a branch in Novgorod's foreign compound of Peterhof. By 1462, however, Novgorod's fur gathering and trade were being undercut by (1) shifts in upperclass European tastes (toward more luxurious skins), (2) trade disputes and

---

[3] See also Chapter 7 for Ivan III's will and examples of Vasili III's possessiveness.

other differences with German merchants, and (3) Moscow's steady encroach-
ment on lands that once paid fur tribute or taxes to Novgorod. The latter two
factors also harmed other aspects of Novgorod's trade and economy.

In Novgorodian politics, the *veche* continued to exist, but the boyar elite,
which had become more powerful than ever, dominated it. Novgorod still selected its own prince and restricted his rights, and with its weak military, it remained susceptible to outside attacks. At first, following in the footsteps of
Alexander Nevsky and other grand princes, the Muscovite princes had occasionally attacked Novgorod as enforcers of Mongol tribute demands. Later,
even though Muscovite princes sought and generally gained Novgorod recognition as its "protector," they still sometimes attacked it, as Vasili II had done
in 1456. To understand why necessitates a more thorough look at Novgorod's
internal and external relations.

Novgorodian society was quite stratified, from boyars and "well-to-do
people" (*zhitye liudi*) at the top to slaves at the bottom. By the mid-fifteenth
century, Novgorodian politics was dominated by several dozen powerful
boyar clans, whose wealth derived both from land and from trade. Also powerful was Novgorod's archbishop, who presided over the otherwise boyar-
dominated Council of Lords and sometimes acted as the city-state's chief representative. As head of the Novgorod Church, he controlled lands worth more
than those of any single landowner. Less significant, but still influential, was
the archimandrite, who had his own jurisdiction as head of Novgorod's
monastic community and its prosperous lands. Yet the political-religious elite
was by no means united, nor were Novgorod's more common citizens, some of
whom occasionally displayed their hostility to boyar wealth and privileges.

Splits within Novgorodian society were heightened by the Lithuanian-
Moscow competition for dominance in the former Rus lands. Caught between
two expanding powers, most Novgorodians believed they had to ally with one
or the other of these "superpowers." The choice of which one divided the boyars as well as other Novgorodians.

Preference for Moscow or Lithuania was partly a question of economics.
Since the days of Ivan I, Moscow had contended with Novgorod for tribute
and tax payments, often in the forms of furs, from peoples in Far Northern
Russian lands. In the late fourteenth century, thanks partly to the missionary
efforts of St. Stephen of Perm, some Finnic Permians switched their fur tribute
from Novgorod to Moscow. Contention and conflicts over other areas of the
Far North followed in the first half of the fifteenth century.

Novgorod's support of the rebellious Dmitri Shemiaka in his civil war
against Vasili II was partly motivated by Novgorodian wishes to regain access
to some of the fur and fur routes it had earlier lost. Vasili's victory against
Dmitri strengthened Moscow's hand in the Far North, however, and Vasili's
subsequent attack on Novgorod in 1456 cost the Novgorodians dearly. By the
terms of the treaty ending the war, Novgorodian boyars had to relinquish to
Moscow all the lands they had obtained from the appanage princes of Rostov
and Beloozero. Novgorod also had to pay a 10,000-ruble fine, agree to Moscow
approval of any documents issued by its *veche*, and cease providing sanctuary
to any enemies of Moscow's grand prince.

During the next decade and a half, Moscow continued chipping away at the Far Northern territories formerly under Novgorodian control. The desire for the area's luxury furs, such as sable, now in fashion in Europe, was one reason for the continuing struggle.

Thus, a sharp economic rivalry for land, fur, and trade routes motivated some Novgorodian boyars who adopted an anti-Moscow stance. Economic considerations, however, influenced other prosperous Novgorodians to believe they would be better off with a pro-Muscovite policy. Good relations with Moscow seemed to offer the possibility of smoother, less disruptive east-west trade, important for Novgorod, which traditionally had acted as an intermediary for such activity. Besides, Novgorod itself depended on Russian lands to its southeast for such valuable imports as grain. Despite some historians' contention that the wealthy were pro-Lithuanian and the commoners pro-Muscovite, the reality was more complex.

Besides economic issues, religious-cultural and political considerations also affected the Lithuanian or Moscow choice. As the center of Russian Orthodoxy, Moscow was undoubtedly a magnet attracting some Novgorodians, whereas Lithuania's dominant Catholicism and increasingly Polonized culture were much more foreign to Orthodox Novgorodians. Yet some clergy supported a pro-Lithuanian policy for political reasons. Like some of their fellow Novgorodians, they feared that embracing the Muscovite grand prince would lead to the end of Novgorodian independence, whereas the Lithuanian monarch would be less interfering in their affairs.

In 1470, with the pro-Lithuanian faction temporarily dominant, Novgorod's government requested Casimir IV of Poland-Lithuania to send them a prince. They also sought his aid in having their archbishop-elect consecrated in the newly established metropolitanate of Kiev, which Casimir had worked so hard to establish. An Orthodox and Slavic prince, Mikhail of Kiev, then arrived in Novgorod, briefly serving as its prince before changing his mind.

Moscow's Ivan III viewed these activities as cause for war and claimed that Orthodoxy was being threatened. He mobilized his troops and attacked Novgorod. In 1471, aided by Novgorod's internal divisiveness and Lithuania's failure to send help—Casimir was then more concerned with Hungarian and Bohemian affairs—Ivan won a major battle on the Shelon River.

Ivan followed up his victory by ordering the beheading of at least four anti-Muscovite leaders. One of them was the son of the widow Marfa Boretskaia, a powerful boyar woman who played a leading role among Novgorod's pro-Lithuanian faction. Chronicle accounts also mention some plundering and burning before Novgorod sent a delegation to Ivan, pleading for mercy.

Considering Ivan's strong position, his terms were restrained. The crux of the treaty was that Novgorod was to remain loyal to Moscow and to the Moscow metropolitan and cease its attempts to deal directly with Poland-Lithuania. Novgorod and its boyars also had to recognize Moscow's claims to the lands east of the Northern Dvina that Muscovites and Novgorodians had been struggling over in recent decades. But traditional Novgorodian institutions such as the *veche* were permitted to continue.

From 1471 until 1477, turbulence gusted in Novgorod. Pro-Moscow and anti-Moscow factions contended with one another in the *veche* and elsewhere. After the *veche* ordered the execution of some of Ivan's Novgorod supporters, he declared war in 1477. This time there was not even a battle. Ivan's large force just surrounded Novgorod. Realizing resistance was hopeless, Novgorod accepted Ivan's humiliating terms, and he returned to Moscow early the following year. His terms stipulated the annexation of Novgorod and its still vast territories; gave him personal control over specified lands, including some of the church; and abolished independent institutions such as the *veche* and office of *posadnik* (mayor). As a crowning humiliation, Novgorodians saw their *veche* bell removed and carted off to Moscow.

Some Novgorodians, however, plotted to regain their freedom. During the next dozen years, Ivan cut down remaining suspected opponents. He imprisoned and exiled thousands of "traitors," mostly of the upper class, and he confiscated their property. But they were more fortunate than others who were tortured and executed. Altogether, Ivan ended up confiscating about 3 million acres of arable land. These lands were then turned over to about 2,000 "service men," allowed to hold them only as long as they served the Moscow prince.[4] This system of mass land confiscation, exile, and resettlement set a precedent for similar actions in future years.

[4] See Chapter 7 on the *pomestie* landholding system.

FIGURE 6.1. Novgorod's kremlin sitting above the Volkhov River. After Ivan III's conquest of Novgorod, the earlier stone walls were replaced by brick ones, and the kremlin appeared much as it does today.

Novgorod's annexation now left Tver surrounded by the expanding Muscovite state. After Tver's Prince Mikhail tried several times to solidify relations with King Casimir of Poland-Lithuania, Ivan invaded and annexed his principality in 1485.

Next, it was the turn of the independent republic of Viatka, located north of Kazan. Like Novgorod, it had offered support to Dmitri Shemiakha against Vasili II, and its independence blocked greater Muscovite control of the fur trade. Although Vasili II defeated the Viatkans and they pledged allegiance to him in 1460, they later reverted to their independent ways until Ivan III finally subjugated them in 1489.

During the late fifteenth century, Moscow also subjugated several Finno-Ugrian tribes east of Viatka. Reacting against the Christianizing attempts of the Russians a century earlier, the Yugra, the Voguly, and some of the Perm had fled eastward as far as the Ob River in northwest Siberia. By 1500, they were all paying sable tribute to Moscow.

After Ivan III's death in 1505, Vasili III continued his father's work by fully annexing Pskov (in 1510) and completing the annexation of Riazan during the following decade. In Pskov, Vasili ordered its *veche* bell removed. In Riazan, he arrested its prince and charged him with negotiating with the khan of the Crimea. In both territories, he repeated the Novgorodian pattern of arrests, confiscations, thousands of deportations, and then resettling lands with faithful "service men." Chronicle accounts of arrested Pskovians and their families being exiled at night with only a few possessions have a chillingly twentieth-century ring.

Moscow Versus Lithuania and the Mongols

Even before the death of Poland's Casimir IV in 1492, Ivan III attempted to win over Lithuanian East Slavic and Orthodox border princes and nobles, along with their hereditary properties. To do this, he used persuasion, raiding parties, and, at times, more full-blown military campaigns. Following Casimir's death, Ivan increased military operations along the whole border area, especially in the Viazma area between Moscow and Smolensk. Casimir had left the Lithuanian part of his kingdom under the direction of his son Alexander, and in 1494, the young man agreed to peace terms favorable to Ivan.

By the treaty, Alexander recognized Ivan's control over Viazma and a large band of territory both east and west of the upper Oka river. That same year, Ivan agreed to the marriage of his daughter Elena to Alexander, provided that she was allowed to continue practicing her Orthodox faith. The marriage occurred the following year. Ivan probably hoped that Elena would act as a Russian Orthodox trojan horse inside the Catholic court of Lithuania.

By 1500, strengthened by an alliance with the Crimean Tatars, Ivan was ready for a full-scale campaign against Lithuania and began his attack that spring. His pretext was Lithuanian mistreatment of Orthodox believers, including his daughter Elena and some border-area princes who announced they were switching their allegiance from Alexander to Ivan. Families were even being broken up, Ivan charged, in the Lithuanian attempt to force Catholicism upon the Lithuanian Orthodox. Alexander's denials of religious persecution and his attempts to prevent war were of no avail.

After great successes in 1500, Ivan made little further headway in the next two years. In 1503, there were peace talks but no peace treaty. Elena's assurances to her father that her husband had not persecuted her or other Orthodox had no softening effect on him. He did, however, agree to a six-year truce. By its provisions, he held on to the areas his armies had taken, including the Belorussian city of Gomel and a northeastern part of Ukraine, including the city of Chernigov. Moreover, he insisted that he had a historic right (exactly how so is not clear) to additional East Slavic lands. During the reign of Vasili III, war broke out again with Lithuania, and in 1514 Russia gained the important city and region of Smolensk.

Although Russian territorial gains from Lithuania were significant, Ivan III's reign is better known for ending the "Tatar yoke." In 1480, the Mongol khan of the Great Horde of the lower Volga, Akhmad, marched toward Moscow with a large army, apparently to force Ivan to renew tribute payments. The khan expected to meet up with Lithuanian forces sent by King Casimir. Ivan was supported by the Mongol khan of the Crimea. Ivan's forces moved south to an Oka River tributary, the Ugra. On the south side of the Ugra, Khan Akhmad waited for the Lithuanian troops, but (as in 1380) they never appeared. Except for a Mongol attempt to cross the river, which Russian arrows and guns beat back, there was little fighting. A little more than a month after reaching the Ugra, Khan Akhmad mysteriously retreated—the Lithuanians' absence plus news of a Russian expedition against his lower Volga headquarters were perhaps the chief reasons.

Whatever the reasons, the retreat marked an important psychological-moral victory for the Russians, even if it was not quite the decisive turning point that some Russian ideologues and historians later made it out to be.

Actually, for about a century, from the mid-fifteenth until the mid-sixteenth, Russian-Mongol relations remained in a state of flux. Russians made incursions into Mongol lands, especially to the east into the khanate of Kazan, and Mongol forces attacked Russian lands. For example, horsemen from the Crimean khanate devastated and plundered southern Russia almost up to Moscow's walls in 1521. Considerable diplomatic activity also went on, with both Russia and Lithuania now allying with one Mongol khanate and then another. Although the Russians no longer paid regular tribute to Mongol khans after 1480, and perhaps had not even done so for decades before, they did in shaky times continue sending "gifts" to various khans.

EVOLUTION OF MUSCOVY'S GOVERNMENT

The government inherited by Ivan III in 1462 was still a fairly primitive one. It had evolved mainly from the grand prince's estate management staff and was primarily concerned with insuring maximum economic gain for the prince. Maintaining law and order was a means to this end.

To assist him and his growing staff, the grand prince depended on five to ten boyars, with the number expanding slightly after 1462. After a man became a boyar, his descendants or clan became part of a boyar elite. By the end of the fourteenth century, the Muscovite prince usually selected his boyars from among the heads of these elite clans. As Kollmann states: "There were fewer than 15 boyar families in existence at any one time in the fourteenth century, and the number of boyars from those families fluctuated between about five and ten."[5]

Although it was possible for new families to break into this exclusive circle, or older ones to lose boyar status, many boyar clans maintained their position for at least several generations. Some boyar families had long resided in the Moscow area, and others were newcomers; some came from princely lines, and others were untitled.

Boyars relied on marriage alliances, kinship ties, and patronage networks to strengthen their families and themselves. Most important, however, in maintaining their status was the valuable service they rendered the grand prince. They were his chief advisers (whether a formal Boyar Council then existed is not entirely clear), provided cavalry troops for battle, and helped him administer Muscovy's internal and foreign policies.

The boyars were the elite of a landed military class, and for their services the Muscovite grand prince generally showered rewards upon them. Gaining such rewards was no doubt one reason for the intense competition for boyar positions. Despite such competition, the boyars generally cooperated to maintain a system that benefited them. Their relationship to the grand prince was a personal one that stressed loyalty. Although they possessed real power and influence, they did not think of themselves as a "class" competing with the prince for political power, and they made no collective efforts to restrict his legal powers, which were unlimited.

As Moscow grew, so too did its court and government. Prior to Ivan III's reign, however, it remained small, especially outside the Kremlin. At first, the Moscow princes depended chiefly on selected individuals to ride around different areas collecting taxes and the Mongol tribute, while also acting as traveling courts of appeal. By the end of the fourteenth century, the grand prince relied more on governors and district administrators—by then there were only about 15 of the former and 100 of the latter. Instead of salaries, they were allowed to "feed themselves" (the infamous *kormlenie* system), which meant that the people they administered were to provide for their maintenance, and in addition these administrators were allowed to keep for themselves a share of court fees and taxes.

The tremendous expansion of Muscovite territory under Ivan III and Vasili III required significant adaptations to this basic system. Ivan III was especially skillful in integrating princes and aristocrats from annexed principalities into his own administration and military. By the middle of the sixteenth century,

---

[5] Nancy Shields Kollmann, *Kinship and Politics: The Making of the Muscovite Political System, 1345–1547* (Stanford, 1987), p. 33.

the "Sovereign's Court" consisted primarily of a few thousand noble landowners who acted as both an elite military unit (the sovereign's bodyguard) and a pool from which he selected important military and government officials. The ruler's court also included an increasing number of scribes (or state secretaries), who were of mixed social origin. Some of them became proficient and influential in areas such as finance and diplomacy, but, compared to the boyar clans, they possessed little power at court.

A final group that at first glance might seem powerful were the younger brothers of the grand prince. By their father's will, they were given appanage territories over which they could rule, as long as they passed the "Tatar tribute" (even if no longer paid to the Mongols) on to their older brother. Strong rulers like Ivan III and Vasili III, however, made sure that none of their brothers became serious challengers to Muscovite rule. These two princes also prevented their brothers from having too many children (possible future rivals to them or their heir) by delaying or prohibiting the marriages of most of their brothers.

While adding new territories, both Ivan III and Vasili III elevated the prestige of the Muscovite grand prince. Ivan was the first Muscovite ruler to refer to himself as "autocrat" and "tsar" (from the Latin *Caesar*, meaning emperor). Autocrat was meant to signify that Ivan was subject to no khan or other foreign ruler. Tsar had been used to designate both Byzantine rulers and Mongol khans, but some Russian churchmen after the Mongol's retreat in 1480 argued that the only true tsar, since the end of the Byzantine Empire, was the Russian ruler.

Besides the 1480 Mongol defeat and the Turks' earlier obliteration of the Byzantine Empire, Ivan's victories over his Russian rivals and Lithuania also contributed to his new exalted image. So too did his marriage in 1472—five years after his first wife's death—to Sophia (earlier Zoe) Paleologue, the niece of the last Byzantine Emperor.

The marriage of Sophia and Ivan had been encouraged by the pope, under whose influence Sophia had been educated. He probably hoped, unrealistically as it turned out, that Sophia would promote church unity based on the Ferrara-Florence accord and help enlist Ivan in a crusade against the Ottoman Turks. Despite Ivan's use of the marriage to bolster his prestige, he did not immediately adopt selected Byzantine symbols and ceremonial practices, as historians have sometimes suggested. The use of the two-headed eagle as a Muscovite emblem, for example, came only in the 1490s and then was occasioned more by imitation and rivalry with the Holy Roman Empire than by a desire to copy Byzantium, which also had used the symbol.

Yet it was no accident that during the reigns of Ivan and his son the theory of Moscow the Third Rome developed. By the 1520s, it meant that the first two Romes (Rome and Constantinople) had both fallen as God's punishment—the Byzantines because of the Ferrara-Florence accords—and that Russia was now the Third (and final) Rome. In other words, the Christian Russians were God's final chosen people. Although most fully enunciated by a Pskov abbot, Philotheus (Filofei), and perhaps having no influence on Vasili III, such ideas had been germinating among some Russian clerics for about a half century.

A contemporary of Philotheus, abbot Joseph of Volokolamsk Monastery (d.

1515), elaborated a theory that further supported Moscow and its ruler. Although he had earlier had his differences with Ivan III and Vasili III, in his final writings he expressed the following ideas: (1) The ruler is God's representative; (2) his main concern should be the spiritual welfare of his people; (3) all his subjects, whether lay or religious, should humbly obey him unless he is clearly acting in a non-Christian manner; (4) even then, however, their disobedience should be passive, willing to suffer at the hands of the unjust ruler.[6]

In his final years, Joseph indicated that he believed Vasili III was a good Christian ruler. Joseph's stance helped strengthen the powers of Muscovy rulers, including those over the Russian Orthodox Church. Following Joseph's death, Vasili III removed a metropolitan who was insufficiently accommodating and replaced him with Daniel, Joseph's successor as abbot of Volokolamsk. Daniel later gave his blessing to Vasili's divorce and remarriage.

The efforts of Muscovite monarchs and churchmen in the late fifteenth–early sixteenth centuries to upgrade the prestige of the Muscovite grand princes and Muscovy built upon an earlier religious-political tradition. Muscovite princes attempted to create an image of themselves as God's instruments in ruling over the faithful Muscovite believers. Vasili II made especially effective use of the cult of the abbot Sergius (d. 1392), who became Russia's most revered medieval saint. Ivan III and Vasili III followed Vasili's example. By such means as pilgrimages to the dead abbot's Holy Trinity–St. Sergius Monastery and lavishing gifts upon it, supporting his recognition as a saint, and making him appear more a backer of the Daniilovich dynasty than he actually was, these monarchs took advantage of a genuine cult that had begun from below. By identifying the Muscovite princely house with such a humble and loving saint, they increased their own prestige.

Many ceremonies at court, including coronations, the observation of religious holy days (sometimes involving public processions), royal weddings, and funerals, reinforced the Muscovite ruler's religious image. One such ceremony toward the end of Vasili III's reign was a three-day affair revolving around the consecration of the Church of the Ascension at the monarch's Kolomenskoe estate near Moscow. Vasili had commissioned the church's construction in 1529 in thanks for the birth of his son Ivan (the future Ivan the Terrible). Its towering tentlike roof was unprecedented in brick or masonry construction. "As an expression of the Muscovite ruler's special relation to the deity, the form of the Ascension at Kolomenskoe can be compared to a votive candle, a fortress tower, a beacon—all serving as metaphors of the authority of the grand prince, the endurance of the princely dynasty, and the centrality of Moscow in the formation of the Russian state."[7]

The acquisition of new territories, the collapse of the Byzantine Empire, and the final overthrowing of the "Tatar yoke," all combined to spur the Muscovite monarchs to expand their government and upgrade their prestige and that of their country. Although Moscow's centralizing efforts were limited by

---

[6] See Chapter 7 for more on Joseph of Volokolamsk and other religious developments.
[7] William Craft Brumfield, *A History of Russian Architecture* (Cambridge, Eng., 1993), p. 119.

FIGURE 6.2. Church of the Ascension at Kolomenskoe royal estate, near Moscow, commissioned in 1529.

certain practical considerations, especially financial ones, these efforts did integrate more thoroughly the Russian people.

In these tasks, the Muscovite monarchs were assisted by the country's political-religious elite. Even though boyar clans or church leaders attempted to increase their own powers or influence, they were content to do so informally, behind what Kollmann has labeled "the facade of autocracy." In dealing with Vasili III's son, Ivan the Terrible, as well as later rulers, the nature of Russian autocracy and whether it was just a facade or a more substantial construction will become clearer.

CAUSES OF MOSCOW'S SUCCESS

In achieving its dominant role in Russia, Moscow benefited from its Mongol policies of cooperation and then later leading the effort to end Mongol controls. It also was aided by the support it received from the Orthodox metropolitans, who resided in Moscow beginning in 1325. Although not agreeing on all issues with the Muscovite prince, the metropolitan generally backed him in his battles with other areas, like Tver or Novgorod. Sometimes a metropolitan relied on persuasion; other times he used spiritual weapons, such as excommunication or the withholding of his blessing from the people of a rebellious prince. The backing of the Moscow metropolitan was also vital in Moscow's conflicts with Poland-Lithuania for the hearts and minds—and territory—of the Orthodox East Slavs who had come under Polish-Lithuanian control.

Moscow's advantage in these two areas, Mongols and metropolitans, becomes even clearer if we look at its two strongest competitors in northern Russia, Novgorod and Tver. Novgorod had an especially uncooperative attitude toward the Mongols. The khans were determined to tap into its rich revenues, however, and Moscow helped in this regard. As for Tver, its rebelliousness against the Mongols in 1327 cost it dearly in the leadership contest with Moscow. Its generally close relations with Lithuania provided another reason for the Golden Horde to favor Moscow over it.

The attempts of Tver and Novgorod to use Lithuania as a counterweight to Moscow failed for many reasons. Certainly religion was one of them. At the end of the 1360s, Metropolitan Alexei excommunicated Mikhail II of Tver for allying with the Lithuanian Olgerd, thought to be a pagan. The subsequent conversion of Lithuanian leaders to Catholicism continued to alienate them from Moscow's metropolitans. Other causes that aided Moscow include its geographic position, economic factors, and the administrative and political abilities of its rulers.

Among Moscow's geographic advantages was its central location amidst the Russian lands, which exposed it less to attacks from outside enemies and furthered its trade and expansion in all directions. Situated on the Moscow River, it had access to the Volga, via the Oka River. It was also close to the sources of two other major rivers, the Dnieper and the Don. It should be noted, however, that Tver, located about 100 miles northwest of Moscow and on the Volga, also was in an extremely good geographic position.

Economic causes for Moscow's rise overlap with its relationship to the Mongols and its geographic position. Although there is no denying the economic burden placed on the Russians generally, Moscow did profit from being the Mongol's chief tax-collector. Furthermore, the Mongols' more frequent punitive raids on other Russian areas hurt them economically and encouraged both their nobles and commoners to seek safer shelter in Moscow. Mongol trade policies also aided Moscow. One example was the rerouting of the Urals' fur trade so that it came to Sarai via Moscow.

The abilities of the Moscow princes were demonstrated in many ways. We have already seen their capacity to outmaneuver their rivals in vying for the Sarai khan's favor. Many Moscow rulers were also sound businessmen, seldom missing a chance to earn a profit. The nickname of Ivan I (Kalita or moneybag) is just one indication of this. The Muscovite grand princes helped insure the financial well-being of their successors by willing them a much larger share of their property than was customary in other principalities. To take just one example, Vasili II bequeathed as many towns to his grand princely heir, Ivan III, as to his remaining four sons combined.

The wills of the Muscovite grand princes demonstrate not only their business sense, but also their eventual desire to deviate from the old collateral principle of succession. As Kollman has indicated, their establishment of primogeniture (succession from father to eldest son) made them unique among the Riurikids. Although it began more by accident—no surviving uncles to contest primogeniture in 1353, 1359, and 1389—it was solidified by Vasili II's victories over the family of his uncle Yuri of Galich in the 1430s and 1440s. Although the Muscovite grand princes would continue thereafter to pass on some territories to their younger sons, the grand princely title went only to the oldest son. Increasingly, so too did most of the Muscovite lands and wealth—upon his death in 1505, Ivan III bequeathed two-thirds of Muscovy's towns to his oldest son, while his other four sons were left with appanages containing only one-third of the towns. This preference for the oldest son helped make Muscovy more stable and less divided than other Russian princedoms.

Medieval supporters of Moscow would have added still another cause for Moscow's success and perhaps even thought it the most important: Divine assistance. Today, historians rightfully are more humble about knowing such things. Whatever the cause, Moscow did benefit from some good fortune. Some examples include the failure of Lithuanian troops in 1380 (and again later in 1480) to appear in time to aid Mongolian forces against Moscow, internal problems in both Poland-Lithuania and the Golden Horde in the fifteenth century, and the generally good health and long reigns of Moscow's rulers. If we discount the challengers to Vasili II in the 1430s and 1440s, Moscow had only five rulers from the accession of Dmitri Donskoi in 1359 until the death of Vasili III in 1533.

SUGGESTED SOURCES*

ALEF, GUSTAVE. *Rulers and Nobles in Fifteenth-Century Muscovy.* London, 1983.

BARBARO, JOSAFA, and AMBROGIO CONTARINI. *Travels to Tana and Persia.* London, 1873 (Reprint, New York, 1964).

BIRNBAUM, HENRIK. *Lord Novgorod the Great: Essays in the History and Culture of a Medieval City-State.* Columbus, Ohio, 1981.

BROWN, PETER B. "Anthropological Perspective and Early Muscovite Court Politics," *RH* 16, No. 1 (1989): 55–66.

CROSKEY, ROBERT M. *Muscovite Diplomatic Practice in the Reign of Ivan III.* New York, 1987.

FENNELL, JOHN. *The Emergence of Moscow 1304–1359.* London, 1968.

———. *Ivan the Great of Moscow.* London, 1961.

GREY, IAN. *Ivan III and the Unification of Russia.* London, 1964.

HARTOG, LEO DE. *Russia and the Mongol Yoke: The History of the Russian Principalities and the Golden Horde, 1221–1502.* London, 1995. Chs. 6–9.

*See also works cited in footnotes.

HOWES, ROBERT C., ed. *The Testaments of the Grand Princes of Moscow.* Ithaca, N.Y., 1967.

MEYENDORFF, JOHN. *Byzantium and the Rise of Russia: A Study of Byzantino-Russian Relations in the Fourteenth Century.* Cambridge, Eng., 1981.

MILLER, DAVID B. "The Cult of St. Sergius of Radonezh and Its Political Uses," *SR* 52 (Winter 1993): 680–699.

OSTROWSKI, DONALD. "The Mongol Origins of Muscovite Political Institutions," *SR* 49 (Winter 1990): 525–542.

PASZKIEWICZ, HENRYK. *The Rise of Moscow's Power.* Boulder, 1983.

PRESNIAKOV, ALEXANDER E. *The Formation of the Great Russian State: A Study of Russian History in the Thirteenth to Fifteenth Centuries.* Chicago, 1970.

———. *The Tsardom of Muscovy.* Gulf Breeze, Fla., 1978.

ROWELL, S. C. *Lithuania Ascending: A Pagan Empire within East-Central Europe, 1295–1345.* Cambridge, Eng., 1994.

SOBEL, LEOPOLD. "Grand Principality of Lithuania," *MERSH* 20: 63–69.

SOLOVIEV, SERGEI M. *The Age of Vasily III.* Gulf Breeze, Fla., 1976.

———. *The Reign of Ivan III.* Gulf Breeze, Fla., 1978.

VERNADSKY, GEORGE. *Russia at the Dawn of the Modern Age.* New Haven, 1959.

ZENKOVSKY, SERGE A., ed. *The Nikonian Chronicle.* Vols. 3–5. Princeton, 1985–1989.

CHAPTER 7

Society, Religion, and Culture, 1240–1533

Russian economic and cultural life suffered from the Mongol impact well into the fourteenth century. Then, like spring after a harsh winter, it began reviving. Despite many woes—Mongol raids, civil wars, famines, and plagues—cities and monasteries grew. From the monastic movement came some of the finest exemplars of Russia's medieval culture, including St. Sergius and the icon painter Andrei Rublev.

Moscow's grand princes helped stimulate and sponsor the economic and cultural revival, and under them their capital became an impressive city and the Kremlin an architectural showpiece. These rulers, however, also tried to shape the revival to their own purposes, thereby keeping it within narrow bounds. They were primarily interested in their own political-military successes and economic gain, and partly for this reason they imposed increasing restrictions on all classes and ideas.

MONGOLS' ECONOMIC IMPACT

The immediate Mongol impact on the economic life of the Rus people was devastating. Cities were especially hard hit, many of them shattered, plundered, and strewn with corpses. Some of the survivors of this carnage, including many skilled craftsmen, were carried off as Mongol captives.

After the initial destruction, heavy Mongol tribute, tax, and labor demands merged with punitive expeditions and slave-gathering raids to keep the common people impoverished. Brick and masonry construction records and other evidence indicate that little improvement occurred in the fifty years following the Mongol invasion.

By the early fourteenth century, however, economic conditions began to improve in Russia and, despite some temporary downturns, continued improving until the second half of the sixteenth century. Although evidence is scanty, it is varied: construction records, archaeological finds, the observations of foreigners, gradually increasing urbanization, and the eventual decrease in tribute payments to the Mongols.

Just as all areas and classes were not equally impoverished in the thirteenth century, so too all did not equally partake of the fourteenth-century upturn. Two regions that did benefit were Novgorod and Pskov, and they continued to sustain healthy economies thereafter. Although Moscow lagged behind the two more affluent northwest territories, at least in the heyday of their independence, it also grew more prosperous. How the upturn affected the average commoner is unclear. The success of the Moscow princes in reducing and eventually eliminating payments to the Golden Horde did not mean that the money they saved trickled down to Muscovite peasants or poor urban dwellers.

Although the Mongols were the chief cause of the initial depression, they also helped stimulate the recovery that followed. Many cities that grew in the fourteenth century benefited from the Mongols' furthering of international trade, especially via the Volga River. These included not only Volga cities such as Nizhnii Novgorod, but also others such as Novgorod, which was linked to the Volga trade and continued under the Mongols to be a center for east-west trade.

As important as Mongol actions and policies were, they do not alone account for Russia's long economic depression and then revival and growth. Many wars—dynastic, between principalities, and against foreign enemies—and the policies of the Moscow princes also influenced the economy. Moreover, there is still much that remains unclear. One of the mysteries of the fourteenth-century economy is the impact of the Black Death. It struck Russia in 1352–1353 and reappeared periodically into the fifteenth century. It killed perhaps as much as a third of the population and hit the people in towns especially hard. Yet, despite the economic damage it must have done, it left few economic footprints for historians to analyze and did not prevent overall economic growth in the late fourteenth century.

Population, Urban Life, and Foreign Trade

Although population estimates vary widely, it seems likely that by 1533 there were no more than 5 to 6 million Muscovites. Considering that the territory under the rule of Moscow was about five times the size of modern France, even 6 million was not many. The most economically advanced areas of Western Europe had five to ten times as many people per acre of land. Especially sparsely populated were the huge, but infertile, Novgorodian lands.

Despite increased urbanization after 1300, the number of town-dwellers by 1533 was also small compared to Western Europe. Even by a generous definition of what constituted a town, the number of urban dwellers was not more than 5 percent of the population. By the late fifteenth century, Pskov had perhaps 15,000 to 20,000 people. The two largest Russian cities were Novgorod (about 30,000 by 1400) and Moscow, which gradually surpassed it. By 1533, Moscow was a huge city. Although it still probably had less than 100,000 inhabitants, some contemporary estimates suggest it had even more. By compar-

Moscow in the Early Sixteenth Century

The following description of Moscow and its Kremlin (fortress) is from Sigismund von Herberstein, *Notes Upon Russia: Being a Translation of the Earliest Account of that Country, Entitled Rerum Moscoviticarum Commentarii*, trans. and ed. by R. H. Major (London, 1851), Vol. II, pp. 4–5. [Ellipses are mine.] Herberstein was in Russia in 1517 and again in 1526 as an ambassador from the Holy Roman Emperor. He was perhaps the most accurate foreign observer ever to visit Muscovite Russia.

The city itself is built of wood, and tolerably large, and at a distance appears larger than it really is, for the gardens and spacious court-yards in every house make a great addition to the size of the city, which is again greatly increased by the houses of smiths and other artificers who employ fires. These houses extend in a long row at the end of the city, interspersed with fields and meadows. Moreover, not far from the city, are some small houses, and the other side of the river some villas, where, a few years ago, the Prince Vasiley built a new city for his courtiers, called Nali (which in their language means "pour in"), because other Russians were forbidden to drink mead and

beer, except on a few days in the year, and the privilege of drinking was granted by the prince to these alone; and for this reason they separated themselves from intercourse with the rest of the inhabitants to prevent their being corrupted by their mode of living. Not far from the city are some monasteries, which alone appear like a great city to persons looking from a distance. . . .

. . . There is a fortress in it built of burnt tiles, which on one side is washed by the Mosqwa and on the other by the River Neglima [Neglinaia]. The Neglima flows from certain marshes, but is so blocked up before the city around the upper part of the fortress, that it comes out like stagnant water, and running down thence, it fills the moats of the fortress, in which are some mills, and at length, as I have said, is joined by the Mosqwa under the fortress itself. The fortress is so large, that it not only contains the very extensive and magnificently built stone palace of the prince, but the metropolitan bishop, the brothers of the prince, the peers, and a great many others, have spacious houses of wood within it. Besides these, it contains many churches, so that from its size it might itself almost be taken for a city.

ison, several Italian cities had reached 100,000 by about 1300 and London reached the same figure by about 1570. Constantinople dwarfed them all, probably reaching a half million before the end of the sixteenth century.

Besides Pskov, Novgorod, and Moscow, other cities were small. At the beginning of the sixteenth century, there were anywhere from about 30 to 160 other towns, depending on one's definition of a town. A narrow definition limits the term to administrative centers that also contained a significant number of craftsmen; a broader one includes almost any fortified site maintained by the government.

It was not size, however, as much as function that separated most Russian cities, by any definition, from those of Western Europe. As Fernand Braudel has pointed out, before 1500, 90 to 95 percent of the cities in the West had less than 2,000 people and most German cities less than 1,000. What distinguished almost all Russian cities from those in Western Europe was that their administrative-military functions so outweighed any independent business transactions and that compared to Western towns they had such little freedom or autonomy. Only Novgorod and Pskov, before their incorporation into the Muscovite state, were noticeable exceptions to these generalizations. By 1533, the old Western European proverb, "city air makes one free," could not be applied to any Russian city.

Like Novgorod and Pskov, some other towns were capitals of separate principalities—until they were taken over by Moscow. Then they usually became regional administrative-military centers. But even before this, free urban workers, artisans, shopkeepers, and merchants were a minority, easily outnumbered by those working for, or directly dependent on, the prince, his servitors, or the clergy. The Mongol expropriation of skilled craftsmen, which continued long after the initial conquest, also contributed to this disproportion.

The great majority of cities had already existed in Kievan Rus, and the newly created ones took on many characteristics of the older towns. Thus, most were still located on a river bank, usually on the higher of the two sides for more protection. The main part of the town, sometimes all of it, was surrounded by fortress walls, usually of wood—although Moscow, Novgorod, and Pskov built stronger stone or brick walls during the fourteenth and fifteenth centuries. With the exception of one or more stone churches, most of the buildings were still wooden. Log houses, scattered among wide dirt (or mud) roads, vegetable gardens, and meadows gave Russian towns a more countrified look than those of Western Europe.

In larger towns, some of the craftsmen and their families lived outside the main fortress. Many worked with leather, metal, textiles, or wood, producing primarily for others in town and the surrounding countryside. Some goods, however, had a wider market. By the fifteenth century, Moscow-produced armaments and armor were sold throughout Muscovy—but Herberstein reported that in his day government permission was required before any could be exported from the country.

Muscovite princes took a proprietary attitude toward commerce, thereby restricting the rights of city-dwellers and business. The will drawn up by Ivan III reflects this. In stipulating what he is leaving to his chief heir, Vasili III, he mentions Moscow, along with "its *tamga* [a city tax paid by artisans and merchants], and with the tax on weighing, and with the tax on measuring dry-measure goods, and with the tax on trading in the market place, and with the tax on trading stands, and with the tax on merchants' courts, and with all its customs."[1]

Herberstein noted several examples of Vasili III's possessiveness. Gifts bestowed upon Russian ambassadors abroad had to be handed over to him. Mer-

---

[1] Robert Craig Howes, ed., *The Testaments of the Grand Princes of Moscow* (Ithaca, N.Y., 1967), p. 269; bracketed material is mine.

chants bringing goods into Moscow had to have them appraised by government agents and offered to Vasili at appraised prices. Only if the ruler had no interest in them could a merchant then freely price his goods and sell them to others. Herberstein also believed that Vasili ordered his subjects to pay foreign merchants in fur skins, or some other form of barter, so as to reduce the gold or silver—the main money metal—leaving the county.

Before turning away from Herberstein's observations, a few more merit mention. He contrasted disreputable business practices in Moscow, such as overcharging foreigners, with more honorable ones that had prevailed, so he heard, in independent Pskov (before 1510). Perhaps, like many foreigners, he was a bit biased against the more Eastern trading and business practices of Moscow; Pskov, like Novgorod, had been part of the Germanic Hanseatic League's trading network and reflected more Western ways. Yet many of Herberstein's observations are corroborated by other sources. Such is the case regarding the usurious interest rates charged in Moscow. Partly because of the difficulty of repaying such loans, indebtedness was common; even princes sometimes were indebted to merchants or monasteries.

Herberstein also mentions some main articles of foreign trade: imports such as jewels, silk, cloths, silver, and gold; exports such as skins, wax, and walrus tusks. He is especially detailed about skins, which included sable, marten, ermine, fox, squirrel, lynx, wolf, and beaver—the export of these fur pelts, mainly from Novgorod and later Moscow, was the chief way of obtaining silver and paying for other imports. Among craft products exported to the Mongols were saddles and bridles.

Along with jewels and silk from the East, the Russians also imported spices, incense, soap, carpets, taffeta, brocade, and horses. From the West, along with cloth, gold, and silver, they imported such goods as metal products, salt, beer, and wine. To both East and West, the Russians exported honey and timber. While many imports were luxury items, used primarily by the upper classes or church, exports were mainly raw materials and semifinished products, along with some finished goods, often bought from the West and then sent East.

Before the Golden Horde's breakup, much Russian trade with the East went through Bulgar on the Volga and from there to Sarai—from Sarai goods moved in various directions, including along the famed silk road through Central Asia to China. After the Horde's breakup, Russian trade with khanates in Kazan and the Crimea (and the Crimean Italian merchants) increased significantly. The Russians imported many horses from another Golden Horde successor group, the Nogai Horde. Most Western trade went through Novgorod, although Pskov and Smolensk also had their share.

EATING AND DRINKING; FAMINES
AND OTHER CALAMITIES

The common people's main food was rye bread. Oats, barley, millet, and wheat were less common than rye. Besides being used for bread, grains were the basis for a variety of other dishes and drinks, such as gruels, kvas (an early "near beer"), beers, porridges, pottages, and pancakes. To supplement bread and other grain-based products, commoners sometimes had lesser amounts of cabbage and other vegetables, dairy products, and fish. Meats and fruits were even less common. Bread, however, and more basically grain, was the basis of life. Lacking grain, most people starved.

The only basic food that most peasants needed to purchase was salt. Otherwise, eating little meat, they would not have enough. It was also a necessary preservative for storing foods like cabbage over the long earth-barren months. Not only was salt imported from abroad, but extracting it—whether from ground-level deposits, seas, salt lakes, or underground salt mines—was the largest single industrial enterprise of Muscovite Russia. All sorts of individuals and groups, from peasants to princes, profited from extracting it. By the sixteenth century, monasteries were especially involved in its production and trade. At Sol (salt) Vychegda before 1533, the Stroganov family, of peasant background, had already become active in the business. By 1550, the Stroganovs owned ten works there. They would later become the most famous merchant family of Russia, and Sol Vychegda, like several other centers for salt extraction, became a sizable town (see map 10.1).

People's eating habits were affected by the Orthodox Church, which mandated many periods of fasting throughout the year, plus every Wednesday and Friday. Altogether there were on average slightly more than 200 fast days a year. Fasting from meat on these days probably did not affect many common people, who could not afford it anyway, but on most of these fast days, they were also forbidden to eat dairy products. Fish was also sometimes prohibited. Herberstein states that during Lent some people ate only bread and water on Mondays, Wednesdays, and Fridays.

The most common drink was probably the hardly alcoholic kvas. Mead, made from honey, and beer were the most available real alcoholic drinks, whereas wine was less common. Of the three, beer seems to have been the most available to poorer classes. Vodka was probably not yet being distilled.

In Herberstein's extract describing Moscow, we have already seen that most Russians were forbidden to drink alcohol except for a few days a year. Up until the late fifteenth century, drinking was more common, especially on feasts, festivals, and important occasions like weddings. Then, according to foreign testimony, successive Muscovite grand princes forbade it except on special days. One Italian stated that a prohibition on producing alcohol stemmed partly from the prince's fear that it interfered with people's work. Beyond these prohibitions, however, the state seems to have done little to interfere in people's private drinking practices.

The elite, of course, ate and drank in ways commoners could only dream about. Herberstein attended princely banquets, sometimes lasting three or four hours, where tables groaned with the likes of roasted swans, brandy, and Greek wines, served on or in silver and gold dishes and goblets. He also described what many a subsequent foreign visitor to Russia has bemoaned—with varying degrees of sincerity. "They do not think that their guests are well received, or hospitably treated, unless they are sent home drunk."

But it was not overindulgence that worried the common people, it was hunger and famine. Between 1270 and 1470, famine occurred in one Russian area or another about once every six years and throughout almost the entire country about once every twelve years. When this occurred, many people died, some perhaps after they first "ate lime tree leaves, birch bark, pounded wood pulp mixed with husks and straw; . . . ate buttercups, moss, horse flesh."[2] Although these words are from a twelfth-century chronicle account, the situation did not change much over the centuries.

Besides famine, and often along with it, came plagues like the terrifying Black Death—a symptom of one strain was black swellings in the groin and armpits. After the appearance of such swellings or after spitting blood, symptomatic of another strain, death came within several days. Spreading from India to Greenland, the plague killed about a third of Western Europe's population and perhaps as high a percentage in Russia. Although epidemics in general were fairly rare in Kievan Rus, Lawrence Langer has estimated that between 1350 and 1450 most of Russia averaged about one every six years, more often than not the Black Death.

RURAL LIFE AND THE MILITARY

Although nature and custom continued to determine much of rural life and most peasants had little contact with any government officials, their lives became increasingly entwined with the military needs of the expanding Muscovite state. Put simply, the state needed money and nobles to fight, and to serve adequately the nobles needed a dependable peasantry on their estates. These combined needs, plus the growth of Russian monastic lands, became the main sources of the increasing demands on the peasants.

During this period, about 85 to 90 percent of Russians were peasant toilers. Most lived in wooden huts in scattered settlements containing only a few nuclear families. Many still cleared their plots in the forests using the old "slash-and-burn" technique and repeated it on new lands when the old became exhausted. By the late fifteenth century, however, peasants, especially in more fertile areas, increasingly used some form of crop rotation.

In northwestern Europe by this time, a three-field system was common, by which one field was planted in the fall, another in the spring, and a third left fallow. The following year the fields were rotated. In Russia, rotation was not as systematic, but a popular method was to rotate fields with rye, planted in the late summer, oats, planted in the spring, and then a fallow period.

For plowing, the peasants most often used a *sokha*, a light plow that cut only a few inches into the ground. It was generally pulled by a horse, although oxen or humans were other possibilities. The peasants made little systematic use of manure except when required to do so, as, for example, on large well-run monastic estates. Besides a workhorse, peasants generally possessed a few

[2] Robert Michell and Nevill Forbes, eds., *The Chronicle of Novgorod, 1016–1471* (London, 1914), p. 11.

other animals, such as chickens and one or two each of cows, pigs, and goats or sheep.

Although not much is known about their form, territorial peasant communes, generally small, continued to exist. So too did confiscation of peasant lands by nobles and monasteries. When this occurred, peasants had to pay—by various combinations of money, produce, or service—to continue farming land from which they could keep the produce, or at least most of it. If they did not like the demands of their new landlord, they could still move somewhere else. Their labor was valuable and much in demand. But obstacles to movement were increasing. By a Muscovite law code of 1497, their freedom to move was restricted to the week before and after St. George's day (November 25th), and even then they had to pay an "exit fee."

Although sometimes evaded, these restrictions were typical of Moscow's increasing demands. The Muscovite grand princes helped remove the "Tatar yoke," only to fashion their own made-in-Moscow one more firmly on the necks of the peasants. Besides restricting their movements, the new yoke imposed more Muscovite taxes, fees, and service requirements and held each commune responsible collectively for paying the total tax levied on commune members.

Peasants' contacts beyond their villages were probably limited. The growth of cities, however, beginning in the fourteenth century, meant increasing urban food needs and a limited number of job opportunities. Archaeological evidence found in villages tells us that some peasants were able to buy such oriental goods as beads and boxwood combs. Thus, some ties, however slight or indirect, existed between some villagers and city buyers and sellers.

Just as the nobles backed by Moscow intensified demands on the peasants, so Moscow also demanded more from the nobles. Formerly, those who owned an inherited estate (*votchina*) had kept it when leaving a prince's service. Now, under Ivan III and Vasili III, Moscow confiscated the estates of such "treasonous" nobles. Ivan III also greatly increased another type of landholding called *pomestie*. When he confiscated 3 million acres in Novgorod and turned it over to his "service men," these 2,000 men held these lands conditionally, in exchange for satisfactory service. From then on, the Muscovite princes used other available opportunities, such as additional land seizures, to increase gradually such conditional (*pomestie*) holdings.

Regardless of what kind of land they held, the nobles' primary obligation, as in many other medieval countries, was to fight as cavalrymen. At first, they fought for the princes of the various principalities recognized by the Mongols and, later, for the Muscovite prince. With all the warfare going on in these centuries, many nobles served each spring through fall (the fighting season), until age or death put an end to their annual call-ups.

Each such cavalryman had to arrive with his own horse, weapons, and supplies. His estate was supposed to provide him the means to do so, but some lands were too poor. One reason for intensifying restrictions upon peasant mobility was to provide such service-class warriors with a stable workforce, freeing them to fight for the Muscovite rulers.

When not fighting, or at least in the field with other troops, many of the nobles lived on estates that were far from opulent. Some even worked in the fields themselves and lived in log cabins not much bigger than those of their peasants. Many nobles were hardly more cultured than the illiterate peasants. Only a small number had more than one estate. Thus, a noble's possessions and lifestyle were often much less grand than we today associate with the term *noble*.

The core of Russia's military during this era remained the cavalry. Influenced by Mongol tactics, cavalrymen attempted to be mobile and fast, relying mainly on their bows, arrows, and swords. To supplement the mostly noble cavalry, Russian princes by the end of the fifteenth century also used, on different occasions, friendly Mongols, artillery, infantry townsmen, and Cossacks (see Chapter 9). As Ivan III and Vasili III expanded Muscovy and tied more nobles to Muscovite service, their armies became stronger.

CLASS STRUCTURE AND SLAVERY

The seizure of land and turning it over to new men provided some social mobility in the expanding Muscovite state. Some who received the new lands in Novgorod, for example, had actually been elite slaves before becoming noble landowners. As Moscow centralized its control, however, there was also a gradual tendency toward more social rigidity.

At the top of the secular class structure were the Riurikid princes and their families. Yet as Moscow slowly achieved dominance, some princes of the formerly independent principalities tumbled into the noble class. By 1500, this class consisted of several layers from the prince's aristocratic Moscow boyar advisors down to the poorest provincial nobles. Beneath the nobles were the various urban classes, which we examine in more detail in the next era, when they become more differentiated. Of lower status were the vast mass of peasants. A final category was that of slaves, who composed perhaps 10 percent of the population by 1533.[3]

By then Russian slavery had much in common with that practiced in other times and places, but it differed in two key ways from later North American slavery. The great majority of slaves were of the same nationality (Russian) as their owners, and most became slaves because they sold themselves into slavery. This later circumstance greatly surprised Herberstein, who noted that the Russians "enjoy slavery more than freedom."

Why did these "self-sellers" outnumber others, such as those who inherited slave status and some war captives who also became slaves? Most of those who sold themselves were at the bottom of society and saw no better option available. By the fifteenth century, the Orthodox Church could not, or would not, provide all the relief necessary. And there was no other agency to serve so-

---

[3] For most of what follows on slavery, I am indebted to Richard Hellie, *Slavery in Russia, 1450–1725* (Chicago, 1982).

ciety's "down-and-outs." Slavery was thus a form of welfare, providing food, shelter, and security in exchange for a loss of freedom.

As might be expected, more people put themselves up for sale during hard or catastrophic times such as winters, famines, or when widowed or abandoned by a husband. Although most of these self-sellers seem to have been lower-class people without available skills—for example, beggars, urban day workers, and landless peasants—this was not always the case. Occasionally, others who could not find or accept their niche in "free" society also sold themselves into slavery.

Most slaves, perhaps two-thirds, were males. Primarily this was because women were much less valued as slaves. Many slaveowners owned only a handful of slaves, often only one, and men could provide more of the functions they wished slaves to perform than could women. In contrast to some other slave societies, slave women in Russia were not often purchased for sexual purposes, and their owners seem not to have been especially licentious in their dealings with them. Second, because girls were less valued than boys, poor parents who sold themselves into slavery were more likely to practice female (rather than male) infanticide. Many slaveowners had no desire to buy slaves with children, especially girls, because they were often seen as more of a liability than an asset.

The slaveowners themselves were primarily nobles in government service. Because owning slaves was a status symbol, the higher one climbed in Moscow society, the more slaves one wanted. Much more rarely, merchants, members of the clergy, peasants, and even elite slaves themselves sometimes owned slaves.

Slaves were used for purposes ranging from working in the fields to serving as musicians or buffoons. Most often, they performed routine jobs in a slaveowner's household, such as being cooks, wet nurses, manservants, and all-purpose lackeys. Male slaves also sometimes went to battle with their masters, either to guard their supplies or to join in the fighting. A small class of elite male slaves acted as stewards, advocates in court trials, treasurers, state secretaries, and in a variety of other important, often supervisory, positions for princes and important nobles. Before the reign of Ivan III, most Russian princes relied chiefly on such slaves to help them administer their principalities.

The price paid for a slave, whether to him or her or to a previous owner, varied according to supply and demand and the sex, age, and skills of the slave. The average price was about what one would pay for a horse. Although this might not seem like much, it was more than many other societies paid, at least in comparison to horses. In Sudan, for example, around 1500, one could buy twelve slaves for the price of a horse. In the United States during the nineteenth century, slave prices varied greatly, but a price of several hundred dollars was common.

As in the Kievan era, there were different types of arrangements made between a slave and a slaveowner. Some slaves were held only temporarily, for example, until a debt was paid. After leaving one slaveowner, either as a result of fulfilling one's temporary obligation or by fleeing, many former slaves sold themselves back into some form of new slavery. Once one got on the slavery treadmill, it was often habit-forming, breeding dependence.

Children could be sold apart from their parents, and when sold, or willed to an heir, children from the same family were often separated. Yet Muscovite slavery was "milder" than many other slave systems. Most slaveowners did not sell their slaves, and husbands and wives were not separated when sold or willed. The relative mildness of Russian slavery was due primarily to (1) most of the slaves working in the home, occasionally in important positions; (2) the desire of slaveowners to keep them contented enough not to flee; and (3) the Orthodox and Russian status of most slaves—even though the Orthodox Church did not condemn slavery, it encouraged humane treatment.

WOMEN AND FAMILY LIFE

As the power of Orthodoxy grew in this era, so too did its influence on women. The most popular devotional readings for the laity were contained in the fourteenth-century collection *The Emerald*. Like earlier Kievan writings, it reflected an Orthodox ambivalence toward women, although now more wary than ever. It advised wives to "obey your husbands in silence" and told husbands: "It is better to suffer from fever than to be mastered by a bad wife."[4]

Part of this wariness of women stemmed from their sexuality. The church acted vigorously to keep even married sex within narrow limits, prohibiting it on many fast days and at least discouraging it on others. It also forbade any sexual position but one—the man on top. Basically the church looked upon sexual activity, even within marriage, as impure. Even though giving birth to children was thought to be in keeping with God's will, the act of childbirth itself—usually carried out in a bathhouse, away from all men—was also regarded as impure. Little wonder that Russians, as Eve Levin points out, were among the medieval people that believed Jesus was delivered through Mary's ear and not her vagina.

To insure compliance to church views, priests relied on detailed and personal questions, which they asked in confessions; on penances, often of a public nature; and on ecclesiastical courts. As Levin has observed, however, we should not think that the church's sexual strictness was always resented in this pre-birth-control era, especially by women, who gained from it more than they lost.

The church's attitude toward sex also partly explains its willingness to allow a woman to seek a divorce because of certain sins of her husband. If he forced her to have sex or (after the mid-fifteenth century) if he were guilty of

---

[4] Quoted in G. P. Fedotov, *The Russian Religious Mind*, Vol. II, *The Middle Ages, The Thirteenth to the Fifteenth Centuries* (Cambridge, Mass., 1966), pp. 76–77.

adultery, she was permitted to petition for divorce, a right not often granted to Russian women.

The biggest change in women's lives was only indirectly influenced by Orthodoxy. Herberstein noticed it in the early sixteenth century. The Muscovites, he said, "consider no woman virtuous unless she live shut up at home, and be so closely guarded, that she go out nowhere. They give a woman, I say, little credit for modesty, if she be seen by strangers or people out of doors." He goes on to say that women are "very seldom admitted into the churches, and still less frequently to friendly meetings, unless they be very old and free from all suspicion."

Herberstein's remarks apply specifically to upper-class Muscovite women, who now often lived in separate rooms, usually high up or in an isolated quarter. Historians have labeled their quarters the *terem*. These women also usually ate separately from the men, and their servants were female.

Exactly why and when these exclusionary practices began no one knows. Some historians have attributed it to the Mongols' influence, but Halperin and others deny that it was due to them. It does not seem to have been the practice in Novgorod before the loss of its independence, and, in fact, noble women there seem to have even gained a few rights. It was most likely due to an increased concern by Muscovite nobles with controlling the sexual lives of their wives and daughters, thereby avoiding any stains on family honor and facilitating politically advantageous marriages.

Upper-class marriages were arranged by the parents. The prospective groom generally was kept away from his future wife until the wedding or at least until he agreed to strong penalties should he change his mind once he was allowed to meet with her. Herberstein says that otherwise if the man tried to catch sight of the young woman, he was usually told: "Learn what she is from others who have known her." The parents of the young woman also arranged for her dowry, which often included such items such as horses, cattle, slaves, weapons, and dresses.

Even though noblewomen were isolated, this did not mean they exercised no power. As human links between different family clans, as wives and mothers, and as friends and acquaintances of other wives and mothers, they no doubt often influenced their husbands and sons.

The military service obligations of most nobles affected marriage and married life in a number of ways. Wars reduced the eligible bachelors and increased widowhood, and military duties also meant that husbands were often gone from home. Wives of cavalrymen, especially in the provinces, must have often played an important part in running the family estate and been less secluded than the Moscow women observed by Herberstein.

As for family life, young couples did not usually live with either set of parents, and parents had absolute powers over their minor children. They could even sell them into slavery if they wished, although this rarely occurred. A young man was considered an adult at fifteen, also the age for nobles to register for military service.

GROWTH OF THE LAW

By comparing the expanded *Pravda* code of the late Kievan era with late four-teenth-century and fifteenth-century charters and law codes from Novgorod, Pskov, and Moscow, we see that the judicial and police powers of governments increased, as did the courts and judicial officials. And courts resorted to more written materials and to harsher methods of investigation and punishment.

Judicial expansion was partly due to the more complex social relations that developed in urban areas such as Novgorod, Pskov, and Moscow. It also re-sulted from the expansion of Moscow and its attempt to exercise centralized jurisdiction over newly acquired areas. Also, the monetary interests of govern-ments and officials in levying judicial fees and fines—and collecting bribes—had an effect on judicial expansion. The Orthodox Church also expanded its jurisdiction into new regions and worked closely with governments to strengthen Christianity and government order in rural and newly conquered areas.

By the time of Ivan III's 1497 law code (the *Sudebnik*), bailiffs sometimes used torture on suspects during pretrial investigations. By then, law codes pre-scribed such punishments as branding, flogging, selling individuals into slav-ery, and death. The 1497 *Sudebnik* mandated capital punishment for robbery, murder, arson, criminal slander, church theft, and certain recidivist crimes such as second-offense theft.

Although the seeking of Divine guidance via iron and water ordeals prob-ably declined, the use of ordeal by battle (a duel) seems to have increased. In Pskov, it could be used, under certain circumstances, to settle land disputes. Sometimes a witness's allegations could be settled by having the defendant and the witness fight a duel. On such occasions, if the defendant were an old man, youth, cripple, priest, or monk, he could hire a substitute to fight the duel for him, but the witness had no like right. Although women in some cases were also allowed to hire substitutes, the Pskov law stipulated that two women could be ordered to fight a duel and neither allowed a substitute.

The hiring of substitutes by clergy occurred despite the church's general disapproval of judicial duels, with or without substitutes. The fact that lower-level clergy could themselves be subject to judicial duels reveals further the growth of governmental jurisdiction. Herberstein observed that priests charged with theft and drunkeness were dealt with in secular, not church, courts. He also saw priests publicly flogged in Moscow.

As to why the law became harsher, several hypotheses have been put for-ward. Some historians have attributed it to foreign influence, Mongol and Western. Others, like Daniel Kaiser, see it stemming more from internal devel-opments. It probably resulted from both. Much blood, however, was also shed during the Kievan era. Death from a vengeful relative, still allowed in the late Kievan era, might not be state-inflicted capital punishment but no less blood flowed. To a large extent, harsher government punishments simply reflected state judicial expansion.

RELIGION

The 300 years following the Mongol invasion was an age of great expansion for the Orthodox Church. But it began slowly. At first, there was the spiritual comfort that religion offered in a time of woe. Within decades after the initial invasion, favorable Mongol policies toward the church assisted its growth. In exchange for prayers for the khan's health and refraining from political opposition, the church was exempted from paying taxes. Mongol tolerance even went so far as to allow the establishment of a bishopric in Sarai, the capital of the Golden Horde.

It was not until a century after the Mongol's conquest, however, that Russian monasticism began its rapid growth. The central figure in this spiritual outburst was St. Sergius of Radonezh (d. 1392), who emphasized humility and love of all God's creation. He founded what was to become the famous Holy Trinity–St. Sergius Monastery, located a little less than fifty miles from Moscow. As we have seen, the Muscovite grand princes did all they could to promote the cult of St. Sergius and identify their own regime with his holy life.

Following St. Sergius's example, others founded additional monasteries. Among the most notable were the Andronikov and Chudov monasteries in Moscow and those of St. Cyril at Beloozero (White Lake) and the Solovetskii on the White Sea. Kliuchevsky has estimated that some 250 monasteries and convents were founded from the fourteenth through the sixteenth centuries. They grew continually more prosperous. By 1533, they operated vast agricultural lands—perhaps one-third of the state's populated land—and some of their agricultural and other enterprises were among the best run in the country. Because many cloisters employed peasants and were located in the countryside, unlike in Kievan Rus, Christianity now made more headway among rural people still strongly influenced by pagan beliefs.

Some monks, such as the fourteenth-century Stephen of Perm, went beyond the ethnic Russians to win other peoples over to Christianity. Going out to the Komi (or Permians), just west of the northern Urals, St. Stephen converted many of them. To further his work, he devised a Komi alphabet and translated religious works into the Komi tongue. In this and other cases, the fanning out of Russian monasteries contributed to Great Russian colonizing efforts.

A further monastic contribution was in introducing the mystical Hesychast movement into Russia. Hesychasm was stimulated by a cultural-religious renaissance that was then occurring in Byzantine and South Slavic lands. As a result of Russian-Byzantine religious ties and the Turkish conquest of part of the Balkans, many Byzantine and South Slav monks and other clergy came to Russian lands in the late fourteenth and fifteenth centuries. The Hesychasm some of them promoted had been practiced in Byzantine and Balkan monasteries, especially Greece's famous Mt. Athos, and aimed at enabling an individual to attain oneness with God, the Divine Light. To accomplish this, various techniques were recommended, including the control of one's breathing and the repetition of the Jesus Prayer—"Lord Jesus Christ, Son of God, have mercy on me."

An outstanding monk whose writings reflect the Hesychast influence was Nil Sorsky (1433–1508). Its impact on him was apparently strengthened by his visit to Mt. Athos in Greece. After returning to the St. Cyril Monastery, he later established his own hermitage nearby. There he taught monks to emphasize mystical union with God. In an age of increasing monastic wealth, often willed to the monasteries by laymen, he espoused a simple life, both for individual monks and for the church in general. He quoted St. John Chrysostom's words, saying that "if a man wishes to donate sacred vessels or other furnishings to a church, tell him to give them to the poor."[5]

A monk who differed with Nil Sorsky on church wealth was another founder of a monastery, Joseph of Volokolamsk, who has already been mentioned as a defender of autocratic powers. He believed that ample church possessions were necessary to help monks perform God's work on earth. He also was active against heretics and, in contrast to Sorsky, advocated violence against them.

A major heresy appeared already a century before Joseph's time. In 1375, some *Strigolniki* were thrown into Novgorod's Volkhov River. The justification given for this act, in the sixteenth-century *Nikonian Chronicle*, was an almost literal interpretation of the words of Jesus (Matthew 18:6): "Whoever causes one of these little ones who believe in me to sin, it were better for him to have a great millstone hung around his neck, and to be drowned in the depths of the sea." The crime of the *Strigolniki* was their criticism of several church practices, including simony—the buying and selling of church offices. They might have even preached against the existence of a priesthood and at least several sacraments, including the Eucharist and confession. They certainly inveighed against the drinking habits of priests.

A century later, another heresy appeared, that of the Judaizers. Although Joseph of Volokolamsk accused them of preaching Judaism and denying the Trinity, they apparently started out attacking abuses such as simony. However they began, they eventually rejected at least the church hierarchy, monasticism, and icon veneration.

Both these heresies were strongest in Novgorod, although a Judaizer party also eventually appeared in Moscow. Both resembled some Western heresies and were dealt with as in the West. In fact, one of Joseph of Volokolamsk's chief allies against the Judaizers appealed to Ivan III to look to the Spanish Inquisition to see how heretics should be treated. After a church council in 1504, Ivan III had several Judaizers burned at the stake.

A final religious phenomenon worth noting is the Russian appreciation of the humble "fool in Christ." Such an individual acted in ways that seemed foolish or crazy to worldly people. Instead of answering a question, for example, he might just echo it back. Or he might make statements that seemed non-

---

[5] G. P. Fedotov, ed., *A Treasury of Russian Spirituality* (New York, 1965), p. 93.

sensical. He would usually dress in a simple, impoverished manner, often barefoot, even in the cold Russian winters. As depicted in hagiography, however, the holy fool was aware of a higher wisdom, often proved by the realization of his prophecies.

The scriptural justification for such behavior was several passages of Saint Paul's First Epistle to the Corinthians, for example: "If any man thinketh that he is wise among you in this world, let him become a fool, that he may become wise. For the wisdom of this world is foolishness with God" (1 Cor. 3:18–19). Although holy fools existed in Byzantium, they were most prominent in Russia, especially from the fourteenth through the seventeenth centuries.

Although the veneration of saints, including some holy fools, was affected by government policies, the desires of the common people also helped shape this veneration. As one example of this, Levin points to the transformation of St. Paraskeva Piatnitsa from a saint venerated by merchants to a special patroness of women and their work (see Fig. 4.2).

LITERATURE AND ART

Like so many other areas of Russian life, literature and art suffered from the Mongol invasion. Only beginning in the fourteenth century do we see much renewed creativity. By the end of that century and thereafter, we also increasingly see the cultural imprint of Moscow.

Literature and Ideas

As in the Kievan era, so too in the period ending in 1533, many Byzantine and South Slavic translations continued to appear. So also did original works such as chronicles, religious writings, and written and oral secular literature.

In the thirteenth and fourteenth centuries, cities such as Novgorod, Tver, and Rostov produced their own chronicles. In the fifteenth century, Ivan III oversaw the compilation of chronicle accounts based on many previous chronicles but touched up to glorify Moscow and its perception of the past.

The chief surviving religious works of the era are the lives of Russian saints. They include lives of saints as different as St. Sergius, St. Dmitri Donskoi, and St. Mikhail, a Fool in Christ. The most accomplished hagiographer was the monk Epiphanius the Wise (d. 1422), who wrote of both St. Sergius and St. Stephen of Perm. Epiphanius was strongly influenced by Hesychasm. This form of mysticism led him as well as many other hagiographers influenced by the Byzantine-South Slavic cultural revival to use an ornate, wordy type of prose, referred to as word-weaving. It sought to uplift and stir readers to a better understanding of the greatness and beauty of a saint's life. As with many hagiographers, Epiphanius was not primarily concerned with factual biographical accuracy. Although his wordiness is not as appreciated today, he was a skilled and poetic writer whose ornate style influenced religious and historical writings for two centuries.

Among secular works, the period is especially rich in military tales. One of the most famous is *Zadonshchina* (see excerpt in Chapter 6). In many ways this tale of Dmitri Donskoi's 1380 victory calls to mind *The Tale of Igor's Campaign* and in some ways imitated it. *Zadonshchina* is marked by similar poetic devices and images and is written in a similar rhythmic prose. Yet it adheres more to the central narrative and has less poetic digressions than does the Igor tale. Despite its undeniable literary merit, however, most critics agree that it is inferior to the Igor epic.

Not only the style, but also the content of *Zadonshchina* is of interest. The author speaks frequently of the "Russian land," of the "Christian faith," of the "infidel Tatars." His message is clear: The "glorious city of Moscow" and its prince Dmitri Donskoi have come forward to unite and lead Christian Russia against its enemies.

In reworked chronicles and in *Zadonshchina*, we see Moscow's ideological stamp or glorification. More openly ideological works, such as those of Joseph of Volokolamsk, and even some hagiography rewritten by Muscovite apologists also furthered Moscow's cause. The life of the Novgorodian Holy Fool

FIGURE 7.1. Transfiguration of the Savior (Spasskii) Cathedral at the Andronikov Monastery, Moscow, early fifteenth century.

FIGURE 7.2. Trinity Cathedral at the St. Sergius Monastery, Sergiev Posad, 1422.

Mikhail, who is made to espouse strong pro-Muscovite views, is a good example.

Western literature and its Humanist roots had little impact on Russia during this era. We encounter no Russian love sonnets like those of Petrarch, no ribald stories like those of Boccaccio. This was not completely due to ignorance of Western ways and ideas. Ivan III's second wife, Sophia Paleologue, had been educated in Italy, and following her, Italian architects, engineers, and craftsmen appeared in Moscow.

The monk Maxim the Greek (c. 1480–1556) came to Russia in 1518 and spent the rest of his life there. Earlier he had lived and studied in Italy and was thoroughly familiar with the Italian Humanist movement. Yet, despite his considerable influence, those he most affected lost out in the political and ideological battles of the day. They included some followers of Nil Sorsky and Prince Andrei Kurbsky, who would become prominent before falling out with Ivan IV. Maxim himself was condemned at a 1525 church council for criticizing Russian Church books and other offenses and spent many of his remaining years in monastic incarceration.

FIGURE 7.3. Church of the Holy Spirit at the St. Sergius Monastery, Sergiev Posad, 1476.

Although possessing much knowledge, Maxim was not a man of secularist sympathies. He admired more Florence's Neoplatonist philosophers and its religious reformer and zealot, Savonarola, than he did Petrarch and Boccaccio. Maxim's ultimate fate, however, indicates that Muscovy's tolerance of foreign ideas, whether religious or secular, was quite limited. The close bond between the Muscovite ruler and conservative theologians was especially important in helping to turn back new ideas just when Russia once again came into increasing contact with the West.

Art and Architecture

In art and architecture, despite some notable works in areas like Novgorod and Pskov, it was again the Moscow region that proved prominent. Its stone and brick constructions owed much to both earlier wooden traditions and borrow-

FIGURE 7.4. Assumption (or Dormition) Cathedral, Moscow Kremlin, 1475–1479.

ings from other regions. Its early masonry architecture is best seen in two early fifteenth-century churches: the Transfiguration of the Savior (Spasskii) Cathedral at the Andronikov Monastery and the Trinity Cathedral at the St. Sergius Monastery. The superimposed arches of the former are especially notable. Such arches are called *kokoshniki* because of their similarity to the *kokoshnik*, a Russian woman's arched headdress. Their first appearance in masonry architecture had been in the Novgorod-Pskov region.

In 1476, Moscow brought Pskov builders to the St. Sergius Monastery, where they built a work combining some of the best Pskov architectural traditions with those of Moscow. This was the Church of the Holy Spirit. Again one notes the many *kokoshniki*. Also of interest is the unusual belfry at the base of the drum, which served a secondary purpose as a watchtower.

The refurbished Kremlin overlooking the Moscow River more than anything clearly symbolized Moscow's dominance and its political-religious significance. The work on it was carried out primarily under Ivan III.

On Cathedral Square, in the heart of the Kremlin, several new churches were constructed to take the place of earlier and smaller ones. The first of these was the Assumption (or Dormition) Cathedral. Although built by the Italian Aristotele Fioravanti (1420–1485?), Ivan wished it to look Russian and therefore instructed Fioravanti to visit Vladimir. While still reflecting some aspects of Fioravanti's Italian background, the new cathedral thus resembled the finest church architecture of twelfth-century Vladimir, especially the original look of

FIGURE 7.5. Cathedral of
the Annunciation, Moscow
Kremlin, 1484–1489.

that city's Assumption Cathedral. The new Kremlin cathedral was a harmo-
nious, simple, yet imposing, five-domed structure that was to serve as the
coronation church of tsars for three and a half centuries.

Next came the Cathedral of the Annunciation and the smaller Church of
the Deposition of the Robe. Both were built by Pskov craftsmen, beginning in
1484. The Annunciation displayed again the *kokoshniki* but this time below
three domes—more domes were added later. This cathedral served subsequent
tsars for weddings and baptisms. The smaller Deposition Church became the
chapel of the metropolitan and later of the Russian patriarch.

In 1487, two Italian architects supervised the building of the Italian-look-
ing Palace of Facets, which was subsequently used for Kremlin court recep-
tions, ceremonies, and banquets. Beginning in 1485, Italian architects also oversaw the replacement of the white stone Kremlin walls built by Dmitri Donskoi
with the great Kremlin brick walls and towers that still stand today.

The final Kremlin cathedral that Ivan planned, but did not live to see com-

FIGURE 7.6. Palace of Facets, Moscow Kremlin, 1487–1491.

pleted, was that of the Archangel Michael. It was designed by another Italian and finished under Vasili III. Although it certainly looks Russian with its five cupolas, an Italian quality is reflected in its exterior decorations and two-story facades. The bodies of tsars prior to Peter the Great are interred in this last cathedral. Before his own death, Vasili III began work on the Ivan the Great Bell Tower but did not live to see its completion (see also Fig. 6.2 for the Church of the Ascension at Kolomenskoe, begun and completed at the end of Vasili III's reign).

Thus, by 1533, the Kremlin walls and cathedrals, despite some later modifications, looked much as they do today. It does not require much imagination to realize how dazzled some Russian from the provinces would be upon first seeing the Kremlin and its beautiful cathedral cupolas extending high above its walls.

Upon entering the cathedrals, a provincial would be further awed by their beautiful mosaics, frescoes, and icons—some, including works of Andrei Rublev (c. 1370–1430), preserved from the earlier Kremlin churches.

In an era that produced Russia's greatest icons, Rublev was that art's greatest practitioner. Even before him, other icon painters from Novgorod to Suzdalia were painting notable works. Novgorodian icons, such as those of the Prophet Elijah and St. George, are justly famous for their simplicity, vigor, and bright red and gold colors. By Rublev's time, and partly as a result of his efforts, Russian churches were also developing a modified iconostasis—a screen

FIGURE 7.7. Cathedral of the Archangel Michael, Moscow Kremlin, 1505–1508.

of icons that divides the sanctuary of an Orthodox Church from the rest of its interior. The new iconostases that emerged were higher and contained more rows of icons that had been traditional in the Orthodox world.

Rublev was a monk who first came to St. Sergius Monastery while its founder was still alive and went on to spend many years at the Andronikov Monastery, where he was buried. As a young man, Rublev worked with Theophanes the Greek, one of the many religious-cultural figures who came to Russia in this period from the Byzantine Empire or South Slavic lands. Although little of Theophanes's art has survived except for some Novgorodian frescos, he was by all accounts the greatest painter of his generation and had a major impact on younger painters like Rublev.

Rublev's most famous icon is one he painted for the Holy Trinity Church at St. Sergius Monastery. It is called the *Trinity*, and at the center of it are three Old Testament angels seated around a cup on a table. In the biblical account, they had come to tell Sarah that she was to have a child despite her old age. In Rublev's icon, as in earlier icons, the three angels symbolize the Holy Trinity of

Father, Son, and Holy Spirit. The icon displays the luminosity, harmony, and deep spiritual serenity that characterize Rublev's great works.

Along with written accounts of saints such as Sergius and churches such as the Kremlin's three cathedrals, Rublev's icons help capture the best of early Muscovy's religious spirit. The increasing political authoritarianism of Moscow, the burning of several Judaizers, and the persecution of Maxim the Greek, however, all were indications that there was a less humane side to this new political-religious capital. This would become even clearer in the reign of the son of Vasili III, Ivan the Terrible.

SUGGESTED SOURCES*

ALEF, GUSTAVE. *Rulers and Nobles in Fifteenth-Century Muscovy.* London, 1983.

ANDREI ROUBLEV. A film directed by Andrei Tarkovsky. Available on videocassette.

ANDREYEV, NIKOLAY. *Studies in Muscovy: Western Influence and Byzantine Inheritance.* London, 1970.

BLUM, JEROME. *Lord and Peasant in Russia, from the Ninth to the Nineteenth Century.* Princeton, 1961. Chs. 4–9.

BRAUDEL, FERNAND. *Capitalism and Material Life, 1400–1800.* New York, 1973.

BRUMFIELD, WILLIAM C. *A History of Russian Architecture.* Cambridge, Eng., 1993. Chs. 4 and 5.

CRUMMEY, ROBERT O. *The Formation of Muscovy, 1304–1613.* London, 1987. Chs. 1, 5, and 7.

FENNELL, JOHN. *A History of the Russian Church to 1448.* London, 1995. Pt. II.

FENNELL, JOHN L., and A. D. STOKES. *Early Russian Literature.* Berkley, 1974.

FLIER, MICHAEL S., and DANIEL ROWLAND, eds. *Medieval Russian Culture.* Vol. 2. Berkeley, 1994.

FRENCH, R. A. "The Early and Medieval Russian Town." In *Studies in Russian Historical Geography,* eds. James H. Bater, and R. A. French. Vol. 2. London, 1983.

HALPERIN, CHARLES J. *Russia and the Golden Horde: The Mongol Impact on Medieval Russian History.* Bloomington, 1985.

HELLIE, RICHARD. *Enserfment and Military Change in Muscovy.* Chicago, 1971.

KAISER, DANIEL H. *The Growth of the Law in Medieval Russia.* Princeton, 1980.

———. *The Laws of Rus': Tenth to Fifteenth Centuries.* Salt Lake City, 1992.

KEENAN, EDWARD L. *The Council of 1503: Source Studies and Questions of Ecclesiastical Landowning in Sixteenth-Century Muscovy: A Collection of Seminar Papers.* Cambridge, Mass., 1977.

———. "On Certain Mythical Beliefs and Russian Behaviors." In *The Legacy of History in Russia and the New States of Eurasia,* ed. S. Frederick Starr. Armonk, N.Y., 1994.

KLEIMOLA, ANN M. *Justice in Medieval Russia: Muscovite Judgment Charters (Pravye Gramoty) of the Fifteenth and Sixteenth Centuries.* Philadelphia, 1975.

LANGER, LAWRENCE N. "The Black Death in Russia: Its Effects upon Urban Labor," *RH* 2, Pt. 1 (1975): 53–67.

———. "The Medieval Russian Town." In *The City in Russian History,* ed. Michael F. Hamm. Lexington, Ky., 1976.

*See also works cited in footnotes and in boxed insert.

LEVIN, EVE. "Childbirth in pre-Petrine Russia." In *Russia's Women: Accommodation, Resistance, Transformation,* eds. Barbara Evans Clements, Barbara Alpern Engel, and Christine D. Worobec. Berkeley, 1991.

————. *Sex and Society in the World of the Orthodox Slavs, 900–1700.* Ithaca, N.Y., 1989.

MARTIN, JANET. *Treasure of the Land of Darkness: The Fur Trade and Its Significance for Medieval Russia.* Cambridge, England, 1986.

MILLER, DAVID B. "Monumental Building as an Indicator of Economic Trends in Northern Rus' in the Late Kievan and Mongol Periods," *AHA* 94 (April 1989): 360–390.

MRECT, Pts. II and III.

OSTROWSKI, DONALD G. "Church Polemics and Monastic Land Acquisitions in Sixteenth-Century Muscovy," *SEER* 64 (1986): 357–379.

PUSHKAREVA, N. L., and E. LEVIN, "Women in Medieval Novgorod from the Eleventh to the Fifteenth Centuries," *SSH* 23 (Spring 1985), 71–87.

RH 10, Pt. 2 (1983). The whole issue is devoted to women in medieval Russia.

RYNDZIUNSKII, P. G., and A. M. SAKHAROV. "Towns in Russia," *MERSH* 39: 127–136.

SMITH, R. E. F. *Peasant Farming in Muscovy.* London, 1977.

SMITH, R. E. F., and DAVID CHRISTIAN. *Bread and Salt: A Social and Economic History of Food and Drink in Russia.* Cambridge, England, 1984.

SOLOVIEV, SERGEI M. *Russian Society in the Age of Ivan III.* Gulf Breeze, Fla., 1979.

TREADGOLD, DONALD W. *The West in Russia and China: Religious and Secular Thought in Modern Times.* Vol. 1, *Russia, 1472–1917.* Cambridge, Eng., 1973. Ch. 1.

VOYCE, ARTHUR. *Moscow and the Roots of Russian Culture.* Norman, 1964.

VERNADSKY, GEORGE. *Medieval Russian Laws.* New York, 1947.

————. *Russia at the Dawn of the Modern Age.* New Haven, 1959.

PART THREE

Muscovy and Its Expansion, 1533–1689

From the beginning of Ivan IV's reign until Peter the Great overthrew his half-sister Sophia in 1689, Muscovite autocracy had many ups and downs but ended up stronger. So too did state control over society, although the government's ambitions often exceeded its still-limited capacities. Ivan IV (the Terrible) was the first Muscovite ruler to be crowned tsar and eventually became a tyrant. His policies weakened Russia, however, and helped lead to a Time of Troubles (1598–1613), in which for a while no tsar ruled. After a *zemskii sobor* (land council) established Mikhail Romanov on the throne in 1613, it continued to meet frequently, especially early in Mikhail's reign. By 1689, however, this consultative body was no more.

There was no other institution or group willing or able to resist actively and successfully the state's growing absolutist demands. For its own reasons, the ruling elite supported the autocratic system. Landowners were appeased by various measures, especially the 1649 Law Code that finally transformed their peasants into serfs. The Orthodox Church, which had generally supported autocracy, suffered a major schism in 1666–1667, which left it in no position to resist successfully further tsarist demands upon it.

Throughout this period, the goals and desires of commoners (overwhelmingly serfs by 1689) were often far different than those of the government or society's elite. Although they resisted serfdom by flight and other methods and sometimes broke into open rebellion, they could offer no real alternative to the autocratic order, only petitions to the tsar or a mixture of tsarist pretenders and anarchy. In 1670–1671, the colorful Cossack

Stenka Razin and his followers—Cossacks, peasants, non-Russian tribesman, and other malcontents—stormed up the Volga, taking one town after another. More disciplined and better armed government troops soon ended the rebellion and the lives of many rebels, including Razin.

If in this era Muscovy's autocracy was strengthened and state power increased, its territorial expansion proceeded by leaps and bounds. By 1689, it was five to six times as large as in 1533 and had reached the Pacific Ocean and acquired Kiev and Ukraine east of the Dnieper. Thus, in about 160 years, it *added* territory slightly larger than the present fifty U.S. states and Mexico combined.

The achievement of such expansion, or even the defense of Russia's ill-defined borders, required substantial military forces and expenditures. Much of the preoccupation of the government was over economic and military needs, which, in turn, had a major impact on molding the Muscovite social order.

These needs, plus the seeking and then gaining of Ukrainian territory under Tsar Alexei (1645–1676), helped to foster Western and other outside influences in Muscovy. These new winds, however, came into conflict with the old belief that Moscow was the true center of the Christian world. By 1689, this cultural conflict was still being waged and would soon escalate under Peter the Great.

CHAPTER 8

Ivan the Terrible: Autocrat

Ivan IV was among Russia's most striking rulers. Some historians think he was even a madman. His centralizing, autocratic, and tyrannical policies influenced Russian politics long after his death. His conquest of Kazan and Astrakhan brought the Volga River under Russian control and opened up new opportunities for further eastward expansion. But his expensive and extended Livonian War (1558–1583), plus his terroristic domestic policies, left a more immediate legacy—impoverishment.

IVAN IV: SOURCES AND PERSONALITY

A central problem in dealing with Ivan IV is the reliability of sources. Until 1971, historians relied heavily on Prince Andrei Kurbsky's *History of Ivan IV* and on a series of letters supposedly exchanged between Kurbsky and Ivan. In that year, however, Edward Keenan's *The Kurbsky-Groznyi Apocrypha* appeared and argued that none of these works were written by Kurbsky or Ivan but were probably seventeenth-century forgeries. Keenan's work ignited a hot debate that still smolders.

One upshot of it has been to befog Ivan's biography. The *History of Ivan IV* charges that when Ivan was twelve or so, he began throwing animals down from the tops of houses and that in his mid-teens he galloped around the squares and markets with his followers beating and robbing the common people. Both actions as well as some passages from the alleged correspondence between Ivan and Kurbsky contribute vivid, but not completely reliable, biographical detail.

Eight years before Keenan's 1971 work, an earlier source affecting knowledge of Ivan IV was unearthed—his corpse. Soviet experts discovered bony outgrowths (osteophytes) and a high level of mercury in Ivan's bones. Keenan has argued that this belated postmortem indicates that Ivan was chronically sick as an adult and that he took large doses of medicines containing mercury as well as abundant alcohol to relieve his pain. Moreover, such a combination of pain and painkillers would make it unlikely that Ivan was quite the forceful, all-powerful autocrat sometimes depicted. Other historians, however, have not read quite so much into these postmortem results.

What primarily remains available to shed light on Ivan's life is the evidence of the policies he approved and enacted. Foreigners have also left accounts of what they witnessed, including some of Ivan's actions. Russian folklore tells both something about Ivan and about the "folk." Of course, all this material, and that in Muscovite chronicles, must be examined with care.

The first thing that strikes us about Ivan IV is the sobriquet "Terrible." It is a somewhat misleading translation of the Russian *"groznyi,"* which might better be translated as awe-inspiring, formidable, or menacing. Some English works have referred to Ivan IV as "the Dread," which also comes close to expressing the original Russian meaning. Certainly, those who linked Ivan IV with *"groznyi"* in Russian folklore usually meant it as a compliment, as an American student might when referring to a football linebacker as "awesome."

The folklore image of Ivan as "awesome," however exaggerated in detail, was based on some solid facts: his victories over Kazan and Astrakhan and his harsh destruction of many of his enemies and presumed enemies. Not only was folklore usually not revolted by Ivan's violence, but also, as Maureen Perrie has written, it is hard to differ with those who describe the commonfolk's attitude in folklore as one of "malicious glee" toward boyar executions.[1]

Granted Ivan was *"groznyi,"* but was he so for sound reasons—as depicted, for example, in Sergei Eisenstein's classic film *Ivan the Terrible*? Or were many of his violent activities motivated by suspicions bordering on paranoia? Or were they not so much a reflection of mental derangement but extreme examples of a ruler's more typical quest for greater power? As often in history, there is no simple answer.

CHILDHOOD, CORONATION, AND EARLY DOMESTIC POLICIES

Ivan IV was born in 1530. He was the long-awaited son that Vasili III had married a second time to obtain. Ivan's mother, Elena, was from the Glinsky clan, part of which had emigrated from Lithuania early in Vasili III's reign. Ironically, this mother of the future conqueror of two Mongol khanates claimed descent from the Mongol Mamai, who was defeated by Dmitri Donskoi in 1380. According to a chronicle account, which we are free to doubt, the wife of the khan of Kazan stated to Russian envoys soon after Ivan's birth that a tsar with two teeth had been born and that "with one he will devour us, and with the other you."

Ivan was only three when his father died—like many princes before him, Vasili was tonsured and became a monk on his deathbed, hoping no doubt it

---

[1] *The Image of Ivan the Terrible in Russian Folklore* (Cambridge, Eng., 1987), p. 60.

would ease his path to heaven. What followed over the next decade and a half, especially after the death of Ivan's mother in 1538, was an insecure childhood for the boy prince. As he looked on while others ruled in his name, various important boyar clan families and their supporters engaged in a chaotic, almost Mafia-like, power struggle. Even before his mother's death, two of Ivan's paternal uncles had died in prison. They were not alone. Both before and after them, others were imprisoned or executed, or both. Between 1539 and 1542, two metropolitans were also successively removed by court factions.

Although the competition of boyar clans was normally kept within stable boundaries, the absence of an adult on the throne upset the political equilibrium. As one faction of clans after another vied for dominant influence at court, the violence escalated, both as a means of weakening rival factions and as retribution against such means. These struggles were power struggles motivated primarily by self-interest, not any ideological or class interests. Whatever their source, the violence they bred probably influenced the young Ivan, permanently scarring him.

In January 1547, after the most important boyar families had apparently reached some sort of settlement, the sixteen-year-old Ivan was crowned tsar. In the four-hour ceremony inside the Assumption Cathedral, this tall young prince was the first Russian monarch to be crowned with this imposing title, which by now implied superiority to all other monarchs. The Metropolitan Makari presided over the ceremony, symbolizing church support for such a powerful God-appointed monarchy.

Three weeks after the coronation, Ivan married Anastasia Romanova of the powerful Zakharin-Yurev clan. But the happy events that began the year gradually gave way to some joyless June days. After a deadly fire leaped from one wooden building to another in central areas of the capital, riots broke out. Rumors circulated that the Glinskys had used witchcraft to start the fire. Enraged townspeople began a witch-hunt for these powerful relatives of the tsar. The mobs were possibly encouraged by some of the Glinsky clan's rivals at court. One of the Glinskys, Ivan's uncle Yuri, was pulled out of the Assumption Cathedral and executed.

After the government had restored order and punished the riots' ringleaders, Ivan began decreeing various measures. They are usually referred to as reforms and were certainly aimed at increasing government and church efficiency and decreasing corruption and other abuses. Yet they were also designed to strengthen the power of the central government. In devising and carrying them out, Ivan was no doubt assisted by trusted advisers. Exactly who these advisers were and how much influence they exercised are unclear.

Like any good politician, Ivan started out by garnering support for his intended initiatives. In 1549, he met with selected church leaders and nobles to inform them of his plans. The nobles included both service gentry and boyars—the number of boyar clans had increased significantly since 1533, and by 1555 about forty individuals held boyar rank. During the next several decades, Ivan sporadically met with such groups and perhaps even added some Moscow townsmen. These gatherings, referred to individually as *zemskii sobor* (assembly of the land), were later idealized by nineteenth-century Slavophiles like Konstantin Aksakov. Under Ivan, however, it was not the representative body of all classes that Aksakov often depicted it as being but an unrepresentative one, called together by Ivan primarily to obtain support for already-made decisions. Although these *zemskii sobory* had no legal rights or powers, Ivan and his advisers were shrewd enough to realize that even an autocratic government needs a certain amount of willing cooperation.

In 1550, Ivan's government issued a new law code (or *Sudebnik*), designed to curb judicial corruption as well as strengthen the central government. The following year, Ivan called together a church council (the Council of a Hundred Chapters) for similar reasons. He wished to strengthen the bishops' and Moscow's control over local churches and to curb church abuses and the moral shortcomings of both clergy and lay Orthodox. Steps toward church centralization were also taken in this early period by recognizing and incorporating many local saints into one Russian church calendar. In the middle of 1551, Ivan forbade monasteries and church leaders to buy nobles' estates and placed restrictions upon the nobles' rights to will property to monasteries. Despite these prohibitions, however, the church continued to obtain new lands.

During the 1550s, Ivan improved the organization of his central government bureaucracy by establishing a number of chanceries—later called *prikazy*. Each, like that of Foreign Affairs, dealt with a single area of government concern.

In 1550, Ivan began creating a permanent force of musketeers (*streltsy*). At about this time, he ordered his officials to provide more lands in the Moscow area for about 1,000 noble military servitors. In 1556, he spelled out the exact military obligation of each landowner, which increased with the size of one's holdings.

In the 1550s, Ivan's government greatly expanded a local government initiative first introduced in 1539. To deal more effectively with widespread banditry, Ivan substantially increased the number of elected district judicial officials. He also created a group of new tax collectors, apparently convinced that the local merchants, well-to-do peasants, and others who received this task would perform it more efficiently and honestly than the governors had. Yet even these apparent decentralizing steps seem to have been designed to strengthen central government control, for the new local officials were made directly responsible to Moscow.

Despite all these Moscow initiatives, however, the central government's control over the country still did not penetrate deeply, especially as compared to more modern governments. It was able to collect taxes, field an army, dispense some justice, and strengthen the powers of landowning nobles and bishops—in exchange for their military or other services to the state. Many people, among both the elite and more common folk, evaded some government impositions and often resisted and frustrated its new initiatives. The issuing of decrees did not always mean that they were carried out the way Moscow intended.

MUSCOVY EXPANSION: SUCCESSES AND FAILURES

In his efforts to expand Muscovy, Ivan the Terrible went beyond his predecessors by concentrating on the conquest of non-Russian areas. In the east, he was successful; in the west, he was not.

Eastward Expansion

In 1552, after several earlier failed campaigns, Ivan captured Kazan. This city was just east of the Volga, about 500 miles from Moscow, and it was the capital of the khanate of Kazan. Political, economic, and religious reasons intertwined to influence Ivan's decision to take it.

Frequent raids from the khanate had resulted in numerous captive Russians in Kazan, most of whom had been, or soon would be, sold in slave markets. Historians differ on the number of Russian captives in Kazan. Vernadsky says more than 100,000 by 1551; Pelenski places the number between 15,000 and 30,000. Russian diplomatic pressure led to the release of many of them in the late summer of 1551, but Ivan insisted on the release of the rest.

Another political consideration was that Russia had exercised sporadic hegemony over Kazan from 1516 to 1546 and continued to compete with the Crimean khanate for influence in the area. Moreover, internal dissension, both among the Kazan Tatars themselves and between the Kazan government and some of the other subjugated peoples of their khanate, provided opportunities too good to pass up. Especially noteworthy was the appeal for Muscovite protection by a large group of the Cheremis (Mari), a Finno-Ugric people northwest of Kazan. Ivan accepted their appeal. His subsequent refusal to recognize Kazan's claims on their territory further worsened relations. In 1550, Ivan founded the fortress of Sviiazhsk on Cheremis territory and used it as a staging ground for his attack on Kazan.

Because the Volga was important for Russia's foreign trade and the khanate was not reliable enough to assist it always, economics also propelled Ivan to take Kazan. The possibility of obtaining new farm lands was another inducement.

One of the biggest supporters of the Kazan campaigns was Metropolitan Makari, who helped mobilize support by depicting the war against Kazan as a religious crusade against Islam. Religious support was rewarded by Ivan's religious policies once he took Kazan. The day after he entered the city, Ivan looked on as the site of a former Moslem mosque was consecrated for a new cathedral. He also granted monasteries and churches land within the city and beyond. In 1555, he, Metropolitan Makari, and other leading churchmen were on hand for the investiture of the first archbishop of Kazan. Ivan strongly encouraged and aided the new archbishop's attempts to win converts from Islam to Christianity but by peaceful means. These proselytizing efforts, however, enjoyed only mixed results.

Meanwhile, the victory of 1552 was followed up by another in 1556, this

FIGURE 8.1. Cathedral of St. Basil the Blessed, Red Square, Moscow. Constructed in 1555–1561 to celebrate Ivan IV's victory over Kazan.

time over Astrakhan, near the mouth of the Volga. The campaign was motivated largely by economics and rebellions against Russian control by some of the Volga tribes. In 1553, English merchants searching for a northern sea route to the Orient were forced by bad weather to land on Russia's White Sea coast. They soon took advantage of their situation to come to Moscow and negotiate a trade agreement with Ivan IV. As a result of England's interest in Central Asian and Persian trade, Ivan was further encouraged to control the whole length of the Volga so as to insure Russian control over, and participation in, any such trade via this mighty river.

Ivan's victories over Kazan and Astrakhan were of enormous significance and not only for trading reasons. As Russian peasants moved into the fertile Volga and Kama river basins, they began a steady advance over steppelands that had once been ruled by mighty nomads.

Perhaps even more importantly, the victories paved the way for further eastward expansion and the development of an increasingly multinational, multicultured empire. The conquered peoples were non-Christian and non-Slavic. Just to their east lie vast, but sparsely populated, Siberia, stretching thousands of miles to the Pacific.

Already in 1581, a small band of Cossacks under their leader Ermak invaded western Siberia. They were hired with Ivan's approval by the rich Stroganov family. Following Ivan's earlier Volga victories, the Stroganovs had developed salt and iron mines from the upper Kama River area to the Urals. Now they used Ermak and his men to establish themselves in western Siberia and take full advantage of the rich furs covering its animals.

Ermak's force advanced into an area that was part of the khanate of Sibir, a Tatar state ruling over various indigenous peoples. By Ivan's death in 1584, Ermak and his colorful Cossacks had captured Sibir, its capital on the Irtysh River (see Map 8.1).

Livonian War

Fueling the Stroganovs' quest for furs were the heightened trading possibilities opened up by both Ivan's conquests and his contact with the English. A Western Europe now glutted with gold from the New World provided ample inducement to expand the fur supply to meet the growing European market. Yet if increased Western trading possibilities helped fuel Russia's successful eastern expansion, it also helped stimulate Ivan to attempt a western expansion in Livonia that ultimately turned out unsuccessful.

At first, Livonia, with its flourishing Baltic ports and fertile farmlands, seemed an inviting target. Its conquest would facilitate trade and appropriate contacts with the West, which the Muscovite government believed were being deliberately hampered by certain Baltic powers. Although the Germanic Knights still ruled over Livonia's Estonian and Latvian peasants, the Knights were no longer that formidable. They now acrimoniously had to share power with Catholic bishops and with Germanic Protestant merchants who dominated various parts of the country.

After a preliminary three-year war with Sweden, Ivan's forces invaded Livonia in 1558 and were at first successful. They captured Dorpat and Narva but then agreed to an armistice to prepare for a campaign against the Crimean Tatars. After the failed Crimean expedition of 1559, Ivan renewed his attack on Livonia. But despite some additional victories, the advances of the Russian army soon came to a halt. Poland-Lithuania, Denmark, and Sweden had no intention of allowing Russia to capture this vital region. Stimulated by Livonian appeals for help—and the chance to dominate areas of Livonia—Poland-Lithuania and Sweden threw themselves into the conflict and became the chief opponents of Russia for control of the region. The Livonian War continued ebbing and flowing until 1583, just a year before Ivan's death. Besides the war battles themselves, several other developments helped determine the final outcome.

In 1569, the loose union between Poland and Lithuania became tighter

Russian Expansion, 1533–1598, and the Livonian War

- Russia in 1533
- Russian expansion to 1598
- Lost by Russia to Sweden in Livonian War; regained in War of 1590–95
- Additional Swedish gains in Livonian War
- Polish gains in Livonian War

0   150   300 Miles

Barents Sea

Narym (1596)

Surgut (1594)   Ob R.

Samoed

KHANATE OF SIBIR (up to final defeat in 1598)

Pechora   *Yugra*

White Sea   Archangel (1584)   Tobolsk (1587)   Irtysh R.

Komi   Tiumen (1586)   Tobol R.

SWEDISH EMPIRE   Karelians   *Perm*   *Ural Mountains*

Kexholm   L. Ladoga   *Cheremis (Mari)*   *Udmurts*

Novgorod   *Bashkirs*

Pskov   Volga R.   Kazan   Ufa (1586)

KHANATE OF KAZAN (up to 1552)   *Kama R.*

Riga   N. Dvina R.   Moscow   Oka R.   Samara (1586)

Livonia   Reman R.   Polotsk   Smolensk   *Mordva*   Saratov (1590)   *Nogai Tatars*

Baltic Sea   Voronezh (1586)   Ural (Yaik) R.   Aral Sea

POLISH LITHUANIAN COMMONWEALTH (after 1569)   Chernigov   Don R.   Tsaritsyn (1589)   Volga R.

Kiev   Dnieper R.   Donets R.   KHANATE OF ASTRAKHAN (up to 1556)   Astrakhan

Zaporozhian Cossacks

KHANATE OF CRIMEA   Terek R.   Caspian Sea

Black Sea

OTTOMAN EMPIRE

MAP 8.1

with the signing of the Union of Lublin. Whereas previously the two nations had been united primarily by their common king, the new agreement created a commonwealth with a common parliament, currency, and foreign policy. In addition, Poland took over Lithuania's Ukrainian lands. The most important effect the new union had on the Livonian War was to bring the dominant Polish part of it more actively into the struggle.

In 1571, the Crimean Tatars attacked Russia and penetrated to the capital itself. Backed by the Ottoman Turks, the Crimean Tatars had not reconciled themselves to the taking of Astrakhan and had made three separate attempts in the 1560s to wrest it from Moscow. In 1571, with most of his military engaged in the Livonian conflict, Ivan's defenses were weak. The Tatars plundered part of Moscow and left much of it in flames and strewn with thousands of Russian corpses. The invaders returned to the Crimea with tremendous booty, including many Russian prisoners. Fearing further Tatar attacks, Ivan was forced to put the Livonian conflict on the back burner and send troops to shore up the southern defenses. Although this hindered his Livonian effort, it did enable him to defeat the Tatars in an important battle when they again invaded Russia in 1572.

That same year offered Ivan additional hope when the Polish king, Sigismund II, died. Several chaotic years followed in which Russia and other foreign powers attempted to influence two different Polish elections. Unfortunately for Russia, however, the Hungarian prince Stephen Bathory emerged in 1575 as the new Polish king.

After a few years of consolidating power in his new commonwealth, Bathory won important victories over the Russians in 1578–1581. At the same time, the Swedes were also pushing Russian forces back in the area south of the Gulf of Finland, both in Livonia itself and in Russian fortress cities to its east. Finally in 1582, Ivan signed an armistice with Poland and in the following year with Sweden. By the first agreement, the prewar borders of the two signatories were reinstated, and Russia turned over its Livonia conquests to Poland. By the second agreement, Russia recognized, at least temporarily, the loss of such fortress-cities as Ivangorod and almost all of Russia's undeveloped coast on the Gulf of Finland and part of Karelia west and north of Lake Ladoga. Ivan was allowed to keep only a small bit of territory around the mouth of the River Neva. Sweden maintained its earlier gains in northern Livonia, including such cities as Reval (Tallinn) and Narva (see Maps 8.1 and 10.1).

Thus, twenty-five years of costly conflict had left the Russians with only losses—and not just territorial ones. To appreciate the war's impact fully, however, we must first examine Ivan's domestic actions during this prolonged war.

DOMESTIC POLICIES, 1558–1584

Most of the terrorist activities for which Ivan IV became infamous occurred after the Livonian War had begun in 1558. These actions were related to Ivan's changing state of mind.

Ivan's Growing Distrust

The boyars' reaction to a severe illness suffered by Ivan in 1553 kindled his progressively violent and suspicious behavior. Although Eisenstein simplified this response in filming *Ivan the Terrible*, his depiction was basically correct. Ivan did ask his boyars to swear their support, should he die, to his infant son, Dmitri. Some, perhaps recalling the bloody feuds of Ivan's youth and not wanting another child on the throne, hesitated and at first preferred Prince Vladimir of Staritsa, a cousin of Ivan's. Although the still sick Ivan was able to change their minds, he seems never to have forgotten this moment of "disloyalty." Yet for a while, his hurt smoldered without breaking into flames.

Foreign policy differences and military failures further contributed to Ivan's distrust. Before the Livonian War, some of his advisers had recommended concentrating instead on defeating the Crimean Tatars. After the start of the Livonian War, Ivan's anger and impatience increased. He blamed defeats on boyars and other officials he had once relied upon and punished them.

In 1560, Ivan's wife Anastasia died. Although still under thirty, she had given birth to six children and seen four of them die, including the baby Dmitri, whose nurse dropped him in a river when a gangplank overturned under her. Rumors, unsupported by any evidence, circulated that Anastasia was the victim of foul play. The loss of his wife further destabilized Ivan. A chronicle account admits that he became wild and lustful.

A year and two weeks after Anastasia's death, he married his second wife, a Circassian princess, who at first knew little of Russia or its language. She and Ivan had a son, who soon died, and she herself died in 1569. Then from 1571 to 1580, Ivan married five more times. Eisenstein once wrote that what stuck in Russians' memories about these wives of Ivan was their peculiar family names, such as Nagaia (naked) and Sobakina (canine).

Shortly after his second marriage in 1561, Ivan began taking harsher measures against those who angered him. From 1562 to 1564, he increasingly resorted to arrests, imprisonments, forced loyalty oaths, exile to monasteries and convents, and executions. Incidents of boyar desertions to Poland-Lithuania also increased. The defection of Prince Andrei Kurbsky in the spring of 1564 was especially significant. The death in late 1563 of Metropolitan Makari, a moderating influence, might also have been important.

In response to the heightened tension that Ivan himself had largely created, he took an unusual step in early December 1564. He loaded up his wife, two sons, and many valuable possessions and took off in a large convoy. After a brief stop at the St. Sergius Monastery, he traveled on to his nearby hunting lodge at the fortressed Alexandrovsk settlement. From there, in early January 1565, he informed the new metropolitan that he was abdicating his throne. For this decision, he blamed primarily the boyars, whom he accused of being disloyal and treasonous. He also had officials read out a proclamation to the common people, absolving them of any blame. His tactics were clearly a populist move designed to drum up support for future actions against his enemies.

As Ivan undoubtedly realized would happen, panic gripped the capital—without any designated or agreed-upon successor, abdication seemed like an invitation to chaos. Church leaders and boyars hastened to Ivan's retreat to plead that he remain tsar. He agreed, apparently on the condition that everyone recognize his right to deal with "traitors" as he saw fit—church intercession for earlier "traitors" had especially annoyed him.

Oprichnina and Its Aftermath

Ivan's new method for dealing with his enemies was to create the most infamous institution of his regime—the *oprichnina*. The most remarkable of its functions was its terrorist one; it was no coincidence that Stalin's NKVD police were sometimes referred to as *oprichniki*. Ivan's *oprichniki* were assigned the job of sniffing out treason and sweeping it away. Although a broom was one of their symbols, an ax might have been more fitting. Not only did they confiscate estates of those charged with treason, but also they slaughtered thousands of innocent people. Kliuchevsky wrote that they rode around dressed completely in black and on black horses with black harnesses. Eventually, there were about 6,000 of these agents of terror.

The *oprichnina*, however, was more than just a group of state terrorists. Directly under Ivan and centered at the Alexandrovsk settlement, it was also a separate royal court and administration. It eventually ruled over about half the country, including part of Moscow and other important prosperous and strategic areas, mainly north of the capital. The rest of the country, now referred to as the *zemshchina*, was run by senior boyars and most of the old government machinery, with Ivan being consulted only on chief issues.

Although it was once believed that the *oprichnina* was a service-gentry bludgeon that Ivan created to beat an autocracy-resisting higher nobility into submission, recent research has swung away from some aspects of this interpretation. Building on the work of historians such as Kliuchevsky and S. Veselovsky, it indicates that both higher nobles and lower nobles (service gentry) were among the persecutors and the persecuted. Furthermore, it denies that the higher nobility was against the tsar's centralization of power.

Yet Ivan's actions do reflect his desire to free himself from too great a dependence on prominent boyar clans and from other constraints. Although neither he nor his predecessors had been legally limited in their powers, custom and tradition had dictated that the monarch rule along with his boyars and in keeping with certain religious principles. The creation and operations of the *oprichnina*, however, also suggest that Ivan had become paranoid, or at least overly suspicious, seeing conspiracies and treason where they did not really exist.

The *oprichnina* galloped on for close to eight years, until Ivan abolished it in 1572. Beset with increasing pathological fears and suspicions—in 1567 he even attempted to arrange asylum in England for himself should it prove necessary—Ivan terrorized all classes. From Prince Vladimir of Staritsa and his mother, so malevolently portrayed in Eisenstein's film, down to poor paupers in Novgorod, thousands perished.

Among other victims were petitioners from a 1566 *zemskii sobor*, who asked Ivan to end the *oprichnina*; many churchmen, including Metropolitan Philip;

many leading *zemshchina* officials; and toward the end, even some of the *oprichnina* leaders themselves. Sometimes when princes or other nobles were killed,
other members of their families and even their servants also were executed. In
1570—about a century after it had been victimized by Ivan III—Novgorod
once again felt a ruler's wrath. Accusing its leaders of treason and Polish sympathies, Ivan the Terrible let loose his *oprichniki* on the city. Although contemporary accounts no doubt overestimated the number executed, it was at least a
few thousand.

As the case of Novgorod makes all too clear, Ivan's victims suffered in just
about every way imaginable. In general, the more fortunate got off with just
the confiscation of their estates and exile, or perhaps, as with some in Novgorod, they just had to endure *oprichniki* plundering and looting. Less fortunate individuals suffered beatings, torture, or rape but still escaped with their
lives. Least fortunate of all were those who suffered gruesome deaths, sometimes after extensive torture. With Ivan sometimes looking on or participating
himself, people were hanged, hacked up, beaten to death by clubs, impaled,
boiled in hot water, roasted by fire, poisoned, or drowned. And this is only a
partial list. It's no wonder Stalin admired Ivan IV so much.

After the *oprichnina* failed to help prevent the Crimean Tatar's successful
attack of 1571, Ivan finally ended it the next year and even forbade mention of
it. Its abolition meant only an easing of state violence, however, not its termi-

FIGURE 8.2. A woodcut of Ivan the Terrible with a head on his lance.
(From Ian Grey, The Horizon History of Russia, *American Heritage Publishing Company,
New York, 1970, p. 98, New York Public Library, Slavonic Division.)*

nation. In his final decade, still occupied with the Livonian War, Ivan continued to display some bizarre behavior. In 1575, he once again announced that he was abdicating, this time to turn Russia over to a Christianized Tatar khan, named Simeon. Ivan himself then posed as a lesser prince to this new grand prince. The charade lasted only about a year.[2]

About this same time, an Austrian ambassador described Ivan as tall, stout, and vigorous, with big darting eyes, a shaved head, and a thick red beard with black streaks. In his final years, however, Ivan displayed less vigor and increasing signs of ill health. But unfortunately for his son Ivan, the Tsar was still healthy enough to strike him a fatal blow, probably with a staff. This occurred in late 1581 and seems to have been occasioned by the son's defense of his pregnant wife, Elena. Apparently the tsar had berated her for being immodestly dressed and had struck her. Not only did the incident lead to the death of Elena's husband, but also to the fetus she soon miscarried.

In the days that followed, the death of his son and the distasteful armistices with Poland and Sweden sucked more life out of Ivan's pained body. Yet he attempted to arrange a marriage with the English Princess Mary Hastings, especially when he became more convinced than ever that he might have to flee Russia. He assured Queen Elizabeth that his present wife could be put away. Even after the queen squelched the idea, he did not abandon hope for an English bride. But before his life could take any more bizarre turns, he died in March 1584. He was only fifty-three.

AUTOCRACY AND THE LEGACY OF IVAN IV

Although disasters such as famines and plagues played a part, Ivan the Terrible's policies were the most significant cause of Russia's late-sixteenth-century miseries. The Livonian War, increased taxes to pay for it, and the ravages of the *oprichnina* helped impoverish and destabilize the country. So too did Crimean Tatar raids, which Ivan had failed to defend against adequately. Moreover, Ivan had given peasant lands and peasants to his growing service gentry, and his demands on the gentry had led them, in turn, to squeeze harder on their peasants. Many peasants responded to the intensifying demands and chaos of Ivan's reign by fleeing south.

At the beginning of the 1580s, Ivan reacted by declaring certain years "forbidden"; during such a year, peasants could not leave their masters, even during the two weeks bracketing St. George's Day (November 25).

By then the oppression and flight had already taken a heavy toll. In many northern areas, populated villages were like lonely islands in a sea of aban-

---

[2] In "Ivan IV's Mythology of Kingship," *SR* 52 (Winter 1993): 769–809, Priscilla Hunt has attempted to demonstrate a relationship between Ivan's behavior and his twisted understanding of certain religious ideas then current in Moscow.

doned lands. Although written two centuries later in different circumstances, some lines of Oliver Goldsmith's "The Deserted Village" seem appropriate:

> Ill fares the land, to hastening ills a prey
> Far, far away, thy children leave the land
> Amidst thy bowers the tyrant's hand is seen

In the region of Novgorod, about 90 percent of the farming land was abandoned; in that of Pskov and Moscow combined, about 84 percent. Some northern cities, especially Novgorod, were also hard hit. The once great northern city lost about 80 percent of its population between the beginning and end of Ivan's reign.

This was not all of Ivan's damage. The unsatisfying armistices he signed with Poland and Sweden almost guaranteed renewed hostilities in the future. His actions against his son Ivan and his daughter-in-law Elena left his dynasty in the weak hands, and loins, of his son Fedor.

This array of deficits might lead students to think that Ivan was "terrible" in more than just the "awesome" sense of the word. Many historians and others, however, have praised Ivan IV for certain "positive" accomplishments. Alexander Yanov in his controversial book *The Origins of Autocracy: Ivan the Terrible in Russian History* (1981) catalogs such favorable assessments, along with more negative ones, throughout Russian history. We have already seen that in Russian folklore Ivan was generally regarded favorably. Even in works of fiction, such as Yuri Trifonov's 1980 novel, *The Old Man (Starik)*, one sometimes comes across characters arguing the plusses and minuses of Ivan the Terrible.

One of the characters in Trifonov's book argues that Kazan and Astrakhan are two plusses. Although the character he is arguing with disputes the value of extending boundaries, many, including historians and some of the "folk" of folklore, have implicitly or explicitly valued Ivan for his territorial gains. His other major service, according to many, was that he ultimately strengthened Russia by increasing both the powers of Moscow and the tsar at the expense of a "feudal" aristocracy. Conversely, its victory over Ivan would have doomed Russia to a more fragmented existence, which would have made the country easy prey for foreign enemies.

This brings us to the question of Ivan's role in strengthening Russian autocracy. We have already seen that Ivan III (the Great) called himself "autocrat" and meant by it that he was not subject to any foreign ruler. In 1547, Ivan IV bestowed upon himself this title (*samoderzhets* in Russian) in addition to that of "tsar." Eventually the term also came to mean a ruler with legally unlimited power, which is how we use it today.

When Ivan the Terrible came to the throne, his powers were already virtually unrestricted by any law. The tsar alone had the right to exercise the ultimate executive, legislative, and judicial powers. This was due to many reasons, some of which have already been indicated. Among the factors contributing to autocracy's development were geography, the militaristic nature of the Muscovite state, internal evolutionary political developments, Byzantine and Mongol influences, the absence of a strong legal tradition, and the political weakness of both the church and other groups.

In Russia, orders or estates, such as the clergy, nobility, and bourgeoisie, had neither the sense of corporate identity nor the legal rights usually existing in Latin Christendom. Nor did Russia have any type of representative parliament, as did most countries in Western Christendom by the end of the fifteenth century. Although few of these parliaments gained the powers of the fourteenth-fifteenth–century *cortes* in Spanish Aragon, where laws could not be made without its consent, most did have the right to block new taxes and some to participate in making laws. Although rights of parliaments declined in many areas of Europe during the sixteenth century, in others, like Poland, they grew stronger.

Although mention is sometimes made of the *zemskii sobor* as a sort of quasiparliament, under Ivan IV it was not even quasi but a powerless group of changing composition, called together on occasion to support Ivan's policies. Most of the small number who openly resisted his plans met with death. Some historians also speak of two other political institutions said to exist under Ivan: the Chosen Council—a small group of Ivan's leading advisers until 1560—and the Boyar Council. Other historians insist that under Ivan no such institutions existed, only boyars and other advisers who either individually or in small groups sometimes gave counsel to the tsar. These differences of opinion are again based in part on the reliability of sources, especially Kurbsky. Either way, however, none of these "institutions" placed any legal limitations on Ivan's powers.

While granting that the tsar operated free from any contemporary Western-type legal limitations, scholars such as Nancy Kollmann and Daniel Rowland have pointed to practical and ideological limitations on the power of medieval Muscovite rulers. Kollmann has emphasized their dependence on their boyars, whose powers were considerable in a patriarchal system based more on personal and family ties than on law. Rowland has argued that most religious and lay thinkers from the mid-sixteenth to the mid-seventeenth centuries shared a consistent ideology that drew the line at obeying a tsar acting contrary to God's will. These Muscovite thinkers also believed that an ideal tsar should be pious, be willing to listen to wise advisers, and be a preserver of both Orthodoxy and the traditional political order. Despite the relative political weakness of the Orthodox Church, as compared to the papacy, Rowland has noted that Metropolitan Philip and others spoke out against Ivan when they thought he acted in a damnable way.

One other minor limitation on a tsar's power that should be mentioned is *mestnichestvo*. This was an order of precedence for aristocrats that came into existence toward the end of the fifteenth century. By the time of Ivan the Terrible, the tsar was expected to abide by it when making appointments to high government and military offices. Doing so would prevent a noble from being "disgraced" by serving beneath someone whose family was lower than his on the precedence ladder.

Yet, if we grant these varied constraints, which Ivan IV was ultimately unable to destroy, we should still be cautious about regarding autocracy as nothing more than a "facade." We can acknowledge the power of boyars (or later on in Russian history of a noble "ruling class") without excessively downplaying that of the monarch. The absence of *legal* limitations on the monarch's powers and the weakness of other safeguards against despotism were important. They lay at the core of autocracy and paved the way for Ivan's despotic actions.

What impact did Ivan's views and policies have on subsequent Russian history? Certainly, autocracy was evolving strongly before Ivan the Terrible, and just as surely he did not strengthen Russia by his victory over a "feudal" aristocracy attempting to prevent Moscow's centralization of power. First, despite increasing centralization on both a secular and a religious level, it is difficult to argue that he left the country stronger. Second, there was no united aristocracy trying to prevent centralization. Although Ivan weakened the country's aristocracy, he did not crush it. Indeed, within a few decades after his death, his policies inadvertently helped lead to the collapse of his dynasty, with boyars and other political forces moving, at least temporarily, into the vacuum.

Ivan the Autocrat Lectures Queen Elizabeth I

The following excerpt from a 1570 letter of Ivan IV to Queen Elizabeth I of England illustrates well Ivan's autocratic personality. Even Keenan has recognized this letter as almost surely a genuine correspondence, although not necessarily actually written by Ivan himself. But whether ghost-written or not, its ideas were Ivan's, and it was part of a large exchange of letters between to two monarchs, dealing primarily with trade. My translation here is indebted to observations made about the letter by Richard Pipes (in his *Russia under the Old Regime*) but is otherwise based mainly on that appearing in George Tolstoy, ed., *The First Forty Years of Intercourse between England and Russia, 1553–1593* (St. Petersburg, 1875; reprint New York, 1963), pp. 111–114; Russian text on pp. 107–109.

And how many letters have been brought to us here [from England] . . . but every letter

has had a contrary seal, which is inappropriate, and such letters in all places are not credited, but every prince in his realm has one proper seal; but we acknowledged these letters. . . .

And after that we had news that a subject of yours had come to Narva, by name Edward Goodman . . . and [we] commanded him to be searched for letters and we found many letters; and in those letters were written words not allowable against our princely state and empire, how that in our empire were many unlawful things done. . . .

. . . And we had thought that you are the sovereign in your domain, and rule alone, and seek your sovereign honor and your country's profit, and therefore we wished to deal with you. But now we perceive that beside you there are men who rule, and not men but low class traders, who look not to our sovereign heads, honor, and profits, but seek their own trading profits. And you abide in your maidenly state like a commoner.

Yet if we look beyond this Time of Troubles (1598–1613), Ivan the Terrible's autocratic and despotic practices left behind a dangerous and tragic precedent. Yanov has written of the "historiographic nightmare," which led many historians from the eighteenth century into the twentieth to consider Ivan IV a force of progress who strengthened Russia. We have already seen that attitudes toward Ivan the Terrible as depicted in folklore were generally positive. Is it any wonder then that many subsequent rulers, such as Peter the Great and Stalin, also regarded him favorably? Although none of these groups completely whitewashed Ivan's "excesses," they did justify many of his policies as necessary for strengthening Russia.

The damaging effects of Ivan IV's legacy have never been clearer than in the twentieth century. The political culture that made Stalinism possible was not solely a result of foreign Marxist influences.

At the beginning of the 1980s, Yanov could still decry the continuing influences of Ivan's autocratic legacy in the country of his birth. After 1991, when nationality problems helped lead to the disintegration of the Soviet Union, even Ivan's pioneering empire-building seemed a tarnished legacy.

SUGGESTED SOURCES*

BERRY, LLOYD E., and ROBERT O. CRUMMEY, eds. *Rude and Barbarous Kingdom: Russia in the Accounts of Sixteenth-Century English Voyagers.* Madison, 1968.

BOBRICK, BENSON. *Fearful Majesty: The Life and Reign of Ivan the Terrible.* New York, 1987.

CRUMMEY, ROBERT O. *The Formation of Muscovy, 1304–1613.* London, 1987. Ch. 6.

———. "Reform under Ivan IV: Gradualism and Terror." In *Reform in Russia and the U.S.S.R.: Past and Prospects,* ed. Robert O. Crummey. Urbana, 1989.

FEDOTOV, GEORGE P. *St. Filip, Metropolitan of Moscow—Encounter with Ivan the Terrible.* Belmont, Mass., 1978.

FENNELL, JOHN, ed. *The Correspondence Between Prince A. M. Kurbsky and Tsar Ivan IV, of Russia, 1564–1579.* Cambridge, Eng., 1955.

———, ed. *Prince A. M. Kurbsky's History of Ivan IV.* Cambridge, Eng., 1965.

GRAHAM, HUGH F. "Mestnichestvo," *MERSH* 22: 8–13.

———, "Prikaz," *MERSH* 29: 211–217.

———, ed. *The Moscovia of Antonio Possevino.* Pittsburgh, 1977.

GREY, IAN. *Ivan, the Terrible.* London, 1964.

GROBOVSKY, ANTONY N. *The "Chosen Council" of Ivan IV: A Reinterpretation.* Brooklyn, 1969.

HELLIE, RICHARD. "Zemskii Sobor," *MERSH* 45: 226–234.

Ivan the Terrible. Pts. 1 and 2. Films directed by Sergei Eisenstein, available on videocassette.

KEENAN, EDWARD L. "Ivan IV and the 'King's Evil': Ni maka li to budet?" *RH* 20, Nos. 1–4 (1993): 5–13.

———. *The Kurbskii-Groznyi Apocrypha: The Seventeenth-Century Genesis of the "Correspondence" Attributed to Prince A. M. Kurbskii and Tsar Ivan IV.* Cambridge, Mass., 1971.

*See also works cited in footnotes and in boxed insert.

————. "Muscovite Political Folkways," *RR* 45 (April 1986): 115–181; Discussion. 46 (April 1987): 157–209.

————. "Vita. Ivan Vasil'evich, Terrible Tsar: 1530–1584," *Harvard Magazine* 80, No. 3 (1978): 48–49.

KLEIMOLA, A. M. "Reliance on the Tried and True: Ivan IV and Appointments to the Boyar Duma, 1565–1584," *FOG* 46 (1992): 51–63.

KLYUCHEVSKY (KLIUCHEVSKY), V. O. *The Course of Russian History*. Vol. 2. New York, 1960.

KOLLMANN, JACK E. JR. "The *Stoglav* Council and Parish Priests," *RH* 7, Pts. 1–2 (1980): 65–91.

KOLLMANN, NANCY SHIELDS. *Kinship and Politics: The Making of the Muscovite Political System, 1345–1547*. Stanford, 1987.

MARTIN, JANET. *Medieval Russia, 980–1584*. Cambridge, England, 1995. Ch. 11.

OWEN, THOMAS C. "Quotations from a Common Source in the Kurbskii-Groznyi Correspondence: A Research Note," *RR* 49 (April 1990): 157–166.

PELENSKI, JAROSLAW. *Russia and Kazan: Conquest and Imperial Ideology (1438–1560s)*. The Hague, 1974.

PLATONOV, S. F. *Ivan the Terrible*. Gulf Breeze, Fla., 1974.

RH 14, Nos. 1–4 (1987). This whole issue, containing many excellent articles, is devoted to Ivan the Terrible.

ROSSING, NIELS, and BIRGIT RONNE. *Apocryphal—Not Apocryphal? A Critical Analysis of the Discussion Concerning the Correspondence Between Tsar Ivan IV Groznyj and Prince Andrej Kurbskij*. Copenhagen, 1980.

ROWLAND, DANIEL. "Did Muscovite Literary Ideology Place Limits on the Power of the Tsar (1540s–1660s)?" *RR* 49 (April 1990): 125–156.

RYWKIN, MICHAEL, ed. *Russian Colonial Expansion to 1917*. London, 1988. Contains several articles dealing at least partly with expansion under Ivan IV.

SOLOVIEV, SERGEI M. *The Reign of Ivan the Terrible: Kazan, Astrakhan, Livonia, the Oprichnina, and the Polotsk Campaign*. Gulf Breeze, Fla., 1995.

SKRYNNIKOV, RUSLAN G. *Ivan the Terrible*. Gulf Breeze, Fla., 1981.

STADEN, HEINRICH VON. *The Land and Government of Muscovy: A Sixteenth-Century Account*. Stanford, 1967.

TROYAT, HENRI. *Ivan the Terrible*. New York, 1984.

VERNADSKY, GEORGE. *Tsardom of Muscovy, 1549–1682*. Vol. 1. New Haven, 1969.

YANOV, ALEXANDER. *The Origins of Autocracy: Ivan the Terrible in Russian History*. Berkeley, 1981.

CHAPTER 9

The Time of Troubles

After the reign of Fedor (1584–1598), Ivan IV's son and the last of Moscow's Daniilovich line, a Time of Troubles began, lasting from 1598 to 1613. Following the Russian historian Sergei Platonov (1860–1933), this period is divided into three successive struggles: dynastic (1598–1606), social (1606–1610), and national (1610–1613). In the first phase, the struggle for the Russian throne was dominant; in the second, social strife; and in the third, foreign intervention and the battle against it. Although each phase had a dominant motif, the struggles overlapped. Finally, in 1613, the Time of Troubles came to an end with the selection of a new ruler, Mikhail Romanov.

BACKGROUND: RUSSIA UNDER FEDOR (1584–1598)

Fedor was born to Ivan IV's first wife Anastasia in 1557. Frail, feeble-minded, and pious—labeled the "bell-ringer" because of his frequent presence at church services—he lacked the strength needed to deal with Ivan the Terrible's sorrowful legacy. Deserted villages and abandoned estates left the government and army short of tax revenues and manpower, and the Crimean Tatars, Poland (or, more exactly, the Polish-Lithuanian Commonwealth), and Sweden remained as threats to Russian security and ambitions.

With a weak tsar at the top, a boyar struggle began to determine who became the power behind the throne. From the outset, Fedor's brother-in-law, the intelligent and resourceful Boris Godunov, then in his mid-thirties, was in a favorable position. He had risen through the *oprichnina* administrative ranks and had favorably impressed Ivan IV. Ivan had not only married Fedor to his sister, Irena, but also named Godunov an executor of his will. By late 1588, Godunov had successfully overcome the challenge of rivals such as the powerful Shuisky clan. For a decade, he remained the power behind the throne.

Godunov dealt with the "deserted village" phenomenon by continuing Ivan's policy of restricting the peasant's right to flee. Godunov also lowered the tax burden on hard-pressed nobles. By 1600, there were clear signs of economic recovery: Cultivated land increased, and as grain became more plentiful, prices decline.

He also strengthened Russia by his dealings with foreign powers and by continuing expansion. In 1589, he persuaded Constantinople's patriarch to ordain Metropolitan Job as the first Russian patriarch. By a war with Sweden, 1590–1595, Russia regained some coastland along the Gulf of Finland that had been lost during the Livonian War. In 1591, Russian forces defeated a Crimean Tatar army that had penetrated almost to the walls of Moscow. Meanwhile, Russia continued advancing and propping up its position south and east of Muscovy. The government built new forts along the Don, Donets, and Volga rivers. It even strengthened its position along the Terek River. But attempts to gain dominance beyond the Terek, in the northern Caucasian regions of Kabarda and Dagestan, ultimately proved fruitless. In Siberia, however, Russia continued to advance. By Fedor's death in 1598, Russian forces controlled the Ob River system, establishing new fortresses along it as they moved southeastward.

Despite Godunov's overall successes up to 1598, one tragic event occurred in 1591. Only in subsequent years would its full significance be understood. This was the death of Fedor's half-brother and possible successor, Dmitri of Uglich, offspring of Ivan's seventh marriage. The young Dmitri died of a knife wound to the neck, and his mother charged that Godunov had masterminded the stabbing. Others, including some in Uglich, believed the charge.

In the nineteenth century, Alexander Pushkin and Modest Musorgsky immortalized Godunov's supposed complicity in a play and opera, both entitled *Boris Godunov*. Yet, Godunov's guilt remains unproven. In 1591, it was far from clear that Dmitri would succeed Fedor upon his death. Fedor himself might yet produce his own heir—in fact, a daughter was born to Fedor and Irena in 1592 (the baby died, however, in 1594). Furthermore, as the son of a seventh marriage, Dmitri's claim as heir might also be challenged by Russian churchmen. It is possible, however, that Godunov did not wish to depend on such eventualities. Whatever the case, the commission Godunov sent to investigate the death concluded that Dmitri had stabbed himself during an epileptic seizure. Of course, the commission's objectivity and verdict remain open to doubt, and Dmitri's death will probably remain one of the great unsolved mysteries of Russian history.

THE DYNASTIC STRUGGLE (1598–1606)

In January 1598, Tsar Fedor died without leaving an heir. Not even a brother survived him. For the first time since 1425, there was now a serious succession crisis. With no rightful heir, who was to succeed Fedor? The Tsarina Irena was a possibility, but soon after her husband's burial, she retired to a convent.

Her brother, Boris Godunov, was in a better position: Most levers of power were already in his hands, and besides his sister's support, he had that of Patriarch Job. His main opposition came from fellow boyars. They could not unite around an alternate candidate, however. According to some reports, soon after Fedor's death, a Boyar Council suggested that it should itself assume authority; but, if so, nothing came of the idea. Godunov, with Patriarch Job's able assistance, orchestrated support from a specially convened *zemskii sobor* and from Moscow townspeople who demonstrated in his favor. At various times, both groups went out to the fortresslike Novodevichii Convent, where Godunov had settled, to petition him to be their tsar. The exact nature of the *sobor* is open to debate, but it seems to have had several sessions and not been especially representative.[1] In September, Boris Godunov was crowned the first non-Riurikid tsar.

He soon dealt with his chief rivals, especially the Romanovs. The most important Romanov, Fedor, was forced to enter a monastery. Despite little enthusiasm for Godunov among many prestigious boyar clans, his intelligence and political skills might have further enabled him to consolidate his power if an adversary more terrible than any human foe had not interceded—famine.

Godunov met the crisis by providing some aid and by restoring, for a year, the peasants' traditional late-autumn right to abandon their landowners' estates. Yet misery and discontent only increased, as did brigandage and other lawlessness. Others in a position to dispense some relief—such as many no-

[1] On the Boyar Council and *zemskii sobor*, see Chapters 8 and 10.

FIGURE 9.1. Novodevichii Convent, Moscow, founded in 1524 to commemorate the gaining of the city of Smolensk.

Famine in Russia

Primarily as a result of bad weather, famine struck Russia like a plague in 1601. One observer of its effects was a French captain in Russian service, Jacques Margeret. The following excerpt is from his *The Russian Empire and Grand Duchy of Muscovy: A 17th-Century French Account*, trans. and ed. Chester S. L. Dunning, pp. 58–59. Copyright 1983 by the University of Pittsburgh Press. Although some dispute exists about the magnitude of inflation and famine deaths, Margeret's figures are on the conservative side, and his general description has been confirmed by other sources. Bracketed material and ellipses are mine.

In the year 1601 began the great famine which lasted three years. A mesure of wheat, which sold for fifteen sols before, sold for three rubles [about a twenty-six-fold increase]. . . . During these years things so atrocious were committed that they are unbelievable. To see a husband quit his wife and children, to see a wife kill her husband or a mother her children in order to eat them—these were ordinary occurrences. . . . In short, this famine was so great that, not counting the number of dead in other towns of Russia, more than one hundred twenty thousand people died from it in the city of Moscow and are buried in three public places outside the city designated for this purpose. This was done by the order of and at the expense of the emperor [Godunov], who even provided shrouds for their burial. The reason for such a great number of dead in Moscow is that the Emperor Boris had alms given every day to as many poor as were found in the city . . . so that everyone, hearing of the liberality of the emperor, rushed to Moscow; this, even though some of them still had enough to live on. When they arrived in Moscow, they could not live. . . . So, falling into even greater weakness, they died in that city or on the roads leading out of it. Finally, informed that all too many hastened to Moscow and that the country was becoming depopulated little by little by those coming to die in the capital, Boris stopped giving alms to them. They could be found in the streets dead or half dead, suffering from cold and hunger. This was a strange spectacle. The sum that the Emperor Boris spent on the poor is incredible. Besides the disbursement which was made in Moscow, there was not a town in all of Russia to which Boris did not contribute something for the care of these poor. I know that he sent to Smolensk by a man known to me twenty thousand rubles.

bles, monasteries, and rich merchants—failed to display much compassion. Some even profited from the famine.

In the summer of 1604, a lodestar appeared in southwest Russia that many people believed would guide them to a better future. This lodestar claimed to be Dmitri of Uglich, son of Ivan the Terrible, and rightful ruler of Russia. Although most historians agree that the real Dmitri died in 1591, this Pseudo Dmitri made believers, or at least followers, out of many of his contemporaries.

The reasons for his popularity are not difficult to discern. Even before the famine, many in the south resented Muscovy's attempts to tighten its control over them. Now many Russians saw the hand of God behind the famine. Why was God punishing Russia so terribly? What better explanation than Boris Godunov's behavior. Rumors spread that he had planned—unsuccessfully it now seemed—the murder of Dmitri and that he had come to power by evil methods and did not belong on the throne. Besides, since Godunov's reign was bringing only misery, some alternative seemed necessary. A legitimate monarch was the only alternative the Russian political culture offered. To paraphrase Voltaire on God: "If Dmitri did not exist, it would be necessary to invent him."

According to Godunov, this is exactly what his boyar opponents had done. He charged that this Pseudo Dmitri was actually a former Moscow monk, named Grishka Otrepev. Many historians have believed this explanation to be a plausible one.[2]

Beyond the support he had from within Russia, Pseudo Dmitri also received Polish and Catholic help. He had been in Poland before crossing the border into Russia, had secretly converted to Catholicism, and had recruited some Polish supporters.

A chief force supporting Pseudo Dmitri was the Cossacks. The term *Cossack* is of Turkish origin and was originally applied to free frontiersmen. Although by 1604, there were Cossacks in various frontier areas, including Siberia, the two largest concentrations were in the lower Dnieper and Don river regions. The first group's center was on an island south of the Dnieper cataracts, then part of Poland's Ukrainian territory (see Map 9.1). Here the Cossacks formed the Zaporozhian Host. Originally, most Cossacks, whether of the Dnieper or Don, were runaway peasants, primarily Ukrainian in the first case and Russian in the second. In both groups, additional nationalities were also present, as were other malcontents and individuals of other classes, including impoverished and adventuresome nobles. The Cossacks lived by various combinations of hunting, fishing, farming, herding, plunder, trade, and mercenary service. Mounted Cossack raids sometimes threatened Muscovite, Polish, or Tatar outposts or traders. Electing their own leaders, called hetmans or atamans, the Cossacks valued above all their free lifestyle.

Pseudo Dmitri crossed the frontier in 1604 and marched northeast with his army of Polish and Russian volunteers. His ranks swelled. Many peasants, townspeople, and soldiers joined him. Yet his army was decisively defeated east of Novgorod-Seversk by better-disciplined Muscovite forces. But Pseudo Dmitri's luck had not yet run out. He escaped to Putivl and continued to generate support in the south. And in April 1605, Boris Godunov died. Although his health had been less than robust since 1602, his death was an unexpected boon for Pseudo Dmitri. Within a few months, he triumphantly entered Moscow. Shortly before, some prominent Moscow boyars had aided his cause

---

[2] While agreeing that Pseudo Dmitri was probably Otrepev, Maureen Perrie in her *Pretenders and Popular Monarchism in Early Modern Russia: The False Tsars of the Time of Troubles* (Cambridge, Eng., 1995), pp. 50–58, rejects the view that Otrepev's challenge was orchestrated by boyars. She thinks it more likely that he initially "acted on his own initiative." Her book is the most comprehensive Western treatment of the more than one dozen pretenders who appeared in Russia from 1598 to 1613, and it examines the phenomenon of pretenders within a broad European context.

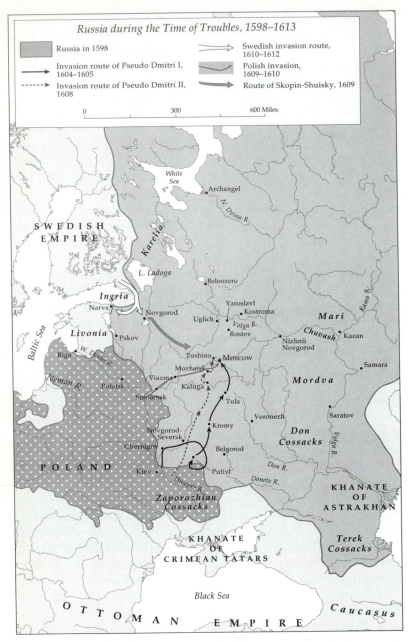

Russia during the Time of Troubles, 1598–1613

- Russia in 1598
- Invasion route of Pseudo Dmitri I, 1604–1605
- Invasion route of Pseudo Dmitri II, 1608
- Swedish invasion route, 1610–1612
- Polish invasion, 1609–1610
- Route of Skopin-Shuisky, 1609

0   300   600 Miles

MAP 9.1

by engineering the overthrow of Godunov's heir and son, Fedor, and killing both Fedor and his mother.

Once in Moscow, the pretender attempted to gain further support from at least some boyar clans, like the Romanovs, but humiliated others, like the Shiuskys. For her own self-serving reasons, the mother of the true Dmitri, Ivan

IV's last wife, Maria Nagaia (now a nun), agreed to recognize Pseudo Dmitri as her true son. In July 1605, in the Kremlin's Assumption Cathedral, he was crowned tsar.

Yet Pseudo Dmitri was not fated to remain in power long. Two main obstacles stood in his way: his own unconventional behavior and the boyars. The more that Muscovites saw of the pretender, the less he seemed a true tsar. For one thing, this short, squat man, with long arms and a short neck, was beardless. Furthermore, he allowed his Polish Catholic followers to alienate Orthodox Moscow's customs and sensibilities. His marriage to the Polish and Catholic Marina Mniszech in May 1606 and raucous postwedding celebrations by the Polish troops who had accompanied Marina to Moscow epitomized this insensitivity. Realizing that the pretender's popularity was quickly waning, some boyars, led by Vasili Shuisky, made their way into the Kremlin and murdered him only nine days after his marriage. Mobs also killed hundreds of his followers. A few days later, backers of Vasili Shuisky declared him the new tsar.

THE SOCIAL STRUGGLE (1606–1610) AND VASILI SHUISKY

Although from an old princely family, this new tsar was hardly in a secure position. Dmitri's supporters remained on the scene, other boyars were envious of Vasili, and the country's mood was becoming progressively more lawless.

To quell rumors that Pseudo Dmitri had miraculously escaped death, the Shuisky government ordered his body dug up, exposed for all to see, and then burned to ashes. To prove that the real Dmitri of Uglich no longer existed, Shuisky also ordered his corpse dug up and brought for reburial to Moscow, where his mother identified it as that of her son—after Pseudo Dmitri's death, she had denounced the pretender as an imposter. Miraculous powers were then attributed to the boy's long-dead body, and Dmitri was canonized a saint. Surely, Shuisky now undoubtedly hoped, people would realize Dmitri was really dead.

To appease his fellow boyars, Shuisky indicated that he would not execute them or their relatives or seize their possessions without a trial involving their peers. If the boyars would have been more united, these promises might have become more significant, but boyar disunity and infighting enabled the new tsar soon to violate his word.

The most serious challenge to Shuisky was that Russian society was becoming unglued. Most discontented southern groups that had supported Pseudo Dmitri—Cossacks, peasants, garrisoned troops, and even many minor nobles—refused to recognize Shuisky as the new tsar. On the middle and lower Volga, Tatars, Mari, Mordva, and Chuvash joined with Russian groups in resisting the new regime.

Although much resistance was spontaneous and without any central direction, several new leaders did emerge, uniting at least some malcontents. The most memorable was Ivan Bolotnikov, who seemed to believe that Dmitri still lived and that he (Bolotnikov) was serving his cause. A Cossack leader (ataman), Bolotnikov appeared in the summer of 1606 in Putivl and directed a rebel attack against government troops at Kromy. By midfall, his forces were entrenched at Kolomenskoe, site of a tsarist summer residence near the outskirts of Moscow.

Only the capable military leadership of Shuisky's young nephew, Prince Skopin-Shuisky, and social dissension within Bolotnikov's ranks helped prevent the rebel from capturing Moscow. Even at the beginning, his supporters had been of mixed composition. After some noblemen, such as the private army of Riazan nobles (under Prokopi Liapunov), joined him on the way to Moscow, class differences became more accentuated.

Without doubt, Bolotnikov attracted peasants, slaves, and other malcontents wishing to liberate themselves from upper-class and government domination. Some historians have claimed that Bolotnikov led a "great peasant rebellion." Others such as Dunning have rejected this position, pointing to Bolotnikov's support from nonpeasant elements as well. To what extent Bolotnikov fanned the flames of class hatred is not clear. Some poor folk certainly used the Bolotnikov rebellion to settle old scores. One nobleman in the Tula region wrote that partly for his past "indiscretions," rebel brigands and peasants had burned down his estate, beat and tortured him, mutilated his hands, and stripped him of all his possessions. Shuisky's government claimed that Bolotnikov spewed out manifestos encouraging Moscow's poor to rise against the rich and to seize their goods and even slavemasters' wives. Such charges, possibly true, along with Shuisky enticements to rebel noble leaders, prompted some, including the Riazan nobles, to switch their allegiance to Shuisky.

The sharpening social rivalries were further underlined in early 1607 when Tsar Vasili issued several decrees intended to win him more landowner support. If obeyed—a big "if"—these decrees would have further solidified landowners' control over their peasants. Not only were peasants forbidden to leave their lords' estates, but also their lords now could recover runaway peasants of the last fifteen years (a 1597 decree had a five-year limit), and those employing runaway peasants were to be assessed fines and damages.

Forced to retreat from Moscow, Bolotnikov's army was besieged first in Kaluga and then in Tula, where it united with other rebels including those of a new pretender. He claimed to be Tsarevich Peter, son of Tsar Fedor. Of course, no such son ever existed. The new pretender seems to have been a Cossack from the Terek region (in the north Caucasus). Whoever he was, he was captured in October 1607, along with Bolotnikov and other rebels in Tula. Taken back to Moscow in January 1608, "Tsarevich Peter" was hanged for all to see. Bolotnikov, however, after being sent into exile, was killed less openly by Shuisky's men.

But Tsar Vasili's troubles were far from over. Even before Tula was taken, still another pretender, Pseudo Dmitri II, had appeared in southwestern Russia. Despite varying claims, it is unclear who this new impostor was. He was, however, neither the true Dmitri nor the one who had ruled briefly, both of whom he claimed to be. In 1608, his army advanced on Moscow. Like that of Pseudo Dmitri I, it was composed of Poles, Cossacks, and other disgruntled elements, some of whom had fought for his predecessor. Although the new pretender suffered some setbacks and was unable to take Moscow, in mid-1608 he did commandeer for his headquarters the large village of Tushino, just a few miles northwest of Moscow.

The Thief of Tushino, as some referred to the new pretender, set up a rival government and began collecting taxes. His authority was strengthened when Marina Mniszech, the wife of Pseudo Dmitri I, now "recognized" the new impostor as her miraculously still-alive husband and began living with him. Some important Muscovite nobles also went over to him, most importantly Fedor Romanov, by now Filaret, Metropolitan of Rostov. In the fall of 1608, Pseudo Dmitri II named him patriarch of Russia.

The Thief of Tushino and his rebels soon overreached themselves. When they tried to impose stiff taxes in northern Russia between the upper Volga and the Northern Dvina, northerners rebelled against them and pushed them back.

Meanwhile, Shuisky had obtained Swedish help in exchange for a border district and fortress. In 1609, his nephew, Skopin-Shuisky, brought Russian troops and Swedish-hired mercenaries from Novgorod toward Moscow. Throughout the rest of 1609 and into 1610, Skopin-Shuisky won numerous victories over supporters of Pseudo Dmitri II, who himself fled from Tushino.

Swedish help stimulated Polish involvement. Poland's King Sigismund III, son of a Polish princess and Swedish king, had for a while held two crowns until ousted in Sweden by his uncle Charles IX. In late 1609, a Polish army invaded Russia and began a siege of Smolensk.

In early 1610, some nobles who had supported Pseudo Dmitri II proposed a deal to Sigismund. In exchange for certain political guarantees, including a prominent role for boyar and church councils, the nobles agreed to recognize Sigismund's son, Wladyslaw, as tsar of Russia. The nobles, who included Patriarch Filaret, also insisted that Wladyslaw would have to convert to Orthodoxy, but Sigismund's response to this demand is unknown.

Despite Polish intervention, Skopin-Shuisky's forces were still winning battles around Moscow, and Smolensk continued to hold out against Polish troops. Then in the spring of 1610, Skopin-Shuisky, still in his mid-twenties, mysteriously died. Support for Tsar Vasili now quickly disintegrated. As Pseudo Dmitri II reappeared with loyal Cossacks near Moscow, conspirators within the city acted to unseat Shuisky. Among the conspirators were Prokopi Liapunov, the Riazan noble who has once supported Bolotnikov, and Prince Vasili Golitsyn, who had led the coup against Fedor II (Boris Godunov's son). The indefatigable Filaret Romanov, who earlier had been taken prisoner by pro-Shuisky forces, also called for Shuisky to step down. Amidst an orchestrated clamor for his abdication, he was seized in July 1610 and forced to become a monk. For the next three years, Russia remained tsarless.

THE NATIONAL STRUGGLE (1610–1613)

After the removal of Shuisky, a council of seven boyars was formed to run the government temporarily until a new tsar could be decided upon—this time with provincial participation. Meanwhile, the council had to face not only social disintegration, but also the Polish and Swedish interventions that now pushed the social struggle out of the limelight.

One of the council's first tasks was to deal with a Polish army that had reached the outskirts of Moscow. The army's commander negotiated with both the Council of Seven and Pseudo Dmitri II, to whom he suggested a coordinated attack on Moscow, but negotiations with the council bore first fruit. They centered on the idea earlier agreed to by Filaret Romanov and others that Wladyslaw of Poland would become the new tsar. Backed by a *zemskii sobor* of influential Russians then in the capital, the council struck a deal with the Polish commander. It included provisions that Wladyslaw convert to Orthodoxy and respect noble rights—for example, nobles were not to be arrested or have their estates confiscated without Boyar Council consent. In exchange for recognizing King Sigismund's son as their tsar, the Council of Seven and its supporters now counted on Polish troops to defeat Pseudo Dmitri II and help restore social order.

To complete the deal, a delegation including Filaret Romanov, Vasili Golitsyn, and monk Varlaam (formerly Tsar Vasili Shuisky) set off for a meeting with King Sigismund, who was with his troops still besieging Smolensk. Sigismund, however, proved less accommodating than his commander near Moscow had been. He wished to rule over Russia himself—and as a strong Catholic ruler. Negotiations soon broke down, and Sigismund arrested most Russian negotiators and dispatched them to Poland.

Moscow now found itself in a more desperate position than ever. Polish troops occupied the capital. Those of Pseudo Dmitri II, now headquartered in Kaluga, south of Moscow, still posed a threat. Social and political divisions were rampant. And in a political culture reliant upon a tsar, no consensus tsarist candidate appeared on the horizon. Nor did any traditional method for selecting a tsar exist. Before Godunov, heredity had taken care of the problem. The Time of Troubles reached its nadir.

Amidst the chaos of the time, and under the threat of a Polish Catholic monarch, one institution ultimately proved capable of leading a Russian revival—the Russian Orthodox Church. Its patriarch, Hermogen, now appealed to the Orthodox faithful to resist Sigismund and the Poles. The murder of Pseudo Dmitri II in December 1610 by one of his own bodyguards helped simplify matters. Early the following year, provincial Russia and many Cossack and other supporters of past pretenders mobilized around the Riazan noble, Prokopi Liapunov, who had earlier supported and then deserted first Bolotnikov and then Vasili Shuisky.

By mid-1611, Liapunov's troops threatened the Poles in Moscow, who with some Russian collaborators ruled over a resentful population. But once again, social divisiveness snatched victory from the hands of the besiegers. It led to the killing of Liapunov by Cossacks and to the disintegration of his coalition army.

Once again social strife, foreign forces, and tsarist pretenders threatened the existence of Russia. In mid-1611, Smolensk finally fell to the Poles and Novgorod to the Swedes. Cossacks under Ivan Zarutsky rallied around a new pretender, Ivan (or the Tiny Thief), the infant son of Pseudo Dmitri II and Marina Mniszech. Others supported a Pseudo Dmitri III, who by the end of 1611 was headquartered in Pskov.

Again, however, Patriarch Hermogen, now a captive of the Poles in Moscow, fueled a new national revival. He secretly encouraged the people of Nizhnii Novgorod, by now a town of some 8,000 people, to reject the Tiny Thief and revive Russia.

Nizhnii Novgorod provided the leadership for a second national army. A town butcher, Kuzma Minin, aroused the townspeople and convinced them to contribute money to help fund a new army. He also persuaded a local nobleman, Prince Dmitri Pozharsky, to head it. Pozharsky had earlier fought under Liapunov.

By early 1612, Minin and Pozharsky had won over the key city of Yaroslavl, only about 160 miles northeast of Moscow. There they set up a provisional government and announced their intention of convening a *zemskii sobor*, representing the country as a whole, to elect a new tsar. Many Volga towns had already supported the Nizhnii Novgorod leaders, and the latter's promise to call a *zemskii sobor* with real provincial representation won them further backing.

The provisional government kept Sweden on the sidelines by clever diplomacy, and it ordered troops out to meet a new Polish army sent to relieve the Polish garrison in Moscow. Before the battle, Minin and Pozharsky persuaded some Cossack forces that had earlier opposed them to come over to their side—other Cossacks under Zarutsky refused to do so and retreated southward. By this time, Pseudo Dmitri III had also been arrested. Augmented by the loyal Cossacks, the provisional government's army defeated the approaching Polish troops. In late October 1612, the Polish garrison in Moscow surrendered.

Minin, Pozharsky, and Prince Dmitri Trubetskoi (leader of the loyal Cossack forces) now moved quickly to summon *zemskii sobor* representatives from throughout Russia. The exact number that gathered in Moscow in January 1613 is unknown, but reliable estimates range from about 500 to 800 delegates. What made this *zemskii sobor* stand out from previous ones was the high percentage of provincial and elected representatives and their social diversity. Merchants and free peasants (those still fortunate enough to have no landowner over them) deliberated along with rich and poorer nobles and clergymen.

In February 1613, they selected as their new tsar Mikhail Romanov, the frail sixteen-year-old son of Filaret Romanov, himself still in Polish captivity. Earlier, Godunov had forced both of Mikhail's parents into cloistered religious life, and for a while the boy had been separated from his parents. He was now with his mother, still a nun, at a monastery a few hundred miles northeast, near Kostroma.

Mikhail was clearly a compromise candidate, chosen only after weeks of debate and maneuvering. He was probably elected for the following main reasons. (1) Unlike some foreign candidates, he was Russian and Orthodox. (2) The Romanovs were a distinguished noble family, who had close ties with the last of the Daniilovich line—Filaret was a nephew of Ivan's "good wife," Anastasia. (3) Many Cossacks supported Mikhail, partly because his father had once

FIGURE 9.2. Monument to Minin and Pozharsky, Red Square, Moscow, in front of St. Basil's Cathedral, 1818, by I. Martos.

been close to Pseudo Dmitri II and his rebel forces, which included many Cossacks. (4) Mikhail was not tainted by charges of being power-grabbing or self-serving or of collaborating with the Poles, as were some other boyars. Russians could see this young man as being, like themselves, a victim of the times. (5) Mikhail had a great advantage his father would not have had: He was young, inexperienced, possibly malleable, and less of a threat than his father might have been to other individuals or political factions.

With the election of Mikhail Romanov and his July coronation, the tumultuous Time of Troubles finally came to an end. Three centuries of Romanov rule now began.

CONCLUSION

Although some Cossack and foreign forces still confronted the new monarch, the worst was over. The accession of Mikhail Romanov in 1613 represented not only a victory of the Russian national spirit and of the Orthodox Church, but also of authority over freedom, of stability over chaos, of the people of the northern forest over those of the southern steppe, and of the upper classes over the lower.

During the Time of Troubles, boyars had attempted to restrain would-be rulers from the type of arbitrariness suffered under Ivan the Terrible—and to a lesser extent under Fedor and Boris. In 1613, a *zemskii sobor* represented the interests of a much broader spectrum of the population. Yet, despite the prominent role of boyars under the new tsar, especially early in his reign, the Time of Troubles did not weaken the foundations of Russian autocracy. Having weathered more than a decade of fierce storms, it now more than ever seemed the only alternative to chaos. The lesson many learned was perhaps similar, although much more painful and protracted, than one the Greek historian Herodotus related: In ancient Persia after a king died, five days of anarchy were allowed to demonstrate the value of kings and laws.

SUGGESTED SOURCES*

AVRICH, PAUL. *Russian Rebels, 1600–1800.* New York, 1972. Pt. I.

BARBOUR, PHILLIP L. *Dmitry, Called the Pretender: Tsar and Great Prince of All Russia, 1605–06.* Boston, 1966.

BERRY, LLOYD E., and ROBERT O. CRUMMEY, eds. *Rude and Barbarous Kingdom: Russia in the Accounts of Sixteenth-Century English Voyagers.* Madison, 1968.

BUSSOW, CONRAD. *The Disturbed State of the Russian Realm.* Montreal, 1994.

CRUMMEY, ROBERT O. *The Formation of Muscovy, 1304–1613.* London, 1987. Ch. 8.

———. " 'Constitutional' Reform during the Time of Troubles." In *Reform in Russia and the U.S.S.R.: Past and Prospects,* ed. Robert O. Crummey. Urbana, 1989.

DUNNING, CHESTER S. L. "Cossacks and the Southern Frontier in the Time of Troubles," *RH* 19, Nos. 1–4 (1992): 57–74.

———. "R. G. Skrynnikov, the Time of Troubles, and the 'First Peasant War' in Russia," *RR* 1 (January 1991): 71–81.

EMERSON, CARYL. *Boris Godunov: Transpositions of a Russian Theme.* Bloomington, 1986.

HOWE, SONIA E., ed. *The False Dmitri: A Russian Romance and Tragedy, Described by British Eye-Witnesses, 1604–1612.* London, 1916.

MASSA, ISAAC. *A Short History of the Beginnings and Origins of These Present Wars in Moscow Under the Reign of Various Sovereigns Down to the Year 1610.* Toronto, 1982.

ORCHARD, G. EDWARD. "The Election of Michael Romanov," *SEER* 67 (July 1989): 378–402.

PLATONOV, S. F. *Boris Godunov, Tsar of Russia.* Gulf Breeze, Fla., 1973.

———. *The Time of Troubles: A Historical Study of the Internal Crises and Social Struggle in Sixteenth- and Seventeenth-Century Muscovy.* Lawrence, Kansas, 1970.

PUSHKIN, ALEXANDER. *Boris Godunov.* In *The Poems, Prose, and Plays of Pushkin,* ed. Avraham Yarmolinsky. New York, 1936.

*See also works cited in footnotes and boxed insert.

SKRYNNIKOV, RUSLAN G. *Boris Godunov*. Gulf Breeze, Fla., 1982.
————. *The Time of Troubles: Russia in Crisis, 1604–1618*. Gulf Breeze, Fla., 1988.
SOLOVIEV, SERGEI M. *The Time of Troubles: Boris Godunov and False Dmitry*. Gulf Breeze, Fla., 1988.
————. *The Time of Troubles: Tsar Vasily Shuisky and the Interregnum*. Gulf Breeze, Fla., 1989.
VERNADSKY, GEORGE. *Tsardom of Muscovy, 1549–1682*. Vol. 1. New Haven, 1969.

CHAPTER 10

The First Romanovs,
1613–1689

From 1613 until 1689, when Peter the Great's reign began, tsarist authority gradually increased. At first, the young Mikhail Romanov relied heavily on institutions like the *zemskii sobor* (land council) and Boyar Council. By 1689, however, the former no longer existed, and the latter had assumed a more ceremonial function.

While tsarist authority was gradually strengthened, so too was the dominant social position of the nobles. The tsars recognized the royal need for noble support in running the country and fighting Muscovy's battles and in exchange for this support were willing to bestow favors upon the nobility. To take just one example, the Law Code of 1649 solidified the nobles' control over their peasants, who now became full-fledged serfs.

There were scattered rebellions against increasing state demands and noble privileges, and Tsar Alexei was forced into making some concessions, especially early in his reign. Yet no ideology was put forth to challenge autocracy. Even the greatest rebel of this period, Stenka Razin, claimed to be acting in the name of the tsar.

While tsarist powers and noble privileges gradually increased, Russia's territorial gains progressed more rapidly. By 1700, Russia was almost three times the size it had been in 1600. Each year of the century, it added on average a territory the size of modern-day Portugal. In the seventeenth century, Russian military force and diplomacy gained most of Ukraine east of the Dnieper as well as most of Siberia.

As always, one of the chief reasons for this expansion was the economic gain the government hoped it would bring. In imposing heavy tribute on native Siberians, for example, the seventeenth-century Muscovite government applied long-established Rus and Russian practices to new peoples.

THE REIGN OF MIKHAIL, 1613–1645

Mikhail's first priority was to restore order and end foreign occupation of territories seized during the Time of Troubles. The first of these two tasks was soon accomplished. Most importantly, in mid-1614, the government captured near Astrakhan the Cossack ataman Zarutsky, his mistress, the Polish Marina Mniszech (wife of the first two Pseudo Dmitris), and her son, the Tiny Thief. This little "family" was brought to Moscow. There the Tiny Thief was hanged; Zarutsky was impaled on a sharp stake; and Marina was sent off to imprisonment and died shortly afterwards.

Regaining lost territory was not so easy. Sweden continued to rule over some northwestern lands, including Novgorod. Only in 1617, with the "eternal peace" of Stolbovo, did the Swedish king, Gustavus Adolphus, agree to give back Novgorod. In exchange, however, he received a 20,000 ruble indemnity and the right to retain Karelia and Ingria, thus keeping Russia back from the Gulf of Finland.

Dealing with Poland was even more difficult. Up until the end of 1618, Polish forces, including Ukrainian Cossacks, attacked Russian lands. After numerous raids, they launched a major campaign under Prince Wladyslaw, who hoped to seize Mikhail's crown. By late 1618, they were besieging Moscow itself; unable to take it, however, Poland agreed at year's end to the armistice of Deulino (a village near the also besieged Trinity Monastery). The truce stipulated the return of war prisoners, especially Mikhail's father Filaret, who returned the following year after eight years in Poland. Again, however, Russia failed to regain its prewar borders. Poland kept a broad belt of western land, including Smolensk and the Ukrainian city of Chernigov, both of which had been won by Russia early in the sixteenth century.

Before Filaret's return in mid-1619, Mikhail received frequent advice from leading boyars and from the *zemskii sobor*. Early in his reign, the latter met almost constantly. Once Filaret returned, however, nonfatherly advice receded, and Filaret was proclaimed patriarch of the Russian Orthodox Church and co-Great Sovereign. In his late sixties when he returned, this tall, energetic father was much more authoritarian than his shorter, more passive son. There is little doubt that Filaret really ran the government up until his death in 1633.

Both father and son, however, relied on important boyars and helped enrich and restore to prominence some of the leading clans of earlier times. Thanks in part to tsarist land grants, the Cherkasskys, Romanovs, Sheremetevs, and Morozovs were among the wealthiest and most influential boyar families in the first half of the century.

To a lesser extent, the early Romanov rulers granted lands to other nobles, including provincial nobles, who were the backbone of the cavalry. In further steps to please the nobles, these monarchs heightened landowners' powers over their peasants and increasingly allowed nobles to treat their conditional landholdings (*pomestie*) as hereditary properties (*votchina*).

Filaret's eight years of captivity had heightened his hostility to the Poles, to their Catholicism, and to their Western culture. His main goal upon returning to Russia was to recover lands lost to Poland during the Time of Troubles. To improve the military, he raised additional revenues and attempted to coordinate Russian anti-Polish moves with those of Sweden and the Ottoman Empire.

King Sigismund III's death in 1632 seemed to present an opportune time for a joint anti-Polish campaign. Russian troops advanced on Smolensk, but unfortunately for them, the great Swedish king and military leader, Gustavus Adolphus, also died, and the new Swedish government rescinded his plans for attacking Poland. The Turks, then at war with Persia, were not much help either, although in 1633 they did order their Crimean Tatar vassals to make peace with Russia. This came, however, only after Tatar raids had reached into the Moscow district itself and diverted some Russian troops besieging Smolensk. Finally, to round off a bad year for the Russian government, Filaret died in the fall of 1633.

After suffering heavy losses, Russia agreed to the "eternal" Peace of Polianovka (1634). In it, Russia agreed to abide by the Polish territorial gains of 1618 and further to pay an indemnity of 20,000 rubles. But at least the new Polish king, Wladyslaw IV, finally abandoned his claim to Mikhail's throne.

The final decade of Mikhail's rule was a lackluster one. Perhaps most significant were the colonizing and fort-building activities sponsored by the government, both in the south and in Siberia. These efforts were later continued by his son Alexei and were important both for improving defenses against costly Tatar raids—which netted the raiders numerous captives to sell in slave markets—and in extending the Russian frontiers.

THE REIGN OF ALEXEI, 1645–1676

Although Alexei came to the throne at the same age (sixteen) his father had, he was better prepared. His body, mind, and character were more lively than those of his father, and his tutor, the boyar Boris Morozov, had encouraged his intellectual curiosity. Many Russian historians, such as Soloviev and Kliuchevsky, have emphasized Alexei's goodness. Fedotov stated that "Tsar Aleksei Mikhailovich was perhaps the only one [tsar] worthy of wearing the sacred crown. Humble, devout, almost a saint—he astounds us with the strength of his faith."[1]

Yet this same tsar admired much of the work of Ivan the Terrible and inflicted brutal punishments on some of his subjects. While encouraging his boyars to take seriously their Christian obligations toward the sick, poor, and homeless, he also told them to be severe with criminals.

The key to Alexei's personality lies in understanding the political conditions and ideas that most influenced him. He lived in a century of European turmoil. Religious differences and increasing demands of centralizing governments, often fueled by military costs, frequently sparked rebellions. In Russia, the century began with the Time of Troubles. When Alexei came to the throne, England was in rebellion against its king, Charles I, and in 1649 executed him.

---

[1] George P. Fedotov, *St. Filip, Metropolitan of Moscow—Encounter with Ivan the Terrible* (Belmont, Massachusetts, 1978), p. 167.

Tsar Alexei: Goodly, Stern, and Pious

One of the best contemporary descriptions of the mature Alexei was by his personal physician from 1660 to 1669, the Englishman Samuel Collins. The following selection is from his *The Present State of Russia: In a Letter to a Friend at London* (London, 1671), pp. 110, 116–117, 121–123. I have modernized spellings and punctuation, and bracketed material and ellipses are mine.

I shall now give you a further description of the tsar. He is a goodly person, about six feet high, well set, inclined to fat, of a clear complexion, lightish hair, somewhat a low forehead, of a stern countenance, severe in his chastisements, but very careful of his subjects' love. . . .

In the night season the tsar will go about and visit his chancellors' desks and see what decrees are passed and what petitions are unanswered. He has his spies in *every corner, and nothing is done or said at any feast, public meeting, burial, or wedding but he knows it. He has spies also attending his armies to watch their motions and give a true account of their actions. These spies are gentlemen of small fortunes who depend on the emperor's favor and are sent into armies and along with ambassadors and are present on all public occasions. Tis death for anyone to reveal what is spoken in the tsar's palace. . . .*

As to the tsar's religion, he is of the Greek [i.e., Orthodox] faith and very strict in the observation thereof. He never misses divine service. . . . On fast-days he frequents midnight prayers . . . standing four, five, or six hours together and prostrating himself to the ground sometimes a thousand times, and on great festivals, fifteen hundred . . . [and] no monk is more observant of canonical hours than he is of fasts.

Alexei was well aware of these events, and in 1648, he himself faced a serious rebellion.

According to Philip Longworth, Alexei's response to his disorderly age was to stress that "everything must be done with good order, discipline, and exact arrangement [for] . . . without good order nothing can be made secure or strengthened."[2] This belief and his conviction that God chose him to rule Russia as a good Christian *autocrat* help explain his emphasis on centralization, obedience, and conformity.

Along with the generally harsh conditions of seventeenth-century Europe, east and west, and government hopes that strong laws would deter crime, these beliefs of Alexei help explain the harshness of his laws and punishments. (See "Crimes, Punishments, and the Law" in Chapter 11.) Although his beliefs, plus his anger, could lead him to inflict severe punishments, he seems to have derived no sadistic delight from torturing or punishing criminals. The autobiography of the rebel Old Believer Avvakum, who was burned at the stake after

[2] Cited by Philip Longworth, *Alexis, Tsar of All the Russias* (London, 1984), p. 229, from Alexei's introduction to his own *The Rules of Falconry*.

Alexei's death, depicts Alexei as sad and burdened by the necessity (as the tsar saw it) of imprisoning and exiling him.

Rebellions and Dissent

From the early days of Alexei's reign to almost its end, Alexei was faced with scattered rebellions. Although they were all unique, they also had at least one thing in common: they reflected resistance to escalating government demands—whether fiscal, military, territorial, or religious. In Russia, as in much of Europe at this time, such demands often stemmed from government centralization efforts.

In the first five years of Alexei's reign, he faced numerous town rebellions. Three were especially serious, one in Moscow in 1648 and then two more in Pskov and Novgorod in 1650.

The first was due primarily to tax increases and resentment against the reputed greed and corruption of the wealthy Boris Morozov and some of his assistants—Morozov had gone from Alexei's tutor to the leader of his government. (Morozov had also become Alexei's brother-in-law by marrying the sister of Maria Miloslavskaia, who ten days earlier had married Alexei.) After petitioning obtained no relief and *streltsy* troops displayed no inclination to stop them, Moscow rioters ravaged and burned boyar homes, including Morozov's. Further, they wanted blood, and Alexei sacrificed two of Morozov's officials to their blood lust. The tsar also promised to exile Morozov, which he finally did for a short time to a White Sea monastery. Further promises and gifts helped quell the rioters.

Although one wealthy boyar, Boris Morozov, was exiled, two others now came temporarily to the political forefront, Yakov Cherkassky and Nikita Romanov, both of whom were rumored opponents of Morozov. Under their leadership, the government convened a *zemskii sobor*, as requested by dissatisfied townsmen and nobles (especially among the service gentry). Moreover, the tsar agreed to issue a new law code (the *Ulozhenie* of 1649) that addressed upper-class interests. After these pacifying measures, Morozov was able to return to the capital and regain some of his lost power.

The Pskov and Novgorod revolts of 1650 were sparked by hunger. At a time when grain was in short supply, people in Pskov discovered that thousands of bushels of grain were being exported to Sweden. That this was being done as part of an earlier agreement made little difference to famished Pskovians. After individuals in Novgorod joined the rebellion, government troops were sent there. Once again, as in the fifteenth and sixteenth centuries, that luckless city felt the wrath of Moscow. Pskov, with the support of local peasants, held out for several more months. Its rebellion ended only after Alexei, prompted by another specially called *zemskii sobor*, promised amnesty.

In 1662, Moscow suffered still another disturbance—the "Copper Riot." In the late 1650s, Alexei's government minted millions of inflated rubles in copper coins. This minting was done to meet pressing fiscal needs, greatly increased by renewed war with both Poland and Sweden. To make matters worse, large quantities of counterfeit copper coins also soon appeared. All this money drove up prices, and many people suffered. Again Muscovites petitioned their tsar. After thousands marched out to his estate at Kolomenskoe and turbulently demanded that he hand over guilty officials, he answered their demands by unleashing loyal *streltsy* upon them, killing many. After returning to Moscow, Alexei ordered more retribution, including the exiling, beating, branding, and amputating of the arms or legs of thousands more Muscovites.

In the same year as the Copper Riot, another rebellion began, and again government attempts to increase revenues helped bring it about. This time it was among the Bashkirs, who lived in an area east of Kazan spreading into western Siberia. Upset over increased tribute payments as well as with corrupt Russian local officials and with colonists moving into their lands, the Bashkirs attacked Russian settlements and churches and sold many of their captives into slavery. After two years, Russian military force, the help of pro-Russian Bashkirs and other tribesmen, and the promise of reforms and concessions helped end the rebellion.

By far the most serious rebellion of Alexei's reign was that begun in the late 1660s by the infamous Don Cossack Stenka Razin. Then in his late thirties, he was tall and his face was slightly pock-marked. He was also strong-willed, brave, energetic, restless, and prone to violence, especially after heavy drinking.

While Razin himself was from a well-established southern Don family, most of his followers were from more northern Don areas where population had swelled in recent decades. As landowners, tax collectors, and army recruiters increased their demands during the costly war against Poland (1654–1667), more peasants and other desperate Muscovites fled southward and became Cossacks. Government search parties trying, with mixed success, to round up runaway serfs only increased antigovernment hostility.

Because the Don Cossacks disdained farming and imported their grain, many newcomers to the Don regions turned from plowing to plundering. Piracy along the Don–Black Sea route and along the Volga–Caspian Sea route, however, made for a precarious existence, especially because the Ottoman Turkish and Russian governments stepped up efforts to curtail it. At the same time, the growing Don population and the needs of the armies fighting Poland drove grain prices up and supplies down. By the late 1660s, many in the northern Don regions were becoming increasingly desperate.

When Stenka Razin appeared on the scene, many in the Don region viewed him as a godsend. He formed a buccaneering band that in 1667 entered the Volga at Tsaritsyn (later Stalingrad and Volgograd) and sailed down to the Caspian. In 1669, he seized Astrakhan and in 1670 moved up the Volga, taking one town after another. He also sent out envoys and detachments to solicit support from other regions, including that of the Ukrainian Cossacks. In September, he attacked Simbirsk. His wrath was directed at nobles and government officials, but not the tsar. On the contrary, he claimed to be working for the tsar in striking out against the oppressors of the common people. He even pretended to have in his midst the tsar's oldest son, who in fact had died at the beginning of 1670. Not only did Razin have someone cloaked in red velvet impersonate the tsarevich, but also he had an impostor in black velvet impersonate the deposed Patriarch Nikon (see Chapter 12).

As Razin stormed up the Volga, he gained support from other discontented groups. Next to the Cossacks, the non-Russians were probably his most important supporters. Russian colonization and Christianization had alienated many among such peoples as the Mari, Mordva, and Chuvash. Razin also gained support from Russian peasants, townsmen, and low-ranking clergymen resentful of the upper classes. Women as well supported Razin. As Paul Avrich has pointed out, they acted not only as nurses, camp followers, and propagandists, but also in a few cases led rebel bands.

Razin's message was freedom and equality. In seized towns, he abolished taxes and established a more egalitarian Cossack-style order. In the process, the Cossacks, non-Russians, and lower classes often took their revenge on upper-class Russians. As tales of burned manor houses, looted property, severed heads, and captured noblewomen reached Moscow, both church and state condemned this brigand who threatened to tear apart the social fabric of Muscovy. More importantly, Tsar Alexei mobilized well-equipped troops to speed toward the Volga.

After besieging Simbirsk for a month, Razin was finally defeated in October 1670. The artillery, *streltsy*, and gentry cavalry of Prince Yuri Bariatinsky relieved the besieged city fortress and routed Razin's more poorly disciplined and equipped Cossacks, commoners, and tribesmen. Although wounded in battle, Razin and most of his Cossacks escaped. But Simbirsk was the turning point. In April 1671, Razin was captured on the Don by more established southern Don Cossack elders and transported to Moscow.

The government's retribution was fierce. Razin was beaten, tortured, and quartered but died courageously and defiantly. While his arms, legs, and head were placed on stakes, what remained was thrown to the dogs. Nor was Razin alone in suffering such indignities. One anonymous English source described the fate of other rebels at the hands of government forces headquartered in the town of Arzamas:

> The place was terrible to behold, and had the resemblance of the suburbs of Hell. Round about it were gallows, each of which was loaded with forty or fifty men. In another place lay many beheaded and covered with blood. Here and there stood some impaled, whereof not a few lived unto the third day, and were heard to speak. Within the space of three months, there were by the hands of executioners put to death eleven thousand men, in a legal way, upon the hearing of witnesses.

Although the government could cut up, hang, and impale the bodies of Razin's rebels, they could not kill off his spirit. Some people refused to believe he was dead, and others thought that he would someday return from the dead.

He became the most popular of Russia's folk heroes and became immortalized in many folksongs.

One final rebellion of Alexei's reign, joined by some of Razin's remaining rebels, was at the Solovetskii Monastery, located on an island in the White Sea. It was kindled by a different fuel than that which had ignited Razin's wildfire. In 1667, it became a crime to maintain the "Old Belief" that went contrary to the new updated practices of the Russian Orthodox Church. Although we will later examine the resistance and repression that the new religious policies occasioned (see Chapter 12), for now we note only that the Solovetskii rebellion (1668–1676) continued until *streltsy* troops finally brought it to an end shortly before Alexei's death.

Ukrainian Developments and War with Poland

One new territory that came under Alexei's control was most of Eastern Ukraine, formerly under Poland. Although Ivan III had gained some Ukrainian territory in 1503, since then Russia had lost more Ukrainian territory to Poland than it had gained—for example, the northeastern Ukrainian area lost in the 1618 armistice of Deulino. By the mid-seventeenth century, Russia held only a frontier area that became known as Sloboda Ukraine (see Map 10.1). In 1653 and 1654, however, Poland's inability to control eastern Ukraine handed Alexei a golden opportunity.

At the root of Poland's failure were religious differences and the Ukrainian Cossacks. Most Ukrainians were Orthodox, and they had seen their church undermined by royal and other lay appointments of their hierarchy and clergy, by conversion to Catholicism of many Ukrainian nobles, and finally by the Union of Brest (1596). The last-mentioned created a Uniate (or Greek Catholic) Church, which allowed Ukrainians to maintain their Orthodox rites and customs, such as the marriage of priests, in exchange for recognizing the supremacy of the pope. Although most of the hierarchy went over to the Uniate Church, the great majority of Ukrainian Orthodox laity and priests, especially in eastern Ukraine, condemned the action of their hierarchy.

While undermining Orthodoxy, the vigorous Catholic challenge, led increasingly by the Jesuit order, also inadvertently stimulated an Orthodox backlash and revival. By the 1620s and 1630s, this was nowhere more evident than in Kiev. A key element in the Orthodox revival was the Ukrainian Cossacks. By the early seventeenth century, they were divided into three categories: the Zaporozhian Host, registered Cossacks, and nonregistered town Cossacks. The first group was composed of about 5,000 to 6,000 men—no women or children were allowed in this brotherhood. Centered in their island fortress south of the Dnieper cataracts, these tough frontiersmen were the least susceptible to Polish control. The second group consisted of only about 3,000 Cossacks. In exchange for being a border militia for the Polish government and restraining the nonregistered Cossacks, they were officially registered as a separate class and granted rights of self-rule. Many of these men were well-to-do and had families. The third group, the nonregistered Cossacks, were by far the poorest and

European Russia, 1617–1689

Russian losses to Sweden recognized by Peace of Stolbovo, 1617

Russian losses to Poland recognized by Armistice of Deulino, 1618

Belgorod Defense Line, completed 1654

Territory ceded to Russia by Poland in Armistice of Andrusovo, 1667

Area declared under joint Russian/Polish control by Armistice of Andrusovo, 1667

0   150   300 Miles

SWEDISH EMPIRE

White Sea

Archangel

N. Dvina R.

Karelia

L. Ladoga

Sol Vychegda

Kama R.

Ivangorod
Narva
INGRIA
Reval
ESTONIA

Novgorod

Volga R.

Mari

LIVONIA

Pskov

Chuvash Tatars

Riga

W. Dvina R.

Smolensk

Andrusovo

Moscow

LITHUANIA
Polotsk

Viazma

Mordva

Vilna

Vitebsk

PRUSSIA

Minsk

BELO-
RUSSIA
Gomel

Briansk

Tambov

Volga R.

POLISH-
LITHUANIAN

Orel

Voronezh

COMMONWEALTH

Chernigov

Kursk

Warsaw
Brest-
Litovsk
Lublin
POLAND

WESTERN
UKRAINE

*Sloboda
Ukraine*

Belgorod

Lvov

Kiev
Zhitomir

Kharkov

Carpathians

Pereiaslavl
Korsun
Bar

Poltava

Donets R.

Don R.

*Dnieper
Cataracts*

Dnieper R.

**Zaporozhian Cossack
Headquarters**

KHANATE
OF
CRIMEAN TATARS

MAP 10.1

largest—some 40,000 to 50,000 by about 1600.[3] Most of them lived in the many frontier towns—often hardly more than wooden fortresses—that had sprung up in recent decades in eastern Ukraine.

The Polish government used Cossacks from all three groups to help protect its borders from Tatar raids, and it sporadically recruited Cossacks in its wars against foreign foes. Cossacks also took it upon themselves to raid Crimean Tatar and even Ottoman Turkish lands. This was especially true of the Zaporozhian Host. Such raids complicated Polish relations with the Tatars and powerful Turks. Polish-Ukrainian tensions were further fueled by Cossacks' resentment of Polish and Polonized Ukrainian nobles' attempts to dominate them and the territories and politics of eastern Ukraine.

In 1620, the hetman of the Zaporozhian Host took two steps that further united and strengthened the two main anti-Polish Ukrainian forces—Orthodoxy and the Cossacks. First, he enlisted the Zaporozhian Host into the Kiev Brotherhood, which was an Orthodox benevolent and enlightenment organization. Second, he helped bring the Orthodox patriarch of Jerusalem to Kiev to consecrate a new metropolitan and bishops, thus further reinvigorating the Ukrainian Orthodox Church.

In 1625, the Kievan metropolitan petitioned Tsar Mikhail of Russia to become overlord of Ukraine. Although the Russian government did not then wish to war with Poland over the matter, it foreshadowed things to come.

From 1620 to 1648, the Ukrainian Orthodox and Cossacks became steadily more difficult for the Polish Commonwealth to control. The 1620s and 1630s were especially marked by Cossack-led revolts and fierce struggles between Uniates and Orthodox over church properties.

After a decade of "peace," the great Ukrainian revolt of 1648 erupted. It was led by the Cossack hetman Bogdan (Bohdan) Khmelnitsky. At about age fifty, he had became involved in a bitter dispute with a Polish nobleman who claimed his estate and killed one of his sons. After fleeing to Zaporozhian headquarters in 1648, he was elected hetman and began his revolt. Before the end of 1648, Khmelnitsky, his supporters, and allied Crimean Tatars had swept over Ukraine like a tornado. Ukrainian peasants and townspeople joined the revolt and attacked Polish noblemen, Catholics, and Jews.

Although gaining major concessions from the new Polish king, John Casimir, in 1649, Khmelnitsky was unable to maintain all his gains after his forces were defeated by a Polish offensive in 1651. After Khmelnitsky attempted to obtain Turkish support by promising to recognize the sultan as overlord in 1651, Russia's Tsar Alexei became more attentive to Khmelnitsky's similar proposition to him. As a result, after consulting in 1653 with the Russian Orthodox patriarch and a *zemskii sobor*, Alexei agreed in 1654 to become overlord of Khmelnitsky's Ukraine.

The crucial agreements reached at Pereiaslavl and in subsequent negotiations later that year have been greatly debated by historians. What does seem

---

[3] All Cossack estimates are from Orest Subtelny, *Ukraine: A History*. 2d ed. (Toronto, 1994), pp. 110–111.

almost certain is the following: (1) Khmelnitsky, his Cossacks, and other Ukrainians in more than 100 towns pledged their loyalty to Alexei and his successors. (2) In exchange for modest revenue from Ukrainian lands, Alexei agreed to provide some financial assistance to Cossack forces and overall military protection. (3) Alexei promised to respect traditional Ukrainian rights, including Zaporozhian rights to their own courts and to elect their own hetman. (4) Alexei recognized the hetman's right, with certain limitations, to receive foreign envoys.

As was expected, the agreements led to a Russian-Polish war, which lasted intermittently from 1654 to 1667. At first, the war went well for Russia. Alexei himself led Russian troops and was joined by Ukrainian Cossacks. Smolensk fell to him in 1654. By mid-1655, most of Belorussia was under his control and part of Lithuania. Then Swedish competition with Russia over Poland-Lithuania and Russian desires to gain a foothold on the Baltic led to a Russo-Swedish war (1656–1661). This conflict and further Ukrainian developments after the death of Khmelnitsky in 1657 helped deflate Russia's Polish gains.

In 1667, after thirteen years of war, plagues, and flight had taken a great toll on Muscovy's population, the Russians and Poles signed an armistice at Andrusovo, south of Smolensk. By it Russia received Left-Bank (east of the Dnieper) Ukrainian lands, plus Kiev for two years, which Russia subsequently refused to relinquish. The Zaporozhian Host was to be under joint Rus-

FIGURE 10.1. Monument to the Reunification of Ukraine with Russia, Kiev. This monument, opened in 1982 by Soviet authorities, glorified the seventeenth-century "reunification."

sian/Polish control. Smolensk was to remain in Russian hands during the course of the armistice, which was set for thirteen years.

Basically the agreement meant that Russia gave up, at least temporarily, most of its claims to Belorussia and the Ukrainian territories west of the Dnieper, but solidified its control over Left-Bank Ukraine. Its Ukrainian gains since 1654 were added to the Sloboda Ukraine region already previously under Russian control. To strengthen frontier defenses, Mikhail and then Alexei encouraged Ukrainian colonizers to enter this latter area and eventually granted them special privileges. Despite subsequent Tatar raids, the Ukrainians and Russians in the area were gradually able to build new defensive lines, extending like an arrowhead south of Kharkov (founded 1656).

Meanwhile, both Khmelnitsky and Tsar Alexei grew increasingly distrustful of each other. Then, after Khmelnitsky's death in 1657, Ukraine underwent a time of troubles of its own. Internal social and political divisions were compounded as different factions sought assistance from different powers, and Polish, Russian, and Moslem Tatar and Turkish troops became involved in Ukrainian struggles. By Alexei's death in 1676, the turmoil in Ukraine had not yet subsided, but his tsarist successors maintained his gains. The political, economic, and cultural effects of this addition to Muscovy proved to be of utmost importance, both for Russians and Ukrainians.

FEDOR III AND SOPHIA, 1676–1689

When Alexei died in 1676 at age forty-six, he left behind a troubling legacy of two marriages and two clans, the Miloslavskys and the Naryshkins. As usually happened following the marriage of one of their clan to the tsar, relatives of each wife had become prominent in the Boyar Council and among the court aristocracy. Alexei's first marriage to the pious Maria Miloslavskaia, who died in 1669, had produced thirteen children, five of them sons. By 1676, only two of these sons, both sickly, were still alive. The oldest was Fedor, who at fourteen became Fedor III.

This third, and last, Tsar Fedor was no more memorable than the first two. Like Fedor I, son of Ivan the Terrible, he was not only frail, but also pious; like Fedor II, the unfortunate sixteen-year-old son of Godunov, he was fond of books and learning. The everyday running of government was left in other hands.

At first his mother's clan, the Miloslavskys, worked with others, like the Khitrovos, who had first come to prominence as a result of Boris Morozov's patronage. Together, this new political grouping ousted the clan of Alexei's second wife, the Naryshkins. Alexei had married the young, vivacious Natalia Naryshkina in 1671, and she bore him three children, the most important of whom was the future Peter the Great, born in 1672. Bitter at the ascendance of the Naryshkins after Alexei's second marriage and especially after the birth of the healthy Peter, the Miloslavsky-Khitrovo coalition wasted no time in convincing Fedor III to exile to the Arctic region the most gifted politician of the Naryshkin clan—Natalia's former guardian, Artamon Matveev—on charges of witchcraft.

But the Miloslavsky-Khitrovo coalition soon came unglued, and by the end of the 1670s, several other enterprising politicians had become more influential. One of them was Prince Vasili Golitsyn, a talented man from a prestigious clan of long-standing. His most important contribution was persuading Fedor to abolish the cumbersome *mestnichestvo* system of precedence (see Chapter 8).

When in the spring of 1682, Fedor's frail life ended, just short of twenty-one, the battle between the Miloslavskys and Naryshkins once again erupted. The Milosvlasky tsarist candidate was Fedor's younger brother, Ivan, the only remaining son of Alexei and Maria Miloslavskaia. He was sixteen, half-blind, and retarded, an unfortunate contrast to the robust Naryshkin candidate, his half-brother, the ten-year-old Peter. At first, the victory seemed to go to the Naryshkins and Peter. The patriarch and a hastily convened assembly—although not a full-fledged *zemskii sobor*—approved of him as the new ruler, with Natalia as his regent. A few weeks later, however, a *streltsy* rebellion reversed the fortunes of the Naryshkins and of the Miloslavskys.

The exact causes of the revolt are difficult to determine. *Streltsy* dissatisfaction with some of their officers and with government officials who refused to act on their complaints was certainly one cause. After Fedor's death, the *streltsy* no doubt realized that the rivalry between the Naryshkins and Miloslavskys provided them an opportunity to redress their grievances. Rumors and *streltsy* fears also played a part. The word spread among the more than 20,000 *streltsy* stationed in Moscow that the Naryshkins had murdered Fedor and Ivan and that Natalia and Artamon Matveev, already on his way back from exile, would favor Western merchants and even Western religious heresies. Because many *streltsy* were engaged in trade when not fighting and because many were also Old Believers, they especially resented any Western competition, whether to their profits or their faith.

Exactly what role the Miloslavskys, especially Ivan's energetic twenty-four-year-old sister, Sophia, played in spreading these rumors remains unclear. They certainly had motive enough. Some accounts also accuse them of dispensing bribes and vodka to the *streltsy*.

Inflamed by rumors, and perhaps by vodka, the *streltsy* marched on the Kremlin and began demanding that Matveev, some of the Naryshkins, and a few other "traitors" be turned over to them. When one of the "traitors," Prince Mikhail Dolgoruky, threatened to beat them, they rushed the staircase where he stood and pitched him down onto the upturned pikes of their comrades below. A similar fate soon befell Matveev and others. Natalia and her son Peter, however, were spared.

Within two weeks, the *streltsy* pressured the Boyar Council, and another quickly convened assembly—again not a real *zemskii sobor*—to name Ivan senior and co-tsar. Peter was designated the other co-tsar and Sophia their regent. Symbolizing the new arrangement was a dual throne especially adapted for the young co-tsars, complete with a curtain and a hiding place behind, from which Sophia or a surrogate could whisper instructions to the boys.

Although many unsubstantiated charges have surrounded Sophia's historical portrait, what we do know is that she was intelligent, forceful, and a most capable politician. She certainly was better educated than most of Moscow's noblewomen, who were still raised and lived out their lives in the *terem*. One of her teachers was the monk, poet, and enlightener Simeon Polotsky (see Chapter 12).

For the next seven years (1682–1689), Sophia remained in power, until finally unseated by her younger half-brother Peter. Despite benefiting from *streltsy* fears of the Naryshkin clan's westernizing sympathies, her internal policies, like those of Fedor III, generally continued the moderate modernizing ones of the earlier Romanovs. Western contacts and influences continued to grow. And her chief adviser, the brilliant and cosmopolitan Vasili Golitsyn, was even more enamored with Western learning than Artamon Matveev had been. Already shortly after coming to power, Sophia made it clear, to the dismay of many *streltsy*, that she had no sympathy for Old Believers. In September 1682, she had the *streltsy* commander and Old Believer, Prince Ivan Khovansky, executed—he was later immortalized in Modest Musorgsky's opera *Khovanshchina*.

Sophia's foreign policy also was in line with that of her father Alexei and her brother Fedor. After more than 100,000 Turks and Tatars had attacked the Russians in Ukraine in 1677, Fedor's armies had retaliated vigorously, in the first major Russo-Turkish war. Following the peace of 1681, which recognized most of Russia's Ukrainian gains, the Turks turned their full force on Austria and Poland in 1682 and besieged Vienna itself in the summer of 1683. In 1686, the Poles appealed to the Russians for help, and in a Russo-Polish "eternal peace," signed that same year, Russia agreed to send an army southward against the Crimean Tatars. In exchange, Poland recognized as permanent the 1667 armistice's territorial terms and the loss of Kiev and Smolensk to Russia.

Thus, in 1687, Vasili Golitsyn led Russian troops to battle the Tatars. Unsuccessful, he tried again in 1689, only again to fail. Although the two campaigns led to tens of thousands of Russian deaths, in the summer of 1689, Sophia proclaimed the returning Golitsyn a victorious hero. Combined with Sophia's increasing pretensions—she had begun calling herself autocrat (*samoderzhitsa*)—and her half-brother Peter's continuing growth and discontent, Golitsyn's failed campaigns helped bring about her fall in the late summer of 1689.

GOVERNMENT AND ADMINISTRATION, 1613–1689

For almost a decade after Mikhail became tsar in 1613, the *zemskii sobor* met frequently, primarily because the government needed help in raising money, especially for military purposes. Delegates (mainly nobles and merchants) probably sometimes voiced their own concerns too. Preventing peasant flight and curtailing foreign business competition were two such matters.

In the decade before 1632, no *zemskii sobor* assemblies are recorded, but then war with Poland (1632–1634) led to sessions in both 1632 and 1634. The possibility of a war against the Turks in 1642 led to still one more important gathering. Most, if not all, the assemblies' delegates from 1632 to 1642 were appointed by the government and initiated no legislation or actions. Mikhail's government, however, did follow their advice in 1634 to seek peace with Poland and in 1642 not to risk war with the Ottoman Empire—after the Don Cossacks offered Tsar Mikhail the fortress of Azov, seized in 1637.

The *zemskii sobor* of 1648–1649, called by Alexei as a partial response to the Moscow riot of 1648, was the most significant since 1613. It featured almost 350 delegates, chosen from more than 100 towns, some in contested elections. They met in two chambers, the upper consisting of representatives of the Orthodox hierarchy and Moscow's elite service class, and the lower and much larger chamber dominated by provincial townsmen and service gentry. The *sobor* considered numerous petitions from disgruntled groups, both in the towns and in the countryside. It also helped mold a new law code (the *Ulozhenie* of 1649). The code's stipulations finalizing serfdom and granting greater trading prerogatives to urban merchants and craftsmen were indicative of the assembly's influence.

Alexei, however, preferred to rule without being pressured by *zemskii sobor* delegates. After a 1653 assembly, called to consider the annexation of Ukraine, no *zemskii sobor* worthy of the name was ever again convened.

A more durable and powerful body than the *zemskii sobor* was the Boyar Council. By the reign of Mikhail, it included not only boyars, but also holders of three lesser ranks including that of state secretary. For most of the seventeenth century, it was the highest advisory body to the tsar, helping him direct his ever-increasing *prikazy* (bureaus) and sometimes acting as a court of appeal. Not all of its members, however, resided in Moscow; for example, some governors of important regions were council members.

Although senior members of long-standing boyar clans frequently sat on this council and helped direct government affairs, they often became members of it only after extensive military or other state service. As the century progressed, however, it became increasingly possible for those without distinguished aristocratic backgrounds to receive council appointments.

The best opportunity for previously undistinguished provincial nobles to rise quickly in Moscow social and political circles was to be part of the clan of a new wife of the tsar—most of the early Romanov brides came from the provincial nobility. Other powerful connections also helped: Patronage was an important part of Muscovite political life, and having an influential dignitary as a patron was probably more important than possessing talent. But such paths of advancement were nothing new. What was new in the late seventeenth century was the increasing number of individuals from nonboyar families who were appointed to the council because of their expertise. Two examples were the statesmen Afanasi Ordyn-Nashchokin and Artamon Matveev, who respectively directed Muscovy's Foreign Office and acted as chief minister during the final decade of Alexei's reign. Although Matveev benefited from the marriage of his ward, Natalia Naryshkina, to Tsar Alexei in 1671, even before then he had a record of extended military and diplomatic service and was already a friend of Alexei and a member of the Boyar Council.

From 1613 to the beginning of 1676, the number of Boyar Council members increased from 29 to 66. Then in the unstable thirteen years that followed Alexei's death, the number shot up to 145. The sharp increase reflected government attempts to deepen and broaden its support by honoring old and new families with council positions. Many of the council members appointed in the late 1670s and 1680s, including some from clans such as the Cherkasskys and Sheremetevs, differed from earlier appointments in being younger and having much less service experience.

Partly as a result of its growth, the Boyar Council grew less influential as the century proceeded. As it became larger, the tsars began depending more on smaller groups of advisers within it, and the functions of the council itself became more ceremonial.

Just as Boyar Council numbers increased, so too did central government officials in the *prikazy*—although these officials still numbered only a few thousand by 1689. The *prikazy* themselves went from twenty-two in early 1613 to about forty by 1682. In the seventeenth century, they were generally headed by a member of the Boyar Council, who supervised a bureau's other officials and clerks. The *prikazy* were created as the need arose, sometimes for only a temporary period. Many dealt with military matters—*streltsy*, Cossacks, armaments—or with collecting revenue, more than half of which was spent for military needs. Other *prikazy* oversaw areas such as justice, slaves, service lands, foreign relations, or administering territories—for example, the Siberian Prikaz. Among the most colorful named *prikazy* were the Prikaz of Big Revenue and the Prikaz of Secret Affairs. Not quite as intriguing as it sounds, the latter was created by Tsar Alexei to deal with private concerns, such as his estates and falcons. Eventually, however, it expanded to become his own private political bureau, which he sometimes used to bypass the Boyar Council.

By the early seventeenth century, local government was overseen by Moscow-appointed *voevody* (military governors), who ruled over about 150 districts or regions of various size. Most often these men were seasoned military officers, and their chief function was to collect revenues for Moscow and suppress serious disorders. For these basic functions, a governor depended on a small military garrison and small administrative staff. Without the cooperation of serfowners, the real day-to-day local government for most Russians, even these basic tasks would have been impossible.

Governors arrived in their provincial capitals with no ties to the areas they ruled and seldom remained more than a year or two. Although Moscow's central government sent them directives, it was much harder to insure their compliance. The governors' reputation for enriching themselves was notorious—the taking of bribes seems to have been more the rule than the exception among government officials, partly because of low government salaries. It is hardly surprising that delegates to the 1642 *zemskii sobor* complained that the governors were stripping them bare.

ABSOLUTISM AND AUTOCRACY

By 1689, despite the broadening of parliamentary rights in England, Europe in general had entered an age of absolutism, personified best by the French "Sun King," Louis XIV. This absolutism was characterized by the weakening or abolition of nonmonarchical elements of government and the growth and strengthening of the central government's powers over financial, legal, political, and cultural aspects of life.

Although Russia's government by 1689 still was relatively small and dependent upon noble landowners to control most of the country's people, it also had become more absolutistic. The fading away of the *zemskii sobor*, the decline of the Boyar Council's importance, and the abolition of *mestnichestvo* were accompanied by the growth of all of the following: bureaucracy, government economic activities and taxes (state revenues approximately tripled during the century), military strength, and power over the Orthodox Church. The Law Code of 1649 and other legal developments helped tighten state as well as landowner control over the population.

If in some ways an evolving Russian absolutism was part of the general European pattern, in other ways it was unique, partly because of its autocratic foundation. The three estates of Europe—clergy, nobles, and townsmen—were much stronger in the West, even in the Age of Absolutism, than in Russia. Partly because of the lack of any substantial Roman legal influence, there was less emphasis on individual or collective rights than in the West. This is one reason why the *zemskii sobor* never developed into a permanent parliamentary body.

Moreover, the Law Code of 1649 went much further than Western legislation in restricting its people. Not only did it permanently enserf landowners' peasants, but also it prohibited most townspeople from leaving their towns (see Chapter 11). Even nobles could not leave the country without government permission. Antigovernment crimes, including economic offenses such as cheating on taxes, had to be reported to authorities. Failure to report a conspiracy against the tsar was punishable by death, even for wives and children of such "traitors."

So ingrained was Russian autocracy that it was not challenged even when weak rulers like Fedor III were on the throne. In 1649, the nobility obtained their primary wish, the enserfment of the peasants. Thereafter, they cooperated in perpetuating and even strengthening the autocratic system. Although some nobles hoped to share in the real exercise of governmental powers, they placed no legal checks on those of the tsar, and only a strong monarch like Peter the Great was needed to expand tsarist authority even further.

CONQUEST OF SIBERIA

Even more dramatic than the growth of tsarist government was that of Russia itself. Although some expansion occurred in the west and southwest, far more occurred in Siberia.

By the mid-seventeenth century, the Russians had reached the Pacific Ocean and had subjugated most of Siberia in less than three quarters of a century. Their feat compares with the Western European overseas explorations and conquests that marked the years 1400 through 1650 and with the later American expansion across the American continent to the Pacific.

In moving Russia's boundary eastward over 3,000 miles, the Russians were aided by an excellent river network (see Map 10.2). Although rivers like the Ob, Enisei, Lena, and Kolyma flowed northward into the Arctic Ocean, they also possessed excellent east-west tributaries. Although frozen half the year, the great rivers and their tributaries even then provided smooth icy road-ways for fast sleigh travel. The eastward movement was also facilitated by the relative flatness of western and central Siberia. Primitive conditions, cold temperatures, and thick forests, however, presented hard challenges.

When the Russians began their advance, there were only some 200,000 natives spread across vast Siberia. These peoples spoke more than a hundred languages or dialects. Except for the Yakuts and the peoples of the southern Siberian steppes, both of whom seasonally migrated with their cattle and horses, most other native Siberians based their economy on the reindeer. It provided not only food, but also skins for clothes and shelter. Some peoples hunted wild reindeer, whereas others relied on domesticated herds. With bows and arrows and spears, native peoples also hunted other game; and they fished and gathered berries, nuts, and roots. Although most were nomadic or seminomadic and private landowning did not exist, differing peoples usually respected each other's traditional hunting, fishing, and grazing grounds.

Most natives except in the far northeast were organized into clans, which recognized a common ancestor. Men generally married outside their clan. The most prevalent native religion was shamanism—the shaman being a combination priest, medicine man, and soothsayer. He was thought capable of communicating with nature's many spirits, including that of the brown bear, venerated by many clans. Like most native Americans, the native Siberians had a great respect for nature and its spirits and generally lived in harmony with it.

Attracted primarily by furs ("soft gold"), Russian entrepreneurs and government forces quickly subjugated native peoples. According to Basil Dmytryshyn, the yearly *yasak* (tribute) quota per adult male native in the early seventeenth century was twenty-two sables and at midcentury, because of sable depletion, five. If sables were not available, the government demanded other forms of tribute, usually other furs. The furs thus collected, plus tithes from Russian hunters and merchants in Siberia, became a major source of tsarist revenue.[4]

---

[4] For much of this section, I am indebted to essays by Dmytryshyn, James Forsyth, and others contained in Alan Wood, ed., *The History of Siberia: From Russian Conquest to Revolution* (London, 1991).

Russia's Expansion in the Seventeenth and Eighteenth Centuries

Seventeenth century acquisitions

Eighteenth century acquisitions

Mid-eighteenth-century defense line (including Orenburg line)

Bashkirs Native peoples

0   300   600 Miles

MAP 10.2

ARCTIC OCEAN

Bering Strait
Bering Sea
Chukchi Sea
East Siberian Sea
Laptev Sea
Kara Sea
Barents Sea
White Sea
Baltic Sea
Black Sea
Caspian Sea
Sea of Okhotsk
Sea of Japan

ALASKA → (gained by Russia in 18th century)
(Not fully subjugated until 19th century)

Kamchatka (gained by Russia in 18th century)
Sakhalin Island (occupied by Russia in 19th century)
Kurile Islands

JAPAN
CHINA
MONGOLIA

Chukchi
Koriak
Itelmens
Tungus
Yukagirs
Yakuts
Buriats
Daurians
Samoeds
Ostiaks
Voguls
Tatars
Bashkirs
Cossacks
Kalmyks
Kazakhs

Stanovoi Mts.
Ural Mts.
Altai Mts.
Lake Baikal

Kolyma R.
Lena R.
Lower Tunguska R.
Upper Tunguska R.
Enisei R.
Ob R.
Irtysh R.
Volga R.
Don R.
Ural R.
Amur R.

Anadyr (1649)
Okhotsk (1647)
Yakutsk (1632)
Nerchinsk (1654)
Irkutsk (1652)
Kiakhta (1720)
Krasnoiarsk (1628)
Tomsk (1604)
Semipalatinsk (1718)
Omsk (1716)
Petropavlovsk (1752)
Tobolsk (1587)
Sibir (1581)
KHANATE OF SIBIR
Orenburg (1743)
Ufa (1586)
Kazan
Samara
Simbirsk
Moscow
Tula
Novgorod
St. Petersburg
Archangel
Tsaryitsyn
Astrakhan
Volga
OTTOMAN EMPIRE

183

FIGURE 10.2. The Tungus from Siberia did not bury their dead in the ground. They sometimes laid them on boards resting in tree trunks, as in the upper left of this picture.
(From Ian Grey, The Horizon History of Russia, *American Heritage Publishing Company, New York, 1970, p. 43.)*

Besides the entrepreneurs and government officials and forces, including Cossacks and *streltsy* troops, a host of other groups also poured into Siberia in the century following Ermak's first incursion. They included state peasants and runaway serfs (Siberia itself remained virtually free from serfdom), clergy, and exiles, such as prisoners-of-war and religious and political dissenters.

Government officials and troops generally resided in strategically placed wooden fortresses that sometimes blossomed into frontier cities. These new outposts advanced along the great river system of Siberia and included Tobolsk (1587), Tomsk (1604), Yakutsk (1632), Okhotsk (1647), and Irkutsk (1652). By 1662, there were some 70,000 Russian men in Siberia.

Because most Russians who went to Siberia were men, there was a shortage of Russian women, especially in the more remote eastern Siberia. This helped lead to a slave trade in native Siberian women and to many children being born of mixed parentage. Native men captured in battle and children also sometimes were enslaved.

Russians treated native Siberians much like other conquerors the world over treated other natives. Superior weapons and state power helped eventually subdue any Siberian natives who dared resist the tribute payment. As in Spanish America, more natives died from diseases contracted from their conquerors than from death in battle. Epidemics like smallpox and measles some-times wiped out more than half a people's population. Although the Russian Orthodox Church wished to convert natives to Christianity, government au-thorities were not so eager because conversion ended the obligation to pay *yasak.*

Yet even if not converted, native Siberians witnessed the undermining of their cultures. In exchange, they obtained the advantages and disadvantages of gradually being absorbed into a more "advanced" civilization.

As with the white conquest of Native Americans, the Russians succeeded in subjugating most Siberians because of scant competition from outside pow-ers. Only China prevented Russia from gobbling up all of Siberia. By the Treaty of Nerchinsk in 1689, Russia agreed to recognize China's claims to the Amur river area and northward up to the Stanovoi Mountains. Only in the mid-nine-teenth century was Russia able to gain the northern Amur region.

*SUGGESTED SOURCES**

AVRICH, PAUL. *Russian Rebels, 1600–1800.* New York, 1972. Pt. II.

BARON, SAMUEL H., ed. *The Travels of Olearius in Seventeenth-Century Russia.* Stanford, 1967.

BROWN, PETER B. "Muscovite Government Bureaus," *RH* 10, Pt. 3 (1983): 269–330.

CRUMMEY, ROBERT O. *Aristocrats and Servitors: The Boyar Elite in Russia, 1613–1689.* Princeton, 1983.

DAVIES, BRIAN. "Village into Garrison: The Militarized Peasant Communities of South-ern Muscovy," *RR* 51 (October 1992): 481–501.

DMYTRYSHYN, BASIL, E. A. P. CROWNHART-VAUGHAN, and THOMAS VAUGHAN, eds. *Russia's Conquest of Siberia, 1558–1700: A Documentary Record.* Portland, Or., 1985.

DONNELLY, ALTON S. *The Russian Conquest of Bashkiria, 1522–1740: A Case Study of Imperi-alism.* New Haven, 1968.

———. "Voevoda," *MERSH* 42: 210–212.

DUKES, PAUL. *The Making of Russian Absolutism, 1613–1801.* 2d ed. London, 1990. Chs. 1–2.

FUHRMANN, JOSEPH T. *Tsar Alexis: His Reign and His Russia.* Gulf Breeze, Fla., 1981.

GRAHAM, HUGH F. "Prikaz," *MERSH* 29: 211–217.

HELLIE, RICHARD. *Enserfment and Military Change in Muscovy.* Chicago, 1971.

———. "Muscovy," *MERSH* 23: 214–228.

———. "Zemskii Sobor," *MERSH* 45: 226–234.

HUGHES, LINDSEY. *Sophia, Regent of Russia, 1657–1704.* New Haven, 1990.

KIVELSON, VALERIE A. "The Devil Stole His Mind: The Tsar and the 1648 Moscow Upris-ing," *AHR* 98 (June 1993): 733–756.

KLIUCHEVSKY, V. O. *A Course in Russian History: The Seventeenth Century.* Armonk, N.Y., 1994.

LINCOLN, W. BRUCE. *The Romanovs: Autocrats of All the Russias.* New York, 1981. Pt. 1.

O'BRIEN, C. BICKFORD. *Muscovy and the Ukraine: From the Pereiaslavl Agreement to the Truce of Andrusovo, 1654–1667.* Berkeley, 1963.

*See also works cited in footnotes and in boxed insert.

PORSHNEV, B. F. *Muscovy and Sweden in the Thirty Years' War, 1630–1635*. Cambridge, England, 1995.

RH 19, Nos. 1–4 (1992). Contains several articles dealing with seventeenth-century frontiers.

RYWKIN, MICHAEL, ed. *Russian Colonial Expansion to 1917*. London, 1988.

SHAW, D. J. B. "Southern Frontiers of Muscovy, 1550–1700." In *Studies in Russian Historical Geography*, eds. James H. Bater, and R. A. French. Vol. 1. London, 1983.

SOLOVIEV, SERGEI M. *The First Romanov: Tsar Michael, 1613–1634*. Gulf Breeze, Fla., 1991.

———. *Rebellion and Reform: Fedor and Sophia, 1682–89*. Gulf Breeze, Fla., 1989.

SOROKIN, IU. A. "Aleksei Mikhailovich," *RSH* 32 (Winter 1993–94): 5–29.

STEVENS, CAROL BELKIN. *Soldiers on the Steppe: Army Reform and Social Change in Early Modern Russia*. DeKalb, Ill. 1995.

VERNADSKY, GEORGE. *Tsardom of Muscovy, 1549–1682*. 2 vols. New Haven, 1969.

CHAPTER 11

Economic and Social Life, 1533–1689

Many of the chief economic and social developments of the late Muscovite period sprung from government's escalating economic and military needs, two needs that were tightly interwoven. The most important social change of the era, the finalizing of serfdom, was instituted primarily to assist the provincial nobles, who were the backbone of the cavalry. And townsmen as well as serfs had their freedom of movement restricted so as to provide a more reliable tax base. New towns sprung up that were initially little more than military fortresses and administrative centers for tax-collecting. Industrial growth, especially that of the iron industry, was stimulated by military as well as economic needs. One reason for the decline of slavery after 1649 was increasing government restrictions on people selling themselves into slavery, for slaves paid no direct taxes. Another reason for its decline was the changing nature of Russian military requirements—by the late seventeenth century, the military required less use of elite slaves.

Even drinking habits and family living patterns were affected by governmental desires. Largely because of the valuable revenues it gained, the government encouraged the sale and consumption of vodka, both of which soon became widespread. In the late 1670s, the government's effort to increase revenues led it to introduce a new household tax. Peasants, however, then attempted to reduce their payments by combining households into larger extended families.

If in some ways government economic and military requirements contributed to social rigidity, in other ways they stimulated more modern social changes. During the late seventeenth century, the government began a serious effort to modernize its military. This modernization effort led to increased Western contacts that affected Russian society in a variety of ways, especially after Peter the Great came to the throne at the end of the seventeenth century.

Of course, other forces besides government needs helped shape the economic and social developments of the era. Russia's low population density, plagues, and famines, and the fleeing of its peasants southward and eastward helped create the scarcity of labor that led to demands for enserfing the peasants. Urban rebellions, especially the one in Moscow in 1648, helped bring about the 1649 Law Code, which not only finalized serfdom, but also introduced other important changes. Russian merchant hostility to foreign traders led to some restrictions on them. Stenka Razin's revolt not only heightened nobles' fears, but also increased their cohesion. The concerns of nobles and other upper-class elements for financial gain, status, and honor are revealed in law codes and in the treatment of women. Finally, at the base of the whole social structure and supporting it with their labor and taxes, and even their drinking, lay the overwhelming majority of the Russian people, the peasants. As the Razin rebellion clearly indicated, they had their own desires and goals, which often differed from those of the government.

ECONOMIC OVERVIEW, POPULATION, URBAN LIFE, MANUFACTURING, AND TRADE

Although the Russian economy suffered severely under Ivan the Terrible, by 1600 it was recovering. Then the 1601–1604 famine and a decade of chaos plunged the economy downward. Following the Time of Troubles, seventeenth-century production (both agricultural and nonagricultural), trade, and government revenues gradually increased. At the same time, however, most peasants were gradually being enserfed. The government's economic demands on the people, primarily to feed military needs, continued growing. So too did Muscovite territory. Yet, whereas it increased fivefold to sixfold between 1533 and 1689, Muscovy's population only doubled to about 12 to 15 million people. About thirty times the size of France, it had fewer inhabitants. Despite some migrations to expanding frontier areas, the central regions surrounding and including Moscow remained by far the most densely populated in the country.

Urban Life

Not only was Russia's population density low, so too was its urban population. It composed a smaller percentage of the total population than in Western Europe, Japan, or even Colonial America. Only Moscow was a large city by world standards. By 1689, it contained about 150,000 to 200,000 people. Although this made it an immense city compared with any in Colonial America, it was only about half the size or less of London, Paris, Naples, or Osaka, Japan.

Moscow's heart was the Kremlin, sitting above the northern bank of the Moscow River, displaying walls, towers, and churches still seen today. To its east lay Red Square and the *Kitai Gorod*. Red Square not only contained the beautifully ornate St. Basil's Cathedral and the nearby *Lobnoe Mesto*, a platform from which official pronouncements were read, but also it was the city's open-air gathering center, and marketplace. Here vendors hawked their wares; entertainers, some with trained bears, entertained; beggars begged; and on mar-

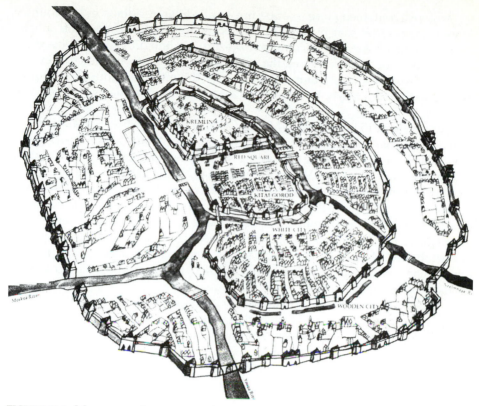

FIGURE 11.1. Moscow, early seventeenth century.
(From Robert Wallace and the Editors of Time-Life Books, Rise of Russia. *Time Inc., New York, 1967, p. 65.)*

ket days, peasants from nearby villages came to sell their produce. *Kitai Gorod* was the main commercial part of the city and its most populated area. Like the Kremlin, it was also protected by stone walls.

North, east, and west of the Kremlin and *Kitai Gorod*, the White City, surrounded by a white stone wall, stretched out and half-encircled them like a horseshoe. Then, further out, the Earthen City (earlier the Wooden City), encircled by an earthen wall, completely surrounded all Moscow, including its southern district, south of the Moscow River.

Beyond the city proper, about five kilometers northeast of the Kremlin, a separate Foreign Suburb (or, more literally, German Suburb) existed after 1652. Increased antiforeign sentiments among the Muscovites helped prompt Alexei to relegate Westerners to this area. He also forbade them to wear Russian clothes or sell alcohol or tobacco to Russians. By 1689, its tree-lined, Western-looking streets contained perhaps 2,000 Western Europeans—especially Englishmen, Scots, Germans, and Dutchmen. Many were soldiers, merchants, or technical experts, but there were also teachers, actors, musicians, Protestant pastors, and others.

Moscow contained close to one-third of all urban residents in the country. Among other cities that by 1689 numbered at least several thousand inhabitants, Archangel, Astrakhan, Yaroslavl, Kazan, Nizhnii Novgorod, Novgorod, Pskov, and Vologda were among the most notable. The newly gained Kiev and Smolensk were also important cities. Even by the most generous definition of what constituted a town, however, less than 5 percent of the population was urban.

Yet between 1533 and 1689, Muscovy's towns and urban population had increased, partly as a result of Russian expansion. Many towns were newly constructed, especially in the expanding southern-southeastern border regions and in Siberia. Typical was Voronezh (near the Don River), founded in 1585, in the mixed zone dividing the forest from the grassy steppe lands to the south. From 1635 to 1654, more than twenty new fortress towns joined Voronezh and about a half dozen other frontier towns to make up the Belgorod Defense Line, which stretched hundreds of kilometers both northeast and southwest of Voronezh (see Map 10.1). Such new towns were mainly military-administrative centers, and most of their men were soldiers and state workers, such as officials or fortress builders and repairers.

There were also, however, new cities in central and northern Russia that were more oriented toward trade and craft production. Some were privately owned by monasteries or nobles. Ivanovo, some 320 kilometers northeast of Moscow, was an example of the latter.

In such towns and in older central-northern ones, the households of craftsmen, merchants, and traders constituted most of the urban tax-paying *posad* community. By the late seventeenth century, the *posad* was no longer so much the urban area outside the city fortress or kremlin but a legal unit responsible for a city's *tiaglo* (burden), a term meaning all the community's tax-paying and labor obligations.

The government's demands on the *posad* people were heavy and included such chores as maintaining roads and fire-fighting. In exchange they received little. Soldiers or those who lived on tax-exempt noble or Orthodox Church properties often competed with them in trades and crafts. To avoid their obligations, some townsmen fled or even sold themselves into slavery, but this just increased, at least temporarily, the *tiaglo* (and discontent) of those remaining.

Following the 1648 Moscow rebellion, the government granted some concessions to the discontented townspeople. The 1649 Law Code strengthened previous stipulations preventing *posad* people from leaving their towns (and their share of the tax burden), either by flight or by selling themselves into slavery; reduced the number of urban tax-exempt properties; and granted merchants, traders, and craftsmen more exclusive rights to town crafts and trade.

Yet it still left most *posad* people in a precarious position—and tied more permanently to their towns than ever before. Heavy burdens remained, along with a lack of autonomy or Western-style rights. Because of loopholes and nonurban competition, even their more exclusive trading rights were as not as significant as they seemed.

Meanwhile the merchants, craftsmen, and other urban workers were becoming increasingly stratified. At the top of the seventeenth-century business class were several hundred men divided into three government-designated groups—the *gosti* (guests) were the smallest and most important of the three. In exchange for assisting the government in buying, selling, and manufacturing products and in collecting liquor duties and customs' revenues, the three groups received exemptions from taxes and from the authority of local governors.

Between these elite merchants and the "free" bottom rungs of urban society were lesser merchants and many craftsmen—some 250 different types in the capital itself, including armorers, blacksmiths, carpenters, coppersmiths, food-producers, furriers, icon-makers, jewelers, tile-glazers, and tinsmiths. At the lower levels of city life were the peddlers of food and wares, manual and menial workers, and yard-keepers.

Although often not as quintessentially urban as the aforementioned groups, some nobles, clergy, soldiers, civilian state employees, slaves, and other dependents also resided in towns. So too did an expanding foreign element in some Russian cities, especially Moscow.

Manufacturing and Trade

In Moscow and most other Russian cities, craftsmen far outnumbered those engaged in manufacturing, but salt production continued to be important. From 1533 to 1689, about fifty iron, copper, glass, gunpowder, leather, paper, rope, textile, and silk-weaving manufactories (manufacturing plants) came into existence. About 50 percent were for producing iron, more than 50 percent were organized by foreigners, and more than 80 percent were begun after 1630. Four water-powered iron (and iron weapons) factories started by the Dutchman Andrei Vinius in the Tula region during the 1630s were indicative of the general trend.

Although perhaps only about twenty-five manufactories were still operating by 1689—and Russia was still importing considerable iron—the iron industry's growth at least enabled the government to provide better for its own military needs. Yet the revolution in manufacturing still awaited a dynamic force—one that soon appeared in the person of Peter the Great.

From the mid-sixteenth century on, Muscovy's dealings with foreign merchants increased. This was especially true in Archangel, where Bushkovitch has estimated foreign trade tripled from the late 1590s to the mid-seventeenth century. Other cities engaged in substantial foreign trade included Novgorod, Pskov, and Astrakhan.

Even though Ivan IV had granted the English Muscovy Company duty-free trading rights, by the early seventeenth century the Dutch had overcome this handicap to become Russia's most valued foreign trading partner. But growing resentment toward foreign merchants was by then chipping away at a century of foreign trading privileges. In 1646, the government terminated duty-free trade for all foreign merchants, and three years later, mad at the English for executing their king, Charles I, Tsar Alexei restricted their merchants to trading only in border cities like Archangel. In his New Trade Regulation of

1667, he further satisfied Russian merchants by similarly curtailing all other foreign traders and by increasing foreign duties.

The pattern of imports and exports continued much as in earlier periods. Russia exported primarily skins, furs, hides and other raw materials, and semi-finished products; it imported such goods as metals—including gold and silver, weapons and other metal products—luxury and household goods, fabrics, and spices. Although most foreign trade was carried on by foreigners coming to Russia, some privileged Russian merchants also traded abroad. One estimate states that in the early 1680s there were forty Russian merchants trading in Stockholm.

The tsar continued to monopolize some trade, for example in caviar, and was (in the words of his doctor, the Englishman Samuel Collins) "the chief merchant in all the empire." Yet neither his agents nor the foreign merchants ever controlled most Russian trade. As Bushkovitch has convincingly demonstrated for the first half of the seventeenth century, most trade—whether in border cities like Archangel or in the interior of the country—was done by Russian merchants and traders for their own benefit. After 1650, as we have seen, Russian merchants were in even a stronger position vis-à-vis their foreign competitors.

Water transport continued to be vital, both for foreign and for internal trade. And many Russians made their living on or near the water. Dukes estimates that in the late seventeenth century, 25,000 boatmen were needed for the transport of salt. Astrakhan was known for its salt marshes, and rowing up the Volga from there was especially difficult and generally done in boats of twenty-six rowers. If transportation was often arduous, so too was communication. It probably took, for example, at least a week to send a message from Archangel to Moscow, a distance of about 1,000 kilometers.

DRINKING, SMOKING, FIRES, FAMINES, AND PLAGUES

Although eating habits remained much the same as earlier, important changes in drinking habits occurred in the late Muscovite period. Most notable were the introduction and growth of vodka (spirits or distilled alcohol) consumption and of government-run taverns (*kabaki*). Both developments owed much to the government's desire for more revenue. By the mid-seventeenth century, alcohol revenues, along with tolls, brought significantly more into government coffers in some cities than did direct taxes.

The government gathered revenues either directly from tavern chiefs entrusted with collecting money from government taverns or by a tax-farming policy that leased the right to run taverns to private entrepreneurs. While continuing to allow upper-class elements to produce their own alcohol, the government attempted to monopolize profits from the drinking of the common people. The Law Code of 1649 stipulated, for example, that illegal sellers of spirits and second-time possessors of such spirits were to be both fined and beaten with a knout.

Occasionally, moral scruples interfered with the government's desire for more alcohol income but usually not for long. Religious leaders complained that heavy drinking often led to moral lapses such as licentious sexual acts and violent attacks on innocent people. They also often linked drinking to the celebration of pagan holidays and customs and to diverting people from Christian services and practices.

Smith and Christian in their excellent book *Bread and Salt* cite a telling example of the government's dilemma in the Stroganov-dominated city of Sol Vychegda. Next to two taverns was the town's main church and its cellars, where spirits (of the alcoholic variety) were stored. Not only were these spirits sold to the taverns, but also they were sold in smaller quantities for on-the-spot consumption. While church services went on above, drinking, singing, and carousing often occurred below. Churchgoers were further reminded of the cellars below by the strong alcoholic smell that wafted upward. Yet the condition continued to be tolerated, no doubt primarily because of the government revenues generated from the church cellars.

Throughout the seventeenth century, foreigners, churchmen, and other Russian sources attest to the heavy drinking not only of laymen, but also of some women and churchmen. In the early seventeenth century, the German official and scholar Olearius observed drunks coming out of taverns; some were "without caps, others without shoes or stockings," or other items of clothing. It seems they had pawned them so that they could keep drinking. Later in the century, Collins, Tsar Alexei's doctor, noted that more than a few drunks passed out on their way home and froze to death in cold weather. He believed that in Russia—as in his native England—drunkenness was an "epidemic distemper."

Foreigners and Russian sources of the time sometimes linked tobacco with alcohol. Olearius testified that in 1634, he saw eight men and one woman lashed for selling spirits and tobacco. The men received twenty-five or twenty-six lashes, the woman, sixteen. They were then marched through the city, receiving more blows on the way. But they were perhaps fortunate because that same year Tsar Mikhail proclaimed the death penalty for anyone buying or selling tobacco. In the 1649 Law Code, Alexei relented somewhat by putting tobacco on about the same level as illicit spirits. As with trafficking in the latter, repeat offenses involving dealing in tobacco brought more severe punishments. Those caught two or three times were tortured and lashed; more than that and the law stipulated that in addition to torture, the offenders should have their nostrils slit and noses cut off and then be exiled.

Yet, partly because of increasing foreigners in Russia, the use of tobacco kept spreading and often went unpunished. In Ukraine it was permitted. Alexei even briefly tried to profit from this habit so strongly condemned by the Orthodox Church: He made its sale a state monopoly. Later, his son Peter the Great, who smoked it in the Foreign Suburb when he was young, finally freed it of any restrictions.

Olearius mentioned that one reason for the strict 1634 prohibition decree on tobacco was because it often led to fires. Undoubtedly, there were already enough fires in Russia without adding smoking to its list of causes. They were primarily due to all the wooden houses and buildings, often crowded together, in both cities and villages. Fire was sometimes symbolized as a "red rooster," and the symbol was painted on buildings in the hope it would keep the dreaded visitor away. Olearius testified that small fires, consuming at least a few houses, were almost a weekly occurrence in Moscow. It also endured many major fires, for example, in 1547, 1571 (when the Crimean Tatars attacked the city), 1611, 1626, and 1671. One late seventeenth-century foreign visitor to Moscow noted that "to make a conflagration remarkable in this country there must be at least seven or eight thousand houses consumed."

Although neither famine nor plague struck as often in the late Muscovy period as they had in the fourteenth and fifteenth centuries, they were still frequent scourges. As we have seen with the 1601–1604 famine, they could be devastating. Other notable famines occurred in 1568–1571 (during Ivan IV's *oprichnina* phase) and in 1650–1652.[1]

Plagues resembling the earlier Black Death often followed in the wake of famine or war, as they did in 1570–1571, 1602–1606, and 1654–1657. The first plague hit the Moscow and Novgorod regions particularly hard; the second was also devastating in these areas, plus the Smolensk region; and the third was severe not only in Moscow and the central regions of the country, but also in Volga cities such as Nizhnii Novgorod, Kazan, and Astrakhan. Some contemporary death estimates for the last plague were close to 1 million but were probably high. Yet there is no doubt it was severe, especially among the congested commoners of Moscow and some of the other cities. Among Moscow's tradesmen, perhaps only 20 percent survived. Three prominent Moscow boyars lost 908 of their combined 950 servants.

The economic and social effects of these famines and plagues were wide-ranging, although difficult to calculate with any precision. At the very least, they contributed to the worsening economic conditions so evident in periods like the 1570s. By reducing the labor supply and tax-payers in towns and villages, they also increased pressures to prevent further population losses by tying commoners permanently to their communities. Having already seen how the 1649 Law Code attempted to do this in the towns, we now need to look at efforts to restrict peasant movement.

PEASANTS AND THE ESTABLISHMENT OF SERFDOM

The peasants continued to make up the vast bulk of Russia's population—about 85 to 90 percent in this late Muscovite period. More of them were obliged to work for nobles or the church, mainly because the government handed over the lands ("black" lands) that peasants had formerly farmed on their own to these more powerful forces. By 1689, about 85 percent of peasants were serfs working on noble or church lands.

The peasants' obligations to their landowners as well as to the state also

[1] See Chapter 10 for the early effects of this latter famine on the Pskov and Novgorod rebellions of 1650.

steadily increased. Although labor obligations (*barshchina*) became more common, money or in kind payments (*obrok*) continued to be the way most peasants fulfilled their landowners' demands.

The most important change that affected these landowners' peasants was their gradual enserfment—that is, their complete loss of freedom to leave a lord's service. We have already seen that laws of 1497 and afterwards restricted peasant rights to exit. Beginning in the early 1590s, the government each year prohibited peasants from exiting except briefly in 1601–1602. In the early seventeenth century, the government gradually extended the period allowed landholders to recover runaway peasants. Finally, the 1649 Law Code completed the enserfing of the peasants. It specified an unlimited time for recapturing runaway peasants, gave serfowners almost unlimited rights over their serfs, and spelled out penalties for those who harbored fugitive peasants.

Although serfs were not slaves and were theoretically tied to the landowner's estates, not to him personally, the master's rights over them and their families and property were extensive and increased even after 1649. By the end of the century, serfowners expected more payments and service, exercised increasing judicial prerogatives, and even—contrary to the law of 1649—bought and sold serfs separately from the land they traditionally worked.

The government's primary purpose in enacting legislation in behalf of serfowners was to insure the military and economic strength of the Russian state. In 1649, the army's core was still the landowning nobility who reported yearly for cavalry duty. These nobles long had insisted that they needed reliable peasant labor if they were going to fulfill their obligation to the state. Poor soil and farming conditions, a scarcity of labor, and peasant flights to frontier regions all exacerbated the problem. The state's awareness of the nobles' need, plus its desire for a reliable tax base, doomed the landowners' peasants to serfdom—this bondage probably would have been finalized even before 1649 if some wealthier nobles and church lands had not benefited from welcoming, enticing, or raiding peasants from many poorer estates.

Neither in the 1649 Law Code nor in other documents of the time does one see any state concern for peasants' rights. As long as they paid their taxes, served their masters adequately, and did not flee or rebel—their only recourse if treated unjustly—the government was happy.

The approximate 15 percent of the peasants who were not the serfs of the nobles or church worked either on crown or "black" lands. Most "black" peasants lived in the sparsely populated far north and in Siberia, where full-fledged serfdom never developed.

SERVICE STATE, SOCIAL STRUCTURE, AND SLAVERY

By the late Muscovite period, everyone was supposed to serve the state, either by military or civil service, tax-paying, or fulfilling religious duties. The government's growing restrictions on townspeople and peasants were part of a larger pattern of more explicitly mandating the obligations of all social categories. This included nobles owning hereditary *votchina* estates, the distinction between *votchina* and *pomestie* landholding having become increasingly blurred.

Muscovite society also became less flexible and more castelike. The 1649 Law Code, with its different penalties for different ranks of society, was just one sign of this intensifying social differentiation.

In 1649, the 52 members of the Boyar Council and their families stood near the top of society, just below the royal family. Below them were the families of the few thousand other members of the upper service class, who helped administer the government and the tsar's court in Moscow. A third group of nobles were the provincial nobility (or middle service class), containing about 35,000 men at this time. Their main job remained serving in the tsar's cavalry forces. All these nobles together possessed about two-thirds of the arable land and pastures in European Russia—the other one-third was held primarily by the clergy, crown, and "black" peasants.

The Moscow nobles, especially the boyars, were generally much wealthier than those in the provinces. Among the Boyar Duma members in 1613, estates ranged in size from about 134,000 acres down to about 850 acres. Such landholdings were usually widely scattered. In 1647, for example, the tsar's chief advisor, Boris Morozov, owned lands in eleven separate districts. His lands contained more than 10,000 peasant household. The next nine richest boyars owned lands possessing between roughly 7,000 down to almost 900 peasant households.

Provincial nobles possessed much less land and even less peasant labor to work their lands. Some provincial nobles controlled no peasant households, many less than five, and only a small percentage over twenty-five. In 1638, they averaged five to six peasant households each. No wonder they so often complained in the early seventeenth century about runaway peasants and insufficient resources to meet their military obligations. Despite the gains they

FIGURE 11.2. In 1576, these boyars, some carrying gifts, acted as diplomatic envoys on a mission to the Holy Roman Emperor.
(From Ian Grey, The Horizon History of Russia, *American Heritage Publishing Company, New York, 1970, pp. 94–95, New York Public Library, Slavonic Division.)*

made in 1648–1649, the great gap between these provincial nobles and those of Moscow continued.

Beneath the nobles was a lower service class of *streltsy*, Cossacks, and other nonnoble military men. The church also had its own social hierarchy from the patriarch (after 1589) on down. Besides the urban classes and the peasants, the only other major group—and the largest after the peasants—was the slaves. Most slaves continued to be Russians who sold themselves into slavery (especially during periods of great economic hardship); men continued to outnumber women by about two to one; and most slaves still worked in noble households and not in the fields.

Yet some important changes also occurred between the early and late Muscovite periods. One was the increasing use of elite slaves in the military after Ivan IV's 1556 Service Decree. Hellie estimates that in the period from 1577 through 1632, provincial nobles and the poorest Moscow nobles brought an average of one slave per noble with them on military campaigns and that more prosperous Moscow nobles brought more. At least half of all these slaves seemed to be used for fighting, while the others guarded the baggage-train. In the middle and latter half of the seventeenth century, because of changing military needs and the consolidation of serfdom, the military use of slaves declined.

In fact, the use of slaves in general decreased by 1689 for some of the same reasons. The final establishment of serfdom in 1649 made owners less dependent on slaves, whether for labor or prestige, and household serfs began taking over many chores earlier performed by slaves.

Another cause of slavery's decline was the state's desire to maintain as many tax-payers as possible. Slaves paid no direct taxes—thus the 1649 law prohibiting tax-paying townsmen from selling themselves into slavery. Although in 1533 most anyone could legally become a slave, by 1689 that "right" was almost limited to those who inherited slave status from their parents, to captives of foreign wars, or to ex-slaves wishing once again to become slaves. Laws were also passed restricting slaveownership. By 1689, only nobles, elite merchants, and clergy could own slaves.

Finally, slavery declined because new alternatives appeared for those too destitute or helpless to survive on their own. Serfdom, almshouses, and the extended family fulfilled some of the relief functions earlier provided by slavery. In the 1670s, almshouses—supported either by the government or by private donors—existed in cities such as Moscow and Yaroslavl. But this was still on a small scale—the almshouses in Moscow could support only about 400 people. More significant was the growth of three-generational households, which offered more support than nuclear families. This growth followed the government's decision by the late 1670s to shift taxes from arable land to households. In the running cat-and-mouse game between tax-payers and tax-collectors, the former immediately began combining into three-generational households because the tax on a household was the same regardless of how many adults lived in it.

THE MILITARY

Like many European countries, Russia spent much of this era at war, both against foreigners and in its own civil conflicts. Until the mid-seventeenth century, the army was dominated by a cavalry composed chiefly of provincial nobles and their slaves. Bows and arrows, swords, spears, and battle-axes remained common weapons, but some cavalry troops gradually began using handguns rather than bows and arrows. Provincial nobles still reported annually—unless they could somehow evade it—and served at least part of the spring-summer season. Unless involved in a major war somewhere else, the southern frontier remained their main responsibility.

To supplement the cavalry, there were the *streltsy* (musketeers), Cossacks, artillerymen, non-Russian native troops (like loyal Tatar units), and, at times, foreign mercenaries. Altogether, there were probably at least 110,000 active troops by the end of the sixteenth century.

In the middle of the seventeenth century, the old-fashioned cavalry lost its predominance. Following the example of Western countries, including its frequent foes Poland and Sweden, Russia began emphasizing new military tactics based more on infantry and guns than on cavalry armed with more primitive weapons. During the Smolensk War of 1632–1634, the government began, with the help of foreign officers and mercenaries, adapting to new-style warfare. Once the war ended, however, the government ordered the mercenaries to leave and once again concentrated on defending the southern frontier, where the old-style cavalry still maintained its significance.

But the completion of the Belgorod Defensive Line and the beginning of the Thirteen Years War with Poland almost simultaneously in 1654 finally helped transform the army. During the war, the government rushed to build up the infantry and modernize the cavalry, thus creating many new-style regiments, usually commanded by Western foreigners. By 1681, about 90,000 troops, two-thirds infantry, were in these new units, composing almost half of the total military forces. New infantry units especially were armed with more modern weapons, such as flintlock muskets, and the government also continued to expand and modernize its use of artillery. Older-style units continued but became less significant. The 55,000 *streltsy* stationed in Moscow and the provinces, for example, were used more for garrison and policing functions and were more poorly armed than new-style infantry units.

As the old-style cavalry declined, so too did the provincial nobles' military significance. Their traditional fighting techniques had proved ineffective in the Thirteen Years War and many nobles perished. Some, under government pressure, gradually joined the new-style regiments, but the government found Cossacks more willing and adaptable. It also relied increasingly on conscripted commoners.

Even before the Thirteen Years War, commoners were made to provide labor support for troops when digging, hauling, and other such work were needed. During the war, they were called up in great numbers (100,000 recruits in all, according to one estimate), and many were used for combat, mainly as infantrymen. Many died or deserted, but those who did not apparently had to remain in service for life. The class composition of the military changed forever.

WOMEN AND FAMILY LIFE

Part of what we know about Muscovite women and family life comes from the observations of contemporary Russian and foreign observers—although the latter must especially be regarded with caution. Despite increasing Western influences, Russian family life did not change much from the preceding era.

In the 1660s, the Russian Grigori Kotoshikhin's observations about separate *terem* quarters and arranged marriages were similar to those made by Herberstein more than a century earlier. The German Olearius and the Englishman Collins both wrote of the Russian women's penchant for painting their faces. Although Olearius thought the women "well proportioned," Collins stated that "the beauty of women they place in their fatness," and that "a lean woman they account unwholesome." Olearius was shocked by women as well as men coming out of Moscow bathhouses stark naked and addressing foreigners in what he considered an immoral manner. He also commented on the frequent swearing, not only by men, but also by women and even children.

The most quoted source about Muscovite family practices is not from an observer, however, but from a mid-sixteenth-century moral guidebook for the upper class, the *Domostroi*. Its chief advice to wives was to subject themselves to their husbands and to seek their advice in all matters, extending even to the wives' choice of friends. Wives were also to keep their houses clean and orderly, to avoid slander and gossip, and to supervise and discipline servants and children (this meant daughters and young boys; older boys were more commonly handled by the father).

Husbands were encouraged to love their wives, but also to instruct and discipline them if they failed to follow the precepts of the *Domostroi*. If a wife refused to follow her husband's guidance, the *Domostroi* recommended that he administer a sensible, not a senseless, beating. He was not to beat his wife with his fist or foot or on the ear or in the face, and afterwards he was to say loving words to his just-beaten mate. This advice reminds one of the old Russian proverb: "Love your wife like your soul, and beat her like your fur coat."

A similar combination of love and beatings was proscribed for the children. The *Domostroi* warned parents that God would hold them responsible on the day of judgment if they failed to bring up their children properly.

Although it is impossible to know how accurately the *Domostroi* reflected everyday upper-class life, wives were probably not as passive as it suggests. All their familial, economic, social, and sexual roles made them too important to be completely subjugated. A thorough investigation of primarily seventeenth-century court cases by Nancy Kollmann has demonstrated that women often sued or had men sue for them. Although it was more common for widows and nuns to litigate for themselves, wives also occasionally did so. Most of

How to Teach Children and Save Them Through Fear

The following excerpt from the *Domostroi* is from Leo Wiener, *Anthology of Russian Literature: From the Earliest Period to the Present Time* (New York, 1902) Vol. I, pp. 127–128. A more recent edition and translation by Carolyn Johnston Pouncy, *The "Domostroi": Rules for Russian Households in the Time of Ivan the Terrible* (Ithaca, N.Y., 1994), pp. 95–97, makes it clear that most of the advice below was taken from the Biblical books of Proverbs and Ecclesiasticus.

Punish your son in his youth, and he will give you a quiet old age, and restfulness to your soul. Weaken not beating the boy, for he will not die from your striking him with the rod, but will be in better health: for while you strike his body, you save his soul from death. If you love your son, punish him frequently, that you may rejoice later. Chide your son in his childhood, and you will be glad in his manhood, and you will boast among evil persons, and your enemies will be envious. Bring up your child with much prohibition, and you will have peace and blessing from him. Do not smile at him, or play with him, for though that will diminish your grief while he is a child, it will increase it when he is older, and you will cause much bitterness to your soul. Give him no power in his youth, but crush his ribs while he is growing and does not in his wilfulness obey you, lest there be an aggravation and suffering to your soul, a loss to your house, destruction to your property, scorn from your neighbors and ridicule from your enemies, and cost and worriment from the authorities.

these suits were due to insults to a woman's honor, either by word or deed—the 1649 Law Code stipulated that the fine for violating a wife's honor was double that for her husband and for a maiden daughter, four times that for her father. The most serious forms of dishonor, rape, often involved much more substantial punishments. Other women sued to protect dowry property or because of abandonment or excessive beatings by husbands.

By allowing such suits, the government and church by no means undermined Muscovite patriarchal society. Indeed, guarding a woman's honor helped perpetuate it. But state and church did allow women some protection and more safeguards than have many other patriarchal societies.

CRIMES, PUNISHMENTS, AND THE LAW

The 1649 Law Code dealt with a wide variety of crimes, from those against the tsar's honor (22 articles) to robbery and theft (104 articles). Judging from the code and from foreign accounts, the last category was especially widespread. Olearius noted that in the 1630s and 1640s it was "unsafe to walk the streets of Moscow in the night time" and that hardly a night passed without robberies and murder. During holiday times, when drinking increased, the unlit

Moscow streets were even more dangerous. And people who were attacked on the streets could expect little help from those inside their houses.

To lessen the danger in Moscow, the government and potential victims took what measures they could. City gates were locked at night. Many who could afford it protected their homes with metal gates, grilles, doors, and shutters and used security guards, although the guards could not always be trusted. Only the foolish ventured out alone at night, even with a torch or lantern. In an effort to improve security in Moscow, Tsar Alexei beefed up patrols in the city. Judging from later seventeenth-century foreign observations, however, Moscow streets remained dangerous.

Alexei's 1649 code called for officials responsible to the Robbery *Prikaz* (Bureau) to ferret out robbers and other criminals. It also spelled out harsh punishments for suspects and offenders. It stated, for example, that if a robber was brought in, he should be tortured, and if he confessed to robbing for the first time, he should have his right ear cut off, be imprisoned for three years, have his property taken away, and then be exiled and made to perform forced labor wherever the tsar dictated. If someone confessed to two robberies, he was to be executed.

Other crimes that merited the death penalty in the code included arson, blasphemy (including preventing a church service from being completed), church theft, counterfeiting of coins (whose practitioners were to have molten metal poured down their throats), forgery of state documents, premeditated murder, several types of rape, and treason or failure to report it.

Because imprisonment was often mandated, the 1649 Law Code required that new prisons be built and staffed. Besides all the punishments mentioned previously (and other types of mutilations), fines and beatings were also often stipulated. Regarding fines for violating someone's honor, the 1649 code built upon the 1550 Law Code. In both codes, the fine for dishonoring the elite *gosti* merchants was fifty rubles, but for peasants only one ruble. Partly because of the more stratified nature of mid-seventeenth-century society, the 1649 code was more detailed about honor violations. For example, more than sixty articles dealt with fines for dishonoring various clerics. For dishonoring bishops, one paid 300 rubles, for most ordinary priests, only 5 rubles. Large fines were often only for those who could afford to pay them. For poorer classes, the law stipulated other punishments, such as imprisonment and beatings.

Beatings, whether for offending someone's honor or for other crimes, were basically of two types: with small wooden rods (*batogi*) or with a knout. The latter, which could slash through to the bone and kill a person, was more damaging. It was used not only for greater offenses, but also at times for lesser persons. Thus, for taking a bribe that resulted in delaying a case, a state secretary was to be beaten with *batogi*, but the lowly scribes beneath him were to be knouted for the same offense.

Like so much else in the late Muscovite period, the laws reflect the hierarchical nature of Russian society, and the determination of the government and upper classes to keep those lower on the social ladder in their "proper" place.

The emphasis on beatings and torture in the 1649 code made it harsher

FIGURE 11.3. Flogging with a knout, seventeenth century.
(*From Ian Grey,* The Horizon History of Russia, *American Heritage Publishing Company, New York, 1970, p. 118–119.*)

than earlier codes. Torture was usually mandated for defendants in criminal investigations, especially, but by no means exclusively, for lower-class suspects. One reason for its increased use by 1649 might have been the disappearance of judicial ordeals. In 1556, the most common remaining ordeal, that by battle, was prohibited. Without ordeals to help a judge determine "truth" and "guilt," he became more reliant on confessions. Even in the West at this time, confession was regarded as the "queen of proofs," and torture was frequently the only means of obtaining it.

Already at the end of the sixteenth century, the Englishman Giles Fletcher reported that defendants were examined by use of such tortures as "scourging with whips . . . or by tying to a spit and roasting at the fire, sometimes by breaking and wresting one of their ribs with a pair of hot tongs, or cutting their flesh under their nails, and such like." A half-century later, Olearius also noted the prominence of torture to obtain confessions. One of the Russian tortures he described, the strappado, was also popular in the West, where it was known as the "queen of torments." It involved suspending the suspect in the air from a rope, attached to his hands, which were tied behind his back. To further increase the strain and pain, some type of weight was often fastened to the feet; in Russia, according to Olearius, it was a "great beam."

Both to obtain confessions of guilt and possibly to implicate others, the government also sometimes used torture on informers if their testimony did not lead to a suspect's confession.

Why then would anyone inform? Primarily because the government mandated denunciation—by the 1649 Law Code even a minor child could be executed for failing to report his father's treasonous activities to the authorities. Collective tax and service responsibilities suggest another incentive, for others had to make up the difference if someone cheated the government.

One crime that was not dealt with in late Muscovite law codes was witchcraft. Traditionally, it had been under church jurisdiction. Ivan IV, however, brought it under civil as well as religious authority, and later tsars dealt with it in separate decrees. In 1653, Alexei mandated burning at the stake for those practicing witchcraft. We know that more than 100 men and women were tried for it in the seventeenth century; in contrast to Western Europe and North America, most (about two-thirds) accused Russian witches were men. At least a dozen of the accused were burned at the stake.

If all of these legal practices seem barbaric, it should be remembered that Russia was not alone in the use of such harsh practices. Most of them were then also practiced in the West. For example, from the second half of the thirteenth century to the end of the eighteenth, torture was part of the ordinary criminal procedure of the Latin Church and of most of the states of Europe.

Although England, Scandinavia, and Colonial America relied on torture much less than did most of Europe, in other ways they were not so enlightened. Richard Chancellor noted after his first visit to Russia in 1553 that the Russian law was more lenient to thieves than in England, where one could be hanged for a first-offense theft—Elizabethan London incidentally was probably no safer at night than Moscow. In Alexei's reign, his English doctor (Collins) stated that capital punishment was less frequent in Russia than in England. In Salem, Massachusetts, in 1692, twenty people were put to death for witchcraft.

In Western Europe, there was even more witch-hunting and hysteria in the sixteenth and seventeenth centuries than in Colonial America or Russia. As for mutilations, the most influential monarch of his day, Louis XIV of France, decreed in 1674 that prostitutes discovered with soldiers in the vicinity of his Versailles palace were to have their ears and noses cut off.[2]

Finally, many Russian "criminals" never were apprehended because the state's crime-fighting capacity was weak. Laws were so harsh partly because the state realized this weakness and hoped severe laws would act as a deterrent. In dealing with crime, as in many other areas, the government's absolutistic desires often exceeded its capacity. Laws reflected not only the state's

---

[2] In "Due Process and Equal Justice in Muscovite Codes," *RH* 51 (October 1992): pp. 463–480, George G. Weickhardt has argued that in the mid-seventeenth century Russia was more "advanced" than Western Europe in regard to certain aspects of the law, specifically in its "procedural norms and concepts of personal inviolability, security of property, and equal justice." Despite different punishments for some crimes, he points out that many of the punishments in the 1649 Law Code were the same for all, regardless of rank.

wishes, but also the intentions of some Russians to evade them. For example, the thirty-one sections of the 1649 Law Code dealing with runaway peasants would not have been necessary if there had not already been so many such "lawbreakers."

SUGGESTED SOURCES*

ALEXANDER, JOHN T. "Plague Epidemics," *MERSH* 28: 100–108.

BARON, SAMUEL H. *Muscovite Russia: Collected Essays*. London, 1980.

———. ed. *The Travels of Olearius in Seventeenth-Century Russia*. Stanford, 1967.

BERRY, LLOYD E., and ROBERT O. CRUMMEY, eds. *Rude and Barbarous Kingdom: Russia in the Accounts of Sixteenth-Century English Voyagers*. Madison, 1968. Includes observations of Giles Fletcher and Richard Chancellor.

BLUM, JEROME. *Lord and Peasant in Russia, from the Ninth to the Nineteenth Century*. Princeton, 1961. Chs. 8–14.

BUSHKOVITCH, PAUL. *The Merchants of Moscow, 1580–1650*. Cambridge, England, 1980.

COLLINS, SAMUEL. *The Present State of Russia, in a Letter to a Friend at London*. London, 1671.

CRUMMEY, ROBERT O. *Aristocrats and Servitors: The Boyar Elite in Russia, 1613–1689*. Princeton, 1983.

DUKES, PAUL. *The Making of Russian Absolutism, 1613–1801*. 2d ed. London, 1990. Chs. 1–2.

FUHRMANN, JOSEPH T. *The Origins of Capitalism in Russia: Industry and Progress in the Sixteenth and Seventeenth Centuries*. Chicago, 1972.

HELLIE, RICHARD. *Enserfment and Military Change in Muscovy*. Chicago, 1971.

———. *Slavery in Russia, 1450–1725*. Chicago, 1982.

———. "Ulozhenie of 1649," *MERSH* 40: 192–198.

———, ed. *The Muscovite Law Code (Ulozhenie) of 1649*. Irvine, Calif., 1988.

HITTLE, J. MICHAEL. *The Service City: State and Townsmen in Russia, 1600–1800*. Cambridge, Mass., 1979.

KAHAN, ARCADIUS. *The Plow, the Hammer, and the Knout: An Economic History of Eighteenth-Century Russia*. Chicago, 1985.

KEEP, JOHN L. H. *Soldiers of the Tsar: Army and Society in Russia, 1462–1874*. Oxford, 1985. Pt. 1.

KIVELSON, VALERIE A. "The Effects of Partible Inheritance: Gentry Families and the State in Muscovy," *RR* 53 (April 1994): 197–212.

KLEIMOLA, ANN M. " 'In Accordance with the Canons of the Holy Apostles': Muscovite Dowries and Women's Property Rights," *RR* 51 (April 1992): 204–229.

KOLLMANN, NANCY SHIELDS. "Women's Honor in Early Modern Russia." In *Russia's Women: Accommodation, Resistance, Transformation*, eds. Barbara Evans Clements, Barbara Alpern Engel, and Christine D. Worobec. Berkeley, 1991.

LONGWORTH, PHILIP. *Alexis, Tsar of All the Russias*. New York, 1984.

PETERS, EDWARD. *Torture*. New York, 1985.

RYNDZIUNSKII, P. G., and A. M. SAKHAROV. "Towns in Russia," *MERSH* 39: 127–136.

RH 10, Pt. 2 (1983). The whole issue is devoted to women in medieval Russia.

SMITH, R. E. F. *Peasant Farming in Muscovy*. London, 1977.

*See also works cited in footnotes and boxed insert.

SMITH, R. E. F., and DAVID CHRISTIAN. *Bread and Salt: A Social and Economic History of Food and Drink in Russia*. Cambridge, England, 1984.

SOLOVIEV, SERGEI M. *The Character of Old Russia*. Gulf Breeze, Fla., 1980.

TORKE, HANS J. "Crime and Punishment in the Pre-Petrine Civil Service: The Problem of Control." In *Imperial Russia, 1700–1917: State, Society, Opposition, Essays in Honor of Marc Raeff*, eds. Ezra Mendelsohn, and Marshall S. Shatz. DeKalb, Ill., 1988.

VOYCE, ARTHUR. *Moscow and the Roots of Russian Culture*. Norman, Okla. 1964.

WEICKHARDT, GEORGE G. "Kotoshikhin: An Evaluation and Interpretation," *RH* 17, No. 2 (1990): 127–154.

ZGUTA, RUSSELL. "Witchcraft Trials in Seventeenth-Century Russia," *AHR* 82 (December 1977): 1187–1207.

CHAPTER 12

Religion and Culture, 1533–1689

In the late Muscovite era, two factors were especially important regarding religion and culture. The first was Moscow's emphasis on itself as the center of true Christian civilization. The second was the growth of foreign influences, mainly in the seventeenth century.

These influences, particularly in the religious sphere, came primarily through more westernized Ukrainian lands and accelerated as Moscow heightened its efforts to acquire Ukrainian territory. Partly because some Ukrainian Orthodox practices differed from Russian ones and were closer to those of other Orthodox believers, Patriarch Nikon decided to bring Russian practices more in line with those of the Ukrainians. But the Ukrainian impact, sometimes transmitting Polish Western influences, extended into other religious and cultural areas as well.

Muscovy's wars with Poland and Sweden and these foreigners' intervention during the Time of Troubles also increased Western contacts. So too did Muscovy's expanded Western trade, diplomatic dealings, and desire for military and technological improvements. As Kliuchevsky noted long ago, adopting Western techniques did not necessarily mean adopting Western cultural values. Yet it was almost impossible to separate the two completely.

Intensified Western and foreign Orthodox contacts and influences, however, inevitably clashed with the prevalent Muscovite Orthodox belief in its own religious-cultural superiority. The Polish and Swedish intervention in the Time of Troubles led to a growing mistrust of foreigners, especially of Polish Catholics. The former Polish captive Patriarch Filaret particularly disliked Catholicism. It was no accident that when foreigners were recruited during and after his sway they were overwhelmingly Protestant and that no Catholic church was allowed in Moscow until Peter the Great's reign.

One of the few prominent Catholics in Russia was the Scottish officer Patrick Gordon. In 1661, he commented on: "strangers being looked upon by the best sort as scarcely Christians, and by the plebeians as mere pagans." In 1688, after he had become a general in the Russian army, he noted that the

Russian patriarch stated that the army could not prosper with a heretic commanding its elite troops.

As Gordon suggests, however, it was not only Catholics and Catholicism that were distrusted. Protestant, Jewish, and secular scientific thought were also suspect and to a lesser extent even certain foreign Orthodox practices. Kliuchevsky illustrated the distrust of foreign secular learning then prevalent by quoting from books that recommended against studying philosophy. One stated: "Impious before God is everyone who loves geometry, and a sin it is to study astronomy." Instead, Orthodox believers were told to love "simplicity more than wisdom" and not to seek that which was above them.

Besides religious-cultural grounds for being wary of foreigners, there were also other reasons. For example, Russian merchants resented Western merchant privileges, and provincial noble officers and others resented Western officers like Gordon. Olearius noted that after the creation of the Foreign Suburb, Russians sometimes obscenely referred to it as "Pricktown." On one occasion vandals attacked Protestant churches there because of rumors that a foreign colonel's wife had thrown Russian icons into a fire. Resentment against foreign influences also played a major part in the Church Schism of 1666–1667.

Early in his reign, Alexei made some concessions to anti-Western sentiments. W. Bruce Lincoln even goes so far as to state that the young Alexei and Patriarch Joseph "railed against all foreigners and their culture as instruments of Satan" and that Alexei "sought to spark a xenophobic upsurge."[1]

Although Alexei never had the mind and heart of a xenophobe, he was devoutly Orthodox. Scarred by rebellions in 1648 and 1650, and soon afterwards about to go to war with Catholic Poland, he was then attentive to conservative Orthodox public opinion. As his reign and confidence progressed, he moved further away from the old Muscovy wariness of the West. His second marriage, to Natalia Naryshkina in 1671, after the death of the pious and conservative Maria, was symbolic of his evolution. As the ward of Alexei's friend and later chief minister, Artamon Matveev, and his Scottish wife, Mary Hamilton, she was brought up in a home full of windows to the West.

Yet Alexei was also no radical westernizer. He remained a devout Orthodox believer and continued to pay some heed to the sensibilities of his people. Kliuchevsky pictured Russia under Alexei at the crossroads, between the old Orthodox culture and the new westernized Russian one that his son Peter the Great would champion. He depicted Alexei as a man who had one foot firmly planted on Orthodox ground and who had raised the other to step over the boundary dividing the old from the new—but instead remained frozen in that position.

RELIGION

By 1533, the great age of Russian monasticism was over. As the sixteenth century progressed, monastic influence waned, and the Russian people, church,

[1] *The Romanovs: Autocrats of All the Russias* (New York, 1981), p. 86.

and government combined to popularize miracle cults. These cults often centered around particular holy shrines and stressed the miraculous powers of relics and icons in aiding communities or individuals in warfare or in peacetime. The state attempted to make use of miracle cults, as it continued to use various Russian Orthodox ceremonies, rituals, and teachings, to strengthen its own ideological hold over the Russian people.

In church councils of 1547, 1549, and 1551 and in writings such as the *Great Menology*, the *Book of Degrees of the Imperial Genealogy*, and the *Tale of the Princes of Vladimir*, Metropolitan Makari and his associates centralized Moscow's church control and bolstered the prestige and claims of the Russian Orthodox Church and the Muscovite tsar. The latter they perceived as the last great Christian monarch. They furthered myths claiming that Ivan IV could trace his genealogy back to the Roman emperors and that a Byzantine emperor had bestowed a crown upon the Kievan ruler Vladimir Monomakh. They also stressed that the Muscovite tsar was the legitimate successor to the former lands of Kievan Rus.

The upgrading of the Russian church by granting it a patriarch in 1589 furthered this sense of religious-cultural superiority. So too did the Constantinople patriarch's declaration to Tsar Fedor: "Your great Russian Tsardom, the third Rome, surpasses all in piety; you alone in all the universe are referred to as the Christian Tsar."

Even though late Muscovite tsars and patriarchs agreed on Russia's superiority, the touchy question of the relative powers of tsar and patriarch remained. The ordaining of Filaret as patriarch in 1619 created a special situation, for the new patriarch was also Tsar Mikhail's father. Until his death in 1633, Patriarch Filaret, who was also co-Great Sovereign, dominated his more passive son. By strengthening the power of the patriarchy over the clergy and over still extensive church lands, he also temporarily halted the growth of state authority over church matters. His example would not be lost on the most dynamic of his successors—Nikon.

Meanwhile, however, following Filaret's death, the government strengthened its powers over the church. For example, the 1649 Law Code forbade sermons to offend the honor of any boyar or official, created a Monastery Bureau (*prikaz*) to oversee litigation against church people, and confiscated church lands located in the cities.

Reforms and Schism

As the state strengthened its controls, two overlapping reform movements occurred within the church. The first was championed by a group, mainly priests, called the Zealots of Piety. While believing in the superiority of Russian Orthodoxy, these men also thought a moral revival was necessary. They attempted to curb drunkenness, smoking, pagan practices and entertainments, adultery, and disrespect of proper liturgical practices. (For their unflinching criticism of their parishioners' moral failings, they were sometimes beaten by those opposed to being so chastised.) The "zealots" also emphasized the Christian's duty to help the poor and needy.

One of their leaders, Stefan Vonifatiev, became Alexei's confessor in the late 1640s, and another, Nikon, became patriarch in 1652. Some of Alexei's early policies were influenced by the group. In 1648, he outlawed *skomorokhi* (minstrels or buffoons), associated by the zealots with paganism. In 1652, besides quarantining Westerners—distrusted by the zealots—in their own suburb, he also enacted an ineffective reform aimed at curbing drunkenness.

The other reform tendency was more of the head than the heart. It attempted to shore up the intellectual defenses of Russian Orthodoxy against other faiths and beliefs. It also aimed at bringing Russian church practices more in line with the rest of the Orthodox world.

Although many zealots also supported the early (and more moderate) efforts of this reform movement, it depended more strongly on Ukrainian churchmen. As part of the Orthodox renewal in Ukraine, the archimandrite of the Kievan Cave Monastery (and subsequently metropolitan of Kiev), Peter Mogila (Mohyla), had founded a Kievan academy in the early 1630s. Ironically, Mogila had studied in Paris and was influenced by Polish Jesuit and other Catholic schools in establishing his new academy. He now adopted some of their educational methods to compete against them better. Most instruction was in Latin, but Greek and Church Slavonic were also studied. So too were theology, philosophy, music, and the natural sciences, often with the help of Western, especially Catholic, writings. In the next several decades, Mogila and his followers produced learned theological works and translations.

By 1652, Kievan monks and writings had made their way to Moscow. Along with other outside Orthodox clergy, they began to help reinvigorate Russian Orthodoxy and champion it in polemics against Catholics and Protestants.

Nikon's appointment as patriarch in 1652 and his radicalization of this second reform movement soon led to a break with many zealots. Well over six feet tall, Nikon was a strong-willed monk of peasant background who earlier had been not only a Zealot of Piety, but also metropolitan of Novgorod. When several zealots objected too vigorously to his 1653 mandating of changes such as the use of three fingers instead of two in making the sign of the cross, he had them exiled.

In the next several years, the uproar continued as Nikon, with the help of church councils and Orthodox from Ukraine and elsewhere, crusaded to bring Russian Orthodox writings and rituals into conformity with those of other Orthodox. He became an enthusiast for Byzantine ways even in church architecture and constructed some new churches in the Byzantine style. To many he seemed to be turning his back on the traditional holy ways of Muscovy. That his reforming activities preceded and coincided with the great plague of 1654–1657 did not help him, for some began saying that the plague was God's punishment for Nikon's deviations from true Christian ways.

For six years, Alexei backed Nikon despite all the turmoil he was creating. In 1658, however, a boyar insulted the dignity of the patriarchal office, and Alexei ignored Nikon's appeal to reprimand the boyar—Nikon, who came from a peasant background, was generally unpopular with the boyars. Nikon then abandoned his position and left Moscow, apparently hoping Alexei would recall him and make amends. Alexei never did. The deeper reason for their split was differences over their respective powers. Probably influenced by Western papal thinking, Nikon resisted state infringement over his spiritual authority.

In 1666–1667, the tsar presided over a church council in which the patriarchs of Alexandria and Antioch participated. While retaining most of Nikon's reforms, it formally deposed and banished him to a northern monastery. It also excommunicated those refusing to go along with such changes as the three-fingered sign of the cross. Furthermore, Alexei made it a crime to continue professing the traditional practices. Thus, the Old Believers (or more accurately, but less commonly, Old Ritualists) became schismatics.

Causes and Effects of the Schism

One of the schismatics' leaders, the archpriest Avvakum, told the visiting patriarchs at the council:

> Among you Orthodoxy has become corrupted by Turkish Mohammedan coercion . . . you have become feeble. Henceforth, come to us to learn: among us, by God's grace, is autocracy. Among us, prior to Nikon, the apostate, the Orthodoxy of our princes and tsars was always pure and unblemished.

While Nikon and Alexei championed conformity with the rest of the Orthodox world, the Old Believers clung to the old Muscovite religious culture. Alexei sanctioned changes partly because he wished to expand Moscow's authority over non-Russian Orthodox in Ukraine and Belorussia and perhaps even beyond to those under Turkish control. But the schismatics—overwhelmingly peasants, traders, and parish clergymen—were more isolationists than expansionists. Even within the old Muscovite state, they were wary of Moscow's expanding centralization, whether ecclesiastical or governmental. Moreover, in the new practices, some saw not only the influence of an impure Byzantine Orthodoxy, but also of Roman Catholicism. During a bewildering era of war, plague, foreign influences, and rebellions, they wished to maintain the rock of their traditional beliefs.

Alexei dealt harshly with prominent schismatics. In his autobiography, Avvakum recounts how some of them had their tongues, fingers, or hands cut off and how others were buried alive, hanged, or burned at the stake—as Avvakum himself eventually was. Among the Old Believers were many women, none more significant than the Boyarina Morozova, the sister-in-law of Alexei's former tutor and adviser, Boris Morozov. In a scene immortalized by the nineteenth-century painter Vasili Surikov, she was bound with chains and taken away to prison in 1671, where she was condemned to die of starvation four years later. Despite such punishments, many Russians still resisted. The longest-lasting active resistance came from the monks and their supporters at the Solovetskii Monastery, located on an island in the White Sea. With their ninety canon and sturdy walls, the monastery held out against the new teachings from 1668 to 1676.

Avvakum and many other Old Believers regarded their opponents as the forces of the anti-Christ that were prophesied to come at the end of history. The year 1666 had special significance for Old Believers because the New Testament's Book of Revelations had ascribed the number 666 to the anti-Christ. During the next two decades, many Old Believers—convinced that the end of the world was at hand and the reign of the anti-Christ underway—gathered together, often in churches, and set themselves on fire, believing that the flames would help purify them for the afterlife. Perhaps some 20,000 schismatics died in this manner. Musorgsky later ended his famous opera *Khovanshchina* with such a scene. Most Old Believers, however, continued living and became the founding generation of a movement that has continued ever since.

The schism's long-term effects were similar to those of religious wars in Europe: They weakened the power of religion and strengthened both state authority over it and secular forces in general. The loss of many ardent believers sapped Orthodox vitality for centuries to come. Alexei now appointed a new, more subservient patriarch and increased his control over the church. His son Peter the Great later took even more advantage of a weakened Russian Orthodox Church. The state, however, also lost something: the heartfelt allegiance of many who once thought the tsar a symbol of true Christian authority. Finally, the reduction of church influence weakened the defenses of those opposed to foreign ways. It was no accident that westernization accelerated following the schism.

POPULAR CULTURE

Although much of Muscovite popular culture involved religion, some of its manifestations were pagan or secular. Popular leisure activities in this era can be divided into two categories: those for regular days and those for special days, such as religious holidays, pagan festive days, and weddings.

Activities of the first type included conversation, story-telling, drinking, smoking, and game-playing as well as seasonal activities such as skating, skiing, sleighing, boating, and swimming. Hunting, although indeed common, could be considered a "leisure" activity only for the wealthy. Among popular games, chess was a favorite, and cards and dice were also played, often for money. People also liked to swing and see-saw. Rougher types of activities were wrestling, fist-fighting, and staged bear fights. One of Muscovites' favorite activities was going to the steam bathhouses. Olearius was especially amazed to see both men and women come out of them naked and rub themselves with snow.

On religious holidays, there were colorful processions. And activities such as drinking and gaming usually became more intensive on these and other special days. Alexei's doctor, Samuel Collins, noted: "In the carnival before the Lent they [the Russians] give themselves over to all manner of debauchery and luxury, and in the last week they drink as if they were never to drink more."

Olearius mentioned a primitive type of ferris wheel that was often set up on holidays.

The *skomorokhi* also became more active on these special days. Some of these entertainers resided permanently in one place (increasingly in the cities) and were considered respectable citizens, sometimes even being permanently employed by a tsar or prominent noble. Less respectable was the reputation of the wandering *skomorokhi*, who were poorer, usually traveled in groups, and were sometimes accused of being thieves.

Although many *skomorokhi* were multitalented, they gradually became more specialized. Their skills included singing, dancing, and playing various musical instruments—flutes, horns, drums, fiddles, and especially the *gusli*, a small harp or zitherlike instrument. They were often accompanied by trained bears and staged puppet and dramatic performances, often with masks.

They were much in demand at pagan festivals, which, despite church and state pressures, continued to be celebrated. A church council of 1551 lamented the presence of *skomorokhi* at weddings, probably because it viewed them not only as entertainers, but also as practitioners of lingering pagan wedding rituals and thus as rivals to priests.

It was not just the church's fear of pagan remnants that led to its criticism of the *skomorokhi* and much of popular culture; it was also a distrust of entertainment itself. The church advised even laypersons to avoid games and laughter—in one seventeenth-century work, *The Life of Yuliania Lazarevsky*, a son relates how his holy mother refrained from games, laughter, and frivolous songs, even when she was a child. Such frivolity was often associated with the devil, who tried to lead Christians away from the serious business of living a good Christian life.

The state had additional fears about popular culture and the *skomorokhi*, especially after the 1648 urban riots. It associated festivals and celebrations with drinking and lawlessness. Samuel Collins observed that the pre-Lenten "drinking bouts are commonly attended with quarrels, fightings, and murders." Gambling could lead to robbery to recoup losses.

Besides their association with such holidays, *skomorokhi* were sometimes irreverent toward authority. These factors, plus the scare of the 1648 riots and the young Alexei's willingness to go along with the church's moral reformers, help explain his decrees of December 1648 banning the *skomorokhi*. In them, Alexei noted how the *skomorokhi* and drunkenness were diverting people from the churches on Sundays and holy days. He also criticized certain pagan holiday activities. He forbade not only *skomorokhi* entertainments, but also all musical instruments associated with them; various pagan rituals; and games such as boxing, cards, chess, and dice. Violators were to be lashed and, after a third violation, exiled.

Although Alexei's decrees were certainly violated after 1648, the *skomorokhi* did decline significantly. By 1800, they seem to have disappeared. No doubt their decline was also caused by changing cultural conditions, including the acceleration of Western influences. Yet, as Russell Zguta and others have pointed out, they left a permanent legacy in such areas as music, dance, and comic and puppet theater.

LEARNING, MORALITY, AND LITERATURE

By 1689, despite growing literacy, few could read, even at a fairly basic level, except government scribes, clergy, and some nobles and merchants. Although the dramatic increase in the printing of primers during the late seventeenth century points to a heightened teaching of reading, no formal educational system existed. Even many priests, who were supposed to demonstrate their literacy before being ordained, did not possess the equivalent of an elementary school education. The embryonic beginning of Muscovite formal education occurred only under Alexei and was influenced by the Kievan Academy founded earlier in the century.

One of the era's most influential educators was the monk Simeon Polotsky (1629–1680). He was a Belorussian who had studied at the Kievan Academy and later at a Jesuit college in Wilno (Vilna or Vilnius). After such exposure to Western influences, and the didacticism that was part of it, he later came to Moscow in 1663. A few years later, he became the director and a teacher of Latin at a short-lived school for government clerks. Following the 1666–1667 church council, he became more influential at court. He tutored three of the tsar's children—Tsarevich Alexei (who died in 1670), Fedor, and Sophia. Latin, Polish, theology, and literature were his specialties, and he was familiar with ancient classical times. He was also a prolific writer, especially of poetry and theological works.

Among his theological writings were two volumes of sermons, which were published shortly after his death, spreading his ideas as far as Siberia. He had apparently first preached most of his sermons at court or at a Moscow monastery where he usually resided. According to Bushkovitch, these sermons, with their emphasis on humility and generosity, were indicative of a new religious trend among the clerical and lay elite. It was a trend away from a public and collective emphasis on liturgy and miracle cults toward a more personal religion stressing morality. Polotsky believed that the elite's Orthodoxy should be grounded on knowledge and learning, including such distrusted subjects as philosophy. By expressing such ideas, he inadvertently helped serve as a bridge between the old religious teachings, suspicious of secular learning, and Peter the Great's emphasis on secular ethics.

Polotsky's stress on humility and generosity was encouraged by Alexei, and these virtues had also been emphasized earlier by several other seventeenth-century clergymen and lay figures. Now that serfdom was firmly in place, all these individuals encouraged a sort of noblesse oblige toward serfs and other social inferiors. At least a few of the boyar elite who came into contact with preachers like Polotsky seem to have made special efforts to treat their serfs, and other social inferiors, with a spirit of generosity and compassion. Although Russian Orthodoxy was used to support Russia's exploitative sociopolitical order, it also exercised more positive influences, which were not completely ignored by Russia's political elite.

Several years after Polotsky's death in 1680, a conflict broke out over the nature of a new academy to be founded in Moscow. Initially the victory went to Patriarch Joachim, who disliked Western and Latin tendencies. In 1685, he helped establish a Helleno-Greek Academy that he hoped would reflect more Greek Orthodox influences. His victory was short-lived, however. The best-educated nobles and the new tsar (after 1689), Peter I, looked not to the Ortho-dox East but to an increasingly secularized West. Although the academy con-tinued—and indeed remained Moscow's leading educational establishment until 1755—it became more westernized and changed its name to the Slavonic-Greek-Latin Academy.

By 1689, literature was also displaying more Western influence and becom-ing more secular, although still often concerned with morality. Because most printings were still controlled by the Orthodox Church, the new trend was most evident in manuscript writings. A century and a half earlier, Muscovite literature was typified by the reworked religious writings in the *Great Menol-ogy* and the rewritten chronicle that appeared in the *Book of Degrees of the Impe-rial Genealogy*. Metropolitan Makari, who oversaw their compilation, at-tempted to glorify Moscow and its Orthodox tsar as symbols of the only true Christian state. Their style, an ornate one thought befitting Moscow's glory, was influenced by Epiphanius's wordy "word-weaving" of a century earlier. Just as Makari's belief in Russia's religious superiority was later undercut by a combination of foreign influences and internal developments, however, so too was the type of literature and language that he championed. Although incom-plete by 1689, the transition between an old Muscovite literature dominated by religious and military works and chronicles and a newer, more secularized and Western-influenced literature, emphasizing new themes and formats, was well underway.

In seventeenth-century biography and autobiography, the transition is best exemplified in *The Life of Yuliania Lazarevsky*, by her son, and in Avvakum's au-tobiography. Although the first shares some characteristics of earlier saints' lives—for example, the occurrence of miracles—it also differs from them in many ways. Yuliania was neither a princess nor a nun, but a devout and com-passionate provincial noblewoman, a wife (later a widow), and a mother. The work is written in a straightforward style, different from the ornate word-weaving previously used for hagiography. The depiction of Yuliania is more realistic, more filled with commonplace details, and more psychologically complex and believable than earlier idealized saints' lives.

Avvakum's autobiography, written about a half-century later, is an even more striking departure. Whereas the language of Epiphanius and his follow-ers was close to Old Church Slavonic, that of Avvakum is the everyday lan-guage of late seventeenth-century Russia. It realistically conveys both his per-sonality and that of other individuals he meets. He depicts, in great detail, his struggles and hardships. No writing better captures the rough tenor of seven-

From the Autobiography of Avvakum

The following selection is translated from the first of three variants as found in *Zhitie protopopa Avvakuma im samim napisannoe* (Petrograd, 1916), Cols. 10–11, 20–21. Translation, ellipses, and bracketed material are mine.

From a widow an official took away a daughter, and I implored him to return the orphan to her mother. But he disdained our plea and raised against me a storm, and to the church he brought a mob that almost beat me to death. And I lay lifeless for more than a half hour, but was then resuscitated by God's will. And he [the official], being frightened, gave up the girl to me. Then the devil advised him, and he therefore came to the church and beat me and dragged me by my legs on the ground in my vestments, while I said a prayer.

Another official, at another time, became furious with me—he came running to my house, beat me, and gnawed my fingers, like a dog, with his teeth.

. . . There arrived in my village dancing bears, with [skomorokhi,] tambourines and domras [stringed musical instruments]. And I, a sinner, but zealous for Christ, chased them away, and their masks and tambourines I smashed in an open field beyond the village, one against many, and two great bears I took away—one I stunned, but he revived, and the other I freed in the field.

. . . Another edict arrived [in 1655] ordering me to go to Dauria, 20,000 versts [1 verst = 1.067 kilometers or 0.663 miles] and more from Moscow. They gave me over to the regiment of Afansi Pashkov—with him were 600 people. To repay me for my sins, he was a stern man: unceasingly he burned, tortured, and beat people. And I had often tried to persuade him [to act less harshly], but now I myself fell into his hands. From Nikon in Moscow, he was ordered to torment me.

When we had left Eniseisk [in Siberia], and were on the great Tuguska River, a storm completely swamped my raft: in the middle of the river it filled full of water, and its sails were torn to pieces—only the deck was above water, all else had gone into the water. My wife, though bareheaded [considered indecent for a married woman], somehow pulled the children out of the water onto the deck. But I, looking to heaven, cried out: "Lord, save us! Lord, help us!" And by God's will, the boat was thrown to shore.

teenth-century Russian life, whether in Moscow, the provinces, or Siberia. It is a first-rate Russian work, perhaps the finest of the century.

The seventeenth century also witnessed the rise of Russian fiction. *The Tale of Sava Grudtsyn* uses Church Slavonic, depicts miracles, and has good triumph over evil—after making a pact with the devil, Sava later is redeemed and becomes a monk. This 1660s' work, however, also points toward the future in being fictional, in relating Sava's affair with a married woman, and in surrounding Sava with concrete details from merchant and military life.

Another fictional work, written a few decades later, is even further removed from the old literature. This is the *Tale of Frol Skobeev, the Rogue*. Written in everyday Russian, it depicts not the triumph of good over evil, but one might almost say the opposite. Frol forces a nobleman's daughter to have sex with him, then wins her love and her parents' begrudging acceptance of him as their son-in-law. The father even gives him an estate, some money, and makes him his heir. This tale also is better constructed and displays a deeper understanding of fictional plotting than does the earlier *Tale of Sava Grudtsyn*.

A final fictional work worthy of mention is the *Tale of Shemiaka's Judgment*. It was written in the late seventeenth century and is an example of what the Russian scholar Dmitri Likhachev has called "democratic literature." It is illustrative of the increasing appearance of satirical tales—in this case directed against a corrupt judge. Although such satires were earlier popular in oral form, their appearance now in writing helped spur the development of fiction and more secularized literature in general.

Although Russian poetry, both oral and written, had certainly appeared before Simeon Polotsky, he was the first major published poet. His poems included odes, occasional pieces, a verse rendition of the Book of Psalms, and satires. He wrote on many topics, including the glory of Russia, and he saw poetry primarily as a teaching tool. Although he wrote poems in a language close to the Old Church Slavonic, the syllabic form he wrote them in resulted from new Polish influences. This form, with each line containing a fixed number of syllables, was much more suitable for Polish than for Russian. This fact, plus his moralistic didacticism and paucity of poetic inspiration, prevents his poetry from having any more than historic interest.

The few dramas Polotsky wrote also have little significance except that they were part of a first wave of such works. Before his time, there had been some dramatic religious presentations in Orthodox churches and varied dramatic presentations by the *skomorokhi* but no real Russian theater. The stimulus now came from two Western sources: Poland via Kiev and Moscow's Foreign Suburb. At the Kievan Academy, where Polotsky had been educated, didactic religious dramas were enacted. In the Foreign Suburb, private plays had also been arranged.

In 1672, Alexei asked a German pastor to put on a play for him about the Biblical Esther at his Preobrazhenskoe estate. Before his death four years later, Alexei had other plays staged for him and his court, both at Preobrazhenskoe and in Moscow. Most dealt with Biblical themes, but they also presented various combinations of large casts and sets, sound effects, music, humor, love, and violence. At the time of Alexei's death in 1676, a much bawdier drama was being prepared, *The Comedy of Bacchus and Venus*, which listed among its roles drunkards, bears, and a brothelmaster. But the new tsar, Fedor, closed the theaters at Preobrazhenskoe and in Moscow, and later the regent Sophia apparently did not feel secure enough to alienate Patriarch Joachim by restoring them. Her half-brother Peter later proved more daring.

ARCHITECTURE AND PAINTING

The late Muscovite period is also an age of transition in architecture and painting. Most illustrative of the beginning of this period is the most famous church in Russia, Red Square's St. Basil the Blessed (see Figure 8.1). Like the literary compilations of Metropolitan Makari, who also suggested building this church, it aimed at glorifying Muscovy's Christian tsardom. The church (actually an ensemble of nine separate churches) was uniquely Russian. Its central tentlike tower was influenced by the Church of the Ascension at Kolomenskoe (see Figure 6.2) and the ensemble as a whole by various other sources including Russian wooden architecture. It was built under Ivan the Terrible in the decade after Russia's victory over the Tatars at Kazan (1552)—the separate churches of the ensemble each commemorating a feast day coinciding with victorious battle days over the Moslem Tatars. Its main church and the ensemble as a whole were originally dedicated to the Intercession of the Virgin, on whose feast day the final attack on Kazan had begun. Only later, after the crypt of the holy fool Basil (Vasili) and a small church to contain it were added to the ensemble in 1588, did people start referring to it as St. Basil's.

Under Ivan the Terrible and his immediate successors, "holy Russia" was also glorified in icons and frescoes. One icon of this period, the *Church Militant*, depicts Ivan, along with Michael the Archangel, leading his victorious troops back from a burning Kazan to the holy city of Moscow. Under Ivan's two immediate successors, Fedor I and Boris Godunov, frescoes were painted in the Kremlin's Palace of Facets depicting what Makari and his associates had tried to demonstrate in their compilations: that the Riurikids were descendants of the Roman Agustus Caesar and that Vladimir Monomakh had received imperial regalia from the Byzantine emperor Constantine Monomakh.

FIGURE 12.1. The tent church on the left is that of Saints Zosima and Savvatii at the St. Sergius Monastery, Sergiev Posad, 1635–1637.

Just as in literature, so in art and architecture, foreign influences increasingly left their mark. In his attempt to reconcile Russian Church practices with those of the rest of the Orthodox world, Nikon called for a return to Byzantine architectural forms, for example, three-domed or five-domed churches. He also renounced the Russian pyramidal or tent roofs that had become popular. The five-domed Church of the Twelve Apostles, which he had constructed in the Kremlin, is more reminiscent of older churches such as the Assumption cathedrals in Vladimir or Moscow.

Nikon's zeal for Byzantine purity also led him to criticize recent Russian tendencies in icon painting. Here it was not native Russian traditions, however, but more recent Western influences on painting that were the subject of his wrath. He smashed some of the icons and ordered the gouging out of eyes and eventual burning of others. Avvakum was even more critical of the Western impact and stated:

> By God's will much unseemly foreign painting has spread over our Russian land. They paint the image of Our Saviour Emmanuel with a puffy face, and red lips, curly hair, fat arms and muscles, and stout legs and thighs. All this is done for carnal reasons, because the heretics love sensuality and do not care for higher things.[2]

[2] Quoted in George Heard Hamilton, *The Art and Architecture of Russia*, 2d ed. (Harmondsworth, England, 1975), p. 170.

FIGURE 12.2. Church of the Twelve Apostles, Moscow, Kremlin, 1652–1656.

FIGURE 12.3. Church of the Transfiguration, Novode-vichii Convent, 1687–1689.

But Avvakum was fighting a losing battle. In the icons of the late seventeenth century, more naturalistic faces and bodies, greater use of perspective, and more realistic and detailed backgrounds all reflected the Western impact. Some iconostases of the period, for example, that in the Novodevichii Convent's Cathedral of Our Lady of Smolensk, also display Western influences in their use of columns and decorative detail.

Within the Kremlin itself, in the Moscow Armoury, many Ukrainian and Belorussian artists and a handful of Western European painters worked along with Muscovites. Here the increasing westernizing tendencies of Alexei's reign were especially evidenced by the growth of secular artists. Lindsey Hughes has noted that whereas in 1675 the Armoury listed thirty icon painters and ten secular painters among its employees, by 1687–1688, it listed twenty-seven of the former and forty of the latter.

Especially indicative of this trend was the rise of portrait painting. Such portraits were evident in more westernized homes, such as that of Sophia's chief adviser, Vasili Golitsyn. Among his more than forty portraits were those of Russian and foreign rulers, one of himself, and ones of patriarchs Nikon and Joachim.

The presence of the latter two was a bit ironic: By agreeing to the painting of their portraits, they were indirectly abetting the growth of that same Western secular artistic influence that they both opposed in other manifestations.

In architecture the new trends can best be seen in the proliferation of elaborate detail and ornamentation—sometimes referred to as the "Moscow Baroque." One example of it is Novodevichii's Church of the Transfiguration (1687–1689). The painted-on false "windows" of the domes and, below them, the shell motifs, richly decorated window surrounds, and Corinthian-type columns of the exterior all reflect new foreign influences (see Figure 12.3).

The estates of the tsars in the Moscow suburbs also took on a more Western appearance in the late seventeenth century. In the late 1660s, Alexei's new wooden palace at Kolomenskoe was constructed. Despite its reflection of many of the unique elements of Russian wooden architecture, the palace, especially its interior, also displayed more modern and Western influences. They could be seen in ornate window decorations, mirrors, imported mechanical devices, portraits of the likes of Alexander the Great and Julius Caesar, a fresco depicting the world as heliocentric, and a throne guarded by two mechanical lions that could be made to roar.

Thus, in art and architecture, as in so many other aspects of seventeenth-century Russian life, a gradual evolution was under way. Later, Peter the Great accelerated the process, changing an evolution into a revolution.

SUGGESTED SOURCES*

BILLINGTON, JAMES H. *The Icon and the Axe: An Interpretive History of Russian Culture.* New York, 1970. Pts. 2–3.

BROWN, W. E. *A History of Seventeenth-Century Russian Literature.* Ann Arbor, 1980.

BRUMFIELD, WILLIAM C. *A History of Russian Architecture.* Cambridge, England, 1993. Chs. 6–7.

BUSHKOVITCH, PAUL. *Religion and Society in Russia: The Sixteenth and Seventeenth Centuries.* New York, 1992.

CHERNIAVSKY, MICHAEL. "The Old Believers and the New Religion," *SR* 25 (March 1966): 1–39.

COLLINS, SAMUEL. *The Present State of Russia, in a Letter to a Friend at London.* London, 1671.

CRUMMEY, ROBERT O. *Aristocrats and Servitors: The Boyar Elite in Russia, 1613–1689.* Princeton, 1983.

———. *The Formation of Muscovy, 1304–1613.* London, 1987. Chs. 5 and 7.

DEWEY, HORACE W., and KIRA B. STEVENS. "Muscovites at Play: Recreation in Pre-Petrine Russia," *CASS* 13, Nos. 1–2 (1979): 189–203.

FLIER, MICHAEL S., and DANIEL ROWLAND, eds. *Medieval Russian Culture.* Vol. 2. Berkeley, 1994. Contains some especially interesting articles dealing with the interrelationship of politics, religion, and religious symbolism.

*See also works cited in footnotes and in boxed insert.

GORDON, PATRICK. *Passages from the Diary of General Patrick Gordon in the Years 1635–1699.* New York, 1968.

HUGHES, LINDSEY A. J. "The Moscow Armoury and Innovations in Seventeenth-Century Muscovite Art," *CASS* 13, Nos. 1–2 (1979): 204–223.

———. "Simeon Polotskii," *MERSH* 29: 8–11.

———. "Zealots of Piety," *MERSH* 45: 213–215.

KARLINSKY, SIMON. *Russian Drama from Its Beginnings to the Age of Pushkin.* Berkeley, 1985.

KLYUCHEVSKY (KLIUCHEVSKY), V. O. *The Course of Russian History.* Vol. 3. New York, 1960.

KORTSCHMARYK, FRANK B. *The Kievan Academy and Its Role in the Organization of Education in Russia at the Turn of the Seventeenth Century.* New York, 1976.

LIKHACHEV, D. S. "Individualism in Muscovite Literature." In *RRH,* 197–205.

LUPININ, NICKOLAS. *Religious Revolt in the XVIIth Century: The Schism of the Russian Church.* Princeton, 1984.

MARKER, GARY. "Literacy and Literacy Texts in Muscovy: A Reconsideration," *SR* 49 (Spring 1990): 74–89.

MEYENDORFF, PAUL. *Russia, Ritual, and Reform.* New York, 1991.

MICHELS, GEORG. "The Solovki Uprising: Religion and Revolt in Northern Russia," *RR* 51 (January 1992): 1–15.

MILLER, DAVID B. "The Viskovatyi Affair of 1553–54: Official Art, the Emergence of Autocracy, and the Disintegration of Medieval Culture," *RH* 8, Pt. 3 (1981): 293–332.

MRECT. Among other seventeenth-century works, this collection contains Avvakum's autobiography and several of the other literary works mentioned in this chapter.

ORCHARD, G. EDWARD. "Filaret," *MERSH* 11: 126–130.

PLATONOV, S. F. *Moscow and the West.* Hattiesburg, Miss., 1972.

SZEFTEL, MARC. *Russian Institutions and Culture up to Peter the Great.* London, 1975.

TREADGOLD, DONALD W. *The West in Russia and China: Religious and Secular Thought in Modern Times.* Vol. 1, *Russia, 1472–1917.* Cambridge, England, 1973. Chs. 2–3.

USPENSKY, BORIS A. "The Schism and Cultural Conflict in the Seventeenth Century." In *Seeking God: The Recovery of Religious Identity in Orthodox Russia, Ukraine, and Georgia,* ed. Stephen K. Batalen. DeKalb, Ill., 1993.

VOYCE, ARTHUR. *Moscow and the Roots of Russian Culture.* Norman, Okla., 1964.

ZENKOVSKY, SERGE A. "The Russian Church Schism," *RR* 16, No. 4 (1957): 37–58.

ZGUTA, RUSSELL. *Russian Minstrels: A History of the Skomorokhi.* Philadelphia, 1978.

PART FOUR

Early Imperial Russia, 1689–1855

During the Early Imperial period, autocracy and serfdom continued to flourish, and the period's last ruler, Nicholas I, staunchly defended autocracy as one of Russia's main pillars. Following the example of the era's first ruler, Peter the Great, his successors generally presented themselves as "reforming tsars," desiring to rule Russia in an enlightened manner. Their reforms, however, like Peter's earlier creation of the Holy Synod to replace the Russian Orthodox patriarch, were not intended to weaken autocracy. Rather they were to be manifestations of an enlightened absolutism that would strengthen Russia.

To help them rule, Russia's rulers depended on the nobility. Peter the Great attempted to broaden access to it so that talented nonnobles could more easily obtain noble status. Throughout most of this period, however, a small number of aristocratic clans dominated Russia's ruling class. But by the early nineteenth century,

growing state needs for more talented military and civilian personnel led Russia's rulers steadily to increase the number of nonnobles able to obtain noble status. Furthermore, by the mid-nineteenth century, a significant minority of high-ranking bureaucrats, even some born into the hereditary nobility, were not serfowners, and they did not especially identify with their fellow nobles who owned estates worked by serfs. By 1855, the nobility was less unified and the landed nobility less powerful than during Catherine the Great's reign (1762–1796).

Although tsarist powers remained legally unlimited throughout this period, there were practical limits. The Russian Empire was simply too large, and the number of faithful government officials too small, for tsarist decrees ever to be complied with to the extent the rulers desired. In Russia's provincial towns and villages, the everyday lives of nobles, townspeople, and peasants were de-

223

termined more by tradition and inertia than by any new laws.

Furthermore, tsars who overstepped the bounds of what the noble elite considered legitimate autocratic behavior could be overthrown, as both Peter III (husband of Catherine the Great) and Paul (father of Alexander I and Nicholas I) tragically discovered. To prevent such coups, most tsars remained mindful of noble interests. Such concern helps explain why no tsar of the era attempted to dismantle serfdom.

Despite opposition to specific tsarist policies, the only notable challenges to the autocratic concept itself were a feeble aristocratic effort in 1730 and a failed conspiracy of 1825. Other opposition to autocracy was limited to the isolated voices of a small number of intellectuals, beginning in the late eighteenth century.

As autocracy and serfdom continued, so too did Russian expansion. From Finland in the north to the Black Sea coast and the Caucasus in the south, the empire added new lands. By 1855, it also included Estonia, Latvia, Lithuania, all of Belorussia, most of Poland and Ukraine, and Bessarabia. Further east, Russia expanded into Kazakhstan, and in the northeast, onto the North American continent.

The government gradually integrated its outlying regions more firmly with its Russian center. Catherine the Great centralized primarily because of her concern for orderliness and efficiency. Nicholas I shared such concerns. But by his time, nationalism had become a greater force, and his emphasis on Russian nationalism and Russian Orthodoxy helped fuel his centralizing policies.

Many of Russia's territorial gains resulted from wars. Peter the Great was almost constantly at war, Catherine the Great fought two wars against the Ottoman Turks, Alexander I withstood and defeated the great Napoleonic challenge, and Nicholas I died in the midst of the Crimean War, a losing effort that helped propel the reforms of his successor, Alexander II.

During this era, Western influences became much stronger in Russia. This was partly because the empire's rulers, court circles, and elite attempted to use Western ideas, methods, and symbols to bolster their authority and strengthen Russia. As Richard Wortman has pointed out, such an adoption of foreign symbols and ceremonies was not new and was a way of underlining superiority: "foreignness established symbolic distance between the ruler and the ruling elite and the subject population."[1]

But Western influences also produced nationalistic reactions. While not abandoning a selective use of Western symbols and methods, Nicholas I reflected the age of nationalism in which he lived by placing more emphasis on Russian traditions. During his reign, a group of intellectuals known as Slavophiles criticized the policies of Peter I for creating a cultural gap between a small westernized elite and the Russian masses, who remained committed to traditional Russian ways. The Slavophiles were answered by another group known as Westernizers, and by the early 1840s, a full-scale debate was under way concerning Russia's relationship to the West.

---

[1] *Scenarios of Power: Myth and Ceremony in Russian Monarchy*, Vol. 1, *From Peter the Great to the Death of Nicholas I* (Princeton, 1995), p. 407.

CHAPTER 13

Peter the Great

No tsar was more dynamic or energetic than that giant of rulers, Peter I. No tsar attempted to accomplish as much. He waged war almost constantly, gained Baltic territory, built St. Petersburg, made Russia a major European power, conquered Caspian territories from Persia, and dreamed of a still greater global role for Russia. In the process, he created a more bureaucratized government, expanded governmental controls and industry, and greatly accelerated westernization and secular ideas, including a new secularized concept of tsarist authority. The burden he imposed was heavy and distasteful to many. There was much opposition to him and his policies, though little of it seemed immediately effective. In the long run, however, inertia, the nobles, and Russian tradition were able to negate or reduce the effects of some of his reforms.

YOUTH AND PERSONALITY

When Peter ousted his half-sister Sophia as regent, he was only seventeen. Years of rivalry between his mother's family (the Naryshkins) and that of Sophia (the Miloslavskys) had exposed him to political intrigue. His formal education was slight. He learned to read, write, memorize scriptural passages, and sing some church songs. He also studied a little arithmetic, geography, and history. His lively curiosity, however, coupled with his dynamic (almost hyperactive) energy and enthusiasm, enabled him to learn much on his own.

His favorite games were military ones. After Sophia became regent in 1682, he spent much time at Preobrazhenskoe, a royal property a few miles northeast of Moscow. There amidst fields and woods, he played at soldiering with other youngsters, both noble and more plebeian. Because Peter was co-tsar—and Sophia at first apparently saw no harm in indulging her half-brother—he was able to order real firearms and cannon from the royal arsenal. His "play" increasingly became like real military training. As his small regiment grew, Preobrazhenskoe could no longer hold all the boy soldiers, so Peter relocated some to another nearby royal property, Semenovskoe. He also turned to foreign officers and technicians residing in the Foreign Suburb to help train his young soldiers and himself.

In these youthful years, he first displayed his willingness to mix with those much less royal than himself. Rather than immediately taking the highest rank, he served first as a drummer in the lower ranks of his Preobrazhenskii Regiment. He ate, slept, and worked along with the other young soldiers. One who drilled with Peter was the commoner Alexander Menshikov—later opponents claimed he had once peddled pirozhki and cakes in Moscow streets. He eventually became Peter's most trusted assistant and the second most powerful man in Russia.

Peter was fascinated with almost all types of "hands-on" activities. He learned stonemasonry, carpentry, printing, metalworking, and, most importantly, sailing and boatbuilding. Later, he boasted of having acquired many other skills, including shoemaking and—probably to the dismay of any around him who unthinkingly complained of a toothache—dentistry. The mature Peter also displayed a lively interest in architecture and other visual arts.

Peter was about six foot, seven inches tall and solidly built. His gigantic stature along with his inexhaustible energy and autocratic powers combined to make him one of history's most unforgettable personalities. The Duke of St. Simon left the following description after observing Peter in France in 1717:

> What he ate and drank at his two regular meals is inconceivable . . . a bottle or
> two of beer, as many more of wine, and, occasionally, liquors afterward; at the
> end of the meal strong drinks, such as brandy, as much sometimes as a quart.

Peter rose early, worked long hours, moving from one place to another with fast, long strides. When his feet were not moving, his hands often were, and his residences were full of model boats, snuffboxes, chairs, and other artifacts he made himself. He even moved at times involuntarily: As an adult, he suffered from an occasional twitching of his face, which sometimes became severe enough also to affect the left side of his neck and his left arm.

Rashness, a bad temper, coarseness, and insensitivity were among Peter's chief faults. When angry, he sometimes knocked to the floor even the best of his friends. In the early 1690s, he created "the Most Drunken Council of Fools and Jesters," which devoted itself to heavy drinking and making fun of the Catholic and Orthodox hierarchy and rituals. It continued to operate throughout his reign. He also liked to force alcohol upon others. He and his second wife, Catherine, even acquired two white bears who had been trained to serve vodka and harass those who refused.

At times, Peter's insensitivity, plus his coarseness and temper, made him seem cruel. The era's harsh laws and customs for dealing with political opposition also contributed to such an image. The imprisonment and torture of his son Alexei, who died in prison in 1718, calls to mind Ivan the Terrible's killing of his son Ivan. But Peter was more rational and less bloodthirsty than this earlier tsar.

Although Peter was far from being a faithful husband (with either of his two wives), his relationship to women was also more stable than that of the

---

Mandatory Drinking for Peter's "Guests"

The following selection is from an ambassador from Hanover, Friedrich Christian Weber, *The Present State of Russia* (London, 1722–1723), Vol. I, pp. 93–94. In this excerpt, he writes of two partial days in mid-1715 spent by him and some other foreign diplomats with Peter at Peterhof, his new summer retreat on the Gulf of Finland. I have modernized the spellings and taken a few liberties with punctuation; bracketed material and ellipses are mine.

[We] were entertained there as usual: For at dinner we were so plied with Tockay wine, though his Tsarist Majesty forbore drinking too much, that at our breaking up, we were hardly able to stand. Nevertheless we were obliged to empty each a bowl holding a full quart, which we received from the Tsarina's own hand, whereupon we quite lost our senses, and were in that pickle carried off to sleep, some in the garden, others in the wood, *and the rest here and there on the ground. . . . At supper [before which Peter had forced them to spend about three hours helping him cut down trees] . . . we received such another dose of liquor as sent us senseless to bed; but having scarcely slept an hour and [a] half, a certain favorite of the tsar's was sent about midnight to rouse us, and carry us, willing or unwilling, to the Prince of Circassia, who was already abed with his consort, where we were again by their bedside pestered with wine and brandy till four in the morning. That next day none of us remembered how he got home. About eight we were invited to court to breakfast, but instead of coffee and tea, as we expected, we were welcomed with large cups of brandy. . . . We had the fourth drinking-bout at dinner [after which Peter displayed his seamanship by sailing off with them in the Gulf of Finland for what proved to be about seven hours, most of it in a frightening storm].*

---

many-wived Ivan the Terrible. Peter's mother arranged his first marriage to Evdokiia Lopukhina in 1689, but ten years later Peter forced her to become a nun. There were apparently only two women that he ever really loved: Anna Mons, daughter of a German merchant and his mistress for over a decade, and Catherine, the daughter of a Lithuanian peasant, whom Peter took up with in 1703, married privately in 1707, and publicly in 1712.

THE OUSTING OF SOPHIA AND THE FIRST DECADE OF PETER'S REIGN, 1689–1699

When in the summer of 1689, Sophia tried to glorify Golitsyn's unsuccessful Crimean campaign, Peter, now seventeen years old, objected. Tensions and suspicions between her followers and those of Peter increased. On August 7, when Peter heard that *streltsy* and soldiers of the guard had been ordered to Preobrazhenskoe (where Peter was residing) "to put certain persons to death," he rode some forty miles to the well-fortified St. Sergius Monastery. For almost a month, a stand-off ensued, but as Peter's support grew, Sophia's diminished, especially among a now divided *streltsy*. Patriarch Joachim also went over to

FIGURE 13.1. The Intercession (Pokrovskii) Convent, Suzdal, the convent where Peter I sent his first wife, Evdokiia. Several other earlier discarded royal wives, including the first wife of Vasili III, also ended up here.

Peter's side. In early September, Peter's supporters forced Sophia into confinement in the Novodevichii Convent and soon afterwards dispatched Vasili Golitsyn to a far northern exile, where he was kept until his death, twenty-five years later.

Although Peter's half-brother, the feeble Ivan V, continued as co-tsar until his death in 1696, Peter's rule was now unchallenged. Yet for the next five years, until his mother's death in 1694, Peter left the running of government to his mother, his uncle Leo Naryshkin, and other boyar supporters. Meanwhile, Peter concentrated his energies on his latest passions, especially shipbuilding. With the help of some Dutchmen, Peter built and sailed ships on Lake Pleshcheevo, near (Northern) Pereiaslavl. In 1693, he headed for larger waters—those of the White Sea. At nearby Archangel, he saw his first big foreign merchant ships, and he began constructing a warship and ordered a forty-four gun frigate (*The Holy Prophecy*) built in Holland.

Peter also became thoroughly at home in the Foreign Suburb and there developed several important friendships. One was with the Swiss Franz Lefort, a charming, adventuresome army officer with a notorious capacity for alcohol. Lefort was frequently surrounded by women, one of whom, the beautiful Anna Mons, soon became Peter's lover. Older and more important than Lefort was the Scottish general Patrick Gordon, who had been the chief foreign officer to support Peter in 1689. He now befriended the young Peter. Lefort was most instrumental in introducing Peter to a light-hearted world of wine, women, and song, whereas the older Gordon was a more sobering influence and became his chief military tutor.

A year after his mother's death in 1694, Peter went to war against Turkey. Following Golitsyn's unsuccessful efforts, there had been a lull but no formal peace. Tatars still sporadically raided Russian territory. And Poland and Austria, still fighting the Turks, encouraged Russia to renew its campaign against them. Peter's own military and seafaring enthusiasms; fears of gaining less than Russia's allies when peace finally came; and Russia's animosity toward the Moslem Turks, who ruled over so many Orthodox Christians, were additional reasons for a new Turkish campaign.

The main target was the fortress town of Azov. It lay at the mouth of the Don River, upstream from where it flowed into the Sea of Azov. Command of the fortress and the nearby sea (which flowed into the Black Sea) would threaten the Crimean Tatars and secure a base for any further moves in the Black Sea and Caucasus.

With Lefort and Gordon among his commanders, Peter and his troops besieged Azov in the summer of 1695. Although a lack of warships hindered Peter from immediately gaining his objective, he was undeterred by this setback. He drafted men to build ships and boats, and he took part in shipbuilding at Voronezh. In late spring 1696, he again attacked Azov; in late July 1696, the Turkish pasha defending it surrendered.

Peter now oversaw the creation of a town, harbor, and naval base at Taganrog, on the sea of Azov. He ordered clerical and lay landowners to contribute to building ships, mostly at Voronezh, where Peter had gathered about fifty Western shipwrights. Moreover, he sent a similar number of Russians to Western Europe to learn shipbuilding techniques and, even more dramatically, decided to learn more himself by a long visit to the West.

Thus, for eighteen months in 1697–1698, Peter traveled in Western Europe, spending about half the time in the two great maritime powers of Holland and England. (He did not visit France until a second, shorter trip to Western Europe in 1717, two years after the death of the Sun King, Louis XIV.) Despite the obvious difficulties of concealing the identity of a six-foot-seven tsar, Peter made Lefort the nominal leader of his traveling "Great Embassy" and started out himself, supposedly incognito, as one "Peter Mikhailov." The main stated purpose of the 1697–1698 embassy was to forge a large anti-Turkish coalition, but not much came of these efforts.

Peter, however, did gain valuable diplomatic experience, and his other goals for the trip were more successful. He learned much, especially in the shipyards of Holland and England, and about applied science and technology generally. He recruited more than 750 Western experts and skilled craftsmen and purchased materials to strengthen his shipbuilding and other military efforts at home. Although he paid little attention to more abstract matters or to political institutions like the British Parliament, the practical Western ways and prosperity he did observe influenced him for the rest of his life.

Peter would have stayed even longer in the West, but while in Vienna in the summer of 1698, he received word of a *streltsy* revolt at home. Even before he returned to Russia in September, however, troops under Patrick Gordon and other commanders had suppressed the revolt. Peter now oversaw six months of gruesome tortures, mutilations, and executions—about 1100 of the latter—and sent most surviving *streltsy* to southern posts. Although he found no proof that his half-sister Sophia was implicated in the plot, he forced her to become a nun at the Novodevichii Convent (see Figure 9.1), where she already had been confined, and hanged three *streltsy* outside her window.

THE GREAT NORTHERN WAR AND
FOREIGN AFFAIRS, 1700–1725

On the way from Vienna to Moscow, Peter stopped in Poland, where he talked of joint anti-Swedish activities with the new Polish king, Augustus II. To Peter's sea-loving mind, Sweden must have seemed a natural target, for it still controlled the Baltic ports that Ivan the Terrible had fought so long and unsuccessfully to win.

By mid-1700, the time for attacking Sweden seemed ripe. Its ruler, Charles XII, was only eighteen. His country's gradual rise to Baltic dominance had created many enemies. Earlier in the year, Poland, Denmark, and Saxony (also ruled by King Augustus II of Poland) had gone to war against Sweden. Realizing that he could not successfully fight the Turks and Swedes at the same time and that Austria was unwilling to join in his anti-Turkish effort, Peter formally ended the Turkish war—keeping Azov and Taganrog—and the next month (August 1700) declared war on Sweden.

Unfortunately for Peter, and unbeknownst to him, while he was declaring war, Denmark was capitulating. A few months later at Narva, without either Lefort or Gordon, both of whom had died the previous year, Peter's troops were routed in a snowstorm. The victory went to a much smaller army under Charles XII, who was already proving to be a great military tactician.

Yet Charles was no genius at strategic planning, for he failed to follow up his victory and for the next six years mired himself in a war with Poland. This allowed Peter time to regroup and build up his forces, which he did with his customary vigor. He drafted more and more peasants and townsmen, reorganized military units, and even ordered some church bells melted down to produce more cannons.

In 1703, Peter captured the mouth of the Neva River along the Gulf of Finland. Nearby, he soon began building a fortress, that of Sts. Peter and Paul (see Figure 18.1), and a new city, St. Petersburg. During the next several years, he won additional victories in the Baltic area, continued his military buildup, and sent an army to Poland to aid in the fight against Charles XII.

But the Swedish king was still able to defeat Augustus II and in 1706 force him to relinquish his Polish crown. Charles then faced Russian troops in Poland and Ukraine. Unhappy with Peter, the Ukrainian hetman, Mazepa, and some of his Cossacks went over to Charles XII's side. Others, however, were opposed to the Protestant Swedish forces, and after Russian forces in 1708–1709 destroyed the hetman's capital of Baturin and the Zaporozhian Sech (main settlement), Ukrainian opposition to Peter's policies diminished.

The decisive Russo-Swedish battle occurred at Poltava, about 200 miles southeast of Kiev. There in late June 1709, a Swedish force of about 22,000 was met and defeated by a Russian army almost twice its size. While the vigorous Peter led the Russian troops into combat, Charles had been seriously wounded in the foot shortly before the big battle and was not able to play his usual active role. Although most Swedish troops were forced to surrender, Charles, Mazepa, and a small force of Swedes and Cossacks escaped to Moldavia and Ottoman protection.

For Peter and Russia, Poltava was a turning point in the war and thrust Russia forward as a major European power. After Poltava, Russia was respected and feared. Foreign rulers became anxious to improve their ties with Russia through regular diplomatic relations and dynastic marriages. Two of Peter's nieces soon married Baltic dukes: Anna, to the Duke of Courland in 1710, and Catherine, to the Duke of Mecklenburg in 1716. In 1711, Peter gained the hand of Charlotte of Brunswick-Wolfenbuttel for his son Alexei. But success also brought the increased wariness of foreign powers like England, concerned about growing Russian ascendance in the Baltic.

Following Poltava, Russia won additional battles against Sweden, including Baltic victories in 1710. Before the fruits of Poltava and these other victories could be fully enjoyed, however, Peter had one more major obstacle to overcome—a new war thrust upon him by the Ottoman Turks. The Ottoman government was upset with Russia's demand that Charles XII be expelled from the Ottoman Empire. For varied other reasons, Charles, Louis XIV of France, and the Crimean khan encouraged Turkish hostility to Russia. Thus, in late 1710, the Turkish sultan arrested and incarcerated the Russian ambassador, Peter Tolstoi, and declared war.

The following summer, Peter I, accompanied by Catherine, found himself in a similar position to that of Charles XII at Poltava. He was also now in enemy territory, some 300 miles southwest of Poltava on the Pruth River. There, short of supplies, he found his troops greatly outnumbered and in danger of complete humiliation. His fate was not to be that of Charles XII's, however; rather than see his army completely crushed, he sought terms from the Turkish commander. Peter's position was so bad that he was prepared to concede a great deal: Azov, Taganrog, his gains from a decade of fighting Sweden (except St. Petersburg), and even additional northern territory such as Pskov.

Yet, for reasons that still remain mysterious, the Turkish grand vizier did not fully press his advantage. He demanded only that Peter give up Azov and other gains of 1696, abandon his Black Sea fleet, evacuate Poland, and allow King Charles XII to return to Sweden.

In the decade after the Russo-Turkish war of 1710–1711, Peter continued the Northern War against Sweden. Charles XII died in 1718, and three years later the war came to an end with the Treaty of Nystad. By its terms, Russia gained a wide stretch of Baltic and northern territory, from just south of Riga to about 200 miles north of St. Petersburg. Peter now officially had his "window

European Russia and Europe during the Reign of Peter the Great

Baltic lands gained from Sweden by the Treaty of Nystadt, 1721

Caspian territory gained from Persia in War of 1722–23; regained by Persia by 1735

Major areas of opposition and revolt against the Russian government

0   300   600 Miles

MAP 13.1

Barents Sea

White Sea

Archangel

Ural Mountains

KHANATE OF KHIVA

PERSIA

Caspian Sea

Baku

Derbent

Caucasus

Ufa

Bashkirs

Kazan

Samara

Ural R.

Kalmyks

Volga R.

Tsaritsyn

Astrakhan

Penza

Tambov

Voronezh

Don R.

Don Cossacks

Azov

Sea of Azov

Taganrog

Yaroslavl

N. Pereiaslavl

Moscow

Lesnaia

Baturin

Poltava

Zaporozhian Cossacks

Sech

Black Sea

Constantinople

OTTOMAN EMPIRE

Novgorod

Pskov

Dnieper R.

Kiev

Dniester R.

Pruth R.

MOLDAVIA

WALLACHIA

BULGARIA

St. Petersburg

Neva R.

Viborg

Gulf of Finland

Reval

Narva

Riga

Courland

Baltic Sea

KINGDOM OF SWEDEN

PRUSSIA

Warsaw

POLAND

HUNGARY

MECKLEN-BURG

SAXONY

AUSTRIA

Vienna

HOLY ROMAN EMPIRE

ITALIAN STATES

Rome

KINGDOM OF NAPLES

KINGDOM OF DENMARK

North Sea

HOLLAND

GREAT BRITAIN

London

FRANCE

Paris

ATLANTIC OCEAN

SPAIN

Mediterranean Sea

on the sea," and the new Latvian and Estonian territories and their peoples, including the Baltic German upper class, would make an important contribution to the Russian Empire in the days ahead—Russia formally became the Russian Empire after Peter celebrated the treaty by adopting the title "Emperor."

In a war of 1722–1723, Peter expanded his empire at Persia's expense. By it he gained control over the western and southern coast of the Caspian Sea—but Russia's hold on the territory was tenuous, disease took a heavy toll on the Russians stationed there, and within a decade Russia relinquished control over it.

In Central Asia, Peter wished to expand Russian influence because of its trade routes and rumored gold. He dispatched a military expedition to the khanate of Khiva, but the Russian troops aroused the ire of the khan and were killed or enslaved in 1717. Attempts in the early 1720s to establish a trade agreement with India and broaden trade with China also failed. Peter was more successful, however, in expanding Russia's holdings in Siberia, even claiming the Kurile Islands, which stretched from the Kamchatka Peninsula to Japan. Shortly before his death, Peter sent out the Danish-born Captain Vitus Bering (dubbed the "Russian Christopher Columbus" by the poet Lomonosov) to explore the area connecting America and Asia. There Bering discovered the strait that now bears his name and stretches fifty-two miles between Alaska and Siberia.

DOMESTIC CHANGES AND REFORMS

Shortly after returning from abroad in 1697–1698, Peter began cutting the beards of his boyars and demanding that they abandon their long Russian caftans and switch to less cumbersome Western attire. He also later demanded or encouraged others to follow suit, although the clergy and peasants, who thought it sinful for a man to be without a beard, were exempted from the new regulations. Others had to pay a graduated tax or fine if they wished to maintain their old ways, and even peasants had to pay a small "beard tax" if they wished to enter a town.

In 1699, Peter insisted that the Russian year no longer begin on September 1 or be counted from the supposed creation of the world, but rather that it begin January 1 and the new year be 1700—not 7208—since henceforth years were to be reckoned from the birth of Christ.

These changes dramatically foreshadowed many others. Indeed some, such as with the military, had already begun. Although these changes are usually called "reforms," many of Peter's subjects did not think of them as improvements.

One motive, above all others, stands out for his reforms (we will use the term for convenience' sake): Peter's desire for a stronger Russia, militarily and otherwise. More a doer than a systematic thinker, Peter often moved intuitively toward this goal. To achieve it, he attacked numerous Russian traditions and attempted to replace them with practices based more on Western ideas.

FIGURE 13.2. An Old Believer is about to lose his beard. The barber is apparently Peter the Great. *(From Ian Grey,* The Horizon History of Russia, *American Heritage Publishing Company, New York, 1970, p. 160.)*

His youthful experiences and his trip to Western Europe disposed him toward such an approach.

Military Reform

New style and better equipped regiments created under Tsar Alexei, plus others like the Preobrazhenskii and Semenovskii Regiments formed early in Peter's reign, created the basis for a more modern army. But the Great Northern War, along with the disbanding of the Moscow *streltsy* after the revolt of 1698, necessitated more extreme measures.

To build his army, Peter at first generated more volunteers by promises of better pay. He also drafted household serfs and slaves, who were delivered by their masters according to a quota system. As the war continued for two decades, one levy after another demanded more draftees—John Keep estimates that during Peter's reign there were altogether fifty-three levies, general and partial, and that more than 300,000 were inducted. The levies often differed on the quota of recruits demanded. One big levy in 1705 required one recruit per 20 households, but from 1713 to 1724 the quota varied from one per 40 to one per 250 households. These draftees were overwhelmingly peasants, both serf and nonserf, and townsmen, and they were drafted for life. By 1725,

Russia had an army of about 200,000 regular troops and about 100,000 others (mainly Cossacks)—roughly 40 percent larger than the army of 1681.

But improved quality more than quantity distinguished the new Russian army. Units were better organized, better trained, and better equipped than earlier. A more professional Russian officer class now reduced dependency on foreign officers. Despite Peter's principle of promotion according to merit, officers were overwhelmingly from the noble class—the disadvantaged backgrounds of commoners usually ill preparing them for competition for officer ranks. Peter also improved the pay and status of officers, especially in elite units like the Preobrazhenskii Regiment.

Infantry were armed with flintlock muskets and relied heavily on the bayonet. Before a bayonet attack (which was accompanied by shouts of "ura!"), artillery fire attempted to soften up the enemy. Domestic production of weapons greatly increased.

Having created a Russian navy, Peter continued its buildup throughout his reign, and it helped him defeat Sweden. By 1725, Russia's Baltic fleet possessed almost 50 large warships and close to 800 other vessels—a much smaller number of ships also remained in the Caspian Sea. Many of Peter's ships were built at the new Admiralty shipyard in St. Petersburg, which employed thousands of workers. Peter also constructed an important naval base, Kronstadt, on Kotlin Island, which guarded the entrance to the Neva River and St. Petersburg.

St. Petersburg and the Government

Although little more than some Finnish huts stood at the Neva's marshy mouth when Peter decided to build a city there, by 1712 St. Petersburg had become the new capital. From Peter's perspective, it had much to recommend it, primarily its access to the Baltic and the West and its newness. It provided Peter a clean slate, free of the tangled traditions of Moscow. But this "Venice of the North" also had many disadvantages: its extreme northern location (comparable to Juneau, Alaska), which kept the Neva frozen five months a year; the frequent flooding that inundated the city at spring thaw; its unhealthy, damp climate; its poor crop potential; and its vulnerability to foreign attack.

Peter, however, was not about to let such considerations stop him. Every year, 10,000 to 30,000 peasants were brought in to help build the new capital. By 1725, besides all the temporary workers, about 40,000 permanent residents lived in the city, most of them brought by Peter's decrees. Here he ordered artisans to settle and wealthy nobles and merchants to build houses. In 1714, in a move to obtain more masons, he even issued a decree prohibiting masonry construction in other parts of the country.

Although some workers brought to the city soon fled and others died in the unhealthy marshy climate, Peter persisted. Influenced by what he had seen in the great port city of Amsterdam, he constructed a Russian city of canals, straight streets, parks, as many stone buildings as possible, and even some streetlamps. To provide for construction, he ordered all carts and ships entering the city to bring in a specified quantity of stones. Gradually, under Peter and his successors, a wondrous new capital emerged—beautifully described by Alexander Pushkin in his poem "The Bronze Horseman." The new capital came to symbolize both Peter and all he stood for, including a government more westernized than its Muscovite predecessor.

By the late 1690s, the government still consisted of a Boyar Council, more than forty *prikazy* (government bureaus), and the *voevody* (local governors or commanders). The Boyar Council's significance continued to decline, however, and after 1700, it ceased to play any meaningful role. From the beginning, Peter had relied more on his own hand-picked group of advisers, who included both men from the old boyar aristocracy and newcomers like Menshikov and Lefort.

By 1708, Peter had appointed those personally close to him to head eight large guberniias (regions) into which he now divided the country. The primary function of the new regional governors was to improve Russia's military capability, but the reform also served to decentralize power from Moscow in the transitional period when the central government was being moved from Moscow to St. Petersburg.

In 1711, before departing to battle the Turks, Peter established a nine-man Senate to run the government in his absence. After his return, he made it a permanent institution, which filled the vacuum left by the now defunct Boyar Council. It soon oversaw provincial administration and tax-collecting and served as the country's highest judicial body. To help it uncover tax evasion and other crimes that would weaken Russia and its military efforts, Peter directed it to appoint an *oberfiscal*. Although the *oberfiscal* and his hundreds of *fiscals* (agents) were responsible to the Senate, they could also investigate senators, leading to some conflict between the two groups.

Although Peter eventually asked the Senate to deal with and advise him on many matters, he never gave it much trust or autonomy. He was forever issuing orders instructing senators how to act and threatening them with fines and worse if they failed to comply. And he did not merely threaten; in 1715, for example, two senators had their tongues branded. Furthermore, Peter appointed various officials to supervise the Senate's work, culminating in the 1722 appointment of a procurator general. The latter was to be the tsar's representative at Senate meetings, and none of its decisions was valid without his approval. He was also placed in charge of the *fiscals* and of newly created procurators, who were to investigate provincial justice to insure it was being applied according to the law.

Meanwhile, Peter created some new *prikazy* and reorganized others. The most interesting new *prikaz* was the Preobrazhenskii *prikaz*. Although Peter initially established it to deal with the Preobrazhenskii Regiment's administrative matters, by 1697 it had become a political police (and sentencing authority) with all-encompassing jurisdiction throughout the country. Often acting on the basis of denunciations, it used torture on both suspects and denouncers to ferret out crimes directed against the tsar and government.

But the overlapping functions of so many *prikazy* offended Peter's sense of order and efficiency. In 1717–1718, he began replacing most of them—the Preobrazhenskii *prikaz* being a notable exception—with "colleges." Similar institutions already existed in Sweden and Prussia. At first, Peter created nine of them, each supervising a certain sphere: foreign affairs, army, navy, justice, and five dealing with different financial and economic matters. In theory, if not usually in practice, they were to be run in a collegial (or collective) fashion—thus their name—by a small group of officials at the top of each college. In 1721, Peter placed the colleges under Senate authority and soon afterward also under the watchful eyes of the procurator general's staff of procurators.

Despite all of Peter's attempts to mold an efficient, hard-working, and honest centralized government, his own chief supervisor, the procurator general, told him: "We all steal, the only difference being that some are bigger and more conspicuous thieves than others."

In 1719, by which time the Northern War was almost over and most of his new centralized government institutions were in existence, Peter decreased the powers of the regional governors he had earlier appointed. During that same year, the guberniias over which they ruled (by now there were eleven of them) were subdivided into forty-five (later fifty) provinces and the provinces into districts. These changes were intended to facilitate the transition from wartime to civilian rule. Peter had ambitious plans for further transforming local government, but little of any lasting value developed, partly because his plans depended too much on foreign models unsuited to Russian reality. Throughout almost all of Russia, local government served as little more than an extension of the central state.

FIGURE 13.3. Medieval towers and churches of Reval. This important Baltic City (modern-day Tallinn in Estonia) was taken by Peter's forces in 1710.

The newly conquered Baltic area, encompassing most of present-day Estonia and Latvia, was somewhat of an exception. Baltic German nobles and merchants had long dominated the region and maintained substantial autonomy under Swedish control. Following Peter's Baltic conquests, he continued to allow considerable local autonomy, despite occasional flashes of autocratic behavior.

Left-Bank Ukraine was not so fortunate. Following Mazepa's defection to Sweden's Charles XII, Peter increased Russian control in Ukraine. He appointed a Russian to command the Cossack forces, gave substantial Ukrainian lands to favorites such as Menshikov, and closely restricted Ukrainian publications. Most significantly in 1722, he established a "Little Russian College," consisting of six Russian officers stationed in Ukraine; they were to share power with the hetman who had taken Mazepa's place. At the same time, the Russian government imposed direct taxes on Ukrainians. By 1724, the chairman of the Little Russian College claimed to be collecting six times the previous revenues taken from the Hetmanate. When the old hetman died in 1722, Peter delayed approving a new one and shortly thereafter imprisoned an acting hetman and others who had petitioned him on behalf of Ukrainian self-rule.

Peter, Political Theory, and the Orthodox Church

In reorganizing Russia's government, Peter often acted hastily, partly because of pressing military concerns. During his last decade, however, as military pressures eased, his changes were motivated by a more comprehensive and articulated political theory.

Muscovite theory had stressed the tsar's conservative role as a maintainer of true Orthodoxy and Orthodox society, but Peter now emphasized a more activist, reformistic, and secular tsarist rule. The imagery and symbols that glorified his power were borrowed more from those of the West, including those of the old Roman Empire, than from the older tsarist tradition. One Russian forerunner he did make good use of was the early Russian warrior-prince Alexander Nevsky. Peter emphasized his own similarity to Nevsky the conqueror and reburied Nevsky's remains in the new capital's Nevsky Monastery.

Peter also viewed himself as the chief overseer and catalyst of economic growth, good citizenship, education, social welfare, and respect for law. In contrast to earlier theorizing about tsarist powers, Peter relied less on religious arguments and more on "Reason."

His westernizing proclivities, his quest for efficiency, and his contempt for many old customs and traditions made him especially susceptible to some rational (and scientific-technological) influences of the European "Age of Reason." Thinkers like Newton and Leibniz were his contemporaries. The latter, although he never set foot in Russia, even acted as a paid consultant to Peter.

Peter's many decrees, issued in unprecedented numbers, reflected the influence of Reason. In them, he mentioned frequently "the general good" and "the interests of the state," and he took great pains to explain how various decrees would serve these ends. He wanted reason—as he interpreted it, of course—to rule Russia, not a ruler's caprice, not the interests of upper-class clans, not the deadweight of custom, and not church authority.

To insure as little church interference as possible, Peter blocked a new patriarchal election when the conservative Patriarch Adrian died in 1700. Instead, for the next two decades, Peter relied on Metropolitan Stefan Yavorsky to administer the church.

Peter also depended on two other important Orthodox clerics, Feodosi Yanovsky and Feofan Prokopovich. Like Yavorsky, both men had been educated at the Kiev Academy but were more sympathetic to Protestant political theory than was Yavorsky. Peter was especially interested in Protestant thinking that justified monarchical control over church affairs.

Protestant influence can clearly be seen in Peter's *Ecclesiastical Regulation* of 1721, mainly drafted by Prokopovich. This statute formally ended the patriarchate, which Peter distrusted, and in its place created an Ecclesiastical College, originally of ten clergymen. Although Peter soon agreed that it could instead be called "the Most Holy Synod," its original name makes its paternity clear: It was to be the branch of government that supervised the Orthodox Church, just as the Foreign Affairs College supervised foreign affairs. To make this even clearer, in 1722 Peter named a chief procurator, a colonel in one of his Guards regiments, to oversee the synod's work.

By Peter's policies, any surviving autonomous church authority was dealt an almost fatal blow. The emperor now appointed the synod's members and had the right to choose, from synod nominees, the Russian Orthodox bishops. Furthermore, documents of the early 1720s indicate that priests were expected to administer loyalty oaths to all but peasants and report information obtained in confession about any intended criminal activity, especially of a rebellious or treasonous nature.

If bringing the clergy under firm state control was one of Peter's goals, another was to pare it down. He thought too many joined the clergy to avoid taxes and state service. He was especially contemptuous of monks, whom he considered lazy, and he issued decrees aimed at limiting their numbers and making them more "productive." Although these measures decreased the number of monks and nuns and increased state revenue from the monasteries, Peter failed to pare the number of priests. In fact, from the early 1720s to the late 1730s, their number grew faster than that of monks and nuns declined.

Toward non-Orthodox religions, Peter was more openly tolerant than previous rulers. His non-Orthodox friends from the Foreign Suburb, his early trip abroad, his desire for more foreign help in Russia, and his own rationalistic and secular absolutistic tendencies all inclined him to support religious toleration, which he did in a 1702 edict. In 1721, he also issued a decree allowing Orthodox Christians to marry Western Christians.

Toleration, of course, did not necessarily mean respect. Although Peter believed in God, his "Most Drunken Council of Fools and Jesters" made fun of Catholic rituals as well as Orthodox ones. Generally, his toleration was based on reasons of state, and when he violated this principle, for example, by decreeing in 1716 that Old Believers were to pay double taxes, it was also for state financial or security purposes.

Economic, Social, and Cultural Policies

Like most European rulers of his day, Peter was a mercantilist. He wished to obtain a favorable balance of trade and increase the government's supply of precious metals. But the mercantilist interest that most appealed to him was its emphasis on a strong state role in building up native industry.

In strengthening Russian industry, Peter used foreign expertise but not foreign capital and sought to reduce greatly Russian dependence on foreign products. At first, he concentrated overwhelmingly on industries that would arm and supply his military, but later, as war pressures eased, he also paid more attention to other industries. Perhaps a little less than 200 new manufactories came into existence under Peter, which compares with about 25 still operating in 1689 (see Chapter 11). Of the new enterprises, more than half produced iron, armaments, nonferrous metals, textiles, or lumber; others made such products as glass, leather, silk, and paper. Especially significant was growth of production in the St. Petersburg area and the rapid development of the iron industry in the Urals. By 1725, Russia was producing more than eight times as much iron as it had a quarter century earlier.

Of the new factories, about half were started by private owners and the other half by the government. Although most of the former came from the merchant class, some nobles also became involved. Because of Russian traditions and the weakness of its middle class, the government's role was greater than in the West, but Peter tried to encourage private enterprise. Partly to offset a shortage of private capital in Russia, the government offered inducements such as loans, subsidies, tax exemptions, tariff protection, and forced labor. Toward the end of his reign, Peter stepped up the practice of turning government-owned factories over to private owners. He also relinquished some government monopolies.

Yet the lot of entrepreneurs was not easy. The many government inducements were themselves evidence of a general reluctance to become involved in the risky business of private large-scale manufacturing. At times, the government even compelled individuals to take over factories.

By the last decade of Peter's reign, Russian exports greatly outnumbered imports, with Great Britain being the chief trading partner. In 1724, Peter introduced protective tariffs that tacked on to the cost of an import a tax ranging up to 75 percent of its value.

By 1725, most Russian foreign trade was going through St. Petersburg and Riga, with Archangel declining rapidly in significance. Astrakhan was a center for the less important trade with Persia and Central Asia. Peter hoped to emulate countries like England and Holland by building up a merchant fleet that would trade abroad, but his efforts bore little fruit. He was more successful in fostering trade by building canals, roads, and bridges. Most significant were the canals that completed the water passage from the Baltic to the Caspian via the Neva-Volga route and also linked, via the Volga's eastern tributaries, the Neva to the Urals' growing industrial complex.

Because of Russia's scarcity of precious metals in this era, Peter decreed that Russian merchants had to exchange gold and silver they obtained from foreigners for Russian money and forbade the export of bullion. The silver content of coinage was also lowered. Finally, Peter encouraged the exploration of new sources of gold and silver, including trade with gold-rich Spain and the disastrous military expedition to Bokhara.

The burden of Peter's economic policies fell mainly on the poorer classes. Russia's stratified society left little room for any free laboring class to develop. Those who built and worked in the new factories were thus overwhelmingly forced to do so. Some were soldiers, criminals, vagrants, beggars, prostitutes, or orphans, but most were state peasants and serfs—a 1721 decree allowed factory owners to purchase serfs for factory work. One estimate is that by 1725, some 54,000 state peasants had been assigned to work in the metallurgical industry alone.

Besides being dragooned into factories and military service—and into other projects like constructing St. Petersburg and canals—commoners paid for Peter's policies with taxes and inflation. Most revenue went for military needs. In 1725, although the Great Northern War was now over, the government was spending 65 percent of its revenues on the army and navy. Although estimates vary considerably, there is little doubt that both revenues and taxes increased significantly during Peter's reign.

Peter even employed "profiteers," whose job it was to think up new sources of revenue. From beards and bathhouses to weddings and watermelons, one new item after another was taxed. The largest gain, however, was in direct taxes and tribute, which made up 55 percent of state income in 1724. In place of the old household tax, Peter introduced a new more burdensome tax in 1718—the poll (or soul) tax. It successfully overcame some evasions of the old tax, for example, the combining of households.

Another source of income, an especially important one in the first decade of the Northern War, was the old tactic of debasing the currency—as Peter's father had done before the Copper Riot of 1662. By 1725, the ruble was worth only about half of what it had been at the beginning of Peter's reign.

Besides these burdens, serfs became more subjugated to their lords. The masters became responsible for delivering recruits to the government and for collecting the new soul tax from their serfs. After the new tax was introduced, it became harder for unhappy serfs to flee their masters because henceforth they had to have their lord's written permission to set foot off his property. Although the government did issue decrees aimed at preventing transactions that broke up serf families and at limiting the masters' rights to beat their serfs, these edicts seem to have had little effect.

Although the serfs were becoming more like slaves, slavery itself disappeared (except in Siberia, where it lingered for another century). Slavery ended not for humanitarian reasons but because by laws of 1680 and 1724 Peter transformed the small number of remaining slaves, who had traditionally not paid taxes, into tax-paying serfs.

Although nobles except for one lowly group were exempt from the soul tax, they also found themselves more subjugated. During the first decade of the Northern War, Peter drafted some nobles along with commoners. Although many nobles quickly became officers, others did not, for Peter thought that rank should be earned by merit. But it was only in the second decade of the war that Peter stepped up efforts to insure that all men served the state, either in the military (which took about two-thirds of those recruited) or in the civilian bureaucracy. Service was to be until death or incapacitation.

In 1710–1711, he ordered new measures to prevent young nobles from concealing themselves from the state. In 1722, he decreed that such men were to be treated as bandits, and could be slain on sight. Realizing that the state, including the military, needed educated nobles, he tried to force at least the rudiments of education upon them. In 1714, he prohibited nobles from marrying unless they could prove their competence in mathematics. That same year, partly in an attempt to deprive most nobles of any alternative to state service, he prohibited fathers from bequeathing their estates to more than one son. At the same time, Peter ended the remaining distinctions between *pomestie* and *votchina* estates, declaring all noble estates both inheritable and necessitating state service.

In 1722, Peter issued one of his most carefully prepared reforms, the Table of Ranks. It listed fourteen parallel ranks for officers and officials in each branch of state service: the military, civil service, and at court. Although mainly nobles rose to these posts, commoners could become nobles upon reaching any of these ranks. Yet, unless they served in the military or reached the eighth rank of civil or court service, they could not pass on the distinction to their children.

The Table of Ranks became one of Peter's most significant reforms. Nobles soon realized it was the only ladder to social status and success and that education was a propellant which helped their sons reach the bottom rank and accelerated their progress upward. In modified form, it lasted until 1917.

Peter viewed education and culture as tools for strengthening the state. When he sent fifty nobles abroad for education in 1697, he told them to learn everything they could about seamanship. The main upper-level schools he founded were technological in nature: for example, one of Mathematics and Navigation (1701), of Engineering (1712), and of Mines (1716). Partly to prepare individuals for such schools, he ordered (in 1714) that mathematical (or cipher) schools be started throughout the provinces, and by 1722 more than forty such schools existed. Peter also laid the groundwork for the foundation of an Academy of Science.

Although Peter's approach to education and culture was utilitarian, the impact of his policies was broad. The architecture of St. Petersburg and Peter's summer retreat of Peterhof, the new calendar, Western clothing fashions, the presence of women at social gatherings, his introduction of Arabic numerals, a simplified Russian alphabet, Western language borrowings, and the first Russian newspaper, which Peter began in 1703, all bore witness to this breadth. In areas like literature and philosophy, his impact was less direct and immediate but still eventually great.

FIGURE 13.4. Peterhof (Petrodvorets), fountains and canal leading to the Grand Palace from the Gulf of Finland.

Peter's educational and cultural policies were often accompanied with his usual threats and force. At the Naval Academy, which he founded in 1715, he recommended that discipline be maintained by retired guardsmen, who could sit in the classrooms and whip anybody, regardless of social status, who got out of line.

OPPOSITION

Given Peter's penchant for forcing his policies upon his people, it is not surprising that many opposed him. Opposition took many forms, overt and covert, active and passive, by word and by deed. It came because of hostility to high taxes and forced service, including conscription. It came because of opposition to Western ways and to Peter's expansionist and church policies. And it came because of his scandalous behavior—smoking, making fun of church rituals, divorcing his Russian wife and taking up with common foreign women, and persecuting his pious son, Alexei.

One response to increased service obligations, whether in factories, on estates, in military units, or on civilian projects like building canals or St. Petersburg, was simply to flee. Partly because of this, the number of peasant households in Siberia between 1678 and 1710 almost doubled. Officers and officials, however, now took additional steps to combat this age-old problem. Army recruits were sometimes chained together on their way to military service. Beginning in 1712, recruits were branded on their left arms, thereby facilitating the apprehension of runaways.

Another form of dissatisfaction was more verbal but still nonviolent. In fact, the most common political offense dealt with by the Preobrazhenskii Prikaz in its first decade was verbal criticism or disrespect toward Peter, his family, or government. Toward the end of his reign, a man was executed for publicly referring to Peter as the anti-Christ—a common belief among many Old Believers.

Violent opposition was less frequent but certainly common enough. Throughout Peter's reign, there were scattered rebellions of peasants (on estates and at industrial sites), of Cossacks, and of non-Russian peoples. On the far-off Kamchatka Peninsula—further east than Japan—many natives lost their lives resisting Russian expansion. Closer to the heartland, east of the middle Volga, the Bashkirs, who had revolted under Tsar Alexei, again revolted from 1705–1711. Upset with increased demands for tribute and horses to help fight the Great Northern War, the Bashkirs attacked Russian troops and forts in their lands and tried to obtain help from their fellow Moslems, the Crimean Tatars and the Turks. After none was forthcoming, the Russians snuffed out the revolt.

The most significant opposition to Peter, whether nonviolent or violent, came from three sources: the *streltsy*, the southern borderlands, and his son, Alexei.

The *streltsy* revolt of 1698 was motivated by opposition to Peter's Western ways and friends, his rejection of traditional customs, and his further downgrading of the *streltsy* in favor of new-style regiments and naval construction. After suppressing the *streltsy* in 1698–1699, Peter sent many of them southward to garrison duty in areas like Astrakhan. Here, in 1705, they became involved in another revolt.

The Astrakhan rebels' grievances were similar to those of 1698. They also opposed new taxes, the policies of local officials and officers (including some foreigners), and the prohibition on beards and traditional Russian clothes. They killed the local governor and several hundred others and set up their own government. In 1706, however, with the help of Kalmyk tribesmen and Don Cossacks, Peter's troops reconquered Astrakhan, and the Preobrazhenskii Prikaz executed several hundred rebels.

In 1707–1708, it was the turn of the Don Cossacks under Kondrati Bulavin. While echoing earlier grievances, such as those against government attempts to recapture runaway peasants, this uprising was also directed at the growing presence and demands of Russian officials, officers, and landowners in the Don region. Opposition to westernization and sympathy for old traditions, especially among some Old Believer communities in the region, also played a part.

As Bulavin's revolt spread in the Don area, it appealed to antinoble sentiments. Although Bulavin died in 1708 and the Don Cossack revolt was finally squashed, again with Kalmyk help, it helped spark scattered peasant revolts to the north and west that continued for over a year.

As already indicated, another instance of southern dissatisfaction was the defection of Mazepa and many of his Ukrainian Cossack followers to Charles XII of Sweden. Mazepa's grievances against Peter, to whom he had once been close, arose primarily from Peter's Ukrainian policies in the first decade of the Great Northern War. While demanding great sacrifices from Ukrainian Cossack troops, Peter curtailed their autonomy (for example, by assigning foreign and Russian officers to their regiments) and in 1707 told Mazepa he could spare no troops to help him turn back a Polish attack. Still another grievance was the behavior of Russian troops quartered in Ukrainian towns and villages.

The opposition of Tsarevich Alexei manifested itself most openly when he resorted to the peasants' favorite method—flight. In 1716, while Peter was in Denmark, Alexei fled to Austria. Born in 1690 and influenced by his conservative mother, Evdokiia, he was separated from her when she was exiled to a convent in 1698. Despite, or perhaps partly because of, Peter's subsequent attempts to mold his son's character, Alexei turned out quite the opposite from his father—as his German mother-in-law put it: "He prefers a rosary to a pistol in his hands."[1] This pious and passive young man became a beacon of hope for those opposed to Peter's newfangled ways.

After over a year abroad, Alexei was persuaded to return by his father's envoy, Peter Tolstoi. Despite assurances that he would be forgiven, Alexei was then imprisoned and tortured. To investigate the whole suspected conspiracy surrounding the defection of his son, Peter established a new office, the Secret Chancellery. Although there was little proof to link Alexei with any anti-Petrine plot, the investigation did reveal considerable opposition to Peter and his policies.

According to the testimony of a young woman Alexei hoped to marry—his wife had died in 1715—the tsarevich told her that, after becoming ruler, "I shall live in Moscow and leave St. Petersburg as a mere provincial town. I shall keep no ships and an army only for defence."[2] What a rejection this must have seemed to Peter! After 128 assembled notables condemned Alexei and recommended execution, he died under mysterious circumstances in 1718 in the capital's Sts. Peter and Paul Fortress.

Among a small number of others who lost their life as a result of this "conspiracy" was the metropolitan of Rostov. The Secret Chancellery also unearthed evidence of additional church antagonism to Peter. This hostility contributed to Peter's decision to abolish the patriarchate, just one of many instances in which political opposition helped trigger new Petrine policies.

PETER'S DEATH AND LEGACY

Although one legend attributed Peter's death to a fever he caught after plunging into icy waters to help save some people, the reality was less dramatic. He

[1] Quoted in B. H. Sumner, *Peter the Great and the Emergence of Russia* (New York, 1962), p. 97.
[2] Quoted in M. S. Anderson, *Peter the Great*. 2d ed. (London, 1995), p. 178.

died in bed in late January 1725, three months after this incident. A serious urinary ailment, from which he had suffered for some time, seems to have been the primary cause.

In 1722, Peter issued a decree announcing that the Russian emperor had the right to name his own successor, but he himself failed to do so. And even though Catherine had borne him several sons, none remained living by 1725.

With his death, one of Russia's most dramatic reigns came to an end. Its significance has been debated ever since, most noticeably by Russian Westernizers and Slavophiles in the early nineteenth century. What is certain is that Russia became a major European power during Peter's reign, that he instituted sweeping domestic changes, and that he was one of history's most important rulers.

Although his wars and diplomacy ultimately gained Russia little in the south, in the north he strengthened Russia at the expense of both Sweden and Poland and made Russia the dominant power in the Baltic.

Peter's domestic policies greatly accelerated the modernization and westernization of Russia and its small elite. He permanently changed the political justification for tsarist rule, and most of his successors at least paid lip service to the concept he established of a "reforming tsar." His policies also strengthened and modernized the idea of state service. His new capital St. Petersburg remained a fitting symbol of these policies.

Despite all his rational explanations for decrees, however, Peter's changes relied more on coercion than persuasion. Besides the heavy burdens and suffering he inflicted on his people, his policies led to a widening cultural gap between a small westernized elite and the rest of the population. Later, individuals such as the novelist Dostoevsky saw this as one of Russia's great tragedies.

This gap was similar to ones later experienced by other countries that attempted westernization and modernization and points to Peter's significance for world history. In his efforts to westernize a technologically underdeveloped country, he was a trailblazer. Furthermore, his relations with the West were not all one-sided. After being influenced by Western thinking on absolutist monarchy, he himself served as a model for some of Europe's later eighteenth-century enlightened absolute monarchs.

Yet, despite all his dynamism and new policies, certain basic characteristics of Russian life did not change or, if they did, not for long. Although active opposition could not stop Peter, custom, inertia, and self-interest eventually frustrated and scaled back some of his policies. The overwhelming majority of the Russian people, the peasants, continued to follow the customs of their ancestors, virtually untouched by any westernizing influences. The nobles gradually chipped away at the obligations Peter had imposed upon them and continued to rule over their serfs as they wished. Despite all the new laws and government institutions created by Peter, patronage and informal networks remained essential ingredients of Russia's political culture.

The chief elements of the Russian sociopolitical order in the late eighteenth century were the same as they had been a century earlier—autocracy, a ruling elite, and serfdom. And the Pugachev revolt that broke out a half-century after the end of Peter's reign occurred for basically the same reasons as the Razin revolt a century earlier—increasing government demands and an unjust social order.

The final evaluation of Peter must to some extent depend on one's own values. Admirers of traditional Russian culture and religion and critics of the West—such as the nineteenth-century Slavophiles—were critical of Peter. Others, who cared little for Russia's pre-Petrine traditions and admired Western culture—such as the westernizing literary critic V. Belinsky (1811–1848)—praised Peter. Opponents of strong state or autocratic powers—such as the novelist and later nonviolent anarchist Leo Tolstoy—criticized him, but admirers of such powers, including Stalin, generally praised him. The nineteenth-century historian Sergei Soloviev, who emphasized the importance of state power to Russia's development, called Peter I "the greatest leader in history."

In the late 1980s, a period in which many Russian intellectuals were criticizing the Communist system, the Soviet historian Evgeni Anisimov faulted Peter for creating a totalitarian, militaristic, bureaucratic, police state and beginning an imperialistic foreign policy. He referred to Peter's reforms as "progress through coercion" and noted a continuity between Petrine Russia and Soviet Russia—a point worth considering later in Russian history.

SUGGESTED SOURCES*

ANISIMOV, EVGENII V. *The Reforms of Peter the Great: Progress Through Coercion in Russia.* Armonk, N.Y., 1993.

AVRICH, PAUL. *Russian Rebels, 1600–1800.* New York, 1976, 1972. Pt. III.

BRUCE, PETER H. *Memoirs of Peter Henry Bruce.* New York, 1970. A reprint of a 1782 edition.

CASS 8 (Summer 1974). This issue contains numerous essays on Peter I's reign.

CRACRAFT, JAMES. *The Church Reform of Peter the Great.* Stanford, 1971.

———, ed. *Peter the Great Transforms Russia.* 3d ed. Lexington, Mass., 1991. Contains an annotated bibliography.

DE JONGE, ALEX. *Fire and Water: A Life of Peter the Great.* London, 1979.

DUKES, PAUL. *The Making of Russian Absolutism, 1613–1801.* London, 1990. Ch. 3.

GASIOROWSKA, XENIA. *The Image of Peter the Great in Russian Fiction.* Madison, 1979.

KAMINSKI, ANDRZEJ SULIMA. *Republic vs. Autocracy: Poland-Lithuania and Russia, 1686–1697.* Cambridge, Mass., 1993.

KEEP, JOHN L. H. *Soldiers of the Tsar: Army and Society in Russia, 1462–1874.* Oxford, 1985. Pt. 2.

KLYUCHEVSKY, VASILI. *Peter the Great.* London, 1958.

MASSIE, ROBERT K. *Peter the Great: His Life and World.* New York, 1980.

MEREZHKOVSKY, DMITRY S. *Peter and Alexis.* New York, 1931. A historical novel.

MULLER, ALEXANDER V., ed. *The Spiritual Regulation of Peter the Great.* Seattle, 1972.

OKENFUSS, MAX, ed. *The Travel Diary of Peter Tolstoi: A Muscovite in Early Modern Europe.* DeKalb, Ill., 1987.

OLIVA, L. JAY. *Russia in the Era of Peter the Great.* Englewood Cliffs, N.J., 1969.

PERRY, JOHN. *The State of Russia.* New York, 1968. A reprint of the 1716 edition.

*See also works cited in footnotes and in boxed insert.

PETERSON, CLAES. *Peter the Great's Administrative and Judicial Reforms: Swedish Antecedents and the Process of Reception.* Stockholm, 1979.

PHILLIPS, EDWARD J. *The Founding of Russia's Navy: Peter the Great and the Azov Fleet, 1688–1714.* Westport, Conn., 1995.

RAEFF, MARC, ed. *Peter the Great Changes Russia.* Lexington, Mass., 1972.

RIASANOVSKY, NICHOLAS V. *The Image of Peter the Great in Russian History and Thought.* New York, 1985.

SCHUYLER, EUGENE. *Peter the Great, Emperor of Russia: A Study of Historical Biography.* 2 vols. New York, 1884; Reprint, New York, 1967.

SOLOVIEV, SERGEI M. *Peter the Great: A Reign Begins.* Gulf Breeze, Fla., 1994.

———. *Peter the Great: The Great Reforms Begin.* Gulf Breeze, Fla., 1981.

SSH (Summer 1989). The issue is devoted to Peter I.

SUBTELNY, OREST. *The Mazepists: Ukrainian Separatism in the Early Eighteenth Century.* New York, 1981.

SUMNER, B. H. *Peter the Great and the Ottoman Empire.* Oxford, 1949.

TOLSTOY, ALEKSEY N. *Peter the First.* New York, 1959. A historical novel.

TROYAT, HENRI. *Peter the Great.* New York, 1987.

VOLTAIRE. *Russia under Peter the Great.* London, 1983.

WHITTAKER, CYNTHIA H. "The Reforming Tsar: The Redefinition of Autocratic Duty in Eighteenth-Century Russia," *SR* 51 (Spring 1992): 77–98.

CHAPTER 14

Three Empresses and Three Emperors: Rulers and Politics, 1725–1762

The third of a century between the reigns of Peter the Great and Catherine the Great was an era of palace coups, court favorites, heightened noble privileges, and six distinctly "nongreat" rulers.

Yet, if less majestic than Peter I and Catherine II, the rulers of this period nevertheless remained absolute monarchs. Even if youth (infancy in one case), inexperience, or indifference led them to pay little attention to matters of state, their officials and favorites acted in their behalf as representatives of absolutism. No legal checks on the monarchs' powers were established. Only in 1730 was there an unsuccessful attempt to limit these powers, and most nobles opposed it.

Nobles supported absolutism for their own self-serving reasons. In exchange for their support, the monarchs rewarded them with positions and opportunities, reduced Peter's strict demands upon them, and increased their control over their serfs. John LeDonne has referred to the eighteenth-century hereditary nobles as Russia's "ruling class" and to their top strata as the "ruling elite."

Although the noble estate was open to talented newcomers, such as those whom Peter I had promoted, members of established noble families were in the most advantageous position. During this era and beyond, two noble constellations were especially influential. The first centered around the Naryshkins, relatives of Peter I's mother; the second united around the Saltykovs, who were often allied with the Dolgorukys (or Dolgorukov clan) and the Miloslavskys (the maternal family of Peter's half-brother, Ivan V). These constellations competed and sometimes cooperated with each other to influence the monarch and dispense patronage. As in earlier Russian history, marriage alliances with other important families, whether "old blood" or "new blood," were an important means for maintaining or strengthening a clan's position.

Although reducing Peter's demands upon the nobles, the era's rulers praised his reforms and maintained most of them. Until 1762, they also maintained, except for a few years, the political police (the Secret Chancellery) he had established. His daughter Elizabeth, who ruled for more than half of this period, especially emphasized the importance of following in her father's foot-steps and did the most to extend his westernization in the cultural realm. The era's rulers also generally pursued similar foreign policies, although because of the greater European role Russia had assumed under Peter, foreign affairs became more complicated. No regions were lost except some weakly held Caspian territories, won in 1723 and relinquished in 1732. To balance these losses, there were further Siberian and Finnish gains.

CATHERINE I AND PETER II, 1725–1730

Because Peter I failed to name a successor, there were several possible candi-dates. One was his grandson Peter, the nine-year-old son of the deceased Alexei. Another prominent possibility was Peter I's wife Catherine, whom he had crowned empress in 1724. Although the royal couple had produced many children—both before and after their marriage—only three daughters survived their father, and one died later in 1725.

Catherine's most important supporter was Prince Alexander Menshikov. This favorite of Peter (and Catherine's lover before him) had ties with the Naryshkin clan. What finally proved decisive—as it often did in future succes-sion crises—was the backing of the regiments Peter I had created while a youth, the Preobrazhenskii and Semenovskii Guards. In 1725, Peter's widow came to the throne as Empress Catherine I of Russia.

At first, Menshikov was the dominant figure behind the half-literate new ruler. In early 1726, however, probably to appease other notables jealous of Menshikov's dominant position, Catherine approved a new institution, the Supreme Privy Council. It was placed above the Senate and consisted of seven members, including Menshikov and Catherine's son-in-law, the Duke of Hol-stein (who was added as an afterthought). Of the seven, only one, Prince Dmitri Golitsyn, was from the old Muscovite nobility, and he had served Peter in various important positions. Furthermore, a Golitsyn was married to Men-shikov's son.

Catherine's reign did not last long. Although only forty-three, she died in the spring of 1727. The logical successor was now Peter's grandson, and he came to the throne as Peter II. Menshikov planned to marry his daughter to the young boy, but this time he had overreached himself. Taking advantage of an illness Menshikov suffered in the late summer of 1727, his opponents helped organize his downfall and later exile to Siberia.

During Peter II's three-year reign, other men were added to the Supreme Privy Council, most importantly several Dolgorukys, descendants of the man credited with founding Moscow. Fittingly enough, there was increased talk of moving the capital back to Moscow, where Peter II transferred some govern-ment agencies and spent most of his reign. Taking a page out of Menshikov's book, the Dolgorukys also now planned to marry one of their own to the young emperor. But on the day set for the wedding, January 19, 1730, Peter II, still only fourteen, died of smallpox.

ANNA, THE NOBLES, AND THE CRISIS OF 1730

The question of succession now became more complex. No males remained with adequate credentials except another grandson of Peter I, the future Peter III. In 1730, however, the Supreme Privy Council dismissed any claim made in his name because his mother—Peter's daughter Anna, by now deceased—was illegitimate. This left Catherine and another Anna, daughters of Ivan V, Peter I's half-brother and co-tsar until his death in 1696 (see Appendix B for this complex genealogy). But the Council also rejected Catherine, Ivan V's oldest daughter, because of her marriage to the Duke of Mecklenburg. Her younger sister, Anna, Duchess of Courland, however, was a widow in her late thirties; and her past behavior made her seem sufficiently pliable to a Supreme Privy Council determined to maintain and even expand its powers.

It therefore offered her the throne but with conditions that, if implemented, would have ended autocracy in Russia. According to them, she was to refrain from marrying or selecting an heir. Without Council approval, she was not to make war or peace; impose taxes or spend revenues; confer titles or high military or civil ranks; grant estates; or deprive nobles of life, property, or honor without a trial. Furthermore, she was to recognize Council control over the Guards and "other regiments."

Of the Council's eight members, four were Dolgorukys and two were Golitsyns. The two most instrumental in drawing up the Conditions seem to have been Vasili Dolgoruky and Dmitri Golitsyn. Both men had traveled abroad, Dolgoruky often as a diplomat, and were familiar with foreign forms of government. Both knew of Poland's limited monarchy and of the limitations placed upon the sister of Charles XII after she succeeded him in Sweden following his death in late 1718. Golitsyn had also been among the fifty nobles sent by Peter to study abroad in 1697–1698. He resided in Venice, notorious for its oligarchic ruling council.

Although knowledge of foreign limited monarchies may have influenced them, they were surely even more affected by their own Russian experiences and fears. They knew that under a new monarch, especially one coming from outside, new favorites could wield tremendous power, as Menshikov once had. They feared that without solid guarantees—and perhaps even with them—distinguished noble families like their own could be swept far from the levers of power by a new regime.

But neither council members nor the nobles in general possessed a corporate sense of noble identity. The Dolgorukys and Golitsyns seemed to be acting as distinguished boyar clans had often acted—to increase their own power, not that of the nobles in general. Thus, their strengthened Council would represent much narrower interests than bodies that limited monarchical power in countries such as England, Poland, and Sweden.

The Council attempted to make the Conditions seem like they came spontaneously from Anna, but other high-ranking officials and officers and some lesser nobles soon discovered who originated the initiative. More nobles than usual were in Moscow because some had come from outside the city to attend Peter II's wedding, but instead remained for his funeral. One estimate is that about 2,000 noblemen—about one-sixth of all noblemen—were then in Moscow. Various groups of them now began writing their own proposals, about a dozen in all.

Two common desires run through them: first, to increase the number of "power-sharers" beyond the eight-member Council and, second, to reduce the demands and limitations Peter I had placed on the nobility. To achieve the first goal, suggestions were made for eliminating or expanding the Council, expanding the Senate, creating other high government bodies, and selecting high office holders by noble vote (one proposal suggested a quorum of at least 100). As a clear sign of dissatisfaction with the four Dolgorukys and two Golitsyns who dominated the Council, it was also proposed that the number of family members on high government bodies be limited. To fulfill the second goal, propositions were put forth for lessening military and civilian service demands, including any service as privates or seamen, and for abrogating Peter's inheritance law, which prohibited the division of estates. None of the proposals suggested eliminating the monarchy.

Meanwhile, Anna had accepted the Council's Conditions, and in the middle of February, amidst pomp and glitter, arrived in Moscow. Although aware of noble opposition to its Conditions and willing to make some compromises, the Council failed to communicate adequately with opposing nobles. Compromise was also hampered—and oligarchic intentions perhaps magnified—by the absence of traditions and institutions for broader "power-sharing."

Ten days after her arrival in Moscow, Anna tore up the document she had signed containing the Council's Conditions. She did so before assembled notables and Guards officers, who had asked her to restore autocratic power.

Russia was not yet ready to limit autocracy. Not only did most nobles resent Dolgoruky and Golitsyn pretensions, but also they feared that their Conditions could lead to political instability, if not outright chaos. At worst, some feared another Time of Troubles, with all its implications of foreign intervention, political disintegration, and peasant revolts. Hence, resentment, fear, the lack of any strong corporate identity or noble institutions, and the nobles' lack of any experience in power-sharing or in representative government helped doom any alternate plan to limit Anna's power. So too did a past that taught most nobles to beware of wealthy Moscow aristocrats, who often acted contrary to the interests of less fortunate nobles. Finally, the support Anna received from the Guards regiments and important figures like former Procurator General Yaguzhinsky, Archbishop Prokopovich, and maverick Council member Andrei Ostermann—all three non-Russians—proved significant.

The reaction of Dmitri Golitsyn, who was perhaps not quite as oligarchic as he then appeared to other nobles, was to say to friends:

Well! the feast was prepared, but the guests were not worthy of it; I know I shall be the victim of this. Be it so. It is for my country I shall suffer. I see before me the end of my career; but those who now make me mourn, will have cause to mourn longer than me.

Whether Golitsyn offered a "feast" that would curtail the evils of autocracy or a minefield that would lead to mayhem is debatable, but he was certainly correct about his own suffering—he died in prison in 1737. As if to support Golitsyn's gloomy prediction, an aurora borealis made the Russian horizon "appear all in blood" the evening after Anna tore up the Conditions.

THE REIGN OF ANNA, 1730–1740

Despite Golitsyn's gloomy prophesying, Anna's reign did satisfy some noble aspirations. She repealed Peter's unpopular law mandating that an estate be passed on to only one son and reduced compulsory military and civil service to twenty-five years. In families of more than one son, one was completely exempted from service so he could administer family estates. To satisfy nobles further, the government established a cadet school, the Corps of Cadets, so that graduates could become army officers without first serving as common soldiers.

Although a decrease in service demands was one main concern of nobles, an increase in their powers over their serfs was another. Here again Anna pacified them. For example, a law of 1736 allowed them to determine the punishment inflicted upon their runaway serfs unfortunate enough to be caught. Because lashes with a knout could lead to death, the state thereby officially, although not explicitly, allowed serfmasters to assume life-and-death powers over captured fugitive serfs.

Although Anna's reign benefited nobles in some ways, most historians have been critical of it. Sergei Soloviev, for example, criticized her for being under the control of Germanic ministers and advisers who wasted funds on unnecessary court expenditures and costly, unprofitable wars. His pupil Kliuchevsky referred to her reign as "one of the darkest pages of our history."

Her bad reputation was due partly to her eccentric personality. She shared her uncle Peter I's taste for crude humor, the most famous example being the wedding arrangements she forced on the middle-aged widower Prince Mikhail Golitsyn, whom she had earlier forced into the role of court jester. She ordered an ice palace (thirty-three feet high and eighty feet long) constructed on the Neva River for Golitsyn and his new bride, a Kalmyk serving woman according to some reports. With great care, it was furnished with ice furniture and furnishings, including a bed, chairs, tables, steps, windows, mirrors, a clock, and even ice logs in an ice fireplace. Outside were more objects, including a cannon, trees, flowers, and birds, all made of ice. Here she had the "newlyweds" delivered in a cage, on the back of an elephant, and forced them, in one of Russia's coldest winters, to spend their wedding night.

Compared to such stunts, the many rumors about Anna's love life and her passion for hunting—she kept hunting guns near her windows to shoot passing birds—seem more normal.

Her domestic policies included restoring St. Petersburg as the unchallenged center of government, replacing the Supreme Privy Council with a smaller Cabinet, and reestablishing the Secret Chancellery (Chancellery for Secret Investigations). Although Baltic and non-Baltic Germans such as E. J. Biron, A. I. Ostermann, and B. C. Münnich (a relative of the Saltykov family) exercised considerable influence over her policies, both domestic and foreign, Russia's historians have often gone too far in depicting her reign as a period of evil foreign domination (*Bironovshchina* or the Biron era) presided over primarily by her lover Biron.

Anisimov's post-Soviet portrayal of Anna's reign, however, is more balanced and accurate. Although he also stresses Biron's strong influence, Anisimov indicates that too much has been made of its "foreign" nature. The policies of Anna, aided by Biron, were generally similar to those of other eighteenth-century Russian monarchs. Furthermore, Anna also relied on Russians, such as her relatives in the Saltykov family and A. I. Ushakov, who headed the Secret Chancellery, which investigated both political and nonpolitical crimes.

IVAN VI AND ELIZABETH, 1740–1761

Before her death in October 1740, Anna named as her successor the infant grandson of her sister Catherine of Mecklenburg and as his regent, Biron. Biron lasted only about three weeks, however, before some guardsmen, under orders from Field Marshal Münnich, invaded his bedroom and arrested him.

The infant Ivan's mother, Anna Leopoldovna, now became regent. Only twenty-two and then pregnant, she immersed herself in passionate affairs—first with her lady-in-waiting and then with the Saxon ambassador—and neither she nor her weak-willed husband was able to prevent the intrigues that swirled around her.

In late 1741, Peter the Great's daughter Elizabeth seized power in a predawn coup at the Winter Palace. She was supported by the Guards, who reflected the sentiments of the nobility and resented German influence at court. Anna and her spouse were allowed to leave Russia, but their infant son, Ivan VI, ended up in the Schlusselburg Fortress, where he languished for more than two decades before being killed.

Elizabeth was thirty-one years old when she became empress. Known for her beauty and charm, she pledged to end "the oppression of foreigners" and to rule according to the laws of her father. For her own political purposes, she overstated the differences between her father's reign and that of Russia's rulers from 1727 to 1741. In some respects, such as her favorable treatment of the nobility, she carried on more in the spirit of the previous fourteen years than in that of Peter I.

The future Catherine the Great, who first met Elizabeth in 1744, thought her frivolous, vain, and lazy. After an initial burst of political activity, Elizabeth

The Inglorious Fall of Regent Biron

The following excerpt describing the arrest of Biron is from C. H. Von Manstein, *Contemporary Memoirs of Russia: From the Year 1727 to 1744* (London, 1968), pp. 278–279. Colonel Manstein was at that time an aide-de-camp to Marshal Münnich. Bracketed material and ellipsis are mine.

Manstein entered the palace, and, to make no noise, had the detachment follow him at a distance. All the sentinels suffered him to pass without any opposition; for, as he was personally known to all the soldiers, they imagined he might be sent to the duke [Biron] upon some affair of consequence, so that he got across the apartment without any difficulty. . . . After he had gone through two chambers, he came to a door that was locked; luckily for him, this was a folding door, and the servants had neglected sliding the bolts at the top and bottom, so that he easily forced it open. In the chamber he found a great bed, in which the duke and the duchess were lying, buried in so profound a sleep that not even the noise he made forcing open the door had woke them. Manstein having got close to the bed, drew the curtains, and desired to speak with the regent. Upon this, they both started up, and began to scream with all their might, rightly judging that he was not come to bring them any good news. Manstein happening to stand on the side on which the duchess lay, saw the regent throw himself out of bed on the ground, apparently with an intention to hide himself under the bed; on which, springing quickly round to the other side, he [Manstein] threw himself upon him, and held him fast locked in his arms till the guards came in. The duke having at length got upon his legs again, and wanting to disengage himself from their hold, distributed blows with his fist to the right and left; which the soldiers returned with strokes from the butt end of their muskets; and throwing him down again on the floor, they crammed a handkerchief into his mouth, bound his hands with an officer's sash, and then carried him, naked as he was, to the guard-room.

left more and more of the running of government to others, such as Nikita Trubetskoi and Alexei Bestuzhev-Riumin, both related to the Naryshkins. The new empress surrounded herself with entertainment: plays and operas, balls and banquets, card-playing and masquerades. She especially enjoyed masquerades where she ordered the men to dress as women and vice versa. Although the men, in crinolines and whaleboned petticoats, were none too happy, Elizabeth (according to Catherine) looked great in male attire, which displayed her shapely legs.

To help run the Russian government, Elizabeth restored the Senate to its former prominence, but she abolished the smaller Cabinet created by Empress Anna. In 1756, she established a Conference of Ten, including the heir (Grand Duke Peter) and high officials, and it became the highest government body under her. The government continued to expand—the number of local and central officials about doubling to around 12,000 in the three decades after Peter the Great's death.

New favorites also influenced state policy. Among them was the illiterate

Field Marshall Alexei Razumovsky, a Ukrainian peasant before his magnificent voice brought him to court as a singer and his handsome looks won the heart of Elizabeth. She may have even secretly married him. Still more influential were the Shuvalovs, whose family roots were in the Kostroma region. The Shuvalovs, like some of the relatives of Alexei Razumovsky, married into leading noble families such as the Saltykovs and Trubetskois. The intelligent and humane Ivan Shuvalov succeeded Razumovsky as the reigning favorite and later founded the University of Moscow. His cousin Alexander became head of the Secret Chancellery, whose earlier head (A. I. Ushakov) Elizabeth had retained until he retired in 1744.

She maintained this security force because she was an extremely cautious ruler and because she felt insecure on the throne she had seized, an anxiety no doubt reinforced by alleged plots uncovered in 1742 and 1743 to restore Ivan VI. Later in her reign, she kept a close eye on her designated heir, Peter, the son of her sister Anna, and his wife Catherine, fearing a plot that might prematurely bring Peter to power.

Elizabeth also had reason to fear disturbances from the peasants. While the court spent lavishly and noble powers increased, the lot of the peasants grew worse. They fled their masters or revolted in increasing numbers; one Soviet historian estimated that major serf revolts, sometimes joined by soldiers and employing field guns, increased more than 300 percent under Elizabeth.

Although accused plotters and rebels—whether peasant or prince, man or woman—were liable, as in earlier reigns, to suffer torture and mutilation, Elizabeth did abolish capital punishment. This seems to have been primarily due to her religious sentiments. For although the English ambassador had once written that Elizabeth "had not one bit of nun's flesh about her," she was quite religious in her own way and sometimes interrupted her amusements with pilgrimages to her country's holy places.

In the cultural domain, where she greatly extended her father's Western orientation, Elizabeth's accomplishments were significant. For example, during her reign, the University of Moscow (Russia's first university) was founded, and many of the architectural wonders of Rastrelli were constructed (see Figures 14.1 and 14.2, and Chapter 17).

DIPLOMACY AND WARS, 1725–1761

Despite the foreign backgrounds of several of the era's rulers, Russia's foreign policy was generally true to Peter the Great's legacy. Russia again fought in Poland (1733–1735) and fought wars with Turkey (1736–1739) and Sweden (1741–1743). Conflict with Persia also broke out anew despite the peace treaty of 1723—by new treaties of 1732 and 1735, Russia gave back the gains Peter had earlier made at Persia's expense. Lending continuity to Russia's foreign policies were two men primarily responsible for directing them: A. I. Ostermann (from 1725 to 1741) and A. P. Bestuzhev-Riumin (from 1741 to 1758).

Russia's most consistent ally was Austria, with whom it signed a treaty of

FIGURE 14.1. The Winter Palace as viewed from Palace Square, St. Petersburg, 1754–1764, architect B. F. Rastrelli. This palace replaced an earlier one on the site and cost about 2.5 billion rubles, derived mainly from salt and alcohol taxes.

alliance in 1726. Ostermann gave careful thought to the treaty and concluded that Russia's long-range interests most coincided with those of Austria, especially regarding Poland, Turkey, and Sweden. Except for a few exceptional periods, Russia and Austria remained allies for more than a century.

Trade and a common distrust of France also brought Russia closer to Great Britain. Russia distrusted France mainly because in the latter's attempt to weaken Hapsburg power in Europe, it supported Poland, Turkey, and Sweden. After Frederick the Great came to power and invaded Silesia in 1740, Russia also became wary of Prussia.

Russia's first major conflict of the era was the War of Polish Succession. In 1733, Russian troops invaded Poland to prevent the French candidate (and father-in-law of the French king), Stanislas Lezczynski, from exercising power after he had been elected king by the Polish nobles. Thus, just as the Russian-backed Augustus II replaced Lezczynski as Polish king back in 1709 (after Poltava), when he had been supported by Sweden, so now the Russian-Austrian-backed son of Augustus II replaced him and became Augustus III.

In 1736, after victory in the War of Polish Succession was assured and peace with Persia finally concluded, Russia declared war on Turkey. Although disputed borders and Crimean Tatar raids on Russian territory were two reasons for the Russian offensive, the Russian government also shared Peter's unfulfilled dream of making Russia a Black Sea power. Because Turkey was then involved in a war with Persia, the timing seemed opportune, and Russian diplomats in Constantinople encouraged the belief that the Orthodox peoples of the Turkish empire would support Russia.

After a cost of many million rubles and some 100,000 dead, Russia concluded the Turkish war in September 1739 by signing the Treaty of Belgrade. Despite winning some important victories on the battlefield, Russian gains were minimized by the defeats of its ally Austria and by French diplomatic support of the Turks. For all its money and deaths, it received only a little territory, primarily Azov, which it had won on the battlefield. Even this gain was minimized because Russia had to agree to destroy Azov's fortifications and to maintain no ships, of any kind, on the Black Sea.

Russia's next war was with Sweden, and France again supported a Russian enemy. This time Sweden began the war (in 1741), hoping to regain territory lost to Russia under Peter the Great. With the infant Ivan VI on the throne and Swedish and French diplomats encouraging Elizabeth to overthrow him, the time seemed ripe.

But Sweden was even less successful than Russia had been in its war with Turkey. By late 1742, Cossacks were in the Finnish capital, Abo, and Sweden agreed to a peace treaty the following year. By it, Russia added a small piece of Finland to its empire and forced Sweden to agree to its choice, a German, as heir to Sweden's old and childless King Frederick.

Russia's last two wars of this era demonstrated that it had become an important piece on the European diplomatic chessboard. In the final years of the War of Austrian Succession (1740–1748), Russia allied itself with Austria and Great Britain against France and Prussia. Although a British subsidy helped persuade Russia to send troops to the Rhine in 1748, peace came before they could fight. The big winner in the war was Prussia, which gained Silesia from Austria.

Partly as a result of the Prussian victory, a European diplomatic "revolution" occurred in 1756. Austria and France, traditional enemies, now became allies, as did Great Britain and Prussia. Realizing that Maria Theresa of Austria now intended to win back Silesia, Frederick the Great of Prussia struck first, and the Seven Years' War (1756–1763) was launched in Europe. (It was also fought abroad successfully by England against France in other areas, including North America, where it was known as the French and Indian War.)

Russia soon came in on the side of her traditional ally, Austria, and played a major part in the war. Russian troops invaded Prussia in 1758, and Russian and Austrian forces occupied Berlin for a few days in late 1760. Despite Frederick's military genius, the coalition against him was too strong. By the end of 1761, he expected little future help from Great Britain and despaired over the possibility of a crushing defeat. Empress Elizabeth seemed close to achieving her recent demand for the annexation of East Prussia. Then on Christmas 1761 (January 5, 1762 N.S.), she died. The new Russian emperor, Peter III, a great admirer of Frederick, returned all Russian-held territories to him—a "miracle" that later briefly gave some hope to Adolf Hitler in his own dark days of besiegement in 1945.

THE SHORT REIGN OF PETER III

Upon Elizabeth's death, she was succeeded by the thirty-three-year-old Peter III. His mother was Empress Elizabeth's older sister, Anna, who had died when he was an infant. His father was the Duke of Holstein-Gottorp. Although Peter was also an heir to the Swedish throne, Empress Elizabeth brought him to Russia and in 1742 declared him heir to the Russian throne. She oversaw his further education and chose his bride for him, the future Catherine the Great. The couple were married in 1745, when he was seventeen and she was sixteen.

In her *Memoirs* Catherine depicts Peter as infantile, ill-mannered, and imprudent, with a passion for military drill. She has him, for example, drilling toy soldiers and hanging a rat for eating some of them. But Catherine was not the most objective of witnesses. A wife who overthrows her husband in a coup, shortly after which he is murdered by one of her followers, can hardly claim impartiality. Her supporters, who also contributed much information about Peter III, likewise were hardly impartial. Catherine and her followers deliberately painted him in dark colors, and he was undoubtedly more intelligent, better educated, and more capable than their collective portrait suggests. As R. Nisbet Bain pointed out at the beginning of the twentieth century and Carole Leonard more recently, most accounts of Peter III have been biased because of their reliance on these early sources.

In Peter III's first few months in office, he reduced the salt tax, abolished the Secret Chancellery, and freed many political exiles. In a Manifesto on the Freedom of the Nobility (February 1762), he ended mandatory state service for nobles and granted them freedom to travel abroad.

True, the manifesto hedged the new freedoms with certain restrictions and stated that compulsion was no longer necessary because education and loyalty had led to an enthusiasm for state service. (Perhaps more significantly, economics prevented most nobles from evading state service; only a small percentage of them owned enough land and serfs to make a decent living without being on the state payroll.) The manifesto also insisted that the nobility in general still had a moral obligation to serve the state and to educate their children, and it encouraged society to ostracize lazy noble shirkers. Finally, it ignored two wishes of the nobles. It did not guarantee their hereditary estates against confiscation, and it did not protect nobles from being subject to corporal punishment. Yet, despite all these limitations, the manifesto marked an important plateau in the ascent of noble gains, and the nobility welcomed it.

But Peter III's popularity soon declined. Following the example of Catherine and her supporters, many historians have attributed his growing unpopularity to his hostility to Russian customs and culture and his preference for foreign ways, especially his admiration of Prussia and its ruler, Frederick the Great.

Peter III's policies directed against the Orthodox Church were cited as one example of this disregard of Russian sensibilities. Catherine II's accession manifesto spoke of his contempt for Orthodoxy and his plan to begin destroying its churches. In this regard, the manifesto spoke some half-truths.

Despite his conversion to Orthodoxy, Peter III had maintained a fondness for the Lutheranism of his childhood and admired the free-thinking ways of Frederick the Great. Most offensive to churchmen was Peter III's command that church lands, along with their peasants, be taken over by the state.

Yet Peter III's sympathy for foreign ways was hardly unique among eighteenth-century Russian monarchs, and Peter the Great had also alienated many clergymen. A more significant cause of Peter III's fall was his military policy. Achieving neither conquests nor compensation, he ended six years of war against Prussia—a step that had both supporters and detractors. Then, however, he gained the reluctant backing of his idol Frederick for a Russo-Prussian war to help Holstein regain Schleswig from Denmark. This was a most unpopular decision, especially among many officials and the Guards regiments. These regiments, which had more than once displayed their ability to interfere in palace politics, now feared being sent to fight against Denmark.

Besides this decision, other military policies of Peter alienated the same two groups. He ordered officials holding high military rank, such as former procurator general Nikita Trubetskoi, to drill troops personally. This was an especially distasteful task for the obese, old Trubetskoi, who often suffered from pained legs. Peter III was contemptuous of the Guards (according to the British ambassador, they had become "accustomed to great idleness and license") and ordered them to dress and drill in the Prussian style. There was some fear among the Guards that they might eventually be disbanded. Meanwhile, Peter III favored his own personal Holstein regiment.

Playing upon such dissatisfactions, Catherine and her supporters overthrew Peter only six months after he had come to the throne.

THE EMPIRE, 1725–1761

In dealing with non-Russian nationalities and borderlands, government policy was generally consistent with that of Peter the Great. Although certainly no religious zealot, Peter had used educational and economic incentives to encourage Moslem Tatar conversions to Orthodoxy. Empresses Anna and Elizabeth went even further: In the early 1740s, about four-fifths of the mosques in the Volga area were destroyed.

Further east, Russia continued to penetrate into Bashkiria. When the Bashkirs discovered a Russian plan to build a major stronghold, Orenburg, and other forts along the Ural River, they once again rose in revolt, for the plan threatened the almost complete encirclement of Bashkiria. From 1735 to 1741, the Russians waged a fierce war against the Bashkirs, who were ultimately outmatched and unable to prevent the construction of the Orenburg Line of forts on their southern border. The Bashkirs were also unable to halt the continuing influx of Russian and non-Russian peoples into their lands. Many new settlers were peasants, including runaway serfs. Thousands of these peasants were converted by the government into Cossacks, some of whom manned the Orenburg Line (see Maps 10.2 and 15.1).

The construction of this line was due not only to concerns about the Bashkirs, but also about the Kazakhs, a nomadic people located to the south of the line in the Kazakh steppe. Seeking help against Western Mongols and Volga Kalmyks, some, but no all, Kazakh leaders turned to Russia for protection in the 1730s. In return, they promised that their tribes would be loyal to Russia. Thus, ironically enough, these Kazakh leaders welcomed the construction of the Orenburg Line, which set the stage for the later Russian penetration of Kazakhstan.

In its quest to maximize fur tribute, the Russian government also continued to strengthen its control over Siberian areas east of Bashkiria. This often led to the abuse of natives, as noted by Heinrich von Fuch, a German who had been instrumental in planning Peter's government reforms but was later exiled to Siberia.

Some mistreatment he attributed to the labor and material demands of the expeditions led by Vitus Bering. After Bering's first trip to the Pacific had helped cause a bloody rebellion among Kamchatka natives in 1730–1731, he arrived in Yakutsk in 1734 to build ships and outfit another major exploratory effort—before it was officially over in 1743, two years after Bering's death, his men reached the Alaskan coast.

Bering's demands on the Yakuts were made worse by dishonest and greedy officials. Fuch stated that in all his years in Siberia he met only one honest official. Overall, Fuch presented a dismal picture of the exploitation of natives who were generally peaceful and punctual payers of tribute. He wrote of Russians stealing and plundering from the Yakuts, providing them little justice from the Russian law, and needlessly exposing them to smallpox, which killed many of them.

Fuch warned that such conditions were counterproductive to Russian interests and would encourage other natives to resist Russian control. He cited the example of the Chukchi in northeastern Siberia, who resisted in the late 1730s—both the Chukchi and the neighboring Koriak also fought against Russian control during the mid-1740s.

Russian mistreatment of natives, of course, was similar to that of other colonizers on other continents, both before and after this era. Worse examples of colonial abuse outside the Russian Empire could certainly be mentioned. Moreover, the Russian government did take steps to end some abuses cited by Fuch; a 1745 decree, for example, mandated an expedition to investigative native suffering stemming from tribute collection.

One new Siberian area annexed by Russia was the Altai Mountain region, just north of the northwest corner of modern-day Mongolia. Here rich mines and smelting works existed, which, before becoming imperial property under Empress Elizabeth, were owned by the Demidov family.

The colonization of Siberia quickened during this era. Native peoples were already a minority in 1720, composing only about 30 percent of Siberia's approximately 1 million people. Colonization was aided not only by voluntary settlers and Cossacks, but also by government exile policies designed to abet a chronic Siberian labor shortage.

Although Moscow had already begun exiling some criminals to Siberia before Peter the Great's reign, Peter slowed the process by diverting many convicts to forced labor on European Russian projects, including manning some of his galleys. After his death, the pace of Siberian exile once again accelerated. A decree of 1728 ordered robbers sent to Siberia if sentenced to three or more years of imprisonment. Another decree of 1735 sent some convicts to Siberian mines. Among those who ended up in Siberia were some individuals convicted of political crimes—for example, a soldier was condemned to lifetime hard labor in Siberia for suggesting that Anna's head be bruised with a brick.

As one ruler succeeded another from Catherine I to Elizabeth, former favorites often found themselves among Siberia's exiles. Menshikov, some of the Dolgorukys, Ostermann, Münnich, and Biron were just some of the more illustrious exiles who shared Fuch's fate.

Although the elimination of the death penalty under Elizabeth in 1753 saved some bodies for Siberian exile, even more significant was a 1760 proclamation that allowed community authorities and serfowners to hand over misbehaving individuals to the state for Siberian exile. In exchange, for every individual so delivered, the community's or serfowner's obligation to provide a military recruit was reduced by one.

At the other end of the Russian Empire, in the Estland and Livland Baltic territories (in modern-day Estonia and Latvia), the Baltic German ruling class continued to enjoy considerable autonomy and was able to strengthen its powers over Estonian and Latvian peasants. This reflected the general growth of noble powers over serfs in the empire. Baltic German nobles, with their knowledge of Western ways, also played an important part in the Russian military and government. After new central government offices were created to deal with Estland and Livland in the late 1720s, the government counted primarily on Baltic Germans to run and staff them.

Further south in Left-Bank Ukraine, government-centralizing pressures ebbed and flowed. Partly because the influential Menshikov had been granted extensive lands in Ukraine and opposed Russian taxes on them, he suddenly became more sympathetic to some measure of Ukrainian autonomy. In 1727, the Little Russian College, established by Peter I, was abolished, and a new hetman, D. Apostol, was appointed. He was able to regain some, but by no means all, the Ukrainian autonomy lost to Peter the Great.

Following the death of Apostol in 1734, Empress Anna again curtailed Ukrainian rights by forbidding the election of a hetman and instead established a new Governing Council consisting of three Russians and three Ukrainians. St. Petersburg directed its new Russian chairman to weaken Ukrainian separateness by encouraging such measures as Russian-Ukrainian marriages. Land-grabbing by Russian officials and officers increased, turning many peasants into virtual serfs. Ukrainians charged with defaming or plotting against the Russian government became liable to investigation, torture, and sentencing by Anna's Secret Chancellery. Finally, under Anna, Ukrainians suffered disproportionate losses (some 35,000 dead) in the Russo-Turkish War of 1736–1739. In addition, the Hetmanate had to pay for the maintenance, including officers' wages, of Russian troops stationed on Ukrainian soil, which was the chief staging area of the war.

The reign of Elizabeth eventually brought about the end of the Governing Council and the appointment of Cyril Razumovsky as hetman in 1750. He was the twenty-two-year-old brother of her favorite, Alexei, and he continued in office until 1764. Orest Subtelny refers to this period as the "golden autumn" of the Hetmanate's autonomy.[1]

[1]*Ukraine: A History.* 2d ed. (Toronto, 1994), p. 170.

FIGURE 14.2. Church of St. Andrew, Kiev, 1747–1767, architect B. F. Rastrelli. The commissioning of the construction by Empress Elizabeth resulted from her visit to Kiev in 1744.

The young hetman, educated in Western Europe, improved the judicial system and brought the Zaporozhians under his control. He was often in St. Petersburg, however, and he left the Cossack nobles free to run the Hetmanate. During this period, many Ukrainians assumed civil government positions in Ukraine and even beyond.

Yet even Cyril Razumovsky could not persuade Elizabeth to allow him to establish separate diplomatic relations, or to restrict the use of Ukrainian soldiers to wars involving Ukrainian concerns, or to dispense Ukrainian lands. Over his objections, Elizabeth colonized Zaporozhian lands with Russian and non-Russian settlers, including thousands of Orthodox Serbs and other Slavs from Hapsburg border regions.

Thus, despite some concessions by Elizabeth to Ukrainian autonomy, the overall thrust of government policy in this era continued the empire-building policies of Peter the Great.

SUGGESTED SOURCES

ANISIMOV, E. V. "Anna Ivanovna," *RSH* 32 (Spring 1994): 8–36. Reprinted in *EER*, pp. 38–65.

———. *Empress Elizabeth: Her Reign and Her Russia*. Gulf Breeze, Fla., 1995.

BAIN, R. NISBET. *Peter III, Emperor of Russia: The Story of a Crisis and a Crime*. New York, 1902.

BRENNAN, JAMES F. *Enlightened Despotism in Russia: The Reign of Elizabeth, 1741–1762*. New York, 1987.

BRYNER, CYRIL. "The Issue of Capital Punishment in the Reign of Elizabeth Petrovna," *RR* 49 (October 1990): 389–416.

CATHERINE II, EMPRESS OF RUSSIA. *The Memoirs of Catherine the Great*. New York, 1957.

CURTISS, MINA. *A Forgotten Empress: Anna Ivanovna and Her Reign, 1730–1740*. New York, 1974.

DMYTRYSHYN, BASIL, E. A. P. CROWNHART-VAUGHAN, and THOMAS VAUGHAN, eds. *Russian Penetration of the North Pacific Ocean, 1700–1799: A Documentary Record*. Portland, Ore., 1986.

DONNELLY, ALTON S. *The Russian Conquest of Bashkiria, 1522–1740: A Case Study of Imperialism*. New Haven, 1968.

DUKES, PAUL. *The Making of Russian Absolutism, 1613–1801*. 2d ed. London, 1990. Ch. 4.

KAPLAN, HERBERT H. *Russia and the Outbreak of the Seven Years' War*. Berkeley, 1968.

LEDONNE, JOHN P. *Absolutism and Ruling Class: The Formation of the Russian Political Order, 1700–1825*. New York, 1991.

LEONARD, CAROL S. *Reform and Regicide: The Reign of Peter III of Russia*. Bloomington, 1993.

LINCOLN, W. BRUCE. *The Romanovs: Autocrats of All the Russias*. New York, 1981. Ch. 4.

LONGWORTH, PHILLIP. *The Three Empresses: Catherine, Anne, and Elizabeth*. New York, 1973.

MADARIAGA, ISABEL DE. "Portrait of an Eighteenth-Century Russian Statesman: Prince Dmitry Mikhaylovich Golitsyn," *SEER* 62, no. 1 (1984): 36–60.

MANSTEIN, CHRISTOF HERMANN VON. *Contemporary Memoirs of Russia from the Year 1727 to 1744*. New York, 1968.

MEEHAN-WATERS, BRENDA. *Autocracy and Aristocracy: The Russian Service Elite of 1730*. New Brunswick, N.J., 1982.

MYL'NIKOV, A. S. "Peter III," *RSH* 32 (Winter 1993–1994): 30–56. Reprinted in *EER*, pp. 102–133.

NAUMOV, V. P. "Elizaveta Petrovna," *RSH* 32 (Spring 1994): 37–72. Reprinted in *EER*, pp. 67–100.

RANSEL, DAVID L. "The Government Crisis of 1730." In *Reform in Russia and the U.S.S.R.: Past and Prospects,* ed. Robert O. Crummey. Urbana, Ill. 1989.

SOLOVIEV, SERGEI M. *Empress Anna, Favorites, Policies, Campaigns.* Gulf Breeze, Fla., 1984.

———. *The Rule of Empress Anna.* Gulf Breeze, Fla., 1982.

———. *A New Empress: Peter III and Catherine II, 1761–1762.* Gulf Breeze, Fla., 1982.

SUBTELNY, OREST. *Ukraine: A History.* 2d ed. Toronto, 1994. Ch. 10.

THADEN, EDWARD C. *Russia's Western Borderlands, 1710–1870.* Princeton, 1984. Pt. 1.

WHITTAKER, CYNTHIA H. "The Reforming Tsar: The Redefinition of Autocratic Duty in Eighteenth-Century Russia," *SR* 51 (Spring 1992): 77–98.

CHAPTER 15

The Reign of
Catherine the Great

Following in the reforming-tsar tradition of Peter I, Catherine II was more a reformer than a reactionary during her thirty-four-year reign (1762–1796). While maintaining absolute power, she increased the number of individuals, especially nobles, included in the political process. Her charters to the nobility and towns (both in 1785) increased the rights of nobles and townspeople. Influenced by the European Enlightenment, she ruled less arbitrarily than most of her predecessors, including Peter I, and fostered respect for law. She encouraged learning and culture and attempted to improve both the economy and the public welfare. In foreign affairs, she pursued policies that greatly expanded the Russian Empire. Within the empire, she systematized government operations.

Yet concessions to the nobles were partly at the expense of most of Russia's population—the peasants. And Catherine's wars and territorial gains were paid for primarily by the blood, sweat, and increasing revenues taken from the common people. Their voices and protests were heard only occasionally, for example, in 1767 through some petitions to delegates of a Legislative Commission and again in 1773–1774 during the Pugachev rebellion.

Although Catherine's final years (1789–1796) brought the extensive territorial gains of the last two partitions of Poland, they also ushered in a tightening of government restraints over intellectuals.

CATHERINE II: BACKGROUND AND THE 1762 COUP

Catherine II was born Sophia Augusta Fredericka in the Baltic city of Stettin on May 2, 1729 (N.S.). She was the daughter of a minor German prince and princess, Christian August of Anhalt-Zerbst and Johanna Elizabeth of Holstein-Gottorp. Johanna was first cousin to the father of Catherine's future husband, Peter III.

In the eighteen years she spent in Russia prior to her husband's reign,

Catherine blossomed into an intelligent and well-read woman. Works of French Enlightenment thinkers such as Voltaire and Montesquieu, which helped cultivate her humane sentiments, were among her favorites.

Catherine was hard-working, vigorous, and optimistic, but also strong-willed, ambitious, and calculating. She realized the importance of not offending Russian sensibilities and learned the Russian language and customs. In preparation for her marriage to Grand Duke Peter, she converted to Orthodoxy from Lutheranism and adopted the name Catherine. She loved to ride horses, shoot wildfowl, and dance, all of which she did well.

When young, she had considered herself ugly, and her mother had not showered affection on her. Throughout her life, she wished to be loved and admired. For reasons that remain unclear, her unloving husband, Peter III, seemed incapable of sexual relations with her, at least in the early years of their marriage.

Eventually, Catherine took up with other men. One of them, Sergei Saltykov, may have been (in 1754) the father of her son—and later emperor—Paul. In her *Memoirs,* she suggests this was so, but Peter III might also have finally consummated his marriage and been the father. She also had a daughter in 1757, and the suspected father was her Polish lover, Stanislas Poniatowski. When Peter III became emperor, she was pregnant with the child of her latest

FIGURE 15.1. Catherine Palace, Tsarskoe Selo (Pushkin), near St. Petersburg. Completed by B. F. Rastrelli in the 1750s and later slightly modified. Catherine II often lived and worked here during part of the spring and summer.

lover, the gigantic Guards officer Grigori Orlov, and a few months later gave birth to a boy later known as Count Alexei Bobrinskoi.

At the time of her accession to the throne in June 1762, Catherine, who was not very tall, was not yet stout and was described as having a noble figure. Although her appearance created a generally favorable impression, at least two foreign observers of the early 1760s noted in her a certain lack of spontaneity. One spoke of her affected walk and smile, and another thought that her projection of goodness and gentleness flowed only from a desire to please. She was especially eager to please in the weeks that followed her coup against her husband because her position was still insecure.

The coup itself was prompted by her fear that Peter III, then residing at his Oranienbaum estate near the capital, was preparing to get rid of her. On the morning of June 28, 1762, she set off by coach from Peterhof to St. Petersburg, where, among others, Grigori Orlov and his brothers had prepared the coup. There she received the allegiance of most of the capital's dignitaries and troops. At the Winter Palace she appeared on the balcony with her young son Paul, delighting the crowd below. Soldiers and civilians celebrated by helping themselves to beer and vodka from the capital's taverns.

That same morning Catherine issued a manifesto. It justified the coup on three grounds: (1) that Orthodoxy had been under siege and was in danger of being replaced by foreign beliefs; (2) that Russia's glory, won by blood and arms, had been desecrated by Peter's dishonorable peace with Frederick the Great, and (3) that the country's internal order had been wrecked. As mentioned earlier, these charges were exaggerated and biased.

That evening Catherine donned the green uniform of the Preobrazhenskii Guards, mounted her white horse, Brilliant, and rode off with her troops back to Peterhof. She ordered Peter III put under guard on a nearby estate, Ropsha, and a week later, on July 6, he was killed.

Although Alexei Orlov (sometimes called Scarface) confessed his guilt for the killing, he may have believed he was acting in Catherine's interest and would not be punished. Indeed, Catherine covered up the crime by declaring her husband had died of colic. She also covered up his throat and part of his face when she had him publicly laid out in his Holstein uniform at the Alexander Nevsky Monastery. Within weeks, she bestowed estates, serfs, and rubles upon her coup supporters, including Alexei and Grigori Orlov.

DOMESTIC POLICIES

Because most of her husband's officials had supported her coup, Catherine began her reign by maintaining most of them in their offices. At the same time, she advanced the careers of new favorites like the Orlovs. She restored some discredited officials, especially Bestuzhev-Riumin, who had directed foreign policy for almost two decades under Elizabeth. Among the rewarded coup supporters were members of important noble families, such as Cyril Razumovsky and Nikita Panin (1718–1783), the tutor of her son Paul. She was also

The Abdication and Murder of Peter III

Catherine's skewed version of Peter III's death can clearly be seen in the letter she wrote a few weeks later to her former lover Stanislas Poniatowski. The source of the letter is R. Nisbet Bain, *Peter III, Emperor of Russia: the Story of a Crisis and a Crime* (New York, 1902), pp. 195–196. Bracketed material is Bain's except for [Fortress]; ellipses are mine.

Peter III. abdicated, at Oranienbaum, in full liberty, surrounded by 5000 Holsteiners, and came . . . to Peterhof. . . . Thereupon I sent the deposed Emperor to a remote and very agreeable place called Ropsha, 25 versts from Peterhof, under the command of Alexius Orlov, with four officers and a detachment of picked, good-natured men, whilst decent and convenient rooms were being prepared for him at Schlusselburg [Fortress]. But God disposed otherwise. Fear had given him a diarrhoea which lasted three days and passed away on the fourth; in this [fourth] day he drank excessively, for he had all he wanted except liberty. Nevertheless, the only things he asked me for were his mistress, his dog, his negro and his violin; but for fear of scandal [sic] and increasing the agitation of the persons who guarded him, I only sent him the last three things.

The hemorrhoidal colic which seized him affected his brain; two days he was delirious, and the delirium was followed by very great exhaustion, and despite all the assistance of the doctors, he expired whilst demanding a Lutheran priest. I feared that the officers might have poisoned him, so I had him opened, but it is an absolute fact that not the slightest trace of poison was found inside him. The stomach was quite sound, but inflammation of the bowels and a stroke of apoplexy had carried him off. His heart was extraordinarily small and quite decayed.

careful not to offend other leading noble clans, such as the Golitsyns, Naryshkins, Saltykovs, and Trubetskois.

Although cautious, Catherine wished to be vigorous and enlightened. Like Peter the Great, she had little tolerance for lazy government officials. Working from a plan submitted by Nikita Panin, in December 1763, she reorganized the Senate to increase senators' knowledge over specific areas of government. She increased the number and pay of provincial officials and more specifically outlined their duties. The following year, she appointed Prince Alexander Viazemsky (whose wife was a Trubetskoi) as procurator general of the Senate. From then until sickness forced him to retire in 1792, he proved indispensable.

Although leading families controlled most important government and military positions, Catherine was careful not to let them obtain too much power. She rejected part of Panin's plan that would have created a small imperial council of lifetime members that would countersign imperial decrees. In appointing Viazemsky, she instructed him not to let the Senate overstep its bounds, and she stated that the size of the Russian Empire necessitated an autocratic ruler. Later, in 1768, when Catherine formed some leading advisers into a small Council of State, she again insisted that it stick to a limited role—advising her when requested.

The Legislative Commission

To create a more efficient absolutistic government, Catherine wished to codify Russia's laws, a task that had not been undertaken since 1649. For that purpose, on July 30, 1767, she convened a Legislative Commission in Moscow and presented them with her *Instruction (Nakaz)* containing 655 articles.

In laboring over this document for almost two years, she borrowed heavily from foreign works, especially Montesquieu's *Spirit of the Laws* and Beccaria's *Crime and Punishment*. By the time the commission met, she was already corresponding with enlightened thinkers, including the Frenchmen Voltaire, Diderot, and Jean d'Alembert.

Indeed, there was much in her *Instruction* that would please them—Voltaire called it the "finest monument of the age." She declared, for example, that "Russia is an European State," that laws should be made only to procure the good of the people, that the use of torture was contrary to Nature and Reason, and that severe censorship led to ignorance. She went beyond Peter the Great by maintaining that government should be constrained by certain fundamental principles.

Although Catherine's *Instruction* was "enlightened" in many ways, it still advocated absolutism and the recognition of Russian realities. One such reality was that serfdom (in LeDonne's words) "was the social creed of the ruling class and the cement of its unity."[1] After being advised to remove some articles from an early draft that suggested improvements in serf conditions, Catherine did so.

The commission was selected according to principles laid down by Catherine. In its more than 200 meetings in a year and a half, its membership fluctuated from a little over 500 members to almost 600. Town corporations, noble assemblies, and government departments provided about 400 delegates. Between 150 and 200 others represented state peasants, Cossacks, and non-Russian nationalities. The serfs were unrepresented, and the clergy had only one representative—from the Holy Synod.

Despite all the time and effort, a new law code was not produced. Catherine's noble-sounding *Instruction* offered little practical guidance, delegates had little practical experience in making laws, and Catherine had little patience with the delegates' divisiveness and inefficiency. The Russo-Turkish War of 1768–1774 made it difficult to continue the Commission's deliberations, and a frustrated Catherine, probably happy to bring their plenary sessions to an end, did so in late 1768.

Yet the whole effort was not in vain, at least for Catherine. She learned much from the process, including how passionately serfowners were ready to

---

[1]John P. LeDonne, *Ruling Russia: Politics and Administration in the Age of Absolutism, 1762–1796* (Princeton, 1984), p. 8.

resist even the slightest tampering with their serfowning privileges. The instructions that electors presented to their delegates told her (and us) a great deal about how the nonserf population felt about their conditions. Although different social groups expressed different feelings, there were also common dissatisfactions and desires. Among all groups, there were complaints of excessive government demands, corruption, and the poor administration of justice. Also widespread was the call for more autonomy and local control. Catherine's later reforms of 1775 and 1785 were a partial response to what she had learned in 1767–1768.

Government Reorganization and the Reforms of 1775 and 1785

After 1768, Catherine's domestic policies were also influenced by her "passion for uniformity" (to use Madariaga's term). In seeking a stronger Russia, however, she differed somewhat from Peter I by relying on a more decentralized structure based on clearly defined social orders (or estates), especially the nobility. (Of course, as absolute monarch she was to remain firmly in overall charge.) Accordingly, she abolished some centralized administrative colleges created by Peter the Great. By the end of her reign, only those of foreign affairs, war, navy, and commerce still existed.

In 1775, Catherine decreed a Statute for the Administration of the Provinces of the Russian Empire. In the two decades that followed, most of its many provisions were enacted. To bring more efficient government to the provinces, the statute recommended increasing their number and redividing the country so that each province contained between 300,000 and 400,000 people. Each province was then to be further subdivided into districts. By the end of Catherine's reign in 1796, there were fifty provinces and almost 500 districts, government officials had more than doubled, and the government was spending about six times as much as previously on local government.

At the top of the provincial leadership were governor-generals, who normally oversaw a few provinces and their governors. Underneath the provincial governors, various officials and boards were responsible for such areas as law and order, taxes and dues collection, and social welfare. Each provincial district had a capital town staffed with officials subordinate to its provincial government. A complex and hierarchical system of law courts was also established in each province, which provided different courts for nobles, townspeople, and state peasants.

Provisions were also made for electing some officials, such as a rural land captain in each district, who was elected by district nobles. His tasks included maintaining public safety and health, law and order, and roads and bridges as well as fostering good agricultural practices.

In 1785, Catherine broadened opportunities for nobles' political participation and heightened their corporate status. According to the 1785 Charter of the Nobility, noble assemblies were to meet every three years to elect officials on both the district and the provincial level. Such officials included a marshall of the nobility for each district and province, judges, land captains, and assessors. Only landowning nobles who had reached officer rank could vote and be elected to such posts. Provincial assemblies were required to keep noble genealogical and service records and were allowed to petition the empress directly.

In the charter, Catherine also praised the nobles for their past service and confirmed various gains made by them in recent decades. She recognized their rights to full legal ownership of their properties; to travel freely or serve friendly governments abroad; and to be free from compulsory state service, corporal punishment, paying the poll tax, and billeting troops. Further, the Charter acknowledged that only a court of peers could deprive a noble of his life, nobility, rank, or property.

In 1785, the empress also issued a Charter of the Towns. It reorganized townspeople into six groups. Although all these groups received some rights, for example, that of trial by their peers and voting for a town council (duma), other rights were restricted to the more privileged town-dwellers. Among the latter's rights were freedom from corporal punishment and from paying the poll tax; they were, however, subject to a tax on capital.

Catherine had earlier stated that Russia possessed no real middle estate and that she wished to help bring one about. The town charter reflected this wish. For various reasons, however, ranging from the small size of some towns to Catherine's reluctance to allow elected town officials much real power, the charter proved less significant than the one for nobles.

The nobles gained the most in 1785. The elected noble officials joined the appointed ones, such as the governors, to make the nobles and their interests dominant in the Russian provinces.

Yet, because Catherine never succeeded in codifying Russia's laws and because none of her legislation created a judiciary independent of state control, even noble rights were precarious and could be violated with impunity. Later, the brief reign of Catherine's son Paul made this all too clear.

Officials, Favorites, and Additional Domestic Policies

In St. Petersburg, Catherine continued relying heavily on her procurator general, A. Viazemsky. After 1775, he issued orders to the provinces dealing with a host of matters relating to finances and law and order. She also depended on her own personal secretariat, especially its leading member, Alexander Bezborodko, and on Grigori Potemkin.

By 1774, Potemkin had become her latest lover—she had split from Grigori Orlov in 1772, compensating him with a palace, a 150,000-ruble annual pension, 10,000 peasants, and other presents. Like Orlov, Potemkin was younger than Catherine—by ten years—and was a military man of noble background. Catherine had promoted him to lieutenant for his faithful service in "guarding" Peter III after the 1762 coup. His gigantic physique and loss of one eye led some to refer to him as "Cyclops." He was intelligent and cultured, familiar with both Western ideas and Holy Scriptures and fluent in Greek. A hero in the

Russo-Turkish War, already a general in 1773, by the end of 1774, Catherine had placed him in charge of the army.

Although Potemkin remained Catherine's lover for only a few years, she continued thereafter to rely heavily on his advice, especially regarding foreign and military policy. He also helped vitalize provincial government. After annexing the Crimea in 1783, Catherine placed him in charge of the southern region called "New Russia," and he contributed much to its growth and development.

Although Catherine had many lovers after Potemkin, none exercised much influence until after his death in 1791. His loss, along with Viazemsky's declining health at about the same time, brought Catherine near to despair. She began relying more on the last of her lovers, Platon Zubov (a protégé of one of the Saltykovs). When she first took up with him in 1789, he was a Guards lieutenant of twenty-two. Although she made him a general, listened to his advice on foreign policy, and gave him some of Potemkin's old positions, including that of governor-general of New Russia, his abilities paled in comparison to those of the one-eyed giant.

In the economic sphere, Catherine attempted to increase agricultural production by sponsoring a Free Economic Society for the Encouragement of Agriculture and Husbandry and by encouraging foreign colonization of government-granted lands. Many of the approximately 75,000 colonists were Germans who settled along the Volga and in the southern lands of New Russia. Catherine opposed monopolies; fostered the growth of towns and economic enterprises, especially in the provinces; and greatly increased foreign trade. Richard Pipes has argued, however, that by opening trade and industry more to nobles and peasants, Catherine greatly weakened—contrary to her announced intention—the development of the middle class.

Her taxation and revenue policies also seemed to act contrary to her announced intention to improve the common good. Increasing government officials in the provinces, lavishing gifts upon her favorites, fighting wars and rebellions, and developing new parts of the empire all cost money. Just as under Peter the Great, increased revenues came primarily from the peasants. Although the poll tax was not increased until 1794, the rent payments of state peasants to the government were tripled by 1783; the state argued it was just keeping up with similar increases that serfowners imposed upon their peasants. The empress also raised more money by the inflationary method of printing more and borrowing abroad. Although it is true that Catherine bequeathed to her successors more rational and effective government accounting methods, she also left them with a large national debt. From 1785 until her death in 1796, every annual budget was in the red.

Of course, the common good cannot be measured just in immediate economic terms. As we shall see, Catherine's educational and cultural policies contributed significantly to the growth of learning in Russia. And with mixed results, she enacted measures to improve public health and to provide for such unfortunates as orphans and the insane. In both these spheres, she displayed more concern than most European monarchs of her day.

POLITICAL OPPOSITION AND CRITICISM

Opposition to Catherine II can be summarized under three categories: (1) a small number of officers who conspired at different times, especially early in Catherine's reign, to bring about a palace coup; (2) frontier groups who opposed the tightening grip of St. Petersburg; and (3) cultured men who voiced criticism of Catherine's policies but did not conspire to overthrow her.

Among the most memorable opposition of the first type was a 1762 plot involving Moscow officers, including a certain Peter Khrushchev, and another conspiracy two years later involving principally Lt. Vasili Mirovich. Both plots involved replacing Catherine II with the imprisoned (and former infant ruler) Ivan VI. The first got no further than talk, which also involved insuring the rights of Catherine's son Paul. The second actually led to the storming of Schlusselburg Fortress, where the unfortunate Ivan VI was held under orders that he should be killed rather than allowed to escape. Thus, it was that the Mirovich-led attack, amidst fog and darkness, inadvertently led to the killing of the man he wished to make emperor.

While Lt. Khrushchev and some of his co-conspirators were exiled to Siberia, Lt. Mirovich was publicly beheaded in the capital, an event not previously witnessed there for more than two decades. Following the death of Ivan VI, military conspirators usually championed Grand Duke Paul, but the second category of opposition, border rebels, usually claimed to be serving emperors who were actually dead—either Peter III or Ivan VI. By the end of Catherine's reign, at least two dozen such pretenders had appeared.

Pugachev Rebellion

By far the most important border rebel was Emelian Pugachev, an illiterate Don Cossack and army deserter who claimed he was Peter III. He began his revolt in September 1773, and it lasted a year before Pugachev was betrayed by some of his own followers and handed over to government authorities in the city of Yaitsk.

The revolt began in Yaitsk, in a steppe area, at a bend in the Yaitsk River, which flowed from the Ural Mountains to the Caspian Sea. The city was the capital of the Yaik Cossacks. (The names of the city, river, and Cossacks were later changed to Uralsk for the city and Ural for the river and Cossacks.) The revolt soon spread beyond these Cossacks, especially among non-Russian nationalities, including the Tatars, Kalmyks, Kazakhs, and, most importantly, Bashkirs. As it progressed, it was joined by many other discontented elements, including army deserters, exiles, Ural factory peasants, and private serfs.

The followers of Pugachev were attracted by his message of opposition to growing government demands. They wished to hack away at the tentacles of the state and its upper-class supporters, tentacles that seemed to be reaching further and further and squeezing harder and harder. This seemed especially true since the beginning of the war with Turkey in 1768, a war in which Pugachev himself had participated.

To the Cossacks, the pretender promised to restore older, freer conditions of military service and fishing rights. To Old Believers, including many Cossacks, he promised tolerance, including the right to maintain their beards, which some had recently lost after being conscripted as regular troops. To all he promised an end to conscription, taxes, officials, serfowners, and other exploiters. He not only held up a vision of earlier, freer days in the border areas, but also pointed toward a golden future. In it, common people would possess the land and elect, as Cossack communities and peasant communes traditionally did, their own local leaders.

Pugachev's promises, petitions to him as the supposed Peter III, and the actions of those who joined him in rebelling against Catherine's government and local nobles all testify to the discontentment and desires of Russia's non-privileged population in the Ural and Volga areas.

Better-disciplined and armed government troops, however, overcame Pugachev's followers. The latter had little in common except their hatred of the government and privileged classes. Even among the Yaik Cossacks and Bashkirs, from whom, along with the Ural factory peasants, Pugachev's most prominent early support came, class divisions prevented unified support.

The cost of the revolt in blood and suffering was heavy on both sides. Pugachev encouraged the "extermination" of serfowners, and many of them, especially among the less affluent, lost their lives. The toll was particularly heavy in the Volga valley area from Kazan southward almost to Astrakhan and in districts west of the Volga, such as Tambov. Often emboldened by both alcohol and past grievances, serfs and others seized and plundered estates, captured and raped noblewomen, and killed estate owners, sometimes with their wives and children.

The cities were not spared either. Volga cities such as Kazan and Saratov and ones further west such as Penza fell to him. In Kazan, which still possessed many Tatars, beardless or Western-attired upper-class men were killed and their wives and daughters captured. Churches were looted, especially by the Moslem Bashkirs and other tribesmen, and most of the city set ablaze. Altogether in the summer of 1774, the rebels probably killed more than 3,000 serfowners, officials, priests, and merchants.

Even more rebel blood flowed, especially in pitched battles against government troops. In March 1774, near Orenburg, the government ended a six-month siege of the city and killed approximately 2,500 in the battle and subsequent pursuit of fleeing rebels. Once rebel areas and prisoners were captured, the government and revengeful nobles shed more blood. Pugachev was brought to Moscow in an iron cage; after being publicly displayed, in January 1775 he was publicly beheaded and quartered. Parts of his body were then displayed in various areas of Moscow. This gruesome ending would have been even worse if Catherine had not overrode the court's sentence that Pugachev *first* be quartered and then beheaded.

Hundreds of other rebels were executed, while still others suffered knoutings and beatings, mutilations (such as the loss of an ear), brandings, and exile. Despite these measures, Catherine II was no Ivan the Terrible. For humane reasons and concern over European public opinion, she prevented the even more severe retribution desired by many of her officials and nobles.

The Panin Party, Radishchev, and Novikov

By the 1760s, the Western Enlightenment had stimulated new political ideas. A few men theorized about the positive aspects of a limited monarchy or even a republic, while still placing hopes in Catherine. Following the failure of the Legislative Commission and the beginning of the Russo-Turkish War in 1768, however, a gap developed between Catherine and some enlightened thinkers.

Some writers, such as Denis Fonvizin (1745–1792), the most gifted playwright of his generation, pinned their hopes on Catherine's son Paul, who turned eighteen in 1772. They also relied on his *oberhofmeister* (governor), Nikita Panin, who supported their careers and was one of the most cultured men of his day.

Early in his career, Panin had spent twelve years (1748–1760) as Russia's ambassador to Sweden, and up to the Russo-Turkish War of 1768–1774, he was the dominant influence on Catherine's foreign policy. Less militaristic than other advisers, such as Grigori Orlov, his influence declined in these war years. During this same period, concerned over growing sympathy for her son Paul, Catherine used the occasion of Paul's marriage to a German princess in 1773 to end Panin's distrusted tutelage of him. Despite these setbacks, however, Panin remained the senior foreign policy official until 1781.

After his enforced retirement that year and before his death in 1783, Panin, along with his brother Peter and Denis Fonvisn, outlined a project for constitutional reform. They hoped Paul would make use of it when he finally came to power.

In their papers relating to the project, they implicitly criticized Catherine for relying on favorites and flatters and for ruling by ever-changing decrees, sometimes mutually contradictory. Instead, they favored a constitutional order based on fundamental natural laws, in keeping with reason and the will of God. They stated their belief in the social contract theory that power originally rested in the nation, not the ruler. More specifically, their project called for some separation of powers, at least beneath the monarch. A separate judiciary was to help insure that the administrative branch complied with the constitution. A regular legislative system, including a State Council and Senate, was also to be maintained. Although all legislation would have to be discussed in the State Council, the ruler would maintain the decisive vote. Finally, the Panin group called for clearly defined rights for each estate, the inviolability of freedom and property, a clear law of royal succession, and religious toleration. Although the constitutional ideas of the Panin group could no be published and had no immediate impact, decades later their project influenced the constitutional ideas of the Decembrist conspiracy of 1825.

Another thinker who was dissatisfied with Catherine's reign was the historian and government official Prince Mikhail Shcherbatov (1733–1790). In his "On the Corruption of Morals in Russia," unpublished until long after his death, he contrasted pre-Petrine days, when he thought boyars had more power, with his own century, when careerists polluted the nobility and moral order. Catherine's 1785 Charter of the Nobility left him far from satisfied, and he believed it necessary to go much further in restoring and strengthening the rights and powers of the old aristocracy.

Despite his criticism of Catherine, Shcherbatov was typical of most eighteenth-century Russian thinkers in supporting Russian autocracy, however differently they interpreted it. In a survey of the views of eighteenth-century Russian historians, Cynthia Whittaker places him in the category of those who stressed that the autocrat should be nondespotic. Shcherbatov, however, was the only one of that group to insist that the key to nondespotic rule was for the autocrat to heed the advice of wise aristocrats.

Toward the end of Catherine's reign and following the French Revolution of 1789, her treatment of two leading intellectuals bore witness to the shrinking limits of her tolerance. But then the first of the two, Alexander Radishchev (1749–1802), was more radical than any of his intellectual predecessors, and his criticism appeared in book form.

As a young man, Radishchev spent five years imbibing Western philosophy and political ideas at the University of Leipzig, where the future great German writer Goethe was also then a student. After returning to Russia in 1771, he entered government service and in 1790 became chief of the St. Petersburg Custom House.

That same year, he printed his inflammatory book, *A Journey from St. Petersburg to Moscow,* which somehow slipped past authorities until remaining copies were snatched up by the government. Catherine declared him worse than Pugachev and believed he was inflicted with "the French madness." He was arrested and condemned to death, but Catherine commuted his sentence to ten years of Siberian exile.

Even a quick glance at the *Journey* indicates why Catherine was alarmed. It criticizes government corruption and injustice, costly wars (Radishchev was not alone in this complaint), censorship, and cruel serfowners. It goes even further by lashing out at the very institution of serfdom. Commenting on enchained serfs sold to crown peasants so they could fulfill the latter's military recruitment quota, Radishchev writes:

> Oh, if the slaves weighted down with fetters, raging in their despair . . . crush our heads, the heads of their inhuman masters, and redden their fields with our blood! What would the country lose by that?[2]

He included in the work part of his "Ode to Liberty," in which he praised Oliver Cromwell for legally executing Charles I of England and thereby teaching people how nations can avenge themselves on unjust monarchs.

Two years after the arrest of Radishchev, it was the turn of the publicist Nikolai Novikov (1744–1818). As a young man, he had been a secretary to Catherine's Legislative Commission and had also served in a Guards regiment. Like Fonvisn, he was influenced by the theory of natural law and shared some

[2]*A Journey from St. Petersburg to Moscow* (Cambridge, Mass., 1966), p. 209.

FIGURE 15.2. The Savior Tower entrance to Fort Il-imsk, where Radishchev spent five years of Siberian exile before his sentence was commuted by Paul I. The tower, with some restored planks, is now located in the outdoor Museum of Wooden Architecture near Irkutsk.

views of both Fonvisn and Nikita Panin. In the late 1760s and 1770s, he edited several satirical journals and eventually became an ardent Freemason, but he remained more a political reformer than a radical.

Novikov's Masonic and publishing activities in Moscow, where he had moved in 1779, led to Catherine's distrust of him. By 1790, Catherine was highly suspicious of Moscow Masons and ordered them watched carefully. She believed Freemasonry had helped bring about the French revolution, and by 1792 she also came to suspect Moscow Masons of being involved in a conspiracy against her. Fueled by suspicious papers found in a search of Novikov's estate, she feared these Masons were conspiring with more senior Rosicrucian Masons in Berlin and with the Prussian court. She suspected they were attempting to recruit Grand Duke Paul and possibly put him on the Russian throne.

Although an investigation failed to unearth enough evidence to substantiate her worst fears, she believed it sufficient to sentence Novikov to fifteen years' incarceration in the Schlusselburg Fortress. He received no trial but was released four years later, after Paul succeeded Catherine.

Radishchev and Novikov were not alone among intellectuals arrested for political opposition in the last years of Catherine's reign. At least a handful of others also suffered. Catherine herself became more conservative—the events in France culminating in the execution of Louis XVI in January 1793 certainly helped propel her in that direction. In 1793–1794, she approved the burning of the works of Voltaire, with whom she had once corresponded. The conflict between monarch and intellectual social critics (later dubbed the intelligentsia), which was to be such a prominent aspect of later imperial history, had begun.

FOREIGN POLICY

If foreign policy success is measured in conquests and territorial expansion, Catherine was very successful. Largely at the expense of Poland and Turkey, she added far more western and southern lands to the empire than Peter the Great had done. And she matched Peter's Baltic conquests, by making Russia a Black Sea power. If her conquests are weighed against their immediate costs, however, in lives and money, and their future costs in suffering, the scales seem less heavily tipped in Catherine's favor. Although the exact effect of Catherine's policies on future events is difficult to discern, there is little doubt that her Polish policies helped strengthen Prussia and eliminate a buffer between it and Russia.

The Early Years, 1762–1774

The major foreign policies of Catherine's first twelve years can be examined under the headings of five "P's": peace, Prussia, Panin, Poland, and the Porte.

Catherine began her reign by pulling back from Peter III's plan for a joint Russo-Prussian offensive against Denmark, but she also reaffirmed his peace treaty with Frederick the Great of Prussia. The Seven Years' War (1756–1763) was a big drain on the Russian budget, and Catherine needed peace for Russia to recover and for her to solidify her rule.

Russia's main ally in the first half of Catherine's reign was not Austria (as usual) but Prussia. The death of King Augustus III of Poland in 1763 and the desire to determine his successor helped bring these two Polish neighbors together. In 1764, Russia and Prussia concluded a treaty promising mutual assistance if attacked and cooperation in the handling of Poland and Sweden.

Nikita Panin, then her main foreign policy adviser, hoped to create a "Northern System" of friendly powers that would include Prussia, Great Britain, Sweden, Poland, and Denmark. Although Prussia was willing enough, and Denmark also signed a defensive alliance with Russia in 1765, Panin was less successful with the other countries. Despite agreeing to a commercial treaty in 1766, Britain was unwilling to meet Russian conditions for an alliance, especially if it meant granting assistance to Russia in the event of a Russo-Turkish war.

Although needing peace, Catherine wished for further gains at the expense of Poland. The nobles of Poland, or more precisely of the Polish-

Lithuanian Commonwealth, elected their own king, but they were susceptible to foreign influences. After the death of Augustus III in October 1763, Russo-Prussian pressure and bribes won out over those of Austria and France, both of whom supported a son of Augustus III. Instead, it was Catherine's former Polish lover, Stanislas Poniatowski, who was elected in 1764.

Poniatowski proved less a puppet than Catherine hoped. He attempted to improve relations with France and Austria and to strengthen Poland through a series of reforms. Catherine II and Frederick II of Prussia opposed him on both counts and insisted on equal rights for Orthodox and Protestant minorities in Catholic Poland.

Many Poles, although not their king, revolted against such foreign pressures. Led by prominent nobles, on February 29, 1768, they formed a rebellious confederation at Bar, in southern Polish Ukraine. For the next four years, the Confederation of Bar waged a civil war against their king and his Russian supporters. Finally, in 1772, after diplomatic events had complicated matters, Russia, Prussia, and Austria imposed a treaty on Poland. It sanctioned the first partition of Poland, by which it lost territories to its three neighbors. Russia's share was primarily in Belorussian lands, but included all previous Polish territory east of the Western Dvina and Dnieper rivers.

Although many historians have suggested that Russia's role in this and Catherine's subsequent partitions of Poland flowed from Russia's expansionist tendencies, Robert Jones has argued that it resulted more from Russia's porous border with Poland. More specifically, he has indicated that Catherine, pressured by serfowning nobles in frontier provinces, wished to prevent serfs from fleeing to Poland, where taxes and other obligations were less than in Russia.

Complicating affairs in Poland from 1768 to 1772 was Russia's relations with the Porte (more formally the Sublime Porte), as the Ottoman Turkish government was then labeled. From the fall of 1768 until the summer of 1774, Russia found itself at war with Turkey.

The main reason for the war was the Porte's dislike of Russian diplomatic and military activity in Poland, their mutual neighbor, and the fear it would further strengthen Russia in its southern expansion toward the Black Sea. Also unwilling to tolerate Russian gains at Poland's expense was France, who encouraged the Turks to fight. After Russian troops poured into Poland and hostilities flowed over the Polish-Turkish border, the Porte declared war on Russia.

Although Turkey began the war, Catherine enthusiastically embraced the opportunity to push Russia's borders southward and add her own name to the list of Russian tsars who led the country to military glory.

During the war, the Russian Baltic fleet sailed to the Mediterranean, and its commander, Alexei Orlov, attempted to incite the Orthodox Greeks against their Turkish Moslem overlords. His brother Grigori, still Catherine's lover and a leading adviser, encouraged Catherine to believe that not only the Greeks, but also other Balkan Orthodox might rebel. Although Orlov's hopes proved overblown, Alexei's fleet did win some Aegean battles, most notably one in 1770 at Chesme, near the Turkish coast. More telling were land victories by the

Russian army, which brought them control over areas such as Moldavia, Wallachia, and the Crimea.

By 1774, with the Pugachev revolt still blazing, Catherine wanted peace. She received it with the Treaty of Kuchuk-Kainarji. By its terms, Russia received a small Black Sea coastal area between the Bug and Dnieper rivers; Azov and control over the Strait of Kerch, which joined the Sea of Azov to the Black Sea; and the Terek and Kuban regions east of these seas. The khanate of Crimea, long a Turkish vassal, was to become independent. For the first time, the Turks agreed to allow Russian merchant ships to enter the Black Sea and to pass through the Straits (the Bosphorus and Dardanelles) en route to the Mediterranean. The Porte paid a secret indemnity of 4.5 million rubles, and in articles that had serious implications three-quarters of a century later, Turkey also granted Russia the right to build an Orthodox Church in Constantinople and to intercede in behalf of those it served (see Map 15.1).

The Latter Years, 1775–1796

Of the five "P's" discussed previously, two continued to be important during Catherine's last two decades, Poland and the Porte. She also maintained peace from late 1774 to 1787 and an alliance with Prussia until 1788. A new "P," Potemkin, soon overshadowed an old one, Panin, in influencing foreign policy.

Even before Potemkin became Catherine's lover and began assuming important posts in 1774, Panin's plan for a Northern System had proved deficient. Besides other problems, Sweden's King Gustavus III, fearful of a fate like Poland's, had managed to strengthen his powers and move closer to France than Russia.

After 1774, despite Britain's desire for Russian assistance in its war against America, France, and Spain, Anglo-Russian relations showed signs of strain. The war led to Catherine's Declaration of Armed Neutrality (1780), which flew in the face of traditional British policy of interfering with neutral merchant ships doing business with Britain's wartime enemies.

The influence of Potemkin contributed not only to Panin's forced retirement in 1781, but also to the final jettisoning of the Northern System. The key element was Catherine's reversion, despite the Russo-Prussian alliance still in effect, to Austria as Russia's main ally. Indeed the negotiating of a secret 1781 Austro-Russian agreement to cooperate against Turkey, despite Panin's advice, coincided with Potemkin's final victory over him.

The main reason for this new agreement was Catherine's sweeping ambitions directed against the Sublime Porte. Austria was in a much better position to help her realize them than was Prussia. The extent of her ambitions, greatly encouraged by Potemkin, are best manifested in her "Greek Project."

Although the practical effects of this grandiose dream are debatable, it involved ending Moslem Turkish rule over European Christians and having Russia and Austria move into the vacuum. Besides allowing the new allies to expand their frontiers at the Porte's expense, the project envisioned creating two new kingdoms. In one, with its capital in Constantinople, Catherine's sec-

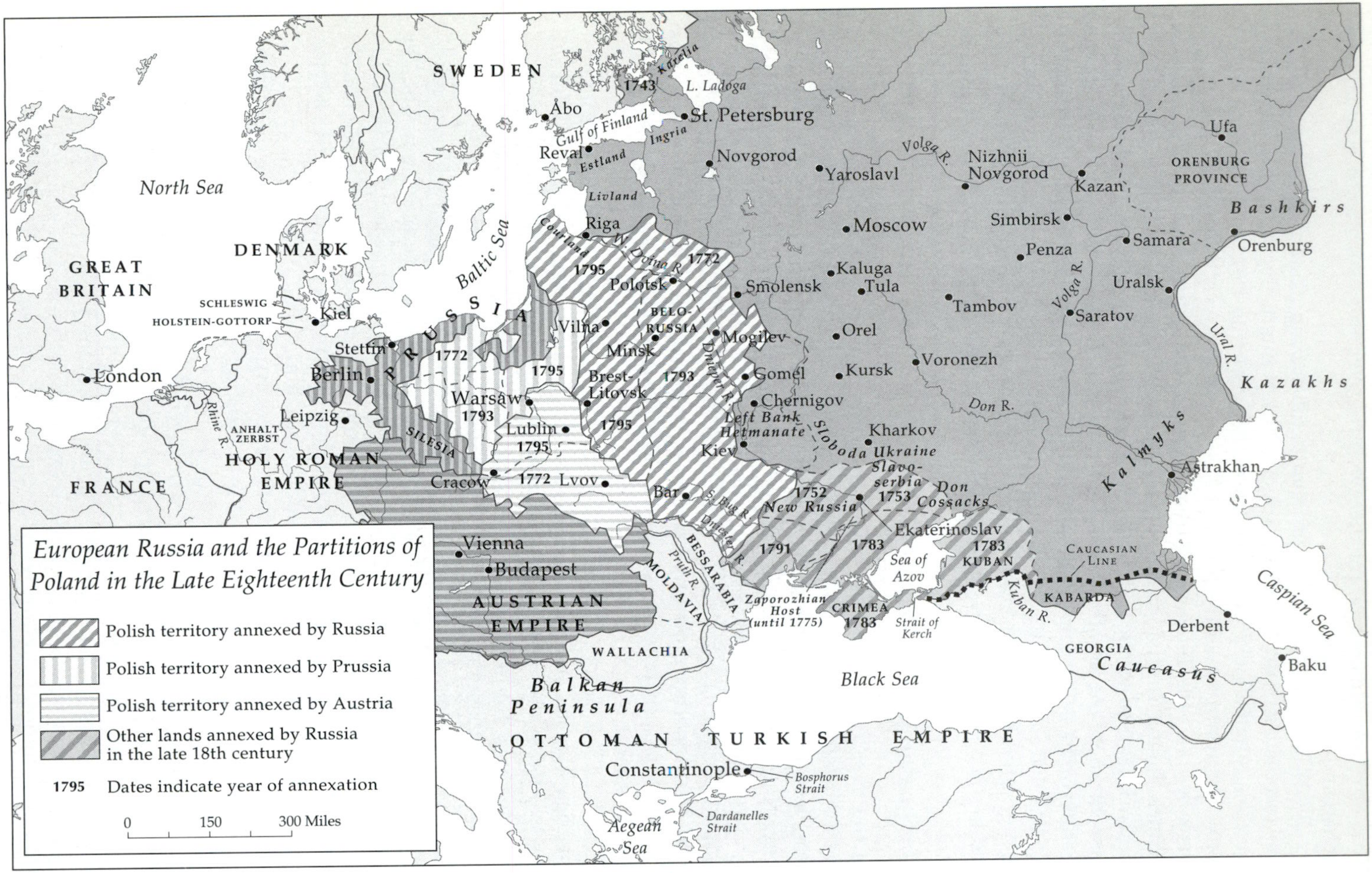
European Russia and the Partitions of Poland in the Late Eighteenth Century
Polish territory annexed by Russia
Polish territory annexed by Prussia
Polish territory annexed by Austria
Other lands annexed by Russia in the late 18th century
1795 Dates indicate year of annexation
0 150 300 Miles
SWEDEN
North Sea
GREAT BRITAIN
DENMARK
SCHLESWIG
HOLSTEIN-GOTTORP
Kiel
London
Baltic Sea
PRUSSIA
Stettin
Berlin
Leipzig
ANHALT-ZERBST
Rhine R.
HOLY ROMAN EMPIRE
FRANCE
SILESIA
Warsaw
1793
1772
1795
Lublin
1795
Cracow
1772 Lvov
Vienna
Budapest
AUSTRIAN EMPIRE
WALLACHIA
MOLDAVIA
Pruth R.
BESSARABIA
Balkan Peninsula
OTTOMAN TURKISH EMPIRE
Constantinople
Bosphorus Strait
Dardanelles Strait
Aegean Sea
Åbo
Reval
Gulf of Finland
Estland
Ingria
Karelia
1743
L. Ladoga
St. Petersburg
Livland
Riga
Courland
1795
W. Dvina R.
1772
Polotsk
Vilna
BELO-RUSSIA
Minsk
Brest-Litovsk
1793
1795
Mogilev
Dnieper R.
Gomel
Chernigov
Left Bank Hetmanate
Kiev
Bar
S. Bug R.
Dniester R.
1791
Zaporozhian Host (until 1775)
CRIMEA
1783
Strait of Kerch
Sea of Azov
Black Sea
1752
New Russia
Slobodа Ukraine
Slavo-serbia
1753
Don Cossacks
Ekaterinoslav
1783
1783
KUBAN
Kuban R.
KABARDA
CAUCASIAN LINE
GEORGIA
Caucasus
Derbent
Baku
Caspian Sea
Astrakhan
Kalmyks
Novgorod
Yaroslavl
Moscow
Smolensk
Kaluga
Tula
Orel
Kursk
Kharkov
Voronezh
Don R.
Tambov
Penza
Nizhnii Novgorod
Volga R.
Simbirsk
Kazan
Samara
Saratov
Volga R.
Uralsk
Ural R.
Kazakhs
Orenburg
Bashkirs
ORENBURG PROVINCE
Ufa

MAP 15.1

FIGURE 15.3. "Imperialistic Catherine," as viewed by an English caricaturist in 1791. (*From Ian Grey*, The Horizon History of Russia, *American Heritage Publishing Company, New York, 1970, p. 208.*)

ond grandson, grandiosely named Constantine, would be the monarch. As ruler of a Kingdom of Dacia, encompassing Bessarabia, Moldavia, and Wallachia, Catherine seemed to have Potemkin in mind.

Although Emperor Joseph II of Austria had his doubts about her project, he did not oppose Catherine's first step in realizing it—Potemkin's annexation of the Crimea in 1783. In 1787, Joseph II joined Catherine in a visit to the Black Sea coast, where Potemkin proudly displayed new buildings and the ships of his new Black Sea fleet.

It was from this trip south and Potemkin's efforts to impress his Empress that the legend of "Potemkin's villages" arose. These were "villages" that looked great as Catherine's galleys passed down the Dnieper, but whose huts were rumored to have been nothing more than painted facades.

In 1783, Potemkin also had expanded Russian influence in the Caucasus. This was done by establishing a Russian protectorate over the Christian kingdom of Georgia.

Russia's 1783 gains, the building of a Black Sea fleet, and the 1787 trip of Catherine and Joseph II all increased tensions between Russia and the Porte. Encouraged by Prussia and Great Britain, Turkey waited until Catherine returned to her capital and declared war in August 1787.

Although Joseph II was far from enthusiastic about supporting Catherine, he lived up to his 1781 commitment and declared war on the Turks in early 1788. That same year, Sweden, wishing to recover lands lost to Peter I and Elizabeth, attacked Russia. The northern fighting had little consequence, however, and two years later Russia and Sweden agreed to a treaty with no gains for either side.

The war against Turkey lasted more than four years for Russia; Austria, faced with more serious troubles elsewhere, signed an armistice with the Porte in 1790. After some impressive Russian victories, especially by General Suvorov, Turkey agreed to the Treaty of Jassy in January 1792 (December 1791 O.S.). By it, the Porte recognized Russia's annexation of the Crimea and handed over an additional chunk of territory north of the Black Sea, between the Bug and Dniester rivers.

Although these gains fell far short of Catherine's Greek Project, she never completely abandoned it. In her final year, 1796, it overlapped an "Oriental Project" associated with the last of her lovers, Platon Zubov. His plan called for conquering the Caucasus and beyond. After a Persian attack on Georgia, Catherine sent Russian troops under Zubov's younger brother down the Caspian coast, where they seized Derbent and Baku. After 1791, however, Catherine's attention turned mainly westward. While Russia was preoccupied with Turkey, the Poles, strengthened by an alliance with Prussia in 1790, had completed fundamental political and social reforms. These reforms were symbolized by a constitution of 1791. Because the reforms would have strengthened Poland, Catherine opposed them and invaded Poland in May 1792, ostensibly in support of a confederation of Polish nobles opposed to the reforms. By then, Prussia and Austria were at war with revolutionary France, and Catherine was able to impose a second Polish partition (January 1793) in which Russia gained the major portion, with a lesser part going to Prussia.

A third partition, which brought an end to the Polish state, occurred in 1795. It followed a 1794 Polish rebellion, led by Thaddeus Kosciuszko, against foreign domination. This time Austria as well as Russia and Prussia once again received a share of Poland.

Overall, in the three partitions of Poland (1772, 1793, and 1795), Russia gained a little over three-fifths of the lands of the prepartition Polish-Lithuanian Commonwealth and a little under half of its population. In 1795, these lands (in size measuring between Texas and modern-day Spain) were peopled by some 7.5 million Belorussians, Ukrainians, Lithuanians, Latvians, Jews, and Poles.

THE EMPIRE: UNIFORMITY, INTEGRATION, AND COLONIZATION

By 1796, Russia's continental empire measured almost 7,000 miles from east to west and contained scores of nationalities. Although Catherine's approach to ruling her lands and peoples displayed some variations, her desire for economic growth and her "passion for uniformity" were the two forces that most propelled her.

Her quest for uniformity was partly prompted by the "enlightened" ideas of the eighteenth century, which emphasized reason and order and valued "civilization," not civilizations or local cultures. In the Caucasus, for example, Catherine thought that Russia offered the advantages of civilization to peoples still swimming in the stagnant waters of Asiatic barbarism. Her stress on uniformity also owed something to tsarist tradition.

This period predated the development of modern nationalism, and Catherine's imperial policies were thus not a manifestation of the latter. This fact, plus her pragmatism and relative religious tolerance, made her less of a "Russifier" than some of her successors.

Catherine's desire for uniformity led her to apply her 1775 and 1785 reorganization plans to as many areas of the empire as possible. Thus, despite major differences between Siberia and European Russia, especially the virtual absence of Siberian serfs and landowning nobles, Catherine applied her 1775 Provincial Reform statute to Siberia in the early 1780s. In 1780, the government mandated it for Sloboda Ukraine; in 1783, for the Baltic Provinces; and after the Polish partitions, for the newly annexed Polish lands. The government also applied the Charter of the Nobility and the Charter of the Towns in some areas such as the Baltic provinces of Estland and Livland. The result of all these steps was to increase fiscal and judicial uniformity.

In other parts of the empire, although sometimes moving more slowly, the government had the same goal. In the large province of Orenburg, essentially old Bashkiria, St. Petersburg reduced Bashkirian autonomy, especially after Bashkirian involvement in the Pugachev rebellion.

In "New Russia" and other southern lands that came under Potemkin's control, he attempted to integrate them more closely with the rest of the empire. In the process, the Don Cossacks fared better than did the Zaporozhian Cossacks. The former were allowed to maintain some autonomy, although Potemkin insisted on certain Russian governmental rights, such as naming the chief Don Cossack leader (the ataman). But the Zaporozhians saw Russian troops destroy their Sech (camp) in 1775. This followed Russia's war against Turkey and the rebellion of Pugachev and his Yaik Cossack followers. New lands gained south of the Zaporozhian territory and the end of Turkish control over the Crimea meant that the Zaporozhian Host lost its raison d'être as a frontier military force. Some Zaporozhians fled to Turkish lands, some were exiled to Siberia, and others remained, but the Host's separate existence came to an end.

Catherine also wasted little time in further integrating the Ukrainian Hetmanate. In 1764, after Cyril Razumovsky and Hetmanate nobles petitioned her for a restoration of lost rights—and Razumovsky even proposed a hereditary Razumovsky hetmancy—Catherine demanded his resignation. In his place, she named an illegitimate son of Peter the Great, General Peter Rumiantsev, to rule over this Left Bank area as governor-general. He was to proceed cautiously but not tolerate movements aimed at restoring earlier autonomy.

In his three decades overseeing the Left Bank, Rumiantsev gradually introduced more Russian fiscal, judicial, and administrative practices. In 1782, the area was subdivided into three Little Russian provinces, each receiving its own governor. In 1783, Left Bank peasants were officially prohibited from leaving the lands of their landowners—thus giving final legal sanction to a serfdom that had gradually redeveloped after Polish serfdom had been ended in the region in 1648.

In integrating the empire, Catherine relied not only on military forces and officials, but also received support from other elements, both Russian and non-Russian. At the Legislative Commission in 1767, for example, her quest for uniformity was shared by those deputies who spoke out against "Baltic privileges" and complained the region was not contributing its fair share of taxes. Coopted native elites also helped further her efforts in the empire.

Catherine's religious policies helped further integrate the empire. On the one hand, she backed Orthodox efforts to win Catholic Uniates to Orthodoxy in the lands won from Poland—by her death more than half of the over 3 million Uniates in this area had converted to the Orthodoxy of their ancestors. On the other hand, she tolerated those who remained Catholic, including many Polish or Polonized nobles in the same region.

Catherine allowed Moslems to construct many new mosques; freed Moslem Tatars from previous trading and commercial restrictions; and, in 1789, established a Moslem Ecclesiastical Council. It was to control Moslem religious life (dogma, marriage, divorce, religious schools), thus legitimizing and further unifying Moslem practices. Centered in the town of Orenburg and later in Ufa, it remained central to Moslem religious life throughout the rest of the Imperial period.

No doubt the Pugachev revolt, involving Bashkirs and other Moslems, and the later annexation of the Crimean Tatar khanate helped stimulate Catherine's concessions to Islam. Her policies, however, fit with her overall goal of integrating native leaders into the empire's command structure. Thus, the government conferred noble status upon the Moslem leader (*mufti*) of the Ecclesiastical Council and other important Moslem officials.

Catherine also increasingly integrated Cossack and native peoples into the Russian military. In the Orenburg Province, they helped man some forty forts by the mid-1790s, three-fourths of them guarding the border with Kazakhstan. In the Caucasus, they helped defend and garrison the new Caucasian Line that stretched between the northern Caspian Sea and the Sea of Azov, guarding against mountaineers to the south and providing a solid line for further advances.

Although Catherine's reforms sometimes forced local non-Russian elites to share influence with Russians and other new "outsiders" in their region, they also helped local elites in various ways. Throughout the empire, Catherine's reforms strengthened noble prerogatives. The reforms also provided new imperial opportunities, especially for Western elites. A more integrated empire required officials familiar with modern Western ways—one of Orenburg's most effective governors was the Baltic noble Osip Igelstrom.

Not only opportunities, but also fears enticed non-Russian elites to cooperate with the Russian government. For example, in the areas Russia took from Poland in 1793 and 1795, there was not only the scare of the French Revolution, but also Kosciuszko's 1794 manifesto freeing serfs who joined his rebellion.

Integrating the empire and encouraging economic development often led to increased colonization. In Siberia, production of precious metals became especially important, and the region was also the base for further explorations, such as to the Alaskan mainland, where Russia had already established a foothold by 1796. Catherine encouraged colonization to Siberia especially to increase its agricultural base, which, in turn, was then better able to support the growing number of officials, military, and mine-workers. By 1796, it contained more than 1 million people.

By then, the Bashkirs made up only about one-fifth of approximately 700,000 people in the Orenburg Province. Besides Russians, who owned the majority of the large estates, other nationalities, especially from the mid-Volga region, continued to pour into this rich area. Among them were the Chuvash and Tatars; the Mari, Mordva, and Udmurts (all three Finnish-speaking); and some Central Asian peoples.

Following the breakup of the Zaporozhian Cossacks, much of their land was distributed to Russian nobles and even German and Serbian colonists. In Eastern Belorussia, after it was gained from Poland in 1772, Catherine made extensive land grants. By 1796, almost one-fifth of the Belorussian peasants were working on estates Catherine had granted to "outsiders."

CATHERINE'S DEATH AND SIGNIFICANCE

The influence of the mediocre Platon Zubov and the empire's growing financial problems marked a sad end to Catherine's reign. In November 1796, she died of a stroke.

Even before her death, some Russians and foreigners referred to her as "Catherine the Great." There can be little doubt she was one of Russia's most significant rulers. Her extensive territorial acquisitions alone merit that designation. But was she also one of Russia's "best" rulers? That is more debatable.

During the nineteenth century, the radical Herzen charged that she ignored the interests of the Russian masses, and the poet Pushkin thought her a hypocrite. Even the more objective historian Kliuchevsky faulted her for her treatment of the vast mass of her people, the peasants. Soviet historians also generally treated her harshly.

Most recent Western scholarship, such as that of Alexander, LeDonne, and especially Madariaga, has been more sympathetic. Although not denying some of Catherine's faults, they insist that Russian conditions often prevented some of her more enlightened goals from being realized. Despite the many roadblocks in Catherine's path, Madariaga maintains she created a more humane, just, and enlightened country.

After examining in subsequent chapters the economic, social, and cultural conditions, both inherited by Catherine II and passed on by her to her successors, we shall be better prepared to judge Catherine's legacy to her adopted country.

SUGGESTED SOURCES*

AKSAKOV, SERGEI. *The Family Chronicle*. New York, 1961. A novel that provides good insights into the Russian colonization of Bashkiria.

ALEXANDER, JOHN T. *Catherine the Great: Life and Legend*. New York, 1989.

———. "Catherine II's Efforts at Liberalization and Their Aftermath." In *Reform in Russia and the U.S.S.R.: Past and Prospects*, ed. Robert O. Crummey. Urbana, Ill., 1989.

———. *Emperor of the Cossacks: Pugachev and the Frontier Jacquerie of 1773–1775*. Lawrence, Kans., 1973.

AVRICH, PAUL. *Russian Rebels, 1600–1800*. New York, 1972. Pt. IV.

BODGER, ALAN. *The Kazakhs and the Pugachev Uprising in Russia, 1773–1775*. Bloomington, Ind., 1988.

CATHERINE II, EMPRESS OF RUSSIA. *The Memoirs of Catherine the Great*. New York, 1957.

CROSS, ANTHONY G., ed. *Engraved in the Memory: James Walker, Engraver to the Empress Catherine the Great, and His Russian Anecdotes*. Oxford, 1993.

DANIEL, WALLACE L. *Grigorii Teplov: A Statesman at the Court of Catherine the Great*. Newtonville, Mass., 1991.

DASHKOVA, E. R. *The Memoirs of Princess Dashkova*. Durham, 1995.

DUKES, PAUL. *Catherine the Great and the Russian Nobility: A Study Based on the Materials of the Legislative Commission of 1767*. London, 1967.

———. *The Making of Russian Absolutism, 1613–1801*. 2d ed. London, 1990. Ch. 5.

———, ed. *Russia under Catherine the Great*. 2 vols. Newtonville, Mass., 1977.

EPP, GEORGE K. *The Educational Policies of Catherine II: The Era of Enlightenment in Russia*. Frankfurt am Main, 1984.

FISHER, ALAN W. *The Russian Annexation of the Crimea, 1772–1783*. Cambridge, England, 1970.

GLEASON, WALTER J. *Moral Idealists, Bureaucracy, and Catherine the Great*. New Brunswick, N.J., 1981.

———, ed. *The Political and Legal Writings of Denis Fonvizin*. Ann Arbor, 1985.

GRIFFITHS, DAVID M. *Russian Court Politics and the Question of an Expansionist Foreign Policy Under Catherine II, 1762–1783*. Ithaca, N.Y., 1967.

GRIFFITHS, DAVID, and GEORGE MUNRO, eds. *Catherine II's Charters of 1785 to the Nobility and Towns*. Bakersfield, Calif., 1991.

JONES, ROBERT E. *The Emancipation of the Russian Nobility, 1762–1785*. Princeton, 1973.

———. *Provincial Development in Russia: Catherine II and Jakob Sievers*. New Brunswick, N.J., 1984.

JONES, W. GARETH. *Nikolay Novikov, Enlightener of Russia*. Cambridge, England, 1984.

KAMENSKII, ALEKSANDR BORISOVICH, "Catherine the Great," *SSH* 30 (Fall 1991): 30–65. Reprinted in *EER*, pp. 135–76.

KAPLAN, HERBERT H. *The First Partition of Poland*. New York, 1962.

KOCHAN, MIRIAM. *Life in Russia Under Catherine the Great*. London, 1969.

KOHUT, ZENON E. *Russian Centralism and Ukrainian Autonomy: Imperial Absorption of the Hetmanate, 1760s–1830s*. Cambridge, Mass., 1988.

*See also works cited in footnotes.

LANG, DAVID M. *The First Russian Radical: Alexander Radishchev, 1749–1802*. London, 1959.

LEDONNE, JOHN P. *Absolutism and Ruling Class: The Formation of the Russian Political Order, 1700–1825*. New York, 1991.

MADARIAGA, ISABEL DE. *Catherine the Great: A Short History*. New Haven, 1990.

———. *Russia in the Age of Catherine the Great*. New Haven, 1981.

MCCONNELL, ALLEN. *A Russian Philosophe, Alexander Radishchev, 1749–1802*. The Hague, 1964.

OLIVA, L. JAY, ed. *Catherine the Great*. Englewood Cliffs, N.J., 1971.

PAPMEHL, K. A. "The Empress and 'un fanatique': A Review of the Circumstances Leading to the Government Action against Novikov in 1792," *SEER* 68 (October 1990): 665–691.

PIPES, RICHARD. *Russia under the Old Regime*. New York, 1974.

PUSHKIN, ALEXANDER. *The Captain's Daughter and Other Great Stories*. New York, 1936. The main story is a novella set against the background of Pugachev's revolt.

RAEFF, MARC. *Imperial Russia, 1682–1825: The Coming of Age of Modern Russia*. New York, 1971.

———. *Political Ideas and Institutions in Imperial Russia*. Boulder, 1994. Contains several reprinted essays dealing with Catherine's reign, including ones on Pugachev and Potemkin. See also other works by Raeff listed at the end of Chapter 16.

———, ed. *Catherine the Great: A Profile*. New York, 1972.

RAGSDALE, HUGH, ed. *Imperial Russian Foreign Policy*. Washington, D.C., 1993. Contains essays by Ragsdale and Robert E. Jones on aspects of Catherine's foreign policy.

RANSEL, DAVID L. *The Politics of Catherinian Russia: The Panin Party*. New Haven, 1975.

REDDAWAY, W. F., ed. *Documents of Catherine the Great: The Correspondence with Voltaire and the Instruction of 1767 in the English Text of 1768*. Cambridge, England, 1931.

SHCHERBATOV, M. M. *On the Corruption of Morals in Russia*. London, 1969.

SOLOVIEV, SERGEI M. *The Reign of Catherine the Great. The Legislative Commission (1767–1768) and Foreign Affairs (1766–68)*. Gulf Breeze, Fla., 1986.

———. *The Rule of Catherine the Great, 1768–1770: Turkey and Poland*. Gulf Breeze, Fla., 1994.

———. *The Rule of Catherine the Great: War, Diplomacy and Domestic Affairs, 1772–1774*. Gulf Breeze, Fla., 1991.

THADEN, EDWARD C. *Russia's Western Borderlands, 1710–1870*. Princeton, 1984. Pt. 1.

TROYAT, HENRI. *Catherine the Great*. New York, 1980.

WHITTAKER, CYNTHIA HYLA. "The Idea of Autocracy among Eighteenth-Century Russian Historians," *RR* 55 (April 1996): 149–171.

CHAPTER 16

Eighteenth-Century Economic and Social Life

The century of Peter I and Catherine II was one of significant expansion not only in territory, but also in population, economic development, and noble privileges. There were also smaller-scale advances in urban development, the status of women and children, social services, fighting famine, and humanizing the law. The century, however, was not one of advancement for Russia's largest group—the serfs.

POPULATION AND TOWNS

Russia's population more than doubled during the eighteenth century, going from about 15 to 16 million inhabitants in 1719 to a little over 37 million by 1796. Although Russia began the century with a smaller population than France, by 1789 it outnumbered France by about 10 million people. Thus, despite its low population density, Russia had become the largest country in Europe.

As colonization and conquests increased, the population spread out more over the entire empire, from former Polish lands to the Pacific Ocean. Although population rose in the center of the empire, it grew even faster in southern areas, such as Left-Bank Ukraine, New Russia, and the lower Volga valley.

Although many new towns came into existence—Catherine II alone claimed credit for 216 new ones in the first twenty-three years of her reign—the percentage of urban dwellers at the end of the century was probably not much higher than at the beginning. Estimates for the 1790s usually range between 4 and 8 percent of the total population, depending on who is counted as urban. Colonization of new lands, certain restrictions on mobility, and unhealthy urban conditions all prevented older cities from growing more rapidly.

By the end of the eighteenth century, St. Petersburg, less than a century old, had become the largest city in the empire. Moscow was a close second.

These "two capitals" together possessed about 400,000 inhabitants. According to Kahan's estimates, no other city of the empire had more than 50,000 people. Astrakhan, Kazan, Tula, and Vilna each had between 30,000 and 50,000; Yaroslavl, Kaluga, Kiev, Kursk, Orel, Riga, and Saratov each had between 20,000 and 30,000. Fourteen other cities had between 10,000 and 20,000. Some large cities were sea or river port towns benefiting from international or domestic trade. Examples of seaport towns were Astrakhan and Riga; river port towns included Yaroslavl and Saratov.

Towns were marked by their walls; their concentrated population; and at least some stone or brick construction, including their churches. Most towns were trading and cultural centers, serving the surrounding countryside, and some also produced goods; some towns of less than 1,000 people were little more than district government centers. Many cities fulfilled several functions. For example, Yaroslavl was not only a Volga port city, but also a provincial capital and a center of textile production.

St. Petersburg and Moscow, both much smaller than London, Paris, or Naples and larger (by 1783) than Berlin, presented an interesting contrast. The first was a planned city of canals and straight roads, reflecting the rationalism of Peter the Great and the eighteenth century. By the end of the century, numerous baroque and neoclassical palaces and other buildings graced the city. Other rich palaces and royal estates surrounded the new capital. By contrast, Moscow had grown more spontaneously, and its many large gardens and old churches made it seem more rural, religious, and "Russian" than the new capital.

Like Peter I, Catherine II preferred St. Petersburg to Moscow. The inhabitants of the first she found more commercial, docile, polite, and open to foreign ideas; those of the second, more slothful and superstitious. She also com-

FIGURE 16.1. City of Tobolsk in the early eighteenth century. By the end of the century, this largest of western Siberian cities contained about 15,000 people.
(*From Ian Grey,* The Horizon History of Russia, *American Heritage Publishing Company, New York, 1970, pp. 146–47.*)

plained of Moscow's thieves and brigands and its heavy concentration of manufactories.

Like Peter I, creator of St. Petersburg, Catherine II was a believer in urban
planning. In both new and rebuilt cities (such as Tver, devastated by fire in
1763), her planners attempted to reduce the constant threat of fire by building
wider streets and more stone buildings. They also tried to improve sanitation
by such measures as locating factories where their pollution would do the least
damage. Catherine II thought that towns had three chief functions. They
should be centers of government, public welfare, and trade and industry. Even
by the end of Catherine's reign, however, institutions such as hospitals,
schools, and orphanages employed and served relatively few.

Townspeople working in crafts, trade, and manufacturing (the earlier
posad people) were still the single largest urban category. They had not increased as fast as other urban dwellers, however. Among the latter were officials and clerks, nobles, soldiers, clergy, and especially peasants, both serfs and
state peasants. Many peasants did not consider themselves permanent city residents, some only staying for the winter season. Many left their families in the
countryside—a partial explanation for why by 1800 the combined male population in St. Petersburg and Moscow was more than double the female. The
peasants, if not serfs belonging to city nobles, took whatever jobs they could
find, for example, manual laborers, water carriers, servants, peddlers, porters,
and horse-carriage drivers.

MANUFACTURING AND TRADE

From Peter I's death in 1725 until 1800, the number of manufactories rose from
perhaps a little more than 200 to about six to ten times that figure. They produced or processed chiefly iron and weapons, precious metals, copper, ships,
salt, linen and wool cloth, silk-wares, cotton textiles, bricks, glass, and paper.

Pig iron was especially important. By 1800, the empire was producing
about twelve times what it had in 1725. It briefly became the largest pig iron
producer in the world, surpassing England, to whom it exported large quantities of this basic metal. By the 1760s, Russia was also in the forefront of European silver and copper production and beginning to accelerate significantly its
output of gold. The increase in precious metals and copper stimulated other industries and trade.

As the century proceeded, a larger percentage of industrial production
was carried on by private enterprise. For example, although the state produced
a little more than one-third of the total pig iron in 1725, in 1800 it produced
only a little more than one-tenth. In most other areas of production, the government was even less involved. It still played a major industrial role, however, by being the chief buyer of many products; by controlling vast natural resources; by granting licenses, monopolies, and subsidies; and by various other
policies that affected the availability of labor and resources.

Despite encouraging some private enterprise both in manufacturing and
commerce, the tsarist government remained ambivalent at best regarding any

large-scale independent business activity. This caution was indicated in various ways including the government's failure to develop adequate corporate laws. As Thomas Owen has noted, between 1700 and 1820 the government allowed only 33 corporations to come into existence, and most of them did not last long.

Even after 1762, when the government prohibited nonnobles henceforth to buy serfs, most factory laborers continued to be either assigned state peasants or serfs owned by the factory owners. In some industries, however, owners gradually came to rely more on hired labor, mainly peasants. Ironically, many of these peasants were privately owned serfs whose noble owners either compelled or allowed them to enter into factory labor contracts. Either way, the serfowners were paid for the loss of their serfs' services.

Russia also made use of many women and children in the factories. After 1725, the government continued to sentence women it considered vagrants, for example, prostitutes and criminals' wives, to factory service. Two decrees of 1762 targeted vagrant wives of soldiers. Children under the age of fifteen, often even younger than eleven, were also employed. Their families needed the money, and the owners could pay them less than adults.

As in most countries' early industrialization, working conditions were often appalling, at least by modern standards. Only Sundays and holidays (together numbering almost 100 days per year) gave much respite. Workers worked twelve hours a day and more and faced unsanitary working and living conditions and harsh factory discipline, including beatings. Only unrest and rebellion, for example, among many Ural workers who joined Pugachev, stimulated the government to take steps (such as pay raises) to appease workers. Such measures, however, had little effect on long-term trends.

Domestic and foreign trade grew rapidly, especially in the second half of the century. The government's abolition of internal customs duties in the early 1750s helped domestic trade. So too did decrees of Peter III and Catherine II ending most merchant privileges in manufacturing and trade, thus opening these spheres up more to other estates and stimulating economic growth in the countryside. Finally, increased industrial and agricultural production fostered trade both between towns and villages and between different regions.

Urban and rural fairs and bazaars were the primary arteries for distributing goods. According to figures of Boris Mironov, the number of fairs increased from 627 in the 1750s to 3,447 within about the same territory in the 1790s.

Fairs lasted several days or longer and varied considerably in size and in the products traded. Although their drawing power varied, the largest fairs attracted people from various regions and even foreign buyers and sellers. Bazaars operated on specific days of the week, and food and craft products dominated the trade. Larger city bazaars offered greater variety, including more manufactured domestic and imported goods.

In foreign trade, Russia continued to export more than it imported. Chief exports were flax, grain, hemp, iron, livestock products, pitch, tar, tallow, timber, and cheap textiles. The opening up of Black Sea ports under Catherine the Great stimulated wheat production and its export from southern regions. Many imports were either for use in Russian industry, such as dyes, lead, raw silk, and tin, or for upper-class use, such as certain clothing, beverages, and food. Only a few imported goods, such as nails and needles, found many buyers among the lower classes.

Russia's chief trading partner throughout the last two-thirds of the eighteenth century was Great Britain, with Russia's exports far exceeding imports. The British bought hemp, flax, pitch, tar, tallow, masts, linen textiles, and iron—such imports helping them fuel Europe's first industrial revolution.

VILLAGES AND HOUSING

Most Russian peasants, whether serfs or not, lived in villages containing anywhere from several to hundreds of households. Most peasant huts were made of wood except in southern areas, where they were built of materials such as clay and stone because of the scarcity of trees. The houses of nobles and townsmen were also often wooden and in the old Russian styles. By the end of the century, however, brick and stone were becoming more common for those who could afford them and so too were Western architectural styles. Both in cities and on noble estates, neoclassical columned buildings especially reflected the new foreign influence.

FIGURE 16.2. A northern peasant village, around 1800.
(From Robert Wallace and the Editors of Time-Life Books, Rise of Russia. *Time Inc., New York, 1967, p. 146, Courtesy of the Free Library of Philadelphia, Rare Book Department.)*

Villages and Housing: A Foreign Observation

One of the best observers of eighteenth-century Russian life was the Englishman William Tooke (1744–1820). The following selection is taken from his *View of the Russian Empire during the Reign of Catherine the Second, and to the Close of the Eighteenth Century* 2d ed. (London, 1800), Vol. II, pp. 40–44. I have modernized spellings and punctuation, and bracketed material and ellipses are mine.

Villages of extremely various dimensions . . . are situated on the margin of rivers, brooks, lakes, and sometimes on mere morasses and springs. . . . Large villages are frequently called slobodes; but many slobodes are less than church villages [the largest of which might contain a thousand or more households]. . . .

The proper Russian architecture is alike in towns and villages. A messuage consists of a dwelling-house, with a few little store-rooms, stables, and a stew, or hot-bath. . . . All these structures are built of bauks, unhewn, placed on one another and notched into each other at the four corners, sometimes, though but rarely, on a brick foundation; these houses are covered with boards, and when the owner can afford it, with oak shingles. The meanest dwelling-houses consist solely of one little room. . . .

In it is an oven, taking up almost one-fourth part of the whole space; adjoining to it, of equal height with the oven, is a broad shelf of board. The top of the oven and this shelf are the sleeping places of the family. The light is admitted into these houses through two or three holes in the walls furnished with shutters, or through a little window of muscovy-glass, or only of bladder, oiled linen or paper. The smoke finds its way out as well as it can through these apertures in the wall. These rooms, as may well be supposed, are as black as a chimney. . . .

The household-furniture, both in town and country, even among people of opulence, is very simple. In the room, which, with very few exceptions, is at the same time the kitchen, are a table, benches, the shelf, which serves for the dormitory, and in the corner one or more holy figures [icons]. . . . Splinters, like laths, of fir or very dry birchwood are much more commonly used for giving light in the room after dark than tallow-candles. . . .

The inferior houses are much pestered with domestic vermin; besides the common house-rat and mouse, they swarm with water-rats, bats, large beetles very frequent, crickets, bugs, fleas in abundance, various kinds of very troublesome flies, gnats, moths, bullmoths, [and] wood-lice.

Besides Tooke's observations, others noted the crowded conditions in the huts, especially in the long winters, when some animals were brought in. Conversely, in the summers, some members of the household, like a young married couple, normally slept in unheated sheds or other areas outside the crowded hut.

AGRICULTURE, NOBLES, AND PEASANTS

Agriculture

Although by 1800 many peasants and some nobles earned supplemental income through crafts, industry, and trade, agriculture still dominated Russia's

FIGURE 16.3. Inside a peasant cabin, around 1800. Note the big oven and the suspended infant cradle.
(From Robert Wallace and the Editors of Time-Life Books, Rise of Russia. *Time Inc., New York, 1967, p. 147, Courtesy of the Free Library of Philadelphia, Rare Book Department.)*

economy. Even some merchants joined nobles and peasants in obtaining new farmlands opened up by Catherine II's conquests. During the eighteenth century, available plow land more than doubled. This growth, plus the stimulus of growing trade, significantly boosted agricultural production, especially under Catherine II.

Activities in the countryside continued to be largely determined by custom and nature. The three-field system of crop rotation and the use of the light *sokha* plow still predominated. From spring to fall, there was primarily plowing, planting, pasturing, mowing, and harvesting. Late fall and winter were chiefly devoted to threshing, repairing, craft production, and what other labor the cold weather would permit.

The Nobles

By 1795, the nobles of the empire made up slightly more than 2 percent of the population. In the previous half-century, they had grown at better than double the rate of the remaining population. This rapid expansion was due primarily to Catherine's partitions of Poland, for in these newly conquered territories nobles were more densely concentrated, consisting of about 8 percent of the population before Russian annexation.

The empire's nobles measured their wealth primarily by the number of male serfs they owned. For those in military or civilian service, their rank also helped determine their wealth and status. LeDonne has divided the noble ruling class into three categories. In the top group, the ruling elite, he places about 8,500 individuals in the 1770s, about 8,000 of whom owned more than 100 male serfs. The second group held lesser ranks or fewer serfs (20 to 100); the third group held still lower ranks or the fewest serfs (less than 20). In the 1770s, about three-fifths of the noble landowners in European Russia possessed fewer than 20 male serfs each, and only about one-sixth of the noble landowners owned more than 100 each, but these wealthier nobles possessed about four-fifths of all serfs.

Most young nobles were forced by economic need to serve in the military or civil bureaucracy, at least until they came into their inheritance. Ironically, however, some complained of being too poor to possess the boots or clothes necessary to enter service. After receiving their inheritance, some nobles resigned from service as soon as possible; at the beginning of Catherine's reign, only about 20 to 25 percent of noblemen served in civil or military service.

Upon a father's death, his sons would normally divide up his property and serfs except for one-seventh, which went to their mother, and an even smaller share to any sisters. Thus, with each generation, noble estates and the number of serfs that went with them tended to decline. (The law in effect from 1714 to 1731 requiring property to be passed on to only one son was often evaded and hardly affected this long-term trend.) Only the purchase or grant of new lands prevented this gradual diminution of landholding, but many nobles were too poor or insignificant to benefit from such remedies.

Some poor nobles lived lives hardly distinguishable from their serfs, often working the fields along with them and sometimes even living together with them in small, crowded huts. Many could not afford to educate their sons, even if they wanted to. S. T. Aksakov in his novel *The Family Chronicle* exaggerates only slightly when he says of his eighteenth-century hero, Stepan Bagrov, "like all his contemporaries of the Russian landed gentry, [he] had little or no education; he could scarcely read or write Russian."[1]

Wealthier nobles, however, increasingly prized education. Some sent their boys away to school, whereas others had them tutored at home. Some also invested in manufacturing. At the top of the noble class, a small number of families, such as the Sheremetevs, the Voronstovs, and the Yusupovs, each owned serfs numbering in the tens of thousands and scattered over numerous provinces. Among such families, visitors might enjoy sumptuous meals in rich surroundings and be entertained by a serf orchestra, ballet, or theater performers.

Because of their many extravagancies, some of the biggest magnates also owed the biggest debts. Count N. P. Sheremetev, the noble with the most serfs (some 186,000 male and female) and land (over 2.5 million acres) owed more than 2 million rubles in 1800. Frugality was not a virtue to many Russian aris-

[1]*The Family Chronicle* (New York, 1961), p. 6.

tocrats. During the late eighteenth century, their profligate ways led the government to set up banks where nobles could borrow money at rates more reasonable than the earlier usurious rates they had paid various moneylenders.

The Peasants

If the wealthy nobles were at the top of the social pyramid, the peasants were at its broad-based bottom, composing about nine-tenths of the population. Throughout the century, most peasants remained the serfs of noble masters. Before 1762–1763, there were three other principal types of peasants: state (a category created by Peter the Great), church, and court, with the first outnumbering the combined total of the other two. Some church holdings rivaled those of the wealthiest landowners; for example, in the middle of the century, Trinity–St. Sergius Monastery possessed more than 100,000 male peasants.

After the secularization of church property in the early 1760s, approximately 1 million male church peasants were transferred to state-peasant status. By 1796, this state-peasant category, which by then contained numerous subgroups, made up close to two-fifths of all peasants and included those earlier referred to as "black peasants" (see Chapter 11). State peasants lived mostly outside the heart of old Muscovy, in the north and in such areas as Siberia and the lower and middle Volga regions. Besides serfs and state peasants, smaller peasant groups still remained, the largest of which were the court peasants, who worked on imperial properties.

By 1796, most peasants, including serfs, worked in repartitional communes that periodically redistributed strips of land in different fields to each peasant household. How many strips were assigned to each household depended on various criteria, for example, its size, its labor strength, or its number of adult males. However it was done, peasants generally did not farm consolidated plots but harvested their crops from scattered strips. The origins of the repartitional commune have been extensively debated, but it seems to have spread rapidly in the eighteenth century. It received noble and governmental backing because both elements wished to insure that all peasants produced at least enough to meet their obligations, whether to the nobles, the state, or both.

In exchange for the right to farm some estate strips for themselves, serfs continued to pay their landowners in primarily one of two ways, *barshchina* or *obrok*. By the late eighteenth century, three days' work for the master on land from which he received the produce was the general *barshchina* practice. But unscrupulous landowners sometimes demanded as much as six days' labor, leaving serfs only nights, Sundays, and holidays to farm the strips they were allotted for their own use. Because *obrok* payments in crops or money did not involve tilling under the supervision of the master or his steward, peasants preferred it to *barshchina*.

Which system any serfowner decided upon—and sometimes a combination of both was required—depended on several variables. Soil quality was always important. Where it was good, as in the southern black-earth region, *barshchina* predominated, whereas to the north, where the soil was less fertile, *obrok* was more dominant. Thus, the better the soil, the more likely the landowner was to set some land aside to be tilled under his or his steward's supervision and from which he received the produce.

One curious aspect of the *obrok* system was that it enabled serfs, if they obtained their master's permission, to leave his estate and work somewhere else—as long as they kept sending back their *obrok* payments. This explains the high percentage of *obrok*-paying serfs in some Russian cities by 1800.

Occasionally a serf even prospered while working in trade or industry, but if he did, his master usually demanded more *obrok*. Because a serf had no legal claim to any property, any or all of it, including his money, could be seized by his landowner. Reluctant to lose a good source of income, serfowners also sometimes demanded exorbitant fees from prosperous serfs who wished to buy their freedom. One of Count Sheremetev's serfs, who had become a rich textile manufacturer, was required to pay more than 130,000 rubles to become a free man.

Besides serfs under *barshchina* or *obrok*, there was still another category—house serfs. They took over many of the jobs earlier performed by slaves; they served as butlers, carpenters, cooks, nannies, seamstresses, scribes, shepherds, and stablemen. Because of their closer proximity to their master and his family—and its whims—the lot of these serf domestics was unenviable, and most peasants dreaded the thought of themselves or their children becoming house serfs.

Overall, the condition of serfs probably worsened in the eighteenth century. Peter Kolchin, who has done a thorough comparison of American slavery and Russian serfdom, states that already by the mid-eighteenth century the power of the Russian serfowner over his serfs was comparable to that of an American slaveowner over his slaves.

By 1796, serfowners could not only beat their serfs, but also have them exiled to Siberia and hard labor or sent to the army for the standard twenty-five years' service. They could force them into marriages and into having sex, and they could sell them, even separate from their families or the land they tilled. (By the late 1780s, 100 rubles was about the average price for a serf, although Potemkin paid 40,000 rubles for a fifty-serf orchestra.) By a 1767 law, serfs were no longer allowed to petition the government about serfowner injustices.

Many historians traditionally believed that serfdom reached its apex under Catherine II. As Jerome Blum stated: "The trade in peasants reached its peak—as did so many of the cruelest aspects of Russian serfdom—during the reign of Catherine II."[2]

Taxes and *obrok* payments demanded by the state and landowners increased during the century, but it is difficult to assess how much, if at all, the economic burden on the serfs (and other peasants) increased. Some historians have even argued that if one factors in inflation, the peasants were probably paying less in real economic terms in the 1790s than they had in the early 1770s.

Isabel de Madariaga has not only indicated this, but also contended that

---

[2]*Lord and Peasant in Russia, from the Ninth to the Nineteenth Century* (New York, 1969), p. 424.

peasant conditions under Catherine II were generally better than usually depicted. She has cited figures, for example, which indicate that about one-fifth of peasant households in the Kursk province possessed substantial numbers of such animals as cows, horses, pigs, and sheep. Her writings as well as some others suggest that Russian peasants were not as impoverished or left as alone and defenseless in hard times as were many poor people in France and some other European countries.

Madariaga has also defended Catherine against charges that she turned over an exorbitant number of state peasants to her favorites, former favorites, and other nobles, thus extending serfdom to hundreds of thousands of previously "free" peasants. According to Madariaga, most of those handed over were already unfree, the chief source being confiscated estates, especially from partitioned Poland.

Catherine did take some minor steps to limit serfdom and alleviate the sufferings of serfs. In 1775, for example, she prohibited re-enserfing any freed serf and allowed provincial governors to seize estates in circumstances in which landowners were treating their serfs cruelly. Fear of upsetting the social equilibrium, however, especially after the Pugachev rebellion, scared her away from any major changes.

Finally, in assessing the life of eighteenth-century serfs, the possible must be distinguished from the probable. Because nobles could confiscate the property of their serfs or have them sent to Siberia does not mean that most serfowners did so. Even Radishchev, a most severe critic of serfowners, recognized that some were noble in behavior as well as title. In his *A Journey from St. Petersburg to Moscow*, he mentioned, for example, a master who educated one of his serfs just as he did his own son. Moreover, some aristocrats during Catherine II's reign established peasant schools that educated a small percentage of their serfs. Finally, in contrast to American slaves, most serfs were of the same race and nationality as their masters, and their ancestors had usually tilled the same soil for many generations. Thus, they were not subject to the racism and degree of alienation suffered by many American slaves.

EATING AND DRINKING; FAMINES AND OTHER CALAMITIES

Although the eating habits of common people changed little in the eighteenth century, those of an increasingly westernized gentry began to reflect growing Western influence. Toward the end of the century, the Englishman Tooke observed that "persons of distinction keep their tables supplied with meats and drinks entirely in the foreign taste, hire French cooks, etc." Indeed by then few Russian aristocrats were without a foreign cook.

Sugar, Tea, and Vodka

One product that became increasingly popular among the nobles was sugar, which gradually replaced honey as their principal sweetener. By the end of

Catherine II's reign, its imported value easily exceeded the combined total of coffee and wines, the next two most imported food or drink items. By then, sugar made up about one-fifth the value of all imports. This growth, in turn, stimulated the establishment of additional sugar refineries after the first was begun in 1723.

One new use for sugar was in tea. Although brief references to tea were made in late seventeenth-century sources, it was only after Peter I's death, and especially during the last third of the eighteenth century, that Russian tea imports from China increased significantly. They came primarily through the border town of Kiakhta. When the Kiakhta trade was occasionally suspended, Russia obtained its tea secondhand from Western Europe.

Under Catherine II, tea drinking, at least in European Russia, was mainly associated with the nobles, some of whom developed the custom of taking afternoon tea. Just as sugar imports stimulated the establishment of sugar refineries, so tea imports encouraged the beginnings of the production of samovars to heat water for tea.

If nobles were the leading tea drinkers, vodka had a more common appeal—and one that continued to grow. Smith and Christian have estimated that spirits consumption went from averaging about four pints per year for every man in the country under Peter I to more than ten pints by the end of Catherine II's reign and that state alcohol revenue went from 11.4 percent of total budget revenue in 1724 to about 30 percent by 1795. The revenue figures explain why the state continued to encourage drinking.

FIGURE 16.4. Village tavern, around 1800.
(From Robert Wallace and the Editors of Time-Life Books, Rise of Russia. *Time Inc., New York, 1967, p. 146, Courtesy of the Free Library of Philadelphia, Rare Book Department.)*

Not only did the government profit from increased vodka consumption, but so too did some merchants and many nobles. Early in the century, both groups, plus the government, operated distilleries, but by the mid-1750s, only the government and nobles could produce spirits. During the last decades of Catherine II's reign, nobles and even their serfs (with noble permission) increasingly joined merchants in the business of leasing from the government the right to sell liquor. Not surprisingly, some of the biggest profits were earned by wealthy noble landowners, including some who helped shape government alcohol policies.

Hunger, Famine, and Plague

The availability of grains for bread and gruel (*kasha*) chiefly determined whether Russia's vast mass of peasants and urban poor suffered from hunger and famine. In normal years, grain was sufficient. But when bad weather was severe and long-lasting, the masses suffered. Russia's low grain yields per acre—less than half that of Western Europe at the end of the eighteenth century—left too little surplus. Grain exports, the use of large quantities of grain for distilling alcohol, and the lack of adequate reserve storage facilities, despite improvements made by Catherine II, further exacerbated the problem. Early frosts, severe winters, excessive rainfall, and drought all endangered the basic food supply.

Although eighteenth-century famines were not as bad as the most severe ones of the past—for example, that of 1601–1603—bad weather still made them a periodic reoccurrence. This was especially true in the first half of the century, when cold weather was the main wrongdoer. Improved weather and expansion into more fertile southern lands helped produce less severe conditions in the second half of the century. Only in the last fifteen years of Catherine II's reign did a substantial number of poor suffer sporadically from famine or near-famine conditions. In this period, drought, the main threat in southern steppe lands, was the chief culprit. Prince Mikhail Shcherbatov reported that in the mid-1780s some poor people were eating hay, leaves, and moss to help sustain themselves.

Although no accurate estimates for famine deaths exist, plague figures are more plentiful. They indicate a heavy toll. Different estimates suggest that plague (primarily bubonic) struck one part of the country or another about one-fifth to one-fourth of the years of the century. It killed tens of thousands in Riga in 1710; struck about half the people in Astrakhan in 1727–1728; and, after killing tens of thousands further south, cut down about one-fifth of Moscow's population in 1771.

The chief disseminators of plague remained rats and the fleas who bit them and then humans. These unknown deadly enemies traveled especially on ships to Russian ports and in the baggage and supplies of moving armies. They proliferated in warm, crowded conditions. Thus, plague struck more in Russia's southern areas and in cities than in the north and in the countryside.

Although the government, especially under Catherine II, often took vigorous measures to avoid the spread of plague, success was greatly limited by ignorance about its source. Isolating and quarantining the affected regions was the most usual method. Once the epidemic hit a city, however, there was little that could be done for the afflicted besides prayer and folk remedies. Even if medical knowledge would have been more advanced, Moscow's fourteen doctors and one fifty-bed public hospital would have still been woefully inadequate to deal with the dreaded disease when it struck there.

Besides plague, the empire also suffered from occasional influenza and smallpox epidemics. The former struck most areas of the country in the late 1750s, in several years of the 1760s, and again in 1781 and 1798. The latter is known to have killed many Siberian natives (less immune to smallpox than European Russians), especially in 1768–1769, and to have killed, and even more frequently left scarred for life, many European Russians. It struck the future Peter III soon after he came to Russia, and it was so common in the eighteenth century that John Alexander has written that Catherine II "was quite exceptional in having attained adulthood without contracting 'the pocks.'"[3]

Largely as a result of Catherine's efforts, some headway was finally made against smallpox. After she set the example by being inoculated against it herself in 1768, clinics were set up in Moscow, St. Petersburg, and several other cities. By 1800, it was reported that about 2 million people had been inoculated.

Hunger, famine, the plague, and other epidemics combined with warfare and other diseases to prevent more rapid population growth. Kahan has estimated that 679,000 persons died in the eighteenth century from combat and diseases while on military campaigns. And it was not only among soldiers and urban residents that death rates were high. Foreign observers and Catherine II herself noted that in the villages, most children died before they reached adulthood. "What a loss for the State!" lamented Catherine.

WOMEN AND FAMILY LIFE

Toward women and children some new Russian attitudes were evident in the eighteenth century, which challenged older ones like those found in the still popular *Domostroi*. These changed sentiments stemmed primarily from the impact of Western ideas and from the policies of Russia's rulers. In many ways, however, the lives of women and children remained as they had for centuries, especially outside of St. Petersburg and Moscow and among the lower classes.

Peter the Great abolished the *terem* and encouraged social mixing of the sexes and the adoption of Western clothing. Following his death, empresses ruled Russia for almost all of the next seventy years. The attitudes, policies, and example of Catherine the Great were especially notable. Along with her friend Catherine Dashkova (see Chapter 17), she bore striking testimony that women could be as well-read and cultured as men. Although other cultured

[3]*Catherine the Great: Life and Legend* (New York, 1989), p. 144.

women also graced high society by the end of the eighteenth century, most noble women were still illiterate.

Foreigners repeated many of the same observations earlier made about Russian women. The Englishman Tooke noted that they "painted" their faces more commonly than women in other countries and that their bodies were more ample than European fashion dictated.

A French abbé traveling in Russia in 1760 found that outside the two capitals most women were not seen in public with their husbands, who treated them more like slaves than loved ones. Although Tooke agreed that wives often suffered from their husbands' "tyrannical treatment," he also stated that in larger towns "many a kind husband sometimes gets a rap of the [wife's] slipper." Despite commenting that many husbands kept their wives isolated, the abbé agreed with Tooke that at least unmarried youngsters mixed quite freely. Tooke noted this especially in the countryside, and both men emphasized that despite the mixing, marriage customs placed great importance on a bride's virginity.

The abbé also believed that this emphasis on virginity helped explain why so many Russians married young, a phenomenon he noted in Nizhnii Novgorod. In 1796, Count Vladimir Orlov argued that early marriage would help prevent the vices to which single people were prone. Based on this rationale, he fined serf women who did not marry by the age of twenty and serf men by age twenty-five. Many other landowners of this time also imposed such fines, some even fining females beginning at fifteen and widows who did not re-marry in their childbearing years.

Other evidence exists of at least peasants marrying young—much younger, for example, than contemporary Western European peasants, who generally did not marry until their mid to late twenties. For the population as a whole, Kahan has estimated that eighteenth-century women generally first married between seventeen and twenty-two and men between twenty and twenty-five.

Despite the type of moral reasons Count Orlov cited for early marriages, more practical considerations were often paramount. The parents of a marriageable male peasant generally were eager to have their son marry and thereby bring another worker (his bride) into the household. Serfowners were anxious to have their serfs begin procreating more serfs as soon as possible. The only consistent peasant opposition to the custom seems to have come from some schismatic and sectarian young women, whose parents sometimes supported their daughter's resistance to early marriage.

In noble households, a daughter was considered marriageable at about sixteen. Although noble parents still sometimes arranged loveless marriages, by the late eighteenth century, marriage without love was becoming less common. By then, even Orthodox Church leaders were placing more emphasis on marriage as a union freely entered into by loving spouses for their mutual betterment. Only these clergymen talked of Christian, not romantic, love. Although they still thought a husband should guide and correct his wife, they encouraged less severe "guidance" than had been advocated in the sixteenth-century *Domostroi*.

For these prelates, marriage was a permanent sacrament. Despite being weakened in many ways, the eighteenth-century Orthodox Church hierarchy gradually increased its control over marriage and divorce. As a result, it became more difficult to dissolve a marriage in Russia, either through divorce or annulment, than in any of the Protestant or Catholic countries of Western Europe.

The everyday life of most women revolved around work. Only aristocratic women had much leisure. Tooke noted that most women "see to the cleanliness of the house, spin, weave linen and coarse cloth on frames . . . make felt, bake bread every day, etc." Peasant women cooked and made clothing, tended vegetable gardens, gathered mushrooms and berries, looked after poultry and other animals, and worked in the fields, especially during harvesting times, when they cut some crops such as rye with sickles, while the men harvested other crops with heavier scythes. Although a well-off noblewoman generally had many servants to do most of the physical labor, she was still responsible for overseeing the household staff.

Of course, Russian women were often pregnant and responsible for caring for their children. Kolchin has estimated that the average serf family probably had more than seven births, although many children did not survive until adulthood.

Most peasant couples and their children did not live alone in their households. It was common for a family's newlywed sons to bring their wives back to their parents' cabin or hut and there live in a three-generational household. Among the nobility and in urban areas, such households, although existing, were less common.

Although peasant children had to work hard from a young age and were often harshly disciplined, eighteenth-century noble children had it considerably better. Noble daughters were brought up primarily by their mother, who was to prepare them for marriage. Until about age seven, noble boys were also mainly the mother's responsibility, after which it shifted to the father. Of course, wealthier noble parents often had governesses, servants, and tutors to help them carry out their child-rearing responsibilities and often spent little time with their children.

Yet despite such infrequent contact, many young noblemen were spoiled. With the father often away from the family estate in government or military service, neither the mother nor the household staff (often composed mainly or exclusively of serfs) provided much discipline for the "young master." Most of his playmates were serfs, whom he could dominate. If he was sent to a parish school for the rudiments of education and misbehaved there, a serf child was often beaten instead of him. Only later, if sent to a boarding school, often of a military character, did his undisciplined days come to an end.

An aspect of parent-child relationships worthy of attention is that of child abandonment. Thanks largely to the work of David Ransel, Western scholars and students now have easy access to a plethora of information about this practice during the Imperial period.

In 1712, Peter I criticized the practice of infanticide and mandated the establishment in all provinces of hospitals where illegitimate children could be left. Like some of Peter's other decrees, however, this one does not seem to have energized provincial officials to beehivelike activity. It was left to Catherine II, a half-century later, to take more forceful steps.

She oversaw the establishment of a Foundling Home in Moscow in 1764 and in St. Petersburg in 1771. By the mid-1790s, more than 1500 children a year were being deposited in each of the two institutions, with more girls being abandoned than boys.

Because a child could be left without the mother being asked anything but whether her child was baptized and, if so, with what name, it is difficult to know all the causes of abandonment. But illegitimacy and poverty were certainly two. The first grew during the century, as more men were separated from their wives (often left back in villages) to serve in the growing military or civil service or work in towns.

Catherine's establishment of the two foundling homes, plus some smaller provincial foundling shelters, was not just due to growing need, but also to the influence of Enlightenment ideas. Both Catherine and Ivan Betskoi, her chief official in charge of the foundling project, were well aware of Enlightenment thinking about unwed mothers and the importance of children, including their economic value to the state. Catherine attached schools to the two major foundling homes, hoping to educate the children to be model urban citizens.

Although the two homes remained showpieces to illustrate Catherine's enlightened ideas, the reality inside, as was often true in Western European foundling homes, was much more grim. Epidemics and the difficulty of attracting sufficient wet nurses to breast-feed all the infants contributed greatly to high mortality rates. According to Ransel's estimates, about 82 percent of the more than 3,000 children admitted to the Moscow home between 1764 and 1768 died before reaching adulthood. After many of the children started being "farmed out" to villages beginning in late 1768, the appallingly high death rate still continued at close to the same level.

RUSSIAN LAW: CHANGE AND CONTINUITY

Western Enlightenment thinking also affected Russian concepts of law. Peter the Great thought that his attempt to base Russia's government more on law—as opposed to the earlier Byzantine-Muscovite autocratic ideology—was compatible with the German natural law theories of Leibniz, Pufendorf, and Christian Wolff. Empress Elizabeth brought a few Western jurists to Russia to teach law. And Peter III attempted to emulate his hero, the free-thinking and "enlightened" Frederick II of Prussia, who began his reign by curbing censorship, torture, and military cruelty. In his half-year of rule, Peter III not only abolished the Secret Chancellery, but also eliminated some forms of corporal punishment in the army and decreed more tolerant measures toward the Old Believers.

But it was Catherine the Great who was most influenced by the humane spirit of the Enlightenment. Her ideas about law were strongly affected by Western thinkers such as Montesquieu, Beccaria (whose *Crime and Punishment* was the most influential work of its kind in Europe), and the English jurist William Blackstone. Isabel de Madariaga credits Catherine with widening recourse to courts and fostering more respect for law, almost eliminating the use of torture, reducing corporal punishment, and generally humanizing penal practices.

Under Catherine, the making of individuals noseless, earless, or tongue-less—or all three, like the old Bashkir described in Pushkin's *Captain's Daughter*—became less common. Under her, not only nobles and upper-level merchants, but also clergy won immunity from beatings. For many lesser crimes, fines were now imposed instead of beatings. During the last half of her reign, foreign observers found Russian prisons no worse than those of many other European countries—not that that was much of a compliment in an age when all sorts of prisoners (male and female, young and old, and suspects and convicted hardened criminals) were often thrown together in crowded and unsanitary conditions.

Even Madariaga acknowledges, however, that Catherine's policies failed to give legal protection to Russia's numerous serfs and that respect for law was hampered by a poor understanding of its significance. When Catherine thought her government seriously threatened, she could still respond with harsh measures—as Pugachev and his followers, Novikov, and Radishchev all discovered.

By the end of her reign, Russian police methods and legal attitudes still reflected many older traditions. The job of maintaining law and order was left to a variety of administrative, judicial, police, and military agencies and forces.[4] Functions were not as delineated as in more modern times. Even after Catherine II's governmental reforms, the judiciary remained part of the country's administrative system, and few "judges" had any legal training. Army troops and townsmen assisted with policing functions, which included not only dealing with crime, but also such other tasks as fire-fighting, disease control, and repairing public buildings. Although Peter III abolished the Secret Chancellery, Catherine II instituted in the Senate a new Secret Expedition in 1763. It performed some of the same political investigative functions as the previous chancellery.

Private rights continued to receive little attention. By the mid-eighteenth century, individuals had to carry printed passports with them if they traveled beyond certain distances—for a peasant, for example, it was required for travel beyond thirty-two kilometers from his village.

Under Catherine II, police duties included insuring that the Orthodox population attended church services on Sundays and holy days and confessed to a priest and received communion at least once a year. The law forbade public assembly or announcements without police approval, and in towns people were supposed to inform the police if guests came to stay in their houses. In

---

[4]For much of this section, I am indebted to John P. LeDonne's excellent treatment of the police and judiciary in *Ruling Russia: Politics and Administration in the Age of Absolutism, 1762–1796* (Princeton, 1984). His *Absolutism and Ruling Class: The Formation of the Russian Political Order, 1700–1825* (New York, 1991) also contains extensive treatment of these subjects.

the capitals, the government opened private mail whenever it wished. It also engaged in censorship, imposed restrictions on clothing and appearance, and prohibited certain card games. Given these sweeping police powers, even if unevenly enforced, it is not surprising that Catherine had several noblewomen whipped for making caricatures of Potemkin.

There were many reasons why Russian legal attitudes and practices evolved more slowly than in the West. Despite all the words of Peter I and Catherine II about being first servants of the state, working for the "general good," and ruling according to law and fundamental principles, Russian monarchs still found it easier than in the West to act in an arbitrary manner. They viewed themselves more as sources of the law than as rulers bound by legal traditions. Their view of law was certainly not that of John Locke, who thought of it as emanating ultimately from the people and as a necessary tool to limit arbitrary monarchical behavior contrary to the common good. Thus, a ruler like Catherine's son Paul could violate with impunity (at least until murdered) rights his mother had bestowed upon the nobility.

Not only did the Russian emperors and empresses fail to appreciate Locke's approach to law, but so too did educated society. As Marc Raeff has pointed out, Russia's eighteenth-century intellectual elites largely ignored the law as a basis for individual rights. The nobles disdained legal institutions and procedures. Because most educated society—and political critics such as Panin, Radishchev, and Novikov—came from the nobility, this is especially significant.

Russia's hierarchical structure and the nobility's dominant social position reduced Russia's need for some of the more complex laws required in more differentiated and freer Western societies such as England. In the latter, law was a more frequent arbitrator between individuals and between groups— even if the scales of justice sometimes tipped toward the rich and powerful. In Russia, rank and power often proved more decisive than the law.

Church-state relations slowed secular legal advances in Russia more so than in the West, where governments generally now displayed more restraint in trying to control their citizen's private beliefs. In Russia, not only did state laws mandate that Orthodox citizens fulfill certain basic church obligations and that priests report criminal intent discovered in confession, but also concepts of punishment continued to be strongly affected by religious ideas.

It had probably been religious more than Enlightenment ideas that led Empress Elizabeth to end capital punishment. The head of Catherine's Secret Expedition, Stepan Sheshkovsky, after daily receiving communion, sometimes personally tortured and beat prisoners and apparently thought of himself as sort of a grand inquisitor defending the moral order. Within a year of coming to power, Catherine II emphasized the importance of suspects confessing to a priest—and thus indirectly to the state. According to new decrees, only if they refused to so confess could they be tortured. Confession was not only the "queen of proofs," enabling courts and officials to be more confident in their judgments, but also it signified acceptance of guilt and repentance. Repentance, in turn, furthered the chances of rehabilitation, a goal of punishment, even if not as important as retribution and deterrence.

Crime and punishment were also viewed in moral terms as involving pride and humility. The criminal was someone who had overstepped his or her humble bounds and violated the political-moral order (as Dostoevsky portrayed a century later with Raskolnikov in *Crime and Punishment*). The chief forms of punishment—knouting or whipping and banishment, including to hard labor for life—were often combined and served to humiliate criminals and remove them from the community whose order they had disrupted.

Finally, Russian legal development was hampered by the lack of professional training and the absence of any substantial body of private law—that which regulated dealings between private citizens or organizations. Although in the West law had been studied and practiced by private citizens for centuries, in Russia before the opening of Moscow University in 1755, formal law studies did not exist. The failure to update the Law Code of 1649 meant that even educated Russians and officials often did not know exactly what the law was. By Catherine's reign, thousands of new laws had been decreed, sometimes contradicting each other or those already in existence in 1649. Not until 1833 was a new codification completed.

*SUGGESTED SOURCES**

ALEXANDER, JOHN T. *Bubonic Plague in Early Modern Russia: Public Health and Urban Disaster*. Baltimore, 1980.

———. "Plague Epidemics." *MERSH* 28: 100–108.

BARTLETT, ROGER P., A. G. CROSS, and KAREN RASMUSSEN, eds. *Russia and the World of the Eighteenth Century: Proceedings of the Third International Conference*. Columbus, Ohio, 1988. The organization sponsoring this conference was the Study Group on Eighteenth-Century Russia, which has sponsored other conferences since then and puts out a periodic newsletter.

BRYNER, CYRIL. "The Issue of Capital Punishment in the Reign of Elizabeth Petrovna," *RR* 49: (October 1990): 389–416.

BUSHNELL, JOHN. "Did Serf Owners Control Serf Marriage? Orlov Serfs and Their Neighbors, 1773–1861," *SR* 52 (Fall 1993): 419–445.

CATHERINE II, EMPRESS OF RUSSIA. *The Memoirs of Catherine the Great*. New York, 1957.

FREEZE, GREGORY L. "Bringing Order to the Russian Family: Marriage and Divorce in Imperial Russia, 1760–1860," *JMH* 62 (December 1990): 709–746.

———. *From Supplication to Revolution: A Documentary Social History of Imperial Russia*. New York, 1988. Pt. 1.

GARRARD, J. G., ed. *The Eighteenth Century in Russia*. Oxford, 1973.

HITTLE, J. MICHAEL. *The Service City: State and Townsmen in Russia, 1600–1800*. Cambridge, Mass., 1979.

KAHAN, ARCADIUS. *The Plow, the Hammer, and the Knout: An Economic History of Eighteenth-Century Russia*. Chicago, 1985.

KOCHAN, MIRIAM. *Life in Russia Under Catherine the Great*. London, 1969.

KOLCHIN, PETER. *Unfree Labor: American Slavery and Russian Serfdom*. Cambridge, Mass., 1987.

*See also works cited in footnotes and in boxed insert.

MADARIAGA, ISABEL DE. See the two books listed in Chapter 15's Suggested Sources.

OWEN, THOMAS C. *Russian Corporate Capitalism from Peter the Great to Perestroika.* New York, 1995. Ch. 2.

RAEFF, MARC. *Origins of the Russian Intelligentsia: The Eighteenth-Century Nobility.* New York, 1966.

———. *Understanding Imperial Russia: State and Society in the Old Regime.* New York, 1984.

———. *The Well-Ordered Police State: Social and Institutional Change through Law in the Germanies and Russia, 1600–1800.* New Haven, 1983.

RANSEL, DAVID L. *Mothers of Misery: Child Abandonment in Russia.* Princeton, 1988.

———, ed. *The Family in Imperial Russia: New Lines of Historical Research.* Urbana, Ill., 1978.

ROZMAN, GILBERT. *Urban Networks in Russia: 1750–1800.* Princeton, 1976.

SMITH, R. E. F., and DAVID CHRISTIAN. *Bread and Salt: A Social and Economic History of Food and Drink in Russia.* Cambridge, England, 1984.

WILSON, FRANCESCA. *Muscovy: Russia Through Foreign Eyes, 1553–1900.* New York, 1970.

WORTMAN, RICHARD. *The Development of a Russian Legal Consciousness.* Chicago, 1976.

CHAPTER 17

Eighteenth-Century Religion and Culture

If in the seventeenth century Western influences slowly flowed into Orthodox Muscovy, in the eighteenth century, they gushed in. Although their greatest impact was on elite culture, which became increasingly secularized, they also influenced aspects of religion and popular urban culture. Russian monarchs, especially Peter I and Catherine II, welcomed many of these influences. For example, they and their supporters made use of baroque and neoclassical literature, art, and architecture to glorify the Russian Empire and its rulers. In doing so, they sometimes suggested parallels with the ancient Roman Empire and its rulers. Writers praised Catherine II as a new Minerva (the Roman goddess of war, wisdom, and learning); the most famous sculpture of the century, "The Bronze Horseman" (Peter I), was modeled on a Roman statue of the Emperor Marcus Aurelius.

Yet many of the religious and cultural developments of the century, whether Western influenced or not, developed more spontaneously and reflected the inspirations and talents of individuals and groups within the empire. The poet Gavriil Derzhavin, for example, not only wrote odes comparing Catherine to ancient goddesses, but also the best lyric poetry of the century. Western ideas influenced some intellectuals, such as Alexander Radishchev, in their criticism of the Russian political system. As the century progressed, institutional and private printing also advanced. Although censorship never completely disappeared, the government exercised decreasing political controls over literature, at least until the more reactionary 1790s reduced printing and increased censorship.

As often happened later in other parts of the world, Western influences eventually produced a reaction, which rebelled against aping foreign ways and stimulated a search for Russia's own roots and cultural uniqueness. This search, in turn, stimulated interchanges between elite and popular folk culture.

RUSSIAN ORTHODOXY

Despite some exceptions, the power of the Orthodox Church decreased during the eighteenth century, and the state's control over it increased. Catherine II, for example, not only took over church lands in 1764, but also eliminated well over half of the country's monasteries and convents. A year earlier, despite having received some church support in her 1762 coup against her anticlerical husband, Catherine made a Freemason the procurator of the Holy Synod. Later in her reign, she forced tens of thousands of individuals out of the clerical estate—almost all sons of priests normally became clergymen themselves—and into other forms of service, including the military.

Although some clergy willingly accommodated themselves to new state policies, others rebelled. Most notable of the rebels was Metropolitan Arseni of Rostov. In 1763, he came out against secularizing church lands and Catherine II's suggestion that the church do more to help educate people in secular as well as religious subjects. The bitterness of his protest caused Catherine to order a Holy-Synod trial for him, in which he was condemned for insulting the Empress and exiled to labor in a northern monastery. After he continued his criticism, he was later transferred to a fortress cell in Reval and officially renamed "Andrei the Liar."

Although the Holy Synod was generally compliant, it did try to improve the church's position. In 1767, it instructed its delegate to the Legislative Committee to seek equal Synod status with the Senate and more state support in forcing Orthodox believers to go to confession and receive communion annually. Its instructions suggested that "incarceration on bread-and-water-rations"[1] be added to the fines already levied on those failing to comply. Among other "instructions" were some calling for the improvement of the parish clergy's living conditions. They noted that even though an imperial decree had stipulated the amount priests could receive for each church rite, many were still impoverished, with most rural clergy supporting themselves primarily by working their small state-allotted plots.

The church's reaction to Western influences was mixed. Under Peter I, it adapted Catholic and Protestant theology and Catholic educational methods to Orthodox needs. As the century progressed, despite the growth of Protestant influences, the curriculum in Orthodox seminaries continued to be based primarily on the Catholic method of Latin studies and scholastic approaches.

As both a student and a teacher in a Novgorod seminary, one of Russia's greatest saints, Tikhon Zadonsky (1724–1783), was exposed to both Catholic and Protestant ideas. Later a bishop and then a monastic recluse in Zadonsk, the strongest foreign influence on his writings seems to have been German Protestant Pietism.

It was unlike Catholic scholastic philosophy, which stressed reconciling reason with doctrine and the writings of Aristotle with those of the early

---

[1]Gregory L. Freeze, *From Supplication to Revolution: A Documentary Social History of Imperial Russia* (New York, 1988), p. 39.

church fathers. Instead, the German Pietists took a more mystical and emotional approach and grounded their Christianity more on faith, love, and scriptures. Pietistic writings began appearing in Old Church Slavonic and Russian translations in the decade after Peter the Great's death.

Pietism's impact did not prevent Tikhon from living and writing within the Russian monastic tradition of Sts. Theodosius and Sergius. His concern for those who suffered, such as prisoners, widows, and orphans, calls to mind Theodosius. He criticized nobles who treated their serfs unjustly and judges more interested in bribes than in justice. He also lamented the heavy suffering endured by the Russian people because of the wars of his day. Although open to Pietistic influences, the Orthodox Church was more critical of European scientific ideas (such as the heliocentric theory of Copernicus), which challenged the traditional Orthodox cosmology.

Churchmen continued to criticize secular amusements. Tikhon once wrote a scolding letter to a man who had put up a see-saw. Such centers of amusement, thought the saint, attracted sinful people. On another occasion, he warned against card-playing, dancing, feasts, banquets, masquerades, and operas.

Despite growing westernization, state control, and secularization, Russian Orthodoxy and its values continued to shape the lives of most of Russia's common people. Among the masses, Orthodoxy was mainly challenged not by Western secular ideas, but by the continuing schismatic Old Belief and by new religious sects.

SCHISMATICS AND SECTARIANS

By the beginning of the eighteenth century, the Old Believers had split into two factions, the Priestly and the Priestless. Their split over whether or not to accept priests ordained in the Orthodox Church was largely motivated by differences over whether the reign of the anti-Christ had yet actually begun. The Priestless took the more radical position and believed no true priests any longer existed. As the century progressed, additional splits developed among the Old Believers. A continuing divisive question for the Priestless was whether, without a priest to preside at their weddings, they could still marry.

At first, the Old Believers were most prominent on the Russian periphery. One of its most notable communities was in the Vyg River region, between the White Sea and Lake Onega. Significant numbers also settled along the lower Volga and in Siberia. Encouraged by Catherine II, who, like Peter III, was more tolerant of them than Empresses Anna and Elizabeth had been, some Old Believers established communities in and around Moscow beginning in the 1770s.

Although no accurate figures exist as to Old Believer numbers in Imperial Russia, some estimates are as high as 20 percent of the peasantry. The hardworking, serious approach of many of them has led to their being compared to the Calvinists in the West. And like the Calvinists, many Old Believers also possessed considerable business talents and became some of their country's most successful businessmen.

Quite different than the schismatic Old Believers were sectarians such as the *Khlysty*, *Skoptsy*, Dukhobors, and Molokane. Because much information about these groups originally comes from hardly objective Orthodox sources, the wilder charges sometimes made against them must be regarded with caution. In general, their main concern was to be filled with the spirit of God, and they practiced various rituals to help bring this about. Although the *Khlysty* were originally stronger in the central regions of the country, by 1800 they and other sectarians were more prominent in the south between the Volga and the Dnieper. Cities such as Tambov and Voronezh were especially rife with sectarians.

The *Khlysty*, the oldest of these sects, apparently began in the seventeenth century. They sang and danced in whirling fashion to bring about religious ecstasy and oneness with God. They rejected the Orthodox view of Jesus and thought that what had made him stand out from other men was that he was full of God's spirit. But he was not the only "christ"; *Khlysty* believed they too could become "christs." Like many sectarians, they espoused rigorous ethical standards. They condemned alcohol, smoking, and sex (even for married couples). A late-eighteenth-century offshoot of the *Khlysty*, the *Skoptsy*, went even further in their fight against sex: they preached self-castration.

The Dukhobors (Spirit Wrestlers) and Molokane (Milk Drinkers) emerged from a common Spiritual Christianity, about which little is known. Although more rationalistic than the *Khlysty*, the Dukhobors became more utopian, radical, and pantheistic than the Molokane, who remained closer to Christian beliefs and placed more emphasis on the Bible than did most eighteenth-century Russian sectarians. But the Molokane still rejected the Orthodox Church structure and many of its doctrines and, in contrast to the Orthodox, they drank milk on fast days.

PHILOSOPHY AND FREEMASONRY

Among Russia's educated elite, however, it was neither schismatic nor sectarian beliefs that most challenged Orthodoxy; it was Western Enlightenment ideas and the hybrid phenomenon of Freemasonry.

Among the most significant Enlightenment concepts were nature, reason, deism, progress, education, and secularism. The previous "scientific revolution" had taught the existence of natural laws, such as Newton's law of gravity, and that by using Reason mankind could discover them. These laws were not limited to the natural sciences. They could also be discovered in other areas of human endeavor, such as what are today labeled "the social sciences"—Adam Smith's economic law of supply and demand being one example.

Many Enlightenment thinkers were deists. They viewed God not as a personal being who answered daily prayers, but as the great lawmaker or "divine clockmaker," who created a marvelous clock (the universe) that would run perfectly if mankind just discovered and applied its laws. Discovering such laws and education in general were two keys to Progress. Not all Enlightenment thinkers condemned the traditional Christian faiths, but they were critical of the religious intolerance that had often accompanied them and were sympathetic to the secularist idea of separating church and state.

We have already seen the impact of some of these ideas on Russian politics. Reason especially could be used by emperors and empresses, like Peter I and Catherine II, in their quest to make Russia a more efficient and stronger power. Yet, interpreted differently, say by a Radishchev, it could become a radical weapon attacking the foundations of Imperial Russia. That was what made Reason so dangerous—no one had a monopoly on it. As Russia's future dramatically indicated, any thinking person could use it—or abuse it. No traditional political, social, cultural, or religious custom or belief was safe from its probes and thrusts.

Originating in the West, Freemasonry was a diverse movement, whose different lodges emphasized different dimensions of the movement. Thus, although Catherine II eventually associated it with political opposition, it could also be embraced by those who supported the monarch's policies. In fact, many government officials of the late eighteenth century were Masons.

In general, however, Freemasonry was a kind of halfway house between the traditional religions and the new Enlightenment ideas. Like the former, it contained ritualistic, social, ethical, and, sometimes, mystical dimensions; like the latter, it preached tolerance, universal brotherhood, education, and progress. Many believed that the pursuit of spiritual truths and moral self-perfection, coupled with love of one's fellow man, could lead to a golden age.

Although Freemasonry began slowly in Russia, it expanded rapidly during Catherine II's reign, especially among the nobility. It fulfilled deep psychological, social, and religious needs among the educated elite, whose traditional Muscovite culture had been uprooted by Peter the Great. It also helped lead some Masons to believe they owed service more to the people than to the state.

Despite Catherine II's growing contempt for the movement—"one of the greatest aberrations to which the human race had succumbed," and "a mixture of religious ritual and childish games"[2]—she did not crack down on it until she arrested Novikov. But the Russian Masons reappeared in strength under her beloved grandson, Alexander I.

Gregory Skovoroda (1722–1794) was perhaps the empire's first real philosopher. He was the son of Ukrainian Cossack parents and was educated at the Kievan Academy, where he studied languages, philosophy, and theology. He also traveled in the West and taught at various seminaries. Sometimes labeled the "Ukrainian Socrates," he was mainly interested in discovering the secrets to happiness and often wrote Socratic-like dialogues. He was knowledgeable about Western scholastic philosophy and ancient writers such as Plato and the Stoics as well as about mystical writers and the Bible. He spent most of his later life as a wandering philosopher in Ukraine. Always teaching

[2]John T. Alexander, *Catherine the Great: Life and Legend* (New York, 1989), p. 299.

and learning, he lived a simple life and was not hesitant to criticize those who exploited the peasants.

Radishchev was also interested in philosophical questions, and his exile in Siberia gave him plenty of time for further contemplation. These reflections bore fruit in his *On Man, His Mortality, and Immortality*, which was published after his death. It displays his knowledge of Western philosophers and argues that man's soul is immortal.

EDUCATION AND SCHOLARSHIP

Besides Peter I's other pioneering educational efforts, including the establishment of mathematical (or cipher) schools (see Chapter 13), in 1721 he also established ecclesiastical schools. Some clergymen's sons attending the former soon switched to ecclesiastical schools. As a result of this and a general lack of enthusiasm for secular education, by 1727 the church schools had six times the 500 students remaining in the mathematical schools, which continued to decline until they came to an end in 1744. At that time the larger remaining ones were merged with garrison schools. These schools for soldiers' children, which Peter I had also been the first to authorize, taught reading, writing, arithmetic, basic artillery and engineering skills, some crafts such as carpentry, and singing and drill.

During the almost four decades that separated Russia's two most vigorous eighteenth-century monarchs, Peter I and Catherine II, education suffered from the lack of a forceful advocate on the throne. Yet even in this period some important advances were made. Long-range economic, social, and cultural developments were working to encourage education, and by the beginning of Catherine II's reign, nobles were increasingly employing tutors for their sons or sending them away to cadet schools. Russia's first university, the University of Moscow, was founded in 1755. Although the majority of its original ten professors were foreigners and instruction was initially in Latin, the use of Russian professors and the Russian language gradually increased. The student body grew slowly, however; in the late 1790s, there were fewer than 100 undergraduates.

With the accession of Catherine II in 1762, education again received a strong boost. She emphasized the necessity of educating foundlings in the Foundling Homes established in the two capitals in 1764 and 1770 (see Chapter 15). In the mid-1760s, she established two lay schools for girls at the Smolny Convent: one a boarding school for noble girls and the other a day school for nonnoble girls.

The Empress's 1775 Provincial Government Statute called for establishing schools in the provinces, but many provinces were slow to act. Meanwhile, a small number of individuals, such as Novikov and some of his fellow Freemasons, were establishing schools on their own initiative. Novikov also contributed to education in a more general way by his extensive publishing activities.

Catherine's most sweeping educational measures came in 1786. In that year, she mandated the creation of five-year higher schools in provincial capitals and two-year primary schools in district towns.[3] She also opened teacher training institutions to provide teachers for them and incorporated some earlier-founded schools into the state system. By the end of the century, these public schools contained about 20,000 students—almost 10 percent of whom were girls—and about 800 teachers.

Meanwhile, church schools and seminaries expanded and improved, more than quadrupling from 1766 to 1799, by which time they were also educating about 20,000 students. Finally, garrison schools increased and contained close to 12,000 students by the end of Catherine's reign.

By the end of the century, these three types of schools—public (five-year and two-year), ecclesiastical, and garrison—contained about 85 percent of those being educated in schools at all levels. Other schools included a few gymnasia, a handful of cadet schools, more than fifty gentry and private boarding schools, a few each of mining and medical schools, and an art academy.

Catherine's public schools opened up educational opportunities to nonnobles; one study suggests that only about one-third of the students in the five-year schools were nobles in 1801. Yet the total percentage of young people receiving formal education was still infinitesimal and far behind most other European countries. France's elementary schools, for example, numbered more than twenty-five times the total of Russia's two-year and five-year schools combined.

Yet eighteenth-century Russia still produced some first-rate scholars and educators. The most noteworthy was Mikhail Lomonosov (1711–1765), the son of a northern peasant fisherman. Because of his many talents, he has been compared to Leonardo da Vinci and Benjamin Franklin. Most important were his discoveries in physics and chemistry—although most of them failed to be appreciated until long after his death. He also contributed to applied sciences such as geology, navigation, and astronomy, and he was an important poet, linguist, literary theorist, and educator. In the last-mentioned capacity, he was a professor at the Academy of Sciences and helped found Moscow University.

Another man of humble origins, Ivan Pososhkov, contributed original economic thoughts in his 1724 work *On Poverty and Wealth*. A merchant's son, Vasili Tatishchev (1686–1750) became Russia's first modern historian with his five-volume *History of Russia* (published posthumously). Later in the century, Prince Mikhail Shcherbatov wrote an even longer *History of Russia*, which eventually appeared in fifteen volumes. The Ukrainian S. E. Desnitsky (1740?–1789) was Russia's first professor of law, at Moscow University, and an eloquent advocate for the importance of law.

Catherine Dashkova (1743–1810) was an early supporter of Catherine the Great and one of the most learned individuals of her day. In 1783, she became first the director of the Academy of Sciences and then, later in the year, the di-

---

[3]The higher schools are sometimes referred to as being "four-year" but actually consisted of four classes, with what we might call "the senior class" taking two years to complete.

rector of a newly established Academy of Letters. In her latter capacity she oversaw the efforts of some of Russia's leading writers in preparing a six-volume Russian dictionary.

LANGUAGE AND LITERATURE

The dictionary overseen by Dashkova was published toward the end of Catherine II's reign and was symbolic of the general support given to language and literature—and culture generally—by Catherine II. She herself had begun a satirical journal in 1769 and later wrote, in Russian or French, enough plays to fill four volumes, including some adaptations or imitations of Shakespeare. (One Shakespeare play that the government forbade being staged in the capital was *Hamlet*; the theme of a son discovering that his mother had helped kill his royal father apparently hit a bit too close to home.)

The dictionary also symbolized a major problem facing eighteenth-century writers—developing an appropriate literary language. This problem, in turn, was connected with another major challenge—that of borrowing from Western culture without becoming mere uprooted, shallow imitators. Dashkova thought the dictionary, and an accompanying grammar, would free the Russian language from dependence on foreign words. Most of the century's leading writers dealt with one or both of the aforementioned major challenges.

The Western culture that so influenced the Russian writers of the century was far from being monolithic. Rationalism and secularism were dominant motifs, but there were also more emotional, sentimentalistic, and religious (Catholic and Protestant) strands in the tapestry. Over the course of the century, the French impact was most prominent, but English, Italian, and especially German influences were also significant.

Indeed, until the reign of Elizabeth, beginning in 1741, the German impact was stronger than the French. Lomonosov, for example, spent almost five years studying in Germany before returning home in 1741, then worked for several decades at an Academy of Sciences dominated by German scientists. He wrote both Russian prose and poetry in a syntax more influenced by the German language than the French. As mentioned previously, another of the century's most important writers, Alexander Radishchev, completed his education in Germany later in the century.

But by Radishchev's foreign-student days (1767–1771), German students and intellectuals were themselves being influenced by French philosophers and thinkers—later in the century, the German Herder would decry the Francomania of his fellow Germans. From France more than anywhere else, the chief cultural influences and Enlightenment ideas emanated.

The dominant eighteenth-century literary movement was neoclassicism, with its emphasis on rationality, clarity, and symmetry and its penchant for satire. Although England produced its share of neoclassical writers—and writings of Pope, Swift, and Defoe, among others, were translated into Russian—the French neoclassical writers exercised the strongest literary influence. In their forefront were the seventeenth-century dramatist Racine and the poet and critic Boileau.

Among Russia's earliest prominent neoclassical writers, four were especially prominent, Prince Antioch Kantemir (1708–1744), Vasili Trediakovsky (1703–1769), Alexander Sumarokov (1718–1777), and Lomonosov. All but Sumarokov, who was educated at the Noble Cadet School in St. Petersburg, attended the Moscow Slavonic Academy and later spent considerable time abroad. Trediakovsky, like Lomonosov, was from humble beginnings (his father being a poor priest) and also finished his education abroad, only in Holland and France rather than in Germany. Kantemir's time abroad was spent mainly in diplomatic service, including more than a decade as Russia's ambassador to England and then France.

The literary reputation of Kantemir rests primarily on his satires; that of Trediakovsky and Lomonosov, mainly on their poetry and contributions to developing an appropriate literary language and poetic forms; and that of Sumarokov, chiefly on his dramas. All four men also engaged in other literary activities, for example, Kantemir and Trediakovsky in translating; Lomonosov in writing a few plays; and Sumarokov in writing fables, poems, journalistic pieces, and literary criticism.

Important as these men were in the development of Russian literature, none of them was a great writer. The three greatest writers of the century came later and built upon the foundations laid out by their predecessors. The century's best dramatist was Denis Fonvizin (see Chapter 15 for his association with the Panin brothers); its finest poet, Gavriil Derzhavin (1743–1816); and its greatest writer of prose, Nikolai Karamzin (1766–1826).

Fonvizin's literary fame rests on two comedies, *The Brigadier* and *The Minor*. Both were popular in their day, especially the latter, which reflected some of its author's political ideas and has continued to be regarded as a classic. Both these comedies were neoclassical in format, poked fun at ignorance and brutishness, preached the importance of education and duty, and satirized Francomania. Such satirization, however, was not new. Even Sumarokov, whose plays owed so much to French models, satirized the aping of French customs. What sets Fonvizin's comedies apart from other plays of the century was his ability to create believable Russian characters—especially the Brigadier's wife and the "minor" and his family—and to write first-class dialogue. Although his more positive characters and their words are often stilted, his satirized characters are rich comic creations.

The poet Derzhavin rose to fame with "Felitsa," a semihumorous ode to Catherine. Soon afterward (in 1784), she promoted him from being a minor bureaucrat to being governor of the Olonets province. Later on, in 1802–1803, he served briefly as Alexander I's minister of justice.

Derzhavin's literary fame rests primarily on his lyric poetry. In such a poem as "A Nightingale in a Dream," the balance, the philosophic reflections, and the technical restraint admired by neoclassicism are seen. We also see and hear concrete images, enjoy his melodious lines, and feel his sadness at death mixed with his love of life and all its pleasures. Like Fonvizin's plays,

Derzhavin's poetry is simply more full of human life than that of any would-be rival.

Like Derzhavin, Nikolai Karamzin was from the provincial nobility of the Volga region. After a good secondary school education in Moscow and a short stint in a Guards regiment, he soon came under the influence of Novikov and Freemasonry and published some early literary works in one of Novikov's journals. In 1789, he began a year and a half trip to Western Europe. From it resulted his *Letters of a Russian Traveler*.

Its publication, plus the brief appearance of Radishchev's *A Journey from St. Petersburg to Moscow* in 1790 and Karamzin's own short tale *Poor Liza* in 1792, was indicative of a strong new trend in Russian literature—sentimentalism. Like Russian neoclassicism, this trend was strongly influenced by Western European writings—in this case, works such as those of Sterne and Rousseau. Sentimentalism emphasized feelings and emotions. They were aroused by such woeful tales as Radishchev's descriptions of mistreated peasants or Karamzin's poor peasant girl ("poor Liza") who, after being seduced and abandoned by her nobleman lover, commits suicide.

Poor Liza: A Tearful Story

The following account is an excerpt from Karamzin's *Poor Liza* as translated by Leo Wiener in his *Anthology of Russian Literature: From the Earliest Period to the Present Time* (New York, 1902), Vol. II, pp. 36–37. Ellipsis marks are mine.

But most frequently of all I am attracted to the walls of St. Siemon's monastery by the memory of the tearful fate of Liza, poor Liza. Oh! I love those objects that touch my heart and cause me to shed tears of tender sorrow! . . .

Liza's father was a fairly well-to-do peasant, for he loved work, carefully tilled the soil, and always led a sober life. But soon after his death his wife and daughter fell into poverty. The indolent hand of the hired servant ploughed the field carelessly, and the grain began to give diminished returns. They were compelled to let their land to a tenant, at an inconsiderable income. At the same time the poor widow, who continuously shed tears for her deceased husband,—for peasant women also know how to love,—grew weaker and weaker from day

to day, and finally could not work at all. Liza alone, who was fifteen years at her father's death,—Liza alone did not spare her tender youth nor her rare beauty, and laboured day and night: she wove hempen cloth, knit stockings; in springtime picked flowers, and in winter berries, and sold them in Moscow. Seeing the indefatigableness of her daughter, the sensitive, gentle old woman frequently pressed her to her feebly beating heart, called her "divine grace, protector, consolation of my old age," and prayed to God to reward her for all she did for her mother.

"God gave me hands to work," Liza would say. "You nourished me at your breast, watched me in my childhood. Now it is my turn to look after you. Only stop grieving, stop weeping! Our tears will not bring father to life."

But often gentle Liza could not restrain her own tears, for oh! she recalled that she had a father, and that he was no more; but to comfort her mother she tried to hide the grief of her heart, and to appear calm and gay.

Sentimentalism was interrelated to several other late-eighteenth-century literary developments. Among them was an increasing emphasis on three interrelated areas: the Russian peasants or "folk," Russian history, and the discovery of Russia's unique national identity. Paradoxically, however, such emphases were not unique. In Germany, Herder, with whose ideas both Karamzin and Radishchev were familiar, was clearly articulating the importance of the "volk" (folk) and national uniqueness.

With all the Western influences flooding into Russia during the eighteenth century, it was only natural that intelligent Russians would begin confronting the question of "Russia and the West." Trips to the West further stimulated such thinking. Before Karamzin's journey, Fonvizin traveled to Western Europe and wrote interesting travel letters. In them, he was quite critical of Western Europe—stating, for example, that the French made a god out of money and that Russians were more human than the Germans.

In the early nineteenth century, when he turned to the writing of history, Karamzin contributed much to the evolution of Russia's sense of historical consciousness. But his own earlier travel letters were less critical of the West than were Fonvizin's, and in 1790 he could still write that the "totally *national* is nothing next to the *all-human*. The chief point is to be *humans*, not Slavs."

Although Karamzin's major contribution to Russia's rising national consciousness still lay ahead, already by the end of the eighteenth century he had placed a permanent stamp on the Russian language. Earlier, Lomonosov and others had struggled with the language question. Because no agreed-upon Russian literary language existed, the struggle involved working toward some consensus on the proper mixture of Old Church Slavonic, vernacular Russian, and foreign borrowings. Lomonosov advocated using mainly different mixtures of the first two, depending on the level and seriousness of the literature being written.

Karamzin moved the Russian literary language further away from Old Church Slavonic, while lacing it with more words borrowed from Western languages, especially French. And he followed the French example by simplifying the Russian syntax. His prose was considerably lighter and more graceful than Lomonosov's had been.

Despite the popularity of his prose, opposition to the "Karamzin style" existed, primarily led by Admiral Shishkov, whose *Discussion of the Old and New Style of the Russian Language* appeared in 1803. The support of the younger generation of writers, however, most notably the great Pushkin, guaranteed the success of Karamzin's new style.

ART AND MUSIC

Because of its nature, major Russian architectural undertakings depended much more than literature on government support. And Russian rulers were more than willing to furnish it.

James Cracraft has written of the tremendous impact of Peter the Great on all aspects of architecture. This effect was mainly seen in his new capital of St.

Petersburg and in the surrounding area, especially at his summer residence of Peterhof. It also extended far beyond the capital and far beyond his lifetime. By supporting the gathering and printing of Western architectural books and prints, by importing thousands of Western experts to help build and teach in Russia, and by sending Russian students to the West to study architecture, Peter helped insure the spread of Western architectural knowledge.

Under Peter's daughter Elizabeth, the best works of the great eighteenth-century architect, Bartolommeo Rastrelli (1700–1771), appeared. Although Parisian born and educated, this Italian came to Russia when he was sixteen with his father, a sculptor invited by Peter I. Among the works that best illustrate his talents are the Catherine Palace at the summer retreat of Tsarskoe Selo (see Figure 15.1), near the capital, and the Cathedral of the Resurrection at the Smolny Convent (see Figure 17.1) and the Winter Palace (see Figure 14.1), both in St. Petersburg. His style is usually viewed as the culmination of the Russian

FIGURE 17.1. Cathedral of the Resurrection, Smolny Convent, St. Petersburg, 1748–1764, architect B. F. Rastrelli.

baroque, but, as with the West's late baroque, it is often graced with the lighter, more joyful variation known as rococo.

Under Catherine II, who preferred neoclassical forms to the more ornamental baroque, new building activity accelerated even more rapidly than under Elizabeth. In the capital alone, stone and brick buildings—many stuccoed over and given facades of yellow, pink, green, and other colors—almost tripled during her first twenty-five years on the throne.

Among the architects who worked for her were the Scottish architect Charles Cameron (c. 1740–1812) and the native Russians Ivan Starov (1743–1808) and Matvei Kazakov (1738–1812). The first designed the Cameron Gallery at Tsarskoe Selo; the second, the capital's Tauride Palace (see Figure 25.2); and the third, various buildings in and around Moscow. Among the last-mentioned were the Senate Building in the Kremlin and the Nobles' Club, later the House of Trade Unions (see Figure 17.2). Although the great Moscow fire of 1812 destroyed many of his buildings, Kazakov left a permanent classical architectural legacy to the city, and much of the rebuilding was done in his style.

Sculpturing and painting also benefited from government support, including the establishment of an Academy of Fine Arts in St. Petersburg in 1757. Perhaps Russia's best native eighteenth-century sculptor, Fedot Shubin (1740–1805), studied there under the Frenchman N. Gillet before completing his studies abroad. After Shubin's return, Catherine and Potemkin commis-

FIGURE 17.2. Nobles' Club (in the Soviet period, House of Trade Unions), Moscow, 1784, architect M. Kazakov.

sioned numerous works from him. His busts of leading figures of the day reflect the era's concern for elegance and his noteworthy ability to capture his sitter's character.

The most famous single work of sculpturing was not by Shubin, but by the Frenchman E. Falconet. It was the bronze equestrian statue of Peter the Great (see Figure 17.3). Looking out toward the Neva River, it almost immediately became one of St. Petersburg's most famous monuments. Baroque in form and modeled after a statue of Emperor Marcus Aurelius in Rome, its boulder base was inscribed "To Peter the First from Catherine II, Summer 1782." Later the subject of Alexander Pushkin' magnificent poem "The Bronze Horseman," it remains to this day a fitting symbol of both Peter the absolutistic emperor and of Russian cultural achievement influenced by the West.

The most famous painter of the era was Dmitri Levitsky (1735?–1822). Son of a Kievan priest, he studied in St. Petersburg, and Catherine later commissioned him to paint many portraits, including some of herself. They reflect different French and English influences, including the light-hearted rococo, and he has been compared to the English painter Gainsborough. Like the sculptor Shubin, he was also adept at psychological characterization.

Although eighteenth-century Russia produced no musical composer of comparable merit to its artists, the groundwork for future composers was developed. Western operas and ballets appeared, and training in both disciplines began. Empress Anna opened the first ballet school in 1738, and the future Emperor Paul I danced in court ballets while still a young man. Some wealthy no-

FIGURE 17.3. The Bronze Horseman, St. Petersburg, 1782, by E. Falconet.

bles even had selected serfs taught ballet for their master's entertainment and that of his guests. Russians also began collecting and printing some of their country's folk songs.

During the reign of Catherine II, Russian composers both imitated Western compositions and began composing works based on Russian folk music. Catherine II herself both encouraged the collection of folk songs and wrote the librettos for a number of operas. Mirroring the increasing interest in Russian history, several of these operas dealt with historical subjects and incorporated Russian folklore and folk songs.

The Problem of Two Cultures

Many historians believe that Russian culture split in two during the eighteenth century. On the one hand, they see a westernized cosmopolitan elite culture; on the other, a traditional national peasant culture that continued many of the ways of Muscovite popular culture. Whereas the former was more secular and rational, the latter was more affected by much older Orthodox and even pre-Orthodox religious and mythical beliefs. The former appeared more in the cities, and the latter appeared more in the villages, especially on holy days and holidays dictated by the church or nature's changing seasons. Elite culture was primarily reflected in written and artistic works, whereas popular culture was more oral and best revealed in folk songs, dances, and tales.

This cultural split was a subject of much concern and debate among Russian intellectuals during the nineteenth century. We must be wary, however, of too rigid a classification. The cultural reality was much more complex. Between elite, partly westernized nobles and illiterate peasants were poorer nobles, merchants, local priests, and others (especially in urban areas) who often did not comfortably fit into either cultural category.

The spread of education and publishing activities helped disperse elite cultural influences more widely and to blur the boundaries between elite and popular culture. Although those who could read still remained only a small percentage of the total population, their reading choices broadened as more newspapers, journals, and books were published. Popular leisure reading included original and translated works. Among the most popular types were moral fables and tales (such as *Aesop's Fables*), biblical and other stories for children, and romance and action stories (such as *Adventures of the English Lord George, The Factual and True History of a Russian Swindler, 1001 Nights,* and *Robinson Crusoe*). Although the works of Russia's best writers did not generally sell as well as the more popular adventure stories of minor or unknown Russian writers, Karamzin's *Poor Liza* as well as Fonvizin's *The Minor* both sold fairly well.

Exactly who read what works is impossible to determine. In an 1802 essay, Karamzin wrote of five bakers, four of them illiterate, who collectively bought Moscow newspapers so that the one literate baker could read aloud to the other four. Karamzin also mentioned illiterate peddlers who went into the countryside and were able to relate, often in a colorful manner, some of the details of the novels and comedies they hoped to sell.

With the expansion of theater at the end of the eighteenth century, the audience for both professional and amateur plays spread, both geographically and further across the social spectrum. By the end of the eighteenth century, popular prints, sometimes satirizing the same subjects as did the satirical journals and plays, had fanned out beyond the poor nobility and merchants to urban workers and peasants.

Conversely, the reawakened late-eighteenth-century interest in the peasants and their tales and songs helped infuse high culture with popular elements. Nobles taught to speak French at home rather than Russian often imbibed popular cultural elements from their nannies and other servants—as would the great Pushkin at the beginning of the next century.

SUGGESTED SOURCES*

ALSTON, PATRICK L. *Education and the State in Tsarist Russia*. Stanford, 1969. Ch. 1.

AVAKUMOVIC, IVAN. "Dukhobory," *MERSH* 10: 30–33.

BAEHR, STEPHEN LESSING. *The Paradise Myth in Eighteenth-Century Russia: Utopian Patterns in Early Secular Russian Literature and Culture*. Stanford, 1991.

BARTLETT, ROGER P., A. G. CROSS, and KAREN RASMUSSEN, eds. *Russia and the World of the Eighteenth Century: Proceedings of the Third International Conference*. Columbus, Ohio, 1988.

BELIAJEFF, ANTON S. "Molokane," *MERSH* 23: 22–24.

"Bezbozhnik" (Priestless), *MERSH* 4: 108–109.

BLACK, J. L. *Citizens for the Fatherland: Education, Educators, and Pedagogical Ideals in Eighteenth-Century Russia*. Boulder, 1979.

BROWN, W. E. *A History of Eighteenth-Century Russian Literature*. Ann Arbor, 1980.

BRUMFIELD, WILLIAM C. *A History of Russian Architecture*. Cambridge, England, 1993. Chs. 8–11.

CRACRAFT, JAMES. *The Petrine Revolution in Russian Architecture*. Chicago, 1988.

CROSS, A. G. *N. M. Karamzin: A Study of His Literary Career, 1783–1803*. Carbondale, Ill., 1971.

CRUMMEY, ROBERT O. *The Old Believers and the World of Antichrist: The Vyg Community and the Russian State, 1694–1855*. Madison, 1970.

DANIELS, RUDOLPH L. *V. N. Tatishchev: Guardian of the Petrine Revolution*. Philadelphia, 1973.

EDIE, JAMES M., JAMES P. SCANLAN, and MARY-BARBARA ZELDIN, eds. *Russian Philosophy*. Vol. 1. Knoxville, 1976.

FARRELL, DIANE ECKLUND. "Medieval Popular Humor in Russian Eighteenth-Century Lubki," *SR* 50 (Fall 1991): 551–565.

FEDOTOV, G. P., ed. *A Treasury of Russian Spirituality*. New York, 1948.

FLOROVSKY, GEORGES. "Western Influences in Russian Theology." In *Aspects of Church History*. Belmont, Mass., 1975.

FONVIZIN, D. I. *Dramatic Works of D. I. Fonvizin*. Bern, 1974.

*See also works cited in footnotes.

FREEZE, GREGORY L. *The Russian Levites: Parish Clergy in the Eighteenth Century*. Cambridge, Mass., 1977.

KARAMZIN, NIKOLAI M. *Letters of a Russian Traveler, 1789–1790: An Account of a Young Russian Gentleman's Tour Through Germany, Switzerland, France, and England*. New York, 1957.

KARLINSKY, SIMON. *Russian Drama from Its Beginnings to the Age of Pushkin*. Berkeley, 1985.

KLIUCHEVSKII, V. O. "Western Influence in Russia after Peter the Great," *CASS* 20, Nos. 3–4 (1986): 467–484; 22, No. 4 (1990): 431–455; 28, No. 1 (1994): 67–98; 28, No. 4 (1994): 419–444. A series of ten lectures translated and edited by Marshall S. Shatz.

MARKER, GARY. *Publishing, Printing, and the Origins of Intellectual Life in Russia, 1700–1800*. Princeton, 1985.

———. "Who Rules the Word? Public Education and the Fate of Universality in Russia," *RH* 20, Nos. 1–4 (1993): 15–34.

MENSHUTKIN, B. N. *Russia's Lomonosov: Chemist, Courtier, Physicist, Poet*. Princeton, 1952.

MOSER, CHARLES A. *Denis Fonvizin*. Boston, 1979.

MUNRO, GEORGE E. "Khlysty," *MERSH* 16: 150–154.

NAKHIMOVSKY, ALEXANDER D. and ALICE STONE NAKHIMOVSKY, eds. *The Semiotics of Russian Cultural History: Essays by Iurii M. Lotman, Lidiia Ia. Ginsburg, Boris A. Uspenskii*. Ithaca, N.Y., 1985.

OKENFUSS, MAX J. *The Rise and Fall of Latin Humanism in Early-Modern Russia: Pagan Authors, Ukrainians, and the Resiliency of Muscovy*. New York, 1995.

RAEFF, MARC. *Origins of the Russian Intelligentsia: The Eighteenth-Century Nobility*. New York, 1966.

ROGGER, HANS. *National Consciousness in Eighteenth-Century Russia*. Cambridge, Mass., 1960.

SAUNDERS, DAVID. *The Ukrainian Impact on Russian Culture, 1750–1850*. Edmonton, Canada, 1985.

SEGEL, HAROLD B., ed. *The Literature of Eighteenth-Century Russia: An Anthology of Russian Literary Materials of the Age of Classicism and the Enlightenment from the Reign of Peter the Great (1689–1725) to the Reign of Alexander I (1801–1825)*. 2 vols. New York, 1967.

SOLOV'EV, O. F. "Freemasonry in Russia," *RSH* 34 (Spring 1996): 27–58.

Walicki, Andrzej. *A History of Russian Thought from the Enlightenment to Marxism*. Stanford, 1979. Chs. 1–3.

WARE, TIMOTHY. *The Orthodox Church*. New ed. London, 1993. Ch. 6.

WORTMAN, RICHARD S. *Scenarios of Power: Myth and Ceremony in Russian Monarchy*. Vol. 1, *From Peter the Great to the Death of Nicholas I*. Princeton, 1995.

CHAPTER 18

The Reigns of Paul and Alexander I

Although the brief rule of Paul, son of Catherine II, contrasted in many ways with that of his mother, the longer reign of Paul's son Alexander I was more similar to his grandmother's. Four similarities are immediately evident: (1) Alexander I came to power as a result of a coup that killed his predecessor. (2) He began his reign talking and planning reforms, but when faced with harsh Russian realities (and his own autocratic inclinations), he discovered that talk of reform was easier than enacting it. (3) He started off with a peace policy but then engaged in wars and diplomacy that helped significantly expand the Russian Empire and Russia's European standing. (4) He became more conservative during the end of his reign and then faced his most serious intellectual opposition, which, after his death, culminated in the Decembrist revolt of 1825.

EMPEROR PAUL AND HIS DOMESTIC POLICIES

When Emperor Paul came to the throne in November 1796, at the age of forty-two, he was determined to undo some of his mother's policies. One reason for this determination was his hostility toward her.

The earlier relationship between mother and son had been an abnormal one. After his birth in 1754, Empress Elizabeth snatched Paul away from Catherine and began overseeing his upbringing. During his first six years, Catherine had little contact with him, and he was left mainly in the care of Elizabeth's female servants. The mysterious death of his "father," Peter III, and Catherine II's fears of conspirators favoring her son also probably helped prevent the development of a normal mother-son relationship.

In 1773, Catherine allowed Paul to choose one of three princesses of Hesse-Darmstadt to be his wife, but she died in childbirth in 1776. Later that same year, he married another German princess, who took the Russian name of Maria Fedorovna. She was an intelligent, cultured woman and a loving wife, who gave birth to ten children, six daughters and four sons.

Primarily because of Catherine's distrust of Paul, the two decades between 1776 and 1796 were frustrating ones for Paul and Maria. Catherine failed to allow Paul much in the way of real responsibility and treated him and Maria much as Elizabeth had treated her and Peter III: Not long after the births of the future Alexander I (1777) and his brother Constantine (1779), she took each boy from his parents and brought him up under her own supervision.

Under such conditions, Paul became increasingly hostile toward his mother. He also became contemptuous of her advisers—on a trip abroad in 1781–1782, he stated, "as soon as I have power, I shall flog them, break them, and kick them all out." Finally, he began to act more like his "father," Peter III, whom Catherine had overthrown. At Paul's Gatchina estate, he started displaying a passion akin to Peter III's for Prussian drill and appearances.

In Catherine's final years, she thought of bypassing Paul and passing the throne directly to her beloved grandson Alexander. But she never got around to it.

Some of Paul's directives after coming to the throne in 1796 seemed belated retaliation against his mother and her advisers. He had Peter III's remains dug up and interred next to her body in the Sts. Peter and Paul Fortress Cathedral, and he freed many persons she had imprisoned or exiled, including Radishchev and Novikov. He also changed Peter the Great's succession law, which had allowed a monarch to select his or her own successor. No doubt wishing to insure that no future monarch could contemplate what his mother

FIGURE 18.1. Saints Peter and Paul Fortress and Cathedral, St. Petersburg.

had—denying him the right to succeed her—Paul decreed a firm male line of succession, topped by the reigning monarch's oldest son.

Other forces, besides squaring accounts with his mother, also shaped his domestic policies. Among the most prominent were his personal insecurities and impetuousness; his political ideas; and contemporary domestic and foreign conditions, especially in France.

Although apparently not insane, Paul was suspicious and at times unstable enough for this charge to surface among some of his contemporaries. Even more fearful of French revolutionary influence than his mother had been, this intelligent and well-read monarch outlawed math and music books because they might contain subversive codes. He increased the Secret Expedition's investigative labors, especially against suspected nobles, and thousands of officers were arrested, including more than 300 generals. Paul violated noble rights, including that of freedom from corporal punishment, and he decreased the government's reliance on elected nobles in the countryside. Partly to improve the sorry fiscal conditions that his mother bequeathed to him, he cut local government spending and began taxing noble estates. He also forbade nobles to work their serfs on Sundays and recommended that they allow them at least three days a week to work their own allotments.

In practice, the lives of the serfs probably changed little during his reign. Although Paul had been more benevolent toward his own peasants at Gatchina than were most nobles, after coming to the throne he continued the practice of turning some state and crown peasants into serfs by giving them away to new favorites.

Yet he was much more popular among the peasants than among the nobles. Many of the latter, after their favorable treatment under Catherine, resented Paul's new decrees, his Prussian ways, and his impetuous temper—on at least several occasions, he became so angry at officers on the drill field that he sent them directly to Siberia.

If such behavior calls to mind Peter III, so too does Paul's removal in 1801. The coup almost seemed a reworked version of that of 1762. In place of the Orlov brothers, there were the Zubov brothers, with Catherine's last lover, Platon Zubov, being one of the chief conspirators. Also involved was another Nikita Panin, the nephew of the same-named man who had tutored Paul and helped Catherine come to power. And like the earlier coup, this one had the support of Guards officers and members of leading noble families (including the Dolgorukovs, Golitsyns, and Viazemskys). Again, there were strong hints of foreign encouragement to remove the reigning monarch and the successor (Paul's son Alexander) knew of the plot, although perhaps not that the overthrown ruler would be killed.

Yet there were also differences between the coups. Catherine was a more active plotter than Alexander, who had to be persuaded to go along with the coup against Paul. (The coup's most visible leader was Count Peter Pahlen, the military governor of the capital.) After Paul was killed in his Mikhailovskii Castle (March 1801), Alexander I—whether or not he ever really believed assurances that his father's life would be spared—was much more troubled by Paul's death than Catherine II had been over Peter III's.

ALEXANDER I AND REFORM, 1801–1812

Alexander I was twenty-three when he became emperor. He was tall and had blue eyes, blond hair, and great charm. Karamzin wrote that he shone "like a divine angel." But his charm masked a personality that has mystified historians ever since—a 1937 French biography of him is subtitled *"un tsar énigmatique."*

One clue to his puzzling personality was that he grew up caught in the middle of the tensions between his grandmother Catherine II and his own parents. He was brought up at his grandmother's court under her solicitous supervision. She appointed the Swiss republican LaHarpe as his principal tutor. When Alexander was barely fifteen, she had him married to a fourteen-year-old German princess, who became Grand Duchess Elizabeth. In his early teens, Catherine's influences were partly counterbalanced by Alexander's regular visits to his parents. At Gatchina, he grew fond of a rougher military life, and Captain Alexei Arakcheev, a strict disciplinarian, introduced him to Paul's Prussian-style military drills.

During his quarter-century reign, Alexander sometimes seemed a split personality, displaying both a LaHarpian side and an Arakcheevian one. When young, seeing that neither his grandmother nor his parents were completely right or wrong, he tried to please both—and in the process furthered his gift for dissembling.

This upbringing partly accounts for the liberalism and conservatism that oscillated within him during his years as emperor. Another cause was the discrepancy between Enlightenment sentiments and Russian reality. LaHarpe had planted noble ideas in his young pupil but had few insights on how to make them bloom in Russia. Finally, although Alexander's ideas for reform were vague, his instinct to resist any outside challenges to his powers was concrete. He wished to be a reformer, but a paternalistic one.

At the beginning of his reign, the youthful Alexander was faced with many problems, both foreign and domestic. The French Revolution, followed by the rule of Napoleon, presented the main foreign-policy challenge. Moreover, by questioning the legitimacy of monarchical absolutism and the noble domination of society, these French developments also helped unsettle Russian internal conditions. To deal with these challenges, Alexander had his high ideals and his absolutist powers. Before he could confidently wield his full authority, however, he had to overcome the attempt of Count Pahlen—leader of the coup against Paul—and others to place limits on his powers (sources of the time are hazy about the exact nature of these limits).

In the face of this challenge, Alexander acted resolutely. He forced Pahlen and others into retirement and surrounded himself with an Unofficial Com-

The Young Alexander

The following excerpt is from the *Memoirs of Prince Adam Czartoryski and His Correspondence with Alexander I.* 2d ed. (London, 1888), Vol. I, pp. 117–120, 128–129. Czartoryski (1770–1861) was a Polish prince brought to court in St. Petersburg in 1794 to insure his family's loyalty to Russia. He soon became a close friend of the young Alexander. Ellipses and bracketed material are mine.

His [Alexander's] opinions are those of one brought up in the ideas of 1789, who wishes to see republics everywhere, and looks upon that form of government as the only one in conformity with the wishes and the rights of humanity. . . . He held, among other things, that hereditary monarchy was an unjust and absurd institution, and that the supreme authority should be granted not through the accident of birth but by the votes of the nation, which would best know who is most capable of governing it. . . . Sometimes during our long walks we talked of other matters. We turned from politics to nature, of whose beauties the young Grand-Duke was an enthusiastic admirer. . . .

. . . His sincerity, his frankness, his self-abandonment to the beautiful illusions that fascinated him, had a charm that was impossible to resist. . . .

Besides our political discussions, and the ever-welcome topic of the beauties of nature, and the dream of a quiet country life after the destinies of free Russia should have been secured, Alexander had also a third ob-ject to which he ardently devoted himself, and which was not at all in accordance with the others, namely, the army, which was his hobby, as it was that of his father, the Grand-Duke Paul. . . .

. . . Alexander's education remained incomplete at the time of his marriage [1793], in consequence of the departure of M. de la Harpe. He was then eighteen years old [in 1795, when La Harpe actually left Russia]; he had no regular occupation, he was not even advised to work, and in the absence of any more practical task he was not given any plan of reading which might have helped him in the difficult career for which he was destined. I often spoke to him on this subject, both then and later. I proposed that he should read various books on history, legislation, and politics. He saw that they would do him good, and really wished to read them; but a Court life makes any continued occupation impossible. While he was Grand-Duke, Alexander did not read to the end a single serious book. I do not think he could have done so when he became Emperor, and the whole burden of a despotic government was cast upon him. . . . The passion of acquiring knowledge was not sufficiently strong in him; he was married too young, and he did not perceive that he still knew very little. Yet he felt the importance of useful study, and wished to enter upon it; but his will was not sufficiently strong to overcome the daily obstacles presented by the duties and unpleasantnesses of life.

mittee, consisting of four of his youthful friends—Adam Czartoryski, Viktor Kochubei, Paul Stroganov, and Nikolai Novosiltsev.

The liberal ideas of these men and Alexander at the beginning of his reign are well documented—especially in recent decades by the St. Petersburg historian M. M. Safonov. They wished, for example, to end serfdom and to ground government firmly on fundamental laws. On the crucial question of limiting tsarist powers, however, there was not only the paternalistic, authoritarian streak in Alexander that would have to be overcome, but also an inescapable dilemma. However desirable it might be in the future, in the early 1800s any "power-sharing" would play into the hands of the nobility, the most educated estate. Nobles might then use their powers to frustrate any reforms that would lessen their powers.

The Unofficial Committee also soon realized, as Catherine II had early in her reign, that serfdom was too dangerous to touch. Attempting to abolish it might create chaos, stirring up, in different ways, both serfowners and serfs. (Ironically, one of the committee members, the ardent Count Paul Stroganov, who had once alarmed Catherine II by his zeal for the French Revolution, came from one of the largest serf-owning families in the empire.)

Yet if such considerations seemed to prevent the most sweeping reforms, they still left the door open for lesser ones. In the first four years of Alexander's reign—before war with Napoleon diverted attention from domestic policies—Alexander began strengthening civil liberties. He freed and brought back into service more than 10,000 individuals whom Paul had jailed or exiled without a trial. He eased censorship and travel restriction. And he reaffirmed Catherine II's Charter of Nobility, some of whose stipulations, such as the nobles' right to be free from corporal punishment, his father had violated. Reflecting his desire to strengthen the rule of law, he abolished the Secret Expedition, whose secret-police work had expanded under Paul.

During this same period, Alexander removed many restrictions on imports and exports and issued several decrees designed to help the serfs. In 1803, for example, he encouraged voluntary emancipation by spelling out the conditions under which it could be undertaken—serfowners, however, freed only about 47,000 male serfs by 1825. Alexander also expanded educational opportunities, most significantly by the 1804 Statute of Schools and the establishment of several new universities (see Chapter 21).

If Alexander and his Unofficial Committee thought Russia was not yet ready for power-sharing and a constitution, education could at least prepare the way. In the meantime, the emperor and his friends attempted to strengthen and streamline his powers so that he could more effectively continue his reforms.

A major step in this direction occurred in 1802, when Alexander established ministries to replace Peter I's system of administrative colleges. Although the ministries (of Foreign Affairs, War, Navy, Commerce, Education, Finance, Interior, and Justice) were legally subject to Senate overview, their eight ministers, in fact, were directly under the Emperor's control.

After an interlude of war (1805–1807) and the signing of peace with Napoleon at Tilsit in 1807, Alexander renewed his concern with domestic reforms. Although the Unofficial Committee no longer operated, Alexander came to rely heavily on Mikhail Speransky (1772–1839), who had served as a secretary to one of its members, Count Viktor Kochubei.

The son of a provincial priest, Speransky was one of the most intelligent men of his day. Despite his earning of hereditary noble rank and the early support he received from the important Kurakin clan, he remained an outsider among the aristocratic ruling elite. His wife was an English governess' daughter, and he made little effort to endear himself to those who considered themselves his social superiors. Although a man of liberal ideas, he realized the need of proceeding cautiously and of pleasing his emperor.

After many discussions with Alexander and with his support, Speransky put forth a plan in 1809 to reorganize the Russian government. Although six years earlier he had shared the Unofficial Committee's belief that Russia was not yet prepared for sweeping governmental changes—and warned of chaos if Russia moved too fast—by 1809, he thought that educated society was ready for his proposed revisions.

Even though the emperor was to keep most of his powers, the plan (and Speransky's summary outline of it) called for the creation of a State Duma that could reject new laws proposed by the administration. Members would be elected to this body by those serving on provincial dumas, who, in turn, would be elected by those on district dumas, who themselves would be selected by those on dumas of the smallest government unit, the *volost* (township).

The plan also called for separate judicial and executive institutions on all four levels, from the national down to the *volost*. The Senate was to act as a supreme court, and the chief national administrative functions would remain in the hands of the ministries. Finally, an appointed State Council was to be established to advise and assist the emperor on legislative, legal, and administrative matters.

Speransky's plan divided society into three estates: the nobility, a middle estate, and "working people." Like most liberal Western thinkers of his time, he believed the right to vote should be restricted to owners of property or sufficient capital. His plan therefore excluded all "working people" from voting. But they would enjoy certain basic civil rights, for example, the right to a trial. The nobles were to enjoy not only these rights, but also certain special rights, such as exemption from military service.

Although opposed to serfdom in principle, Speransky, in his final 1809 draft, did little more than suggest the *possibility* of abolishing it. No doubt, he believed Alexander much more willing to risk governmental reform than the emancipation of the serfs.

Circumstances and Alexander's ambivalence, however, prevented him from implementing Speransky's plan. In 1810, he created a Council of State but with more limited advisory functions than Speransky had intended. In 1810–1811, he reorganized some of his ministries as suggested in the 1809 plan. Yet, despite Alexander's failure to do more, Speransky remained close to him until 1812. A French diplomat referred to Speransky in 1811 as a sort of "minister of innovations" and stated that he influenced everything.

Meanwhile, many leading nobles were trying to undermine Speransky. They disliked some of his initiatives, such as an 1809 law requiring a university degree or the passing of a difficult examination as a prerequisite for holding certain upper-level positions. They were upset with an 1812 decree stipulating an emergency progressive tax on estate incomes. And they feared continuing Speransky-generated innovations and that the expanding military forces and civilian bureaucracy were creating too many opportunities for outsiders like him. Their aristocratic dominance of the country's most important military and governmental positions seemed to be eroding. Rumors that Speransky was pro-French also helped weaken him. In March 1812, just a few months before Napoleon's invasion of Russia and at a time when Alexander greatly needed noble support, he dismissed Speransky.

RUSSIAN FOREIGN POLICY, 1796–1812

When Paul came to the throne in late 1796, French armies had been advancing for several years and were then, under Napoleon, in the midst of a successful Italian campaign. At one time or another during the mid-1790s, a coalition of forces, including Austria, Prussia, Great Britain, the Netherlands, Spain, and Sardinia, had fought against France. Although under Catherine II Russia had stayed out of the wars, both Paul and Alexander I were swept into the conflict. Until 1815, Russia alternated between warring against France or allying with it.

Foreign Policy of Paul I

Although Paul began his reign by emphasizing peace and recalling troops sent to the Caucasus as part of Platon Zubov's Oriental Project, in 1798 he went to war against France. Paul hated revolutionary France and feared its advances in the eastern Mediterranean. Strangely enough, it was Napoleon's takeover of the island of Malta in mid-1798, en route to seizing Egypt, which most galvanized Paul into allying against Napoleon. In 1797, Paul had become a protector of a Catholic order that ran the island, the Maltese Order of the Knights of St. John.

Thus roused, Paul played a leading role in a Second Coalition against France. It included Russia, Austria, Great Britain, Turkey, Portugal, and Naples. Russian forces fought on both land and sea. Most notable were General Suvorov's victories against the French in Italy and Switzerland. Almost seventy years old, Suvorov surprised the French with one daring attack after another in 1799 and became legendary by cutting through a larger French force and crossing the Alps.

But discord among coalition members led to Russia's withdrawal from the Second Coalition in 1799. In 1800, Russia and Sweden played the leading roles in reviving an Armed Neutrality League to protect their shipping trade against British interference. That same year, Paul moved closer to France. Napoleon's political takeover in late 1799 had encouraged Paul to believe that France's revolutionary challenge to more traditional regimes had ended, and Napoleon pursued a diplomacy designed to win Paul over to his side. Hoping, with Napoleon's backing, to gain Constantinople and Balkan territories, Paul agreed to support France against England. Shortly before his overthrow, Paul ordered more than 20,000 Cossacks to cross Central Asia and invade British

India. The order was just more fuel for the flames of domestic resentment already burning against him.

Peace and Wars, 1801–1812

Like Paul, Alexander I began his reign by calling for peace and recalling troops sent out by his predecessor on a far-fetched scheme—in this case, the Cossacks dispatched toward British India. Also like his father, he then entered a coalition against France, only to make peace later with Napoleon and turn against England.

While Napoleon's boundless ambitions propelled him toward conflict with Russia, Alexander was also nudged toward war by other considerations. Among them were frustrations with the difficulties of implementing reforms at home, Russia's traditional trade ties with Great Britain, and Alexander's own personality. He was attracted both to military heroics and to idealistic international "grand designs." He outlined his first such plan in 1804. It called for an end to French "tyranny" and the establishment of just European frontiers.

The Third Coalition against France began in 1805 and included Russia, Great Britain, Austria, and Sweden. Late that year at Austerlitz (northeast of Vienna), Napoleon crushed a Russian-Austrian force. The defeat forced Russia to withdraw her remaining troops from Austrian lands and led Austria to negotiate a peace with Napoleon.

The following year, however, Prussia joined the coalition against France. It did not stop Napoleon, now labeled the anti-Christ in Orthodox sermons. In October, he routed Prussian troops and occupied Berlin. Alexander increased Russian forces but was woefully short of muskets for them. In June 1807, Napoleon's army defeated Russian troops at Friedland. Less than a month later, near Tilsit in East Prussia, Napoleon and Alexander signed a peace treaty on a raft in the Nieman River.

Although Alexander did what he could for his Prussian ally, this agreement, and another Tilsit treaty between France and Prussia, recognized significant French gains at Prussia's expense. Included in France's gains were Prussia's previous Polish holdings. Alexander also secretly agreed to ally with France against Britain if he could not persuade the British to accept a French-offered peace.

Unable to do so and angered by several British actions, Alexander kept his promise and broke off diplomatic relations with Britain in late 1807. Early the next year, encouraged by Napoleon and fearful of any possible threat from Britain's ally Sweden, Alexander sent Russian troops to attack Swedish forces in Finland. In 1809, Sweden ceded Finland to Russia, and it remained part of the Russian Empire for over a century (see Map 18.1).

The first decade of Alexander's reign witnessed even longer periods of war in the south. Russia's enemies in that region included some Caucasian peoples, Persia, and Turkey.

In September 1801, Alexander issued a proclamation annexing Georgia—it reinforced a similar one issued by Paul in late 1800. Although many Georgians, including its king, had wished for Russian protection against Georgia's many

Europe and European Russia, 1796–1856

Russian Empire in 1796

Territories gained under Alexander I, 1801–1825, and retained

Territory gained under Alexander I, but lost in Treaty of Paris, 1856

Territories gained under Nicholas I, 1825–1855, and retained

Territories gained in 1829, but lost in Treaty of Paris, 1856

German Confederation following the Congress of Vienna, 1815

0   300   600 Miles

French Invasion June–Sept.(O.S.) 1812
French Retreat Oct.–Dec.(O.S.) 1812
X Major Battles

Area gained between 1801 and 1855

Baltic Sea

Moscow
BORODINO
SMOLENSK
Vitebsk
DRISSA
Borisov
Vilna
Riga
Kovno
Königsberg

RUSSIA
PRUSSIA

Caspian Sea
Baku
Derbent
CHECHNIA
CAUCASUS
GEORGIA (1801)
ABKHAZIA
ARMENIA
KARABAGH
Erevan

Kazan
Saratov
Nizhnii Novgorod
Penza
Ivanovo
Vladimir
MOSCOW
Tambov
Kaluga
Riazan
Tula
Kursk
Kharkov
Ekaterinoslav
Taganrog
Nikolaev
Kherson
Odessa
CRIMEA
Sea of Azov
Strait of Kerch
Black Sea
Bosphorus Strait

St. Petersburg
Novgorod
BORODINO (1812)
SMOLENSK (1812)
Kiev
Berdichev
UKRAINE
BELO-RUSSIA
Ladoga

FINLAND (1809)
Gulf of Finland
Estland
Livland
Riga
W. Dvina R.
Courland
LITHUANIA
Vilna
Volga R.
Don R.
Dnieper R.
S. Bug R.
Dniester R.
BESSARABIA (1812)
Kishinev
MOLDAVIA
WALLACHIA
Danube R.
Ural R.

SWEDEN
DENMARK

Tilsit
FRIEDLAND (1807)
Posen
KINGDOM OF POLAND
LEIPZIG (1813)
AUSTERLITZ (1805)
Vienna
Warsaw
Berlin
P R U S S I A
AUSTRIAN EMPIRE
ITALY
SPAIN
FRANCE
Paris
London
GREAT BRITAIN
WATERLOO (1815)
DUCHY OF OLDENBURG
Elba
Corsica
Sardinia
KGDM. OF THE TWO SICILIES

OTTOMAN TURKISH EMPIRE
Constantinople

MAP 18.1

Moslem neighbors, they did not wish to be annexed. This action, plus the presence of the arrogant General Paul Tsitsianov (d. 1806) as commander of the Caucasus, led to further campaigns in the region. In an area of many nationalities and local varieties of both Christian and Moslem beliefs, Russia played upon tribal rivalries, religious differences, and the absence of any coordinated Persian-Turkish assistance for their fellow Moslems. As a result, Russia was able to annex or create vassal states in additional Caucasian lands.

Annexing territory was one thing; keeping it another. Besides sporadic rebellions against Russian control, Russia had to fight wars with both Persia (1804–1813) and Turkey (1806–1812). Both countries resented Russian expansion in the Caucasus. By the Treaty of Golestan in 1813, however, a defeated Persia recognized Russian gains extending from Georgia eastward to the khanate of Baku.

Russia's war with the Ottoman Turks resulted not only from Russian moves in the Caucasus, but also from Balkan Turkish-Russian tensions. The latter were partly stimulated by Napoleon, who in 1806 wished Turkish help against Russia. Then, after the Tilsit peace of 1807, he suggested to Alexander a plan for partitioning the Ottoman Empire, but the two emperors could not agree on control over Constantinople and the Black Sea Straits. Only in mid-1812, fearing war with Napoleon, did Alexander make peace with the Turks. By the Treaty of Bucharest, Russia received Bessarabia, formerly part of Turkey's Moldavian principality.

NAPOLEON AND RUSSIA, 1812–1815

After Tilsit, Russian-French tensions gradually increased. Not only did the two emperors disagree on how to partition the Ottoman Empire, but also further Napoleonic gains in Germany and, at Austria's expense, in Poland alarmed Alexander. He was especially upset when in 1811, contrary to the Tilsit treaty, Napoleon annexed the Duchy of Oldenburg—Alexander's sister Catherine was married to its heir. Conversely, Napoleon was angered by Russia's gradual withdrawal from his Continental Blockade against the British.

In June 1812, Napoleon led a massive army across the Nieman River. With later reinforcements, it numbered almost 600,000 men, including troops from allied and occupied countries stretching from Portugal to Poland. The Russian forces that met it were outnumbered about three to one.

But even before the war, Alexander had stated that in case of a French attack Russia had space, time, and weather on its side and that he was prepared to retreat all the way to the Kamchatka Peninsula rather than accept defeat.

The first major battle was in early August at Smolensk. Both sides lost heavily, and the Russians retreated, pursuing a scorched earth policy to deny Napoleon needed supplies. This policy helped debilitate and demoralize Napoleon's troops, and many of them died or were weakened, especially from intestinal illnesses.

On August 26, about seventy-five miles west of Moscow, at the village of Borodino, Napoleon sent some 130,000 men against a slightly smaller Russian force. It was led by Mikhail Kutuzov, an old one-eyed general recently appointed supreme commander. Earlier labeled General Slowpoke by some of Alexander's advisers, he eventually proved to be a wily strategist. By nightfall at Borodino, bullets, bayonets, shells, and swords had done their job: On the fields perhaps 100,000 dead and wounded lay, almost evenly divided between the two opposing forces.

After the battle, Kutuzov retreated toward Moscow but soon abandoned it. When Napoleon entered it at the beginning of September, Moscow was nearly deserted. Almost immediately, homes and other buildings began going up in flames, started perhaps either by careless French troops or patriotic Russians desiring to leave little to the French "anti-Christ."

With most of the city burned, winter approaching, and short on supplies, Napoleon was forced to retreat after only thirty-five days in Moscow. Faced with Kutuzov's army to the more fertile south, Napoleon's troops had to retreat nearly the same war-scarred way they had come, via Smolensk. Russian partisans, cold weather, hunger, sickness, and Kutuzov's pursuing army, avoiding any major battles, decimated them as they retreated. By the time they left Russian territory in early December, this once Grand Army of 600,000 was only a small fraction of what it had been. The rest had deserted, been taken prisoner, or perished. The invasion had also taken hundreds of thousands of Russian lives. Kutuzov advised Alexander not to lose more in pursuing Napoleon once he had left Russia.

Alexander, however, decided otherwise. Prussia and Austria, seeing Napoleon now in retreat, joined Russia, Great Britain, and Sweden in a new coalition. Although Napoleon recruited a new army and won some minor victories, he was defeated in October 1813 at the decisive battle of Leipzig, in which Alexander himself played a major role. On March 31, 1814, allied forces paraded through Paris. Alexander, atop a horse once given to him by Napoleon, was cheered by many Parisians as he rode by on this sunny day.

Indeed, Parisians had good reason to cheer: Alexander and the other allied leaders did not impose a vindictive peace. Despite Napoleonic wars that had cost several million lives, the allies restored the French monarchy and the French borders of 1792, which included gains made after 1789. They also encouraged the new king, Louis XVIII, to issue a constitution. Napoleon was banished to the island of Elba.

From September 1814 to June 1815, allied statesmen, and eventually even Talleyrand of France, met in Vienna to draw up a postwar settlement. Their work was temporarily interrupted by Napoleon's return from Elba and the start of his "Hundred Days" rule in France from March until the end of June 1815. Even before Napoleon was finally defeated at Waterloo, however, the Congress of Vienna had concluded its work. Alexander I gained about four-fifths of the Polish territory that Napoleon had fashioned into the Grand Duchy of Warsaw. Under the agreement, this portion became the Kingdom of Poland (also known as Congress Poland), with Alexander I as its king. He willingly granted the Poles a constitution that promised various liberties, their own bicameral assembly (the *Sejm*), and an independent judiciary.

In Napoleon's final defeat during June 1815, Russia played little part.

FIGURE 18.2. The Alexandrine Column (1830–1834), to the left, on St. Petersburg's Palace Square commemorates the Russian victory over Napoleon in 1812. On the top of the column, Alexander is symbolized by an angel. In the left rear is the dome of St. Isaac's Cathedral and on the right the golden spire of the Admiralty Building.

Therefore, it was primarily Prussia and Britain that decided the harsher terms of a second Peace of Paris (November 20, 1815). It scaled the French borders back to those of 1790 and forced France to pay a $700 million indemnity and the cost of an allied occupation of seventeen French fortresses for up to five years.

RUSSIAN FOREIGN POLICY, 1815–1825

During the last decade of his life, Alexander's diplomacy was primarily concerned with safeguarding the post-Napoleonic arrangements he had been instrumental in creating. Thus, his objectives generally coincided with those of the influential Austrian foreign minister, Metternich. But they also sometimes displayed a more utopian, mystical side than those of the ever-pragmatic Metternich.

Alexander's mysticism was best exemplified in his September 1815 proposal for a Holy Alliance. Although by no means a man completely of the spirit—for more than a decade, he had been having an affair with a beautiful Polish princess—Alexander had gradually become more interested in mystical matters during the 1812–1815 period. In the months immediately preceding his

Holy Alliance proposal, he had numerous conversations with Baroness von Krüdener, a woman of strong mystical inclinations. Although historians have debated the degree of influence she had on his proposal, it did call upon his fellow European monarchs to rule in the spirit of the Scriptures and be guided by charity, peace, and justice. Although most European powers, including Austria, signed this pious declaration, Metternich thought it a "loud-sounding nothing," and Britain's foreign minister, Lord Castlereagh, refused to sign—"a piece of sublime mysticism and nonsense."

Again in 1816, Alexander put forth another pious proposal in a letter to this same Castlereagh. It called for a joint Russo-British effort to bring about disarmament. Again Castlereagh was skeptical, and nothing came of the project.

On a more practical level, Russia did renew (on November 20, 1815) its Quadruple Alliance with Austria, Prussia, and Great Britain. The signatories pledged themselves to preserve the post-Napoleonic order for the next twenty years and to meet regularly to discuss European concerns. In 1818, the rulers of this Concert of Europe met at the Congress of Aix-la-Chapelle, where they agreed to end the occupation of France and admitted it into a new Quintuple Alliance.

Three more congresses were held between 1820 and 1822, primarily to deal with revolutions in Spain and Italy. These years were ones of revolution, with outbreaks also occurring in Portugal and Greece. Alexander believed that the monarchies of Europe had to work together to stamp out such revolts. He offered Russian troops to help Austria quell a rebellion in Naples and aid to the Spanish monarch to throttle revolution in both Spain and Latin America. Meanwhile, Britain began parting company from its more conservative allies, especially regarding Spain and its possessions in South and Central America; in the Monroe Doctrine (1823), the United States also announced its opposition to European intervention in the Americas.

Although firmly opposed to rebellions against the Christian monarchies of Europe, the Russian government was more ambivalent toward the Greek rebellion against the Moslem Turks. Greeks in the Russian city of Odessa had founded a "Friendly Society" in 1814, devoted to obtaining Greek independence. They backed one of Alexander's generals and aides-de-camp, the Greek Alexander Ypsilanti, who personally began the armed revolt in March 1821, when he led a small force across the border from Russia into Moldavia. The Greek John Capodistrias, who together with K. Nesselrode was acting as joint Russian foreign minister when the rebellion began, tried to convince Alexander that Russia should send troops to support the Greeks. Despite these pressures and Russians' natural sympathy for their Orthodox brethren, the tsar repudiated Ypsilanti, allowed a disappointed Capodistrias to resign (in 1822), and did not unilaterally intervene.

RULING THE EMPIRE, 1796–1825

The addition of Finland, Congress Poland, Bessarabia, and new areas in the Caucasus was comparable to the imperial gains made in the previous three decades by Catherine the Great. Alexander I, however, was less concerned with imposing uniformity than his grandmother had been. Among the most important reasons for this were Alexander's interest in federalism and constitutional projects, the increasing differences between newly annexed peoples and the Russian majority in the empire, and the political and economic demands of the Napoleonic era.

New Territories

Although the Grand Duchy of Finland and Congress Poland were brought into the Russian Empire, they were granted considerable autonomy. Finland's was less solidly grounded, more based on Alexander's good will, than was Congress Poland's, where Alexander granted a constitution in 1815. In Finland, he did not grant one; and after 1809, he never allowed another diet to meet, as he did in Poland. But he did grant the duchy more self-rule than had Sweden; appointed a Finnish governor-general, who was advised by a duchy Government Council (in 1816 renamed the Finnish Senate); and generally abided by the traditional laws of the region.

By a statute of 1818, Alexander also approved of considerable Bessarabian autonomy. This statute reflected an idealistic belief that by respecting local laws and customs and by working through the Rumanian noble class, Russian administrators could use Bessarabia for the overall good of the Russian Empire. By 1823, however, enough bad reports from Russian officials in Kishinev had reached Alexander to convince him that his plans were not working. Rumanian nobles and Russian officials simply had not worked well together, each group being wary of, and often hostile toward, the other.

To improve the administration of Bessarabia, Alexander turned to Mikhail Vorontsov (1782–1856). In 1823, the tsar made him the first Russian civilian to govern it; he was also given jurisdiction over the provinces of Kherson, Ekaterinoslav, and the Crimea. Vorontsov had been brought up in England, where his father was the Russian ambassador, and later, before leaving the military, he commanded Russian troops occupying post-Napoleonic France. Upset by local corruption and overburdened peasants, he reduced Bessarabian autonomy in the hope of establishing a more humane, efficient government. Later, this process was greatly accelerated after Alexander's death in 1825.

The situation in the Caucasus was more bellicose. Between 1802 and 1806, Russian authority was in the hands of General Tsitsianov, himself a Georgian. Contemptuous of Moslems and even of most non-Moslem peoples of the region, and believing in fear as an instrument of rule, he angered many by his policies. In 1804—when war with Persia also began—an anti-Russian rebellion broke out in Georgia as well as in several other areas of the Caucasus.

Additional rebellions occurred in subsequent years, especially in 1812, against Tsitsianov's stern military successors. For the remainder of Alexander's reign, Russian troops often attacked Moslem mountaineers in an attempt to pacify them.

Annexed areas, such as Georgia, were ruled more directly than Caucasian vassal states such as Karabagh. But each of the latter states usually was re-

FIGURE 18.3. From 1828 to 1848, Mikhail Vorontsov had the above palace in Alupka (in the Crimea) built based on plans by English architects. The southern portico pictured here, reflecting Islamic influence, looks out on to the Black Sea.

quired to turn over control of its foreign policy to Russia, to pay tribute (although economic difficulties sometimes prevented this), and to allow the garrisoning of Russian troops in its capital. Although in most respects vassal rulers were free to rule according to traditional methods, they were liable to be overthrown and replaced if they angered Russian authorities. And sooner or later, either in Alexander's reign or in subsequent decades, their states completely lost their autonomy.

In both vassal states and in directly annexed areas, Russia was forced to rely at least partly on native elites and sometimes to advance native pro-Russian commoners to elite status. Attempts were made, through such means as education and the awarding of Russian ranks, to co-opt the old non-Russian elites into willingly serving Russian interests. To the extent money would allow—and it would not allow much—Russian officials and Russian troops were also increased in the Caucasus. By 1819, there were about 50,000 to 60,000 Russian troops there. Despite some limitations on both Islam and Georgian Orthodoxy (for example, the Georgians lost their right to their own patriarch), the Russian government generally did not interfere with the religious beliefs and practices of the Caucasian peoples.

Older Western Regions

Although in ethnic Russia, both Paul and Alexander I supported more government centralization than had Catherine II, in most non-Russian western regions conquered before Paul's reign the two male tsars were less rigorous centralizers than Catherine had been. As in Finland and Congress Poland, concessions to local sentiments resulted partly from the desire to gain local support in the Napoleonic wars and partly from other personal and administrative reasons.

In the areas of Livland, Estland, and Courland, the Baltic German elite regained some local controls lost under Catherine II. Although pressured by St. Petersburg to emancipate their serfs, when it occurred (1816–1819), the serfs received no land, and the Baltic nobles benefited in many ways more than the serfs. By 1825, the Germanic nobles, along with Lutheran pastors, also dominated an educational system more developed than Great Russia's.

In Lithuania, Belorussia, and part of Ukraine, education was overwhelmingly under Polish influence, and St. Petersburg ceased actively supporting the conversion of Catholic Uniates. One of Alexander's influential young friends and Unofficial Committee members, the Polish Prince Adam Czartoryski, served for two decades as educational curator over this large region—all encompassed in the Vilna School Region. From its language of instruction and textbooks to its administrators, it was basically Polish.

Only toward the end of Alexander's reign, when he became more conservative, did Russian policies, educational and otherwise, become less tolerant of Polish influence in the partitioned territories.

Among Alexander's Unofficial Committee, there was a Ukrainian as well as a Pole. The Ukrainian, Viktor Kochubei (also Alexander's first minister of interior), was not an ardent spokesman for his nationality. In fact, he shared the Little Russian mentality of many Ukrainian nobles: He was opposed to any talk of Ukrainian autonomy. Partly as a result of such attitudes, the government continued its policy of gradually integrating Ukraine into the empire's administrative structure. Paul introduced military conscription to the area in 1797, and many Ukrainians, including Ukrainian Cossacks, loyally supported the tsar against Napoleon.

Siberia and Russian America

Under Alexander I, Siberia experienced one of its worst governor-generals and one of its best. The first was Ivan Pestel, who, from 1806 to 1818, despotically ruled over both native peoples and Russians alike. The second was the reformer and former chief adviser of the tsar, Mikhail Speransky. Although he was governor-general for only two years, he drew up a series of reforms that Alexander promulgated in 1822. They outlined certain native rights and represented a distinct improvement in bringing a more orderly, less corrupt, and less arbitrary administration to Siberia. Yet even these reforms continued to aim toward the eventual Russification of Siberia.

The reigns of Paul and Alexander were full of Russian activity in Alaska and even further south on the American Continent. In 1812, the Russian-American Company founded Fort Ross, some hundred miles north of San Francisco

Bay. The Monroe Doctrine of 1823 was aimed not only at European interference in Latin America, but also at Russian expansion in North America.

The main Alaskan attractions were sea otters and fur seals. In 1799, Paul granted the Russian-American Company a monopoly to exploit Russian possessions in North America. From its regional capital of New Archangel (later Sitka), it oversaw an increasingly profitable operation until, by the end of Alexander's reign, government interference contributed to reversing profitability.

DOMESTIC POLICIES, 1815–1825

In the last decade of his reign, Alexander's enthusiasm for reform proposals waned but did not completely disappear. With few exceptions, such as Speransky's Siberian reform plan, even less came of them than earlier ones.

One such plan, finalized in 1820, was composed by a former Unofficial Committee member, Nikolai Novosiltsev, who also had participated in drawing up the constitution for Congress Poland in 1815. Although similar in some respects to Speransky's 1809 constitutional project—but even more firmly maintaining tsarist powers—it proposed a more decentralized administrative structure for the tsar to oversee. His empire was to be divided into large administrative areas, each containing at least several provinces.

Novosiltsev's plan was probably promoted not only by Alexander's interest in constitutions, but also by the addition of so many new non-Russian areas to the empire. With Congress Poland, Finland, and Bessarabia already receiving considerable autonomy, and other new peoples from the Caucasus becoming part of the Russian Empire, some new thinking about how to rule such a heterogeneous empire seemed fitting. Yet, except for creating a few new large administrative areas and putting strong administrators in charge of them—such as Vorontsov in the south-southwest—Alexander introduced little from this reform plan.

Instead, partly because of his escalating fear of rebellious forces, both at home and abroad, and because of his growing mysticism and religiosity, he became more conservative. He began relying more than ever on General Alexei Arakcheev, the man who had introduced him to military life at Emperor Paul's Gatchina. The radical Alexander Herzen later described Arakcheev as: "without a doubt, one of the most vile characters emerging after Peter I to the heights of the Russian government." His character traits, thought Herzen, included "superhuman devotion, mechanical exactness, the precision of a chronometer, [and] no feeling whatsoever." Although Herzen was not being completely objective and Alexander I once wrote of Arakcheev's "sensitive soul," Herzen's remarks mirrored the feeling of many intellectuals of the general's own era.

Arakcheev's influence on domestic policies was extensive during Alexander I's last decade, and he is best known for his association with Military Settlements. They were begun by the tsar in 1810 and greatly expanded beginning in 1816. Estimates of the percentage of Russian soldiers serving in these settlements by 1825 vary, but some place them as high as about 30 percent of the total army. Most were in the areas of Novgorod and in the south between the Dnieper and Bug Rivers.

Alexander began the settlements with the best of intentions. They were to save the government money and create a more humane environment for soldiers. The savings—much needed by a government heavily in debt—were to come primarily by combining farming and military training, thus supplying the settlements' food. Some able-bodied men were to be primarily farming peasants, others primarily soldiers, but all were to do at least some drilling and farming. The more humane environment was to come chiefly by allowing the families of the soldiers to live in the settlements—normally soldiers were separated from their families during their twenty-five years of service. Health care, sanitary conditions, and education were to be superior to that normally provided for either soldiers or peasants.

Once again, however, reality thwarted good intentions. As implemented by Arakcheev and his subordinate officers, military savings (and even profit making) far outweighed humane considerations in dealing with perhaps as many as 750,000 colonists (including men, women, and children). Given Arakcheev's emphasis on stern discipline, this is hardly surprising. The lives of the settlements' peasants, women, and children became more militarized and regimented, and those of the soldiers more laborious. Huts were all uniform—and crowded—and their inhabitants uniformed. Living conditions were harsh. When rebellions broke out, as they often did, the usual punishment for ringleaders was running the gauntlet (where thousands of blows often resulted in death) or being sent to Siberia—and sometimes, if one survived the gauntlet, both.

If Arakcheev appealed to Alexander's military side and love of order, Alexander Golitsyn (1773–1844), his procurator of the Holy Synod, appealed to his growing religiosity. In 1812, the tsar had followed Golitsyn's recommendation to create a Bible Society, and by 1824 it had close to 300 branches spread over the Russian Empire. Both Golitsyn and Alexander were quite ecumenical in their Christian mysticism, and the society included Christians of different denominations. In 1817, the tsar named Golitsyn to head a new Ministry of Education and Religious Affairs.

Golitsyn's goal was to base education on religious principles. This goal was sometimes applied in an extreme manner, especially by the opportunist Mikhail Magnitsky, who began purging the University of Kazan of "Godless" professors and books. This began in 1819, soon after he was named as curator of the Kazan educational district.

By 1824, Magnitsky had become part of a plot to oust Golitsyn. The most prestigious plotter was Arakcheev, who had long resented Golitsyn's influence over Alexander. Already in 1822, Arakcheev had introduced the tsar to a fiery Orthodox monk, named Photius, who had little tolerance for either Enlightenment ideas or Golitsyn's more ecumenical religious views. Alexander soon came to regard Photius as divinely inspired and followed his advice to dissolve Masonic lodges (1822) and, in 1824, to dismiss Golitsyn, who was rumored to be sympathetic to Freemasonry.

POLITICAL OPPOSITION AND THE DECEMBRISTS

By the time Masonic lodges were prohibited, educated opinion had grown and become more independent. The growth of education, social and cultural organizations, student "circles," private clubs and salons, and fraternal societies (including Masonic lodges) all helped bring educated people together and fostered discussions and thoughts about civic concerns. In the first half of Alexander's reign, the problem of Napoleon was often central to such concerns—as Tolstoy's opening chapters in *War and Peace* remind us. Although social standing affected political attitudes, it did no determine them. Among aristocratic families, for example, both conservatives and radicals could be found.

The growth of educated society and public opinion gave more breadth to political opposition. Before 1812, it came primarily from conservative aristocratic nobles, some of whom were senators (there were ninety-one senators in 1809). These conservative aristocrats were resentful of the Unofficial Committee, of Speransky, and of the failure of the Senate to play a more important governmental role. They found allies at court among relatives of Alexander and in the writer and historian Karamzin. The latter's 1811 *Memoir of Ancient and Modern Russia* reflected conservative opposition to reform schemes such as those of Speransky, which were believed to be foreign-inspired. Karamzin argued that historical continuity demanded the maintenance and support of autocracy, noble privileges, serfdom, and Orthodoxy.

Within educated society (*obshchestvo* in Russian), there was a smaller group, sometimes later labeled the intelligentsia. Although debates have existed for more than a century on just who should be included in this category, it certainly included radical critics of autocracy and serfdom and had come into being by 1825. Most of its members were of noble origin, and many of them later became involved in the Decembrist conspiracy of 1825, the seeds of which were sown much earlier.

Most Decembrist leaders were from the upper nobility, including Prince Sergei Trubetskoi (1790–1860); Prince Sergei Volkonsky (1788–1865); Paul Pestel (1793–1826), son of the former governor-general of Siberia; and several Muravievs and Muraviev-Apostols. Many of the leaders had been young Guards officers who fought against Napoleon, both in Russia and in other parts of Europe, and remained officers afterwards.

The Decembrists belonged to a sequence of secret societies between 1816 and 1825. The first was the Union of Salvation (or Society of the True and Loyal Sons of the Fatherland), founded in 1816 in St. Petersburg. At its maximum, its membership consisted of about thirty Guards officers. In early 1818, it was succeeded by the Union of Welfare, which expanded to about 200 members (still mainly Guards officers). Partly because of increasing government pressure and the dispersion of military officers, it, in turn, was transformed into two new societies in 1821: the Northern Society and the Southern Society. A final group, the Society of United Slavs, was formed in 1823 and had about fifty members, almost all junior officers, when it merged with the Southern Society in 1825.

Ultimately, almost 600 men were implicated in the Decembrist conspiracy, almost half of whom received sentences. These Decembrists differed considerably in their political ideas but agreed in their opposition to serfdom and autocracy. Illustrative of their differences by 1825 are two chief documents: a draft constitution drawn up by the Northern Society's Nikita Muraviev and another, more radical one, called *Russian Justice*, written by the Southern Society's leader, Colonel Paul Pestel.

Among the inspirations for Muraviev's draft was the U.S. Constitution and Nikita Panin's eighteenth-century reform ideas. The draft called for a federation of thirteen states and two provinces. It would have a hereditary emperor, but his powers would be limited, more analogous to those of a U.S. president. He would have to share federal powers with a bicameral People's Assembly. Serfdom, censorship, and official classes and titles were to be abolished and civil liberties, such as freedom of assembly, recognized.

This document, although liberal, was not democratic: The right to hold office and vote was based on property qualifications. (This, however, is hardly surprising at a time when neither Great Britain nor the United States yet allowed all white men full suffrage rights.)

It also did not threaten noble landholding rights. Although the serfowners were to loose their serfs, they were to keep their estates. This would guarantee that many former serfs would continue laboring on their former masters' estates.

Although Muraviev's constitution was willing to grant considerable local powers to his proposed states and regions, some of which contained primarily non-Russians, Pestel's draft called for rigid centralization and even Russification. It stated that its proposed new administration should "constantly aim at making them [the nationalities] into *one* single nation and at dissolving all differences into one common mass."[1] Only for Poles and Jews was Pestel willing to make concessions. He held secret negotiations with some Poles and suggested in his draft the possibility of Polish independence under certain conditions. For Jews who would not wish to assimilate, Pestel's document suggested helping them emigrate to Asia Minor, where they could establish their own state.

Pestel's *Russian Justice* also differed from Muraviev's plan in calling for a republic. In it, power would be divided between a unicameral People's Assembly, a 5-person State Duma, and a 120-member Supreme Council. To bring about his system, Pestel counted on a military coup, followed by a temporary dictatorship; like most Decembrists, he did not intend to stir the masses to rebellion.

Although Pestel's document also called for eliminating serfdom, censorship, and official class distinctions, its insistence on a secret political police and

---

[1]Marc Raeff, ed., *The Decembrist Movement* (Englewood Cliffs, N.J., 1966), p. 147.

a ban on private organizations and societies was hardly liberal. The radical and rationalistic French Jacobean thinking seemed to influence him more than did the moderate and pragmatic American or British traditions.

This can be seen further in Pestel's granting of full citizenship rights—to all men over twenty—and in his radical land reform plans. Half of all land of the country's wealthiest property owners was to be confiscated, and every citizen was to have the right to enough public land (from communes) to provide for his family.

The ideas in the two documents were generated by many causes, especially the turmoil of the Napoleonic wars and their aftermath, which exposed some Decembrists to foreign lands and ideas. Early expectations and later frustrations also played their part. The first were stimulated by Alexander's initial and lingering liberal sympathies and his rhetoric against the "universal tyrant" Napoleon, by the philanthropic ideas of Freemasonry, by foreign revolutionary and patriotic examples (stretching from Spain to Germany and Greece), and by the heroic Romanticism of the period. Later Decembrist frustrations were created by seeing post-Napoleonic France and Congress Poland receive constitutions while Russia did not; by the contrast between a freer, more prosperous West and Russia; and by hatred of Arakcheev and all he stood for, including the military colonies and harsh, cruel discipline in the army. The final fuel to the fire was unexpected and occurred in Taganrog, on the Azov Sea. There, on November 19, 1825, a visiting Alexander I died after a brief illness. (Later unfounded rumors claimed he did not then die but lived on for many years—some said as a hermit.) His death, followed by almost a month of dynastic uncertainty, seemed to present the Decembrists with an opportunity not to be missed.

Alexander and his wife had no sons and accordingly—as decreed by Emperor Paul—the emperor's oldest surviving brother was to become the next ruler. This was Constantine, but he had secretly given up his right to the throne several years earlier. Yet the next oldest brother, Nicholas, although aware of this renunciation, still thought it proper to swear allegiance to his older brother. Only after Constantine, the governor-general in Congress Poland, again renounced his claim did Nicholas set December 14 as the date for officially proclaiming himself emperor.

On that day, the Northern Society attempted to incite a rebellion that would impose a new constitutional regime on Russia. Their specific plans were hazy, however, and hindered by the last-minute defection of several conspirators, including the movement's so-called temporary dictator, Prince (and Colonel) Sergei Trubetskoi.

Nevertheless, Decembrist officers did muster about 3,000 troops to march to the Senate Square, where the famous statue of Peter the Great stood looking out over the Neva River. The officers convinced their troops not to swear allegiance to Nicholas because he was usurping his brother's crown. To counter them, Nicholas, who was forewarned of a conspiracy, massed a force at least three times as large. Before unleashing his loyal troops on the rebels, Nicholas sent both the capital's governor-general and its metropolitan to persuade them to cease their rebellion. The first was shot and the second told to stay out of

politics and stick to prayer. After several hours, and with late-afternoon darkness approaching in this northern capital, Nicholas ordered a Horse Guards'
attack. Partly because of the slippery ice, it was ineffective. Finally in despera-
tion, he began his reign as he hoped he would not have to—he ordered his cannons to fire on the rebels.

The cannons did their job. Some rebels were killed or wounded; others
fled, especially toward the Neva, where cannon shots broke through the ice,
causing some drownings. Although no exact death toll is known, most estimates place the number under 100. Almost immediately the roundup of conspirators began. One prominent Decembrist had even been arrested the day
before the outbreak in the capital. This was Colonel Paul Pestel, leader of the
Southern Society. Within a few weeks, that society's Sergei Muraviev-Apostol,
with the help of other southern conspirators, led troops in an armed uprising
in Ukraine. They too, however, were soon suppressed.

For their plotting and insurrections, close to 300 men were sentences to imprisonment or exile. Most of them were officers, including a total of more than
thirty colonels and generals. Among them were the princes Colonel Sergei Trubetskoi and General Sergei Volkonsky, whose wives followed their husbands
to the Siberian mines of Nerchinsk. Five men were hanged, including Kondrati
Ryleev (a poet and secretary of the Russian-American Company), Pestel, and

FIGURE 18.4. The grave site of Princess Catherine Trubetskaia, at the Znamenskii Convent, Irkutsk. She died in 1854, a year and a half before her husband, Sergei, was finally
permitted to leave Siberia.

Sergei Muraviev-Apostol. In the hanging, three of the five nooses slipped. After falling to the scaffold floor, and before being lifted up for a second, more successful attempt, Muraviev-Apostol uttered: "Poor Russia! We can't even hang someone decently!"

SUGGESTED SOURCES

ATKIN, MURIEL. *Russia and Iran, 1780–1828.* Minneapolis, 1980.

BARRATT, GLYNN. *The Rebel on the Bridge: A Life of the Decembrist Baron Andrey Rozen (1800–84).* London, 1975.

CATE, CURTIS. *The War of the Two Emperors: The Duel Between Napoleon and Alexander—Russia, 1812.* New York, 1985.

CHRISTIAN, DAVID. "Mikhail Mikhailovich Speranskii," *MERSH* 37: 41–46.

CZARTORYSKI, ADAM. *Memoirs of Prince Adam Czartoryski and His Correspondence with Alexander I.* 2 vols. 2d ed. London, 1888.

FITZGIBBON, EDWARD M. *Alexander I and the Near East: The Ottoman Empire in Russia's Foreign Relations, 1801–1807.* Ann Arbor, Mich., 1981.

FEDOROV, VLADIMIR ALEKSANDROVICH. "Alexander I," *SSH* 30 (Winter 1991–1992): 49–91. Reprinted in *EER*, pp. 217–255.

———. ed. *The First Breath of Freedom.* Moscow, 1988.

GOODING, JOHN. "The Liberalism of Michael Speransky," *SEER* 64 (July 1986): 401–424.

GRIMSTED, PATRICIA K. *The Foreign Ministers of Alexander I; Political Attitudes and the Conduct of Russian Diplomacy, 1801–1825.* Berkeley, 1969.

HARTLEY, JANET M. *Alexander I.* London, 1994. Contains an excellent annotated bibliography.

JELAVICH, BARBARA. *Russia's Balkan Entanglements, 1806–1914.* Cambridge, England, 1991.

JENKINS, MICHAEL. *Arakcheev: Grand Vizier of the Russian Empire, a Biography.* New York, 1969.

JEWSBURY, GEORGE F. *The Russian Annexation of Bessarabia, 1774–1828: A Study of Imperial Expansion.* Boulder, 1976.

KEEP, JOHN L. H. *Soldiers of the Tsar: Army and Society in Russia, 1462–1874.* Oxford, 1985. Pts. 3–5.

KLIER, JOHN. *Russia Gathers Her Jews: The Origins of the "Jewish Question" in Russia, 1772–1825.* DeKalb, Ill., 1986.

KLIMENKO, MICHAEL. *Notes of Alexander I, Emperor of Russia.* New York, 1989.

LEDONNE, JOHN P. *Absolutism and Ruling Class: The Formation of the Russian Political Order, 1700–1825.* New York, 1991.

MAZOUR, ANATOLE G. *The First Russian Revolution, 1825: The Decembrist Movement, Its Origins, Development, and Significance.* Stanford, 1961.

MCCONNELL, ALLEN. *Tsar Alexander I: Paternalistic Reformer.* New York, 1970.

MCGREW, RODERICK E. *Paul I of Russia, 1754–1801.* Oxford, 1992.

O'MEARA, PATRICK. *K. F. Ryleev: A Political Biography of the Decembrist Poet.* Princeton, 1984.

ORLOVSKY, DANIEL T. *The Limits of Reform: The Ministry of Internal Affairs in Imperial Russia, 1802–1881.* Cambridge, Mass., 1981.

PALEOLOGUE, MAURICE. *The Enigmatic Czar: The Life of Alexander I of Russia.* Hamden, Conn., 1969.

PALMER, ALAN. *Alexander I: Tsar of War and Peace.* New York, 1974.

———. *Napoleon in Russia.* New York, 1967.

PIENKOS, ANGELA T. *The Imperfect Autocrat: Grand Duke Constantine Pavlovich and the Polish Congress Kingdom*. Boulder, 1987.

RAEFF, MARC. *Michael Speransky: Statesman of Imperial Russia, 1772–1839*. 2d ed. The Hague, 1969.

———. ed. *The Decembrist Movement*. Englewood Cliffs, N.J., 1966.

RAGSDALE, HUGH. *Detente in the Napoleonic Era: Bonaparte and the Russians*. Lawrence, Kan., 1980.

———. *Tsar Paul and the Question of Madness: An Essay in History and Psychology*. New York, 1988.

———. ed. *Paul I: A Reassessment of His Life and Reign*. Pittsburgh, 1979.

RHINELANDER, A. L. H. *Prince Michael Vorontsov: Viceroy to the Tsar*. Montreal, 1990.

RIASANOVSKY, NICHOLAS V. *A Parting of Ways: Government and the Educated Public in Russia, 1801–1855*. Oxford, 1976.

RYWKIN, MICHAEL, ed. *Russian Colonial Expansion to 1917*. London, 1988.

SAUL, NORMAN E. *Russia and the Mediterranean, 1797–1807*. Chicago, 1970.

SAUNDERS, DAVID. *Russia in the Age of Reaction and Reform 1801–1881*. London, 1992. Chs. 1–4. Contains an extensive bibliography of books and articles.

SEGUR, PHILIPPE-PAUL. *Napoleon's Russian Campaign*. New York, 1965.

SOROKIN, IURII ALEKSEEVICH. "Paul I," *SSH* 30 (Winter 1991–92): 3–48. Reprinted in *EER*, pp. 178–215.

STARR, S. FREDERICK, ed. *Russia's American Colony*. Durham, 1987.

TARLE, E. V. *Napoleon's Invasion of Russia, 1812*. New York, 1971.

THACKERAY, FRANK W. *Antecedents of Revolution: Alexander I and the Polish Kingdom, 1815–1825*. Boulder, 1980.

THADEN, EDWARD C. *Russia's Western Borderlands, 1710–1870*. Princeton, 1984. Pt. 2.

TOLSTOY, LEO. *War and Peace*. New York, 1960. A great nineteenth-century novel dealing with Russia in the Napoleonic era. A six-hour film based on the novel and directed by Sergei Bondarchuk is available on videocassette.

TROITSKII, NIKOLAI ALEKSEEVICH. "The Great Patriotic War of 1812: A History of the Subject," *RSH* 32 (Summer 1993). Whole issue.

TROYAT, HENRI. *Alexander of Russia: Napoleon's Conqueror*. New York, 1982.

WOODHOUSE, C. M. *Capodistria: The Founder of Greek Independence*. London, 1973.

ZAWADZKI, W. H. *A Man of Honour: Adam Czartoryski as a Statesman of Russia and Poland, 1795–1831*. Oxford, 1993.

CHAPTER 19

Nicholas I: Despotism, Reform, and Legitimacy, 1825–1855

The radical Alexander Herzen once called Nicholas I "Chinghis Khan with telegraphs." The judgment of the nineteenth-century historian Sergei Soloviev, a more moderate contemporary of Herzen, was just as harsh. Although Soloviev was an advocate of strong monarchy and believed Peter the Great the greatest leader in history, he compared Nicholas to the despotic Roman emperor Caligula. In his memoirs, Soloviev faulted Nicholas for turning the Russian people into "sticks"; for suppressing individual and social initiative; and for failing to realize that national strength depended on the realm of the spirit, not just material might. Most leading historians after Soloviev, whether Russian or foreign, were also critical of Nicholas.

There are solid reasons for such negative assessments. Both minority nationalities and independent-minded thinkers suffered from his distrust of diversity and free thought. Although he fought successful wars against Persia and the Ottoman Turkish Empire early in his reign and expanded Russian territory in the Caucasus and Asia, he ultimately weakened Russia by alienating even moderate intellectuals and, in 1853, by entangling Russia in the Crimean War. By the time it ended in 1856, however, he was dead, and his son Alexander was left in the unenviable position of having to conclude it.

Yet there is another side to Nicholas's reign. In his 1978 biography of him, W. Bruce Lincoln provided a needed corrective to balance the prevailing negative view. Lincoln pointed out that Nicholas was also responsible for many initiatives that prepared the ground for the "Great Reforms" of his son Alexander II. Like most of Peter's successors, Nicholas wished to be an enlightened, although absolute, ruler, and he realized that some reforms were necessary if Russia was to remain a great power.

NICHOLAS I: THE MAN AND HIS POLITICAL VIEWS

Nicholas was twenty-nine when he became tsar. He was tall, stern, and humorless and invariably dressed in military uniform. His father, that lover of Prussian-like drill, Paul I, had made him a colonel when he was only four months old and surrounded him with tutors who reinforced a militaristic mentality.

Yet Nicholas's imposing and severe appearance concealed an insecure, nervous man who adopted a military approach to life partly because of the unbending structure and assurance it provided. He was not quite five when his father was murdered in the palace coup that brought his older brother Alexander to the throne. As a youngster, Nicholas displayed a special interest in *defensive* fortifications and eventually became Alexander I's commander of army engineers. The Decembrist revolt, which attempted to prevent his accession, reinforced Nicholas's insecurity.

Many women, including a young Queen Victoria of England, thought that Nicholas was a handsome, charming, and courteous man. Not surprisingly, he was attracted not only to Prussian-like drilling, but also to a Prussian princess, whom he married and who took the Russian name Alexandra Fedorovna. They had seven children, four boys and three girls. Nicholas the father—like Nicholas the ruler—stressed the virtues of hard work, duty, and patriotism. Despite his sternness and exacting standards, he was, in his own way, a loving father. From his marriage in 1817 until the early 1840s, when Alexandra's poor health seems to have ended their sexual relations, he also apparently was a faithful husband. Even after establishing a lasting liaison with one of his wife's ladies-in-waiting, he continued to value his wife's companionship.

Despite his later infidelity, Nicholas emphasized the importance of family life and thought of himself as a faithful servant of God. It was his religious convictions and high sense of duty, not any love of his work, that kept him laboring at the increasingly difficult job of running his empire. Especially toward the end of his reign, he regarded his obligations as his Christian cross to bear.

His political doctrine (later labeled Official Nationality) was summarized in three words: Orthodoxy, autocracy, and nationality. Count Uvarov, his minister of education from 1833 to 1849, first articulated and consistently reiterated the importance of this triad.

Nicholas was a firm believer in autocracy. He once told the French Marquis de Custine that he could not understand representative monarchy because it was typified by "lies, fraud, and corruption."

Orthodoxy was important to Nicholas and his followers not only because it provided a system of personal religious beliefs, but also because it propped up autocracy. Orthodox priests annually proclaimed a curse on "those who do not believe that the Orthodox monarchies have been elevated to the throne thanks to God's special grace."[1] The Fundamental Laws of the country stated that God ordained that Russians should obey their tsar. Orthodox reminders of human weakness, sinfulness, and the fallible nature of reason served well a regime attempting to keep its subjects in their proper humble places. They were to be loyal subjects, and the all-powerful autocrat was to be their stern but loving ruler. Russian conservatives also valued Orthodoxy because it was so intricately intertwined with Russian traditions and helped ward off unwanted Western influences.

---

[1] J. S. Curtiss, *Church and State in Russia* (New York, 1940), p. 28.

FIGURE 19.1. Statue of Nicholas I, St. Petersburg, 1859, by P. Clodt. On the pedestal, Faith, Wisdom, Justice, and Might are represented by the faces of Nicholas's wife and daughters.

Nicholas's emphasis on nationality meant, of course, the Russian nationality. Like many Russian conservative nationalists, he believed "Holy Russia" was superior to a Western Europe more infected with individualism, class struggle, and free-thinking anti-Christian and revolutionary behavior. Although Nicholas's besieged-fortress mentality led him to take many steps to *defend* Russia against certain Western influences, some of his nationalist followers, such as the historian and publicist M. P. Pogodin (1800–1875), were more offensive-minded and dreamed of spreading Russia's "holy" influence and hegemony, especially over other Slavic peoples.

ADMINISTRATION AND INTERNAL POLICIES

Nicholas's desire for control and order led him to involve himself personally in numerous aspects of government. This became evident at the start of his reign when he questioned many Decembrists and decided their fates. Sometimes he even ordered St. Petersburg's firemen about as they sought to put out the capital's fires. He especially liked "pop-in" inspections, not only of military units, but also of government offices, schools, prisons, and hospitals. The government official Alexander Nikitenko recounted how Nicholas's visit to a secondary school in 1833 led to the dismissal of a history teacher and the superintendent of the St. Petersburg school system, primarily because two students were not sitting up straight.

Nicholas's penchant for control and discipline also led to increasing government centralization; the appointment of trusted military men to run civilian offices and ad hoc committees; and the expansion of the emperor's own private Imperial Chancery, which eventually comprised six divisions and often bypassed the established bureaucracy.

Nicholas's drillmaster personality and his suspiciousness often won out over his better qualities and hindered Russian modernization efforts. Of course, the desires of powerful interest groups, such as the wealthy landowning nobles, and Nicholas's desire not to alienate them also blocked the path to some needed changes.

A year after coming to power, Nicholas established the Committee of 6 December to propose minor government reforms. Although no changes of substance were enacted as a result of the committee's work, the fact that it held many meetings over the next five years and that the reform-minded Mikhail Speransky was a member of it indicated that Nicholas was at least open to the possibility of limited reforms. He kept the committee's existence secret, however, wishing to discourage any suggestions from the educated public. Like his brother Alexander, he was not against paternalistic reform, but he wanted only solicited advice and reforms that would not threaten the existing social order.

More fruitful than the efforts of the Committee of 6 December were Nicholas's actions in increasing the size of the government and appointing some capable individuals to serve it. As compared with Western countries such as Great Britain, France, and Prussia, Russia's government was woefully short of personnel when Nicholas came to the throne. Although it would remain comparatively understaffed and many of its top positions would continue to be dominated by aristocrats, Nicholas increased the ratio of civil servants to population, and from 1836 to 1843 about two-thirds of those who reached the rank that brought with it hereditary-noble status were from non-noble backgrounds.

Among Nicholas's appointments were Counts L. Perovsky and P. Kiselev. These two men, in turn, made use of the talents of reform-minded men such as Nikolai Miliutin, who was Kiselev's nephew and worked under Minister of Interior Perovsky. As head of a section for reorganizing municipal government, Miliutin worked to prepare a statute that was accepted for St. Petersburg in 1846 and later served as a basis for Alexander II's municipal reforms. Miliutin himself would later be a principal force in helping to bring about the emancipation of the serfs in 1861.

Despite these positive steps, Nicholas's desire for more control contributed to drowning his officials in paperwork. In 1850, Perovsky's Ministry of Interior alone processed more than 30 million documents.

Nicholas's most important reform was overseeing the collecting, codifying, and publishing of almost all the laws enacted since 1649. This herculean task was carried out under the direction of Speransky and the Second Section of Nicholas's Imperial Chancery. By 1833, *The Complete Collection of the Laws of the Russian Empire* and a fifteen-volume *Digest of the Laws of the Russian Empire* were completed. Now it was possible, with a few exceptions, to know what the law was. This helped curtail, but certainly did not end, governmental arbitrariness and was a necessary first step if Russia were to become a state governed by laws. The founding in 1835 of the Imperial School of Jurisprudence was another step forward.

Again, however, Nicholas's fears prevented him from going further. He deliberately withheld from Speransky some secret decrees that he did not want published, and he rejected Speransky's early suggestion that once the old laws were gathered and systematized, the tsar should draft a new law code more in keeping with modern demands. In 1845, Nicholas did issue a new Criminal Code, but it was hardly a step forward. Forty-five pages of it dealt with crimes against the government, including any attempts to limit autocracy. The code stipulated that even failing to report such attempts made one liable to capital punishment. Mere disrespect toward the tsar could lead to confiscation of property and as many as a dozen years' hard labor.

Nicholas's censorship policies and infamous Third Section of his Imperial Chancery (created in 1826) also reflected both his desire to be an enlightened absolute monarch and his fears of disorder and revolutionary ideas. A censorship law of 1828 was more moderate than an earlier one of 1826 or than conditions prevailing during Alexander I's final years, and Nicholas wished to encourage literature as long as it was not subversive. Yet censorship later became more intense, especially after European revolutions in 1848–1849 alarmed Nicholas more than ever. Ludicrous examples of censorship were numerous; for example, a cookbook was prohibited from using the term "free air," although only referring to oven space.

The Third Section systematized political-police functions that had earlier been haphazard, and it directed paid informers and several thousand blue-uniformed and white-gloved gendarmes. Early in its existence, it suggested to Nicholas certain reforms that might decrease dissatisfaction with the government. Its main job, however, was to prevent, or at least ferret out, subversive activities.

In his approach to Russia's serfs and state peasants, Nicholas again mixed limited reform and extreme caution. In 1842, he recognized that serfdom, as it then existed, was "an evil, palpable and evident to all." But he added that "to attack it now would be even more disastrous." Nicholas had no wish to anger the serfowning nobles by taking away their most prized right, and he did not wish to awaken peasant expectations. He did approve, however, of some minor steps to ameliorate serf conditions. For example, a law of 1842 *allowed* serfowners to transform their serfs into freer, but still "obligated," peasants.

Unfortunately for the serfs, however, any such measures depending on serf-owner benevolence were unlikely to have much overall impact.

In dealing with state peasants, Nicholas had less to fear and therefore accomplished more. In 1836, he appointed Kiselev to head a Fifth Section of his Imperial Chancery, charged with directing state peasant affairs. In late 1837, Nicholas created the Ministry of State Domains, with Kiselev as its head, to take over and upgrade the Fifth Section's functions. For the rest of Nicholas's reign, Kiselev tried to improve the lot of the state peasants. He broadened their involvement in local affairs, promoted better farming methods, eventually made more government land available to communes with insufficient amounts, and improved sanitary and educational conditions. Kiselev's reforms, however, brought some unwanted government intrusions into peasants' lives.

By 1848, Nicholas had presided over almost a quarter century of educational growth—both secondary and university students had more than doubled since 1825. Yet his fears following the European revolutionary outbreaks of 1848–1849 led to new educational policies that decreased university enrollments and imposed standard uniforms and haircuts. The government also prohibited the teaching of constitutional law and all philosophy but logic, which was henceforth to be taught only by priests. In addition, professors now had to submit their lecture notes for prior administrative approval.

NICHOLAS AND THE WESTERN NATIONALITIES

In dealing with his empire's non-Russian nationalities, Nicholas's Official Nationality policy blended with his suspicious and order-loving personality to impose more centralized control. Being a cautious man, however, he restrained his centralizing tendencies at times when he feared that imposing them might stir up still waters. Finland was a good example. Appreciating the stability and loyalty of this area won by Alexander I, he continued to allow it considerable autonomy.

Nicholas also displayed restraint in the Kingdom of Poland (Congress Poland) before a rebellion there in 1830. His sense of honor prevented him from violating its 1815 constitution, but his distaste for the limitations it placed upon him was clear enough.

Although economic and political conditions were better in this "kingdom" than in Russia itself, this offered little solace to Poles inflamed by the spirit of revolution and romantic heroism then in the European air. Coupled with the Poles' accumulated grievances—including the late-eighteenth-century partition of their country and more minor, but still galling, recent complaints—this spirit sparked a rebellion in November 1830. Students from a Warsaw school of cadets attacked Grand Duke Constantine's Warsaw palace. Warsaw workers also soon joined the young rebels. Besides other complaints, the workers were upset by recent increases in grain and alcohol prices.

In the days that followed, the rebellion spread throughout the Kingdom of Poland and beyond to the "western provinces," which had been part of Poland before the late-eighteenth-century Polish partitions. The Polish national army, which had been under Grand Duke Constantine, joined the rebels. But the Poles were hurt by divisiveness between Polish radicals and moderates and by a lack of substantial peasant support. England and France offered only vocal support to the rebels, and by the fall of 1831, superior Russian forces had defeated the Poles.

In 1832, Nicholas replaced the 1815 constitution with an Organic Statute. It no longer permitted a Polish Sejm (Diet) or national army but did allow the Poles to retain separate laws and some participation in government. Although Nicholas gradually increased his control over Polish administration and education, the Poles retained their legal code and right to use Polish in their schools, courts, and lower government offices.

In the Lithuanian, Belorussian, and Ukrainian provinces, where he never had to worry about constitutional scruples, Nicholas now accelerated Russification. He closed the University of Vilna—as he also did the University of Warsaw. Instead, he founded a new university in Kiev (1833). Minister of Education Uvarov made it clear that its task was "to disseminate Russian education and Russian nationality in the Polonized lands of western Russia."[2]

To further this goal in the western provinces, Nicholas and his officials also closed Polish schools and curtailed instruction in Polish, substituting Russian

[2]Quoted in Orest Subtelny, *Ukraine: A History.* 2d ed. (Toronto, 1994), p. 210.

FIGURE 19.2. Kiev University, 1837–1842, by V. I. Beretti. Nicholas I himself decided it should be the same color as his Winter Palace, which was then red.

schools and more instruction in Russian. By the end of 1840, Nicholas had abolished in the region the Lithuanian Statute (a law code rooted in Western medieval law) and the Magdeburg Law, which had allowed a city like Kiev certain autonomous legal rights. He also struck at the dominant Polish nobility in these provinces, depriving many thousands of them of their lands and noble status and exiling some far into Russia. Finally, Nicholas chipped away at the Uniate form of Catholicism. He pressured its practitioners to revert to Orthodoxy and ultimately, in 1839, forbade it except in the former Kingdom of Poland.

All these measures inadvertently stirred nationalist reactions. In 1847, a small group of Ukrainian nationalists were arrested. They were members of the secret Brotherhood of Sts. Cyril and Methodius. Although it contained only about a dozen active members and a few dozen sympathizers, two leading Ukrainian figures were associated with it. One was its central founder, Nikolai (Mykola) Kostomarov (1817–1885), who just months before his arrest had begun teaching Russian history at Kiev University. The other was the poet Taras Shevchenko (1814–1861), whose writings did more than those of any other nineteenth-century Ukrainian to foster a Ukrainian literary language and a sense of Ukrainian nationhood.

Kostomarov wrote the constitution and guidelines for the society. They stipulated that its members would work toward the creation of a Slavic federation in which nationalities such as the Ukrainians would have their own autonomous national governments. Kostomarov also called for abolishing both serfdom and class distinctions, and he said that the federation should contain democratic institutions similar to those in the United States.

For his activities, Kostomarov was imprisoned in the capital's dreaded Sts. Peter and Paul Fortress for a year and then exiled to Saratov on the Volga. But his punishment was minor compared to that of the better-known and more radical Shevchenko, who was sentenced to ten years in a Siberian military labor battalion. Another response of the government was to issue an imperial decree calling on scholars, writers, and educators to promote loyalty to the Russian Empire over non-Russian nationalist sympathies.

Nicholas's centralizing tendencies also spelled trouble for another nationality residing primarily in the western provinces—the Jews. There were about 1.5 million Jews living in the area and in the Kingdom of Poland. In 1827, Nicholas decreed that henceforth Jews would no longer be allowed to pay a tax in lieu of military service. Henceforth, they were to be subject to the standard draft of twenty-five years and even longer if they were drafted when under eighteen. In the next three decades, as Michael Stanislawski has noted, "Some seventy thousand Jewish males, most of them children [many younger than twelve], were drafted into an army that swore to eradicate the Jewishness of any of its soldiers who managed to survive. Few returned to their families; most either converted or died."[3] No other nationality saw such a high percent-

[3]*Tsar Nicholas I and the Jews: The Transformation of Jewish Society in Russia, 1825–1855* (Philadelphia, 1983), p. 185.

age of its children treated in such a way. By forcing Jewish communities to select such recruits and by imposing additional restrictive cultural, economic,
and educational policies upon Jews, Nicholas undercut the stability of Jewish
communities.

Toward Baltic Germans, Nicholas was more tolerant, probably because of
their conservatism, their record of distinguished state service, and his own
Prussian inclinations. For these reasons, he continued to allow separate institutions and laws in the Baltic provinces where the Baltic Germans dominated
other nationalities. Yet even here his Official Nationality triad made some in-
roads, especially the principle of Orthodoxy. The Orthodox Church established
a bishopric in Riga in 1836, and the new bishop and other Russian authorities
strongly encouraged Latvian and Estonian conversions to Orthodoxy. This was
especially true between 1845 and 1847, when some 75,000 of them occurred.

PUBLIC OPINION AND OPPOSITION

Despite Nicholas's harsh treatment of the Decembrists (including members of
some of Russia's leading families) and his distrust of educated public opinion,
most Russians supported autocracy. Nicholas's reign looked worse in retrospect, after his death and Russia's defeat in the Crimean War, than it did during the heyday of his rule, when Russia still basked in the glory of a military
that had defeated Napoleon. Serfs might wish to throw off their shackles, but
they blamed the nobles and not the tsar for their plight. Some writers such as
Gogol and the poet Tiutchev were ardent supporters of Nicholas's Official Nationality principles. Although most moderates or liberals were critical of some
policies, such as Nicholas's stringent post-1848 censorship, they wished a
strong, albeit reforming, monarch.

Before 1848, most opposition to Nicholas's government came from a small
group of men, mostly nobles, who had once been friends or acquaintances in
Moscow. In salons and in academic circles, students of Moscow University
and their friends gathered to find meaning for their own lives and that of their
country. Two circles were especially prominent in the 1830s. One was headed
by Nikolai Stankevich (1813–1840) and included Mikhail Bakunin (1814–
1876), Vissarion Belinsky (1811–1848), T. Granovsky, M. Katkov, and C. Aksakov. The other was headed by Alexander Herzen (1812–1870) and his good
friend Nikolai Ogarev.

The dominant influence on the Stankevich circle was a succession of German philosophers—Schelling, Fichte, and Hegel. Herzen later ironically described the impact of Hegel and German philosophy:

> People who loved one another parted for whole weeks because they disagreed
> on the definition of [Hegel's] 'transcendental spirit.' . . . All the insignificant
> brochures on German philosophy—published in Berlin and other provincial
> and district towns—where Hegel was only mentioned were written for and
> read to shreds. . . . A man who went to walk in Sokolniki [Park] went in order
> to give himself up to the pantheistic feeling of his oneness with the cosmos.

Although influenced by Hegel himself, Herzen's circle was more politically oriented. In 1834, when the government discovered that Herzen and Ogarev were sympathetic to the ideas of the French utopian socialist St. Simon, they were arrested, imprisoned, and later exiled to the provinces.

By late 1842, Herzen was back in Moscow interpreting Hegel in a new and revolutionary way, and Bakunin and Belinsky also now realized the revolutionary potential of Hegel's ideas, especially the dialectic. Like Karl Marx in Germany, all three men in the early 1840s were influenced by the German Left Hegelianism of individuals such as Ludwig Feuerbach and the ideas of French Utopian socialists such a Charles Fourier.

While Herzen was still in exile in 1836, he read an amazing article that had slipped past the censors and into the journal *Telescope*. It was, said Herzen, "a shot that resounded through the dark night." It was the first "Philosophical Letter" of the Moscow nobleman Peter Chaadaev. It stated that Russia was a wasteland that had contributed nothing of value to civilization, partly because Orthodoxy was not the positive civilizing force that Catholicism was in the West. After Nicholas declared Chaadaev insane and put him under medical and police surveillance, Chaadaev wrote the *Apology of a Madman* (1837). In it he conceded that thanks to Peter the Great's westernizing policies, Russia could still make significant contributions in the future.

Chaadaev's letter began a debate with a group calling themselves Slavophiles. Belinsky, Bakunin, and Herzen, among others, later joined Chaadaev's side and were labeled Westernizers by their opponents. All four men rejected the Slavophiles' belief in the superiority of Orthodoxy and pre-Petrine Russia as well as their contention that Peter I had greatly harmed Russia by trying to westernize it. On the contrary, the Westernizers believed that Peter the Great had performed a great service by attempting to put Russia on the track of Western civilization.

But Belinsky, Bakunin, and Herzen did not share Chaadaev's appreciation of Catholicism or his belief that a "universal mind" was evolving toward the Kingdom of God on earth. They also did not share the moderate westernizing views of others such as the Moscow historian Timothy Granovsky. As the 1840s progressed, the three radical Westernizers became more critical of religion and increasingly sympathetic with socialist ideas that aimed at creating a more humane, reasonable, and just society.

Belinsky was the son of a poor provincial doctor and had been kicked out of the University of Moscow. Thereafter, he made his living as a journalist and as his generation's most influential literary critic. Herzen has left us an excellent portrait of him:

> But in this shy man, in this sickly body dwelt a powerful gladiator's nature. . . . When his deepest convictions were touched upon, when the muscles of his cheeks began to tremble and his voice to break, then he was something to behold. He threw himself on his opponent like a snow leopard, he tore him into pieces, made him look ridiculous and pitiful, and in doing so developed his own thought with unusual strength and poetry. The argument ended very often with blood, which flowed from the sick man's throat [Belinsky had tuberculosis].

In 1847, Belinsky wrote a scathing letter to Gogol criticizing him for his *Selected Passages from a Correspondence with Friends,* where he had glorified Orthodoxy, autocracy, and even serfdom. The letter soon circulated in "underground" copies, and only Belinsky's death the following year apparently saved him from prison.[4] Even without the martyrdom of prison, his passionate stand for human dignity guaranteed his reputation among free-thinking youth.

The more robust Bakunin spent the 1840s in Western and Central Europe. By 1842, he was preaching the complete destruction of the old order. He met and was influenced by revolutionary thinkers, including Karl Marx and the French anarchist Pierre-Joseph Proudhon. In 1848, he summarized his views at the time in an *Appeal to the Slavs.* It called for Slavic workers and peasants to rise up and dismantle the Austrian, Russian, and Turkish empires by forming a free and democratic Slavic federation.

In the revolutionary years of 1848–1849, Bakunin was a whirlwind of revolutionary activity. He took part in revolutionary activities from Paris to Prague, and he was eventually arrested and then condemned to death by two governments before being handed over to Russian authorities in 1851. He soon found himself in solitary confinement in the Sts. Peter and Paul Fortress.

In 1847, Herzen left Russia and never returned. The failure of the 1848–1849 European revolutions greatly disillusioned him, and like his former Slavophile rivals, but for different reasons, he began glorifying the Russian peasant commune. With its self-governing structure and its periodic redistribution of land, he now saw it as the best hope in the world for developing democratic socialism. First, of course, it would have to be liberated from the shackles of an oppressive state and class system.

But Herzen was also mindful that illiterate masses and their leaders might oppress individuality if they came to power. Thus, he stressed the importance of respecting individual rights and warned against subordinating the individual to abstract concepts and ideals.

The Slavophile rivals of the Westernizers, some of whom had participated in the same salons and circles, were not as reactionary as many of the defenders of Nicholas's Official Nationality. Essentially Moscow nobles, the group included Alexei Khomiakov, Ivan and Peter Kireevsky, Constantine and Ivan Aksakov, and Yuri Samarin. Although they defended the principles of Orthodoxy, autocracy, and nationality, they were wary of St. Petersburg—that city of the westernizing Peter the Great—and its government. They were opposed to serfdom, thought government censorship went too far, and occasionally crossed Nicholas's rigid line of the permissible. One of the younger Slavophiles, Yuri Samarin, was even imprisoned for twelve days (in March 1849) in the Sts. Peter and Paul Fortress for suggesting that the power of the Baltic Germans should be curtailed. Following this sobering experience, Nicholas—always the scolding father figure—had this young noble brought directly from prison to the royal palace, where the tsar reprimanded him.

A month later, Nicholas's Third Section uncovered what it considered far

---

[4]For excerpts from this letter and more on Belinsky as a literary critic, see Chapter 21.

more serious opposition—the Petrashevsky Circle. Its leader was a colorful minor official in the Ministry of Foreign Affairs who sometimes walked around St. Petersburg in a cape and sombrero. He was an ardent believer in the utopian socialist principles of Fourier and in Feuerbach's conviction that humans could transform their lives to a higher plane if they liberated themselves from their religious myths. Petrashevsky hosted freewheeling Friday night discussions at his home in the capital.

Although Petrashevsky was willing to wait until talk, persuasion, and legal reforms changed society, a more conspiratorial, revolutionary group formed among some of his Friday-night visitors. One of its members was the young writer Fedor Dostoevsky (1821–1881). He agreed to help set up a secret printing press and read, on several occasions, Belinsky's famous forbidden letter to Gogol.

For their participation in the Petrashevsky Circle, fifty-one individuals were sentenced to exile. Twenty-one more, including Petrashevsky and Dostoevsky, were condemned to death. After eight months in the Sts. Peter and Paul Fortress, the condemned men were brought to a public square at dawn where a firing squad awaited them. Only at the last minute, after convincing them that they were soon to die, did Nicholas let them know their real sentences— for Dostoevsky it was to be four years in a Siberian prison and then forced military service.

For the rest of Nicholas's reign, few intellectuals dared openly express any radical ideas. Yet the diverse dissatisfaction with the present order, which was already growing among Russian intellectuals during the 1840s, was only exacerbated by Nicholas's increasingly reactionary policies after 1848. The Crimean War, which he began but did not live to finish, further discredited him by its failure. By 1858, three years after Nicholas's death, many intellectuals shared the sentiment that the moderate official and lover of literature A. V. Nikitenko expressed in his diary: "Nicholas's reign . . . was all a mistake."

FOREIGN AFFAIRS AND RUSSIAN EXPANSION

Although Nicholas's fear of revolutionary movements and his adherence to Orthodoxy, autocracy, and nationality carried over into his foreign policy, it was harder to apply the three principles internationally. Moreover, considerations such as trade and geopolitics also affected his dealings with other countries and peoples. In general, in dealing with foreign countries, he supported the status quo and "legitimate" rulers as the best defense against revolution.

His reign began with a war with Persia (1826–1828). The conflict started when Persian troops, hoping to regain Caucasian territories lost to Alexander I, crossed into Russian territory. But the Treaty of Turkmanchai, which ended the war after a series of Russian victories, only added to Russia's Caucasian gains. Persian Armenia, including the city of Erevan, now became part of the Russian Empire.

Further north in the Caucasus, Moslem mountaineer tribesmen rebelled against Russian incursions. In the late 1820s, their leaders proclaimed a "holy war" against the Russian infidels. The rebellion centered in Chechnia and Dagestan. The mountaineers resented the advance of fortified government settlements and Cossacks, and they feared the loss of their winter pasturelands in the plains. Nicholas was determined to pacify the mountaineers even if it meant the "extermination of the unsubmissive."[5]

In the mid-1830s, after the death of several Moslem leaders, a remarkable warrior named Shamil assumed leadership. Despite having more than 200,000 troops in the Caucasus in the 1840s, the Russians could not stamp out the Moslem holy war. Only after the death of Nicholas was Shamil finally captured and the war brought to an end.

In Central Asia, Nicholas had to face hostility from Moslem Kazakhs, who numbered about 1.5 million and were largely nomadic and pastoral. As in the Caucasus, the native peoples resisted the advance of Russian settlers (still relatively small in number) and the building of Russian forts. They also resented the imposition of centralized Russian authority and taxes. Yet, despite several open rebellions, Russia extended its control over the Kazakh steppe throughout Nicholas's reign. By 1855, Russia had advanced to the western portions of the Syr-Daria River and in the east to Fort Vernoe (later Alma-Ata).

Further to the east, the dynamic governor-general of Eastern Siberia, N. N. Muraviev, pushed forward along the Amur River region claimed by China. In the early 1850s, Russia established Nikolaevsk at the mouth of the Amur and laid claim to the island of Sakhalin (see Map 24.1).

In foreign affairs, Russia, Prussia, and Austria supported the status quo and "legitimism" in repressing Polish revolutionary sentiments. In 1849, Nicholas displayed his fidelity to legitimism by sending more than 350,000 troops to put down Hungarians (and some Poles) rebelling against their "legitimate" Austrian sovereign.

But support for legitimism sometimes conflicted with Nicholas's other priorities. This was especially true in dealing with the Ottoman Turkish Empire, where a Moslem sultan ruled over many non-Moslems, including Balkan Orthodox Christians. Turkish control of the straits (the Bosphorus and Dardanelles) leading from the Black Sea to the Aegean further complicated Russo-Turkish relations, for access through them to the Mediterranean had become vital to Russia's economic interests.

Nicholas's first war with the Ottoman Turks (1828–1829) was a legacy of unfinished business left to him by Alexander I. At the time of Nicholas's accession to the throne, the Greeks were continuing the rebellion they had begun against the Turks in 1820–1821. Acting in concert with the British and French, and contrary to his usual defense of legitimism, Nicholas assisted the rebelling Greeks. In October 1827, in the battle of Navarino Bay, Russian, French, and British naval squadrons destroyed most of an Egyptian fleet sent by the sultan to put down the Greek rebels.

Yet Nicholas's actions leading up to Navarino Bay were not motivated by

---

[5]Cited in Firuz Kazemzadeh, "Russian Penetration of the Caucasus," in *Russian Imperialism from Ivan the Great to the Revolution,* ed. by Taras Hunczak (New Brunswick, N.J., 1974), p. 253.

sympathy for the Greeks, even though they shared his Orthodox beliefs. He thought them reprehensible rebels. He violated his own belief in legitimacy primarily to further Russia's aims. Making use of the sultan's precarious position in the face of the coalition against him, Nicholas, in 1826, forced the sultan to accept several ultimatums. By the Akkerman Convention, the sultan agreed to honor previous treaties, which Nicholas thought the Turks had been violating, and to grant navigation rights to Russian merchant ships through the Straits and in Turkish waters.

Two months after the battle of Navarino Bay, the sultan, hoping to take advantage of loosening ties between Russia and its two Western allies, repudiated the Akkerman Convention and called for a holy war. He then closed the Straits to Russian merchant ships. In April 1828, two months after concluding peace with Persia, Nicholas declared war against Turkey and shortly thereafter sent troops into the Turkish Danubian principalities of Moldavia and Wallachia.

After Russian victories in the Balkans, where Nicholas personally participated, and the Caucasus, the sultan agreed to peace terms. By the Treaty of Adrianople (1829), he once again pledged to honor the Akkerman Convention, ceded territory to Russia in the Caucasus and at the Danube's mouth on the Black Sea, and recognized Moldavia and Wallachia as a temporary Russian protectorate (see Map 18.1). Greek independence, which was greatly facilitated by Russia's victory, was insured the following year by a conference in London, where Russia, Britain, and France agreed to guarantee it.

FIGURE 19.3. Moscow Gate in St. Petersburg, 1834–1838, by V. P. Stasov. This triumphal arch commissioned by Nicholas I was to commemorate his successful campaigns against Persia and Turkey.

In 1832, Nicholas was able to show his support for legitimism by supporting the sultan against his rebellious Egyptian vassal, Mohammed Ali. For helping to turn back the challenge of the rebel armies, Nicholas received new gains in the Treaty of Unkiar-Skelessi (1833). By its provisions, good for eight years, the Turks agreed to close the Dardanelles to foreign war ships, and Russia agreed to support Turkey if attacked by another power.

After another revolt by Mohammed Ali (1839–1840) and the expiration of Unkiar-Skelessi, it was replaced by a broader Straits Convention (1841). In it, the five major European powers (Austria, Britain, France, Prussia, and Russia) and Turkey agreed on the Turkish prohibition of foreign warships through the Straits during peacetime.

THE MILITARY AND THE CRIMEAN WAR

Russia's army looked much better on paper and on the parade ground than it did in battle. On the eve of the Crimean War (1853–1856), it had about 1 million men and was the largest in Europe. Partly because of Nicholas's penchant for discipline and order, he and his officers strongly emphasized inspections and parades. They also thought that parades were good preparation for battle, and battlefield tactics emphasized marching in formation into battle and defeating the enemy with a bayonet attack.

Conditions in the army were not good, however, and its quality was not high. The enlisted men were overwhelmingly illiterate peasants who had to serve fifteen or more years of active service (at the beginning of Nicholas's reign, twenty-five years had been the requirement). Nobles, merchants, and some others were exempt from mandatory service. Moreover, many of the conscripts had been selected because they had displeased one authority or another, often on the communal level. Army discipline and punishments were severe. Especially draconian was the punishment of running the gauntlet, which consisted of passing through rows of soldiers who beat the offender with wooden rods. These beatings—as many as 2,000 blows might be delivered—sometimes led to death. If battles or beatings did not end conscripts' lives prematurely, diseases often did. In the twenty-five years before the Crimean War, about 1 million soldiers died other than in battle, mostly from diseases.

Partly because of Nicholas's experience with the Decembrists, he and his command staff distrusted innovative and intellectual officers. Neither the training nor the military thinking of Nicholas's officers was up to the challenge of the Crimean War. Officers were also frequently involved in graft. Nicholas himself cited one case in which an officer used enlisted men and even some soldiers' wives in various personal enterprises ranging from stealing and processing lumber to caring for his oxen, sheep, and camels.

An untypical officer was the writer Leo Tolstoy, who was an artillery sublieutenant in the Crimean War. He recognized many of the abuses in the army and in early 1855 planned to write a *Plan for the Reform of the Army*. Although he soon abandoned the idea, he did write, "We have no army, we have a horde of slaves cowed by discipline, ordered about by thieves and slave traders." The most intelligent officers and enlisted men were found in the artillery and the engineers—where Dostoevsky had briefly served as a young officer in the early 1840s.

The deficiencies in the army also extended to animals and equipment. Cavalry horses, fattened with oats and beer, looked healthy enough on the parade ground but were often far from the tip-top shape required for war duty. The situation in regard to rifles was even worse. In the Crimean War, Russian infantrymen were armed overwhelmingly with outdated muskets that were no match for the more accurate, rapid, and longer-range percussion rifles carried by many French and British troops.

The most obvious cause of the war was a dispute between Russia and France over Orthodox and Catholic rights in the Holy Lands, then part of the Turkish Empire. Partly because Orthodox pilgrims to Jerusalem and other Holy Lands overwhelmingly outnumbered Catholic ones and because the Orthodox spent generously to keep up the holy shrines, Russia had been able to persuade the sultan to allow the Orthodox special privileges there. From the late eighteenth century until the mid-nineteenth century, France had not seriously challenged the Orthodox claims backed by Russia. In 1851, President— soon to be Emperor—Louis Napoleon, in a bid for Catholic support at home, attempted to persuade the sultan to grant Catholics more rights. By late 1852, he had wrung some concessions from the sultan, including a promise to grant Catholics possession of a key to Bethlehem's Church of the Nativity.

Nicholas was displeased by this course of events and in February 1853 sent a special envoy, Prince A. S. Menshikov, to Constantinople. He remained for several months attempting to gain formal Turkish recognition of Orthodoxy's superior rights in the Holy Land—thus repealing France's recent gains—and Russia's right to protect Turkey's 12 million Orthodox subjects. The latter claim was based upon a debatable interpretation of the 1774 Treaty of Kuchuk-Kainarji and was especially worrisome to the Turks, who saw it as a wedge for further Russian interference in the internal affairs of their empire.

Believing, with justification, that France and Great Britain would not stand idly by if Russia attacked Turkey, the sultan refused Menshikov's demands. In the beginning of July 1853, Russian troops crossed the Pruth into Turkey's Danubian principalities (Moldavia and Wallachia). Despite a flurry of unsuccessful diplomatic activity in the next few months, Turkey declared war in October. After Nicholas ignored a British-French demand that he withdraw from the Danubian principalities, the two Western powers declared war on Russia in March 1854. In early 1855, Sardinia also entered the allied side against Russia.

Besides Russia's intercession for Orthodox Christians in the Ottoman Empire, there were other causes of the war. They included miscalculations and mistrusts fostered by rising nationalism in Europe, a phenomenon that made it increasingly difficult for the powers to continue the post-Napoleonic concert system of cooperation.

Nicholas's past diplomatic and military successes, especially in dealing with Turkey, made him overconfident. He failed to foresee Britain's resolve in backing Turkey, and he later expressed bitterness toward such nations that called themselves Christian but supported his Moslem Turkish foe. He insisted, apparently sincerely, that he had no desire to dismantle the Turkish Empire, only that if this "sick man" of Europe expired on its own, he wished to share the spoils.

But British mistrust of Russia was high by 1853, both among its diplomats and among the British public. Britain's interests in the Eastern Mediterranean and India made it wary of any expansion of Russian influence or territory southward. British as well as French public opinion was also hostile toward Nicholas (the "gendarme of Europe") because he was perceived as the chief opponent of freedom in Europe. Thus, Western animosity to Russia in the early 1850s bore some resemblance to Cold War hostility to the "Russian bear" a century later.

As so often happens, innumerable smaller details also tipped the scales to-

---

The Marquis de Custine on Russian Imperialism

Public opinion in the West was strongly influenced by the publication in 1843 of Marquis de Custine's classic *La Russie en 1839*. It was a "best-seller" in France and soon afterwards also appeared in translation in other countries, including England. Even though prohibited in Russia, copies found their way into the hands of intellectuals like Alexander Herzen. Custine's scathing criticism of Russia entered into the debate between Slavophiles and Westernizers. The following excerpt is taken from the English translation, *Russia* (New York: D. Appleton & Co., 1854), pp. 482, 488–489. It illustrates well both the dislike of Russia's autocracy and an almost paranoid fear of its intentions toward the rest of Europe. Ellipsis marks are mine.

I have found among the Russians that the principles of absolute monarchy, applied with inflexible consistency, lead to results that are monstrous. . . .

An ambition inordinate and immense, one of those ambitions which could only possibly spring in the bosoms of the oppressed, and could only find nourishment in the miseries of a whole nation, ferments in the heart of the Russian people. That nation, essentially aggressive, greedy under the influence of privation, expiates beforehand, by a debasing submission, the design of exercising a tyranny over other nations: the glory, the riches, which it hopes for, console it for the disgrace to which it submits. To purify himself from the foul and impious sacrifice of all public and personal liberty, the slave, upon his knees, dreams of the conquest of the world.

It is not the man who is adored in the Emperor Nicholas—it is the ambitious master of a nation more ambitious than himself. The passions of the Russians are shaped in the same mould as those of the people of antiquity: among them every thing reminds us of the Old Testament; their hopes, their tortures, are great, like their empire.

There, nothing has any limits—neither gifts, nor rewards, nor sacrifices, nor hopes: the power of such a people may become enormous; but they will purchase it at the price which the nations of Asia pay for the stability of their governments—the price of happiness

Russia sees in Europe a prey which our dissensions will sooner or later yield to her.

ward war. For example, Menshikov forgot to bring maps of the Ottoman Empire with him when he came to Constantinople in February 1853. This delayed negotiations for three crucial weeks, weeks in which the British ambassador was absent from Constantinople and the sultan might have been more compliant.

Once the war began, Russia became more diplomatically isolated. A month after Britain and France declared war, Austria and Prussia agreed to oppose any Russian attempt to annex the Danubian principalities, and Austria leaned increasingly in an anti-Russian direction, even demanding Russia's evacuation of the principalities. Nicholas became furious toward Austrian Emperor Franz Joseph, whom he had helped in Hungary in 1849. After hearing of Austria's demand, Nicholas turned a picture of the Austrian Emperor against the wall and wrote on the back of it *"Du Undankbarer!"* (You Ingrate!) After Russia withdrew from the principalities in August 1854, Austrian troops moved in.

In September, allied forces landed on the Crimean peninsula and a month later began the bombardment of Sevastopol. Thanks largely to the engineering fortifications of Colonel Todleben, Sevastopol was able to hold out for almost a year. Yet, despite the heroism and sacrifices of the Russian defenders of Sevastopol (realistically portrayed by Tolstoy in his *Sevastopol Sketches*) and despite some Russian victories in the Caucasus, Russia's handicaps were too great. Besides its outdated muskets, it was hampered by its perceived need to protect the Russo-Austrian border and St. Petersburg, by a backward transportation system, and by poor military leadership.

About a year after Nicholas's death in early 1855, his son and heir Alexander II was forced to agree to the Treaty of Paris. By its terms, Russia had to give up the mouth of the Danube, a chunk of Bessarabia (to Moldavia), and its claims to act as an exclusive protector in either the Danubian principalities or over all of Turkey's Orthodox subjects. Most galling of all were the clauses that prohibited any Russian (or other) warships or coastal fortifications in the Black Sea. Thus, after sacrificing 0.5 million Russian lives in the war, many to diseases, Russia gained only a humiliating peace treaty.

SUGGESTED SOURCES*

BAUMGART, WINFRIED. *The Peace of Paris, 1856: Studies in War, Diplomacy, and Peacemaking.* Santa Barbara, Calif., 1981.

CARR, E. H. *Michael Bakunin.* New York, 1961.

CHRISTOFF, PETER K. *An Introduction to Nineteenth-Century Russian Slavophilism.* 4 vols. The Hague, Princeton, and Boulder, 1961–1991.

CURTISS, JOHN S. *The Russian Army Under Nicholas I, 1825–1855.* Durham, 1965.

———. *Russia's Crimean War.* Durham, 1979.

CUSTINE, MARQUIS DE. *Empire of the Czar: A Journey through Eternal Russia.* New York, 1989.

*See also works cited in footnotes.

GAMMER, MOSHE. *Muslim Resistance to the Tsar: Shamil and the Conquest of Chechnia and Daghestan.* Portland, Ore., 1994.

GLEASON, ABBOTT. *European and Muscovite: Ivan Kireevsky and the Origins of Slavophilism.* Cambridge, Mass., 1972.

GOLDFRANK, DAVID M. *The Origins of the Crimean War.* London, 1993.

JELAVICH, BARBARA. *Russia's Balkan Entanglements, 1806–1914.* Cambridge, England, 1991.

KAPUSTINA, TAT'IANA A. "Nicholas I," *RSH* 34 (Winter 1995–96): 7–38. Reprinted in *EER*, pp. 257–293.

KEEP, JOHN L. H. *Soldiers of the Tsar: Army and Society in Russia, 1462–1874.* Oxford, 1985. Ch. 14.

LINCOLN, W. BRUCE. *In the Vanguard of Reform: Russia's Enlightened Bureaucrats, 1825–1861.* DeKalb, Ill., 1982.

———. *Nicholas I, Emperor and Autocrat of All the Russias.* Bloomington, 1978.

MONAS, SIDNEY. *The Third Section: Police and Society in Russia Under Nicholas I.* Cambridge, Mass., 1961.

MOON, DAVID. *Russian Peasants and Tsarist Legislation on the Eve of Reform: Interaction Between Peasants and Officialdom, 1825–1855.* New York, 1992.

NIKITENKO, ALEKSANDR. *The Diary of a Russian Censor,* abridged, ed. and trans. Helen Saltz Jacobson. Amherst, Mass., 1975.

PALMER, ALAN. *The Banner of Battle: The Story of the Crimean War.* London, 1987.

PINTNER, WALTER M. *Russian Economic Policy Under Nicholas I.* Ithaca, N.Y., 1967.

PRESNIAKOV, A. E. *Emperor Nicholas I of Russia, the Apogee of Autocracy, 1825–1855.* Gulf Breeze, Fla., 1974.

RIASANOVSKY, NICHOLAS V. *Nicholas I and Official Nationality in Russia, 1825–1855.* Berkeley, 1961.

———. *A Parting of Ways: Government and the Educated Public in Russia, 1801–1855.* Oxford, 1976.

———. *Russia and the West in the Teaching of the Slavophiles: A Study of Romantic Ideology.* Gloucester, Mass., 1965.

RICH, NORMAN. *Why the Crimean War?: A Cautionary Tale.* Hanover, N.H., 1985.

ROBERTS, IAN W. *Nicholas I and the Russian Intervention in Hungary.* New York, 1991.

Saunders, David. *Russia in the Age of Reaction and Reform, 1801–1881.* London, 1992. Chs. 5–7.

SEATON, ALBERT. *The Crimean War: A Russian Chronicle.* New York, 1977.

SEDDON, J. H. *The Petrashevtsy: A Study of the Russian Revolutionaries of 1848.* Manchester, England, 1985.

SQUIRE, P. S. *The Third Department: The Establishment and Practices of the Political Police in the Russia of Nicholas I.* London, 1968.

THADEN, EDWARD C. *Russia's Western Borderlands, 1710–1870.* Princeton, 1984. Pt. 3.

WALICKI, ANDRZEJ. *The Slavophile Controversy: History of a Conservative Utopia in Nineteenth-Century Russian Thought.* Oxford, 1975.

WIRTSCHAFTER, ELISE KIMERLING. *From Serf to Russian Soldier.* Princeton, 1990.

ZIMMERMAN, JUDITH E. *Midpassage: Alexander Herzen and European Revolution, 1847–1852.* Pittsburgh, 1989.

CHAPTER 20

Economic and Social Life, 1796–1855

In the six decades from the death of Catherine II to that of Nicholas I, the population of the expanding Russian empire almost doubled, urban areas grew even faster, and industry and trade continued to expand. Yet by 1855, Russia was still Europe's most agrarian country and the industrial gap between it and Europe's other leading powers had widened.

In the countryside, life remained much as it had under Catherine II. Although agricultural goods produced for market and agricultural innovations increased, most estate owners continued relying on traditional methods and farming primarily for their own needs. Although some noble rights over serfs were curtailed—under law, if not always in practice—the nobles' treatment of their serfs remained much the same. Although no massive Pugachev-like revolts occurred, smaller-scale peasant disturbances increased.

Russia's high death rate persisted into the nineteenth century. Although plague no longer killed large numbers, other diseases such as cholera killed many. About half of Russia's children died before age six.

Russian law continued to mandate a patriarchal society, in which women and children had few rights, and the plight of Russian peasant women, especially widows, remained harsh. The law discriminated not only between male and female, but also between different social estates. Although Russian laws were codified under Nicholas I, there was little genuine legal reform. Yet there was an increase in juridical training, a training that produced some independent-minded experts who made important contributions to legal reform later in the century.

POPULATION AND TOWNS

Between 1796 and 1855, the Russian Empire's population grew from about 37 million to about 73 million. Although some growth was due to new annexations in areas such as Finland, Poland, and the Caucasus, most was not. The percentage of natural increase alone in the empire was slightly higher than Europe's overall growth.

Russia's more rapid increase was due mainly to much earlier marriages and higher birth rates than the European average (see Chapter 16). They barely compensated, however, for a Russian death rate that failed to decline as much as that of the French, English, and some other Europeans. Partly because of high child-mortality rates, by 1855 the average Russian's life expectancy (at birth) was probably less than thirty years, compared to roughly forty years for a French or English citizen.

Population growth in Russia, as in the West, was boosted by the availability of more food. Food became more plentiful in Russia, however, primarily because of the expansion of sown areas, not because of new agricultural practices and techniques, as was generally the case in Western Europe.

Although its population doubled, Russia remained sparsely populated. In 1855, France contained only about half as many people as the Russian Empire but had six times as many individuals per square kilometer as did European Russia. In the Siberian part of the empire, the discrepancy was much greater: Less than 3 million people were spread out over an area about twenty-five times the size of France.

The empire's towns grew at a faster rate than the overall population, and by the late 1850s, town-dwellers made up as much as 10 percent of the total population. St. Petersburg contained almost 500,000 and Moscow almost 370,000 people by 1856. Warsaw had a little over 150,000 and Odessa a bit over 100,000. Only ten other cities had over 40,000: Riga, Kishinev, Kiev, Saratov, Kazan, Tula, Berdichev, Vilna, Nikolaev, and Kursk.

In comparison, Great Britain by then was already over 50 percent urban and France over 25 percent. London was more than six times and Paris more than three times as populated as St. Petersburg. Berlin was the only other European city that was larger—and just barely.

Observers, especially conservatives, continued to contrast Moscow and St. Petersburg. The writer Nikolai Gogol, for example, in his "Petersburg Notes of 1836" wrote of the former as more Russian, the latter more German-like, or even akin to a "European-American colony." In a similar vein, Anna Tiutcheva, a lady-in-waiting at court, contrasted (in 1855) the freedom, spontaneity, irregularity, and colorfulness of the European-Asiatic Moscow with the order, discipline, and military and official uniforms that characterized St. Petersburg. Despite their bias, these characterizations did point to some real differences.

The "two capitals" together also differed in many ways from other towns of the empire. The capitals' large size and opportunities made them magnets attracting ambitious people from throughout the empire. Smaller Russian provincial towns were viewed by many of the capitals' cultured elite as being terribly backward, a view strengthened by such unflattering literary portraits of them as Gogol's *Inspector General* and *Dead Souls*.

Some of the empire's biggest cities were located outside of Russia proper, and the Russians in them found themselves outnumbered by other nationali-

FIGURE 20.1. The port of Odessa and the Potemkin steps leading down to it. The steps were constructed from 1837 to 1841 and later made famous in Sergei Eisenstein's film *The Battleship Potemkin.*

ties. In cities such as Warsaw and Odessa, Jews were an important minority and contributed to their cosmopolitan nature.

Most large towns were also provincial capitals and therefore government outposts. Government activities, along with commerce, continued to dominate Russian town life. Most of the fastest-growing cities in the empire, such as the port cities of Odessa and Nikolaev, benefited from accelerated trade, which still relied mainly on waterways. But as cities and trade grew, the government found it increasingly difficult to mold towns into the islands of tsarist order and civilization dreamed of by Catherine and her urban planners.

Although some city centers had geometrically designed streets and some impressive modern buildings, less central city areas remained less ordered. There one found huts, cabins, or houses, some with gardens or courtyards, situated haphazardly among streets that were usually dusty or muddy (when not snow-covered), unlit, and often foul-smelling. Even in central Moscow, one might encounter a cow headed for pasturing on the city outskirts.

As Daniel Brower has indicated, cities frustrated the autocratic penchant for order for both monetary and human reasons. Scarce funds often hampered the government from more building or rebuilding, from maintaining adequate city services, and from hiring enough officials and police to create the streamlined, orderly Russian city of which rulers could only dream. As people poured into cities looking for work, they created large transient populations.

The government attempted to maintain strict classifications of urban residents, with corresponding obligations. Yet both the transients and more permanent townspeople often succeeded in evading government-imposed responsibilities, including taxes and fees. Although many transients were *obrok*-paying serfs, legally permitted by their owners and the government to work in a city, others were "illegals" who had fled to a town without proper authorization.

Urban populations were classified by estate. The largest estate in most Russian cities was the *meshchane*. Its most affluent members were men of business and commerce just below the much smaller and better-off merchant estate. Other members engaged in petty trade and crafts. The poorest *meshchane* eked out a precarious living any way they could: as peddlers, servants, workers in factories or other businesses (including prostitution), or even on arable land on town outskirts. In St. Petersburg, however, the *meshchane* were smaller by 1843 than three other estates. The peasants (overwhelmingly *obrok*-paying serfs) outnumbered them three to one and made up more than a third of St. Petersburg's population. The military estate was almost twice as large and the nobility slightly larger than the *meshchane*. Seven other categories, including a miscellaneous one, made up the rest of the population. Although St. Petersburg was atypical in many ways, the peasant population of Moscow was also increasing rapidly during this era.

INDUSTRY AND TRADE

During the early nineteenth century, the industrial-development gap between Russia and other leading powers increased. Although it is sometimes argued that too much has been made of Russia's "backwardness" compared to the West's most developed countries, it was these countries that were Russia's chief rivals. The production of pig iron, a most important industrial product, exemplifies Russia's problem. For a brief period around 1800, it produced more pig iron than England (or any other country), but by 1855, it produced less than one-tenth England's output. Although England's industrial development was clearly exceptional, it was by no means the only country industrializing more rapidly than Russia. By 1860, seven countries produced more iron than it did.

Undoubtedly, there were many reasons, including economic, social, and political ones for this increasing gap. The attitude of the Russian government, especially under Nicholas I, was certainly among them. Although Russian tariff policies in this era were generally protectionist, this was more for monetary and fiscal reasons—such as collecting more taxes—than because of any ardor for domestic industrial development. Nicholas I was primarily concerned with domestic order and military strength. He feared rapid industrialization would destabilize society, and he failed to appreciate adequately industry's military significance.

Russia's minister of finance from 1823 to 1844, Count E. F. Kankrin, wrote of entrepreneurs being "oppressors of the workers, whom they force to toil for their benefit." He also declared that "factory production engenders in the lower classes immorality, humiliation, stupidity, revolts, and demands for higher wages."[1] Both he and Nicholas hoped to protect Russia from such ills, partly by regarding most industrial workers as legally still peasants—only temporarily working outside their native villages—and by encouraging cottage industry.

This same Count Kankrin also distrusted railways and failed to perceive their freight-carrying potential. He said they "prompt frequent journeys without any need and thus heighten the inconstant spirit of our age."[2] Such attitudes help explain why by 1855 Russia had less than one-tenth the railway track of Britain—primarily the recently completed 400-mile St. Petersburg–Moscow line.

Despite such thinking, Russian industries and factory workers still increased noticeably in this period. Official figures, excluding mining and metallurgical workers, indicate about a fivefold increase in factories and factory workers between 1800 and 1855. By 1855, factories numbered approximately 11,000 and workers in them about 500,000. Yet even counting mining and metallurgical workers, in 1855 only about 1 percent of the population could be classified as industrial workers.

The greatest percentage growth and most modernized production was in cotton mills and sugar refineries. Cheap British yarn and, after 1842, the import of British spinning machinery boosted the growth of the mills. So too did capable Russian workers and entrepreneurs, foreign investment and know-how, and sufficient domestic and foreign markets, such as those of China and the Middle East. The sugar industry grew (according to official figures) from 108 workers in 1804 to almost 65,000 by 1860. By then, many refineries were steam-driven.

Despite the refineries' dramatic increase, factories producing cotton or woolen textiles each still outnumbered them by 1860. Other factories produced such items as linen textiles, silk, paper, leather, metal goods, tobacco products, tallow, soap, candles, and wax.

In textile production, the provinces of St. Petersburg, Moscow, and Vladimir were all leaders, as were the Warsaw and Lodz areas in the Polish part of the empire. St. Petersburg produced much of the country's sugar made from imported sugar cane, but Ukraine developed and dominated refining from home-grown sugar beets. The Urals remained the chief mining and metallurgical center.

By mid-century, the city of Moscow had about twice as many factory workers—overwhelmingly in textiles—as St. Petersburg's approximate 20,000 workers. The capital, however, employed more people in metalworking, an industry that was becoming increasingly important.

By no means did all industrial production occur in cities. Factories also ex-

---

[1]Cited in M. I. Tugan-Baranovsky, *The Russian Factory in the 19th Century* (Homewood, Ill., 1970), p. 240.
[2]Ibid., p. 241.

isted in the countryside, often owned by nobles or even serfs. Count Sheremetev's Ivanovo, called by one visitor of the 1840s the Russian Manchester, was
still then legally a village. Located in the Vladimir Province, some 125 large
cotton printing plants already existed there by 1825. They were owned by
Sheremetev serfs and former serfs, most of whom paid a dear price for their
freedom. Some of the count's serf factory owners themselves possessed hundreds of serfs. Cottage industry, especially the weaving of textiles, also flourished in the countryside. By 1855, the overwhelming majority of weavers and
looms operated in villages, often in small peasant huts and often working for
mill owners using the "putting-out" method.

The fact that the empire's industrialists appeared from so many different
social estates—most notably nobles, peasants, and merchants—hampered their
coalescing into a capitalist class. Moreover, nationality and religion further divided them. As Blackwell has noted: "Religious outcasts, such as the Old Believers and Jews, were among the earliest of industrial capitalists and
bankers."[3] The Old Believers were significant in such industrial centers as
Moscow and Ivanovo; the Jews were significant in western provinces of the
empire and primarily in textiles and beet sugar.

The conditions of industrial workers remained harsh but probably no
worse than those of other countries in the early stages of industrialization. It
was not unusual for workers to work more than twelve hours a day—a law of
1845 attempted to limit the factory workday to twelve hours for children
under twelve but was unenforced and ineffective. Especially harsh were the
conditions of so-called "possessional" peasants, whom the government had assigned to certain factories. In his *The Russian Factory in the 19th Century*, Tugan-
Baranovsky devoted a whole chapter to their "unrest," mainly due to low pay,
in the first half of the century. Many factory owners came to prefer hired workers—often someone else's *obrok*-paying serfs—and in 1840, the government allowed owners to free possessional peasants. Many did so, further contributing
to the gradual shift from forced to hired workers.

The growth in manufacturing was interwoven with an increase in trade.
Urban and rural fairs and bazaars continued to multiply. The largest fair was
that of Nizhnii Novgorod. Throughout most of this period, it was located facing the city proper, at the confluence of the Volga and Oka rivers, and lasted
from mid-July to mid-August. There, in permanent buildings and temporary
pavilions, goods were bought and sold and various support services provided,
including religious services.

In Ukraine, the biggest of many fairs by the late 1830s was in Kharkov. J. G.
Kohl, a meticulous German observer of Russian life, estimated that by then
"independently of the merchants themselves, some 15,000 drivers, and perhaps 80,000 horses, have been required to convey the various articles of mer-
chandise in sledges to the fair."

Such large fairs were mainly for purchasing materials for resale. Textile

---

[3]William L. Blackwell, *The Industrialization of Russia: An Historical Perspective.* 3rd ed. Arlington
Heights, Ill., 1994), p. 21.

goods were usually the most important commodities, but the sale of horses often began the fairs. Numerous other items from books and bells, through food products, furs, and furnishings, to weapons and wheels also changed hands.

In the cities, extensive trade was also carried on in open-air markets, in shops, and by peddlers. A common practice was for many shops to cluster together in one large enclosed structure. In St. Petersburg, this was the Gostinii Dvor, a colossal building, fronting on the Nevsky Prospect, in which about 10,000 sellers (Kohl's estimate) offered a great array of products. In Moscow, Kohl estimated that at least 1,200 shops gathered under one roof across from Red Square facing the Kremlin. In such shops, and in buying and selling generally, prices were determined by bargaining. Only in some of the more fashionable shops, often operated by foreigners, were prices fixed. Along city streets, peddlers hawked food, drinks, toys, and other items.

Peddlers and buyers also traveled in rural areas. On foot or by wagon, they bought, sold, or bartered goods often first purchased or later sold at fairs. Often these peddlers were linked to a trading network of wealthier merchants and other peddlers.

Russia's foreign trade remained similar in many ways to that of the late eighteenth century. It continued to grow—although Russia's percentage of world trade remained about the same at a little under 4 percent—and it remained overwhelmingly in the hands of foreign traders. Russia still generally exported more than it imported. Its chief exports continued to be food products and raw materials (especially grains, flax, hemp, fat, and lard); its main imports remained manufactured and luxury goods (including nonessential foods and drinks); and its principal trading partner also stayed the same— Great Britain.

Yet, there were some new developments. The export of grains became more important, accounting for a little more than one-third of all exports by the late 1850s. As the Russian cotton and beet-sugar industries began using more modern technologies in the 1840s, more machinery and raw cotton and less yarn and sugar were imported. By 1860, machinery made up 8 percent of total imports—up from 2 percent in 1820.

With few railways by 1855, most Russian trade and travel continued to rely on horse-drawn transport and ships and boats. Kohl estimated that in the capital alone there were some 50,000 to 60,000 horses. Despite the hard-surfacing of some 5,000 miles of roads during Nicholas I's reign, the empire's roads remained in poor shape and made traveling arduous. Only snow provided much relief from mud or ruts. Water travel was facilitated, but not greatly altered, by a spurt of canal building from the late 1790s to about 1830. Russia's first steamboat was built in 1815, but only in the 1840s did steamboats begin appearing with any frequency on the Volga and then mainly for passengers, not freight. Because by the end of the 1850s only some 200 steamers sailed the Volga, most cargoes continued to be pulled up it by the back-breaking labor of hundreds of thousands of boat-haulers.

NOBLES AND PEASANTS

Because most Russian nobles and peasants continued to farm in the old ways, the gap widened in agricultural yields between Russia and Western countries adopting more advanced techniques. By the mid-nineteenth century, Russia grain yields were probably not much more than one-third the per acre yields of the latter countries. Most Russian estate owners produced food chiefly for their own needs. Even absentee noble landowners, who resided mainly in the cities, often had supplies delivered to them by sleighs and carts from their country estates.

Yet, motivated partly by a desire for luxury goods, some nobles began producing more for the open market. This was especially true in the south, where the soil was richer, and among wealthier nobles, who owned large numbers of serfs. Agricultural production also became more diversified, and crops such as sugar beets and potatoes became more important.

Nobles

Although the number of nobles increased during the early nineteenth century, their rate of growth was not as rapid as that of the rest of the population. By the late 1850s, there were about 1 million nobles (of both sexes), or roughly 1.5 percent of the population. Their total would have been larger if the government, prompted by the nobles, had not taken steps to make noble rank harder to gain.

Even though almost all serfowners of the early nineteenth century were nobles, many nobles (including an increasing number of high officials) did not possess serfs. For example, beginning early in Alexander I's reign, those who had gained nonhereditary noble status—a little more than one-third of all nobles by the end of the 1850s—were no longer allowed to buy serfs. And in 1841, nobles without landholdings were ordered to get rid of their serfs. Partly for this reason, the number of serfowners in European Russia (according to Blum's figures) declined from 127,103 to 1834 to 103,880 by 1858.

As in previous centuries, many of the serfowning nobles were far from wealthy. In the early nineteenth century, about half of them possessed between one and twenty serfs and landowners possessing such a meager number were considered poor. A Riazan noble spokesman in 1857 claimed that one-fourth of all his province's noble households were so impoverished that they lived in the same hut and ate at the same table as their serfs.

At the other end of the scale were a small number of serfowners who each owned more than 1,000 serfs. In 1834, they composed 1 percent of all serfowners and collectively possessed one-third of all serfs. They generally lived in grand style, even if beyond their means. In 1810, John Quincy Adams, then U.S. ambassador in St. Petersburg, wrote of Russian aristocratic ways as being "marked by an excess of expenses over income." Around mid-century, D. N.

A Wealthy Noble Family in Town and Country

Wealthy nobles usually possessed both landed estates and city residences. One such noble, possessing 1,200 serfs, was the father of the future anarchist rebel Peter Kropotkin (1842–1921). In his *Memoirs of a Revolutionist* (New York, 1899), pp. 28, 31, 44, 45, the younger Kropotkin describes his family's life in the late 1840s and early 1850s, in both town (Moscow) and country (their Nikolskoye estate about 160 miles from Moscow). Besides the material excerpted here, Kropotkin also mentions that every winter before Christmas, twenty-five peasant sledges would arrive at their Moscow home from the Nikolskoye estate loaded with provisions to help them make it through the winter. Ellipses are mine.

We were a family of eight, occasionally of ten or twelve; but fifty servants at Moscow, and half as many more in the country, were considered not one too many. Four coachmen to attend a dozen horses, three cooks for the masters and two more for the servants, a dozen men to wait upon us at dinner-time (one man, plate in hand, standing behind each person seated at the table), and girls innumerable in the maid-servants' room,—how could any one do with less than this? . . .

Nearly every night we had visitors. The green tables were opened in the hall for the card-players, while the ladies and the young people stayed in the reception-room or around Hélène's piano. When the ladies had gone, card-playing continued sometimes till the small hours of the morning, and considerable sums of money changed hands among the players. Father invariably lost. . . .

Dancing-parties were not infrequent, to say nothing of a couple of obligatory balls every winter. Father's way, in such cases, was to have everything done in a good style, whatever the expense. But at the same time such niggardliness was practiced in our house in daily life that if I were to recount it, I should be accused of exaggeration. . . . "The old prince," it was said, "seems to be sharp over money at home; but he knows how a nobleman ought to live." . . .

For the quiet life of the landlords of those times Nikolskoye was admirably suited. . . . Besides the main house, which father had recently built, there were, round a spacious and well-kept yard, several smaller houses. . . . An immense "upper garden" was devoted to fruit trees, and through it the church was reached; the southern slope of the land, which led to the river, was entirely given up to a pleasure garden, where flower-beds were intermingled with alleys of lime-trees, lilacs, and acacias. From the balcony of the main house there was a beautiful view of the river. . . .

Large parties were organized, also, in which all the family took part, sometimes picking mushrooms in the woods, and afterward having tea in the midst of the forest.

Sheremetev possessed both more serfs (almost 300,000 males and females) and larger debts (6 million rubles in 1859) than his profligate father had (see Chapter 16).

Besides Kropotkin, others writers such as S. Aksakov, Pushkin, Lermontov, Gogol, Herzen, Nekrasov, Saltykov-Shchedrin, Tolstoy, and Turgenev were all born into the nobility and left behind them works that shed light on the nobility of the era.

Their literary works reveal a portrait varied and insightful: From Pushkin's or Lermontov's discontented young noblemen, such as Evgeni Onegin, to innocent and pure young rural noblewomen, such as *Evgeni Onegin*'s Tatiana; from the honorable Bolkonskys and Rostovs of Tolstoy's *War and Peace* and the kindly Nikolai Kirsanov of Turgenev's *Fathers and Sons* to the less lovable, sometimes downright dislikable, provincial nobles of Gogol's *Dead Souls* or Saltykov-Shchedrin's *The Golovlevs*.

Along with the miserliness and boorish provincial backwardness satirized by the last-mentioned two writers, literature also often depicted nobles leading a superficial, superfluous, and slothful life. One notable such depiction was by a man born into the merchant class. This was Ivan Goncharov's *Oblomov* (1859). It takes the fictional Oblomov the entire first chapter to get out of his bed in the morning. Almost immediately the term *Oblomovshchina* (Oblomovism) was coined to characterize such noble slothfulness.

Despite the poverty of some nobles, the nobility was truly a privileged estate. Speransky thought of it as "a handful of idlers who, God knows why and to what end, have grabbed all the rights and advantages."[4] They were not subject to direct taxes or military recruitment. Despite some merchant landholding by 1855, the nobles, along with the royal family and state, still owned almost all the land in the empire and were lord and master over their serfs. And despite an increasing number of "outsiders" such as Speransky, men born of noble parents dominated the upper military and governmental ranks. Certain schools, such as the Imperial Corps of Pages and the lyceum at Tsarskoe Selo, were established to prepare noble sons for such eventual service. Partly as a result of government policies aimed at giving them privileged educational access, nobles also dominated the world of literature and ideas.

Such a privileged life produced, at least for some wealthier nobles, not only a life of nannies and tutors, of city clubs, balls, gambling, and carousing, of hunting and other pleasures on their country estates, and of travel abroad, but also it contributed to a climate that fostered eccentric behavior. There was, for example, the nobleman Fedor Tolstoi, who took a pet ape with him on a Pacific Ocean expedition, during the course of which he had himself covered with tattoos. On another occasion, he displayed his marksmanship by firing through the heel of the shoe of his wife (a gypsy singer) as she stood on a table.

Because of property divisions among many heirs, poor soil, insufficient serfs, backward agricultural techniques, poor estate management, and profligate ways—in various combinations—many nobles found it necessary to supplement estate income. Entering civil and military service, selling land and serfs, and borrowing from the government were a few such ways. Leo Tol-

[4]Cited in Daniel Field, *The End of Serfdom: Nobility and Bureaucracy in Russia, 1855–1861* (Cambridge, Mass., 1976), p. 8.

FIGURE 20.2. Nobles gambling away serfs (as depicted in a French book, 1854).
(From Otto Hoetzsch, The Evolution of Russia, *#108, p. 128. Harcourt, Brace & World, 1966
[© Thames & Hudson of London].)*

stoy's paternal grandfather (who sent linen to Holland for cleaning) took the
post as governor of Kazan to help meet his many expenses. Leo himself sold
some land, serfs, and even the house he was born in to pay off gambling debts.

The nobles' dependence on the government for jobs, loans, and maintaining serfdom hindered them from developing greater corporate political power.
Often gone from their estates, they displayed little of the local authority often
evidenced by other European nobles. On the national level, nobles were more
concerned with competing for ranks and favors and maintaining their privileges than with demanding more political power.

By mid-century, some enlightened bureaucrats (who were nobles by rank,
whether born to the nobility or not) were highly critical of serfowning
landowners. Other nobles, including the writer Turgenev (himself a wealthy
serfowner), were critical of both the government and the majority of their more
conservative fellow serfowners. This division among nobles was symptomatic
of Nicholas's reign. From its beginning, with men from some leading noble
families such as the Volkonskys and Trubetskois being involved in and punished for Decembrist plotting, divisiveness among the nobility had been on the
increase. By 1855, the Russian nobility was much less cohesive than it had been
under Catherine the Great, and aristocratic serfowning families were a less
dominant political force.

Peasants

Peasants continued to be the backbone of Russia. By 1855, five of every six inhabitants in European Russia were still peasants. By then, however, the serfs had become a slight minority of all peasants.

About the living standards of serfs and other peasants in this era, it is difficult to generalize. As population increased and good land became scarce, the size of serf allotments declined in many areas, but regional variations, increased agricultural prices, and opportunities for supplemental income—usually greater in the north—must also be taken into account.

In contrast to Jerome Blum, who cited sharp decreases in land allotments in several provinces, Steven Hoch, in his detailed examination of the Petrovskoe estate in southern Tambov (in the black-earth belt), found little change. From 1810 to the late 1850s, in exchange for labor on the master's strips, the estate continued to allot about fifteen acres of plowland strips—not counting those left fallow—to a serf and his wife. Each household, usually larger than a nuclear family, also had a garden, whose size varied but generally seems to have been a few acres. Other indices of serf living standards—such as their livestock holdings—remained fairly consistent for the Petrovskoe serfs except for crises years resulting from exceptionally bad weather. In normal years, according to Hoch, these serfs ate better than French or Belgian peasants had at the turn of the century.

As the nineteenth century progressed, however, Russia's ability to curtail "crises years" fell further behind that of Western European countries. Years of serious Russian grain deficiencies were more common from 1830 to 1855 than earlier in the century, reinforcing the perception that serf economic conditions deteriorated under Nicholas I.

Although the allotments of Petrovskoe serfs did not decline like many in the north, they were probably less fortunate than most northern serfs regarding housing. Forests and woodlands were less abundant than further north, and most Petrovskoe households, averaging about eight persons, had huts of less than 500 square feet, plus unheated structures for storage and other purposes. Even in areas rich with timber, most serfs and other peasants spent their winters in one heated, crowded room.

The center of serf and other peasant life throughout the country remained the village and the commune—in central Russia, still mainly the repartitional commune (see Chapter 16). Villages varied in size from a few households to many hundreds. Larger villages usually had a church of their own, plus other buildings like a tavern. If the village was composed of serfs, they might be owned by different serfowners. Each village was most often represented by a single commune, but one commune sometimes represented more than one village or just a portion of one, with one or more other communes representing the other villagers. Although nineteenth-century intellectuals coined the term *obshchina* for commune, peasants used the word *mir*, and it was no accident that it also meant "the universe." Despite the increasing movement of peasants to cities and other areas, looking for temporary work, the village and commune remained the essence of most peasants' world. And villagers tended to be suspicious of outsiders.

Serfowners or their stewards generally dealt with the communes and not with individual serfs, and the heads of households in a commune elected their own communal officials. Although serfowners or their surrogates could punish their serfs by beatings or having them exiled to Siberia, it was in the owners' interest to obtain as much cooperation as possible from the communes.

Because a serfowner needed serf cooperation to run a successful estate, serfs were not completely powerless. They could be made to work for the lord but not with 100 percent effort. If they felt he was being unjust, they could use many stratagems to give much less: foot dragging, stealing, lying, work stoppages, fleeing, petitioning higher authorities, and occasionally even open rebellion or murder.

Even under normal serf conditions, it would not be surprising if a serf poached or stole wood from his master's lands—if he believed he would not be caught—or (if under *barshchina*) he worked harder on his own allotment than on the lord's lands. If serfs believed that a master was imposing new, unfair conditions or going beyond what they considered normal or customary, they frequently resorted to extraordinary means. Such new conditions might be an increase in the serfs' *obrok* or *barshchina* or the failure of a master to reduce his demands when a major crop failure occurred. (In recompense for the bonds of serfdom, serfs believed that a master should at least be charitable in times of disaster, and, indeed, according to custom and law, he was supposed to provide for them when catastrophe left them helpless.)

Serfs were generally suspicious of innovations imposed by a master, fearing the changes would harm them. Even when he wished to change his serfs' conditions for the better, they often distrusted and frustrated his goals—a phenomenon the young Leo Tolstoy discovered and captured in his story, "A Landowner's Morning."

Although there were no massive revolts in the early nineteenth century, the number of small-scale serf and other peasant disturbances (*volneniia*) increased significantly. If the 60 years between 1796 and 1855 are broken into four 15-year periods, each successive period witnessed more officially recorded disturbances than the preceding one.

Besides the specific actions of serfowners or their stewards, another major cause of many disturbances was the rumor that the tsar wished to free the peasants but that the serfowners were blocking his will. It helped lead to over 100 disturbances per year in 1797 and 1826, both years immediately following the accession of a new tsar.

The first step aggrieved serfs often took against a landowner was to have a communal petition prepared and then hand-carried to a higher authority, usually on a local or provincial level but occasionally to the tsar himself. Serfs also might refuse to work for their landowner. In case of serious trouble, local authorities, and sometimes troops, were often brought in to restore a master's authority. Although a disturbance was often ended before any deaths occurred, if they did occur, the victims were most likely to be serfs. From 1835 to 1854, less than 200 owners or stewards were recorded as having been killed in such outbreaks.

Among other peasant groups, the state peasants were by far the largest, and by the late 1850s, they alone outnumbered the serfs in the empire. Although their lot was certainly better than that of the serfs and further improved in some respects after Nicholas I placed the reform-minded General Kiselev over them (see Chapter 19), it is more difficult to generalize about any changes in their living standards. They certainly suffered, like others, from the more frequent "crises years" that occurred under Nicholas I. Moreover, their delinquency rate on paying taxes increased greatly during the last twelve years of Nicholas's reign, which might suggest a reduced capacity to meet their obligations. Yet peasants in general were buying significantly larger quantities of manufactured goods at the end of this era than they were at the beginning.

Although state peasants were responsible for only about one-sixth as many disturbances as the serfs, they shared the serfs' distrust of innovations imposed from above. The changes introduced by Kiselev's reforms, including his efforts to have them grow potatoes, spurred the most unrest and clashes with government troops.

EATING AND DRINKING; FAMINES AND DISEASES

The peasants' eating habits remained basically the same as they had for many centuries.[5] Grains, especially rye, were the basis of not only home-baked bread—the main item of their diet—but also of other foods such as *kasha* (porridge). Vegetables from their gardens, especially cabbages and cucumbers, were second in importance. The most popular Great Russian soup was *shchi* (cabbage soup)—Kohl called it their "chief national dish." Up until General Kiselev mandated potato-growing among the state peasants in the early 1840s, the potato was of minor significance. Despite strong peasant resistance, however, potato production increased fivefold between 1840 and 1843. Mushrooms and berries were the most often-gathered foods and, like some vegetables, were sometimes preserved.

Although variations of wealth, possessions, and food intake certainly existed among the peasantry, most peasants possessed at least some animals. In the Tambov province, peasant households typically owned at least a few horses and cows and slightly more pigs, sheep, and domestic fowl. Horses were the most common plow animals. Hoch has written that meat was available at least weekly for the serfs of Petrovskoe, but in more northern provinces weekly meat-eating was less common among the peasants, although animal fat used in cooking helped supplement their diets. Dairy products were an-

[5]For Russian food and drink customs, I am strongly indebted to R. E. F. Smith and David Christian, *Bread and Salt: A Social and Economic History of Food and Drink in Russia* (Cambridge, England, 1984).

other supplement but not as commonly consumed as in Western Europe. Fish was eaten especially during fasting periods and by people near rivers and lakes or by those who could afford it at markets.

Diets were greatly affected by seasonal changes and the Orthodox Church calendar, which continued to mandate many fast days (see Chapter 7). Food was most available in the late summer and early autumn, which was appropriate, for this was the harvest season, when most energy was needed. Once winter set in, food became more scarce, and matters got worse in the spring as food supplies dwindled. It was fitting that the winter-spring months were the period of greatest fasting, including the Lenten Great Fast.

The drinking habits of the Russians remained much as they had been. The barely alcoholic kvas remained the most common everyday drink—water being too impure and regular tea-drinking still too expensive for the average peasant. The chief drink for special occasions remained vodka (spirits or distilled alcohol). Beer-drinking was much less common, although it increased as one traveled west in the empire toward the Baltic provinces and Congress Poland. Although beer consumption was higher per capita in the Belorussian and Ukrainian provinces than in Great Russia, so also was vodka-drinking. Vodka was more affordable and available in these provinces, partly because of greater competition. In Great Russia, liquor dealers, leasing the right to sell from the government, monopolized its sale throughout most of this period.

As in earlier centuries, the profits of the government and liquor profiteers, including noblemen, remained more important than any moral concerns about the ill effects of alcohol. Liquor revenues in this period continued to provide roughly 30 percent of all regular government income. About all that government officials were willing to do was suggest more moderate regular consumption as opposed to excessive occasional drinking. But such suggestions flew in the face of custom, for vodka drinking was primarily for special occasions and for getting drunk and could not be regularly afforded by the masses.

Russians and foreign observers alike made frequent mention of the country's drinking problem. An aide to General Kiselev who investigated the lives of peasants wrote that drunkenness was one of the chief causes of peasant poverty. The Marquis de Custine wrote: "The greatest pleasure of the people is drunkenness." He added, however, that "unlike the drunkards of our country, who quarrel and fight, they [the peasants] weep and embrace each other." Although such generalizations must be regarded with caution, the observant German Kohl made similar comments, although admitting that occasional quarrels did occur.

Observers of the time speak less commonly of famine, but it occurred. The worst years on a national scale were 1821–1822, 1832–1834, and 1848–1850. Spring frosts and drought were the chief causes of the bad harvests that made food more scarce and expensive. Locusts also destroyed part of the 1822 crop. At such times, people ate substances such as tree bark, straw, and pine cones. Although no accurate estimate of famine death exists, the number must have been considerable. National population growth figures and more local evidence—including Hoch's account of the Petrovskoe serfs in Tambov—certainly suggest large losses.

Some areas were hit harder than others. In 1848, the Penza province, northeast of Tambov, was especially unfortunate. That year, its net harvest of grains and potatoes was only one-twentieth of what it would be in 1851. Generally the south-southeastern steppe areas of European Russia were most susceptible to drought.

Although bad weather was the chief cause of famine, it was not the only one. Russia's relatively low yields, widespread impoverishment, transportation difficulties, and insufficient emergency supplies—despite government efforts to increase grain reserves for emergencies—all made coping more difficult when food shortages developed.

The 1848–1850 famine struck at a time when the cholera epidemic of 1847–1849 was taking more than 750,000 lives in the empire. The cause of this bacterial disease, transmitted by impure water and food, was then unknown. Like another catastrophe 600 years earlier—the Mongols—it appeared first in the south (this time in 1823 in the Caspian Sea area) and then reappeared (1829–1833) after some years to strike the country a major blow. This first cholera epidemic killed about 250,000 people and was part of a global outbreak that began in 1816 and lasted for two decades. Ineffective government measures sparked riots in some areas. Besides the major epidemics of 1829–1833 and 1848–1850, cholera claimed additional lives in many other years after 1823.

One of the most hard-hit cities was St. Petersburg. Official figures, perhaps low, placed the cholera deaths in 1848 at about 12,000, one-thirty-sixth of the capital's population. Many who did not die and were able to leave the city did so. With its canals and rivers, polluted by human and other wastes, and its frequent floods, St. Petersburg was a natural breeder of diseases such as cholera. In the 1850s, the city's death rate greatly outnumbered its birth rate.

Luckily for Russia, the bubonic plague outbreaks that had so troubled the country in previous centuries became less serious in the nineteenth century, partly because of more effective government policies. Rarely now did the plague kill more than a 1,000 people in any single year.

WOMEN AND FAMILY LIFE

The 1836 Code of Russian Laws read, "The woman must obey her husband, reside with him in love, respect, and unlimited obedience, and offer him every pleasantness and affection as the ruler of the household."[6] Although a woman was not supposed to be married against her will, it certainly occurred. After marriage, the power that her father possessed—to decide if, when, and where she could study, travel, or work—now fell to her husband. If he beat her, the law gave her no recourse unless she was seriously injured. A divorce, especially for those considered Orthodox Christians, was possible only in unusual

---

[6]Cited in Richard Stites, *The Women's Liberation Movement in Russia: Feminism, Nihilism, and Bolshevism, 1860–1930* (Princeton, 1978), pp. 6–7.

circumstances, such as proven adultery or lengthy abandonment of one's spouse. Nor could Orthodox Christians legally separate. Of course, such strict divorce and separation laws offered married women some safeguards as well as constraints.

Although marriages were more difficult to disband in Russia than in Western Europe, Russian property and inheritance laws were generally more favorable to women than were European codes, especially those influenced by the Code Napoleon. For example, Russian women retained the rights to any dowry property brought into a marriage, and a nonpeasant widow was generally entitled to receive one-seventh of her husband's landed property.

The lot of Russian peasant women was more difficult, and not only in regard to property rights. A peasant proverb stated: "A hen is not a bird, a woman is not a person."

Several studies suggest that most Russian peasant women still married before age twenty; women who did not marry were few and treated with contempt. These marriages were commonly arranged by parents with the help of matchmakers.

Once married, the wife went to live with her husband, generally in his parents' hut. There she was subject not only to her husband, but also to her father-in-law, who ruled supreme over the whole household, and to her mother-in-law, who supervised the female household duties. At worst, the young wife might have to suffer considerable abuse, including forced sexual relations with her father-in-law (a practice called *snokhachestvo*). Yet, even when young hus-

FIGURE 20.3. An aristocratic wedding, around 1800. The crowning of the couple is a traditional part of Orthodox weddings.
(From Robert Wallace and the Editors of Time-Life Books, Rise of Russia. Time Inc., New York, 1967, p. 148. Courtesy of the Free Library of Philadelphia, Rare Book Department.)

bands were gone for long periods of time—for example, to work in a city—this practice was likely much more the exception than the rule.

Even in a good household or in one in which she had no father-in-law and mother-in-law, a peasant woman still had a hard life, working at her many tasks (see Chapter 16). If she later became a mother-in-law herself, a wife still possessed only the authority her husband was willing to grant her. And it could not have been easy to help keep peace in a large household—but small hut—which might include several daughters-in-law and many grandchildren.

Because of high male death rates (partly due to military service), Russian villages contained many widows. In his study of the serfs of one large estate in the Tver Province, Rodney Bohac found that in seven censuses between 1813 and 1851 serf households containing widows averaged almost 30 percent of the total. On the estate in 1851, 17 percent of the serf women over age twenty were widows.

Ample evidence, including many peasant proverbs, indicates that the life of a peasant widow was often difficult. What she inherited from her husband varied greatly, depending especially on her circumstances and the will of the commune, which in some cases exploited her. If childless, she might receive nothing and return to her parents. Otherwise, she might receive one-seventh of the household property or become a trustee over the inheritance of minor sons. In either case, she often remained with her in-laws, who might be reluctant to let her return to her parents or remarry because it would reduce total household property. Conversely, however, communes and serfowners often encouraged or pressured widows to remarry, especially if they were still young enough to produce more children.

Despite strong handicaps, some widows, especially older ones, became household heads, even though one or more adult sons lived in the household. Although as heads they sometimes participated and voted in *mir* assemblies, they were seldom treated as true equals. Attitudes like those expressed in the proverb "A woman is like a mindless bird" explain why.

The lives of other women varied considerably according to their social backgrounds and occupations, ranging from being a nun to being a prostitute. Some were urban workers in industries such as textiles or tobacco, and at the end of this period, during the Crimean War, 163 women became "sisters of mercy" (nurses). One extraordinary woman, Nadezhda Durova, disguised herself as a young man, served with distinction as a cavalry officer against Napoleon, and decades later published her journals describing her adventures.

More noblewomen now received "finishing-school" education at female institutes modeled on St. Petersburg's Smolny Institute. Some cultured women presided over salons, as did Caroline Pavlova (1807–1893), who was also an excellent, but then unappreciated, poet. By the 1840s and 1850s, women such as Avdotia Panaeva were following the lead of France's most famous woman novelist, George Sand. In her writings, Panaeva dealt with injustices suffered by women, and in her life she followed the example of Sand's heroines, who believed in following the promptings of the heart. Despite her marriage to I. Panaev, she lived with his fellow editor, the poet Nikolai Nekrasov.

Sand's influence was widespread by then, and Westernizers such as Bakunin, Belinsky, and Herzen greatly admired Sand's ideas and became critical of marriage as an institution. To some, Sand's women now became more heroic than Pushkin's heroine Tatiana (in *Evgeni Onegin*), who in the end rejects Evgeni, whom she still loves, and remains faithful to her husband.

Overall, however, Russia remained an overwhelmingly patriarchal society, and this affected child-rearing practices as much as male-female relationships. To many, the precepts of the sixteenth-century guidebook, the *Domostroi*, remained the best guide for the treatment of children. Like this book, many peasant proverbs advocated harsh discipline for children, including beatings when necessary.

Shortly after birth, Russian children of all classes were bound by tight swaddling clothes—a condition that generally lasted six months to a year. Although done for mistaken health reasons, swaddling was a foretaste of other types of parental constraint that would follow. A folk proverb stated: "When the earth receives the parents, the children receive their freedom."

This was especially true for male peasants, who often remained under the father's roof and authority until he died. Peasant children, whether male or female, were born, usually in a bathhouse, into a harsh world. About half of Great Russia's children died before age six, and such an appalling high death rate continued throughout the century. As David Ransel has pointed out, it was due to both unhealthy conditions and certain peasant attitudes toward children.

A child's exposure to unsanitary conditions began from the time a midwife with unclean hands began helping the mother give birth. From then on, an unclean environment surrounded the child, who was soon placed in a cradle in a hut that was often filled with smoke or flies. Some diseases that killed children were the same that killed adults and, like cholera, were connected with unsanitary practices. Children also died in great numbers as a result of their own unique circumstances.

Because peasant mothers had to work in the fields, especially during the summer, infants were often not breast-fed during the day and were sometimes watched over by a young child or left alone. To pacify and nourish infants, they were given partially chewed food covered in cloth. The dangers to the baby of such a practice included catching germs from the food-chewer, the food spoiling while the baby was still sucking on it, or the cloth breaking, leaving the baby to ingest, and perhaps choke, on the food. Partly because breast milk was believed insufficient sustenance for babies, even when the mother was available, they also often received solid food long before their systems could handle it.

Because of frequent pregnancies, the high death rates for children, and certain cultural attitudes—like an emphasis on the collective rather than the individual—the death of a child was taken more in stride than in many other cultures. In fact, it even seems likely that unhealthy, crippled, or illegitimate children that were considered a burden on the family were neglected more than others. Ransel has noted that in a certain town in the Novgorod Province, between 1836 and 1855, not one out of more than 2,000 illegitimate children survived.

The growing number of infants deposited in the foundling homes of St. Petersburg and Moscow also suggested that many children were unwanted, often because of illegitimacy or a family's impoverished condition. At the St. Petersburg Foundling Home in the early 1850s, the admittance rate was well over a third of the number of births in the city. Even though not all admitted infants were born in the city, the overwhelming proportion probably were. This proportion of admittances and births was not unusual for the era of Nicholas I. The death rates of those admitted, especially among the majority who were "farmed out" to village peasants, continued to be appallingly high.

Children of peasants and many urban dwellers were put to work as soon as possible. On city streets, children peddled a variety of wares, and other youngsters, including some foundlings, worked in factories and shops. Not until 1845 did a law restrict child factory labor, and then only for children twelve and under, who could still work all day but no longer after midnight.

LAWS, COURTS, AND PUNISHMENT

The *Digest of the Laws of the Russian Empire* published under Nicholas I made clear what had long been the case: Different laws and punishments applied to different social estates. And within these estates, other legal distinctions existed, for example, in the peasant estate between serfs and state peasants.

With few exceptions, serfowners had the final say in determining the law for their serfs, although they frequently allowed the commune and its customs to decide specific cases. State peasants also settled many differences according to custom, with the village elder or assembly often making the final decision. Although there were already courts specially designed for disputes between state peasants, Kiselev's reforms of the late 1830s attempted to strengthen them and make them more responsive to peasant needs. Peasant judges were to be elected by the peasantry on both the village and the canton (*volost*) level—with the canton court acting as a court of appeal. The peasant courts were to rule according to peasant customs. Yet, despite Kiselev's intentions, these peasant courts were often corrupted by local administrative interference, and many peasants distrusted them.

On all levels of the court system, Russian administrators, including governors, left their stamp, and the courts protected their interests more than those of the people. The police, court secretaries, and bribes also affected court decisions and judges, who were overwhelmingly without any legal training and often illiterate.

In a criminal case, the accused could be jailed indefinitely, pending the police investigation and preparation of written proofs. Confession remained the "queen of proofs." Although Alexander I and Nicholas I prohibited the use of torture to help obtain it, there is little doubt that strong pressures were sometimes applied to encourage confession. The accused had no right to a legal defense or counsel and was not even permitted access to judges, who deliberated and arrived at verdicts in secret.

Once convicted, a person could appeal to a higher court, but this was generally a lengthy process, and a failed appeal could bring a harsher sentence. The dependence on written materials, bureaucratic red tape, and a shortage of adequate personnel and financing greatly hampered the Russian court system, whether in criminal or civil cases. The latter sometimes stretched out over many years, and in 1842 there were more than 3 million undecided cases before the courts.

Although serfowners had serfs fined, beaten, or assigned extra work for such offenses as drunkenness and brawling, the government generally exiled major criminal offenders, of all social estates, to Siberia. For some nonnobles, such as serfs who led revolts against their masters, exile often followed a beating. And exile often included imprisonment or forced labor. Although the experiences of many Decembrists and later Dostoevsky—who recounted his Siberian prison experiences in his *The House of the Dead*—are best known, the great majority of exiles to Siberia were murderers, robbers, and thieves. Official figures of the Exile Bureau at Tobolsk indicate that almost 80,000 criminals were sent to Siberia from 1827 to 1846.

Although both Alexander I and Nicholas I approached law in a fairly traditional manner, there was—as Richard Wortman has noted—a growing legal consciousness in Russia during this era. Although the government hoped to use law to strengthen and systematize its authority, its encouragement of the study of jurisprudence did not always have the desired effect. Many professors and students of law came to think of it as more of a science, with its own rules and dictates, rather than simply a tool of the government.

Most law students studied at either the Imperial School of Jurisprudence, founded in 1835, or at one of Russia's universities, especially Moscow University. Among those who taught law at this largest of Russian universities were two moderate Westernizers and Hegelians, Peter Redkin and Constantine Kavelin. Redkin, who had studied in Germany, gave an introductory lecture in which he stated: "There is nothing higher than truth and science is its prophet. But like everything sacred and great in the world truth demands selflessness and self-renunciation. Take your cross and come to me."[7]

Even some officials who had not formally studied law came to regard it in a similar way. The most outstanding of these individuals was Sergei Zarudnyi, an idealistic Ukrainian who had studied mathematics at Kharkov University before going to work in the Ministry of Justice. He was yet another example of the increasing number of college-educated individuals who entered civil service under Nicholas I, some of whom became influential "enlightened bureaucrats." He taught himself law, including some Western law, while working in the ministry. In the 1860s, he spearheaded Alexander II's judicial reform.

---

[7]Cited in Richard Wortman, *The Development of Russian Legal Consciousness* (Chicago, 1976), p. 224.

SUGGESTED SOURCES*

ALEXANDER, JOHN T. "Plague epidemics," *MERSH* 28: 100–108.

BARTLETT, ROGER, ed. *Land Commune and Peasant Community in Russia: Communal Forms in Imperial and Early Soviet Society.* New York, 1990.

BATER, JAMES H. *St. Petersburg: Industrialization and Change.* Montreal, 1976.

BLACKWELL, WILLIAM L. *The Beginnings of Russian Industrialization, 1800–1860.* Princeton, 1968.

BLUM, JEROME. *Lord and Peasant in Russia, from the Ninth to the Nineteenth Century.* Princeton, 1961.

BOHAC, RANDY. "Widows and the Russian Serf Community." In *Russia's Women: Accommodation, Resistance, Transformation,* eds. Barbara Evans Clements, Barbara Alpern Engel, and Christine D. Worobec. Berkeley, 1991.

BROWER, DANIEL R. *The Russian City between Tradition and Modernity, 1850–1900.* Berkeley, 1990.

CRISP, OLGA. *Studies in the Russian Economy Before 1914.* New York, 1976.

CUSTINE, MARQUIS DE. *Empire of the Czar: A Journey through Eternal Russia.* New York, 1989.

DUROVA, NADEZHDA. *The Cavalry Maiden: Journals of a Russian Officer in the Napoleonic Wars.* Bloomington, 1988.

FALKUS, MALCOLM E. *The Industrialisation of Russia, 1700–1914.* London, 1972.

FEDOR, THOMAS S. *Patterns of Urban Growth in the Russian Empire during the Nineteenth Century.* Chicago, 1975.

FITZPATRICK, ANNE L. *The Great Russian Fair: Nizhnii Novgorod, 1840–90.* New York, 1990.

GATRELL, PETER. *The Tsarist Economy, 1850–1917.* New York, 1986.

HAMM, MICHAEL F. *Kiev: A Portrait, 1800–1917.* Princeton, 1993.

———, ed. *The City in Late Imperial Russia.* Bloomington, 1986.

———, ed. *The City in Russian History.* Lexington, Ky., 1976.

HOCH, STEVEN L. *Serfdom and Social Control in Russia: Petrovskoe, A Village in Tambov.* Chicago, 1986.

KAHAN, ARCADIUS. *Russian Economic History: The Nineteenth Century.* Chicago, 1989.

KINGSTON-MANN, ESTHER, and TIMOTHY MIXTER, eds. *Peasant Economy, Culture, and Politics of European Russia, 1800–1921.* Princeton, 1990.

KOHL, J. G. *Russia.* London, 1844 (Reprint, New York, 1970).

KOLCHIN, PETER. *Unfree Labor: American Slavery and Russian Serfdom.* Cambridge, Mass., 1987.

LEDONNE, JOHN P. "Criminal Investigations before the Great Reforms," *RH* 1 (1974): 101–118.

LEWIN, MOSHE. "Customary Law and Russian Rural Society in the Postreform Era," *RR* 44 (January 1985): 1–43.

MCGREW, RODERICK E. "Cholera in Russia," *MERSH* 7: 73–77.

RANSEL, DAVID L. "Infant-Care Cultures in the Russian Empire." In *Russia's Women: Accommodation, Resistance, Transformation,* eds. Barbara Evans Clements, Barbara Alpern Engel, and Christine D. Worobec. Berkeley, 1991.

———. *Mothers of Misery: Child Abandonment in Russia.* Princeton, 1988.

*See also works cited in footnotes and in boxed insert.

————, ed. *The Family in Imperial Russia: New Lines of Historical Research*. Urbana, 1978.

RIEBER, ALFRED J. *Merchants and Entrepreneurs in Imperial Russia*. Chapel Hill, N.C., 1982.

VUCINICH, WAYNE, ed. *The Peasant in Nineteenth-Century Russia*. Stanford, 1968.

WILMOT, MARTHA, and CATHERINE WILMOT. *The Russian Journals of Martha and Catherine Wilmot, 1803–1808*. London, 1934.

WOROBEC, CHRISTINE. *Peasant Russia: Family and Community in the Post-Emancipation Period*. Princeton, 1991.

CHAPTER 21

Religion and Culture, 1796–1855

As earlier, religious and educational developments were strongly influenced by government policy. The state also exercised major influence over art and architecture, primarily by its control over the St. Petersburg Academy of Fine Arts and by its granting of commissions. And it attempted to reign over literature by censorship and its treatment of writers. Some it favored, some it exiled, and one—the promising young poet Kondrati Ryleev—it executed for his part in the Decembrist conspiracy. Western cultural movements and study abroad affected many Russian writers and artists. Western influence on Russia and, partly in reaction, Russia's search for its own roots and uniqueness became central cultural issues.

Yet, as significant as government policies, Western influences, and the reaction to them were for the era's religion and culture, they did not provide the vital force, the breath of life, that made this period such a rich one in Russian cultural history. That came from individuals, including Alexander Pushkin, Nikolai Gogol, and Mikhail Glinka, whose minds were fed by both Western influences and the rich traditions of their own country.

RELIGION

In the final years of Alexander I's reign and throughout that of Nicholas I, the state displayed little religious toleration. Nicholas's curtailment of Catholic Uniate rights was perhaps the most dramatic example of this intolerance. Usually, government methods were more subtle, such as increasing the economic incentives for non-Russians who converted to Orthodoxy. In 1849, for example, the government decreed a lifelong exemption from the soul tax, a six-year exemption from other taxes, and a monetary reward of up to 30 rubles for anyone who converted among the *inorodtsy*—a category including many eastern nationalities such as the Volga Tatars.

But the government's championing of Orthodoxy and its discrimination against non-Orthodox religions often failed to win permanent converts. Many Moslems who converted to Christianity soon returned to Islam. Despite new measures that Nicholas took against Old Believers and sectarians, their numbers remained large. In 1859, the Ministry of Interior estimated that their true number was about 9.3 million, more than ten times the official figure.

From 1836 until 1855, Nicholas I relied on a former army officer, N. A. Pratasov, to oversee the Orthodox Church. As procurator of the Holy Synod, he strengthened the power of his office while weakening the role of the Synod's clerical hierarchy.

Although government policies tightened state control over religions, including Orthodoxy, they did little to strengthen the Orthodox faith. By 1855, despite some positive Orthodox developments, dissatisfaction with the condition of the Orthodox Church and the state's religious policies was widespread among educated people.

Bishops were most concerned with their loss of power to Procurator Pratasov and other lay government officials. Even some strong lay supporters of Orthodoxy and autocracy, such as the historian M. P. Pogodin, believed church reforms were needed. In early 1855, he encouraged a parish priest, I. S. Belliustin, to write a description of the clergy's condition. After the priest did so and the manuscript was published abroad a few years later, it stimulated a debate in the Russian press.

Although ignoring the state's increased control over the Orthodox Church, which was at the root of some church problems, Belliustin strongly criticized many aspects of church life. He thought the education and housing conditions at ecclesiastical schools, which were open only to the sons of clergy, were woefully inadequate. He decried the dominance of the unmarried, black (monastic) clergy, who alone could become members of the church hierarchy. He thought that the parish priests' lack of any regular salary and dependence on fees for certain religious services led to corruption and the people's hatred of their priests. And this hatred, in turn, stimulated hostility to religion and perpetuated spiritual ignorance. Belliustin wrote: "Our *Orthodox* folk, and I say this without the slightest exaggeration, do not have the *remotest conception of anything spiritual.*"[1]

Although Belliustin was critical of Westernizers like Belinsky and did not share his negative views on autocracy and Orthodoxy, some of this parish priest's criticisms call to mind Belinsky's famous letter to Gogol (see Chapter 19 and p. 397).

Like Belinsky, many other intellectuals, although being baptized into Orthodoxy, no longer felt any allegiance to it. Some searched for new religious answers. The writer Leo Tolstoy, while serving in the Crimean War, noted in his diary that he felt capable of devoting his life to the founding of a new religion based on Christ's teachings, but one seeking happiness on this earth and free from church dogma and mysteries.

[1] I. S. Belliustin, *Description of the Clergy in Rural Russia: The Memoir of a Nineteenth-Century Parish Priest,* translated with an Interpretive Essay by Gregory L. Freeze (Ithaca, N.Y., 1985), p. 125; italics are Belliustin's.

Belinsky's Criticism of the Orthodox Church

Vissarion Belinsky's 1847 letter to Niko-lai Gogol remained unpublished until Alexander Herzen published it abroad in 1855. Even before this, however, it circulated in thousands of underground copies, although circulating it was a se-rious crime—it was, for example, one of the government charges against Dosto-evsky in 1849. Ivan Aksakov, a member of the Slavophile camp opposed to Be-linsky, wrote in 1856: "There is not a single high-school teacher in the guber-nia towns who does not know Belin-sky's letter to Gogol by heart." This quotation and the following excerpt from the letter are taken from V. G. Belinsky, *Selected Philosophical Works* (Moscow: Foreign Languages Publish-ing House, 1948), pp. 506–507, 530. Brackets and ellipses are mine.

It [the Orthodox Church] has always served as the prop of the knout and the servant of despotism; but why have you mixed Christ up in this? What in common have you found between Him and any church, least of all the Orthodox Church? . . . Do you really mean to say you do not know that our clergy is held in universal contempt by Russian society and the Russian people? Of whom do the Russian people relate obscene stories? Of the priest, the priest's wife, the priest's daughter, and the priest's farm hand. Does not the priest in Russia repre-sent for all Russians the embodiment of gluttony, avarice, servility and shameless-ness? Do you mean to say that you do not know all this? Strange! According to you the Russian people is the most religious in the world. That is a lie! The basis of reli-giousness is pietism, reverence, fear of God. . . .

Take a closer look and you will see that it [the Russian people] is by nature a pro-foundly atheistic people. It still retains a good deal of superstition, but not a trace of religiousness. . . . Religiousness with us ap-peared only among the Schismatic sects who formed such a contrast in spirit to the mass of the people.

Yet, along with such alienation from traditional Russian Orthodoxy, there were also signs of Orthodox renewal. Theology advanced, both in clerical quarters such as the four theological academies of St. Petersburg, Moscow, Kiev, and Kazan, and among some educated laymen. It was stimulated both by earlier Orthodox thinkers and by recent Western philosophical ideas.

The most important lay contribution was made by the Slavophile Alexei Khomiakov (1804–1860), sometimes called Russia's first original theologian. His most significant idea—and one that influenced later thinkers like Dosto-evsky—was that of *sobornost* (conciliarism). According to Khomiakov, the Catholic Church had overemphasized unity and authority at the expense of freedom, and the Protestant churches in reaction had overemphasized individ-ualism. The Orthodox Church, however, had maintained *sobornost*, or the free unity of its members through a love grounded on the love of Christ. Although mindful of the harm state interference in church affairs had caused in Russia, Khomiakov believed it had not undermined the essential nature of Orthodoxy.

Russian monasticism was reinvigorated by the disciples of Paissi Veli-chkovsky (1722–1794), a Ukrainian who had studied at Mount Athos in Greece and later became the head of a monastery in Moldavia. From there, his followers brought to Russia his contemplative and mystical ideas, the practice of living under a common (cenobitic) rule and obeying a *starets* (a wise elder), and some translations of long-neglected works of early Eastern Orthodox thinkers.

A monastery greatly influenced by these followers was Optina, located in the Kaluga Province, south of Moscow. It became known for its *startsi* (elders), especially Leonid and Makari—and later in the century, Ambrose. In the late 1840s, Makari became, and remained thereafter, the main spiritual guide of one of the chief Slavophiles, Ivan Kireevsky (1806–1856). During this period, Makari and Kireevsky collaborated in publishing a number of Eastern Orthodox spiritual works. Although not relying primarily on Makari for spiritual guidance, the writer Gogol also visited Optina and conferred with him. As the nineteenth century proceeded, more such laypersons turned to the *startsi* for advice.

One *starets* later canonized an Orthodox saint was Seraphim of Sarov (1759–1833). In 1825, after many years of seclusion, he began seeing all that wished his help, including sick people hoping for cures. In his mysticism and love of the Jesus prayer—also stressed by Velichkovsky—he calls to mind the hesychasts and Nil Sorsky (see Chapter 7). He preached that the acceptance of the Spirit of God would bring joy and the transformation of human life.

A strong supporter of monastic reform was Filaret, the Archbishop of Moscow from 1821 until 1867. Despite clashes with the Holy Synod's procurator, Pratasov, he was the most influential religious leader of his era. He not only supported Optina's publications, but also strongly encouraged the adoption of a more communal life in the monasteries and convents. Despite Velichkovsky's influence at places such as Optina, communal sharing was not the rule in most Russian monasteries and convents. Each person was responsible for his or her own support by such means as making handicrafts or begging. Although Filaret's reform efforts met considerable resistance from already established monasteries and convents, he was more successful with new ones, especially those upgraded from the status of "women's communities."

These communities had begun as a way of circumventing the government's limitation on the number of convents. From 1764 to 1894, 156 such communities were founded, often by widows. They included women from varying classes, from the nobility to the peasantry, and often performed charitable works. Some of the founders and heads of these religious communities were valued by laypersons for their practical and spiritual wisdom. Two-thirds of these communities ultimately were raised to convent status and operated on the basis of communal principles.

The religiousness of the Russian Orthodox peasant has been greatly debated. Although Belinsky and others denied it, others such as Gogol, the Slavophiles, and later Dostoevsky attested to it. Such differences were partly due to individual definitions of "religiousness"—what one regarded as a superstition, another thought of as a religious practice or belief.

On more specific points, however, a scholarly consensus does exist: The peasants had little knowledge of many Orthodox dogmas and teachings, but church rituals and customs were important to them. The priest Belliustin wrote that none of his parishioners could intelligently relate even a portion of

Christ's life and that no more than two or three out of 1,000 knew the ten com-
mandments. One reason for this was that priestly sermons were rare.

When it came to church practices, however, the peasants were dutiful.
Their observances in the early nineteenth century were probably little different
than those observed later in the century by Donald Mackenzie Wallace. He
wrote:

> It must be admitted that the Russian people are in a certain sense religious.
> They go regularly to church on Sundays and holy-days, cross themselves re-
> peatedly when they pass a church or Icon, take the Holy Communion at stated
> seasons, rigorously abstain from animal food—not only on Wednesdays and
> Fridays, but also during Lent and the other long fasts—[and] make occasional
> pilgrimages to holy shrines.[2]

The peasants also venerated icons, both at church and in the icon corner of
their huts. Many of the icons that made up the iconostasis at church were the
illiterate peasants' chief windows to the Bible.

The peasants' Christianity, however, remained interwoven with older pre-
Christian beliefs and practices. Spirits like the *domovoi* (house spirit) and the
rusalki (water and tree nymphs) continued coexisting in the peasant mind with
the saints they revered. The belief in magic and sorcery lived on alongside that
in miracles and faith in the power of icons, sacraments, and prayer.

This mixture of beliefs was mirrored in the peasants' yearly cycle of holy
days and festivals and in the important events of their lives, from birth
through marriage to death. Even Easter, the greatest Orthodox Christian holy
day, was tinged with remnants of older pre-Christian practices, whereas other
days such as those of the late winter festival *Maslenitsa*—during which winter
was urged to depart by setting afire a straw dummy—were clearly dominated
by pre-Christian vestiges. Such pagan customs were often intricately connected with the peasants' agricultural life and their attempts to influence the
workings of nature positively. The peasants also appealed to certain Christian
saints for help with different facets of nature and had patron saints for rain,
cattle, horses, and so forth.

Thus, if religion is defined broadly to include both "primitive" and Christian beliefs and practices, the Russian peasants' world was far more religious
than secular. Not only their fasts, feasts, and festivals were primarily religious,
but also their everyday farming and social life was filled with practices that
testified to their belief in spiritual and magical forces. Because of the close
church-state connection in Russia, even the wishes of their tsar and government were often clothed in religious garb.

EDUCATION AND SCHOLARSHIP

Although educational opportunities advanced considerably in this period,
they still lagged far behind those available in Western Europe. By 1856, the

---

[2]*Russia* (New York, 1877), p. 63. For more on him and this book, see Chapter 22, in which a selection from it is included.

FIGURE 21.1. A village church (the Church of the Transfiguration, from the village of Kozliateva, 1756, presently in the Suzdal Outdoor Museum of Wooden Architecture and Peasant Life).

number of students receiving some form of public education in European Russia (excluding Poland and Finland) had increased about sevenfold from the approximately 62,000 students in 1801.

Certain characteristics of Russian education became clearly evident in this period. According to Ben Eklof, they included a suspicion of any private schooling and an emphasis on advanced (beyond basic) education and educational uniformity. Although the government believed in educating enough people to enable Russia to meet the needs of nineteenth-century international competition, it did not want education to destabilize the social order. This meant that peasants generally were to receive no more than a very basic education. The government feared that too much education for peasants would stimulate discontent.

During Alexander I's first decade of rule, this fear was not nearly as evident as it became later. In fact, Alexander's educational decrees and statutes of 1803–1804 were marked by his early liberal enthusiasms and aimed at restructuring the educational system to provide a "ladder" of linked schools from basic ones to universities. One's degree of ascent was to be based not on class but on talent. As Alexander's policies became more conservative, however, this dream faded.

The one-year parish schools, established in some towns and villages under Alexander I, were at the bottom of the ladder. Then came the district and provincial schools, originally created by Catherine II but transformed during this era into three-year district schools and seven-year gymnasiums—yet many district towns (over 130 in European Russia in 1825) remained without a school. At the top were the universities, which were granted considerable autonomy under the University Statute of 1804. By 1825 (and still by 1855), there were six of them in the European Russian provinces: in Moscow, St. Petersburg, Kharkov, Kazan, Dorpat, and Vilna (replaced by one in Kiev in the 1830s). In addition, there was one each in Congress Poland (until the uprising of 1830–1831) and Finland.

Although Alexander I intended these different level schools to be the main rungs of the educational "ladder," by 1855, the lower rungs only rarely led any higher and indeed were not intended to for most of the common people. In all the gymnasiums and universities, there were by then only a little over 21,000 students, with about one-sixth of the total attending a university.

Besides these main institutions, other schools continued to grow or were newly created. The largest number of the former were the schools for military children and the church schools and seminaries for the sons of priests. The new schools that educated the most students, including a small percentage of girls, were primary church schools under the Holy Synod and the three-year schools that General Kiselev began establishing for state peasants in the late 1830s.

At a higher level, about twenty new women's institutes came into existence in this era, mostly modeled on the Smolny Institute created by Catherine the Great. These institutes, plus some private women's boarding schools, were mainly the preserve of the daughters of nobles and, less frequently, of wealthy merchants. For men, there were other secondary and higher educational institutions besides the gymnasiums and universities, including the four theological academies in St. Petersburg, Moscow, Kazan, and Kiev. Nicholas I was especially fond of technical and applied learning, and under him a number of institutions teaching such subjects as architecture, technical drawing, agronomy, and veterinary medicine began operation. For noblemen particularly, other new schools were opened. They included cadet schools and special institutions such as the Imperial Lyceum on the royal grounds of Tsarskoe Selo, opened in 1811, and the School of Jurisprudence, founded in 1835.

The quality of education in Russia's schools varied widely. At the basic level—for example, the parish, district, and church schools, and those Kiselev established for state peasants—the three Rs and religion were supposedly stressed. Because of insufficient government financing, inadequate books and teachers, poor classrooms, and peasant reluctance to send their children to school, the actual learning that occurred often fell short of expectations. The best-financed and best-run primary system was that of Kiselev's Ministry of State Domains, yet in 1855, empty seats in many of its schools led the ministry to conscript male and female orphans to fill them. The learning that did occur was often characterized by memorization without comprehension.

Because priests did much of the teaching, including that in Kiselev's schools for state peasants, Belliustin's comments on ecclesiastical schools are noteworthy. The preseminary schools stressed Latin, Greek, catechism and biblical history, and Russian grammar. Belliustin sums up this education by writing: "the entire course of study amounts to nothing more than rote memorization, a science of cramming."[3] He thought that the more advanced six-year seminaries were little better and that nothing in them was taught or learned thoroughly. Besides faulting the instruction given future priests, Belliustin also complained of inadequate textbooks, instructional buildings, and dormitories.

Secondary lay education in the gymnasiums (seventy-four of them in 1851) and more advanced schooling seems to have been better, no doubt partly because such education was designed mainly for the sons of the nobility. By the 1830s, the gymnasiums stressed a classical education. The program followed by the future historian Sergei Soloviev at a Moscow gymnasium in the 1830s indicates how demanding the best of them could be. Besides heavy doses of Latin and Greek, he took courses in German, Russian language and literature, history, religion, mathematics, and physics. The students attended classes six hours a day, six days a week, and summer vacation lasted a month at the most. Only a minority of Soloviev's fellow students made it all the way through to graduation.

Women's "secondary schooling" at the Smolny and other institutes and boarding schools was much less rigorous. They were primarily "finishing schools" designed to produce young noblewomen who could speak good French, play the piano, and otherwise serve the social and domestic needs of their future husbands.

Under Alexander I, many university professors were foreign and did not speak Russian, instead giving their lectures in Latin, German, or French, and thereby being poorly understood by some of their students. As late as 1835, about a fourth of the professors lacked graduate degrees. At the University of St. Petersburg in 1834 and 1835, the writer Nikolai Gogol, who possessed not even an undergraduate degree, was an assistant professor of medieval history and demonstrated to his students that he knew little about his subject.

Gradually, however, instruction improved. This was especially true under Sergei Uvarov, who served as Nicholas I's minister of education from 1833 to 1849, and before Nicholas's fears of the 1848–1849 revolutions led him to place new restrictions on the universities and cut back their enrollments. From 1848 to 1854, the number of university students fell from about 4,600 to about 3,600. Although new regulations and policies of the mid-1830s curtailed some of the considerable university autonomy earlier granted by Alexander I, they also strengthened faculty qualifications and improved faculty salaries. Many new faculty were hired, including more than a few who had studied abroad. The improvement was especially marked at Russia's largest university, that of

[3]Belliustin, p. 83.

Moscow. By 1855, it had about 1,200 students, or about a third of the total university population.

Of the new Moscow professors, Timothy Granovsky (1813–1855) was particularly popular and influential. Many of the era's outstanding writers, thinkers, and educators were either his students (such as Sergei Soloviev and the historian and juridical scholar Boris Chicherin) or his friends (such as Ivan Turgenev and Alexander Herzen). After studying abroad for three years and absorbing European history from such scholars as the great German historian Leopold von Ranke, Granovsky became a professor of medieval and European history in 1839. Although influenced, like most of his generation, by Hegel's views on history, he emphasized not only the German philosopher's laws of history and its march toward progress, but also the individual's moral responsibility and role in history. In the fierce Slavophile-Westernizer debate over Russia's past and future, he stood with the Westernizers but was far more moderate than Belinsky, Bakunin, or Herzen. This debate's importance and Granovsky's humane personality and lecturing skills won him large audiences for the public lectures he gave during the 1840s.

Although some of Russia's great writers and thinkers who came to maturity under Nicholas I never attended Moscow University, many did, although not all graduated. Among its students, at least briefly, were the novelists Turgenev and Goncharov; the poets Lermontov, Ogarev, and Fet; the Slavophile K. Aksakov; and the Westernizers Herzen and Belinsky. Among influential professors at the university, there was also the conservative and nationalist historian M. P. Pogodin and Sergei Soloviev, who replaced him in 1845 as professor of Russian history.

Other universities also possessed some noteworthy professors and students. At the University of Kazan, the great pioneer in non-Euclidean geometry, Nikolai Lobachevsky (1793–1856), both taught and served as rector of the university from 1827 to 1846, helping it to recover from Magnitsky's disastrous policies. A student who entered Kazan University while Lobachevsky was rector later became one of world literature's greatest writers, Leo Tolstoy. But like another famous later student of the university, Vladimir Lenin, he left before graduating.

Yet Tolstoy's experiences at Kazan University tell us a good deal about both Tolstoy and Russian higher education in this period. In the spring of 1844, months short of his sixteenth birthday, Tolstoy took the entrance examinations for one of the university's most distinguished and difficult programs, the Faculty of Oriental Languages. Although doing well enough to pass in German, French, English, Arabic, Turko-Tatar, math, and literature, his scores in history, geography, statistics, and Latin were poor, and he was denied admission.

Months later, he tried again, was successful, and began his studies in the fall of 1844. But he soon became more concerned with his social life than classes, missed many lectures, and failed to complete his first year successfully. He then transferred to the university's easier Faculty of Jurisprudence, but after less than two years in it decided to leave the university. Once, while being locked up overnight for missing a history lecture, he fumed that "history is nothing other than a collection of fables and useless details, interspersed with a mass of unnecessary dates and proper names."

Like many noblemen of the era, Tolstoy's early education was provided by tutors, some of them foreign. Whether educated by tutors or schools or both, the education of many noblemen never advanced beyond an elementary level. Only a minority of nobles graduated from cadet schools, gymnasiums, or private schools or (like Tolstoy and Herzen) received a secondary education primarily from their tutors and their own reading.

Many noble parents resisted the rigors of a classical gymnasium education for their sons, and the government allowed some less demanding five-year gymnasiums to be established by noblemen at their own expense. Among other courses they could take at these abbreviated gymnasiums were ones thought especially fitting for noblemen, such as fencing, horsemanship, and ballroom dancing. When they did attend the regular seven-year gymnasiums, they often lived in separate dormitories where commoners were excluded. The government of Nicholas I was willing to make such concessions because it believed that gymnasium and university education should be primarily for the sons of nobles. In the first decade of Nicholas's reign, about three-fourths of the gymnasium students were from the nobility.

Yet nobles who were both willing and able to complete a gymnasium or even more advanced schooling did not exhaust the government's need for well-educated individuals, especially officials; thus, the door to talented commoners, unless serfs, was never completely shut. From 1840 to 1848, no more than 55 percent of university students were from the nobility. Among nonnoble laymen, those from the urban tax-paying groups had the best chance to obtain postelementary education. The government also allowed some sons of priests, such as Sergei Soloviev, to pursue advanced secular schooling. In his memoirs, Alexander Herzen noted the democratic mix of students at Moscow University before the 1848–1849 European revolutions, after which Nicholas took new measures to restrict the entrance of poorer commoners.

LITERATURE

The early nineteenth century was a great age for Russian literature. It witnessed the Golden Age of Russian poetry; the writings of Alexander Pushkin, Mikhail Lermontov, and Nikolai Gogol; and the beginning of the careers of Fedor Dostoevsky, Leo Tolstoy, and Ivan Turgenev. Although Western authors and movements influenced all these writers, the poems, prose, and plays they wrote breathed of Russia and reflected its own uniqueness.

In the West, romanticism was the dominant literary movement of the time, until replaced by realism in the middle of the nineteenth century. Although sharing some characteristics of the earlier sentimentalism, romanticism went much further in its rebellion against neoclassicism's emphasis on rationality and restraint.

Western romanticism emphasized individualism, imagination, emotion, the wonders of nature, the medieval, the strange, and the mysterious. Romantic writers often seemed discontented and alienated, unable to find satisfaction in common beliefs, whether of an everyday religious or secular nature. Thus, they looked for happiness and meaning in other places—in nature, the past, romantic love, music, mysticism, the German philosophy of Schelling, heroic action (Napoleon was a hero to some)—or the *Volksgeist* (folk-spirit) of their nation.

Although not as strong and long-lasting as in some Western countries, romanticism in Russia shared these characteristics but combined and displayed them in a way that reflected the Russian identity. The alienated heroes of Pushkin or Lermontov, although bearing some similarities to the heroes of the English poet Byron, exist in and are influenced by a Russian environment. The exotic settings of Russian romantic literature were often different (for example, the Caucasus) than those of Western romanticism. And the Russian romantic concern with national originality was greater than in other countries.[4]

One Russian writer who reflected romantic tendencies was Vasili Zhukovsky (1783–1852). This poet and tutor of the future tsar Alexander II was also one of the world's finest translators of poetry. Among his many English and German translations were some romantic works, including Byron's *The Prisoner of Chillon*. He was the first major poet of poetry's Golden Age, and his melodic poems were known for their "enchanting sweetness." Building on Karamzin's language reforms, he molded a poetic language that influenced later poets.

Two other excellent poets that were strongly influenced by romanticism were Evgeni Baratynsky and Fedor Tiutchev. The romantic element appears especially in their philosophical pessimism and in the subjects they treated.

Tiutchev often wrote about the sea, sky, and seasons but used them as a basis for philosophical reflections—he has often been labeled a "metaphysical poet." His romanticism owed something to the German philosopher Schelling, whose works he read and whose lectures he attended while stationed as a diplomat in Munich. He also wrote perhaps the greatest Russian tragic love poetry. In addition, this diplomat by profession and conservative panslavist by conviction wrote conservative political poems and prose, expressing his belief in the West's decline and Orthodox Russia's historical uniqueness and future historical mission.

The greatest Russian poet was Alexander Pushkin (1799–1837). After an upbringing that included being taught to speak French before Russian, learning Russian folktales from his nanny, and being educated at the Imperial Lyceum at Tsarskoe Selo, Pushkin spent the next three years (1817–1820) enjoying the prerogatives of a youthful nobleman in St. Petersburg. He went to balls and theaters, gambled, drank, and womanized. He also began to write poetry that was clearly superior to his schoolboy poems, some of which had been good enough to be praised by Derzhavin and Zhukovsky. Unfortunately for Pushkin, however, some of his political poems helped get him into trouble, and the government exiled him to southern Russia.

[4]Nicholas I's stress on Russia's national uniqueness (as well as Alexander I's earlier interest in mysticism) was thus in keeping with the romantic spirit of the era.

After four years of southern exile, Pushkin spent two more years of exile on his family's estate. In 1826, Nicholas I summoned Pushkin, talked with him, and told him that henceforth his writings would be subject only to the tsar's personal censorship. From then on, however, Pushkin's activities and writings were closely watched by the Third Section.

Pushkin married the beautiful Natalia Goncharova in 1831. After a few years, he grew increasingly jealous of her many admirers. Finally in 1837, incensed by the ardent courting of Natalia by the adopted son of the Dutch ambassador, Pushkin challenged the young man to a duel. Wounded in it, Pushkin died two days later.

Some of Pushkin's writings, especially his poetry, reflect his own stormy life and strong emotions. And there are certainly romantic elements in some of his works, especially those written in the south under Byronic influence. Yet Pushkin's style was generally more restrained, simple, and objective—more classical some would say—than that of the European romantic writers of his day.

His reputation rests not only on the quality of his poetry, but also on the wide spectrum of his writings, both poetry and prose. He wrote short poems on subjects from love, friendship, freedom, nature, and death, to poems on a water-nymph (*rusalka*), his own genealogy, his inkwell, and to slanderers of Russia. He wrote longer narrative poems, among the greatest of which are *Evgeni Onegin, The Gypsies,* and *The Bronze Horseman.* In them, he touched on a broad range of topics, including freedom and fate, the individual and the state.

He wrote poetic folktales such as the *Golden Cockerel* and *King Saltan* and plays such as *Boris Godunov* and *Mozart and Salieri,* the latter one of a number of "little tragedies." He penned fictional prose narratives: short stories such as "The Queen of Spades" and "The Stationmaster" and longer works such as *A Captain's Daughter* (set against the background of the Pugachev revolt). Finally, if we skip over his letters, critical essays, and other minor categories, we come to his historical works. Although his *The Moor of Peter the Great,* about Pushkin's African great-grandfather, took some artistic liberties with the facts, his *History of the Pugachev Rebellion* and an unfinished work on Peter the Great were more purely historical.

Not only have Pushkin's works been widely read and appreciated by Russians, but also his writings have had a great impact on many subsequent writers. The language of his poetry and prose, his artistic realism, his fictional plotting and story construction, and his characters—especially Onegin and his love Tatiana—strongly influenced such writers as Lermontov, Dostoevsky, and Turgenev. Composers and choreographers were also greatly indebted to him. They used works such as *Evgeni Onegin, Boris Godunov,* and *The Queen of Spades*—to name just a few of many—as the basis for ballets and operas.

A more romantic and Byronic writer was Mikhail Lermontov (1814–1841). In one of his early and best short poems, "The Angel," he expresses his longing for a better world than the tedious human world of sorrow and tears. This sense of alienation, sometimes unrelieved by romantic hopes or dreams, continued until his brief life ended in a duel. In "The Last House-Warming," in which he contrasts a despicable and shallow France of 1840 with the greatness of Napoleon, it is evident that his contempt for society was not limited to Russia.

Like Byron's poetry, Lermontov's sometimes expressed rebellion not only against society, but also against religion and God. Aspects of this rebellion can be seen in such long poems as *The Demon* and *The Novice* and in his late short poem "Gratitude," in which Lermontov cynically thanks God for his bitter life.

A good part of the romantic atmosphere in Lermontov's mature writings came from his exile to the exotic Caucasus, where he died. On two occasions, the government sent him to serve in the military there, once for his poem on Pushkin's death, which criticized Nicholas I's regime, and later for a duel with the son of the French ambassador.

Lermontov's poetry was generally more emotional and unrestrained than that of Pushkin's and has been valued especially for its melodious qualities. In some poems, however, especially of his last years, his style became more concise and his approach less romantic and more realistic.

This greater realism can also be seen in Lermontov's prose masterpiece, *A Hero of Our Time* (1840). Although the Caucasian setting is romantic and the hero, Pechorin, is typical in many ways of the alienated romantic hero who is at odds with his society, Lermontov's treatment of him is more objectively realistic than romantic. Some have referred to this work as Russia's first novel of psychological realism.

Another writer who displayed both romantic and realistic characteristics was Nikolai Gogol (1809–1852). Born in Ukraine, he came to St. Petersburg in 1828, hoping to become an actor, but instead achieved fame in 1831–1832 with a collection of stories called *Evenings on a Farm Near Dikanka*. These and a later collection, *Mirgorod* (1835), were primarily romantic in their use of legends, folklore, horror, and supernatural elements such as demons, witches, water spirits, and ghosts. One of the stories in *Mirgorod* was "Taras Bulba," which Gogol later expanded and revised. In writing this piece of historical fiction, he was influenced not only by Ukrainian folk legends, but also by the historical romances of Walter Scott, which were then popular in Russia. Yet some of the stories in his two collections also displayed a great talent for depicting realistic details and dealt with rather unromantic characters whose lives were marked by banality.

One of Gogol's favorite writers was the German Romantic E. T. A. Hoffmann. In later stories set in St. Petersburg, Gogol continued, like Hoffmann, to display an ability to mix everyday life with the weird and supernatural. In "The Nose," a barber finds the nose of an official, one of his customers, in a loaf of bread; the official goes hunting for his nose, and it takes on a life of its own. In one of Gogol's most famous and influential stories, "The Overcoat," a poor copyist is robbed of his overcoat, appeals to an important official to urge a more robust police investigation but is thrown out by him, and dies grief-stricken shortly afterwards. His ghost, however, has his revenge, going on an overcoat-stealing rampage, including the theft of the important official's coat.

Two of Gogol's most famous works were the comedy, *The Inspector General*, first performed in 1836, and the novel *Dead Souls*, which appeared in 1842. Both reflect Gogol's unique satirical genius, are set in Russia's provinces, and revolve around a dishonest outsider who appears in an insignificant provincial town, full of banal characters. Both works helped establish Gogol's reputation as a social critic, a reputation that this supporter of Nicholas's Orthodoxy, autocracy, and nationality found uncomfortable.

This reputation owed a great deal to Belinsky, the most important literary critic of his day. In his short life, this Westernizer praised many of the works of Pushkin, Lermontov, Gogol, the young Turgenev, and the young Dostoevsky. And he established a trend in Russian literary criticism which advocated that literature should be of social value and true to life. In his famous 1847 letter to Gogol, which attacked him for the conservative views of his *Selected Passages from a Correspondence with Friends,* Belinsky wrote: "Yes, I loved you with all the passion with which a man, bound by ties of blood to his native country, can love its hope, its honor, its glory, one of the great leaders on its path of consciousness, development and progress." Belinsky's anger with Gogol in 1847 stemmed largely from feeling betrayed by a man whose previous works he had so greatly admired. What Belinsky valued in Gogol was his "naturalism," or as he put it: [that his] "works deal exclusively with the world of Russian life and he has no rivals in the art of portraying it in all its truth."

For Belinsky, this "truth" was that Russia was backward, her political and social system was unjust, and the masses suffered as a result of it. Because works such as "The Overcoat," *The Inspector General,* and *Dead Souls* called attention to these conditions, they were, to Belinsky, important steps in the direction of progress.

Gogol's later work did little to change perceptions of the social value of his earlier writings. But more modern Gogol criticism, although disagreeing on many points, has indicated that Gogol was a much more complex writer than Belinsky had suggested. This newer criticism has revealed a tormented personality, and it has pointed out that Gogol did not approach literature primarily as a realist.

Like Tiutchev and the Slavophiles, Gogol came to believe that the West was mired in sin and falseness and that humanity needed to base its culture on Christian truth, a truth safeguarded properly only in the Orthodox Church. This belief developed primarily between 1836 and 1848, years spent chiefly abroad, especially in Italy. During the latter part of this period, Gogol worked hard over an uplifting sequel to *Dead Souls,* but he eventually burned it.

Besides Zhukovsky, Pushkin, Lermontov, and Gogol, there were other writers of note during this era. One was Ivan Krylov, whose satirical verse fables were extremely popular. Many of his lines became proverbs. This was also true of many lines of Alexander Griboedov's comedy *Woe from Wit* (written in the early 1820s). It stands alongside Gogol's *The Inspector General* as one of the two greatest plays of the early nineteenth century. Although its hero, Chatsky, like many a Romantic hero, was alienated from the society of his day, this work could no more be labeled a manifestation of romanticism than could Pushkin's *Evgeni Onegin.* Both works mixed classical, realistic, and romantic elements.

Along with Lermontov's Pechorin, both Chatsky and Onegin became part of a tradition of Russian "superfluous men," a category not limited to the alienated heroes of romanticism. What these superfluous men had in common was being alienated from society but being unwilling or unable to act to change it.

ART AND MUSIC

In Russian architecture, painting, and music, as with its literature, romanticism was a weaker force than in the West. Despite some romantic manifestations, early nineteenth-century Russian architecture continued mainly in the classical (or neoclassical) tradition of the late eighteenth century, at least until the 1830s. The dominance of classicism is evident primarily in public buildings, including some famous churches.

Three examples should suffice to indicate classicism's dominance and then decline in early nineteenth-century architecture. All three were built in the capital and made ample use of columns, which were central to the era's architecture. The first was Kazan Cathedral, (1801–1811) (see Figure 21.2). Its architect was Andrei Voronikhin, who was born a serf but later studied in St. Petersburg, Rome, and Paris. The second was the semicircular General Staff Building (1819–1829), which faced the Winter Palace and was constructed by one of the period's most prolific architects, Carlo Rossi (see Figure 25.1). The third was St. Isaac's Cathedral, which took four decades to build and was not completed until the late 1850s (see Figure 21.3). Although it was designed by a French-

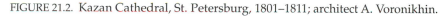

FIGURE 21.2. Kazan Cathedral, St. Petersburg, 1801–1811; architect A. Voronikhin.

FIGURE 21.3. St. Isaac's Cathedral, St. Petersburg, 1818–1848, architect A. Montferrand.

man, Avgust Montferrand, Nicholas I often interfered in the project, resulting in the cathedral becoming larger, heavier, more "authoritarian," and less graceful and classical than originally intended.

It is ironic that both Kazan Cathedral, which housed General Kutuzov's remains and memorabilia from the victorious war against Napoleon, and St. Isaac's, which reflected the interference of the nationalistic Nicholas I, still looked more Western than uniquely Russian. But such buildings existed primarily because both Alexander I and Nicholas I believed them appropriate manifestations of Russian autocracy.

By the 1830s, however, Nicholas I, who prided himself on his knowledge and interest in architecture and whose tastes were more eclectic than Alexander I's, was sponsoring new construction that moved further away from the classical. Reflecting his desire to stress the Russian nationality, he encouraged more uniquely Russian, or at least Russo-Byzantine, constructions. The Cathedral of the Savior in Moscow, later blown up by Stalin, was a good example of this emphasis (see Figure 27.1).

The most famous painter of his era was Karl Briullov (1799–1852) and his most famous painting was the enormous (and then overrated) "The Last Day of Pompeii." Like many of the painters of his day he studied at the Academy of Fine Arts in St. Petersburg and later went to Italy, where he painted his acclaimed canvas. Although it dealt with a classical event and contained ample realistic detail, its scene of terror-struck people fleeing crumbling buildings and volcanic lava was more typical of romanticism.

A painter whose reputation has better stood the test of time is Orest

Kiprensky (1782–1836). His many portraits, including numerous self-portraits and ones of Pushkin and Zhukovsky, reflected romanticism's increased emphasis on the individual, the unique, and the heroic.

Two other interesting painters of the era were Alexei Venetsianov and Alexander Ivanov. Venetsianov emphasized the importance of working from nature and painted many rural scenes and peasants. Although his peasants are too peaceful, neat, and contented to be fully realistic, he is often viewed as a founder, or at least an important forerunner, of Russian realistic painting.

Ivanov is often compared to his friend Gogol. Like Gogol, he came to believe in a special Russian spiritual mission, wished to create a spiritually uplifting piece of art, was politically conservative, and is difficult to place within any single artistic movement. For a quarter of a century, Ivanov worked in Rome over his "Appearance of Christ to the People." At one point (1845), he was encouraged by Nicholas I, who stopped by his studio on a trip to Rome—the tsar liked to encourage religious art and thought it in keeping with his emphasis on the principle of Orthodoxy. But by the time Ivanov's canvas was finally exhibited in St. Petersburg in 1858, its creator was dissatisfied with it, and its public reception was only lukewarm.

Like many painters, Russia's most famous composer of the era, Mikhail Glinka (1804–1857), studied in Italy. After returning to Russia, he composed his opera *A Life for the Tsar* (also called *Ivan Susanin*), which dealt with a peasant (Susanin) who gave his life for young Mikhail Romanov. Its 1836 appearance was much more successful than his subsequent *Ruslan and Liudmila,* which was later recognized as Glinka's masterpiece. The libretto of this latter opera was taken from Pushkin's poetic romance set in Kievan Rus. Glinka's use of Russian material, including elements of Russian folk music, helped set the stage for the brilliant generation of Russian national composers who would later follow him.

Like Venetsianov's paintings of Russian rural scenes and peasants, Glinka's reliance on old Russian settings and folk music was in keeping with Nicholas I's stress on the principle of *nationality.* Interest in the Russian "folk" had begun in the eighteenth century and then been stimulated by the romantic nationalism that developed after the defeat of Napoleon. Among the industrious collectors of unwritten folk songs was the Slavophile Peter Kireevsky.

The appearance of Glinka's *A Life for the Tsar* in 1836 helped make that year a special one for Russian culture. It was also the year that Pushkin's *A Captain's Daughter* appeared, Gogol's *Inspector General* was staged, and Briullov's masterpiece was first exhibited in Russia. And it was the year that the Slavophile-Westernizing debate began, as Chaadaev's first "Philosophical Letter" resounded, as Herzen said, like a shot in the night. Russian culture became caught up in the debate. Indicative of this were opposing views of Briullov's masterpiece, some saying the destruction of Pompeii was a foreshadowing of the descent of the West and the rise of Russia, and others countering that it foretold the destruction of autocratic Russia.

Two decades later, amidst the ashes of the Crimean War, Russia's future destiny became a pressing concern for the government as well as for the cultural elite.

SUGGESTED SOURCES*

ALSTON, PATRICK L. *Education and the State in Tsarist Russia.* Stanford, 1969.

BROWN, W. E. *A History of Russian Literature of the Romantic Period.* Ann Arbor, 1986.

BRUMFIELD, WILLIAM C. *A History of Russian Architecture.* Cambridge, England, 1993. Chs. 12 & 13.

CHRISTOFF, PETER K. *An Introduction to Nineteenth-Century Russian Slavophilism.* 4 Vols. The Hague, Princeton, and Boulder, 1961–1991.

CIZEVSKIJ, DMITRIJ. *History of Nineteenth-Century Russian Literature.* 2 vols. Nashville, 1974.

DIMNIK, MARTIN. "Monasticism in Russia," *MERSH* 23: 29–34.

EKLOF, BEN. *Russian Peasant Schools: Officialdom, Village Culture, and Popular Pedagogy, 1861–1914.* Berkeley, 1986. Ch. 1.

FEDOTOV, G. P., ed. *A Treasury of Russian Spirituality.* New York, 1948.

FLYNN, JAMES T. *The University Reforms of Tsar Alexander I, 1802–1835.* Washington, D.C., 1988.

FREEZE, GREGORY L. *The Parish Clergy in Nineteenth-Century Russia: Crisis, Reform, Counter-Reform.* Princeton, 1983.

HERZEN, ALEXANDER. *My Past and Thoughts.* 4 vols. London, 1968.

KAHAN, ARCADIUS. "Social Structure, Public Policy, and the Development of Education." In *Russian Economic History: The Nineteenth Century.* Chicago, 1989.

LEWIN, MOSHE. "Popular Religion in Twentieth-Century Russia." In *The Making of the Soviet System: Essays in the Social History of Interwar Russia.* New York, 1985.

MATHES, WILLIAM L. "Education in Russia Prior to 1917," *MERSH* 10: 132–140.

MEEHAN-WATERS, BRENDA. "Metropolitan Filaret (Drozdov) and the Reform of Russian Women's Monastic Communities," *RR* 50 (July 1991): 310–323.

———. "To Save Oneself: Russian Peasant Women and the Development of Women's Religious Communities in Prerevolutionary Russia." In *Russian Peasant Women,* eds. Beatrice Farnsworth and Lynne Viola. New York, 1992.

ORCHARD, G. EDWARD. "Filaret," *MERSH* 11: 126–130.

REDDEL, CARL W. "Sergei Mikhailovich Solov'ev: The Early Years (1820–1848)." Ph.D. dissertation. Indiana University, 1973.

ROOSEVELT, PRISCILLA R. *Apostle of Russian Liberalism: Timofei Granovskii.* Newtonville, Mass., 1986.

RYDEL, CHRISTINE, ed. *The Ardis Anthology of Russian Romanticism.* Ann Arbor, 1984.

STAVROU, THEOFANIS GEORGE, ed. *Art and Culture in Nineteenth-Century Russia.* Bloomington, 1983.

WARE, TIMOTHY. *The Orthodox Church.* New ed. London, 1993. Ch. 6.

WHITTAKER, CYNTHIA H. *The Origins of Modern Russian Education: An Intellectual Biography of Count Sergei Uvarov, 1786–1855.* DeKalb, Ill., 1984.

*See also works cited in footnotes and general works on literature cited in the General Bibliography at the back of this volume. In addition, there are numerous biographies in English of Russia's writers, and many of their works have been translated into English.

PART FIVE

Late Imperial Russia, 1855–1917

Late Imperial Russia calls to mind the tsarist symbol, the two-headed eagle, for like it, Russia in this era looked in two different directions. One face stared backward toward the old autocratic and patriarchal order, and the other peered forward into a future whose exact outlines could not be discerned.

The tsarist symbol, the two-headed eagle, over the St. Peter's Gate, Sts. Peter and Paul Fortress, St. Petersburg.

The period began and ended with Russia at war—first the Crimean War and later World War I. The Crimean defeat forced the tsarist government to look forward and accelerate economic modernization, for if it did not, it would eventually cease to be a Great Power. This realization helped spur the Great Reforms of Alexander II's reign (1855–1881), the most important of which was the emancipation of the serfs in 1861. It also spurred an acceleration of railway building and manufacturing. Other signs of modernization were significant increases in the number of industrial workers and professionals and in urbanization, life expectancy, and literacy.

Yet, if one face of tsarist policy looked forward, another looked nostalgically backward. The era was not only one of reforms, but also of counterreforms. The policies of the last two Russian emperors reflected an ideology similar to that of Alexander II's father, Nicholas I, with its emphasis on Orthodoxy, autocracy, and the Russian nationality. Like Nicholas I, the last two Romanov rulers as well as the reforming Alexander II hoped to maintain autocracy. All three of Nicholas I's successors felt uncomfortable dealing with the new elements strengthened by modernization, for example, the growing cities, industrial workers, professionals, and proliferating private organizations.

Nicholas II especially liked to think of himself as following in the old-fashioned tsarist tradition—his favorite tsar was the Muscovite ruler Alexei (father of Peter the Great). In his own mind, he was the tsar-*batiushka* (the affectionate father) of the peasant masses. Although he believed in the myth of the benevolent

tsar and (like his predecessors) relied upon ceremonies, symbols, and the Russian Orthodox Church to reinforce it and his God-ordained right to rule over his people, the myth itself was losing its hold over the masses. In this disintegrating process, events during 1905 and World War I were especially important.

Another element of traditional Russia, the nobility, became more diverse during this era. A decreasing percentage remained agricultural landowners. The majority of nobles lived by other means, such as government service, business activities, or professional occupations. Some, such as Vladimir Lenin, whose father had earned hereditary noble status, even became full-time revolutionaries.

The government's attitude toward the landed nobles reflected its basic dilemma. On the one hand, the desire to modernize led it sometimes to act contrary to their needs, for example, in emancipating the serfs. On the other hand, the desire to maintain autocracy and social stability inclined the tsars, especially Alexander III and Nicholas II, to rely upon these nobles as a bedrock of tradition.

For their part, the landed nobles also faced a dilemma. They resented their declining influence and St. Petersburg's modernizing bureaucrats such as Sergei Witte, who served under both Alexander III and Nicholas II. To gain more power, many of them were willing to curtail that of the tsar. At the same time, they were dependent on tsarist authority to help maintain their social position, a fact that the events of 1917 made all too clear.

The tragedy of Late Imperial Russia was that the old and the new were not harmoniously blended. Given the

Romanov rulers' desire to maintain autocracy, it is difficult to see how such a blending could have occurred, even if the last emperors had been more effective autocrats. Although Nicholas II agreed in 1905 to the creation of an elected legislative body, he did it in the midst of a revolt and under duress. Although four legislative Dumas met from 1906 to 1917, Nicholas never gave up the belief that he was still an autocrat and that he could take away rights he had once granted, whether to a Duma or any other body.

Besides tsarist policy and the condition of the nobility, other aspects of Russian political, economic, social, religious, and cultural life manifested the tension between old traditions and new ways. Like many other aspects of Russian life, modernization trends were only partly because of government initiatives. Moreover, the government's impact outside the capital remained limited by its relatively small number of civil servants. Whatever its causes, however, modernization contributed to the increase of political opposition across a broad spectrum of Russian society.

So too did Russia's unsuccessful wars. After gaining enough territory in Asia during this era to more than offset the sale of Alaska in 1867, Russian expansion halted in 1904–1905, when Russia was defeated in the Russo-Japanese War. The Russian Empire even shrank a bit when it was forced to cede Southern Sakhalin to Japan.

While the failures of the war against Japan helped spark the 1905 revolt and force concessions from the autocracy, the failures of World War I helped lead to its overthrow in early 1917. The tensions of the latter war, along with Marxist propaganda regarding class conflict, also heightened resentment and opposition to the upper classes. Eight months after the fall of the Romanov dynasty, they were toppled from the heights of the social pyramid by the Marxist Bolsheviks, who came to power and launched a new era.

CHAPTER 22

Alexander II, Reformism, and Radicalism

Alexander II was the "tsar liberator," the ruler who finally freed the serfs in 1861. He also instituted other important reforms, especially in local government, the judiciary, and the military. Mindful of Russian weaknesses displayed during the Crimean War and faced with serious economic problems, he hoped the reforms would strengthen Russia without weakening autocracy. Fulfilling such a combined goal, however, was an almost impossible task, even if Alexander II had been a stronger and more visionary leader than he was.

Although the reforms helped modernize Russia, the climate that bred them also fostered discontentment and discord. Reactionaries, conservatives, liberals, radicals, and government officials battled against each other and among themselves. In a famous dream sequence in his novel *Crime and Punishment*, Dostoevsky wrote apropos of this period: "All were in a state of unrest and did not understand one another. Each thought that he alone possessed the truth." Alexander's reign ended tragically when he was assassinated in 1881 and his reactionary son, Alexander III, came to the throne.

ALEXANDER II: THE MAN AND HIS TIMES

When he came to the throne, Alexander II was thirty-six. Although his father, Nicholas I, had attempted to educate and train him for his future responsibilities, the new tsar was not a man who relished his work except perhaps when reviewing his troops. Although fairly intelligent, he did not possess an agile, curious mind, and as tsarevich his thinking had seemed little different than his father's. As tsar, during Russia's Golden Age of Literature, he displayed more interest in hunting and whist (an early form of bridge) than he ever did in the writings of Dostoevsky, Tolstoy, or Turgenev. He did, however, possess some humane sentiments and once told the writer Turgenev that his *Sportsman's Sketches*, with its sympathetic treatment of the peasants, had influenced his decision to free the serfs.

Although Alexander's boyhood tutors had noted that he was easily discouraged by difficulties, he did, like most of the Romanovs, have a high sense of duty. This sense of obligation, coupled with the demands of the time, helped energize him to carry out the bulk of his reforms during the first decade of his reign. After that, however, his energy waned. By the end of his reign, he was a tragic figure, criticized by much of the educated public and hunted by assassins. His tragedy and Russia's was that he possessed no clear ideas, no grand vision, on how to reconcile his basic conservative instincts with the modernizing demands of the second half of the nineteenth century. Without such a vision, he seemed irresolute and weak to many contemporaries—at times a reformer, at others, an opponent of reform. The judgment of the Moscow historian, professor, and occasional tutor to Alexander's children, Sergei Soloviev, is harsher than some but still valid: "Fate did not send [Alexander II] a Richelieu or a Bismarck; but the point is that he was incapable of using a Richelieu or a Bismarck; he possessed pretensions and the fear of a weak man to seem weak."

Yet, despite his personal flaws, circumstances propelled Alexander II toward enacting the "Great Reforms." After the Crimean War ended in early 1856, the country's main problem was its economic and social backwardness. Indeed, it had been a major cause of Russia's loss to its enemies. In 1856, for example, the Slavophile Yuri Samarin wrote:

> We were defeated [in the Crimean War] not by the external forces of the Western alliance but by our own internal weakness. . . . Now, when Europe welcomes the peace and rest desired for so long we must deal with what we have neglected. . . . At the head of the contemporary domestic questions which must be dealt with, the problem of serfdom stands as a threat to the future and an obstacle in the present to significant improvement in any way.[1]

EMANCIPATION OF THE SERFS

Causes and Background

The Crimean defeat called into question not only Russia's military prowess, overestimated since the defeat of Napoleon four decades earlier, but also economic traditions that were thought to affect it adversely. Thus, any economic factor that stood in the way of increasing Russia's overall strength was now examined with a new urgency. Many thought, like Samarin, that serfdom was a major impediment to a whole range of economic as well as social improvements.

Nikolai Miliutin, who participated in bringing about the reform, believed that it was necessary to end serfdom to increase agricultural productivity and thereby increase the capital required for industrialization. His friend the legal

---

[1]Martin McCauley and Peter Waldron, eds., *The Emergence of the Modern Russian State, 1855–81* (Totowa, N.J., 1988), pp. 99–100.

historian and Westernizer Constantine Kavelin, who had good connections with reform-minded relatives of the tsar, maintained that serfdom was the chief cause of poverty in Russia. Although historians have debated to what extent serfdom retarded economic development, what is crucial is that Alexander II and important figures such as Samarin, Nikolai Miliutin, and Kavelin believed that ending serfdom would strengthen the Russian economy and thereby the country as a whole.

In 1856, General Dmitri Miliutin, the brother of Nikolai, composed a memorandum on army reform in which he indicated the necessity of reducing the size of Russia's traditionally large and costly standing army and creating instead a large trained reserve. He pointed out, however, that this could be done only if serfdom were first eliminated. The historian Alfred Rieber has plausibly argued that Miliutin's thinking, and military considerations in general, strongly influenced the tsar's decision to emancipate the serfs. In 1861, Alexander II made Dmitri Miliutin his minister of war.

Also related to Russia's strength was its great-power status. Larisa Zakharova has written that its loss and diplomatic isolation were the ruling elite's chief fears emanating from the Crimean defeat. These fears, along with a desire to create a more positive view of Russia abroad, helped propel Alexander and his officials toward ending serfdom.

Another cause was the increase in peasant disturbances in recent decades and the fear of massive rebellions in the future. In early 1856, Alexander II told a group of Moscow nobles: "It is better to begin to abolish serfdom from above than to wait until it begins to abolish itself from below." Although Alexander might have alluded to the possibility of dangers "from below" partly to scare Russia's serfowners into working with him to abolish serfdom, he also took the threat seriously himself.

Two additional factors helping to bring an end to serfdom were public opinion and enlightened bureaucrats. Although most serfowners were opposed to losing their serfs, and some land along with them, most leading opinion makers, from the influential radical émigré editor Alexander Herzen to the conservative publicist M. P. Pogodin, were for emancipation.

From 1857 to 1861, reforming officials such as the tsar's brother, Grand Duke Constantine, and Nikolai Miliutin, deputy minister of interior, were instrumental in preparing for the emancipation of the serfs. The Interior Ministry pressured Lithuanian and then other nobles to establish gentry committees to draft proposals for freeing the serfs. Although most lords wished to free their peasants without providing them land, Alexander II made it clear by the end of 1858 that some gentry land would have to be made available to former serfs.

In the capital, a Main Committee directed the work of the newly established provincial gentry committees, whose various reports were considered by Editing Commissions established in 1859. It was in these commissions, soon combined into one, that Nikolai Miliutin was especially influential in drafting the emancipation legislation of 1861.

FIGURE 22.1. The Kremlin's Grand Palace and churches, Moscow. In August 1856, with the Crimean War now over, Alexander's official coronation took place in the Kremlin.

Emancipation Statutes

On February 19, 1861, Alexander II signed the legislation into law. The government did not issue Alexander's emancipation manifesto and have it read in the churches until two weeks later—after the annual pre-Lenten carnival-week drinking had come to an end and the populace was, it was hoped, in a sober Lenten mood. The new law was a political compromise between the interests of the nobles and those of the peasants and their supporters, and the government was unsure of the response of either side.

The nearly 400 pages of statutes and annexes that made up the new law were terribly complex, but the emancipation provisions can be summed up as follows: (1) "the right of bondage" over serfs was "abolished forever" (except in some outlying areas of the empire such as the Caucasus, where separate emancipation legislation came later); (2) new arrangements regarding gentry-peasant relations and landholding were to be worked out in stages during the next few decades; (3) peasants who had previously farmed gentry land, as opposed to household serfs, were eventually to receive land, the exact amount to be determined by a combination of negotiation, government maximum and minimum norms for each province, and the use of mediators; (4) most of this new land was to go to peasant communes, not directly to individual peasants; (5) landowners were to be compensated for their loss of lands by a combination of government notes and peasant payments; and (6) peasants, unless they chose a free and minuscule "beggars' allotment," were obligated to repay the government with annual redemption payments spread over a 49-year period.

This legislation applied only to the country's serfs—about 40 percent of the total population and slightly less than half of all peasants. By the end of 1866, however, the government had promulgated further legislation to bring the status of other peasants more into line with that of the freed serfs. In general, all these peasants were still treated as a separate class: They were judged on the basis of common law, the powers of the communes and households over individual peasants were strengthened, and peasants continued to pay a head tax from which the nobles were exempt.

Reaction of the Peasants and Analysis

As was to be expected, the reaction to the emancipation manifesto was mixed. Many of the emancipated serfs were confused about the complex new statutes and disbelieving or disappointed when told they would have to make payments (for half a century) for land they received. Many peasants believed that

FIGURE 22.2. Serfs on a Moscow noble's estate hear the provisions of Alexander's emancipation decree.
(*Novosti Press Agency.*)

the fault lie with evil officials and nobles who were frustrating the tsar's real intentions. They thought that as soon as he overcame these troublemakers, new, more favorable, legislation would be forthcoming. Before the year was over, nobles reported more than 1,000 disturbances, most of which required troops to quell. In the summer of 1861, Alexander felt it necessary to admonish a delegation of peasants: "There will be no emancipation except the one I have granted you. Obey the law and the statutes! Work and toil! Obey the authorities and noble landowners!"

Collectively the former serfs received less land than their pre-emancipation allotments. More than one-fourth of them received allotments insufficient to maintain their households—former serfs of Polish landowners, especially after the Polish rebellion of 1863, and imperial and state peasants came off better. Overall the noble serfowners kept roughly two-fifths of their lands, whereas the ex-serfs, greatly outnumbering them, received the rest. And the

---

Peasant Opinions on the Emancipation

The following selection is from D. M. Wallace, *Russia* (New York, 1877), pp. 500–501. This is from the first edition of the Englishman's first-hand observations and reflections. This selection offers valuable insights not only into the peasants' reaction to the emancipation, but also into their general mentality. Ellipses are mine.

It might be reasonably supposed that the serfs received with boundless gratitude and delight the Manifesto. . . . In reality the Manifesto created among the peasantry a feeling of disappointment rather than delight. To understand this strange fact we must endeavor to place ourselves at the peasant's point of view.

In the first place it must be remarked that all vague, rhetorical phrases about free labor, human dignity, national progress, and the like, which may readily produce among educated men a certain amount of temporary enthusiasm, fall on the ears of the Russian peasant like drops of rain on a granite rock. The fashionable rhetoric of philosophical liberalism is as incomprehensible to him as the flowery circumlocutionary style of an

Oriental scribe would be to a keen city merchant. The idea of liberty in the abstract and the mention of rights which lie beyond the sphere of his ordinary everyday life awaken no enthusiasm in his breast. And for mere names he has a profound indifference. What matters it to him that he is officially called, not a "serf," but a "free village inhabitant," if the change in official terminology is not accompanied by some immediate material advantage? What he wants is a house to live in, food to eat, and raiment wherewithal to be clothed. . . . If, therefore, the Government would make a law by which his share of the Communal land would be increased, or his share of the Communal burdens diminished, he would in return willingly consent to be therein designated by the most ugly name that learned ingenuity could devise. Thus the sentimental considerations which had such an important influence on the educated classes had no hold whatever on the mind of the peasants. They looked at the question exclusively from two points of view—that of historical right and that of material advantage—and from both of these the Emancipation Law seemed to offer no satisfactory solution of the question.

peasants eventually paid more for their land than it was worth and received land less suitable than that retained by the owners.

On a more positive note, the ending of the serfs' personal bondage to serf-owners was an important step forward, and relatively little bloodshed resulted from the emancipation. Finally, in assessing the settlement, the practical difficulties and realities of the economic and political situation should be noted. The tsar feared to force a more equitable settlement upon a resentful gentry that made up the backbone of the country's elite.

ADDITIONAL REFORMS

Although censorship remained in place, Alexander II eased up on some of its restrictions—during the first seven years of his reign, the number of Russian periodicals increased about eightfold. Furthermore, Alexander II's government enacted measures to improve state financing, allowed more freedom to the empire's universities, expanded educational opportunities, and enacted other minor reforms. Three other major reforms in addition to emancipating the serfs dealt with local government, the judiciary, and the military.

Zemstvo Reform

The zemstvo (or local government) reform was enacted in early 1864 to help fill the void left by the collapse of the gentry's control over their serfs. As with the emancipation legislation, it did not immediately apply to all areas of the empire; Belorussia and western Ukrainian provinces, for example, were not allowed to establish zemstvo institutions until 1911, and the tsars never permitted them in Siberia. Nevertheless, by the end of Alexander II's reign there were zemstvo institutions in thirty-four of the country's fifty European provinces and in more than 300 districts within these provinces.

District assemblies were elected by three separate electorates: private rural landowners, peasants, and industrial property owners and merchants. These assemblies, which varied in size but averaged almost forty delegates per assembly, met annually for no longer than ten days. Gentry representatives slightly outnumbered those from the vast peasantry, and together the two estates made up about 80 percent of district assembly representatives.

One of the main jobs of a district assembly was the election to a three-year term of a district board of three to six members. This board operated year-round, overseeing the work of the zemstvos. Another job of a district assembly was the election of delegates, again for a three-year term, to participate in an annual provincial assembly, which, in turn, elected a provincial executive board. For a variety of reasons, including the gentry's greater education, leisure, and wealth—zemstvo assembly and board service was not remunerated—the gentry furnished a clear majority of the members of zemstvo boards and an even greater majority of provincial assembly representatives.

To carry out their work, boards hired administrative staff and specialists.

The latter included teachers, physicians and other medical personnel, veterinarians, agronomists, and statisticians. In areas such as primary education, the zemstvos made a major difference. By the end of Alexander's reign, they were involved in the running of some 18,000 primary schools in European Russia—twenty-five years earlier, there had been only 8,000 in the whole empire. Professional medical and veterinary services often became available to peasants for the first time. The insane, paupers, and orphans also received meaningful assistance from zemstvo workers. By organizing fire brigades and other measures, the zemstvos helped peasants deal with village fires, in addition to offering them fire insurance.

Although the zemstvos were primarily known for these services, the central government required additional functions from them: They had to assist in recruiting and housing troops, maintaining local roads, and operating the postal system. Local taxes were the main source of zemstvo revenues, although they were limited to a small amount compared with central government taxation. Despite the uplifting work of the zemstvos, peasants often blamed them for problems and complained of the additional burden of zemstvo taxes. In Chekhov's story "The Peasants," he writes: "The zemstvo was blamed for everything—for the arrears, the unjust exactions, the failure of the crops."

In 1870, many of the zemstvo principles were copied when the government established town councils (dumas) in the cities. The delegates were selected by three electorates divided by wealth. Again, improvements, especially in education, were soon evident. In St. Petersburg, for example, spending on municipal schools increased tenfold during the last ten years of Alexander II's reign.

Judicial Reform

In late 1864, the judicial reform became law after several years of strenuous effort. It replaced the old arbitrary, backlogged (over 3 million undecided cases before the courts in 1842), corrupt, and despotic judicial system with one based largely on Western principles. As with the previous two "Great Reforms," however, it was not applied immediately in all parts of the empire. Some of its provisions, for example, trial by jury, were not introduced at all in Belorussia, parts of Ukraine, Poland, and the Caucasus.

Where it was applied fully, the following principles came into effect: (1) the creation of two separate court systems—for major civil or criminal cases, there were regular courts, and for minor cases, there were courts presided over by a Justice of the Peace, elected by a zemstvo or city duma; (2) rights to appeal under either system to higher courts; (3) the independence of the judiciary from administrative interference and the appointment of judges for life except when removed for moral misconduct; (4) trial by jury for serious criminal cases unless considered crimes against the state; (5) the right to a lawyer; (6) the open publicity of court proceedings; (7) the use of oral testimony and pleadings—as opposed to the use of exclusively written evidence as under the old system; and (8) the establishment of a professional bar.

In addition to the new courts, separate military, ecclesiastical, and peasant courts continued to exist. Because the country's peasants made up about four-fifths of the population, their *volost* courts were especially significant. Following the emancipation, the government reconstituted these courts, which had previously existed for state peasants. In each *volost* (an administrative unit generally containing several village communes), peasants now elected from among themselves their own judges. These judges dealt with minor peasant criminal offenses and most civil disputes involving only peasants. They could impose small fines, imprisonment for short periods, and even sentence a peasant to be flogged with a rod for up to twenty blows. Their decisions were to be based upon customary practices, as opposed to written law.

Although the Russian official Nikitenko complained in his diary that the new laws failed to generate widespread discussion or enthusiasm, the new judicial profession that it created did prove popular with university students. By the end of the 1860s, more than half of them were majoring in law.

Military Reform

The fourth major reform, that of the military, was actually a series of reforms culminating in the Universal Military Service Statute of 1874. The driving force behind them was Dmitri Miliutin, who for two decades (1861–1881) served as Alexander II's war minister.

The motivation for reform was the clear necessity of modernizing Russia's military and in a manner as economically efficient as possible. The country's many conquered territories, its continuing expansion, its extensive borders, and its great-power ambitions all seemed to necessitate a strong military. But rubles to finance improvements were scarce. By 1863, the military was already soaking up about one-third of the state's budget.

Therefore, influenced by both military and economic considerations, Miliutin attempted to create a more efficient, streamlined army. To accomplish this, he reorganized the army structure and improved the training and education of both officers and enlisted men. The pre–Crimean War army had emphasized parade ground maneuvers and ignored such basics as target practice. Miliutin rectified this and had recruits taught the basics of reading and writing. Moreover, he set out to improve morale by abolishing the worst abuses of the old military justice system, for example, running the gauntlet, whereby soldiers sometimes died from thousands of blows. Because of rapidly changing armaments and high costs, rearming the military with the latest weapons was more difficult, but Miliutin made some progress even in this area.

One of his greatest desires was to create a large, efficiently trained reserve and to reduce the length of service in the regular army. By the 1870s, he thought that such a reduction would bring about savings, which could be used for further expansion of the railways—from 1855 through 1870, there had already been about a tenfold increase in the country's railway track. The success of the Prussians in using their railways to mobilize troops during the Franco-Prussian War of 1870–1871 seemed to strengthen his case, and in 1874 he won a major victory with the enactment of the Universal Military Service Statute.

Its provisions reduced to six years the maximum period of required active service—at the beginning of Alexander II's reign, fifteen or more years was the norm. After a six-year stint, the new law required nine more in the reserves and five in the militia. Lesser amounts of time, however, were usually served. Reductions could be achieved for volunteering or for educational attainment; university graduates, for example, had to serve only six months. Another major change was that now men of all estates could be drafted upon reaching the age of twenty if their names were selected in a draft lottery. Previously the upper classes had been exempt, and pre-reform enlisted men had come almost entirely from the peasants, often from those considered minor criminals or at least troublemakers.

As with the emancipation of the serfs, some nobles fought this reform, especially the stipulation making young noblemen liable to the draft. Alexander II stated, however, that military service was a task that should be "equally sacred" for all.

AUTOCRACY AND ITS OPPONENTS

Although willing to grant sweeping reforms, Alexander II was unwilling to limit his autocratic powers. In 1865, he reacted forcefully to an assembly of Moscow nobles who urged him to create an elected General Assembly to discuss state needs. He dissolved the noble assembly and responded with a document that stated:

> The right of initiative . . . belongs exclusively to ME, and is indissolubly bound to the autocratic power entrusted to ME by God. . . . No one is called to take upon himself before ME petitions about the general welfare and needs of the state. Such departures from the order established by existing legislation can only hinder me in the execution of MY aims.[2]

At about the same time, he privately stated that he would sign a constitution if he were convinced that it was good for Russia, but that he knew that the result would only be Russia's disintegration.

Moderate Reformism and Radicalism, 1855–1865

The great Russian writer Leo Tolstoy later described the year 1856 in this way: "Everyone tried to discover still new questions, everyone tried to resolve them; people wrote, read, and spoke about projects; everyone wished to correct, destroy, and change things, and all Russians, as if a single person, found themselves in an indescribable state of enthusiasm." Although ideas and projects

[2]As quoted in Terence Emmons, *The Russian Landed Gentry and the Peasant Emancipation of 1861* (London, 1968), p. 411. Although Alexander II resisted legal limits on his autocratic powers, the Great Reforms and other changes helped weaken his actual controls. See Alfred R. Rieber, "Interest-Group Politics in the Era of the Great Reforms," in *Russia's Great Reforms, 1855–1861*, eds. Ben Eklof, John Bushnell, and Larissa Zakharova (Bloomington, 1994), pp. 79–80.

were plentiful in the first decade of Alexander II's reign, moderate reformers and radicals were the chief proponents of change.

In 1856, the historian Boris Chicherin wrote: "Liberalism! This is the slogan of every educated and sober-minded person in Russia. This is the banner which can unite about it people of all spheres, all estates, all inclinations." Liberalism, he thought, would also cure Russia of its social ills and enable it to take its rightful place among the nations of the world. In this one word, he wrote, lies "all the future of Russia." Chicherin identified liberalism with various freedoms, including freedom from serfdom, and with due process of law and openness (*glasnost*) regarding government activities and legal procedures.

But the hopes of Chicherin and other liberals were soon smashed on the rocks of Russian reality. Rather than becoming a rallying flag, liberalism increasingly became a target of scorn. Its failure was crucial for the future of Russia.

In the West, liberalism had been supported by a strong middle class and by those wishing to reduce monarchical and governmental powers. In Russia, the middle class was weak, and its businessmen were not especially liberal. In addition, men such as Chicherin and the Miliutin brothers wanted a reforming monarch but did not wish to weaken his powers. In fact, they wanted a strong monarch who would stand above class interests and champion progressive policies in the interest of the entire empire. Thus, as paradoxical as it might seem, Constantine Kavelin (Chicherin's fellow reformer and former professor) wrote about the "complete necessity of retaining the unlimited power of the sovereign, basing it on the widest possible local freedom."

These liberal "statists" soon came into conflict with another group of moderate reformers. They were gentry liberals, whose appetites for political participation had been whetted by involvement in the provincial assemblies set up to discuss emancipation. Already in the late 1850s and early 1860s, most liberal statists had opposed gentry requests for more extensive participation in formulating public policy. Although ideas such as convening an elected national assembly might seem to be liberal, the liberal statists feared such an assembly would be dominated by the gentry and their own narrow interests.

The split between liberal statists and liberal gentry was one reason why a Western-style liberalism was not more successful in Russia. Although the liberal statists correctly feared gentry bias, they failed to perceive adequately the inherent unlikeliness of any lasting marriage between an unlimited monarchy and reform.

If the two liberal groups could not be held together, it was even more unlikely that the radical Alexander Herzen, then publishing in London, would long cooperate with divided reformers. But this founder of Russian agrarian socialism, who had left Russia in 1847, temporarily toned down his radicalism, hoping to encourage reform. His periodical, *The Bell*, was smuggled into Russia and became essential reading for many liberals and radicals. Each of its few thousand copies passed through countless hands, even those of members of the royal family. It alone delivered news and opinions not subject to censorship. Among its Russian contributors were not only radicals, but also some government officials writing anonymously—for example, Nikolai Miliutin.

From 1857 until 1862, Herzen continued to exert a major influence on Russian public opinion. Although many educated people disagreed with him, not many chose to ignore him. Visiting him in London became a must for Russian intellectuals traveling to Europe, including the writers Tolstoy, Turgenev, and Dostoevsky.

If moderates such as Turgenev tried to restrain Herzen's more militant tendencies, radicals such as Herzen's co-editor Nikolai Ogarev and the fiery Mikhail Bakunin encouraged such leanings. After being imprisoned and exiled for more than a dozen years, Bakunin escaped from Siberia and arrived in London at the end of 1861 eager for revolutionary action. Alluding to his penchant for believing revolution ever imminent, Herzen later wrote that he always "mistook the second month of pregnancy for the ninth."

The influence of Ogarev and Bakunin contributed to Herzen's stepped-up criticism of the government and his increasing support of radical ventures. At the end of 1861, he charged that the government consisted of "riffraff, swindlers, robbers, and whores." In 1862, he aided in the formation of a revolutionary organization called "Land and Liberty." One of the causes supported by this organization was Polish independence. When a full-scale Polish rebellion broke out in January 1863, Herzen supported it in *The Bell*. (For the Polish rebellion, see Chapter 24.) As a result of this support, his popularity and that of his journal plummeted in Russia.

The Polish revolt was the culmination of several years of rising radicalism in the Russian Empire. Student demonstrations led to the closing of St. Petersburg University in 1861, and when mysterious fires broke out in the capital in 1862, many people blamed them on radical students. Blood-thirsty pamphlets such as one entitled "Young Russia" increased the alarm. It called for revolution, for socialism, for the abolition of marriage and the family; and if the defenders of the imperial party resisted, it proclaimed: "We will kill [them] in the streets . . . in their houses, in the narrow lanes of towns, in the broad avenues of cities, in the hamlets and villages."

As a result of Turgenev's controversial novel *Fathers and Sons* (1862), a new word was popularized that some soon applied to such radical beliefs. The term was *nihilism*, and nihilists thought that nothing (*nihil*), including family, society, or religion, should be accepted that was not based on Reason. Many nihilists were noteworthy for their utter contempt for traditional authorities and for their unconventional behavior and appearance (for example, long hair for men or short hair for women).

Although there is some debate as to whether Nikolai Chernyshevsky and Nikolai Dobroliubov should be considered nihilists, they are usually linked with the nihilist Dmitri Pisarev as the most important of the new radical thinkers. All three men were journalists. Pisarev was the son of a landowner, and Chernyshevsky and Dobroliubov were the sons of priests and members of the *raznochintsy*—a term applied to those who did not fit into any other legal estate.

All three men thought that progress lay in following the path of Reason, science, philosophic materialism, and an enlightened utilitarianism, or "rational egoism," which saw no real conflict between the true good of the individual and that of society. All three also preached the necessity of emancipating women.

Chernyshevsky and Dobroliubov generally believed that the liberals' concern for "rights" and participation in government was not nearly as important to the peasant masses as was climbing out of poverty and stopping a situation whereby "one class sucks another's blood." As the radical Belinsky had earlier put it: "The people need potatoes, but not a constitution in the least."

Pisarev's writings were less political than those of Chernyshevsky and Dobroliubov, who were not only champions of the peasant masses, but also of socialism. Although Chernyshevsky's view of the peasants was in general sober and realistic, the younger Dobroliubov tended more toward idealizing them.

Alarmed by the growing radicalism, the government arrested both Chernyshevsky and Pisarev in mid-1862. Chernyshevsky's two-year imprisonment in the capital's infamous Sts. Peter and Paul Fortress, his subsequent trial, and his nineteen-year exile to Siberia—all based on flimsy and fabricated evidence—were glaring examples of the injustice of the pre-reform legal system. Pisarev's treatment was less scandalous but still harsh; he was jailed for four and a half years for trying to have an illegal article printed. Amazingly, both men were allowed to write while in prison and have some of their works printed legally. While in prison, Chernyshevsky wrote his most famous work, *What Is To Be Done?* (see Chapter 27).

Yet it was the Russian nationalistic reaction to the Polish rebellion of 1863–1864, rather than the earlier arrests of Chernyshevsky and Pisarev, that was most important in slowing, at least temporarily, the growth of radicalism. In the new climate, flirting with radicalism became less popular.

Liberalism was another casualty of the reawakened Russian nationalism and one that did not bounce back as quickly. The nationalist reaction ripped apart any tattered hopes of rallying public opinion around a liberal banner. Just as many liberals in Germany in the 1860s opted for the nationalist policies of Bismarck over their own earlier liberal principles, so too in Russia some liberals became more nationalistic and less liberal as a result of the emotions generated by the conflict with the Poles.

Reformism and Radicalism, 1866–1881

During the last fifteen years of Alexander II's reign, reformism from below made little headway. As the judicial and zemstvo reforms were gradually implemented, many lawyers and zemstvo workers, including physicians and teachers, supported further reforms. So too did several journals, such as *The Messenger of Europe*. Yet, having already implemented most of his major reforms, Alexander II was disinclined to go much further. In fact, after an assassination attempt on him in 1866, a period of reaction set in.

The would-be assassin, Dmitri Karakozov (subsequently hanged), had been influenced by the ideas of a cousin who headed a revolutionary group in Moscow called "Organization." A small cell within it, labeled "Hell," advocated terrorist methods and talked of freeing Chernyshevsky from Siberian exile. Before trying to shoot the tsar, Karakozov composed a manifesto which stated that the tsar was the greatest enemy of the "simple people" and that he enabled the rich to continue exploiting them.

Although Karakozov was acting on his own and the "Organization" that influenced him had only about fifty members, the attempted assassination led to a major government shake-up. The most prominent new appointments, both conservatives, were Dmitri Tolstoi as minister of education and General Peter Shuvalov as head of the Third Section (secret police). Shuvalov often represented the interests of wealthy landowners, and he soon became the second most powerful man in Russia. He remained as head of the Third Section until 1874, when he became ambassador to England. In the eyes of War Minister Miliutin, Shuvalov overemphasized the dangers facing Alexander and was primarily responsible for impeding new reforms.

After Karakozov's arrest, the next big revolutionary case stemmed from a murder committed in 1869 by the revolutionary Sergei Nechaev. After a trip to Switzerland, where he had impressed Bakunin and Ogarev, Nechaev returned to Russia and, with some accomplices, murdered a young revolutionary named Ivanov, who had refused to subordinate himself to Nechaev. Whether there were other causes is not certain. The subsequent publicity given to the murder helped to discredit Nechaev and some of his more unsavory and authoritarian beliefs and tactics—many of these were spelled out in *The Revolutionary Catechism*, a pamphlet he had prepared with the help of Bakunin.

The populist radical movement of the 1870s emerged partly in reaction to Nechaev's methods. One of its first groups, the "Chaikovsky Circle," was opposed to having a single leader and thought of itself as a group of friends working together for their own improvement and for the good of the people. At first, the group confined itself primarily to distributing radical literature to various parts of the country and to teaching and propagandizing among city workers and peasants.

The two strongest influences on these young populists were Bakunin and Peter Lavrov. By the beginning of the 1870s, Bakunin had completed the development of his anarchistic philosophy. He believed that any centralized government was incompatible with human liberty and that the state and religion were humankind's two greatest enemies.

Bakunin's ideal, similar to that of Herzen's, was a system of free federated communes. In contrast to Herzen, who by his death in 1870 had foreseen that a revolution of blood would have to be maintained by blood, Bakunin wanted violent revolution. He encouraged young Russians to become brigand-rebels among the peasant masses. Whereas Herzen admired the Russian peasants primarily for their socialistic and democratic tendencies, Bakunin also saw in them potential rebels. Like those who had joined the Razin and Pugachev rebellions of earlier centuries, Russia's peasants, he thought, were just waiting for an opportune time to rebel.

Peter Lavrov was a more moderate man than Bakunin. Like Bakunin, he was from the wealthy gentry and escaped from Russian exile and settled in Western Europe. From there, he continued to influence young Russian radicals. Both before and after his 1870 escape, he stressed the *debt* of the educated and privileged minority to the masses, a debt they owed because their privileges, including education, had come at the expense of the peasants, who had been exploited for centuries. Although he desired an agrarian socialist society, he emphasized patient educational and propagandistic work among the peasants, rather than trying to incite them to any premature upheaval.

The influence of both Bakunin and Lavrov was especially evident in 1874. That spring and summer, more than 1,000 radicals went into the countryside to work among the masses, to repay their debt to the people. Depending upon the varied inclinations of the radicals, "work" took on various forms: for example, carpentry or cobbling, giving smallpox inoculations, teaching literacy, propagandizing, and fomenting revolution. Many also believed that there was much they themselves could learn from the peasants.

But centuries of oppression had made the peasants naturally wary and cautious. Although they did not generally denounce the radicals to the authorities, they realized that being too receptive to these outsiders might get them in serious trouble. In addition, the mental gap between the peasants and newcomers was often great. And the local gentry and others were often not as reluctant as the peasants to report them to the police. Before the year was out, more than 700 of these populists were arrested.

As a result of the failure of this spontaneous, poorly organized movement, radicals began to emphasize more organization and in 1876 formed a new "Land and Liberty" group. In 1879, however, this group split in two.

It did so primarily because of differences over the use of terrorism. One of the new groups, the Black Repartition, opposed emphasizing it, believing it would distract them from further work among the masses. The other group, the People's Will, thought such tactics were now necessary.

Even before 1879, as the radicals saw their friends arrested, some of them turned to violent methods out of frustration and to facilitate escapes. A forerunner of things to come was the famous case of Vera Zasulich. Because she had heard that General Trepov, the military governor of St. Petersburg, had ordered the flogging of a prisoner, she walked into his office one day in 1878, pulled a revolver out of her muff, and shot him.

Another motivation for now stressing terrorism was the fear of some radicals that capitalism was rapidly developing in Russia and that it would increase the misery of the people. Members of the People's Will blamed the government for being "the greatest capitalist force in the country" and for excessively taxing the peasants to pay for this development. They thought that their best hope of reversing the situation was to overthrow the tsarist government and work toward the establishment of a socialist society. They hoped that terror, especially the assassination of Alexander II, would demoralize the government and awaken the masses to the realization that the government could indeed be overthrown.

Meanwhile, dissatisfaction with the tsarist government had increased. Passions unleashed in the 1876–1877 crusade to help the South Slavs in their battle against the Ottoman Turks were further inflamed by a Russo-Turkish War of 1877–1878 (see Chapter 24). But the eventual peace settlement agreed upon at the 1878 Congress of Berlin left many nationalists critical of the government. And the liberal zemstvo assembly of the province of Tver passed a resolution noting that the tsar had helped the Bulgarians establish a liberal constitutional order, which included an elected assembly. The Tver assembly hoped, fruitlessly as it turned out, that Alexander would see fit to grant his own people a similar benefit.

Alexander's personal life was also a source of dissatisfaction to many in royal circles. Some were privately critical of his treatment of his wife Maria and his continuing relationship with the young Catherine Dolgorukova, with whom he maintained a second family. Constantine Pobedonostsev, the chief advisor to Tsarevich Alexander, referred privately to Alexander II as a "pitiful and unfortunate man" whose will was exhausted and who wanted "only the pleasures of the belly" [sic].[3] Only six weeks after the Empress Maria's death in mid-1880, Alexander married his mistress of fifteen years in a morganatic marriage.

By this time, he was being hunted in earnest by the People's Will, who had already organized a couple of failed assassination attempts. The first had blown up an imperial train but not the one the tsar was on, and the second had killed eleven people in his Winter Palace. After the second explosion, wild rumors spread around the city. The tsar's brother, referring to the terrorists, lamented in his diary: "We do not see, do not know, do not have the slightest idea of their numbers."

To deal with the increase of terrorism after the Russo-Turkish War, Alexander resorted to more authoritarian measures and curtailed some of the previous freedoms of the zemstvos, educational institutions, and the press. Following the explosion in the Winter Palace in early 1880, he appointed a Supreme Administrative Commission. Its head was General Loris-Melikov, who became extremely powerful. Although the commission remained in place only for several months, Loris-Melikov retained his power by then becoming minister of interior.

Loris-Melikov allied himself with Alexander's more progressive ministers, such as Dmitri Miliutin, and combated the influence of more reactionary ministers, such as Tolstoi who was both minister of education and procurator of the Holy Synod Dmitri. Loris-Melikov also pursued a two-pronged policy of trying to fight terrorism more effectively, while gaining public support for the government. To accomplish the latter, he lessened government restraints on the zemstvos and press and even recommended going one big step further. In early 1881, he presented a plan that provided for the creation of several commissions that would make legislative recommendations in the areas of finance and administration to the tsar's advisory State Council. Moreover, some of the delegates of the commissions would be elected, as would fifteen others who would sit with the State Council to consider the recommendations.

---

[3]As quoted in Robert F. Byrnes, *Pobedonostsev: His Life and Thought* (Bloomington, 1968), pp. 143–144.

FIGURE 22.3. The Church of the Resurrection of the Savior on the Blood, St. Petersburg, 1883–1907, architect A. Parland, was built on the spot where Alexander II was assassinated near the Catherine Canal.

Although this project was a long way from granting an elected national assembly or a constitution to his country, Alexander II expressed fears after approving it that he was "going along the road toward a constitution."

As it turned out, however, the road he went down later that day, March 1, 1881, was the road to his death. Directed by the diminutive Sophia Perovskaia, daughter of a former civilian governor of the capital, People's Will assassins finally killed him. After a first home-made bomb rocked his carriage and mortally wounded a few people, Alexander got out of his carriage but was then hit by another bomb, thrown by another assassin. It knocked him to the ground and ripped his legs apart. Bleeding profusely, he was rushed to the Winter Palace, but his life could not be saved. Later that same afternoon, the reign of the "tsar liberator" came to an inglorious end.

SUGGESTED SOURCES*

ALMENDINGEN, E. M. *The Emperor Alexander II: A Study.* London, 1962.
BERGMAN, JAY. *Vera Zasulich: A Biography.* Stanford, 1983.

*See also books cited in footnotes.

BROIDO, VERA. *Apostles Into Terrorists: Women and the Revolutionary Movement in the Russia of Alexander II.* New York, 1977.

BROWER, DANIEL R. *Training the Nihilists: Education and Radicalism in Tsarist Russia.* Ithaca, N.Y., 1975.

CARR, E. H. *Michael Bakunin.* New York, 1961.

———. *The Romantic Exiles: A Nineteenth Century Portrait Gallery.* Boston, 1961.

CHERNYSHEVSKY, N. G. *What Is to Be Done? Tales about New People.* New York, 1961.

EMMONS, TERENCE, ed. *Emancipation of the Russian Serfs.* New York, 1970.

EMMONS, TERENCE, and WAYNE S. VUCINICH, eds. *The Zemstvo in Russia: An Experiment in Local Self-Government.* Cambridge, Eng., 1982.

ENGEL, BARBARA ALPERN, and CLIFFORD N. ROSENTHAL, eds. *Five Sisters: Women against the Tsar.* New York, 1975.

FIELD, DANIEL. *The End of Serfdom: Nobility and Bureaucracy in Russia, 1855–1861.* Cambridge, Mass., 1976.

———. *Rebels in the Name of the Tsar.* Boston, 1976.

FOOTMAN, DAVID. *The Alexander Conspiracy: A Life of A. I. Zhelyabov.* LaSalle, Ill., 1974.

GLEASON, ABBOTT. *Young Russia: The Genesis of Russian Radicalism in the 1860s.* New York, 1980.

HAMBURG, GARY M. *Boris Chicherin and Early Russian Liberalism, 1828–1866.* Stanford, 1992.

HARDY, DEBORAH. *Land and Freedom: The Origins of Russian Terrorism.* New York, 1987.

HERZEN, ALEXANDER. *My Past and Thoughts.* 4 vols. London, 1968.

KROPOTKIN, PETER. *Memoirs of a Revolutionist.* New York, 1971.

LINCOLN, W. BRUCE. *The Great Reforms: Autocracy, Bureaucracy, and the Politics of Change in Imperial Russia.* Dekalb, Ill., 1990.

MENDEL, ARTHUR P. *Michael Bakunin: Roots of Apocalypse.* New York, 1981.

MILLER, FORRESTT A. *Dimitrii Miliutin and the Reform Era in Russia.* Nashville, 1968.

MOSSE, W. E. *Alexander II and the Modernization of Russia.* Rev. ed. New York, 1962.

NIKITENKO, ALEKSANDR. *The Diary of a Russian Censor,* abridged, ed. and trans. Helen Saltz Jacobson. Amherst, Mass., 1975.

ORLOVSKY, DANIEL T. *The Limits of Reform: The Ministry of Internal Affairs in Imperial Russia, 1802–1881.* Cambridge, Mass., 1981.

PEREIRA, N. G. O. *Tsar-Liberator: Alexander II of Russia, 1818–1881.* Newtonville, Mass., 1983.

POMPER, PHILIP. *Sergei Nechaev.* New Brunswick, N.J., 1979.

RIEBER, ALFRED J. "Alexander II: A Revisionist View," *JMH*[†] 43 (March 1971): 42–58.

———, ed. *The Politics of Autocracy: Letters of Alexander II to Prince A. I. Bariatinskii, 1857–1864.* Paris, 1966.

SAUNDERS, DAVID. *Russia in the Age of Reaction and Reform, 1801–1881.* London, 1992. Chs. 8–11.

SCHAPIRO, LEONARD. *Rationalism and Nationalism in Russian Nineteenth-Century Political Thought.* New Haven, 1967.

ULAM, ADAM B. *In the Name of the People: Prophets and Conspirators in Prerevolutionary Russia.* New York, 1977.

VENTURI, FRANCO. *Roots of Revolution: A History of the Populist and Socialist Movements in Nineteenth Century Russia.* New York, 1966.

WCISLO, FRANCIS WILLIAM. *Reforming Rural Russia: State, Local Society, and National Politics, 1855–1914.* Princeton, 1990.

WORTMAN, RICHARD. *The Development of a Russian Legal Consciousness.* Chicago, 1976.

ZAIONCHKOVSKII, PETER A. *The Abolition of Serfdom in Russia.* Gulf Breeze, Fla., 1978.

————. *The Russian Autocracy in Crises, 1878–1882.* Gulf Breeze, Fla., 1979.

ZAKHAROVA, L. G. "Alexander II," *RSH* 32 (Winter 1993–94): 57–88. Reprinted in *EER*, pp. 295–333.

————. "Autocracy and the Abolition of Serfdom in Russia, 1856–1861," *SSH* 26 (Fall 1987). (The whole issue is devoted to this work except for the useful introduction of the editor and translator of it, Gary M. Hamburg.)

CHAPTER 23

Reactionary Politics, Economic Modernization, and Political Opposition, 1881–1905

In the quarter century after the death of Alexander II, tsarist domestic policy combined reactionary policies designed to safeguard the autocratic order with modernizing economic measures intended to strengthen Russia in the world. Yet the two aspects were difficult to harmonize and frequently undercut each other. Modernization, for example, greatly increased the number of educated people, but by 1905 opposition to Nicholas II's autocracy was widespread among them and took primarily two forms: socialist and liberal.

ALEXANDER III AND POBEDONOSTSEV: THE AUTOCRAT AND HIS CHIEF ADVISER

Just a few days after his thirty-sixth birthday, Alexander III succeeded his assassinated father. He was a bearded, herculean man who liked to entertain the friends of his twelve-year-old son Nicholas by twisting iron pokers into knots. In a train wreck in 1888, he protected his wife and children by holding up a collapsing dining car roof. His approach to ruling was similar. By the strength of his will and crown, he tried to prevent the collapse of the autocratic political order and showed no more mercy to its opponents than he did to iron pokers.

The new tsar was honest, dutiful, and forthright. He was also often ungracious and could be blunt to the point of rudeness. Once at a state dinner, after the Austrian ambassador had mentioned the possibility of mobilizing a few army corps because of Balkan differences with Russia, the tsar bent a fork into a knot and pitched it toward him, saying: "That is what I am going to do to your two or three army corps."[1]

Alexander III's straightforward, unswerving approach to problems was made simpler by his lack of intellectual discernment, curiosity, or flexibility. Yet, unfortunately for him and Russia, the country required a ruler with just

---

[1]Aleksandr Mikhailovich, Grand Duke of Russia, *Once a Grand Duke* (New York, 1932), pp. 66–67.

such intellectual qualities as well as a strong will. Only such a ruler stood much of a chance of successfully overseeing Russia's modernization, while maintaining stability and order.

The chief adviser to the new tsar was Constantine Pobedonostsev, a tall, thin, humorless man. He was the grandson of a priest and considered himself fortunate to have graduated from the noble-dominated Imperial School of Jurisprudence. In addition to other positions, he had been the chief tutor and guide of Alexander since 1865. Although as tsar Alexander sometimes took competing advice from other advisers, his policies most often mirrored Pobedonostsev's ideas, which coincided with the tsar's basic instincts.

Pobedonostsev spelled out his ideas most clearly in 1896 in *Moskovskii Sbornik,* a book published in England two years later with the title *Reflections of a Russian Statesman.* His view of the human condition was pessimistic. ("From the day that man first fell falsehood has ruled the world.") He divided men into two groups: a small intellectual aristocracy and the vulgar "herd," incapable of higher thinking. Because he believed that humans were by nature sinful and the masses ignorant, and because of Russia's historical development, he thought that autocracy was the only form of government for it.

He stated that parliamentary bodies were "one of the greatest illustrations of human delusion." Universal suffrage is "a fatal error, and one of the most remarkable in the history of mankind." The press, the organ of public opinion, "is one of the falsest institutions of our time." Also, "faith in abstract principles is the prevailing error of our time." Parliaments, democracy, the press, and rationalism, like the ideas of human perfectibility and secular progress, led to discontentment and misery. So too, he thought, did education beyond one's needs.

Because the natural, organic development of a nation was important to Pobedonostsev, he was more tolerant of parliamentarism in England, where it had slowly evolved, than he was of it in other countries where it was not an organic growth. He thought it had no place in Russia, however, and Western imports such as liberalism, legalism, and religious tolerance did not belong there either. He believed the Orthodox Russians should dominate the empire.

Pobedonostsev took his religion most seriously and from 1880 until 1905 served as the procurator of the Holy Synod. He believed that the true religion and faith were the only hope for sinful humanity, but happiness was to come primarily in heaven, not on earth.

The Orthodox Church was not only to help Russians save their souls and get to heaven, but also it was "to inspire the people with respect for the law and for power." Orthodoxy was to be the moral glue that bound people to their Orthodox tsar. For the non-Orthodox of the empire (counting Old Believers and sectarians, probably more than a third of the population), Pobedonostsev could offer no effective "moral glue," only coercion.

REACTIONARY POLICIES OF ALEXANDER III

Although the oppression of ethnic and religious minorities was one characteristic of Alexander III's reign (see Chapter 24), his first task was to deal with his

father's assassins and other members of the People's Will. A panel of government-appointed officials, acting as both judges and jury, condemned six individuals, including two women, to be hanged. After it was discovered that one
of the women was pregnant, her sentence was changed to life imprisonment.
The other woman was the noble-born Sophia Perovskaia, who had directed the
assassination.

Before the sentences could be carried out, two prominent individuals appealed to the tsar to act like a true Christian monarch and forgo applying capital punishment. One was the famous novelist Leo Tolstoy; the other was the
philosopher and religious thinker Vladimir Soloviev, whose father, the University of Moscow's Sergei Soloviev, had once tutored Alexander III in history.
Upon hearing of the appeals, Pobedonostsev wrote to the tsar, advising him
not to heed the requests of those possessing "weak minds and hearts." The tsar
did not. Despite one of the condemned twice hitting the scaffold floor before
being strung up for a third try—shades of the Decembrists' slipshod hangings
in 1826—all five were hanged on April 3, 1881.

FIGURE 23.1. The hanging of Alexander II's assassins on Semenovskii Square, St. Peters-
burg, April 3, 1881.
(From Ian Grey, The Horizon History of Russia, *American Heritage Publishing Company,
New York, 1970, p. 287, New York Public Library.)*

In the next several months the new tsar made it clear that he intended to rule with an iron hand. Siding with Pobedonostsev, who (according to Dmitri Miliutin) called the Great Reforms of Alexander II a "criminal mistake," the tsar rejected Loris-Melikov's earlier plan for the establishment of advisory commissions and issued a manifesto affirming the necessity of maintaining absolute power. Upset at this course of events, Loris-Melikov, Miliutin (who thought Pobedonostsev a "fanatic-reactionary"), and a few other reform-minded ministers resigned.

In August, in an effort to root out revolutionaries still at large, the tsar approved a "Regulation on Measures for the Safety of the State and the Protection of Public Order." Strictly speaking, it was not a "law," arrived at by normal bureaucratic procedure (through the Council of State), but an emergency ordinance. Although applying to only some provinces and supposedly lasting only three years, these "temporary regulations" were gradually extended and continued to exist for more than three decades. They squelched the hopes of reformers who wished to see Russia build upon Alexander II's judicial reforms and become a country in which the due process of law was a recognized right of citizens.

The "temporary regulations" recognized two types of emergencies and permitted governors to bypass regular courts and laws. Under varying conditions, they could fine, imprison for three months or less, turn over to military courts, or banish from their province any suspected person. They could also prohibit meetings and gatherings, including those of zemstvos, shut down factories or schools, suppress newspapers, and fire certain officials.

Throughout his reign, Alexander III attempted to strengthen the state's control over society. The University Statute of 1884 curtailed university autonomy. From 1889 to 1892, the government cut back on rights of peasants and local governing bodies. Most significant of Alexander's "counterreforms" was the creation of land captains in 1889. By 1895, there were about 2,000 of them. These government-appointed noblemen received sweeping administrative and judicial powers over the peasants. Each land captain was responsible for overseeing part of a district's peasants, their elected peasant officials, and institutions such as the village and canton (*volost*) assemblies and cantonal courts. He could overturn assembly decisions and suspend peasant officials and cantonal court rulings. He could even fine or briefly jail such officials. He also became a judge in civil and minor criminal cases involving peasants beyond the cantonal court level, replacing for them the elected Justices of the Peace created by the 1864 judicial reform.

In 1890, a new law strengthened the government's powers over the zemstvos. It stipulated that henceforth zemstvo heads had to be confirmed by the minister of interior and zemstvo boards and employees by their provincial governor. The latter also received new powers, including that of appointing the peasant members of the district zemstvos from lists of candidates submitted by canton assemblies. Not only did peasants lose their previous right of electing delegates to the district zemstvos, but also they saw their proportion of delegates decline to less than one-third of the total delegates in district assemblies.

Conversely, noble representation in them increased, and the 1889–1890 changes are sometimes taken as a sign that Alexander III wished to rely more on the nobles as a bulwark of the regime. Thomas Pearson's study of the autocracy's local government policies in this era indicates, however, that the 1889–1890 changes polarized and alienated the nobles. Although the policies were intended to strengthen Ministry-of-Interior control while making local government more efficient, St. Petersburg also hoped they would gain it more provincial support. It proved an illusory hope, as peasants as well as nobles became more disillusioned with the government.

In 1892, town councils, officials, and voters experienced the government's heavy hand. A new law stipulated the government confirmation of elected officials, regulated the number of council meetings, and, by increasing property qualifications, shrunk the electorate. For example, the already small number of eligible voters in St. Petersburg and Moscow was reduced by more than 60 percent. This meant that in the two cities combined, less than 1 percent of the total population could now vote.

Other measures also reflected the government's distrust of the masses. In 1887, for example, the government increased gymnasium fees in the hope of keeping lower-class children out of the gymnasiums.

POLICIES OF ECONOMIC MODERNIZATION, 1881–1903

Although reactionary measures were one aspect of tsarist policy, economic modernization, which had begun earlier but accelerated most rapidly in the century's final two decades, was another. Not all government economic policies contributed to modernization, however, and it occurred for many reasons in addition to governmental actions.

The government pursued modernization chiefly by investing or encouraging investment in railways, mining, and manufacturing. This policy necessitated building up capital for investment, which, in turn, spurred other increases: in tax revenues, the balance of payments, the gold reserve, and foreign loans.

Alexander III's first of three finance ministers was N. K. Bunge. He inherited a national budget drained by heavy military expenditures and servicing a high foreign debt. To build up Russia's gold reserve, he set out to improve its balance of payments by raising import tariffs. By thus boosting the prices of foreign products, Bunge aided competing Russian industries. He also reorganized the railway system, which in 1880 was overwhelmingly in private hands, and increased the state's role in constructing and operating new lines. Believing that Russia's tax policy placed an unrealistic burden on the peasants and that it had to be overhauled if the Russian economy was to be healthy, he reduced peasants' taxes, even eliminating the long-standing soul tax. Although careful not to drive capital out of Russia, he introduced new taxes that affected mainly the upper classes, for example, on inheritance, profits, and savings. Finally, he oversaw the establishment of a factory inspectorate and peasant and noble land banks to provide loans.

Compared to the policies of his two successors, Bunge's initiatives were fairly moderate, but they did not generate enough income to enable the government to balance its budget or reduce its foreign debt. He resigned in 1886.

Alexander III's second finance minister (1887–1892) was I. A. Vyshnegradsky. As with Bunge, not all his policies were directly motivated by the modernizing impulse, but collectively they did move Russia further down that road. To balance Russia's budget, increase gold reserves, and produce a healthy trade surplus, he increased indirect taxes and exports, especially grain, and upped import tariffs to higher levels than those of any other power.

These policies contributed to both positive and negative results. The most devastating of the latter was the famine of 1891–1892. Increases in indirect taxes on basic goods, along with other government measures, led the peasants to sell more grain, leaving them little surplus if an emergency arose. Vyshnegradsky's statement of 1887 that "we may undereat, but we will export" now took on a grim reality. The resulting famine and the public outcry it created forced him to resign. (For more on this famine, see Chapter 26.)

His successor from 1892 to 1903 was one of the most dynamic ministers of late imperial Russia, Sergei Witte, a man who came to symbolize Russia's modernization drive. After studying mathematics at Novorossiisk University in

FIGURE 23.2. Peasants depicted taking thatch from their roof to feed their animals during the famine of 1891–1892.
(From Otto Hoetzsch, The Evolution of Russia. Harcourt, Brace & World, New York, 1966, #137, p. 161. © Thames & Hudson of London.)

MAP 23.1

Odessa, he began a successful career in railway administration. By the time he became minister of finance, he had gained a reputation for his practical business sense, his hard-working habits, and his passionate belief in the necessity of rapid Russian industrialization.

To achieve it, he continued and expanded some of his predecessors' policies regarding high import tariffs, indirect taxes (on such items as sugar, matches, tobacco, and kerosene), and the maintenance of a favorable trade balance. Although grain exports had to be reduced in 1891 and 1892, by 1894 they accounted for more than 50 percent of the value of all Russian exports. During his eleven years in office, the state's annual revenue doubled. To facilitate foreign loans and make the ruble convertible, in 1897 he put Russia on the Gold Standard. Not only foreign loans, but also foreign investment rose quickly while he was in office, and he estimated that in 1900 about half of all industrial and commercial capital was of foreign origin.

The results of all these financial moves were impressive. Partly because of them, government investment in industrial modernization increased significantly, as did industrial production, which more than doubled in the 1890s. Especially notable was the growth of iron and petroleum production and of railways. As the government's railway head and then minister of finance, Witte oversaw the building of most of the Trans-Siberian Railway, begun in 1891 and almost completed by the time he left office in 1903.

But Witte's policies also had negative consequences. For almost a century, the dominant view was that his policies—along with those of Vyshnegradsky before him—led to an extended agrarian or peasant crisis. Some recent research, however, has challenged this view. Yet there still seems little doubt that at least sectors of the peasant economy and parts of the country (for example, the central black-soil provinces) suffered increased economic hardship, that government financial policies had something to do with it, and that many of Witte's contemporaries believed his policies were helping to cause an agrarian crisis.

His policies certainly helped accelerate changes, such as the rapid growth of industrial workers, and helped fuel the rising manifestations of public discontent. The landed nobility were critical of him, and in the late 1890s, industrial and student strikes became more prevalent. In 1902, peasant disturbances broke out in the provinces of Kharkov and Poltava. Other sectors of the public were also becoming more restive.

Partly to further industrialization and keep foreign loans (primarily French) and investments coming, Witte advocated an easing of government repression. This displeased many of Nicholas II's more reactionary ministers and advisers, especially his minister of interior, V. K. Plehve, who blamed much of the increased dissatisfaction in the country on Witte. Witte's standing was further undercut by an economic depression that began around 1900. Finally, in 1903, Nicholas replaced him as finance minister. Although the tsar appointed him chairman of the Council of Ministers, the council seldom met, and the position was largely honorific.

NICHOLAS II AND THE POLITICS OF REACTION, 1894–1904

When Alexander III died unexpectedly of nephritis in October 1894, his oldest son, Nicholas, was only twenty-six. His reaction to his father's death is described by Grand Duke Alexander Mikhailovich (then twenty-eight) to whom Nicholas addressed the following words:

> What is going to happen to me, to you, to Xenia, to Alix, to mother, to all of Russia? I am not prepared to be a Czar. I never wanted to become one. I know nothing of the business of ruling. I have no idea of even how to talk to the ministers. Will you help me, Sandro?[2]

These words revealed much of Nicholas's character. Much shorter and thinner than Alexander III, he was also much less confident and outspoken. Although adoring and in awe of his father, he was closer to his solicitous mother, Maria, who had been born a Danish princess. He grew up surrounded by his parents, his large extended family of relatives, and a faithful array of servants and tutors. Partly as a result of the terrorism that brought the terrible death of his grandfather, Alexander II (which he had witnessed as a twelve-year-old boy), Nicholas was raised in a sheltered environment.

Whatever the complex reasons, he grew up a dutiful son, showing few signs of rebellion or independence. As his later life made clear, he was often fatalistic, resigned to suffering what he felt was inescapable—a feeling reinforced by the fact that he was born on St. Job the Sufferer's day. After he became tsar, observers commented on his politeness and charm, but they often failed to discern the personality behind these external appearances. He was cautious and suspicious and could be stubborn, but he hated confrontation. He also hated complexity and lacked the intellectual stamina, although not the intelligence, to work through complex problems. Like most of the Romanovs, however, he possessed a high sense of duty and believed in autocracy. Moreover, his mother had emphasized to him how important it was to display the correct imperial behavior. So he did his best, but he probably spoke from the depths of his soul when he said he never wanted to become tsar.

If one looks at his course of studies and the positions he held as tsarevich, it seems, at first glance, that he was adequately prepared to be tsar, but a deeper look reveals serious deficiencies. He became proficient in French, German, and English; studied history, geography, math, science, religion, drawing, music, and military matters; and was tutored by Pobedonostsev in law and by Bunge in economics and finance. Yet, except for history and especially military matters, he displayed little enthusiasm for learning. The pattern was similar in the positions the young tsarevich assumed after reaching adulthood. Only military duties, and not very taxing ones at that, elicited much sustained enthusiasm from him. His sheltered upbringing, coupled with the belief that Alexander III (only forty-nine at the time of his death) still had many years to rule, further contributed to his unpreparedness for the awesome task of becoming autocrat of the Russian Empire.

One reason for the tsarevich's interest in the military was his preference for the outdoors. He enjoyed pastimes such as riding, hunting, skating, and sledding and chores such as chopping wood. He also enjoyed other pleasures common among young officers. For several years in the early 1890s, he had an af-

[2]Ibid., pp. 168–169.

fair with a young ballerina, while simultaneously hoping that a marriage could be arranged between him and Princess Alix (later Alexandra) of Hesse-Darmstadt. Not only did he spend much time at the ballet, but also he enjoyed the theater and the operas of such composers as Glinka, Musorgsky, and Tchaikovsky.

Joining Nicholas at his father's deathbed was Princess Alix, who by then had agreed to give up her Protestant faith and convert to Orthodoxy to marry Nicholas. Although four years younger than he and in a foreign country, she did not hesitate to advise the tsarevich to be firm, show his own mind, and demand the respect due to him from his father's doctors and others. This was typical of the advice this tall, proud woman often gave him after their marriage, which occurred a month after Alexander III's death.

At first, Nicholas II maintained most of his father's officials, including Pobedonostsev as procurator of the Holy Synod and Witte as finance minister. Even though Pobedonostsev's influence on Alexander III had waned somewhat in the final years of his reign, it was reportedly Pobedonostsev who advised Nicholas in January 1895 to object to zemstvo hopes for a greater political role. At a reception of zemstvo delegates and others who had come to congratulate the new tsar, Nicholas referred to wishes of zemstvo government participation as "senseless dreams." And he stated his intention to maintain "the principle of autocracy just as firmly and unshakably" as had his father. Not possessing his father's iron will, however, and in the face of rising opposition, this was easier said than done.

Also exercising influence on the tsar were his uncles, especially his father's brother Grand Duke Sergei, governor-general of Moscow. He was primarily responsible for planning the traditional coronation distribution of presents to commoners and for choosing the site, a large field full of ditches, where this would occur. Some of the large crowd who rushed forward on that May morning in 1896 fell in the ditches and were trampled on by others. Estimates of the number of dead varied from hundreds to thousands. Although some advised Nicholas to display his sympathy for the dead and cancel further festivities, Sergei and his brothers argued against canceling anything. The attendance of Nicholas and Alexandra at a ball that night left a bad impression on many, and Nicholas missed an important opportunity to display his concern for the common people.

Once Nicholas settled into the routine of trying to run the empire, he found the task difficult and often distasteful. Although influenced by his own beliefs and personality, his work life reflected primarily traditional autocratic practices. It consisted of innumerable meetings with individual ministers and others who reported on and received his instructions on everything from promotions to divorce applications. Sensing that he was a much weaker man than his father, ministers and relatives competed to win his backing for various causes, schemes, and ideas.[3] He had to read many reports and correspondence, and,

---

[3]Tuomo Polvinen in his *Imperial Borderland: Bobrikov and the Attempted Russification of Finland, 1898–1904* (Durham, N.C., 1995), pp. 269–271, quotes numerous primary sources to indicate this competition for Nicholas's favor during his first decade of rule and how it contributed to the perception that a firm autocratic hand was lacking.

FIGURE 23.3. Nicholas II and family early in the century.
(UPI/Bettmann Newsphotos.)

unwilling to trust a private secretary, he personally wrote out his own letters. There were also the countless formal and ceremonial appearances, military reviews and parades, and social gatherings that a tsar was expected to attend.

His main solace in such a world was his family, especially his wife and children, four girls and a boy, all born between 1895 and 1904. Alexandra grew increasingly weary of the social aspects of being an empress and never mixed comfortably in Russian high society.

Nicholas's domestic policies in the first decade of his rule followed the pattern set by his father: a continuation and extension of the "temporary regulations," further restrictions on local government, more Russification and persecution of ethnic and religious minorities, and support of Witte's industrialization program. Although never personally close to Witte, he recognized his ability and therefore retained him as finance minister until 1903.

Yet there was one important way in which Nicholas was not able to imitate his father, and that was in dealing with opposition to his autocratic regime.

PUBLIC OPINION AND POLITICAL OPPOSITION, 1881–1904

Nicholas's failures to squash political opposition as effectively as his father had done was not just a result of his being a weaker man. The modernizing needs of the country had increased the number of opponents to traditional autocratic practices, making repression more difficult.

In early 1905, the historian Paul Miliukov noted "the enormous growth of the politically conscious social elements that make public opinion in Russia." Among these elements were more professionals, artists and writers, men of business, government officials, and zemstvo workers. Especially notable was the growth of zemstvo employees, which by 1905 numbered about 70,000 individuals spread out over 358 districts. Although more than half of them were teachers, there were also zemstvo doctors; paramedics; midwives; veterinarians; pharmacists; insurance agents; statisticians; librarians; agronomists; and administrative, technical, and clerical personnel.

Earlier, in 1881, Alexander III had heard two voices giving him the same unsolicited advice to forgo inflicting capital punishment on his father's assassins. In the decades ahead, Leo Tolstoy and Vladimir Soloviev continued to criticize government policies, primarily from an ethical-religious perspective.

Tolstoy's specific criticisms of the government were many, ranging from its persecution of religious and ethnic minorities to its failures to deal adequately with famine needs in 1891–1892, a famine that Tolstoy personally did much to alleviate. In 1901 and 1902, he wrote to Nicholas II advising him on certain minimum steps he should take. But since the early 1880s, Tolstoy's ultimate desires had gone much further. He wanted to abolish centralized governments, which he believed acted in behalf of the upper classes, and he evolved a philosophy of nonviolent anarchism. His main methods for bringing an end to government were for people to refuse to pay taxes or serve the government in any manner, including military service.

Tolstoy especially irritated Pobedonostsev, still the procurator of the Holy Synod, by rejecting many basic Orthodox teachings and doctrines. In 1901, a Holy Synod edict all but excommunicated him for his heresies. If Tolstoy had not by then possessed such an imposing worldwide reputation, there is little doubt that the government would have dealt with him more severely.

The unconventional religious philosopher Vladimir Soloviev also irritated Pobedonostsev. He polemicized with Russian nationalists and criticized religious and ethnic persecution. An early ecumenical thinker, he was especially eloquent in his criticism of Russian antisemitism. Although primarily a philosopher, he was also a gifted poet. He possessed a utopian temperament and was not especially interested in political details. But to further such goals as religious toleration, he allied from the late 1880s until his death in 1900 with secular liberals and contributed to their most popular journal, *The Messenger of Europe.*

Yet despite Soloviev's strong philosophic and poetic influence (see Chapter 27) and the "Tolstoyan" followers of Tolstoy's ideas, most of educated society's political opposition was more secular. Although it was diverse, Miliukov was essentially correct in identifying its two chief currents as socialist and liberal.

Russian Socialism: The Populist Strain

From 1881 until the beginning of 1905, there were basically two types of Russian socialism. One was an eclectic homespun brand in the populist tradition, and the other was Marxist.

After the assassination of Alexander II, the Executive Committee of the populist People's Will printed thousands of copies of an open letter to Alexander III. The committee promised that their organization would disband if the new tsar agreed to certain conditions. These included an amnesty for all past political crimes and the calling of a freely elected constituent assembly to remodel Russia's government in accordance with the wishes of the people. If Alexander III failed to agree to their demands, they promised increased terrorism.

Arrests, however, helped prevent them from carrying out any extensive terrorism, and despite efforts of revolutionaries to keep the People's Will alive, it slowly withered and died. By 1887, when a group of St. Petersburg students attempting to assassinate Alexander III claimed to be part of the People's Will, no such organization still existed. There were only some individuals, like the older brother of Vladimir Ulianov (Lenin), who wished to follow in its tradition. For their plans and actions, which included preparing assassination bombs, Alexander Ulianov and some of his co-conspirators were arrested. Ulianov and four others were hanged.

Before his death, Alexander Ulianov had been troubled by the question of whether Russia had to undergo a capitalist era before inaugurating socialism. For decades to come, this issue remained vital to many Russian socialists, including Alexander's brother Vladimir.

Among other socialists concerned with this question were the legal populists. The government permitted them to publish "legally" because they advocated no political overthrow or major political reforms. A major figure in whose journals they often published was the populist writer and editor N. K. Mikhailovsky (1842–1904). Already at the end of the 1860s, he had written an article entitled "What Is Progress?" It spelled out his belief that progress was not the type of capitalist development and increasing division of labor that was occurring in the West. Rather it was whatever contributed to the fullest development of the individual personality and the full use of one's physical and mental capacities. Like most populists, Mikhailovsky stressed the importance of free will and rejected the belief that any historical laws predetermined Russia's future.

Two of the most important legal populists of the 1880s and 1890s were V. P. Vorontsov and N. F. Danielson. What both men wanted was to avoid a fully developed capitalism in Russia, a capitalism both men believed would only increase the suffering of the Russian masses. Indeed, they believed its early stages were already doing so. Instead, they desired a state-sponsored industrialization that would be carried out not for the profits of a minority, but for the good of the masses, including small producers and peasants.

The famine of 1891–1892 helped stimulate a revival of populist activists in the 1890s, especially in the black-earth provinces stretching from Ukraine to the Urals. Until 1901, there was no large populist party, only a small number of groups and individuals working in the populist tradition. In 1901, however, several of these groups came together to form the party of Socialist Revolutionaries (SRs).

The SRs main theoretician was Viktor Chrenov, who had organized a populist peasant group in the Tambov Province. In the populist tradition, the SR program emphasized a dislike of capitalism, the belief that Russia's future was not determined by any "historical laws," that it could follow its own unique path of development, and that the interests of small producers and peasants had to be safeguarded. Although the SRs were active in the cities and propagandized and recruited urban workers, SR leaders considered the peasants and their welfare their chief concerns. Peasant disorders in the Kharkov and Poltava provinces in 1902, including attacks on noble estates, strengthened the SRs' belief in the revolutionary potential of the peasants.

The SRs' immediate goals were raising the revolutionary consciousness of workers and peasants and undermining tsarist rule. Ending autocracy would allow the free will of the masses to be expressed, and SR leaders were confident the masses would favor socialism. Because some SRs strongly believed in the use of terrorism to help accomplish party goals, an autonomous "Combat Organization" was formed that was ultimately responsible for killing many officials. From 1902 to 1905, its members killed, among others, Grand Duke Sergei (Nicholas II's uncle) and two interior ministers, including the much hated V. K. Plehve.

After the collapse of autocracy, the SRs envisioned a transition period in which land would be socialized and farmed by individuals or collectives and capitalist practices gradually limited. While predicting a final socialist order, marked by collective cultivation and the socialization of industry, the SRs claimed they would not try to dictate future developments.

Many populists of this period, although not considered Marxists, were familiar with Karl Marx's ideas and admired him for his criticism of capitalism. Danielson had helped translate *Das Kapital* into an 1872 Russian edition. In this work, Marx had quoted British factory inspectors' reports to expose such evils as the exploitation of child labor. To take just one short example, Marx quoted a father who said: "'That boy of mine . . . when he was 7 years old I used to carry him on my back to and fro through the snow, and he used to have 16 hours [of work] a day . . . I have often knelt down to feed him as he stood by the machine, for he could not leave it or stop.'"

Russian Socialism: The Marxists

The "father of Russian Marxism," Georgi Plekhanov, was a former populist and leading member of the Black Repartition. By 1883 (the year of Marx's death), Plekhanov had come to believe that full-scale capitalism was inevitable in Russia. In that year, in Geneva, he and some other former populists, including Vera Zasulich, formed the first Russian Marxist organization, the Emancipation of Labor. For them, the essence of Marx's self-proclaimed scientific socialism was his theory of "the materialist conception of history," or "historical materialism."

Marx spelled out its essence most succinctly in 1859 in a preface to his *A Critique of Political Economy:*

In the social production which men carry on, they enter into definite relations
that are indispensable and independent of their will; these relations of production correspond to a definite stage of development of their material productive
forces. The sum total of these relations of production constitutes the economic
structure of society—the real foundation, on which arises a legal and political
superstructure and to which correspond definite forms of social consciousness. The mode of production in material life determines the general character
of the social, political, and spiritual processes of life. It is not the consciousness
of men that determines their existence, but, on the contrary, their social existence determines their consciousness. At a certain stage of their development
the material forces of production in society come into conflict with the existing
relations of production. . . . From forms of development of the forces of production these relations turn into fetters. Then comes the period of social revolution.

More specifically, Marx stated that such productive forces as technology,
material resources, and labor determined economic relationships. The productive forces and economic relationships together made up the foundation (or
base) of society and, in turn, determined—or at least conditioned—the *superstructure* of government, laws, religion, and culture used by the dominant class
in any historical period to strengthen its position.

Productive forces, Marx declared, had evolved in the course of history—
which he divided into five stages: primitive communism, slavery, feudalism,
capitalism, and socialism\communism. The general pattern was that a new
class supported productive forces that evolved out of the old society, and this
new class came into conflict with the class that dominated the older relations
of production and superstructure. The old dominant class, however, never relinquished its power without a struggle. Thus, class conflict was inevitable and
would continue until the establishment of socialism\communism—although
Marx often used the two terms interchangeably, he sometimes used *socialism* to
indicate the transitional period between capitalism and communism, a practice
later adopted in the Soviet Union.

Marx and his frequent collaborator, Friedrich Engels (1820–1895) had
begun their famous *Communist Manifesto* with the sentence: "The history of all
hitherto existing society is the history of class struggles." In his own era in
Western Europe, Marx believed the capitalist class of merchants and industrialists had proved victorious over the old feudal landowning class. Just as inevitably, said Marx, the industrial working class or "proletariat" would associate itself with still newer productive forces, even then evolving out of capitalist
society. This working class would clash with the capitalist class and would
eventually overthrow it.

Following the overthrow of the capitalists, the proletariat would establish
a "dictatorship of the proletariat." It would deal with any remaining class enemies, end private control over productive forces, and introduce a classless socialist society. Since the main role of the state had previously been to protect
class interests, the dictatorship of the proletariat and all the machinery of government would then no longer be necessary. Thus, it would gradually wither

away and be followed by a Communist age of equitable social relations, humanized labor, and increased leisure.

Although Marx himself was unclear on the subject, Plekhanov interpreted Marx's writings, as did many others, to mean that Russia had to go through a fully developed capitalist stage before it could reach socialism.[4] In contrast to most of the populists who, following Lavrov and Mikhailovsky, believed that free will created various future possibilities, Plekhanov emphasized deterministic laws of development that humankind could not avoid. In the Marxist tradition, he emphasized the importance of the proletariat rather than the peasants. And because he believed a capitalist era would have to precede a socialist one, he was willing to cooperate with liberals to bring an end to the tsarist regime.

While Plekhanov and the other founders of the Emancipation of Labor remained abroad, by 1896–1897 Marxist circles operated in numerous cities of the Russian Empire. Many of these circles recognized a debt to Plekhanov and his comrades in Switzerland. This was partly because of the Russian censors' willingness to allow works penned by Plekhanov (but under various pseudonyms) to be published in Russia—the government viewed theoretical Marxist works, which often attacked the Populists, as not especially dangerous.

Among those impressed by Plekhanov was Vladimir Ulianov or Lenin, who traveled to Switzerland and met with him in 1895. Lenin was born in the Volga town of Simbirsk in 1870, where his father was a school inspector and passionate believer in education. By the time of his father's death in 1886, his civil service rank was equivalent to that of a general and had earned him and his family hereditary noble status. After graduating at the top of his gymnasium class (shortly after his brother was executed), Lenin enrolled at the University of Kazan, where he was soon expelled for taking part in a demonstration. From 1888 to 1893 he read, studied, and discussed radical ideas, first in Kazan and then in the Samara Province. In 1891, authorities permitted him to take the law examination at St. Petersburg University, which he passed, and in 1893 he moved to the capital, supposedly to practice law.

It was there that he first became involved with leading young Russian Marxists such as Peter Struve and Yuli Martov and began encouraging industrial workers to strike for their rights. Arrested at the end of 1895, he spent the next several years in prison and Siberian exile.

Meanwhile, despite organizing a founding congress of the Russian Social Democratic Labor party (RSDLP) in Minsk in 1898, Marxists within Russia were already becoming divided. Plekhanov was especially troubled by what he perceived as Russian variations of the Marxist revisionism of the German Eduard Bernstein, who believed that some commonly held Marxist assumptions had proven false.

At the end of Book I of *Kapital*, Marx had written of the diminishing num-

---

[4]For more on Lenin's interpretation of this and other Marxist doctrines by the end of 1917, see my *History of Russia: Since 1855*, Vol. II (New York, 1997), Chapter 8.

ber of capitalists and the increasing misery and class consciousness of the masses that would precede and help trigger the final collapse of the capitalist system and the "expropriation of the [capitalist] expropriators." He also believed that this collapse would be brought about by the inability of the impoverished masses to purchase the growing number of goods turned out under advanced capitalism. But Bernstein argued that too much emphasis was placed on this one section of Marx's writings and that even it was open to different interpretations.

Regardless, however, of what Marx's true views were, Bernstein maintained that the facts were that the number of capitalists was increasing, that many workers now were better off, and that class conflict was decreasing. As a result of these developments and the growing political role that the proletariat was beginning to play in some countries, Bernstein argued that the dream of a Marxian socialist revolution was outdated and that workers were right to use trade unions and democratic and parliamentary means to improve their everyday lives and gradually evolve toward socialism.

Plekhanov believed that "Economism" was the Russian variant of these ideas, for Economism's adherents also emphasized, above all, the workers' economic struggle. To some extent, they were merely mirroring the priorities of the growing number of radical workers. In Siberian exile, where Lenin had completed *The Development of Capitalism in Russia* and married a fellow Marxist, Nadezhda Krupskaia, he was also troubled by Economism and other signs of Bernstein's influence in Russia. Like Plekhanov, Lenin was fearful that Bernstein's influence might lead Russian workers from revolutionary thoughts to a trade-union mentality.

Upon being released from Siberian exile in 1900, Lenin joined Plekhanov in Switzerland, and the two men plus Martov and three others began publishing a Marxist journal, *Iskra* (*The Spark*). In it they defended what they considered Marxist orthodoxy against revisionism—besides Economism, they also thought that the "Legal Marxism" of Struve and others was tainted with Bernsteinism.

By 1903, *Iskra,* smuggled into Russia, was having a strong influence on the growing Marxist (or Social Democratic) movement, and Economism was all but smashed. To unify the Social Democrats better, the *Iskra* editors prepared a second congress of the RSDLP. It was held in the summer of 1903 in Brussels and then, for better security, in London. Forty-three delegates represented twenty-six local groups, among them the Jewish Bund.[5]

By then, however, Lenin and Martov disagreed over the nature of the RSDLP. In *What Is To Be Done?*, published in 1902, Lenin stated: "We have said that *there could not have been* Social Democratic [i.e., Marxist] consciousness among the workers. It would have to be brought to them from without. The history of all countries shows that the working class, exclusively by its own effort, is able to develop only trade union consciousness."

Although Marx at times wrote of a leading role for Communist intellectu-

5On the Jewish Bund, see Chapter 24.

als, Lenin went much further in downplaying the role of the proletariat and increasing that of the revolutionary intelligentsia. He feared that if workers were left to their own devices, they would be co-opted by the capitalists and sell their potentially revolutionary souls for better working conditions and wages.

The battle between Lenin and Martov at the congress revolved around party membership and centralized control over the party. Lenin's basic mistrust of workers' instincts and his fear of revisionism prodded him to attempt to limit membership to active participants in party organizations. Martov wanted a more broad-based party, which would include not only full-time revolutionaries, but also less active supporters.

Lenin lost the vote on membership to Martov, but he won out over his rival when the congress agreed to stronger controls over the RSDLP by a reduced *Iskra* board including Lenin and Plekhanov (who had supported Lenin). At the congress, Lenin labeled his faction the Bolsheviks (the majority) and Martov's the Mensheviks (the minority). It was not immediately evident that the split and names would long continue after the congress ended, but they did. Plekhanov's support of Lenin, however, did not last long. Within months, Plekhanov was trying to reconcile the factions, and when his efforts failed, he increasingly blamed Lenin and charged him with trying to establish a "dictatorship over the proletariat."

Liberalism and Reformism

In the era of counterreforms, the meaning of liberalism continued to be as elusive as it had been under Alexander II. Historians still disagree on whether some men were *liberal* or not, and the term was not one that individuals frequently applied to themselves. Be that as it may, it is used here to characterize the chief nonsocialist opposition of Alexander III and Nicholas II.

The liberalism of the 1880s and early 1890s has often been referred to as a liberalism of "small deeds." Many reformers were connected with the zemstvos or city councils, as representatives, members of the boards, or hired employees. In their local work, they tried to improve the lot of peasants and urban residents through such means as improving education, sanitation, and health care.

At times, local leaders suggested additional steps. From late 1881 to mid-1883, Boris Chicherin, who in 1856 had called Russians to rally around the banner of liberalism, served as head of Moscow's municipal government. For giving a speech in which he called for "crowning" the zemstvo and municipal structure by establishing a national body, Alexander III forced him to give up his position.

Such government reactions and the counterreforms of Alexander III weakened the voices of moderate reform and ultimately turned many to more radical measures. The government's ineffective response to the famine of 1891–1892, followed by Nicholas II's signals that he intended to follow in his father's footsteps, further stimulated liberals to switch from "small deeds" to more radical demands.

After Nicholas had warned the zemstvos against "senseless dreams" in 1895, some liberals wrote an open letter to the tsar indicating the effect of his action:

> You challenged the zemstvos, and with them Russian society, and nothing remains for them now but to choose between progress and faithfulness to autocracy. Your speech has provoked a feeling of offense and depression; but the living social forces will soon recover from that feeling. Some of them will pass to a peaceful but systematic and conscious struggle for such scope of action as is necessary for them. Some others will be made more determined to fight the detestable regime by any means. You first began the struggle; and the struggle will come.

By 1900, even the "conservative liberal" Chicherin had despaired of autocratic government and was now calling for a "limited monarchy." In 1904, the emerging liberal leader Professor Paul Miliukov called Chicherin's proposed limitations "the minimum program of contemporary liberalism." Along with Miliukov, Peter Struve, a former Marxist, became another liberal leader more radical than most of the liberals of Chicherin's generation. Backed by zemstvo financial support, in 1902 Struve began editing abroad a new liberal Russian-

---

Chicherin's Call for a Limited Monarchy

In 1900, Boris Chicherin's *Russia on the Eve of the Twentieth Century* was published in the Russian original in Berlin. The present English language excerpt of it is taken from Paul Miliukov's *Russia and Its Crisis* (Chicago, 1906), pp. 329–330. Ellipsis marks are in the Miliukov text.

It is impossible to limit bureaucracy without limiting the power whose weapon it is, or—as more often happens—which itself serves as a weapon in the hand of bureaucracy. I mean the unlimited power of the monarch. As long as this exists, unlimited arbitrariness at the top will always generate like arbitrariness in the dependent spheres. Legal order can never be affirmed where everything depends on personal will, and where every person invested with power may put himself above the law, while sheltering himself behind an imperial order. If the regime of legality may be said to form *the most urgent need of the Russian society, we must conclude that this need can be satisfied only by the change of the unlimited monarchy into a limited. . . . It is necessary that the elective assembly should be invested with definite rights. A consultative assembly, whose decisions may or may not be followed, will always be swayed by the ruling bureaucracy, though it is just bureaucracy that must be limited. Only such an organ as would be entirely independent and possess a deciding voice in state affairs can counterbalance the officials surrounding the throne. Only such an assembly, possessing some rights, can limit the will of the monarch—which is the first condition of the legal order. As long as the monarch will not grow accustomed to the idea that his will is not almighty, that there exists a law independent of his will, and that he must defer to it, every hope to overrule the arbitrariness of the officials, every dream about "guaranties," are vain and futile.*

language journal, *Liberation*. The following year, in Switzerland, he and 19 others founded the Union of Liberation.

The ideas of Miliukov, Struve, and others were spelled out in the program the new organization adopted in October 1904. Like Chicherin and Constantine Kavelin in 1856, the new leaders hoped to rally the nation around a liberal banner. Among other demands, including an eight-hour day and more land for peasants, this program called for elections to a Constituent Assembly. This would mean that the future government of Russia would be decided by elected delegates—for Russia a radical step indeed.

Meanwhile, zemstvo leaders, including some Union of Liberation members, prepared for a zemstvo congress to be held in St. Petersburg in November 1904. The assassination of Plehve in July and early setbacks in the Russo-Japanese War (see Chapter 24) had been followed by the appointment of a new reform-minded minister of interior, Prince P. D. Sviatopolk-Mirsky. He allowed the congress to proceed, as long as it met in private residences.

The results of the congress were a clear sign that the majority of zemstvo representatives were becoming more radical. Besides basic freedoms, equal rights, and expanded zemstvo rights, they recommended that elected representatives be empowered to legislate (and not just consult), control the budget, and determine the legality of administrative actions.

Following this early November congress, groups of students, businessmen, and others met to discuss the zemstvo recommendations. The Union of Liberation arranged for a series of banquets to discuss them. While some banquet gatherings supported the recommendations, others went further and called for a Constituent Assembly.

Mirsky realized that Nicholas II would never agree with the majority of the zemstvo congress but tried to convince him of the necessity of at least some reforms, including allowing elected representatives a consultative role in formulating legislation. The minister believed that 99 percent of educated opinion favored some sort of participation by elected individuals. Nicholas did sign a decree in December 1904 that promised a reduction of both censorship and the "emergency rule" begun in 1881, more religious toleration, and an expansion of zemstvo activities. After considerable wavering, however, he followed the advice of Witte, his uncle Sergei, and Pobedonostsev: He refused to go along with his minister of interior's suggestion for a consultative role for elected deputies. Thus, almost a quarter century after his grandfather Alexander II had agreed to allow some elected delegates to offer advice on new legislation, Nicholas II, like his father, refused such a concession.

*SUGGESTED SOURCES**

ANAN'ICH, BORIS V., and RAFAIL SH. GAMELIN. "Nicholas II," *RSH* 34 (Winter 1995–96): 68–95. Reprinted in *EER*, pp. 370–402.
BARON, SAMUEL H. *Plekhanov: The Father of Russian Marxism.* Stanford, 1963.

*See also books cited in footnotes.

BASIL, JOHN D. "Konstantin Petrovich Pobedonostsev: An Argument for a Russian State Church," *CH* 64 (March 1995): 44–61.

BILLINGTON, JAMES H. *Mikhailovsky and Russian Populism.* New York, 1958.

BYRNES, ROBERT F. *Pobedonostsev, His Life and Thought.* Bloomington, 1968.

CHERMUKHA, VALENTINA G. "Alexander III," *RSH* 34 (Winter 1995–96): 39–67. Reprinted in *EER,* pp. 335–368.

DALY, JONATHAN W. "Emergency Legislation in Late Imperial Russia," *SR* 54 (Fall 1995): 602–629.

FERRO, MARC. *Nicholas II: The Last of the Tsars.* London, 1991.

GALAI, SHMUEL. *The Liberation Movement in Russia, 1900–1905.* Cambridge, England, 1973.

HAMBURG, GARY M. *Politics of the Russian Nobility, 1881–1905.* New Brunswick, N.J., 1984.

JUDGE, EDWARD H. *Plehve: Repression and Reform in Imperial Russia, 1902–1904.* Syracuse, 1983.

JUDGE, EDWARD H., and JAMES SIMMS, eds. *Modernization and Revolution: Dilemmas of Progress in Late Imperial Russia: Essays in Honor of Arthur P. Mendel.* New York, 1992.

LIEVEN, DOMINIC. *Nicholas II: Emperor of All the Russias.* London, 1993.

LINCOLN, W. BRUCE. *In War's Dark Shadow: The Russians Before the Great War.* New York, 1983.

MCLELLAN, DAVID. *Karl Marx.* New York, 1975.

MEYER, ALFRED G. *Leninism.* New York, 1957.

MILIUKOV, P. N. *Russia and Its Crisis.* Chicago, 1905.

NAIMARK, NORMAN M. *Terrorists and Social Democrats: The Russian Revolutionary Movement Under Alexander III.* Cambridge, Mass., 1983.

OFFORD, DEREK. *The Russian Revolutionary Movement in the 1880s.* Cambridge, England, 1986.

PEARL, DEBORAH L. "Marxism's Russian Centennial: Soviet Scholars and the Emancipation of Labor Group," *RR* 49 (April 1990): 189–198.

PEARSON, THOMAS S. *Russian Officialdom in Crisis: Autocracy and Local Self-Government, 1861–1900.* Cambridge, England, 1989.

PIPES, RICHARD. *Struve: Liberal on the Left, 1870–1905.* Cambridge, Mass., 1970.

POBEDONOSTSEV, KONSTANTIN P. *Reflections of a Russian Statesman.* Ann Arbor, 1965.

ROBBINS, RICHARD G. *The Tsar's Viceroys: Russian Provincial Governors in the Last Years of the Empire.* Ithaca, N.Y., 1987.

ROGGER, HANS. *Russia in the Age of Modernization and Revolution, 1881–1917.* London, 1983.

SERVICE, ROBERT. *Lenin: A Political Life.* Vol. I, *The Strength of Contradiction.* Bloomington, 1985.

SNOW, GEORGE E., ed. *The Years 1881–1894 in Russia—a Memorandum Found in the Papers of N. Kh. Bunge: A Translation and Commentary.* Philadelphia, 1981.

TIMBERLAKE, CHARLES E., ed. *Essays on Russian Liberalism.* Columbia, Mo., 1972.

ULAM, ADAM B. *The Bolsheviks: The Intellectual and Political History of the Triumph of Communism in Russia.* New York, 1965.

VERNER, ANDREW M. *The Crisis of Russian Autocracy: Nicholas II and the 1905 Revolution.* Princeton, 1990.

VOLKOGONOV, DMITRI. *Lenin: A New Biography.* New York, 1994.

VON LAUE, THEODORE. *Sergei Witte and the Industrialization of Russia.* New York, 1963.

WALICKI, ANDRZEJ. *The Controversy Over Capitalism: Studies in the Social Philosophy of the Russian Populists.* Oxford, 1969.

WHELAN, HEIDE W. *Alexander III and the State Council: Bureaucracy and Counter-Reform in Late Imperial Russia.* New Brunswick, N.J., 1982.

WILDMAN, ALLAN K. *The Making of a Workers' Revolution: Russian Social Democracy, 1891–1903.* Chicago, 1967.

WITTE, S. IU. *The Memoirs of Count Witte.* Armonk, N.Y., 1990.

ZAIONCHKOVSKII, PETER A. *The Russian Autocracy under Alexander III.* Gulf Breeze, Fla., 1976.

CHAPTER 24

Russian Imperial and Foreign Policy, 1856–1905

Tsarist policies toward the empire's minority nationalities reached their Russifying and reactionary pinnacle during this era. Because many nationalities (such as the Poles, Ukrainians, and Armenians) existed not only in Russia, but also in large numbers in neighboring countries and because of Russia's poorly defined southern and southeastern borders, nationality policies often overlapped with foreign affairs. Those who were "foreigners" one year might become part of the empire the next, as happened in certain Asian areas during this era. It is hardly surprising, therefore, that the government's Asiatic Department dealt with both imperial and foreign policies.

After the Crimean War (1853–1856), the Russian government attempted to maintain its empire and great-power status by modernizing its economy and avoiding costly wars with major European powers. It did not, however, forgo its perceived right to expand in Asia, which it did until checked by Japan in the Russo-Japanese War of 1904–1905. Also, it did not cease to believe that it had a special ethnic and religious relationship to the Balkans. This belief helped drag it into the Russo-Turkish War of 1877–1878. Although Russia's victories won it substantial gains in the Treaty of San Stefano, they were soon reduced by other European powers at the Congress of Berlin.

Although imperial and foreign policy goals during this half-century were generally consistent, the means of implementing them fluctuated. Such changes were due primarily to changing circumstances and to the difficulties of reconciling major goals with each other and determining the best means to achieve them. These uncertainties left the door open for different ministers and public voices to influence tsarist policies.

THE FAR EAST, THE CAUCASUS, CENTRAL ASIA, AND ALASKA, 1856–1895

Alexander II's policies regarding China, the Caucasus, and Central Asia manifested the long-held Russian conviction that it had a right to Asian expansion and to civilize "backward" peoples. Alexander's actions in these areas built upon those taken by his father, Nicholas I. They also reflected Russian desires to compensate for the loss of the Crimean War and to battle against any further English gains in Asia.

Alexander II's China policy was strongly influenced by the Amur River gains of the early 1850s made by the governor-general of Eastern Siberia, Nikolai Muraviev (later Muraviev-Amursky in honor of his acquisitions). Muraviev had argued that the Amur was needed to insure Russian control of Eastern Siberia and to subvert any possible British moves to control the mouth of the Amur. He also argued that Russian possession of the Amur would enable Russia to strengthen its control over the Kamchatka Peninsula, expand trade with China, and maintain its influence there.

Alexander II allowed Muraviev to continue strengthening Russia's position along the Amur and even to advance into the area east of the Ussuri River. At the same time that British and French troops and diplomats (along with U.S. diplomats) were trying to force concessions of their own from the Chinese emperor, Russia was able to win recognition of its territorial gains. By the Treaties of Aigun and Tientsin (both in 1858) and the Treaty of Peking (1860), Russia gained territories from China about the size of Germany and France combined. Although containing few inhabitants, these lands strengthened Russia's Pacific position, placing it on the Sea of Japan and giving it a border with Korea. On that sea and near that border, Russia founded, in 1860, Vladivostok (meaning Ruler of the East) (see Map 24.1).

Russia's other major gain in the Far East under Alexander II was the island of Sakhalin, over which Japan and Russia contested before finally coming to an agreement in 1875. By the Treaty of St. Petersburg, Japan recognized Russia's claim to the island in exchange for Russia's recognition of Japanese control over the Kurile Islands.

In 1859, Russian forces in the Caucasus defeated Chechen and other Moslem forces and captured Shamil, who for a quarter of a century had led the Moslem "holy war" against Russia. This broke the Moslem resistance in the eastern Caucasus. Russian forces were now able to concentrate on the Circassians in the northwest Caucasus. By 1864, Circassian opposition was crushed, and the Circassians were forced to move to other Russian territories or leave the country. Most of them, some 400,000, left for Turkey, but many never reached it because of the difficulties of the journey. More importantly to the Russian government, after more than a half century of repeated warfare, almost all of the Caucasus was finally under Russian control (see Map. 24.3).

The focus now shifted to Central Asia and its Moslem peoples. Russian military moves in this region were part of an ongoing rivalry with the British, who controlled India and frequently interfered in Afghanistan. British protests in 1863 against Russia's treatment of the rebelling Poles seemed to many Russians just another sign of British hostility toward Russia. Russian gains in Central Asia were one means of countering British strengths elsewhere and of forestalling any British attempts to move north from India.

From 1864 to 1885, Russian troops south of the Kazakh steppe conquered the khanates of Kokand, Khiva, and Bukhara and the Turkmen or Transcaspian

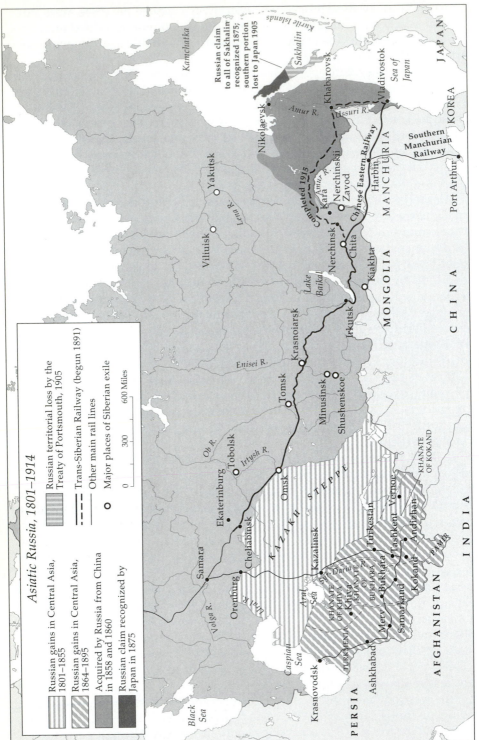

MAP 24.1

Asiatic Russia, 1801–1914

Russian gains in Central Asia,
1801–1855

Russian gains in Central Asia,
1864–1895

Acquired by Russia from China
in 1858 and 1860

Russian claim recognized by
Japan in 1875

Russian territorial loss by the
Treaty of Portsmouth, 1905

Trans-Siberian Railway (begun 1891)

Other main rail lines

Major places of Siberian exile

0   300   600 Miles

Kamchatka

Russian claim
to all of Sakhalin
recognized 1875;
southern portion
lost to Japan 1905

Sakhalin

Kurile Islands

JAPAN

Sea of
Japan

Khabarovsk

Vladivostok

KOREA

Nikolaevsk

Amur R.

Ussuri R.

Southern
Manchurian
Railway

Port Arthur

Yakutsk

Lena R.

Completed 1915

Kara

Nerchinskii
Zavod

Nerchinsk

Chita

Chinese Eastern Railway

Harbin

MANCHURIA

CHINA

Viliuisk

Lake
Baikal

Kiakhta

MONGOLIA

Irkutsk

Krasnoiarsk

Enisei R.

Minusinsk

Shushenskoe

Tomsk

Ob R.

Irtysh R.

Tobolsk

Ekaterinburg

Omsk

KAZAKH   STEPPE

KHANATE
OF KOKAND

Vernoe

Andizhan

Turkestan

Tashkent

PAMIR

INDIA

Samara

Cheliabinsk

Kazalinsk

Syr Darya

KHANATE
OF
BUKHARA

Bukhara

Kokand

Samarkand

AFGHANISTAN

Orenburg

Ural R.

Aral
Sea

Darya

KHANATE OF KHIVA

Khiva

Mery

Volga R.

Caspian
Sea

TURKMENIA

Ashkhabad

Krasnovodsk

PERSIA

Black
Sea

region, east-southeast of the Caspian Sea and northeast of Persia. In 1884, Russia took over the city of Merv and the Merv region, and the following year Russian forces moved further south and engaged Afghan troops along the Afghan border.

For a while in the spring of 1885, it looked as if this latest Russian advance might lead to war with Great Britain. Not only were the British agitated over Russia's decades-long southern advance, but also they regarded Afghanistan as a buffer state to protect India. But the powers soon stepped back from the crisis and agreed to arbitrate the Russo-Afghan border. In 1895, Russia and Britain settled the disputed Pamir frontier, completing Russia's Central Asian expansion.

Although the Central Asian advances were partly motivated by Russia's rivalry with Great Britain, there were other factors at work. Some of these were explained by Foreign Minister Alexander Gorchakov in a memorandum intended to clarify Russia's policy to foreign powers.

A Justification for Russian Advances in Central Asia

The following selection is excerpted from Gorchakov's memorandum of November 1864, which was to be communicated to foreign governments. This excerpt was taken from Alexis Krausse, *Russia in Asia: A Record and a Study, 1558–1899* (London, 1899), pp. 224–225. A few spellings have been modernized.

The position of Russia in Central Asia is that of all civilized states which are brought into contact with half-savage nomad populations possessing no fixed social organization.

In such cases, the more civilized state is forced in the interest of the security of its frontier, and its commercial relations, to exercise a certain ascendancy over their turbulent and undesirable neighbors. Raids and acts of pillage must be put down. To do this, the tribes on the frontier must be reduced to a state of submission. This result once attained, these tribes take to more peaceful habits, but are in turn exposed to the attacks of the more distant tribes against whom the State is bound to protect them. Hence the necessity of distant, costly, and periodically recurring expeditions against an enemy whom his social organization makes it impossible to seize. If, the robbers

once punished, the expedition is withdrawn, the lesson is soon forgotten; its withdrawal is put down to weakness. It is a peculiarity of Asiatics to respect nothing but visible and palpable force. The moral force of reasoning has no hold on them.

In order to put a stop to this state of permanent disorder, fortified posts are established in the midst of these hostile tribes, and an influence is brought to bear upon them which reduces them by degrees to a state of submission. But other more distant tribes beyond this outer line come in turn to threaten the same dangers, and necessitate the same measures of repression. The state is thus forced to choose between two alternatives—either to give up this endless labor, and to abandon its frontier to perpetual disturbance, or to plunge deeper and deeper into barbarous countries, when the difficulties and expenses increase with every step in advance.

Such has been the fate of every country which has found itself in a similar position. The United States in America, France in Algeria, Holland in her colonies, England in India; all have been forced by imperious necessity into this onward march, where the greatest difficulty is to know where to stop.

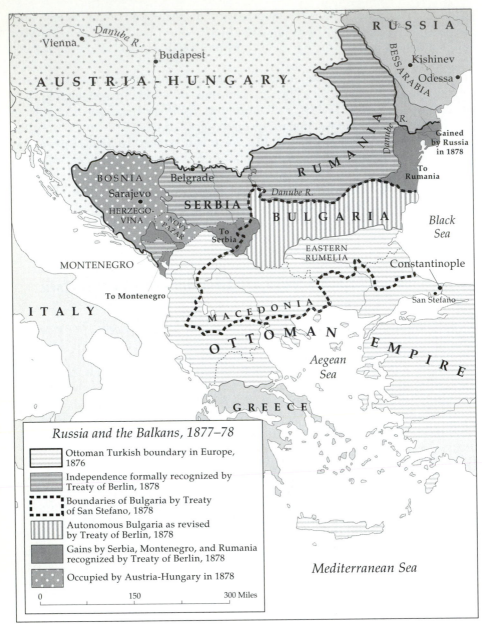

MAP 24.2

Despite the justifications for advancing in Central Asia, the 1864 memorandum stated that Russia's advancement in Central Asia would be limited. When, in succeeding decades, Russia continued to advance far beyond the limits suggested by the memorandum, the cautious Gorchakov sometimes blamed it on adventurous generals who went beyond the orders of the tsar.

Although there was some truth to this excuse and Alexander II apparently

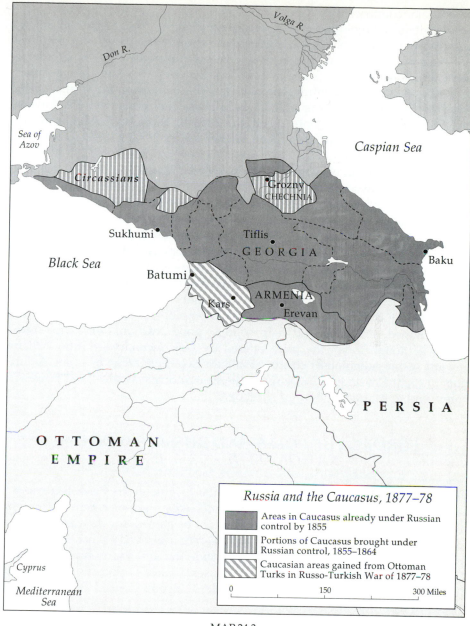

MAP 24.3

possessed no master plan to take all the lands gained in subsequent decades, both he and Alexander III supported cautious, piecemeal advancement. The tsars believed (correctly as it turned out) that such a policy could be pursued without leading to a war with Britain.

The memorandum's comparison of Russia's situation with that of Western powers reflected the belief that Russia's policies were consistent with those of other major countries. War Minister Dmitri Miliutin believed that Russia owed Great Britain no apology for its advancement, noting that the British did not consult the Russians before expanding their empire. But the advance in Central Asia was perhaps more comparable to the American white man's movement westward at the expense of Native Americans. Like the Native Americans, the Moslems in Central Asia lost out to a better organized and united force that possessed superior military technology and moved steadily forward on contiguous territory. Only when the British, along with high southern mountain ranges, rose up to impede further advances did Russia's southern thrust come to an end.

Although hope of economic gain also enticed Russia southward, this aspiration was not a major factor. In fact, Minister of Finance Reutern warned about the costs of expansion and made every effort to keep them to a minimum.

Concern about state finances also influenced Russia's decision to sell Alaska to the United States in 1867. Although the new Asian territories gained in the Far East and Central Asia more than compensated for the amount of land lost by the sale of Alaska, it was still a large area to relinquish. By 1867, however, the Russian government considered it more of an economic liability than an asset, and it badly needed the $7.2 million the U.S. government was willing to pay. Besides, Alaska was all but impossible for Russia to defend, and Russia hoped its sale would help solidify good relations with the United States. Although today the price offered by U.S. Secretary of State William Seward seems ridiculously cheap—less than two cents an acre—some Americans thought Russia got the better of the deal and referred to it as "Seward's Folly" and to Alaska as "Seward's Icebox."

EUROPE, THE POLES, AND RUSSIA'S WESTERN NATIONALITIES, 1856–1875

From 1856 until 1870, the regaining of military rights in the Black Sea was an important goal of Russian diplomacy. Gorchakov's appointment as foreign minister in 1856 indicated how this end might be gained, for he was known to favor a rapprochement with France. Yet, despite improved Franco-Russian relations, France's Napoleon III failed to provide the diplomatic support Russia needed to overturn the hated Black Sea clauses. France's opposition to Russian actions during the Polish revolt of 1863–1864 further doused hopes for any Black Sea help from the French.

The full-scale rebellion that broke out in Warsaw in January 1863 was due to many reasons, including permanent Polish resentment against Russian control, rising Polish nationalism, and Alexander II's relaxation of the Russian reins on Poland. This easing fueled Polish expectations that exceeded the concessions Alexander II was willing to grant.

Because of Polish guerrilla tactics and the rebellion's spread to other western borderlands, it took more than a year for Russian forces to restore order. But restore it they did, and with a special vengeance in the Lithuanian area, where the governor-general, Mikhail Muraviev, became known as "the hang-man of Vilna."

In Lithuania, Belorussia, Ukraine, and Kingdom of Poland (which now lost this special designation), the government instituted new Russification policies that went further than those of Nicholas I. They involved primarily the further Russification of the schools and government. For example, Russian now became the principal language of instruction in Poland's secondary schools. In the nine western provinces Catherine II had gained from Poland, a law of 1865 forbade people of Polish descent from acquiring further land except through inheritance. Catholicism was also subjected to new discriminations, and, in 1875, the government forced Catholic Unites in Poland to cease their separate existence and "reunite" with Russian Orthodoxy.

Yet for peasants in Poland and in the Lithuanian, Belorussian, and western Ukrainian provinces, some good did emerge from the revolt. To win them over to the Russian side, the government enacted more generous land provisions for emancipated peasants than it did for Russian peasants. Because so many lords in the western provinces were Polish or Polonized, the government had few qualms about demanding greater land sacrifices from them than from the Russian landowners.

Russification in Ukraine was stimulated not only by the Polish rebellion, but also by signs of growing Ukrainian nationalism among Ukrainian students and intellectuals. In 1863, Minister of Interior Peter Valuev prohibited educational, scholarly, and religious publications in the "Little Russian dialect"—he refused to admit that a separate Ukrainian language existed. In 1876, the government went further by prohibiting Ukrainian from being spoken on the stage or by teachers in the classroom. Furthermore, Ukrainian could not appear in any new or imported publications or in school libraries.

Other nationalities fared better, especially the Finns, who were permitted considerable autonomy. In 1863, in the midst of the Polish rebellion, Alexander II allowed the first Finnish Diet to meet since 1809 and continued thereafter to allow regular sessions of that legislative body. In the Baltic provinces, the Baltic Germans retained their privileged status throughout Alexander II's reign. But resentment of them grew in this nationalistic age, especially on the part of some Great Russian nationalists. In 1867, the use of the Russian language was required by imperial officials in the Baltic provinces, and ten years later Baltic towns were required to adopt Russian municipal institutions and the use of Russian in official activities.

Jewish life under Alexander II improved in some ways but in others foreshadowed the more oppressive conditions that would follow under Alexander III. The hated special draft of Jewish boys was ended in 1856, and more Jews were allowed opportunities outside the Jewish Pale of Settlement and Congress Poland (see Map 24.4). Nevertheless, in 1881 about 19 out of every 20 legally registered Jews continued to reside in these restricted areas. When new municipal rules were enacted in 1870, it was mandated that no more than one-third of any town council could be composed of Jews and that no Jew could serve as a mayor.

FIGURE 24.1. Statue of Alexander II on Senate Square, Helsinki. This statue was erected in 1894 by the Finns and still stands today, a tribute to Alexander II's relatively tolerant attitude to Finnish autonomy.

In 1871, an anti-Jewish pogrom occurred in Odessa, a city about one-quarter Jewish. Eight people were killed, and hundreds of Jewish apartments and shops were looted or vandalized. By the end of Alexander II's reign, Judeophobia was on the rise. The writer Dostoevsky was just one of many individuals who expressed his prejudices. In 1880, he wrote: "The Jew and the bank now dominate everything: Europe and Enlightenment, the whole civilization and socialism—especially socialism, for with its help the Jew will eradicate Christianity and destroy the Christian civilization."[1]

Meanwhile, internationally, France's strong objections to Russia's crushing of the Polish rebellion, along with Prussia's support of Russian actions, led Alexander II to move closer to Prussia. While Prussia's Wilhelm I (Alexander's uncle) and his indispensable minister, Otto Von Bismarck, were fighting three

---

[1]Quoted in Hans Kohn, *Prophets and Peoples: Studies in Nineteenth Century Nationalism* (New York, 1961), p. 181, n. 27.

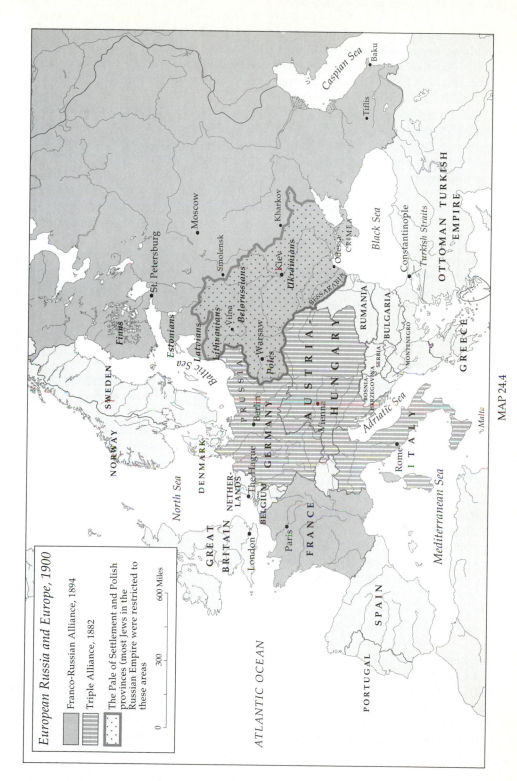

European Russia and Europe, 1900

Franco-Russian Alliance, 1894

Triple Alliance, 1882

The Pale of Settlement and Polish provinces (most Jews in the Russian Empire were restricted to these areas)

0   300   600 Miles

MAP 24.4

Caspian Sea
Baku

Tiflis

Black Sea

OTTOMAN TURKISH EMPIRE

Constantinople

Turkish Straits

Moscow

Kharkov

Kiev

CRIMEA

Odessa

Ukrainians

Smolensk

BESSARABIA

St. Petersburg

Belorussians

RUMANIA

BULGARIA

GREECE

Finns

Estonians

Latvians

Lithuanians

Vilna

Warsaw

Poles

MONTENEGRO

SERBIA

SWEDEN

Baltic Sea

PRUSSIA

Berlin

AUSTRIA-HUNGARY

BOSNIA

HERZEGOVINA

Adriatic Sea

Vienna

NORWAY

DENMARK

GERMANY

Malta

North Sea

NETHER-LANDS

The Hague

BELGIUM

ITALY

Rome

Mediterranean Sea

GREAT BRITAIN

London

FRANCE

Paris

ATLANTIC OCEAN

SPAIN

PORTUGAL

wars and uniting Germany between 1864 and 1871, Alexander II and Russia remained benevolently neutral. In 1870, Russia used the occasion of the Franco-Prussian War to abrogate the hated Black Sea demilitarization clauses of the Treaty of Paris—a move allowed to stand by an international conference in London the following year.

Russia therefore gained an immediate benefit from Prussia's wars and its own benevolent neutrality. After the tremendous German devastation of Russia in two twentieth-century wars, however, the question must at least be posed whether aiding the creation of a strong, united Germany was in Russia's long-term interest.

Once Prussia had defeated France in 1871, Bismarck worked to insure diplomatic arrangements that would enable the new Germany to keep its gains. Again, Alexander II was willing to cooperate. In 1873, Russia and Germany agreed to come to each other's aid, with an army of 200,000, if attacked by another European power. Later that year, Alexander II and Franz Joseph of Austria signed an agreement pledging consultation and cooperation in case of another power's aggression. The two agreements together created the Three Emperors' League, which was aimed at any major threat that would destabilize the three empires.

CRISIS IN THE BALKANS AND THE RUSSO-TURKISH WAR OF 1877–1878

Despite the Three Emperors' League, cooperation between Austria and Russia proved difficult. This was primarily because of Russo-Austrian competition in the Balkans, where rising Slavic national movements threatened to overthrow Turkish control. Both Austria and Russia had strong special interests in the area. Containing many Slavic nationalities itself, the Austro-Hungarian Empire feared that unchecked nationalism south of its borders would carry over into its own empire and act as a disintegrating force. Russian interest in the area stemmed primarily from Balkan domination by the Moslem Turks, Balkan linkage with the Black and Mediterranean seas, and Orthodox-Slavic Russia's traditional role as an intermediary for its Balkan co-religionists.

As Russian nationalism grew stronger during and after the Polish rebellion, so too did Russian panslavism. Its most ardent champions, including the historian M. P. Pogodin, dreamed of a Slavic union under Russian hegemony that would stretch from the Pacific to the Adriatic. For more than a decade before his death in 1875, Pogodin had been the president of the Slavonic Benevolent Committee, which reached the height of its influence in the late 1870s. By 1877, Moscow committee and its branches in St. Petersburg, Kiev, and Odessa possessed more than 1,000 members. They included the journalist and Slavophile Ivan Aksakov, who succeeded Pogodin as president; the influential editor Mikhail Katkov; the writer Dostoevsky; General (retired) R. A. Fadeev;

the botanist N. Danilevsky; and Russia's ambassador to Constantinople, N. P. Ignatiev. Fadeev's *Opinion on the Eastern Question* and Danilevsky's *Russia and Europe* both appeared in 1869 and called for Russia to battle her enemies and unite the Slavs.

In mid-1875, Herzegovina and then Bosnia revolted against Turkish rule. The following spring, Bulgaria joined them in revolt; and early in the summer of 1876, Serbia and Montenegro declared war on Turkey.

At first, Alexander II worked with other European rulers to deal with the crisis. The major powers, with the exception of Great Britain, agreed upon a program of land, tax, and religious reform in the Balkans that Turkey would administer under their watchful eyes. But British Prime Minister Disraeli distrusted Russian intentions and hoped to drive a wedge between the members of the Three Emperors' League. His attitude encouraged Turkish resistance to European diplomatic efforts.

Meanwhile, Russia's enthusiasm for the heroic struggle of its fellow Orthodox Slavs spread rapidly. The Slavonic Benevolent Committee and Orthodox Church leaders were in the forefront of relief efforts. The tsarina and the tsarevich also helped. Russian officers were allowed to take furloughs to serve as volunteers in the Serbian army. Other Russian volunteers also assisted the Serbs. The semiretired Russian General Cherniaev, called the "Lion of Tashkent" for his Central Asian conquest, soon became the head of the Serbian army. Leo Tolstoy, who was then writing *Anna Karenina* and who was unsympathetic with the mood of educated society, described it in his novel (as translated by Aylmer Maude).

> Among the people to whom he belonged, nothing was written or talked about at that time except the Serbian war. Everything that the idle crowd usually does to kill time, it now did for the benefit of the Slavs: balls, concerts, dinners, speeches, ladies' dresses, beer, restaurants—all bore witness to our sympathy with the Slavs. . . . The massacre of our co-religionists and brother Slavs evoked sympathy for the sufferers and indignation against their oppressors. And the heroism of the Serbs and Montenegrins, fighting for a great cause, aroused in the whole nation a desire to help their brothers not only with words but by deeds.

In Constantinople, still another force acted to encourage Russian assistance to the Slavs—Russia's ambassador to the Ottoman Empire, Nikolai Ignatiev. Apparently without tsarist authority, he encouraged the Serbs to believe they could count on Russian aid if they went to war with Turkey.

In the autumn of 1876, after the Serbs had suffered a series of defeats and the Turks were threatening Belgrade, Alexander sent an ultimatum to the Turks, demanding a truce. They agreed to a six-week armistice.

With his finance minister, M. K. Reutern, warning of the economic consequences of a war, Alexander continued to seek a diplomatic solution. He assured the British ambassador to Russia that British fears of Russian intentions regarding Constantinople and India were ludicrous. But Disraeli remained uncooperative, and Alexander remained under pressure from various quarters, including his wife Maria and his oldest son, the future Alexander III. After several more months of futile diplomatic efforts and fearful of alienating public opinion, Alexander II decided on war. In April 1877, after obtaining Austria's assurance of neutrality by assenting to a future Austrian occupation of Bosnia and Herzegovina, Russia declared war on Turkey.

Russia's educated public cheered the declaration. Many liberals and radicals supported the Slavs rebellions in the Balkans because they saw them as a struggle of freedom-fighters against Turkish tyranny. Others, such as Dostoevsky, thought that Russia was fighting for a sacred cause and that the war would help to unite Russia around the true Orthodox ideas it should be following.

Although Russian troops suffered some setbacks in Bulgaria and the Caucasus, they generally advanced, and in early 1878 Turkey agreed to an armistice. In March, the two powers signed a treaty at San Stefano, a little village occupied by Russian troops only about six miles from the walls of Constantinople.

Among others, Ignatiev and Dostoevsky had wanted Russia to seize Constantinople, but fear of English and Austro-Hungarian intervention restrained the tsar. British ships had already advanced to within a few miles of the Turkish capital, and Britain threatened war if Russia seized it.

The Treaty of San Stefano allowed Russia to regain southern Bessarabia (lost in the Crimean War); created a large autonomous Bulgaria with a sizable Aegean coastline; provided for Russian territorial gains in the Caucasus and a Turkish indemnity to Russia; recognized the independence of Serbia, Montenegro, and Rumania; stipulated territorial gains for Serbia and especially Montenegro; and mandated Turkish reforms in Bosnia and Herzegovina.

Russian nationalists and panslavists were generally happy with the treaty, although some thought it was the minimum Russia could accept. Austria and Britain were far from pleased, however, and exerted diplomatic pressure for modifications to it. Fearing war and its effects on an already strained Russian budget, Alexander II agreed to a peace congress in Berlin, where Bismarck was to act as an "honest broker."

The Congress of Berlin met in mid-1878. By the Treaty of Berlin, the enlarged Bulgaria that Russia hoped to dominate was greatly reduced in size; Austria-Hungary obtained the right to occupy Bosnia and Herzegovina and Britain to administer the island of Cyprus. In Asia Minor, Russia retained most of its gains at Turkey's expense. The powers also recognized Russia's right to annex southern Bessarabia.

Although territorial gains, an indemnity, expanded rights for the peoples of the Balkans, and a weakening of the Ottoman Turkish Empire remained as real accomplishments, Russians realized that the new treaty was a diplomatic setback and a blow to Russian pride. Although he felt helpless to prevent it, Alexander II considered it one of the darkest moments of his reign. Russian nationalists were especially upset. The panslav leader Ivan Aksakov openly criticized Russian actions in Berlin, a criticism that led to his exile in the countryside and the closing of the Moscow Slavonic committee.

EUROPEAN RELATIONS, 1881–1905

Although angered at Germany and Austria-Hungary for their part in the Berlin settlement of 1878, Alexander II once again pressed these two neighbors to renew the Three Emperors' League. This was after he received word that they had entered negotiations for a new treaty, which they soon signed in 1879. In this alliance, they promised to come to each other's aid if either were attacked by Russia. Later, in 1882, they would join with Italy to sign a a Triple Alliance, which stipulated that if one or two of the three signatories were attacked by two or more powers, the other member(s) of the alliance should render assistance. Alexander II feared diplomatic isolation, and the conservative monarchies of Germany and Austria-Hungary still seemed the best potential allies.

In 1879, however, Bismarck was in no hurry to renew the Three Emperors' League. It was not until mid-1881, after Alexander III had come to the throne, that a secret Three Emperors' Alliance was finally signed. Its most important clause stipulated benevolent neutrality in case any of the three powers became involved in a war with a fourth power. If that fourth power happened to be Turkey, the agreement became operative only if the three signatories first agreed on the results of a Turkish war. Other clauses reaffirmed recognition of the closure of the Straits to warships—Russia especially wished to keep British naval vessels out of the Black Sea—and addressed Russian and Austro-Hungarian interests in the Balkans, which were to come at the expense of Turkey. These clauses allowed for the eventual enlargement of Bulgaria (by the addition of Eastern Rumelia) and the Austro-Hungarian annexation (when opportune) of Bosnia and Herzegovina. The treaty was for three years and was renewed for another three in 1884.

The fact that the Three Emperors' Alliance called for neutrality, not military aid, is worth emphasizing because Russia's fragile economy necessitated avoiding war with any major power. To put its economic house in order and invest more in the basic industrial structure so important for modern war, Russia cut back on direct military spending in 1882. For more than two decades after that, Russia avoided any major conflict.

As a result of clumsy policies and practices, Russia lost the leverage it had possessed in Bulgaria, and Austrian and British influence in that country increased. Tensions between Russia and Austria-Hungary over Bulgaria helped prevent the renewal of the Three Emperors' Alliance when it expired in June 1887. Yet that same month Germany's Bismarck concluded a secret Reinsurance Treaty with Russia, binding for three years. He was mindful of France's desire to win back what it had lost in 1870–1871 and feared a Russo-French alliance. The Reinsurance Treaty stipulated neutrality if either country became involved in a war with a third power, but if Germany attacked France, or Russia attacked Austria, the neutrality clause would not apply. The treaty also declared that Germany recognized Russia's right to predominant influence in Bulgaria, once again reaffirmed the two powers' support of the closure of the Straits, and promised German "moral and diplomatic support" if Russia found it necessary to defend the entrance to the Black Sea against foreign warships.

German support regarding Bulgaria and the Black Sea had minimal practical effect and cost Bismarck little. Russia's predominant influence in Bulgaria was already disappearing, and the closure of the Straits had already been agreed to many times by the European powers.

Until the mid-1880s, Russo-German relations were buttressed by close economic cooperation. German capital, industrial goods, and technical expertise flowed into Russia, while Germany received large amounts of Russian grain. Already by 1887, however, a tariff conflict between the two powers was underway, as protectionism became more prominent in both countries. Toward the end of that same year, Germany seriously curtailed its loans to Russia. In 1890, two years after coming to the throne, the young Emperor Wilhelm II of Germany dismissed Bismarck and refused to renew the Reinsurance Treaty. The Russian government finally overcame its ideological scruples toward republican France and moved toward a Franco-Russian alliance.

Already in 1888 and 1889, republican France and autocratic Russia had begun to move closer. French bankers furnished loans, helping to fill the vacuum created by the tightening of German credit in 1887, and French officials agreed to furnish information about, and allow the purchase of, a new French rifle then being developed.

After Emperor Wilhelm's rebuff, Franco-Russian cooperation accelerated. In July 1891, Alexander III greeted a French naval squadron and its admiral at Kronstadt, the naval base guarding St. Petersburg. A Russian band played the "Marseillaise," the anthem of the French Revolution, while the autocratic Alexander III stood at attention. The following month, the two countries signed an agreement promising to consult if peace was endangered.

In 1892, the French presented the Russians with a draft military convention. After considerable changes and delays, it was ratified in January 1894 (N.S.). The heart of this Franco-Russian secret agreement was the mutual promise to assist each other, with all available forces, in case of a German attack on either country. German support for Italy against France or for Austria against Russia obligated the nonattacked ally (Russia or France) to fight Germany. The French were so pleased with the new treaty and Alexander III that in 1896, two years after his death, they began building the Alexander III bridge over the Seine River in Paris.

Yet the Russian government remained hopeful that war with Germany would not occur, and it continued attempting to improve relations with both Germany and Austria. In 1894, Russia and Germany signed a new tariff treaty, and during the next decade, Russia's trade with Germany exceeded that with any other country. In 1897, Russia and Austria agreed not to disturb the status quo in the Balkans.

Russia's desire for peace was partly motivated by its realization of its weak economic and military position at a time when world military spending and military technology were advancing rapidly. In 1898, this same realization helped prompt the Russian government to call for an international conference to limit armaments. Out of this Russian initiative, two peace conferences (in 1899 and 1907) eventually resulted, both held in The Hague. But in this militaristic era, there was little chance of any serious arms limitation agreement. All that the delegates could agree on were the rules of war and the establishment of an international (but not compulsory) court of arbitration.

NATIONALITIES, RUSSIFICATION, AND DISCRIMINATION, 1881–1905

By 1897, Great Russians were a minority in the Russian Empire, and together with the Ukrainians and Belorussians (both mainly Orthodox Slavs), they still constituted only about two-thirds of the empire's population.

Russification Policies

Despite some Russification of Russia's nine western provinces and the former Kingdom of Poland after the Polish revolt of 1863, Russification and discrimination against non-Russians did not reach their height until 1881–1905. Although in retrospect such policies seem foolish and counterproductive, there were many factors nudging the government in the direction it took.

Among European powers, Germany's growing strength after 1870 most impressed its neighbors. In minority areas, such as its Poland lands, it imposed Germanization by such measures as demanding the use of German in administration and schools. Austria-Hungary was weaker than Germany, and some Russian nationalists believed this was partly because of the Dual Monarchy's inability to impose a unifying nationality policy upon its peoples. Besides the German example, there was a growing fear of Germany, especially by the 1890s, and Russification measures were especially prevalent in border areas that could be threatened by Germany.

Other causes also stimulated Russification. Economic modernization sped up centralizing tendencies that were often accompanied by Russifying measures. In a more backward direction, Russification was part of the counter-reform mentality of the times, a reaction to the growing forces threatening autocracy and the empire's political stability. In some ways, this reaction hearkened back to the Official Nationality policies of Nicholas I. By the 1880s, however, nationalism in Russia and throughout Europe (as the philosopher V. Soloviev noted and decried) had taken on harsher tones. The new mood was evidenced by the increased popularity of Danilevsky's Europe-bashing *Russia and Europe,* which was published in new editions in 1888 and 1889.

Certainly one cause of the increased Russification of the 1881–1905 period was Pobedonostsev. As procurator of the Holy Synod and a tsarist adviser, he

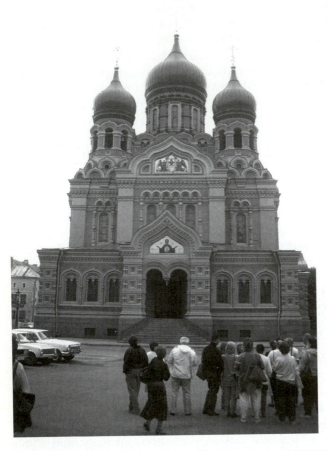

FIGURE 24-2. Alexander Nevsky Cathedral, Reval (Tallinn), 1894–1900. The construction of this Orthodox Cathedral exemplified Pobedonostsev's policy of trying to strengthen Orthodox influence among the predominately Lutheran Estonians and Latvians.

pushed Russification policies along with ones designed to win converts to Orthodoxy and discourage other religions in the Russian Empire.

Pobedonostsev realized the danger of national movements to the unity of "composite states" such as Austria-Hungary and Russia. One reason he gave for rejecting parliamentary government was that in multinational states, a parliament became a forum for "racial hatred, both to the dominant race, to the sister races, and to the political institution which unites them all." Russian autocracy, he claimed, had "succeeded in evading or conciliating" racial or national "demands and outbreaks, not alone by means of force, but by the equalization of rights and relations under the unifying power."

The problem was that Pobedonostsev's "equalization of rights and relations" too often meant forcing Russian ways and the Russian language upon national minorities. Such standardization, which was often supported by other government bureaucrats and military leaders, including some co-opted non-Russians, was a far cry from equal rights. Although some ministers, such as Finance Minister Witte, opposed extreme Russification, thinking it counterproductive to stability and financial growth, their opinions on the subject had little impact.

Both government nationality policies and opposition to them, however, were quite complex and varied from one region to another. Pobedonostsev, for example, although generally pushing Russification, opposed some of the specific measures applied in Finland. And if non-Russians often suffered from Russification, the ethnic Russians—less urbanized, less literate, and with lower life expectancies than many of the non-Russian western nationalities—could hardly be considered a privileged people.

In many areas, the nationality issue was complicated by the presence of more than one non-Russian nationality. Russia's Jews, for example, resided mainly in the former Kingdom of Poland, Lithuania, Belorussia, Ukraine, and Bessarabia. The Baltic Germans were the dominant class in the Baltic region but were still a minority among native Latvians and Estonians. The Caucasus were a hodgepodge of nationalities. Armenians, for example, were outnumbered by the combined total of other nationalities in most of their own provinces, but Armenian merchants, traders, and artisans were important to the economic life of non-Armenian Caucasian cities such as Tiflis and Baku.

The presence of large numbers of Armenians, Poles, Ukrainians, and other non-Russian nationalities outside as well as inside the empire's borders further complicated Russia's nationality policies. So too did the overlapping of non-Orthodox faiths with non-Russian peoples. Powerful and influential Catholic and Lutheran voices abroad, for example, could not be completely ignored as Russia pursued its policies in its Polish and Baltic lands.

Despite these foreign voices, however, the Russification policies instituted by Alexander II in the western provinces and Poland continued, and his two successors went even further. For example, in 1885, the Russian government extended to Polish primary schools the use of Russian as the language of instruction for almost all subjects. As relations with Germany grew cooler, Russian anxieties about Baltic security increased and helped usher in the most extensive Russification policies the region had ever witnessed. The government enacted them in Estland, Livland, and Courland primarily between 1887 and 1894 and in Finland from 1899 to 1904.

Because of the previous tolerance of Finnish autonomy, the attempted Russification in Finland was especially significant. For five years, until his assassination in 1904, Governor-General N. I. Bobrikov administered a policy that curtailed the rights of the Finnish Diet, decreed Russian the official administrative language, and proclaimed a new conscription law that made Finns susceptible to being drafted directly into Russian units. The law also aimed at integrating the small (and previously separate) Finnish military into the Russian army. After these policies awakened massive resistance, Bobrikov, in 1903, suspended remaining traditional rights and assumed strengthened emergency powers.

In contrast to the Baltic area, there was little direct Russification in Central Asia and among the Turkic and Moslem peoples. Any large-scale Russification effort among these peoples would have been extremely expensive. Largely for this reason, the khanates of Bukhara and Khiva retained autonomy and responsibility for their own internal affairs, and even the directly annexed parts of Central Asia retained considerable control over local affairs.

Yet, aided by the growth of railways, Russian colonists migrated to cities like Tashkent and Samarkand and even to some rural Central Asian areas. This colonization facilitated the growth of Russian schools and other institutions in the region and offered some competition to native Moslem traditions.

Opposition Among the Nationalities

Opposition to Russian nationality policies was sometimes spurred by religious grievances. In 1898, a Moslem religious leader and his followers proclaimed a holy war against the Russians and marched on the Central Asian city of Andizhan, where they were defeated by Russian troops. After the Russian government confiscated Armenian Church property in 1903, Armenians launched a massive passive resistance campaign.

Opposition movements among the non-Russians were also fueled by more secular forces. Accompanying increased urbanization was the growth of socialist parties. Although some non-Russians, including Joseph Stalin, joined the Russian Social Democratic party (later split between Bolsheviks and Mensheviks), others joined more local national Marxist or socialist organizations. Among those formed between 1887 and 1904 were the Jewish Bund and socialist parties in Armenia, Georgia, Poland, Ukraine, Belorussia, Latvia, and Lithuania. An important issue to many of these parties was whether national or socioeconomic goals should receive a greater priority. This debate sometimes led to a split and the formation of new parties.

Organized political opposition, whether fueled by religious or secular ideas, developed more slowly among Russia's Moslem population. Nevertheless, the Crimean Tatar Ismail Bey Gasprinsky (1851–1914), an influential publicist and educator, advocated the development of a single Turkic language and furthered a sense of unity among Russia's Turkic Moslems.

National consciousness and participation in national opposition to Russification varied considerably. Among Poles, Finns, and Armenians, opposition was at times widespread. Among Ukrainians and Belorussians, overt opposition was more limited, involving primarily students and intellectuals. And some non-Russians among virtually all nationalities were willing to pay the price of Russification for the benefits they believed it brought them.

Jews

Russification and reactions to it do not tell the entire story of Russia's nationality policy. Russia's treatment of its Jewish population was less a question of Russification and more a case of exclusion.

After anti-Jewish pogroms broke out in Ukraine in spring 1881, the panslavist Ignatiev became minister of interior. He blamed the anti-Jewish violence (eventually some 20,000 Jewish homes were destroyed) on the Jews themselves. Like Dostoevsky earlier, he complained of Jewish monetary influence, and he thought the pogroms were a reaction to "Jewish exploitation."

Although scholars such as Rogger have challenged the traditional belief of strong government complicity in the pogroms of this period, there remains little doubt that Judeophobic attitudes were widespread in government and conservative nationalist circles, starting at the top with the era's last two tsars. Pobedonostsev was especially hostile to Jews. Although he knew it was unlikely, he hoped—in the words of his leading biographer—"one-third of the Jews would emigrate, one-third would be assimilated, and one-third would die out."[2] Such attitudes fertilized the soil out of which both pogroms and antisemitic measures germinated.

To curtail "Jewish exploitation" and thereby remove what he considered a main cause of the pogroms, Ignatiev prepared new "temporary regulations." By the May Laws of 1882, any new Jewish settlement in villages or rural purchase of property was prohibited, as was doing business on Sunday mornings or Christian holy days.

Other prohibitions and restrictions soon followed. Jews were limited to no more than 5 percent of army medical personnel. By a law of 1887, Jewish students could make up no more than 10 percent of the total secondary and higher school enrollments within the Pale of Settlement (the restricted western areas where the overwhelming majority of Russia's Jews resided); in St. Petersburg and Moscow, the limit was 3 percent and in other areas 5 percent. In 1889, Jews were excluded from practicing law without special ministerial permission; and in 1890 and 1892, they were denied voting rights in zemstvo and municipal elections. In 1886, many Jews were expelled from Kiev and in 1891 from Moscow.

The series of pogroms that began in 1881 finally sputtered to a halt in 1884. Another wave hit Russia from 1903 until 1906, accelerating in frequency with the Russo-Japanese War of 1904–1905 and the rebellion of 1905.

The 1903 pogrom in the Bessarabian city of Kishinev became infamous. Because Jews were overwhelmingly confined to an urban existence, Kishinev, like most cities in the Pale of Settlement, contained many Jews—about 50,000 or roughly one-third of the city's population. Enflamed by a local antisemitic paper that spread rumors that religious ritualistic needs had led Jews to kill a Christian boy, mobs attacked the city's Jews, killing about forty-seven of them, wounding hundreds of others, and burning or looting about 1,300 houses and shops.

The response of Jews to all this discrimination and violence (plus economic misery) varied, but it did drive some to revolutionary activities. The most significant Jewish radical group was the Jewish Bund (General Jewish Workers' party of Russia and Poland), founded in 1897 and containing some 25,000 members by 1903. Following the Kishinev pogrom, it urged resistance against pogroms and organized self-defense groups. Many other Jews became Bolsheviks, Mensheviks, or members of other radical groups.

As more Jews became revolutionaries, the Russian government overestimated and magnified their impact, contributing to further antisemitism.

---

[2]Robert F. Byrnes, *Pobedonostsev: His Life and Thought* (Bloomington, 1968), p. 207.

Among others, Nicholas II and Plehve believed that Jews were the head and heart of the revolutionary movement.

Although some Jews stayed and became radicals, many more left the country, helping fulfill at least one-third of Pobedonostsev's formula for solving the "Jewish Problem." By 1914, almost one-third of Russia's Jews (who had totaled roughly 5 million in 1897) had emigrated, mostly to the United States. The strong appeal of Zionism, which encouraged emigration to Palestine, was another manifestation of the same phenomenon.

Russian Advances in Asia and the Russo-Japanese War of 1904–1905

After it was humiliated by other European powers at the Congress of Berlin, Russia began focusing more attention on Asia. General M. D. Skobelev's victory over Turkmen forces at the fortress of Gok Tepe in January 1881 delighted panslavists such as Dostoevsky, who now believed Russia should concentrate, at least temporarily, on Asia. He suggested that because Europeans hated Russia, and Russia was part Asian, it should leave Europe to its own squabbles, while it expanded its civilizing influence and control in Asia.

In the next few decades, a number of scholars, publicists, statesmen, and military men echoed Dostoevsky. The focus gradually changed, however, from Central Asia to the Far East. Even Vladimir Soloviev, the philosopher, poet, and eloquent critic of Russian nationalism and antisemitism, wrote in the 1890s about the necessity of Russia advancing in East Asia.

Siberia and Russian Far Eastern Policies

In a report in late 1892, Witte argued that the completion of the Trans-Siberian Railway would greatly facilitate Russian trade with China. At the same time, it would allow Russia to operate a fleet in the Far East, which could dominate the area's Pacific coastline. To supply future Far Eastern Russian forces, whether on land or sea, was certainly one reason for proceeding with the difficult construction of what was to be the world's longest railway.

The laying of some 4,000 miles of track began simultaneously: westward from Vladivostok, and eastward from Miass in the Urals (about 60 miles west of Cheliabinsk). Tens of thousands of workers, including convicts and Chinese laborers, worked in often appalling conditions. Winter brought subzero temperatures and summer enough daylight for seventeen-hour workdays. To lay track across or through plains, mountains, marshes, and rivers, workers had to chop down millions of trees, transport countless tons of dirt, and cut through miles of rocks. The most daunting task was constructing bridges over Siberia's wide rivers, including the Irtysh, the Ob, and the Enisei, and completing the final mountainous link around the southern shore of Lake Baikal.

By the beginning of the Russo-Japanese War in early 1904, all but the Baikal link was completed, although most of the railway's eastern section, the Chinese Eastern Railway, cut across northern Manchuria. (Not until World War I would an all-Russian Trans-Siberian line link Vladivostok with European

Russia.) The Trans-Siberian greatly facilitated migration to Siberia. In the two decades before the start of World War I, some 3 million people moved to Siberia, which was about the same number of people living in all of Siberia around 1860.

Along with the Trans-Siberian construction, the Chinese-Japanese War of 1894–1895 stimulated more Russian involvement in the Far East. Alarmed by Japanese gains in the war, Witte led a campaign in 1895 to deny Japan the Manchurian Liaotung Peninsula, gained from China in the treaty ending the war.

In 1896, Witte won Chinese permission to have the Russian-run Chinese Eastern Railway constructed, a shorter and easier way of linking the cities of Chita and Vladivostok than completing the eastern Trans-Siberian on Russian territory. In 1898, in the midst of other great-power pressures on China, Russia wrenched from the hapless Chinese what it had denied Japan—the Liaotung Peninsula and, at its tip, the ice-free Port Arthur. Not only did Russia receive a lease to the peninsula, but also permission to build a railway branch (the Southern Manchurian Railway) linking the Chinese Eastern Railway at Harbin with Port Arthur.

These steps of 1898 went beyond Witte's more moderate approach to Chinese penetration, but Nicholas II had by now begun listening to more impa-

FIGURE 24.3. Railway Station at Krasnoiarsk. On the Trans-Siberian Line, the population of Krasnoiarsk almost tripled from 1897 (when Lenin spent five weeks of his Siberian exile there) to 1911.

tient and reckless advisers who fed his belief that Russia could dominate the Far East. During the next five years, Russia increased its forces in Manchuria, partly as a response to the Boxer Rebellion of 1900, and stepped up its challenge to Japan's hope to dominate Korea. Japan attempted to negotiate a compromise on Far Eastern spheres of influence but received little positive response from Russia. Nicholas II underestimated both Japanese determination and strength. He thought Russia could pursue its policies without risking war. Even if war came, his minister of interior, V. Plehve, apparently believed that such "a successful, little war" would help dampen revolutionary sentiments at home.

Russo-Japanese War of 1904–1905

In early February 1904, exasperated by Russian unwillingness to negotiate, the Japanese launched a surprise attack on the Russian squadron at Port Arthur. Although a few Russian ships were damaged, none sank. Nicholas II shrugged the attack off as a flea bite and was confident Russia would successfully end the war Japan had begun.

But the Japanese "flea" proved more than a match for the Russian bear. Japan profited from modernized military forces operating close to their home base and enthusiastically supported by the civilian population. In contrast, Russian Far Eastern forces were undermined by overconfidence, by poor governmental and military leadership, by insufficient weapons, by great distances from the Russian industrial heartland, and by quickly dissipating societal support for the war.

Symbolic of Russia's frustration was the fate of its Baltic Fleet, sent halfway around the world to link up with its ships at Port Arthur. After more than seven months at sea, during which time Port Arthur had surrendered to Japan, the Baltic Fleet was met by a Japanese fleet before it could reach safe harbor in Vladivostok. In May 1905, at the battle of Tsushima Straits, the Baltic Fleet was sunk, scattered, or forced to surrender. The loss shocked Russian society and contributed to growing discontent back home. Despite Russia's improving capacity to ship men and equipment to the Far East and its ability eventually to far outnumber Japanese forces, public opinion and financial considerations led it to seek peace.

U.S. President Theodore Roosevelt, not wishing either side to grow too strong, offered to host a peace conference at Portsmouth, New Hampshire. By the Treaty of Portsmouth (September 1905), Russia ceded to Japan the southern half of Sakhalin, its lease of Port Arthur and the rest of the Liaotung Peninsula, and the Southern Manchurian Railway. It also recognized Japan's paramount interests in Korea. Russia was permitted to retain control over the Chinese Eastern Railway and maintain predominant influence in northern Manchuria. Despite considerable pressure on Witte, who negotiated for Russia, he refused to go along with Japanese demands for monetary indemnity. Yet there was little doubt that Japan had won the war against one of Europe's major powers.

Besides its treaty losses, the war cost Russia billions of rubles and hundreds of thousands of dead and wounded. Rather than deflating revolutionary ardor, as Plehve had hoped, this "little war" helped spark it.

SUGGESTED SOURCES*

BECKER, SEYMOUR. *Russia's Protectorates in Central Asia: Bukhara and Khiva, 1865–1924.* Cambridge, Mass., 1968.

BOURNE, KENNETH, and D. CAMERON WATT, eds. *British Documents on Foreign Affairs: Reports and Papers from the Confidential Print.* Part I: *From the Mid-Nineteenth Century to the First World War.* Series A: *Russia, 1859–1914,* ed. Dominic Lieven. Frederick, Md., 1983.

CARRÈRE D'ENCAUSSE, HÉLÈNE. *Islam and the Russian Empire: Reform and Revolution in Central Asia.* London, 1988.

CLAY, CATHERINE B. "Russian Ethnographers in the Service of Empire, 1856–1862," *SR* 54 (Spring 1995): 45–61.

DOSTOEVSKY, F. M. *The Diary of a Writer.* New York, 1949.

FADNER, FRANK. *Seventy Years of Pan-Slavism in Russia: Karamzin to Danilevskii.* Washington, D.C., 1962.

GEYER, DIETRICH. *Russian Imperialism: The Interaction of Domestic and Foreign Policy 1860–1914.* Leamington Spa, N.Y., 1987.

HABERER, ERICH. *Jews and Revolution in Nineteenth-Century Russia.* Cambridge, England, 1995.

HOPKIRK, PETER. *The Great Game: The Struggle for Empire in Central Asia.* New York, 1992.

JUDGE, EDWARD H. *Easter in Kishinev: Anatomy of a Pogrom.* New York, 1992.

KAZEMZADEH, FIRUZ. *Russia and Britain in Persia, 1864–1914: A Study in Imperialism.* New Haven, 1968.

KENNAN, GEORGE F. *The Fateful Alliance: France, Russia, and the Coming of the First World War.* New York, 1984.

KLIER, JOHN DOYLE. *Imperial Russia's Jewish Question, 1855–1881.* Cambridge, England, 1995.

KLIER, JOHN, and SHLOMO LAMBROZA, eds. *Pogroms: Anti-Jewish Violence in Modern Russian History.* Cambridge, England, 1992.

LANGER, WILLIAM L. *European Alliances and Alignments, 1871–1890.* 2d ed. New York, 1964.

LESLIE R. F. *Reform and Insurrection in Russian Poland, 1856–1865.* London, 1963.

LONG, JAMES W. *From Privileged to Dispossessed: The Volga Germans, 1860–1917.* Lincoln, Nebr., 1988.

MACKENZIE, DAVID. *The Lion of Tashkent: The Career of General M. G. Cherniaev.* Athens, Ga., 1974.

———. *The Serbs and Russian Pan-Slavism, 1875–1878.* Ithaca, N.Y., 1967.

MARKS, STEVEN G. *Road to Power: The Trans-Siberian Railroad and the Colonization of Asian Russia, 1850–1917.* Ithaca, N.Y., 1991.

MCDONALD, DAVID M. *United Government and Foreign Policy in Russia, 1900–1914.* Cambridge, Mass., 1992.

MCNEAL, ROBERT H. *Tsar and Cossack, 1855–1914.* New York, 1987.

MOSSE, W. E. *The European Powers and the German Question, 1848–1871, with Special Reference to England and Russia.* Cambridge, England, 1958.

*See also books cited in footnotes.

PETROVICH, MICHAEL B. *The Emergence of Russian Panslavism, 1856–1870.* New York, 1956.

PIERCE, RICHARD A. *Russian Central Asia, 1867–1917: A Study in Colonial Rule.* Berkeley, 1960.

POLVINEN, TUOMO. *Imperial Borderland: Bobrikov and the Attempted Russification of Finland, 1898–1904.* Durham, 1995.

QUESTED, R. K. I. *The Expansion of Russia in East Asia, 1857–1860.* Kuala Lumpur, Malaysia, 1968.

RAGSDALE, HUGH, ed. *Imperial Russian Foreign Policy.* Cambridge, England, 1993.

ROGGER, HANS. *Jewish Policies and Right-Wing Politics in Imperial Russia.* Berkeley, 1986.

———. *Russia in the Age of Modernization and Revolution, 1881–1917.* London, 1983. Chs. 8–9.

SUMNER, B. H. *Russia and the Balkans, 1870–1880.* Oxford, 1937.

TAYLOR, A. J. P. *The Struggle for Mastery in Europe, 1848–1918.* Oxford, 1954.

THADEN, EDWARD C. *Conservative Nationalism in Nineteenth-Century Russia.* Seattle, 1964.

———, ed. *Russification in the Baltic Provinces and Finland, 1855–1914.* Princeton, 1981.

WESTWOOD, J. N. *Russia Against Japan, 1904–1905: A New Look at the Russo-Japanese War.* Albany, 1986.

WOOD, ALAN, ed. *The History of Siberia: From Russian Conquest to Revolution.* London, 1991.

CHAPTER 25

Revolution or Evolution? Politics and War, 1905–1917

In 1905, the largest general strike the world had ever witnessed forced Nicholas II to issue a manifesto promising fundamental reforms. The manifesto indicated that an elected Duma (or legislative council) would be created and be given power to approve or reject all laws.

The elections to the four Dumas that met between 1906 and 1917, especially to the last two, were far from democratic. From the beginning, the powers of the Duma were weak and had to be shared with a conservative State Council. Yet the Duma's existence could have led to Russia's gradual evolution from autocracy into a true constitutional monarchy with a parliamentary type of government. That it did not was due primarily to Nicholas II (and his wife, Alexandra), although there were also numerous other causes for this failure, including World War I. The war itself displayed Nicholas's lack of leadership as never before; by the end of 1916, his disillusioned subjects were on the verge of rebellion.

THE 1905 REVOLUTION: FROM BLOODY SUNDAY TO THE OCTOBER MANIFESTO

In the same month (December 1904 O.S.) that Nicholas II refused to appease a swelling opposition by allowing for elected deputies to advise the government, Port Arthur fell to the Japanese. This embarrassing defeat fueled still further opposition. By the beginning of the second week of January, more than 100,000 St. Petersburg workers were on strike. On Sunday, January 9, 1905, many of them, still believing in the old myth of the benevolent tsar, marched to his Winter Palace to present him with a petition.

Their leader was a priest in his mid-thirties, Father Georgi Gapon. Hoping to turn workers away from socialist influences, the government had allowed him to head a new organization called the St. Petersburg Assembly of Russian Factory and Mill Workers. Gapon, however, had ideas of his own.

Although the men, women, and children who marched toward the palace carried pictures of Nicholas II and Alexandra as well as icons, and Gapon's petition contained no direct criticism of his monarch, it was nevertheless a radical document. It mirrored both general political concerns and specific worker grievances. It criticized capitalists and bureaucrats for exploiting the people, and it called for a Constituent Assembly elected by universal suffrage. It also listed as indispensable full civil liberties; universal, state-financed education; equal legal treatment; the separation of church and state; an end to the Russo-Japanese War; the abolition of peasant redemption payments; the transfer of more land to the peasants; an eight-hour workday; and numerous other provisions, mainly empowering workers in their battle with employers.

The tsar never received the petitioners, for he was outside the city at his Tsarskoe Selo residence. But troops near the palace and on snowy avenues leading to it did greet them—with shots and swords. More than 100 men, women, and children were killed and hundreds of others wounded on this "Bloody Sunday."

The events of this day ignited still more opposition, both within the capital and in other areas such as the Volga city of Saratov. Bloody Sunday also undercut the common people's trust in the goodness of the tsar. As the year proceeded, and bad news kept arriving from the Far East, the turbulence increased. Students voted to boycott classes. Workers struck in cities around the

FIGURE 25.1. General Staff Building (1819–1829, architect C. Rossi) and Palace Square, St. Petersburg, looking down from the Winter Palace. Scene of bloodshed on Bloody Sunday.

empire. Nationalities voiced their grievances, formed new parties, and increasingly called for autonomy. Peasants began appropriating landowners' goods and sometimes burning their houses. Some military units mutinied—the most famous example (later immortalized in an Eisenstein film) being the June mutiny of the sailors aboard the battleship *Potemkin*.

In May, a Union of Unions, under the chairmanship of the Union of Liberation's Paul Miliukov, was formed of fourteen unions. They represented agronomists, clerks and bookkeepers, doctors, engineers, journalists, lawyers, pharmacists, professors, railway workers, teachers, veterinarians, zemstvo-constitutionalists, and two organizations dedicated to Jewish and women's emancipation. That same month, peasants met in Moscow and agreed to form a Peasants' Union that became a reality two months later. Although its main concern was obtaining more land for peasants, it also agreed with the Union of Unions on the necessity of convening a Constituent Assembly.

In the months from Bloody Sunday through the end of the summer of 1905, the response of an often perplexed Nicholas II was to make concessions he thought would not touch the autocratic core. He decreed greater religious toleration, curtailed some censorship and university restrictions, and made limited concessions to the nationalities—for example, rescinding the confiscation of Armenian Church property. In August, he finally issued a manifesto stipulating procedures for electing and convening what he had resisted before Bloody Sunday: an elected, yet purely consultative, assembly, the Duma.

Such measures, however, were no longer enough. Many groups were unhappy with the proposed unequal and discriminatory election procedures and with the limited role proposed for the Duma. Although some moderate liberals were willing to accept such a Duma as a first step, the Union of Unions recommended boycotting elections to it. Most socialist parties went even further. They called for a general strike that they hoped would lead to an armed revolt that would end monarchical rule.

Although the Bolsheviks, Mensheviks, and Social Revolutionaries by no means controlled the workers, their socialist ideas were now falling on increasingly receptive ears. Many workers perceived that their everyday economic and labor grievances could no longer be separated from larger political issues.

In September and October, a Moscow printers' strike spread to bakeries, factories, and railroad shops. Sympathy strikes were held in St. Petersburg. In early October, railway strikes spread from Moscow to other areas of the empire, shutting down the country's rail traffic and igniting the biggest general strike in history. It involved roughly 2 million people. Most of them were industrial and railway workers, but they were joined by many government employees and others, including actors, ballet dancers, doctors, lawyers, professors, shop clerks, stockbrokers, students, and teachers.

In St. Petersburg, where regular activities and electricity were suspended, workers and socialist intellectuals formed an organization to direct strike activities. In less than a week, it was calling itself the Soviet (or Council) of Workers' Deputies and had decided to publish its own newspaper, *Izvestiia*.

On October 17, the same day the Soviet adopted its official name, the tsar issued a manifesto. He was convinced by Witte and others that he had little other choice. His manifesto directed his ministers to grant civil liberties and expand the electorate and rights for the already planned Duma. Previously excluded classes were now to participate in electing it, and thereafter no law was to be issued without Duma confirmation. The manifesto also promised that Duma members would be allowed to participate in overseeing the legality of government actions. Although Nicholas II did not wish to admit it, the manifesto seemed to signal an end to autocratic rule.

CONTINUING DISORDERS AND DUMA PREPARATION

Although the tsar hoped his October Manifesto would end the turmoil, it did not. Nor did the appointment of Witte as a prime minister with real powers, including the right to replace ministers (such as Pobedonostsev) with ones more to his liking. Although these steps mollified some moderates and ended most strikes, the manifesto was also followed by a proliferation of soviets, ethnic and national disturbances (including anti-Jewish pogroms), and peasant violence.

Following the example of the St. Petersburg Soviet, roughly fifty other soviets sprang up in the next few months. Overwhelmingly, they were in cities, but several also appeared among peasants and soldiers.

The St. Petersburg Soviet itself continued to push demands such as an eight-hour workday and the convening of a Constituent Assembly. And it took upon itself certain governmental responsibilities, for example, decreeing freedom of the press, which it attempted to enforce by having printers refuse to print censored papers.

The most dynamic force in the capital's soviet and an author of many of its proclamations and appeals was Leon Trotsky. Born Lev Bronstein into a Ukrainian Jewish family in 1879, he later was exiled to Siberia for revolutionary activity. After he escaped abroad, he impressed Lenin, who in early 1903 recommended him for inclusion on the editorial board of the journal *Iskra*. But during and after the Russian Social Democratic Congress held later that year, Trotsky sided with the Mensheviks in denouncing Lenin's plans for the party, claiming they would lead to dictatorship.

On December 2, 1905, the St. Petersburg Soviet called upon people to withhold their taxes. The government responded by arresting and jailing about half the more than 500 Soviet members, including Trotsky and most other Executive Committee members. Later in the month, it crushed a ten-day strike and insurrection led by the Moscow Soviet and followed it up with severe reprisals, including immediate executions.

In late October 1905, Nicholas II wrote to his mother that "nine-tenths of the troublemakers are Jews." Although he grossly exaggerated Jewish involvement, there were enough revolutionary Jews to make them convenient scapegoats and victims at a time of dissatisfaction and anxiety.

In Odessa, where Trotsky had earlier received most of his formal education, news of the October Manifesto was followed by a fierce pogrom that lasted several days. About one-third of Odessa's approximate half-million people were Jews. Some were involved in anti-tsarist demonstrations, which were countered by patriotic processions. In one of the latter, a boy carrying an icon was shot. Soon afterwards, mobs began attacking Jews, killing hundreds of them. Thousands more were victimized by beatings; rapes; and pillaging and destruction of their apartments, houses, and businesses.

Odessa's Jews were not alone in their suffering. In the two months following the October Manifesto, more than 500 other pogroms occurred, taking approximately another 2,000 Jewish lives and destroying additional Jewish property. Overwhelmingly, they occurred in other Pale of Settlement locations, including Kiev and Minsk.

Local officials, police, and soldiers sometimes encouraged the pogroms through either actions or inactions (such as standing aside while Jews were beaten). Although there is no evidence to support claims that the pogroms were directed by Witte's government—which was wary of any lawlessness—nevertheless, the antisemitic attitudes of Nicholas II and some of his ministers encouraged, at least inadvertently, such developments. Toward the end of October 1905, Nicholas II wrote that the pogroms were a case of "loyal people" attacking "bad people."

Proliferating right-wing antisemitic organizations and publications played a more direct role in the 1905 pogroms. Such groups, especially their more activist, violent followers, were often labeled "the Black Hundreds."

Strong national and ethnic feelings were also displayed among other groups. Shortly after the October Manifesto, Nicholas II attempted to appease the Finns by restoring rights he had earlier taken away. He was less willing, however, to accommodate other nationalities. In late November, he imposed martial law on Estonians and Latvians in response to their unrest and demands for greater autonomy and a reduction of Baltic German prominence. When rebellions continued in the region, the government dispatched fresh Russian troops to crush them.

Some of the Baltic rebels were peasants, and peasant disturbances increased dramatically after the October Manifesto. They were especially prevalent in the mainly black-earth, south-central region, including the provinces Chernigov, Poltava, Voronezh, Tambov, Penza, and Saratov. They reached their peak in November–December 1905 and again in June–July 1906 but continued into 1907. Even the termination of the hated emancipation redemption payments in 1905–1906 proved unable to stem the tide of peasant dissatisfaction.

Although the peasants looted, destroyed, and sometimes seized noble estates, they took almost no noble lives. Their aim was primarily to drive nobles and other nonpeasants off rural lands so that, by one way or another, they could obtain them. They hoped the government would grant them these lands and appealed to various sources, including the Peasant Union and new Duma, to help them realize their hope.

To restore order, both in the countryside and in scattered rebellious cities around the empire, Nicholas II sent in more punitive military expeditions like those sent to the Baltic region. Fortunately for him, Russia's troops generally remained loyal.

Meanwhile the government prepared new laws to carry out the changes indicated in the October Manifesto. In December, it spelled out election procedures for the new Duma. Although the exclusion of women and young people (those under twenty-five) was typical of the era, the denial of voting rights to some subgroups of commoners and the grossly disproportionate weight of peoples' vote was less common: One landowner's vote was to equal that of 15 peasants or 45 workers—believing that the peasants still revered their tsar, Nicholas trusted them more than urban workers.

In April 1906, the tsar accepted the resignation of Witte as prime minister. Although in moments of crisis Nicholas sometimes turned to strong and determined men reminiscent of his father, reactionary voices eventually convinced him that they were undermining his autocratic prerogatives, and he ceased offering them much support. Such was the case with Witte and later with Peter Stolypin.

On April 23, just one day after officially accepting the frustrated Witte's resignation, Nicholas made public "The Fundamental Laws." They were to provide the legal framework for the new era promised in the October Manifesto, but they also reflected Nicholas's desire to make as few concessions as possible. Although the laws stipulated that no new law could be passed without Duma approval, they also declared that the Emperor retained "supreme autocratic power." Because Nicholas viewed the Fundamental Laws and the Duma as favors he bestowed, he thought they could be revoked whenever he wished.

The powers granted to the new Duma were few. Although it could initiate new legislation, it was normally expected to react to proposed laws submitted to it. Although it could reject proposed laws, the tsar had the right to determine the length of annual Duma sessions and the interval between them, or to dissolve a Duma before its members served a normal five-year term, provided that he scheduled new elections. Between Duma sessions, he could (by the infamous Article 87) decree emergency laws that could continue in force for up to sixty days after a new session convened. Duma-passed legislation could not become law unless approved by the State Council, now transformed into an upper legislative house, and the tsar. The State Council was to be partly appointed by the tsar and partly elected, primarily by groups that insured upper-class, ethnic-Russian domination of the council. Only the tsar could review or revise the Fundamental Laws and exercise control over foreign policy and military affairs, including the decision to go to war.

Contrary to the statement in the October Manifesto, the Duma received no real powers in overseeing the legality of government measures. It could question ministers about the legality of their actions but could not force compliance.

Along with the State Council, the Duma was allowed to review the proposed annual state budget. But both houses were exempted from exercising any control over certain areas, including traditional Imperial Household expenses and most military spending and state debt payments. If a new state budget were not approved, the government could operate according to the previous year's budget.

THE FIRST TWO DUMAS, 1906 AND 1907

On April 27, 1906, four days after the promulgation of the Fundamental Laws, the first Duma gathered in St. Petersburg. During the next few months, its number and composition varied slightly but hovered near 500 members.

The left-liberal Constitutional Democrats (or Kadets) had the largest number of delegates (approximately 180). Founded in late 1905, its leader was Paul Miliukov, although he was not among its delegates. The government had charged him with violating censorship and disqualified him from running. More radical than the Kadets, especially on the land question, was a coalition of leftist factions, called the Trudoviks or Laborites. They possessed about 100 delegates, many of them peasants.

Other parties and factions had much smaller representation. Most radical leftists had boycotted the elections. To the right of the Kadets were the Octobrists (moderate liberals who had accepted the October Manifesto) and other smaller parties. Altogether they constituted about 45 delegates. The rest of the delegates were from national or religious minorities or had no clear affiliation. Many of the latter were peasants, and these and peasants in the other groupings composed about two-fifths of the total delegates.

From the beginning, it was clear that the tsar and his new prime minister, the loyal but undistinguished bureaucrat I. L. Goremykin, intended to prevent any meaningful power-sharing with the Duma. Conversely, Duma members were unsatisfied with the small role Nicholas II intended for them and insisted on expanded powers. They wanted ministers to be responsible to them, democratic suffrage, the abolition of the State Council, amnesty for political offenses, the rule of law, and land reform, including the confiscation of private lands over a certain maximum, for which compensation would be paid. Alarmed at such radical demands, especially regarding land transfers, Nicholas dissolved the Duma on July 8, 1906.

Fearful the police would prevent their further actions, Miliukov and about 200 delegates, mostly Kadets, retired to the Finnish city of Vyborg. There, most of them signed a manifesto calling on people to refuse paying taxes or providing military recruits until another Duma met. The manifesto had little effect except for getting the Duma members who had signed it arrested and barred from running in the next election.

The activities of the signatories were later criticized extensively by V. A. Maklakov, a Kadet lawyer who disagreed with his party's majority. Many later historians also faulted Miliukov and others for their impatience and unrealistic expectations in late 1905 and 1906. In his memoirs, Miliukov responded to such criticism by contending that if the Kadet party would have become as "moderate" as Maklakov and others desired, it would have lost authority, many followers, and become insignificant.

On the same day that Nicholas II dissolved the First Duma, he replaced

A Description of the First Duma

The following selection is from Bernard Pares, *Russia and Reform* (London, 1907), pp. 550–552. Pares spent much time in Russia, observing its life and institutions, and became England's first professor of Russian history. Ellipses are mine.

If the Duma did nothing else, it brought together for the first time representatives of every class and of every interest in Russia. It was of course far more Imperial than any other European Parliament. It would be difficult to imagine a more picturesque gathering. Each man wore the costume of his class. The country gentry of the Intelligents dressed very simply, but there were Russian priests with long beards and hair, a Roman Catholic bishop in skull-cap lined with red, finely accoutred Cossacks from the Caucasus, Bashkirs and Buryats in strange and tinselled Asiatic dress, Polish peasants in the brilliant and martial costumes of their people, and a whole mass of staid, bearded, and top-booted Russian peasants. Strangers easily obtained admittance; and amongst the most picturesque visitors were the so-called "walking deputies" who were sent by peasant constituents to look after their members, and others who had tramped for hundreds of miles to ask the Duma to settle their private disputes. Groups of members and non-members formed in the corridor to discuss without reticence any question of the moment. Small party conferences, sitting in the committee-rooms, seemed in no way disturbed by passing strangers. Milyukoff [Miliukov], in the simple dress of an English country gentleman, walked up and down the corridor receiving the suggestions of various party leaders, which seldom induced him to deviate a yard from the tactics upon which he had determined. One noticed that the Cadets as a body quite failed to get hold of the non-party members. These peasants, who would not sink their individuality in any party formula, expressed the most fresh and interesting opinions of all. . . . but Milyukoff was hardly ever to be seen talking to a non-party man. . . . The Duma was allowed to discuss the franchise, and it of course declared in favour of the well-known formula "universal, direct, equal, and secret." The debate on women's suffrage excited a lively interest. On this day the corridor was invaded by an active band of suffragettes, who evidently thought that they could give the necessary lessons to the non-party peasant. It was amusing to watch the peasants dealing with these young ladies. One very typical peasant admitted that it was most unfair that women should receive lower pay than men for similar work. "We will put that right for you," he said "let us get on our legs first, then we will give you some rights." But the young ladies wanted not to receive, but to take, and claimed that women ought to be sitting in the Duma. "Look here," said he, "I will tell you what: you go and marry! You will have a husband and children, and your husband will look after you altogether." "Look after, indeed!" said the young ladies; but the peasant would not promise anything more. Equally interesting was the attitude of the Non-party group towards the Jews: they spoke without any ill-will, but remarked: "Even without rights, the Jews are on the top of us."

Goremykin with his minister of interior, Peter Stolypin. Only months earlier, Stolypin, still in his early forties, had come to St. Petersburg, previously having served several years as a provincial governor.

His first task as prime minister was to restore order. Peasant disturbances

FIGURE 25.2. Taurida Palace, St. Petersburg, 1783–1789, architect I. Starov. Commissioned by Catherine II for Prince Potemkin, this building was where the Duma met.

had again risen sharply in June 1906. In the cities, SR Maximalists (members of the Combat Organization) and other revolutionaries often assassinated police and government officials. Stolypin claimed that in the eight months preceding June 1906, almost 300 Ministry of Interior officials and police had been killed. In August, a few SR Maximalists threw explosives into his own residence, injuring his two children and killing about thirty others, including the terrorists themselves.

Forceful man that he was and mindful of Nicholas II's impatience to end such terror, Stolypin used Article 87 to set up special new military courts to deal with civilians accused of antigovernment crimes. Within three days of a crime, a court was to meet and conclude its verdict. Proceedings were secret, and no defense lawyer was allowed. If execution was the verdict (as it was in about 1,000 cases over the next eight months), it was to occur within twenty-four hours. After the Second Duma convened in late February 1907, the special courts failed to gain Duma approval and thus expired in April. They had left an indelible impression, however—the ropes used to hang the condemned became known as "Stolypin's neckties"—and other military courts continued to sentence civilians to be executed. Altogether, from 1906 to 1909, many more Russians were executed than in the previous eighty years combined.

Stolypin also used other methods to counter violence and unrest in the country. Much of Russia continued to be ruled by martial law; while unrest and assassinations continued, so too did exiling and death sentences. Although rural unrest declined considerably in 1907, urban terrorism, while slowing somewhat, continued to be a major problem. From late 1905 until mid-May 1910, more than 6,000 officials and police were killed or wounded.

Elections to the Second Duma brought no comfort to Stolypin and Nicholas II: It was more radical than its predecessor and had no intention of cooperating with Stolypin's policies. The Bolsheviks, Mensheviks, and Socialist Revolutionaries had decided to participate in elections and together gained almost as many delegates as the Trudoviks (or Laborites). All these leftist delegates, including the Trudoviks, outnumbered the Kadets by more than two to one. The Kadets themselves were becoming more moderate and centrist. Deputies to the right of the Kadets also outnumbered them but more slightly. The antisemitic and far-right Union of the Russian People, which had more than 200 branches in the country, gained ten Duma seats.

Stolypin was no reactionary and believed law and order had to be accompanied by reforms. Like Bismarck earlier in Germany, he hoped to deflate leftist appeals by taking away some of their grievances. He proposed to the Duma land and tax reforms, advancement toward compulsory primary education, workers' insurance and the recognition of their right to unionize and strike, and the strengthening and extension of local government and the rule of law.

But cooperation was doomed primarily by one fundamental difference between Stolypin and a majority of the Duma delegates: land confiscation of nonpeasant lands to benefit the peasants. Nicholas II and Stolypin were firmly against confiscation; the socialists and Kadets were for it, although the Kadets on a more modest scale and with compensation for confiscated noble lands. In early June, three and a half months after it was convened, the Second Duma was dissolved.

STOLYPIN'S LAND POLICIES

In 1906, between the First and Second Dumas, Stolypin began a bold new agricultural policy, later furthered by legislation of 1910 and 1911. He made more state and crown lands available for peasant purchase, made Peasant Bank mortgages easier to obtain, and facilitated resettlement to areas such as Siberia where more land was available. He also freed peasants from some legal restrictions (for example, on domestic travel) that separated them from the rest of society. Most significantly, he empowered peasants to withdraw from the commune and obtain title to the strips of land they had previously farmed or, where possible, to a consolidated plot of equal land.

In 1905, a little more than three-fourths of peasant households in the country's European provinces farmed in communes; most of those who did not reside in Ukraine and other western areas. By 1916, approximately half of European Russian peasant households owned their land outside the communes, but only about one-tenth possessed consolidated plots, and most of these owners did not reside on their farmland but in nearby peasant villages.

Stolypin's measures were designed to create a strong class of individual peasant proprietors who would respect private property and support the government. In 1908, he stated that the government had staked its future "on the sober and strong" peasants, not the "drunken and the weak."

He knew that an agricultural transformation would take several peaceful decades of determined implementation. The outbreak of World War I in 1914, three years after his own assassination, deprived Russia of peace. Besides time and government determination, peasant attitudes toward Stolypin's policy were also crucial. Although some peasants took advantage of the new opportunities, many others did not. One thing they all agreed on, however, was that they needed more land.

THE THIRD AND FOURTH DUMAS, 1907–1914

The dissolution of the Second Duma was accompanied by a new electoral law that violated Nicholas's own Fundamental Laws. It strengthened the already weighty vote of large landowners and reduced that of most peasants, workers, and non-Russian nationalities. The failure of Duma peasant delegates to support tsarist policies had been especially disappointing to Nicholas II, a failure he blamed on outsiders who misled the peasants. The electoral changes meant that most future Duma delegates were elected by landowners who made up only about 1 percent of the population. As Stolypin said in 1908: "If you took an assembly which represented the majority . . . sane ideas would not prevail in it. . . . We want not professors but men with roots in the country, the local gentry, and such like."

Given the new electoral laws, the composition of the Third Duma, labeled the "Masters' Duma," is hardly surprising. Nobles outnumbered peasants by more than two to one, and there were ten times more Great Russians than all the other nationalities combined. The Octobrists became the largest party, with slightly more than one-third of the delegates. Other more conservative parties totaled an almost equal fraction. The remaining deputies were from parties to the left of the Octobrists, including the Kadets, and from the non-Russian nationalities and unaffiliated. The SRs had no deputies, having once again boycotted Duma elections.

The Third Duma opened on November 1, 1907. Its composition facilitated more cooperation with Stolypin and Nicholas II, and in its five-year term it initiated more than 200 pieces of legislation and voted on more than 2,500 bills introduced by the government.

The value of its work varied greatly. Besides backing Stolypin's agricultural policies, the Duma passed legislation designed to expand educational opportunities and literacy, provide workers' health insurance, and extend women's inheritance rights. Other acts helped bring zemstvos to new provinces (although discriminating against non-Russians in them) and restored justices of the peace, while concurrently reducing the powers of the land captains. The Duma passed additional legislation that never found its way into law, much of it never getting past the State Council, which was more conservative than Stolypin.

If at times progressive, at other times the Third Duma was more reactionary, especially when it came to nationality issues. Among other steps, it helped Stolypin roll back Finnish autonomy, restore and expand Russification measures in Poland, repress Ukrainian nationalism and desires for cultural autonomy, and increase colonization and Great Russian interests in Moslem areas of the empire.

Despite heightened cooperation with Stolypin, the Third Duma often differed with him as well as with the State Council. In early 1911, he managed to alienate the overwhelming majority of both houses, plus the tsar.

By late 1911, Nicholas II had lost confidence in Stolypin, and his effectiveness was waning. Rumors circulated that the tsar was about to replace him. A bullet saved him the trouble. At an intermission to a performance of *The Story of Tsar Saltan*, Stolypin was shot in a Kiev opera house and died several days later on September 5. Strangely enough, although such circumstances were by no means unique under Nicholas, the assassin had been a police informant who shot Stolypin to prove his loyalty to fellow revolutionaries.

Nicholas II replaced Stolypin with his finance minister, Vladimir Ko-

FIGURE 25.3. Opera House, Kiev, scene of Stolypin assassination in 1911.

kovtsov. Miliukov considered him a faithful servant of the tsar with a deserved reputation as an "honest bookkeeper." He remained in office until early 1914, when Goremykin, like an "old fur coat," was brought out once again to become prime minister.

The Fourth Duma, with a makeup as conservative as the Third, first met in November 1912. In the less than two years that remained before World War I, however, the Duma found it increasingly difficult to cooperate with tsarist policies that were becoming more rigid. Indicative of the Duma's sentiments was a resolution it passed in 1913, condemning the Ministry of Interior for its arbitrary actions, its "illegal acts," and its delay of reforms.

Minister of Interior N. A. Maklakov responded by asking Nicholas to warn the Duma to correct its ways and if it did not, to dissolve it. The tsar was prepared to go even further. He asked his ministers to consider a plan requiring the Duma to submit majority and minority reports to him for selection and confirmation—essentially turning the Duma into a consultative body. Although his Council of Ministers thought this was going too far, Nicholas's request indicates that he still opposed any real power-sharing.

Also indicative of the government's tone in 1913 was the Belis case. Spurred on by the antisemitic Union of the Russian People, the government brought a Jewish clerk (Belis) to trial for allegedly committing a ritual murder against a Christian boy. It thus furthered antisemitism and the myth that Jews committed such murders.

THE RADICAL OPPOSITION, 1907–1914

Following the turbulent 1905–1907 period, Stolypin's "necktie" and other measures helped weaken the radical opposition. Popular support of the major socialist parties declined. Factionalized and living mainly abroad, the socialist leaders looked at times like impractical, squabbling émigrés living on the fringes of reality. In 1911, the government found it necessary to exile only about one-quarter the number of political opponents exiled two years earlier.

During this period, criticism of the revolutionary intelligentsia, including the leaders of the socialist parties, reached new heights. For some time, right-wing groups had accused them of being too cosmopolitan, antireligious, and anti-Russian. Now the most famous criticism came from a group of leading intellectuals, most of them former Marxists, who had participated in the Union of Liberation. It appeared in a book of essays called *Vekhi* (*Landmarks*), which appeared in 1909, and was hotly debated for years afterward. The crux of their critique was that the intelligentsia had placed too much faith in political revolution, been too dogmatic, and failed to realize that the transformation of society depended first on the inner spiritual transformation of each individual.[1]

The *Vekhi* essays were symptomatic of an emphasis on idealism, religious

---

[1]Although debate has existed for more than a century on just who should be included in the category "intelligentsia," it was generally used to indicate critically thinking people who expressed the belief that Russia's sociopolitical order was unjust, especially to the lower classes.

thinking, and new cultural approaches that marked the period. The intellectual spirit of the times reflected more the influence of the poet and philosopher Vladimir Soloviev, who died in 1900, than it did Karl Marx or Mikhail Bakunin.

Yet the festering social and political problems of Russia left the door open for a resurgence of the radical left. Workers and peasants remained more susceptible to socialist agitation than Solovievian ideas. A replay of 1905, this time with a different ending, remained a distinct possibility.

News that troops had killed some 200 unarmed strikers at the Siberian Lena goldfields in April 1912 helped spark a new wave of worker unrest. Strikes, which had declined considerably between 1907 and 1911, now increased dramatically. During the month following the killings, twice as many workers struck as had done so during the entire previous four years. The number kept increasing until it reached well over 1 million in the first half of 1914. Moreover, the increasing influence of the Bolsheviks on workers during the 1912–1914 period boded ill for those desiring stability.

RUSSIAN FOREIGN POLICY, 1906–1914

In November 1913, Octobrist leader Alexander Guchkov feared that the new labor militancy and, even more, the government's reactionary and incompetent policies were leading Russia to disaster. Russia's only hope, he thought, lie with those whose first desire was to see Russia remain a major power.

Such patriotic sentiments were typical of this period and not just in Russia. Thus, it is hardly surprising that maintaining great-power status (and the military might needed to guarantee it) was a goal the Russian government shared with much of educated Russian society, including most Duma members. Yet, given Russia's defeat in the war against Japan and its own internal conditions, maintaining such a status required great skill and leadership. Unfortunately for Russia, Nicholas II could not provide them.

Nicholas was wise enough, however, to realize the dangers of war before a major Russian rearmament program could be completed. In 1911, he declared that "it would be out of the question for us to face a war for five or six years." What he lacked were the skills to manage a cautious but forceful diplomacy, or at least to find someone who could. He was fatalistic and, although stubborn at times, rather weak-willed—during World War I, Alexandra wrote to him: "How I wish I could pour my will into your veins." These were not the most desirous qualities for a leader on the eve of World War I.

After a decade in office, Nicholas illustrated in July 1905 that he was still a babe in the diplomatic woods. His bullying cousin, Kaiser Wilhelm II of Germany, had little respect for him—once referring to Nicholas as "only fit to live in a country house and grow turnips." He personally persuaded Nicholas to sign a defensive alliance, the Treaty of Björkö, that shocked his foreign minister and Witte, who together discussed whether Nicholas had forgotten about the Franco-Russian treaty. Convinced by his ministers that he had made a mistake, Nicholas was forced to inform Wilhelm that the treaty they had just signed could not become operational without major changes. Wilhelm responded, "What is signed is signed!" But the treaty was dead.

In 1908, it was Foreign Minister Izvolsky's turn to be duped and then reverse himself. He agreed that Russia would look benevolently upon Austria's annexation of Bosnia-Herzegovina (consisting mainly of ethnic Serbs), which it had occupied since 1878. In exchange, Austria's foreign minister agreed to provide diplomatic support for Russian efforts to open up the Turkish Straits to Russian warships. It remains unclear what, if anything, was agreed to regarding when these activities might occur.

When Austria acted more quickly than Izvolsky thought it would, he was left unprepared. France and Great Britain were angered at the Austrian move and with Izvolsky's assistance in making it possible. Gaining further diplomatic support for his Straits' policy now proved impossible. Moreover, Serbian and Russian nationalists were incensed over the Austrian annexation, and Stolypin informed Izvolsky to oppose it, which he now did. Germany promised Austria its backing and bluntly demanded recognition of the annexation. Humiliated, but unwilling to risk the consequences suggested by Germany if it did not comply, Russia yielded. Neither Russia nor Serbia forgot the incident, and both became determined not to suffer such humiliation again.

Although France and Britain were angered at the course of events and left wondering at the reliability of Russia, the three countries had moved closer together in recent years. In 1904, Britain and France concluded an entente, or understanding, concerning North African spheres of influence. Kaiser Wilhelm's belligerence toward the entente and a continuing German naval buildup pushed Britain to improve its ties with France further. Britain also moved closer to France's ally, Russia. By the Anglo-Russian Entente of 1907, the two long-time rivals agreed over the status of Persia, Afghanistan, and Tibet. Most significantly, they agreed that Britain would have dominant influence over southeast Persia; Russia over northern Persia; and that a neutral zone would exist between the two other Persian spheres. The growing closeness of Russia, Britain, and France (the Triple Entente), however, only increased Germany's fear of encirclement and its determination to maintain its Austro-Hungarian alliance by vigorously supporting its ally.

The next major trouble in the Balkans came in 1912–1913. Warfare there involving Turks and Balkan nations chipped away more Turkish territory in Europe, nudged the Ottoman Empire closer to Germany and Austria-Hungary, and increased tensions and hostilities between Serbia and Austria-Hungary. Although Sergei Sazanov, who had replaced Izvolsky as foreign minister in 1910, attempted to prevent war, his vacillating policies inadvertently contributed to bringing it about.

Then, on June 28, 1914, a Bosnian of Serbian nationality assassinated Austrian Archduke Franz Ferdinand. Austria was convinced that the Serbian government was implicated but feared Russia would support Serbia in case of a conflict. Austria therefore sought and received German backing (the infamous "blank check") before it proceeded to send an ultimatum to Serbia on July 23. If fully complied with, the ultimatum would have guaranteed Austrian dominance over Serbia.

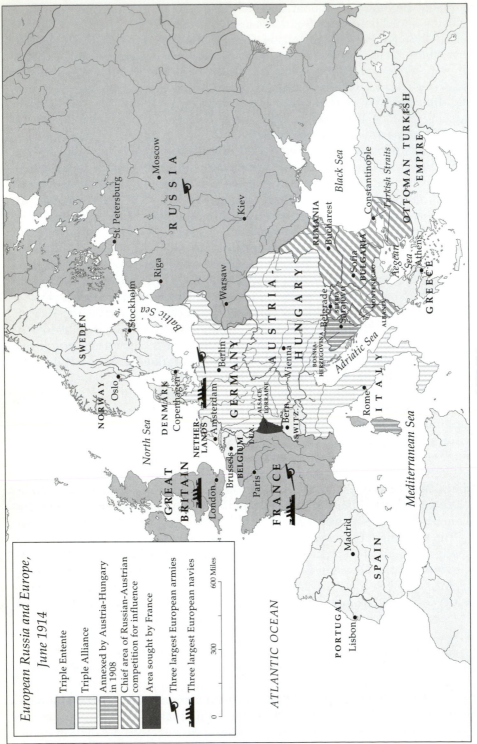

European Russia and Europe,
June 1914

Triple Entente

Triple Alliance

Annexed by Austria-Hungary
in 1908

Chief area of Russian-Austrian
competition for influence

Area sought by France

Three largest European armies

Three largest European navies

0   300   600 Miles

ATLANTIC OCEAN

PORTUGAL
Lisbon

SPAIN
Madrid

Mediterranean Sea

GREAT
BRITAIN
London

NETHER-
LANDS
Amsterdam

DENMARK
Copenhagen

NORWAY
Oslo

SWEDEN
Stockholm

North Sea

Baltic Sea

BELGIUM
Brussels

LUX.

FRANCE
Paris

ALSACE-
LORRAINE

GERMANY
Berlin

SWITZ.
Bern

ITALY
Rome

AUSTRIA-
HUNGARY
Vienna

BOSNIA-
HERZEGOVINA
Sarajevo

SERBIA
Belgrade

MONTENEGRO

ALBANIA

Adriatic Sea

GREECE
Athens

Aegean
Sea

RUMANIA
Bucharest

BULGARIA
Sofia

Black Sea

Constantinople

Turkish Straits

OTTOMAN TURKISH
EMPIRE

RUSSIA
Moscow

St. Petersburg

Riga

Warsaw

Kiev

MAP 25.1

498

Neither Serbia nor Russia could tolerate this. It would have ended Russian hopes for major Balkan influence and sealed Austrian supremacy in the area. After hearing of Austria's ultimatum, Sazanov declared: "That means a European war!" Although advising Serbia to proceed cautiously, on July 25 (N.S.), Russia approved preliminary military preparations, hoping to alarm Austria into a compromise or, failing that, to be ready to help Serbia. France backed Russia's stand.

Encouraged by Russian support, Serbia, although somewhat conciliatory, did not accept all the Austrian demands. On July 28, Austria declared war on Serbia and bombarded Belgrade, the Serbian capital.

After some indecisiveness about how to mobilize, on July 30 (N.S.), Russia ordered a general mobilization of its troops. France encouraged this action because it knew of the general thrust of Germany's Schlieffen Plan, which called for a fatal German blow against France before Russian mobilization would force Germany to divert more troops to its eastern front.

Because of Germany's plan, its response to Russia was no surprise. On July 31, after several warnings on previous days, it sent an ultimatum with a twelve-hour limit demanding that Russia end its war preparations along the German frontier. On August 1, having received no reply, Germany declared war on Russia. Two days later, certain that France was preparing to aid Russia, Germany declared war on France. It directed its attack through neutral Belgium, thereby alarming Britain, which declared war on Germany on August 4.

The responsibility of Russia and other powers in beginning World War I has been greatly debated. Certainly Russia played its part in the combustible nationalistic-militaristic-imperialistic climate of the era. And its decision to mobilize fully on July 30 was especially important. Along with the other powers, Russia valued security, prestige, influence, and allies more than peace.

Yet, shortly before he ordered full mobilization on July 30, Nicholas told one of his ministers that "everything possible must be done to save the peace. I will not become responsible for a monstrous slaughter." Nicholas made his fateful decision because he was assured by his generals that no partial mobilization plan existed to mobilize troops just against Austria-Hungary and not Germany. This fact reflected more the Russian government's ineptness and lack of flexibility than any lust for war.

Moreover, many historians have followed Fritz Fischer's lead in placing the primary blame for World War I on Germany. For example, Lieven has argued that even without the Russian general mobilization, war would have come and "the major immediate responsibility for the outbreak of the war rested unequivocally on the German government."[2]

TSARIST RUSSIA AND WORLD WAR I, 1914–1916

In Russia, as in most European countries, the beginning of World War I brought a lessening of political opposition and a patriotic rallying around the

---

[2]D. C. B. Lieven, *Russia and the Origins of the First World War* (New York, 1983), p. 151.

government. This was especially true among Great Russian urban dwellers. The strikes that had been surging for two years now ended. Symbolic of the new spirit was the crowd of close to a quarter-million that jammed the vast Palace Square on August 2 (N.S.). After Nicholas appeared on the Winter Palace balcony overlooking the square and swore he would make no peace while enemy troops remained on Russian soil, the crowd sang "God Save the Tsar" and the hymn "Lord, Save Thy People and Bless Thine Inheritance."

Russia began the war by rushing troops into East Prussia, a move critical to relieving German pressure on France. The campaign proved a disaster for Russian troops, who were defeated at the battles of Tannenberg (August 26–30) and Mansurian Lakes (September 6–15). In December, the Russians lost the Polish industrial city of Lodz to the Germans. Against Austria, the Russian army had been more successful, moving into Galicia and capturing its capital of Lemberg (Lvov or Lviv) in September (see Map 25.2). Overall, by the end of 1914, the war had cost Russia more than 1 million dead, wounded, or captured, plus hundreds of thousands of weapons.

During 1915, German and Austrian forces attacked over a broad area from the Baltic to the Rumanian frontier. By October 1915, they had captured Vilna (Vilnius), Pinsk, and Lemberg; Riga and Minsk were not far away. As Russia retreated, it practiced scorched-earth policies, attempting to leave as little as possible to the enemy, but also swelling the number of refugees into the millions. Some victories in the Caucasus against Turkey, which had entered the war in the fall of 1914, hardly compensated for huge losses in Russia's western provinces.

In the late spring of 1916, one of Russia's most able generals, A. A. Brusilov, launched an offensive against Austrian forces, pushing them back, inflicting many casualties. His success encouraged Rumania to join the war on the Entente side, but it also led Germany to divert troops to halt the Russian advance, which they did.

Meanwhile, Russian losses continued to mount. By the end of 1916, killed, wounded, missing, or captured numbered about 7 million. As losses steadily rose, morale just as steadily fell.

Even during the first year of war, many soldiers deserted. By the beginning of 1917, the number reached perhaps 1 million or more. As more new men replaced those killed or otherwise lost, discipline declined. In November 1916, Paul Miliukov, leader of the Progressive Bloc, which was formed in August 1915 and contained a majority of Duma deputies, surveyed the state of affairs at home and on the front and asked his fellow Duma members: "Is this stupidity, or is this treason?" At the front, rumors incorrectly favored the latter explanation.

There was also discontent brewing among minority nationalities. After the government attempted to draft a half-million Central Asians for labor service in mid-1916, scattered rebellions broke out in their region, resulting by year's end in thousands of Russian civilian and military deaths. Central Asian losses were much higher.

Although many Russian villagers were by now condemning the war, the greatest dissatisfaction was displayed in the cities, where population had in-

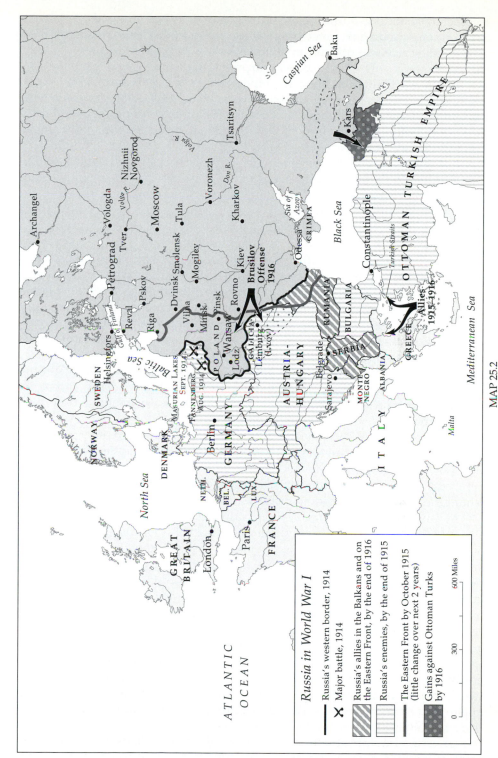

Russia in World War I

— Russia's western border, 1914
✕ Major battle, 1914

▨ Russia's allies in the Balkans and on
   the Eastern Front, by the end of 1916

▥ Russia's enemies, by the end of 1915

— The Eastern Front by October 1915
   (little change over next 2 years)

▦ Gains against Ottoman Turks
   by 1916

0   300   600 Miles

MAP 25.2

ATLANTIC
OCEAN

GREAT
BRITAIN
London

NORWAY

SWEDEN

Helsingfors
Gulf of Finland
Reval
Riga
Pskov
Vilna
Minsk

DENMARK

NETH.
BEL.
LUX.

Berlin

GERMANY

Paris

FRANCE

ITALY

Malta

Mediterranean Sea

North Sea

Baltic Sea

TANNENBERG
AUG. 1914
MASURIAN LAKES
SEPT. 1914

POLAND
Warsaw
Lodz

GALICIA
Lemburg
(Lvov)

AUSTRIA-
HUNGARY

Belgrade
Sarajevo
SERBIA
MONTE-
NEGRO
ALBANIA

RUMANIA

BULGARIA

GREECE

Allies
1915-1916

Constantinople
Turkish Straits

OTTOMAN TURKISH EMPIRE

Pinsk
Rovno
Kiev
Brusilov
Offense
1916

Dvinsk
Smolensk
Mogilev

Archangel

Vologda
Tver
Volga R.
Nizhnii
Novgorod

Petrograd
Moscow
Tula
Voronezh
Kharkov
Tsaritsyn

Don R.

Sea of
Azov
CRIMEA
Odessa
Black Sea

Caspian Sea
Baku

Kars

Volga R.

501

creased by about one-fourth between 1914 and 1916. In Petrograd (no longer the German-sounding St. Petersburg), Moscow, and other cities, food and fuel grew more scarce and difficult to afford. Workers' pay failed to keep up with the soaring prices of basic needs. Not surprisingly, the lull in strike activity that greeted the war did not last long. In September 1915, there were 100,000 strikers in Russia; in October 1916, there were about 250,000 in Petrograd alone. In the Duma, many shared Miliukov's disgust. Police reports and memoirs from the period indicate that by the end of 1916, many in the capital thought revolution was just around the corner.

The military's poor showing was a major cause of discontentment. At first, it was primarily because of shortages of supplies and poor leadership—the priorities of Russia's prewar rearmament program overemphasized some items, such as battleships, at the expense of more vital needs. By the end of 1914, Russia was almost 2 million rifles short of what it needed to arm its 6.5 million men. For a while in 1915, the situation grew worse. Many men were forced into combat without rifles, unless or until they were able to pick them up from their fallen comrades. Not only rifles, but also machine guns, bullets, cartridges, artillery shells, motorized vehicles, uniforms and boots, telephone and telegraph equipment, airplane spare parts, and other supplies were all insufficient. What Russia did possess, including manpower, it could not get to the front as quickly as Germany. This was due largely to the greater distances Russian supplies needed to travel and because per square mile of territory, European Russia possessed less than one-tenth the railway of Germany. Yet by the spring-summer of 1916, dramatic domestic production increases and more supplies from its allies and the United States had helped surmount most of the supply problems.

The problem of poor leadership was more difficult to overcome, primarily because at the top of the pyramid stood Nicholas II. He was ultimately responsible for appointing and retaining so many inept military and civilian leaders. Time and again he ignored or refused good advice to get rid of poor leaders, while listening to poor advice to dismiss good ministers and generals.

Although already displaying this poor lack of judgment before August 1915, the problem worsened after that because Nicholas was absent from the capital. Despite the alarm it caused some of his ministers, he went to army headquarters in the Belorussian city of Mogilev to take command of his troops personally. Henceforth, he was increasingly influenced by his generals and the unlimited advice sent to him from his wife, Alexandra, who remained on the outskirts of Petrograd, at the nearby tsarist retreat of Tsarskoe Selo.

Even under normal circumstances, she was less capable than he of making good political judgments, but by now she had fallen under the sway of the notorious Grigori Rasputin. He was a self-proclaimed holy man of Siberian peasant background—he was also a great lecher and carouser, but Alexandra refused to believe it. His influence over her was due chiefly to his ability, apparently hypnotic, to alleviate the bleeding of her only son, the hemophiliac Alexei, an ability she attributed to Rasputin's closeness to God. His peasant background also appealed to the royal couple, who wished to believe they were still loved by the peasants. Alexandra's influence on Nicholas, and

Rasputin's on her, is illustrated in her letters to Nicholas and in his subsequent actions. Rasputin helped bring about the dismissal of some ministers and the appointment of others, a major criteria being whether or not they favored him.

One of his recommendations was Boris Sturmer. After Alexandra recommended him to replace Goremykin as prime minister, Nicholas appointed him in January 1916. The French ambassador, Maurice Paléologue, described Sturmer as: "worse than a mediocrity—a third rate intellect, mean spirit, low character, doubtful honesty, no experience, and no idea of state business. The most that can be said is that he has a rather pretty talent for cunning and flattery." Nicholas entrusted such a man not only with the office of prime minister, but also he served concurrently for part of 1916 as minister of interior and then foreign minister.

Sturmer failed to remain as close to Rasputin and Alexandra as they had hoped, so they backed the appointment of Alexander Protopovov as minister of interior. Appointed in September 1916, he proved to be a disastrous choice.

The "ministerial leapfrog" now at its height especially disgusted one of the Duma's right-wing leaders, the Union of Russian People's Vladimir Purishkevich. For it, he placed much of the blame on Rasputin and decided that the so-called holy man had to go before he brought down the monarchy itself. By now the most scandalous rumors were common, for example that Rasputin and Alexandra were lovers and that they were both working for the Germans. Rasputin's negative effect on the monarchy's image was perhaps more damaging than his actual influence. Purishkevich and Prince Felix Yusupov, one of Russia's richest men and related to the tsar by marriage, decided to kill Rasputin. The murder was to take place at Yusupov's palace along the Moika Canal.

On December 17, 1916, in one of history's most bizarre deaths, the two conspirators poisoned Rasputin, shot him several times, beat and kicked him, and finally tied up his body and disposed of it beneath icy waters. News of Rasputin's death brought joy to many in Petrograd and Moscow. Upon hearing it, an audience at the Imperial Theater in Moscow burst out in applause and demanded the singing of the national anthem.

CONCLUSION

Although the actual fall of the monarchy was still a few months away, the ground was well prepared by the end of 1916. Andrew Verner believes that Nicholas's negative attitude toward Duma cooperation and his failures to address properly the crisis of 1905–1906 were crucial. "Russian autocracy was doomed, or rather, had doomed itself. With the crisis of 1905–1906, its ultimate fate had been decided; the ten years remaining until 1917 were little more than a death rattle."[3] Other "pessimists" agree with Verner that developments be-

[3]Andrew M. Verner, *The Crisis of Russian Autocracy: Nicholas II and the 1905 Revolution* (Princeton, 1990), p. 6.

fore World War I made the monarchy's fall at least likely. Many emphasize long-range developments such as the incompatibility between economic modernization and autocracy, the gap between autocracy and educated society, or the government's continuing failure to address nationality and peasant concerns adequately. From such a perspective the influence of Rasputin, as Read insists, was more a symptom than a cause of the monarchy's downfall.

Although not necessarily denying Nicholas's hostility to power-sharing, other historians have emphasized the progress Russia was making in the years 1906 through 1914. They point to indicators such as economic growth; Stolypin's agricultural reforms; and increases in education, participatory government, political patience, and civil rights. Despite the increased strikes of 1912–1914, these "optimists" believe that if the war had not intervened, Russia might have continued a gradual evolution toward a true constitutional monarchy.

Yet, even many "optimists" recognize that Nicholas II bore a heavy responsibility for Russia's failures and declining morale during the war. True, he inherited many of his problems, including an outmoded autocratic system and a country less economically developed than other European powers, but his own wartime failings were costly.

From the criticism of V. A. Maklakov and the *Vekhi* contributors to more recent criticism by Alexander Solzhenitsyn and Richard Pipes, the intelligentsia have also been faulted for their pre-1917 behavior. Pipes, for example, writes: "Had the Russian intelligentsia been politically more mature—more patient, that is, and more understanding of the mentality of the monarchic establishment—Russia might perhaps have succeeded in making an orderly transition from a semi-constitutional to a genuinely constitutional regime."[4]

Despite such criticism, Pipes by no means ignores the many failings of Nicholas II. In the final analysis—despite the increased sympathy displayed in post-Soviet Russia for this tragic tsar, this loving husband and father—Nicholas II was a poor ruler. As Lincoln's lengthy study of Russia during World War I illustrates again and again, the tsar himself was a major cause of his own, and the Romanov dynasty's, demise.

SUGGESTED SOURCES*

ASCHER, ABRAHAM. *The Revolution of 1905.* 2 vols. Stanford, 1988, 1992.

Battleship Potemkin. A 1925 film directed by Sergei Eisenstein. Available on videocassette.

BUSHNELL, JOHN. *Mutiny amid Repression: Russian Soldiers in the Revolution of 1905–1906.* Bloomington, 1985.

EDELMAN, ROBERT. *Gentry Politics on the Eve of the Russian Revolution: The Nationalist Party, 1907–1917.* New Brunswick, N.J., 1980.

[4]Richard Pipes, *The Russian Revolution* (New York, 1990), p. 156.
*See also books cited in footnotes.

————. *Proletarian Peasants: The Revolution of 1905 in Russia's Southwest.* Ithaca, N.Y., 1987.

EMMONS, TERENCE. *The Formation of Political Parties and the First National Elections in Russia.* Cambridge, Mass., 1983.

ENGELSTEIN, LAURA. *Moscow, 1905: Working-Class Organization and Political Conflict.* Stanford, 1982.

FERRO, MARC. *Nicholas II: The Last of the Tsars.* New York, 1991.

FULLER, WILLIAM C. *Civil-Military Conflict in Imperial Russia, 1881–1914.* Princeton, 1985.

GAPON, GEORGE. *The Story of My Life.* London, 1905.

GASSENSCHMIDT, CHRISTOPH. *Jewish Liberal Politics in Tsarist Russia, 1900–1914: The Modernization of Russian Jewry.* New York, 1995.

GATRELL, PETER. *Government, Industry, and Rearmament in Russia, 1900–1914: The Last Argument of Tsarism.* Cambridge, England, 1994.

GEIFMAN, ANNA. *Thou Shalt Kill: Revolutionary Terrorism in Russia, 1894–1917.* Princeton, 1993.

GURKO, VLADIMIR I. *Features and Figures of the Past: Government and Opinion in the Reign of Nicholas II.* Stanford, 1939.

HOSKING, GEOFFREY A. *The Russian Constitutional Experiment: Government and Duma, 1907–1914.* Cambridge, England, 1973.

KORROS, ALEXANDRA SHECKET. "Activist Politics in a Conservative Institution: The Formation of Factions in the Russian Imperial State Council, 1906–1907," *RR* 52 (January 1993): 1–19.

LIEVEN, D. C. B. *Nicholas II: Emperor of All the Russias.* London, 1993.

————. *Russia's Rulers under the Old Regime.* New Haven, 1989.

LINCOLN, W. Bruce. *Passage through Armageddon: The Russians in War and Revolution, 1914–1918.* New York, 1986.

MAKLAKOV, VASILII A. *The First State Duma: Contemporary Reminiscences.* Bloomington, 1964.

McDONALD, DAVID M. *United Government and Foreign Policy in Russia, 1900–1914.* Cambridge, Mass., 1992.

McKEAN, ROBERT B. *St. Petersburg between the Revolutions: Workers and Revolutionaries, June 1907–February 1917.* New Haven, 1990.

MELANCON, MICHAEL. *Stormy Petrels: The Socialist Revolutionaries in Russia's Labor Organizations, 1905–1914.* The Carl Beck Papers . . . , no. 703. Pittsburgh, 1988.

MILIUKOV, PAUL N. *Political Memoirs, 1905–1917.* Ann Arbor, 1967.

OLDENBURG, S. S. *Last Tsar: Nicholas II, His Reign and His Russia.* Vols. 2–4, Gulf Breeze, Fla., 1975–1978.

PALÉOLOGUE, MAURICE. *An Ambassador's Memoirs.* 3 vols. New York, 1972.

PARES, BERNARD. *The Fall of the Russian Monarchy: A Study of Evidence.* London, 1939.

PORTER, THOMAS, and WILLIAM GLEASON. "The Zemstvo and Public Initiative in Late Imperial Russia," *RH* 21 (Winter 1994): 419–437.

RADZINSKY, EDVARD. *The Last Tsar: The Life and Death of Nicholas II.* New York, 1992.

Rasputin. A 1985 film directed by Elem Klimov. Available on videocassette.

READ, CHRISTOPHER. *From Tsar to Soviets: The Russian People and Their Revolution, 1917–1921.* New York, 1996. Chs. 1 & 2.

————. *Religion, Revolution and the Russian Intelligentsia, 1900–1912: The Vekhi Debate and Its Intellectual Background.* London, 1979.

REICHMAN, HENRY. *Railwaymen and Revolution: Russia, 1905.* Berkeley, 1987.

SAZONOV, S. D. *Fateful Years, 1909–1916: The Reminiscences of Serge Sazonov.* New York, 1928.

SHANIN, TEODOR. Russia, 1905–07: Revolution as a Moment of Truth. New Haven, 1986.

SHATZ, MARSHALL, and JUDITH ZIMMERMAN, eds. Signposts: A Collection of Articles on the Russian Intelligentsia. Irvine, Calif., 1986.

SHOWALTER, DENNIS E. Tannenberg: Clash of Empires. Hamden, Conn., 1991.

SHULGIN, V. V. The Years: Memoirs of a Member of the Russian Duma, 1906–1917. New York, 1984.

STAVROU, THEOFANIS GEORGE, ed. Russia under the Last Tsar. Minneapolis, 1969.

STONE, NORMAN. The Eastern Front, 1914–1917. New York, 1975.

SURH, GERALD D. 1905 in St. Petersburg: Labor, Society, and Revolution. Stanford, 1989.

SWAIN, GEOFFREY. Russian Social Democracy and the Legal Labour Movement, 1906–1914. London, 1983.

SZEFTEL, MARC. The Russian Constitution of April 23, 1906: Political Institutions of the Duma Monarchy. Brussels, 1976.

WARTH, ROBERT D. "Peter Arkad'evich Stolypin," MERSH 37: 152–156.

WEINBERG, ROBERT. The Revolution of 1905 in Odessa: Blood on the Steps. Bloomington, 1993.

WEISSMAN, NEIL B. Reform in Tsarist Russia: The State Bureaucracy and Local Government, 1900–1914. New Brunswick, N.J., 1981.

ZENKOVSKY, A. V. Stolypin: Russia's Last Great Reformer. Princeton, 1986.

CHAPTER 26

Economics and Society, 1855–1917

In the Late Imperial period, the Russian Empire remained overwhelmingly agrarian, but some dynamic changes occurred: its population, cities, industry, trade, and middle and urban working classes all grew significantly. In contrast, noble landholding decreased. Although some changes (such as Alexander II's reforms) stemmed from government policies, such policies were themselves affected by a global modernization trend. To remain a major power, Russia had to modernize.

Reaction to Russian modernization varied greatly, both then and later. Some applauded the growth of capitalism in Russia; others, such as the populists or Leo Tolstoy, believed it did not represent true progress. Some historians have emphasized statistics indicating Russia's rapid economic growth or the eventual decline in its high death rate; other scholars have stressed Russia's continuing lag behind the major Western powers.

Although officials and nobles supported some modernizing developments, they often resisted others that threatened to undermine autocracy or Russia's patriarchal social system. While perceiving the necessity of modernization, the tsars remained more comfortable with the old world of social estates, especially nobles and peasants, than they did with emerging classes and urban society. Thus, Russia's economic and social order entered World War I with one foot in the modern world, while the other remained imbedded in traditional Russia.

POPULATION, TOWNS, AND URBAN SOCIETY

From 1855 until 1913, the population of the Russian Empire increased from about 73 million to about 168 million. Although new territories were annexed, population growth was due more to other factors, especially a declining death rate and, despite some decline, a birth rate that remained much higher than Western Europe's. The most dramatic population growth occurred in areas of significant in-migration, for example, southern European Russia, Siberia, the former Kingdom of Poland, and urban areas in general.

From 1856 until 1913, the urban population increased from about 10 percent to about 18 percent of the total population.[1] Based on Thomas Fedor's figures, from 1856 to 1910, St. Petersburg's population more than tripled and Moscow's more than quadrupled, bringing the capital to slightly more than 1.5 million people and Moscow to a little under that figure. Growth in the empire's third to fifth largest cities by 1910 was even more rapid, increasing more than fivefold in Warsaw and Odessa and more than eightfold in Kiev. Beneath these cities, Fedor lists eight others with more than 200,000 people by 1910. They included, in descending order of population: Lodz, Riga, Tiflis, Kharkov, Baku (which increased almost thirtyfold), Saratov, Ekaterinoslav, and Tashkent.

Although still considerably less urban by 1913 than Western Europe or the United States, Russian cities were large by world standards. Although smaller than Tokyo, both Moscow and St. Petersburg were much larger, for example, than any city in China or Latin America.

The cities grew faster than the countryside primarily because trade and manufacturing made more jobs available in them, and the growing transportation system, mainly railways, provided the means to reach them. By 1897, more than half of the inhabitants of large cities (those with over 50,000 people) were born elsewhere, mainly in the countryside. When seasonal or temporary work was completed, or disillusionment set in, peasants sometimes made their way back to their villages or headed for other cities. Daniel Brower has compared the empire's cities to "great revolving doors."[2]

The empire's major cities at the turn of the century were vibrant, dynamic places, teeming with different nationalities and social groups. (Smaller provincial towns, in contrast, often seemed boring and stagnant, at least to many intellectuals, such as the writer Chekhov.) In Warsaw and Odessa, Jews made up one-third of the population. In Riga, the Latvians made up about two-fifths of the population, as did the Germans and Russians combined. In the booming oil town of Baku, Russians were the largest nationality but were outnumbered by the combined total of Azerbaijani Turks and Armenians. In the Georgian city of Tiflis (later Tbilisi), Armenians made up almost two-fifths of the population. Although nationalities often lived side-by-side in harmony, pogroms and other ethnic conflicts sometimes occurred.

Even on St. Petersburg's fashionable Nevsky Prospect, where before World War I stood a Singer Sewing Machine building and an Equitable Life Insurance office, so many of the empire's nationalities were visible that one tourist called it "a valuable lesson in ethnography." In the capital one could see, for example, Moslems in white turbans; Hasidic Jews with earlocks hanging down beneath their skullcaps; Russian factory workers with peaked caps; bearded Russian

---

[1] As earlier, conditions of the time make almost all statistics merely rough approximations. Unless indicated otherwise, they are for the Russian Empire as a whole.

[2] "Urban Revolution in the Late Russian Empire," in *The City in Late Imperial Russia*, ed. Michael F. Hamm (Bloomington, 1986), p. 327.

peasants fresh from the countryside; kerchiefed women and more elegantly dressed ones with their hands enveloped in muffs; and uniformed officials, students, and military men.

Partly for the benefit of illiterates (still an urban majority in 1900), many shops displayed signs picturing what they carried, and street vendors and peddlers still hawked their goods on city streets. In the center of major cities, horse-drawn trams and gas lighting were just beginning to give way to electric trams and lighting. But horse-drawn sleighs and carriages still far outnumbered trams of any sort or automobiles, although by 1914 both St. Petersburg and Moscow offered motorized taxi service, and some cities had motor clubs.

While the rich shopped in the elite foreign and domestic shops on streets such as the capital's Nevsky Prospect, the poor were more likely to do their buying in areas such as that of Moscow's Khitrov market. Set in one of Russia's most infamous slums, it was surrounded by flophouses, penetrated by foul smells, and often enveloped in river mists.

While the rich lived in palaces or roomy, richly decorated apartments, the poor lived in factory dormitories, slums, or attics or basements of buildings whose other occupants were better off. As migrants streamed into the big cities and housing became more scarce, the practice of renting out small corners of rooms, often in basements, became increasingly common. By 1900, about one-sixth of Moscow's population lived in such corners. The conditions were similar in St. Petersburg. Cities, especially the largest, were beginning to make some progress in regards to water supply and sanitation. By 1900, roughly three-fourths of St. Petersburg's apartments possessed piped water, and about two-thirds had toilets.

During this era, the social profile of cities became more diversified. The government continued to classify people by social estate (*soslovie*). This classification, however, was becoming more cumbersome each year—industrial workers, for example, had no category of their own and were chiefly included in the peasant category. In Moscow, where many businesses were owned by those listed as "peasants," Leo Tolstoy discovered some nobles living in flophouses.

ENTREPRENEURS AND CIVIL SOCIETY

By 1914, Russia's small entrepreneurial elite numbered only a few thousand individuals. Yet, during this period, it became a more dynamic social force, both in behalf of its own interests and in relation to larger public issues. This elite came from different backgrounds, including the peasant, merchant, and noble estates; showcased its goods at major exhibitions; and organized regional and, less commonly, national meetings and organizations. The most public-spirited entrepreneurial families resided in Moscow. They had generally made a fortune in textiles and then branched out into other areas such as railways, mining, and banking. At first, they displayed their civic-mindedness primarily in the city's duma (council) and by patronizing the arts (see Chapter 27).

National political involvement came more slowly. Ethnic, religious, and re-

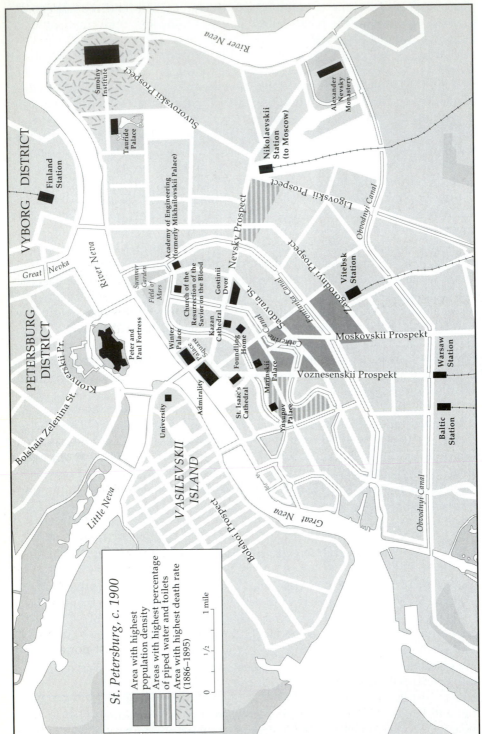

St. Petersburg, c. 1900

Area with highest
population density

Areas with highest percentage
of piped water and toilets

Area with highest death rate
(1886–1895)

0   1/2   1 mile

MAP 26.1

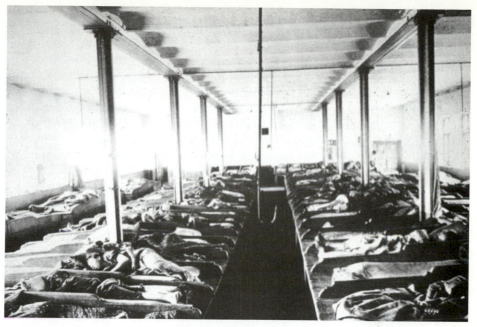

FIGURE 26.1. A workers' dormitory around the turn of the century, Trekgornaia Textile Mill, Moscow.
(From Chloe Obolensky, The Russian Empire: A Portrait in Photographs. *Random House, New York, 1979, #292.)*

gional differences continued to divide business leaders, as did their differing social backgrounds, making it difficult for them to speak with one voice. Before 1904–1905, government actions were not threatening enough to spur more unity—the administration's tariff and tax policies and its contracts and guarantees were generally favorable to the business elite.

Intelligentsia hostility to capitalism and the bourgeoisie also hindered the major entrepreneurs from exercising more national political influence. Herzen's sentiment—"God save Russia from the bourgeoisie"—was shared by most intellectuals. Despite the Marxist belief that capitalism was a progressive stage on the way to socialism, both Marx and many of the Russian Marxists were contemptuous toward the capitalists. Most liberals also were unsympathetic to them. Historian and Kadet party leader Paul Miliukov warned industrialists in 1905–1906 that he did not wish his newly formed party to be sullied by narrow class interests. In 1906, Leo Tolstoy, neither a socialist nor a liberal, referred to the bourgeoisie as "a class of people living idly on others' labor."

Despite these impediments to a more dynamic national role, the outbreak of political opposition in 1904–1907 spurred industrialists and financiers to greater political activity. In early 1906, for example, business leaders formed a Council of Representatives of Industry and Trade to represent their interests.

During the next decade, the council often objected to the government's competition with private enterprise and its interference in business.

Between 1906 and 1916, there was one major attempt to create a strong entrepreneurial-led political party. The most dynamic force behind this effort was the Moscow manufacturer, banker, and publisher Paul Riabushinsky. His family belonged to the schismatic Old Believer religious community, and he was initially sympathetic to the Octobrists, whose principal leader, Alexander Guchkov, was a fellow Moscow industrialist also from an Old Believer background. Along with some other industrialists, however, Riabushinsky soon became disenchanted with the Octobrists, believing them too accommodating to the government.

In 1912, Riabushinsky and some like-minded liberal Moscow industrialists formed the Progressive party. His publications and party activities indicate that Riabushinsky was a nationalist who harbored panslavist dreams but criticized St. Petersburg bureaucrats. He advocated freedom of thought, religious belief, and legal safeguards. He and his like-minded colleagues thought of themselves as forward-looking capitalists who had the practical knowledge and energy to lead Russia into a more democratic, enlightened, and prosperous future.

Although the Progressive party had fewer delegates in the Fourth Duma than the Octobrists or Kadets, they became an important moderate voice in that body. They were a vital part of the Duma's Progressive Bloc, formed in 1915. That same year, Riabushinsky called for the creation of a War Industries Committee (WIC) to help supply the military. Nicholas II permitted its creation, and Alexander Guchkov became its chairman and the industrialist V. I. Konovalov, Riabushinsky's close political ally, its vice-chairman. Riabushinsky became chairman of its Moscow District branch.

Many of the civic activities of Riabushinsky and other progressive entrepreneurs reflected the growth of an embryonic civil society—a social sphere standing between the government and the family or individual, in which people could freely interact and create their own independent organizations. Its rapid evolution before World War I was closely connected with the growth of urban life. Joseph Bradley has noted that Moscow's 1912 City Directory "listed more than six-hundred societies, organizations, clubs, and associations, covering a wide range of charitable, technical, literary, sporting, artistic, educational, and learned activities."[3] Such organizations were essential for the development of an autonomous civil society and for the growth of middle-class values.

Yet any continued development of the public sphere (and the respect for law and pluralism that was linked to it) was threatened by two major fissures that grew wider during World War I. One was between the tsar's government and educated society, the other between educated society and the urban and rural masses. Like some others in educated society, Riabushinsky and his publications attempted to lessen both these gaps. But the revolutionary earthquake

[3]"Voluntary Associations, Civic Culture, and *Obshchestvennost'* in Moscow," in *Between Tsar and People: Educated Society and the Quest for Public Identity in Late Imperial Russia,* eds. Edith Clowes, Samuel Kassow, and James L. West (Princeton, 1991), pp. 136–137.

of 1917 toppled both the liberal aspirations of urban leaders such as Riabushinsky and the autonomous civil society that had been slowly developing.

ECONOMIC GROWTH

The increase of entrepreneurial influence by 1917 reflected the rapid growth of Russian industry and trade during the half-century before World War I. This growth was especially evident in the 1890s and again from 1909 to 1913. In 1913, fourteen times as much pig iron and 120 times as much coal was being produced as in 1860. In this same period, 44 times more railway track came into existence. The textile industry also accelerated its already rapid growth of the early nineteenth century. By 1913, it and the metal-machine industry were the largest employers of factory workers, with the former being dominant in Moscow and the latter in St. Petersburg. Overall, Russian factory and handicraft production increased at least tenfold from 1860 to 1913.

The reasons for this rapid development include Russia's significant population growth, which led to greater demand and a larger work force. State policies and practices both hampered and helped industrial growth. Largely as a result of government actions and inactions, the number of Russian corporations in existence by 1913 trailed far behind that of other European powers. By emancipating the serfs and spurring railway construction, however, the government helped stimulate the economy. Western Europe's example and the growing realization of the connection of industrial might and military power prompted the state to take additional steps, including encouraging foreign investment.

On the eve of World War I, about one-third of the capital of Russian companies was owned by foreigners, primarily the French, British, and Germans. Foreign capitalists were especially prominent in the oil industry, which the Nobel brothers helped launch in Baku during the 1870s. Along with two U.S. Corporations, International Harvester and Singer Sewing Machine, Nobel Brothers Petroleum was still by 1914 one of the largest businesses operating in Russia. Foreigners also figured prominently in Russian mining and metallurgy. In 1869, the Welshman John Hughes received a government concession to produce coal, iron, and rails in the Donets Basin. The Lena goldfields, site of the 1912 tragedy that killed strikers and helped reenergize Russian labor militancy, were owned by a British firm.

The prominence of foreign capitalists in Russia, plus that of capitalists of minority nationalities such as Armenians, Germans, Jews, and Poles, led many Russians to think of capitalism as foreign to Russia's traditions. From the Late Imperial period into the 1990s, as Thomas Owen has pointed out, Russian anti-capitalism has frequently been heightened by Russian xenophobia.

Among Russian workers who labored in foreign-owned factories was future Soviet leader Nikita Khrushchev, who, in 1908, came to Yuzovka (a city of almost 50,000 named after John Hughes). By this time the area had become a vital part of Ukraine's quickly developing heavy industry. Along with the Krivoi Rog area west of it, the Donets Basin by 1914 had overtaken the Urals as

Russia's leading metallurgical center. Besides these areas and the St. Petersburg and Moscow provinces, the former Kingdom of Poland and the Baltic area, especially Riga, were other important industrial regions (see Map 26.2). In general, Russian industry was more concentrated than in other major countries.

Despite Russia's impressive industrial growth, in 1913 it still ranked behind the leading Western countries. By then, it produced only about one-eighteenth the coal, one-thirteenth the electricity, and one-seventh the steel produced by U.S. industry. Although Russia's total industrial output by 1913 trailed only that of the United States, Germany, Britain, and France, on a per-capita basis it also ranked behind several other countries, including Belgium and Sweden. Per mile of land, even countries such as Serbia and Bulgaria had more railway track.

Although growing more slowly than its industry, Russia's domestic trade also expanded. Wholesale and retail sales, for example, more than tripled between 1885 and 1913. Trade fairs continued to be important and grew in number, but they generated a decreasing percentage of total trading volume. Regular trading establishments remained primarily small scale—in 1912, small stores, chiefly family owned and operated, and market stalls made up more than 80 percent of the total. Haggling and bargaining over prices remained customary, especially outside the more modern and fashionable stores and shops.

Foreign trade grew faster than domestic commerce and by 1913 constituted just a little over 4 percent of world trade. Most of it continued to be transported in and out of Russia in foreign ships. Government policies generally insured that the value of exports (still mainly food products and raw materials) exceeded imports (still chiefly industrial and luxury goods).

Yet within this broad continuity, there were some new variations. Wheat, eggs, butter, sugar, and petroleum all became more important export goods, as did industrial products sent to Asia. Among imports, machines and machine tools became more significant; and in 1913, almost five times as much cotton was imported as the yearly average in the late 1860s. Because of the textile industry's need for cotton, imports would have been much greater had it not been for a sharp increase in the supply of domestic cotton, primarily from the new Central Asian regions.

Perhaps more importantly, Germany replaced Great Britain as Russia's leading trading partner. By 1913, it furnished almost half of Russia's imports and more than one-third of its exports; this prewar reliance on German trade was an additional reason for Russia's supply problems during World War I.

As important as industry and trade were, agriculture remained the backbone of the Russian economy and continued to employ most of the empire's workforce. An expansion of sown areas and improved per-acre yields helped agricultural output outdistance population growth and provide more agricultural produce, whether for export or domestic consumption. Nevertheless, agriculture grew much less rapidly than industry, lessening the rate of overall economic growth.

According to Paul Gregory's figures, Russian national income in 1913 was about quadruple what it had been in 1861, although on a per-capita basis it had less than doubled. By 1913, Gregory estimates that Russia's per capita national income was roughly one-tenth the U.S. figure, one-fifth the United Kingdom's, and less than two-fifths Germany's or France's. Overall the gap between Russian per capita income and that of the major Western powers increased from 1861 to 1913.

Yet, despite some bad years and economic zigzags, consumption levels and living standards gradually improved. There were sharp regional variations, however. In the last few decades of the era, the central Russian provinces seemed to suffer more economic want than peripheral areas such as the Baltic provinces, Siberia, and Russian Poland.

A much greater disparity existed among social groups, whether living in the cities or countryside. The municipal statute of 1870 divided voting rights and direct taxpayers into three categories. The top group was the smallest and richest and had to pay the most taxes, which might be many thousand times more than the kopecks paid by some of the poorest members of the third and largest group. Yet few urban dwellers owned or made enough even to be included in the third group. In Moscow during the 1870s and 1880s, all three groups constituted less than 1 percent of the city's population.

INDUSTRIAL AND URBAN WORKERS

According to the 1897 census, slightly more than half of Russia's manufacturing laborers worked outside the empire's cities. Inside them, they composed only one-fourth of the urban workforce, and many of them were artisans not factory workers. In 1902, Moscow shops, stores, and the lodging and restaurant business combined to employ tens of thousands more people than did the factories. Domestics and transportation workers (such as those working on docks and railways and driving horse-cabs) were another significant grouping. In the decade after 1902, Moscow's office and sales clerks, teachers, bookkeepers, and cashiers grew at a faster rate than its factory workers.

Yet, although urban factory workers remained greatly outnumbered by all the other laborers in the cities, they still increased rapidly in the final decades of this era, especially in the larger cities. In St. Petersburg by 1902, one of four hired employees worked in a factory; in Moscow, about one in five worked in factories. Compared to other industrialized countries such as the United States or Germany, a higher percentage of factory laborers worked in large factories employing more than 1,000 workers. During crisis years such as 1905 and 1917, such concentrations proved significant.

Before labor legislation of the 1880s and 1890s, both factory workers and artisans often worked more than twelve hours a day. Women and children, many under ten years old, worked for less wages than men. At the workplace, working conditions were usually unsafe; workers were often fined, paid late, and sometimes forced to buy food at inflated prices from company stores. Workers had no rights and were forbidden to form unions. Whether they lived

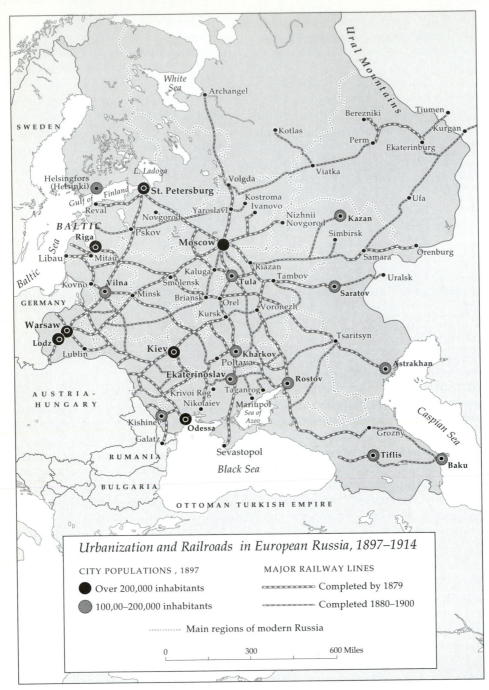

SWEDEN

White Sea

Archangel

Kotlas

Berezniki   Tjumen

Perm   Ekaterinburg   Kurgan

Ural Mountains

Viatka

L. Ladoga

Helsingfors (Helsinki)

Gulf of Finland

St. Petersburg

Reval

Volgda

Kostroma

Ivanovo

Yaroslavl

Ufa

BALTIC Sea

Novgorod

Nizhnii Novgorod

Kazan

Riga

Pskov

Simbirsk

Libau

Mitau

Moscow

Orenburg

Kovno

Vilna

Kaluga

Riazan

Samara

Uralsk

Smolensk

Tambov

Baltic Sea

Minsk

Briansk

Tula

Saratov

GERMANY

Orel

Voronezh

Kursk

Warsaw

Tsaritsyn

Lodz

Kiev

Lublin

Kharkov

Poltava

Astrakhan

Ekaterinoslav

Rostov

Caspian Sea

AUSTRIA-HUNGARY

Krivoi Rog

Taganrog

Nikolaiev

Mariupol

Sea of Azov

Kishinev

Grozny

Odessa

Galatz

Tiflis

Baku

RUMANIA

Sevastopol

Black Sea

BULGARIA

OTTOMAN TURKISH EMPIRE

Urbanization and Railroads in European Russia, 1897–1914

CITY POPULATIONS , 1897   MAJOR RAILWAY LINES

⬤ Over 200,000 inhabitants   Completed by 1879

🔘 100,00–200,000 inhabitants   Completed 1880–1900

.... Main regions of modern Russia

0   300   600 Miles

MAP 26.2A

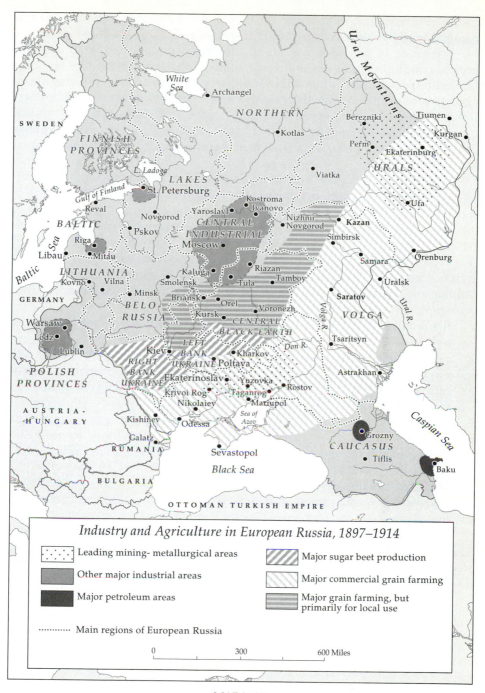

Industry and Agriculture in European Russia, 1897–1914

:·:·:·: Leading mining- metallurgical areas	///// Major sugar beet production
▓ Other major industrial areas	Major commercial grain farming
▓ Major petroleum areas	Major grain farming, but primarily for local use
·········· Main regions of European Russia	

0   300   600 Miles

MAP 26.2B

inside or outside factory dormitories, they were crowded together and had to contend with the twin scourges of urban inflation and fear of being fired.

Beginning in the 1880s, legislation, although often evaded, gradually improved conditions, more in the factories than among artisans. An 1882 law prohibited factories from hiring children under twelve or from employing those aged twelve to fifteen more than eight hours a day. By the end of the century, factory inspectors, who began operating in the 1880s, attempted to enforce other new legislation that limited the factory workday to 11.5 hours (ten hours on Saturdays) and prohibited or limited mining and night work for women and adolescents.

By mid-1914, factory workers, still less than 2 percent of the empire's population, had made additional gains. Most now toiled only about ten hours a day, six days a week (except for the forty-some religious and other holidays). A sickness and accident law of 1912 provided some pay while off the job. (Non-factory workers were less fortunate; for example, many of Kiev's bakers still worked nineteen hours a day.) Factory workers also won wage gains, although inflation and inadequate statistics make it difficult to compute any changes in purchasing power. The proliferation of workers' consumer cooperatives did, however, help make some items more affordable.

A fundamental gain was the right to unionize, which the government finally granted in 1906. In the revolutionary year of 1905, 165 unions sprang up in St. Petersburg and Moscow. Although some had been crushed by early 1906, 137 unions in the two cities received legal status in the fifteen months after a law of March 1906 made this possible. From mid-1907 until the Lena goldfields shooting of April 1912, the government and employers reacted against the developing unions and took successful steps to reduce them. Even the prewar resurgence of union activity following the Lena massacre failed to bring the number of unions and union members close to the totals of 1906–1907.

World War I further reduced earlier gains. Employers lengthened workdays but cut back on safety regulations and protections for women and adolescent workers. As urban inflation increased faster than wages, many workers discovered they had to work longer to buy less.

All these generalizations, however, just hint at the workers' broad diversification. Besides regional, gender, age, ethnic, and rural-urban distinctions, workers differed in regard to education, skills, and experience. Such differences also affected wages. St. Petersburg's metal workers, for example, were overwhelmingly male and 90 percent literate by 1913, and they averaged almost twice the income of textile workers, among whom women and illiterates were more common.

NOBLES AND RURAL PEASANTS

As in earlier times, great economic diversity also continued to exist among the nobles. The extent of economic differences among the peasantry was hotly debated by Lenin and the Populists in the 1890s and still remains murky.

Nobles

In 1897, nobles made up about 1.5 percent of the empire's population, with about two-thirds being hereditary nobles. About half the nobility was non-Russian, with the Polish nobles alone accounting for slightly more than one-quarter the total. Some nobles remained wealthy and influential. In 1905, 155 nobles possessed more than a 135,000 acres each, with the wealthiest possessing more than a half-million acres. But most nobles did not make their living from the land. Indeed, by 1905, a majority of even the hereditary nobility no longer owned an estate. Although some nobles became wealthy by other means, most did not.

Seymour Becker has correctly warned against overstating the nobles' decline and emphasized that many of them left the land for better opportunities elsewhere. Nevertheless, many nobles (such as the fictional Madame Ranevskaia in Chekhov's 1904 play *The Cherry Orchard*) were forced to sell their land because of their improvident ways. By 1905, the nobility of European Russia (exclusive of Finland, Poland, and the Caucasus) had sold roughly two-fifths of the land it had held after the 1861 emancipation. This left nobles with less than one-sixth of the total public and private land (arable and nonarable) in European Russia; the peasants, communally or individually, by then owned almost three times as much land as did the nobles. The peasant disturbances of 1905–1907 prodded more nobles to sell their land. By 1914, they possessed only about half the land they had kept after the 1861 settlement, and the peasants now possessed more than four times as much as the nobles and rented some of the rest. The challenge to noble preeminence was not limited to landholding. As never before, individuals from other social groups chipped away at their dominance of the officer corps, high officialdom, and the universities.

A major difficulty for noble landowners was adjusting to postemancipation developments. Although a minority of them modernized their estates, most made little changes except for relying on hired or sharecropping labor instead of serfs. Hans Rogger has noted that in 1911 there were only 166 tractors being used in all of European Russia, whereas in the United States there were then 14,000 in use. A worldwide decline in grain prices during the 1880s and 1890s, partly because of increased American productivity, also hurt most noble landowners.

Considering military needs and other pressures to industrialize, the government did what it could to arrest the nobles' decline. A manifesto of 1885, drawn up by Pobedonostsev, stressed the desirability of maintaining the nobles' leading position and announced the creation of a state-funded Nobles' Land Bank to help them retain and operate their estates successfully. By early 1904, the Nobles' Bank had lent out more than 700 million rubles, almost twice the amount loaned out by the Peasants' Land Bank (created in 1883) and on cheaper terms. Other government actions, such as the changed Duma electoral laws of 1907, also favored the nobility.

Despite the mutual dependence of the government and nobility on each other, conflicts occurred. They resulted partly from the diversity of the nobility. Many nobles were among the professionals and zemstvo spokesmen who pushed for changes the government considered too radical. Other nobles, especially landowning ones, opposed many of Witte's policies that they considered unsympathetic to their needs—in his memoirs, Witte refers to the majority of the nobility as a group of "degenerates," attempting to gain privileges at the expense of the common people.

Frightened by the rural disturbances of 1905–1906, many landholding nobles agreed on the need for law and order and the preservation of noble rights. In 1906, some large landowners formed a group known as the United Nobility to represent their interests. Despite their advocacy of law and order and the breakup of peasant communes, the organization criticized Stolypin whenever it believed he was not sufficiently heeding its needs. And despite its support for tsarist autocracy, it joined with many other groups in late 1916 and criticized the tsar's disastrous policies.

Yet, even in the 1906–1916 period, the nobility as a whole was too diverse in nationality, occupations, wealth, and political views to unify. The United Nobility represented primarily the interests of Great Russian large landowners and was hostile to "alien" elements; in the Duma, noble deputies joined different parties and factions.

Rural Peasants

In Anton Chekhov's short story "The Peasants" (1897), he depicts a three-generational peasant family of thirteen living in one heated room. It was dark, dirty, and filled with flies. As with most peasant huts, it contained a large stove of clay or brick, the top of which was a favorite sleeping spot. Although the average family according to the census of 1897 contained only 6.3 members and was probably not a three-generational one, the peasant housing conditions described by Chekhov were otherwise fairly typical of those that had prevailed for several centuries.

Considerable continuity in peasant life, however, coexisted with accelerating changes. The emancipation of the serfs in 1861 ended the major difference among peasants—that between serfs and state peasants. As trade, industrialization, and urbanization accelerated and rural population growth increased the demand for farmland, more peasants moved into nonagricultural occupations. Whether engaged in such work temporarily or permanently, part-time or full-time, in the city or in the countryside, most of these workers officially continued to be classified as part of the peasant estate. Yet despite some peasant departures from farming, by 1913 seven out of ten working Russians were still primarily farming peasants.

Although the emancipation legislation attempted to modify the old communal structure, it did not wish to destroy it, and most peasants continued to operate within its confines. Many different types of communes remained, and new ones were sometimes created. Although most village communes were engaged in agriculture, there were also some made up primarily of artisans or other types of workers. Some communes represented one village, others more than one, and still others only part of one. Some periodically redivided the land, others part of it, and still others none at all. Regional variations existed, and changes occurred over time.

Most typical in central Russia was the small or medium-sized repartitional agricultural commune that represented a single village. As described by Boris Mironov, such a commune (in the 1860s and 1870s) contained anywhere from four to eighty households and mediated between the outside world, especially the state, and individual peasant. The commune (including its assembly and elected officials) regulated land distribution; exercised legal, administrative, and police powers; and helped coordinate cultivation and the religious, cultural, educational, and social aspects of village life.

Despite many pressures on the communes, especially Stolypin's attempt to break them up, they survived and even grew stronger in the turmoil of 1917. Although often blamed for the backwardness of Russian agriculture, the communes were much more flexible, pragmatic, and adaptable than most outsiders realized and provided a basic security in a fast-changing world.

The adherence of many peasants to the commune did not preclude their taking a strong interest in improving their own household's position. Household attempts to gain either more communal or noncommunal lands were ongoing, and some peasants found ways to prosper within the communal structure. The influence of wealthier peasants within the communes was strong, and many such peasants were firmly opposed to their breakup.

The mention of wealthy peasants leads to two related questions: How did the peasants as a whole fare between 1861 and 1916? To what extent did economic diversification among the peasants increase?

The evidence and range of opinions on peasant welfare are mixed. The traditional historical view stressed the economic decline of the peasantry, especially from the 1860s until 1905. The decline was attributed primarily to the reduction of land held by the average peasant household. The emancipation settlement provided ex-serfs with smaller allotments on average than they had earlier farmed, and the rapid rise of rural population thereafter further decreased the size of the average household allotment. Although resettlement and new peasant land purchases occurred, they were believed insufficient to compensate for the increased pressure that population growth placed upon the limited lands available. The perceived deterioration of the peasants' condition was made worse in the 1880s and 1890s by an increase in Russia's chief form of taxation—indirect taxes on items such as sugar, tea, kerosene, matches, tobacco, and vodka.

This picture of growing peasant misery, however, has been challenged by more recent and convincing revisionist views (such as those of Gregory and Gatrell). These views indicate that the rural peasantry *as a whole* shared in the overall increase in Russian living standards from 1861 to 1913. The revisionist perspective maintains that the traditional view had too often concentrated on specific regions and years, rather than considering the entire empire and the era as a whole. The older view had also underestimated the importance of peasant families' nonfarm income (some of it sent from family members in the cities).

Significant differences also exist on the second question mentioned previously: To what extent did economic diversification among the peasants increase? In his *Development of Capitalism in Russia* (1899), Lenin stated that the percentage of rich and poor peasants was increasing at the expense of middle-level peasants, and many historians later accepted this view.

Certainly differences existed in peasant wealth, measured by such criteria as landholding and the possession of animals and farm machinery. Although some peasant households possessed no land and worked for others or possessed just a few acres, other peasant households possessed more than 100 acres, sometimes considerably more.

Such differences, however, were neither notably increasing nor permanent. They were often correlated to household size and went up or down as it changed over a family's life cycle. Generally the more adult male workers per household, the greater the landholdings and the total household wealth. After

FIGURE 26.2. Women dressed in traditional peasant costumes standing outside the large cabin of a prosperous late-nineteenth-century peasant, the Suzdal Outdoor Museum of Wooden Architecture and Peasant Life.

a detailed review for the years 1880–1905, Heinz-Dietrich Lowe found: "In central Russia (black soil and non-black soil regions) and down the Volga, there were practically no trends to a greater differentiation of peasant society."[4] A number of other studies also indicate that Lenin overestimated differentiation increases. That economic differences did not increase rapidly was partly due to the communes. Although not preventing peasant economic differentiation, they did help to restrain it.

FOOD AND DRINKING; FAMINE AND DISEASES

People's eating habits during this era remained much the same as earlier. Grain, especially in the form of bread, continued to provide most of the calories for most of the population. The most significant change was probably the increase in the consumption of potatoes, tea, and sugar. The use of samovars spread increasingly to the villages, often becoming one of a household's most prized possessions. Foreign visitors commented on the masses' practice of drinking tea through a piece of sugar held in the mouth.

Both statistical and anecdotal evidence make it clear that alcoholism increased during this era. One reason for this was an increase in modern drinking habits. As David Christian has pointed out, increased urbanization and wage work stimulated more regular drinking, especially on weekends and in the taverns, which were overwhelmingly male domains. In St. Petersburg and Moscow, many workers by the turn of the century reported for work on Mondays hung over from weekend drinking and then spent part of such "Blue Mondays" drinking more.[5] At the same time, especially in the villages, traditional drinking customs, which stressed communal and festive drinking and in which women participated more fully, also continued.

As always, governmental alcohol policies continued to influence vodka consumption. In 1858 and 1859, the increasing vodka prices charged by liquor dealers were countered by mass vodka boycotts and attacks on taverns in many areas of European Russia. Partly as a result of these disturbances, in 1863 the government opened up the production and sale of alcohol and ended the old "farming-out" method, by which it had sold these liquor rights to selected entrepreneurs (tax farmers). At the same time, it introduced an excise tax, which in subsequent years more than made up for government revenues lost by ending the old system. At first, the changeover led, at least in Great Russia, to a decrease in vodka prices and an increase in consumption.

Despite subsequent increases in the excise taxes levied by the government, alcoholism showed few signs of abating. According to Minister of Finance

---

[4]"Differentiation in Russian Peasant Society: Causes and Trends, 1880–1905," in *Land Commune and Peasant Community in Russia: Communal Forms in Imperial and Early Soviet Society,* ed. Roger Bartlett (New York, 1990), p. 191.

[5]For an excellent treatment of workers' drinking habits (and other material conditions) outside the two major cities, see Theodore H. Friedgut, *Iuzovka and Revolution,* Vol. 1, *Life and Work in Russia's Donbass, 1869–1924* (Princeton, 1989).

Witte, Alexander III wished to decrease alcohol consumption and backed a plan of Witte's that established an Imperial Vodka Monopoly. It was enacted in 1894 and gradually applied throughout the empire. Once again, however, both alcohol consumption and resulting government revenues increased.

Despite the government's continuing reliance on liquor revenues—about 30 percent of total revenues from 1905 to 1913—the government was not completely two-faced in dealing with the alcohol problem. It continued to hope that it could maintain its alcohol revenues by encouraging people to spread their drinking out and thereby engage in less binge drinking. Drunkenness might thereby be decreased without decreasing alcohol revenues. As part of its effort to deal with increased drunkenness, the government offered some encouragement and support to a temperance movement, which sputtered along for a while and then became a conspicuous phenomenon beginning in the 1890s.

Later the Duma studied ways to reduce government dependence on vodka revenues. But the Ministry of Finance remained unsympathetic to any attempts to reduce this reliable source of income. World War I, however, accomplished what peacetime could not—prohibition. The selling of vodka was first curtailed during the mobilization of troops, and in August 1914 prohibition was decreed for the duration of the war.

Besides war, Russia also suffered in this era from the traditional scourges of hunger and famine. Drought and poor environmental policies and practices—including deforestation (especially stimulated by railway development), overploughing, and overgrazing—contributed to frequent food shortages. After a severe drought in 1891, such shortages produced a major famine in the Central Black-Earth and Volga regions in 1891–1892. (See Chapter 23 for how government economic policies helped bring it about.)

In confronting it, peasants turned to their traditional method of dealing with grain shortages: They made "hunger bread," stretching out their grain by adding such ingredients as acorns, bark, leaves, straw, and weeds to it before baking. Often unable to feed their animals, they sold many of them.

Although at first attempting to downplay the crisis and prevent too much private involvement, the government did temporarily suspend grain exports and begin its own massive relief efforts. Working largely through local officials, including the land captains and those of the zemstvos, it dispersed grain to millions of Russians. Private and foreign assistance, especially from the United States, also helped meet the crisis. Writers such as Vladimir Soloviev and Leo Tolstoy helped awaken public opinion, with Tolstoy taking an especially active role including the establishment of food kitchens.

No reliable figures are available as to how many deaths the famine caused. As was often the case, many people died prematurely as a result of reduced resistance to diseases. In 1892, typhus and cholera epidemics struck the famine-stricken provinces especially hard, and the death rate in these provinces was higher than normal.

Despite Russia's gradually declining death rate in the Late Imperial period, by 1913 it was still much higher than Western Europe's and roughly 40 percent higher than Japan's. Infant and child mortality rates remained especially high. Among the European Russian Orthodox population at the end of the 1890s, more than one-fourth of the infants died before their first birthday. Between 1907 and 1911, the European Russian death rate in the same age group was about twice as high as those born in England and France.

Although susceptibility to diseases varied from towns to villages, the frequent movement back and forth between them by peasants looking for work helped spread infectious diseases in both areas. The alarming spread of syphilis to the villages by returning peasants was just one example. Besides cholera, typhus, and syphilis, other diseases that killed significant numbers were consumption and pneumonia (the two leading killers in St. Petersburg around 1900), diphtheria, dysentery, influenza, malaria, measles, scarlet fever, and smallpox. In the countryside, many Russians also died painful deaths from eating contaminated grain.

WOMEN AND FAMILY LIFE

In 1912, women's inheritance rights were extended, and in 1914 marital separation was made easier, but overall Russian women made few legal gains before 1917.

Throughout this era, the "woman question" was intertwined with that of radicalism, reform, or reaction. Radicals tended to be most sympathetic with female equality, whereas reactionaries resisted proposals for equalizing women's rights. Following Chernyshevsky's lead, most women radicals concluded that female equality depended upon the overthrow of the existing system and made that their first priority. By the 1870s, about 20 to 25 percent of the active revolutionaries were women.

After feminists founded the All-Russian Union for Women's Equality in 1905 and began pushing for female suffrage, they discovered that many liberals were hesitant to commit fully to their cause. Although more supportive than some liberals, Paul Miliukov, head of the Kadet party, attempted at times to soften proposals of his wife Anna, who was active in the women's union.

As with political opposition generally, feminist political activity was strong between 1905 and 1907 but then ebbed in the more reactionary period that followed it. Nevertheless, although unable to obtain many goals such as suffrage, by 1914 women had still made substantial educational and professional gains (see Chapter 27).

Most of these advances affected upper-class and middle-class women, but lower-class women, both in the villages and in the towns, also made gains. Some peasant women used the new township courts to obtain justice, especially in property disputes with their in-laws. And peasant women often were responsible for three-generational family breakups. Considering the unfavorable position of the daughters-in-law within these large peasant households, it is hardly surprising that, despite the economic risks involved, many of them preferred to go off with their husbands and establish their own nuclear families.

As more husbands went to the cities in search of work, wives assumed more tasks traditionally performed by their spouses. In addition, in the decades immediately following the emancipation of the serfs, more village women, especially in Russia's Central Industrial Region, engaged in domestic production for markets outside their village. Working in their own huts or in village workshops or small factories, they supplemented their family income by working at such tasks as weaving, knitting stockings and gloves, gluing cigarette tubes, and unwinding cotton. Often they worked for merchants who provided materials and disposed of the products of their labor. They also worked for manufacturers who put out work to village women and children because they could pay them less than regular factory workers.

By the end of the nineteenth century, however, this labor started to be undercut by new factory machinery, and more village women moved to the cities in search of income. Before World War I, most of them who found work did so as domestic servants, but a growing number became factory or shop workers. In St. Petersburg's textile industry, women workers increased from 57 percent of the total in 1900 to 68 percent in 1913. In food processing, they went from 33 percent to 47 percent in the same period. Generally, women entered into the lower-paying, less skilled jobs and were less likely to become unionized.

As cities grew and more peasant women entered them, prostitution increased. The government used special police and urban medical-police committees to ferret out, medically inspect, and license prostitutes. But unregistered prostitutes continued to outnumber "yellow-ticketed" ones—a registered prostitute had to exchange her internal passport for a "yellow ticket," which more sharply restricted her movements. Poverty was a major cause of girls and women entering the profession.[6] Feminists and others debated how to end, or at least reduce, prostitution and founded philanthropic organizations such as the Russian Society for the Protection of Women, established in 1900. Despite vigorous lobbying, however, reformers were unable to stem the growth of prostitution. Most radicals believed the only solution to the problem was the overthrow of tsarist autocracy.

Despite the small percentage of women in labor unions, women workers gradually became more radical. In 1913, socialist women in Russia observed International Women's Day for the first time. A prime mover in encouraging this participation and an advocate of socialism as the only valid response to the woman question was Alexandra Kollontai, herself of noble background. Lenin's wife, Nadezhda Krupskaia, who authored the pamphlet *The Woman Worker* (1900), and Inessa Armand, another Marxist close to Lenin, were two other women who helped launch a working-women's movement in Russia. They established an underground journal, also called *The Woman Worker*, which appeared in seven issues in the first half of 1914.

Although World War I brought great hardships to Russian women, many of whose husbands were called to military service, it also brought new oppor-

[6]A concise summary of prostitution and the intrusive medical police, especially in St. Petersburg, is presented in Barbara Alpern Engel, *Between the Fields and the City: Women, Work, and Family in Russia, 1861–1914* (New York, 1994), pp. 166–197. A more exhaustive study can be found in Laurie Bernstein, *Sonia's Daughters: Prostitutes and Their Regulation in Imperial Russia* (Berkeley, 1995).

tunities. As in other participating countries, women now sometimes served in occupations that previously had been closed to them, making it harder to maintain stereotypical beliefs about women's proper roles in the country's economic and social structure.

Most of the changes affecting women also affected family life in general. Changes came most slowly in the countryside, where the patriarchal order remained least affected by modern developments and thinking. Even in rural areas, however, education and urban influences were making dents in the old system. Particularly after 1905, signs of youthful hostility to authority, especially in the form of rural hooliganism, alarmed many defenders of traditional society.

In the cities, challenges to old family ways came earlier and more forcefully. The radical pamphlet *To the Younger Generation* (1861) called upon the young to overthrow the old order. It was distributed by M. I. Mikhailov, a young poet and essayist, who a few years earlier had begun the first major press discussion of the woman question by advocating female equality. Turgenev's novel *Fathers and Sons* (1862) mirrored the new generational conflict and stimulated discussion about it. From the 1860s until 1917, urban youth were the chief followers of radical ideas, including those that challenged traditional patriarchal authority.

Besides radical challenges, other forces were also eroding traditional family life. As peasants flocked in growing numbers into the cities, housing space became increasingly scarce. Many married couples were even forced to live separately. Housing scarcity was one reason why many male peasants left their wives and children back in the villages. This shortage also helps explain why more permanent town-dwellers married later and had fewer children than did villagers. Family life was further changed by the increasing number of unmarried peasant women who went to the cities. If they eventually married, they usually did so later than village women.

Partly because of the growing number of single women entering the cities, more illegitimate children were born. Only around the turn of the century did the trend begin to level off and finally go down—an increasing use of birth control, especially abortion (which was illegal), being perhaps one explanation. The number of children left at the foundling homes of St. Petersburg and Moscow displayed a similar pattern, although a tightening of admission procedures at the beginning of the 1890s had a more dramatic immediate effect in finally reducing admissions.

Although urban youth of all classes had better educational opportunities than villagers, poor children raised in the cities led a difficult life. Both parents often worked long hours outside their miserable lodgings, and children were often left with little or no supervision. Furthermore, children themselves often began working at a young age. Although labor laws of the 1880s and 1890s reduced exploitation of child labor, by the early 1900s most artisan, sales, and service apprenticeships still began before, or shortly after, children had reached their teens.

As these young apprentices put in their long work days—fourteen to sixteen hours were still common for nonfactory workers—they soon became exposed to adult ways, including drinking and smoking. As young workers learned new skills, earned money, and spent most of their time away from home, they had more opportunity to develop independently than did youth raised in village families, whose values were often reinforced by village institutions such as the commune.

The overall decline in marriage, birth, and death rates, which was especially notable in European Russia during the last two prewar decades, affected and reflected rural as well as urban developments. But female peasants who remained in their villages generally continued to marry young and give birth to many children. In 1897, the mean age that women first married in the Russian areas of European Russia (rural and urban) was 20.4, and peasant women seem to have averaged around a half dozen births or so, although this varied from province to province.

Changes in family life concerned many Russian writers, Dostoevsky and Tolstoy being two who lamented a decline in family values. The most sweeping proposals for changes in family life came from socialists such as Lenin, Krupskaia, and Kollontai, who were only able to put some of their ideas into practice after 1917.

LEGAL DEVELOPMENTS

The Late Imperial period was one of important legal developments, including the Judicial Reform of 1864 (see Chapter 22). By 1914, almost 19,000 registered attorneys and assistant attorneys existed. The number of civil cases heard by district courts increased faster than population growth, with about 300,000 cases being submitted in 1914.

According to Walicki "the main concern of Russia's liberal thinkers was the problem of the rule of law."[7] A growing number of professionals, entrepreneurs, and even some reform-minded officials desired to transform the empire into a state in which the rulers as well as the ruled would be bound by the country's laws (a *Rechtsstadt,* to borrow the German term). In 1905, for example, industrialists from the Ural area stated that only under such conditions could business life adequately develop. The traditionalist officials dominant under Alexander III and Nicholas II, however, viewed law primarily as an instrument to help maintain government control, not as a guarantor of individual or corporate rights.

Russian rule under the last three Romanovs was characterized by concessions, usually under pressure, to the rule of law and then "takebacks" when the pressure eased or threats to the autocratic order seemed too great. Alexander III's long-lasting "temporary regulations" of 1881 were just the most egregious circumvention of the spirit of the 1864 legal reform.

The political turmoil surrounding 1905 produced new concessions. In the October Manifesto of 1905, the government appeared ready to meet some de-

---

[7]Andrzej Walicki, *Legal Philosophies of Russian Liberalism* (New York, 1987), p. 1.

FIGURE 26.3. The 1881 trial of the assassins of Alexander II. In this trial, government-appointed officials acted as both judges and jury.
(From Ronald Hingley, Nihilists: Russian Radicals and Revolutionaries in the Reign of Alexander II. *Weidenfeld & Nicolson, London, 1967, p. 1102.)*

mands for the rule of law and the expansion of civil liberties. The manifesto promised to grant the population "the unalterable foundations of civic freedom based on the principles of real personal inviolability, freedom of conscience, speech, assembly, and association." During subsequent months, the government took some steps to fulfill this commitment by issuing new laws on matters such as censorship and freedom of assembly and association. But the Fundamental Laws of April 1906 indicated that Nicholas did not intend to fulfill all the promises of the October Manifesto. During the next decade, the tsar along with the conservative State Council blocked most measures that would have fully implemented the rights promised in late 1905. The electoral law of 1907, guaranteeing more conservative Dumas than the first two, was perhaps the best example of "takebacks" during the Duma era.

In 1907, the perceptive Bernard Pares stated that "the Government has, in principle, capitulated to the principle of law, but has, in practice, so multiplied the exceptions that they altogether swamp the principle. Thus it has not yet been possible for the ordinary Russian to have any confidence in the principle of law as protecting him from arbitrary and exceptional chastisement."

As the legal profession expanded, along with legal journals and societies, so too did debates about legal approaches. Many members of the Russian intelligentsia, including Russian Marxists and Tolstoy, disparaged law, considering it an instrument of the state and of class domination. Intellectuals who emphasized the importance of law for securing individual freedoms and rights were in the minority.

Although the Third Section was abolished in 1880, its Corps of Gendarmes continued under the jurisdiction of the Ministry of Interior, which also oversaw other antisubversive sections such as the Okhrana. The latter often recruited agents to infiltrate revolutionary organizations. In pursuing its tasks, the political police did not hesitate to violate basic civil rights. Even members of the nobility complained of having their mail opened by police officials, and the practice did not cease after 1905.

Although new laws eliminated or reduced some of the harshest corporeal punishments, the number of exiles sent to Siberia increased. By 1898, more than 300,000 exiles were living in Siberia. Only about 1 percent could be considered political exiles, and almost half the total exiles had been legally sent there by their communities. One could be exiled to Siberia as a convict, necessitating imprisonment or hard labor, or as exile-deportee. The convicts in Siberia, such as those described in Dostoevsky's *House of the Dead* or Chekhov's *Sakhalin Island*, were much worse off than those simply exiled. Lenin, for example, spent a comparatively comfortable three years in exile in southern Siberia, where he was free to live in a peasant cottage and spend his days, indoors or outdoors, much as he wished. During the Communist era, such an exile would have seemed more like a vacation to the millions who found themselves exiled to Siberia under Stalin.

With some justification, tsarist Russia's critics sometimes called it a "police state." Yet ratio of its police to citizens remained far smaller, especially in small towns and rural areas, than in more liberal and democratic countries such as France and England. Because of this shortage, the state did a poor job protecting its citizens.

From about 1900 to 1914, the problem of hooliganism—the term was borrowed from England—was continually reported on and debated. It was believed to be rising and spreading from towns into the countryside. It most often implied brazen, insulting, disrespectful behavior, especially toward authority or "respectable" people. At times, it went beyond verbal assaults, cursing, and lewd suggestions and involved violent actions such as window breaking, assaults, muggings, rape, and murder. The problem seemed especially acute in the Great Russian areas of the empire.

Despite efforts to increase the number of policemen, especially in major urban areas, the perception in villages and towns alike by the early twentieth century was that crime was on the rise. Policemen and officials were thought to be either unwilling or unable to do much to protect the common people. One problem was that the police spent a disproportionate amount of time on victimless crimes and security measures. Hans Rogger cites figures for St. Petersburg that indicate that of the 115,000 people detained by the police in 1896, more than half were for passport violations, beggary, and "idleness." Furthermore, low police salaries contributed to police corruption, and hatred of the police was common among workers.

In the villages, the peasants' customs dominated their legal dealings. Most legal matters were settled outside of court or according to "customary law" in

Policing the Russian Empire in the 1880s

The following selection is from George Kennan, "The Russian Police," *The Century Illustrated Monthly Magazine* 37 (April 1889): 890–891. Kennan spent considerable time in Russia and later wrote the two-volume work *Siberia and the Exile System*. To keep the selection short, I have abbreviated the list of required "permissions" that Kennan mentions, indicating these omissions and others by ellipses.

Matters that in other countries are left to the discretion of the individual citizen, or to the judgment of a small group of citizens, are regulated in Russia by the Minister of the Interior through the imperial police. If you are a Russian, and wish to establish a newspaper, you must ask the permission of the Minister of the Interior. If you wish to open a Sunday-School, or any other sort of school . . . you must ask the permission of the Minister of Public Instruction. If you wish to give a concert or to get up tableaux for the benefit of an orphan asylum, you must ask permission of the nearest representative of the Minister of the Interior, then submit your programme of exercises to a censor for approval or revision, and finally hand over the proceeds of the entertainment to the police, to be embezzled or given to the orphan asylum, as it may happen. If you wish to sell newspapers on the street, you must get permission, be registered in the books of the police, and wear a numbered brass plate as big as a saucer around your neck. If you wish to open a drug-store, a printing-office, a photograph-gallery, or a book-store, you must get permission. If you are a photographer and desire to change the location of your place of business, you must

get permission. If you are a student and go to a public library to consult Lyell's "Principles of Geology" or Spencer's "Social Statics," you will find that you cannot even look at such dangerous and incendiary volumes without special permission. . . . If you are a peasant and wish to build a bath-house on your premises, you must get permission. If you wish to thresh out your grain in the evening by candlelight, you must get permission or bribe the police. If you wish to go more than fifteen miles away from your home, you must get permission. . . . In short, you cannot live, move, or have your being in the Russian Empire without permission.

The police, with the Minister of the Interior at their head, control, by means of passports, the movements of all the inhabitants of the Empire; they keep thousands of suspects constantly under surveillance; they ascertain and certify to the courts the liabilities of bankrupts; they conduct pawnbrokers' sales of unredeemed pledges; they give certificates of identity to pensioners and all other persons who need them; they superintend repairs of roads and bridges; they exercise supervision over all theatrical performances, concerts, tableaux, theater programmes, posters, and street advertisements; they collect statistics, enforce sanitary regulations, make searches and seizures in private houses, read the correspondence of suspects, take charge of the bodies of persons found dead, "admonish" church members who neglect too long to partake of the Holy Communion, and enforce obedience to thousands of multifarious orders and regulations intended to promote the welfare of the people or to insure the safety of the state.

courts on the village and canton (*volost*) levels. Out-of-court methods for solving disputes included arbitration, compromise, swearing oaths, and casting lots. Community-decided punishments, part of the peasants' world of *samosud* (self-adjudication or taking the law into one's own hands) included requiring an individual to treat the village to vodka, expulsion from the village, beatings, shaming rituals, and worse. Although villagers might punish petty thievery with a mild punishment, they were not as tolerant with horse thieves, especially habitual ones, who might be subjected to maiming that would permanently mark them or to gruesome tortures and murder.

Such violent acts were contrary to statutory law, but the peasants believed that statutory law and the official courts were too lenient with horse thieves. In this respect and in others, the peasants and the authorities' views of law often differed. The peasants were more concerned with what they considered justice than with obeying any outside-imposed law. They had little ability or desire to apply abstract principles to specific cases. Their main concern was the practical one of maintaining their own security, interests, and way of life. Such an act as stealing wood from a state or noble's forest was considered laudable, permissible, or no more than a minor offense by most peasants.

In the battle that sometimes ensued between state law and peasant "justice," the state was often at a disadvantage because of its paucity of police and police officials in the countryside. As earlier in Russian history, a gap continued to exist between the government's desires and its abilities to control the population.

SUGGESTED SOURCES*

BATER, JAMES H. *St. Petersburg: Industrialization and Change*. Montreal, 1976.

BECKER, SEYMOUR. *Nobility and Privilege in Late Imperial Russia*. DeKalb, Ill., 1985.

BONNELL, VICTORIA E. *Roots of Rebellion: Workers' Politics and Organizations in St. Petersburg and Moscow, 1900–1914*. Berkeley, 1983.

BRADLEY, JOSEPH. *Muzhik and Muscovite: Urbanization in Late Imperial Russia*. Berkeley, 1985.

BROWER, DANIEL R. *The Russian City between Tradition and Modernity, 1850–1900*. Berkeley, 1990.

CHEKHOV, ANTON. "The Peasants." In *Great Stories by Chekhov,* ed. David H. Greene. New York, 1959.

CHRISTIAN, DAVID. *"Living Water": Vodka and Russian Society on the Eve of Emancipation*. New York, 1990.

CLEMENTS, BARBARA EVANS, BARBARA ALPERN ENGEL, and CHRISTINE D. WOROBEC, eds. *Russia's Women: Accommodation, Resistance, Transformation*. Berkeley, 1991. Pt. II.

CONROY, MARY SCHAEFFER. *In Health and in Sickness: Pharmacy, Pharmacists, and the Pharmaceutical Industry in Late Imperial, Early Soviet Russia*. Boulder, 1994.

CRISP, OLGA, and LINDA EDMONDSON, eds. *Civil Rights in Imperial Russia*. New York, 1989.

EDMONDSON, LINDA H. *Feminism in Russia, 1900–17*. Stanford, 1984.

*See also books cited in footnotes.

ENGELSTEIN, LAURA. "Combined Underdevelopment: Discipline and the Law in Imperial and Soviet Russia," *AHR* 98 (April 1993): 338–352.

FARNSWORTH, BEATRICE, and LYNNE VIOLA, eds. *Russian Peasant Women.* New York, 1992. Pt. I.

FEDOR, THOMAS S. *Patterns of Urban Growth in the Russian Empire during the Nineteenth Century.* Chicago, 1975.

FITZPATRICK, ANNE L. *The Great Russian Fair: Nizhnii Novgorod, 1840–90.* New York, 1990.

FREEZE, GREGORY L. "The Soslovie (Estate) Paradigm and Russian Social History," *AHR* 91 (February 1986): 11–36.

———. *From Supplication to Revolution: A Documentary Social History of Imperial Russia.* New York, 1988. Pts. 2–3.

FRIEDEN, NANCY. *Russian Physicians in an Era of Reform and Revolution, 1856–1905.* Princeton, 1981.

FRIEDGUT, THEODORE H. *Iuzovka and Revolution.* 2 vols. Princeton, 1989–1994.

FRIERSON, CATHY A. *Peasant Icons: Representations of Rural People in Late Nineteenth Century Russia.* New York, 1993.

———, ed. *Aleksandr Nikolaevich Englegardt's Letters from the Country, 1872–1887.* New York, 1993.

GATRELL, PETER. *The Tsarist Economy, 1850–1917.* New York, 1986.

GEYER, DIETRICH. *Russian Imperialism: The Interaction of Domestic and Foreign Policy 1860–1914.* Leamington Spa, N.Y., 1987.

GLICKMAN, ROSE L. *Russian Factory Women: Workplace and Society, 1880–1914.* Berkeley, 1984.

GREGORY, PAUL R. *Before Command: An Economic History of Russia from Emancipation to the First Five-Year Plan.* Princeton, 1994.

HAIMSON, LEOPOLD. "The Problem of Social Stability in Urban Russia, 1905–1917," *SR* 23 (December 1964): 619–642; 24 (March 1965): 1–22; Discussion. 24 (March 1965): 23–46.

HAMM, MICHAEL F., ed. *The City in Late Imperial Russia.* Bloomington, 1986.

HOCH, STEVEN L. "Russian Peasant Standard of Living," *SR* 53 (Spring 1994): 41–75.

HOGAN, HEATHER. *Forging Revolution: Metalworkers, Managers, and the State in St. Petersburg, 1890–1914.* Bloomington, 1993.

HUTCHINSON, JOHN F. *Politics and Public Health in Revolutionary Russia, 1890–1918.* Baltimore, 1990.

JOHNSON, ROBERT E. *Peasant and Proletarian: The Working Class of Moscow in the Late Nineteenth Century.* New Brunswick, N.J., 1979.

KINGSTON-MANN, ESTHER, and TIMOTHY MIXTER, eds. *Peasant Economy, Culture, and Politics of European Russia, 1800–1921.* Princeton, 1990.

LINDENMEYR, ADELE. *Voluntary Associations and the Russian Aristocracy: The Case of Private Charity.* The Carl Beck Papers . . . , no. 807. Pittsburgh, 1990.

MACEY, DAVID, A. J. *Government and Peasant in Russia, 1861–1906: The Prehistory of the Stolypin Reforms.* DeKalb, Ill., 1987.

MANNING, ROBERTA. *The Crisis of the Old Order in Russia: Gentry and Government.* Princeton, 1982.

MCCAFRAY, SUSAN P. *The Politics of Industrialization in Tsarist Russia: The Association of Southern Coal and Steel Producers, 1874–1914.* DeKalb, Ill., 1996.

MCKAY, JOHN P. *Pioneers for Profit: Foreign Entrepreneurship and Russian Industrialization, 1885–1913.* Chicago, 1970.

MIRONOV, BORIS. "The Russian Peasant Commune after the Reforms of the 1860s," *SR* 44 (Fall 1985): 438–467.

NEUBERGER, JOAN. *Hooliganism: Crime, Culture, and Power in St. Petersburg, 1900–1914.* Berkeley, 1993.

OWEN, THOMAS C. *Capitalism and Politics in Russia: A Social History of the Moscow Merchants, 1855–1905.* Cambridge, England, 1981.

———. *Russian Corporate Capitalism from Peter the Great to Perestroika.* New York, 1995. Chs. 3 & 5.

PARES, BERNARD. *Russia and Reform.* New York, 1907.

PLAGGENBORG, S. "Tax Policy and the Question of Peasant Poverty in Tsarist Russia, 1881–1905," *CMR* 36 (1995): 53–69.

RANSEL, DAVID L. *Mothers of Misery: Child Abandonment in Russia.* Princeton, 1988.

RIEBER, ALFRED J. *Merchants and Entrepreneurs in Imperial Russia.* Chapel Hill, 1982.

ROBINSON, GEROID T. *Rural Russia under the Old Regime: A History of the Land-Lord-Peasant World and a Prologue to the Peasant Revolution of 1917.* New York, 1932.

ROGGER, HANS. *Russia in the Age of Modernization and Revolution, 1881–1917.* London, 1983. Chs. 5–6.

ROOSEVELT, PRISCILLA. *Life on the Russian Country Estate: A Social and Cultural History.* New Haven, 1995.

RUCKMAN, JO ANN. *The Moscow Business Elite: A Social and Cultural Portrait of Two Generations, 1840–1905.* DeKalb, Ill., 1984.

SEMYONOVA, TIAN-SHANSKAIA, OLGA. *Village Life in Late Tsarist Russia.* Bloomington, 1993.

STITES, RICHARD. *The Women's Liberation Movement in Russia: Feminism, Nihilism, and Bolshevism, 1860–1930.* Princeton, 1978.

THURSTON, ROBERT W. *Liberal City, Conservative State: Moscow and Russia's Urban Crisis, 1906–1914.* New York, 1987.

TOLSTOY, LEO. "On the Moscow Census." In *The Complete Works of Count Tolstoy.* Vol. 17. New York, 1968.

TROYAT, HENRI. *Daily Life in Russia Under the Last Tsar.* London, 1961.

VUCINICH, WAYNE S., ed. *The Peasant in Nineteenth-Century Russia.* Stanford, 1968.

WAGNER, WILLIAM C. *Marriage, Property, and Law in Late Imperial Russia.* New York, 1994.

WALLACE, DONALD MACKENZIE. *Russia on the Eve of War and Revolution.* New York, 1961.

WITTE, S. IU. *The Memoirs of Count Witte.* Armonk, N.Y., 1990.

WOROBEC, CHRISTINE. *Peasant Russia: Family and Community in the Post-Emancipation Period.* Princeton, 1991.

WYNN, CHARTERS. *Workers, Strikes, and Pogroms: The Donbass-Dnepr Bend in Late Imperial Russia, 1870–1905.* Princeton, 1992.

YANEY, GEORGE. *The Urge to Mobilize: Agrarian Reform in Russia, 1861–1930.* Urbana, Ill., 1985.

ZELNIK, REGINALD E. *Labor and Society in Tsarist Russia; the Factory Workers of St. Petersburg, 1855–1870.* Stanford, 1971.

ZUCKERMAN, FREDERICK S. *The Tsarist Police in Russian Society, 1880–1917.* Washington Square, N.Y., 1996.

CHAPTER 27

Religion and Culture, 1855–1917

In the Late Imperial period, the Russian government continued to rule over religious organizations and education. It also exercised censorship over literature and other cultural spheres. Yet government controls were increasingly being resented and challenged, and the state's own modernizing needs seemed to demand less authoritarian approaches, especially in education, which expanded rapidly in this era. In the face of such challenges, government policy oscillated between reform and reaction. The former was most evident under Alexander II and then again between 1905 and 1917; the latter coincided almost exactly with Pobedonostsev's tenure as procurator of the Holy Synod from 1880 to 1905.

In the realm of high culture, this was Russia's greatest era, first producing a Golden Age for the Russian novel and a little later a more diffuse Silver Age of the arts. The names of writers, painters, and composers, including Turgenev, Dostoevsky, Tolstoy, Chekhov, Kandinsky, Chagall, Musorgsky, Tchaikovsky, Scriabin, and Stravinsky, eventually became familiar to people around the world.

The works of these and other artists often reflected similar concerns, such as Russia's past and its uniqueness or kinship with the West. In the late nineteenth century, realism predominated in the arts, and many works dealt with the common people. During Russia's Silver Age, which coincided with the reign of Nicholas II (1894–1917) and was a great age for poetry, many artists became more concerned with their own fulfillment. They experimented with a multiplicity of styles and often dealt with topics such as religion, mysticism, sexuality, demonology, and humanity's transformation or collapse.

As cities, technology, and education expanded, high culture became more diffused; popular culture, especially in the cities, more modern; and the lines between high culture and popular culture more blurred. Yet the gap between Russia's elites and the urban and rural lower classes was not closed and in some ways even widened. During the reigns of Alexander III and Nicholas II, most writers, painters, and composers displayed less concern than under Alexander II with awakening sympathy for "the people" (*narod*).

RUSSIAN ORTHODOXY AND THE STATE

Despite the restoration of certain powers to the hierarchy of the Holy Synod in the late 1850s, it and the church in general remained strongly subject to state control. Although the tsar and his government did not interfere in questions of church dogma and ritual, he did sometimes personally decide which clergyman to appoint to a high position or make "suggestions" with which the Holy Synod complied. And the government still expected Orthodox clergymen to help act as its ears and voice. If they heard of a crime against the state, even in the privacy of confession, they were supposed to report it. They were also to encourage obedience to government decrees and to preach the sinfulness of disobeying the tsar's will.

Not only did the state depend on the Orthodox Church, but also the church depended on the state, for both income and support against other religions.

By the mid-1890s, Pobedonostsev, the Synod's lay procurator from 1880 to 1905, had tightened most restraints over the hierarchy that had been loosened in the late 1850s. Some churchmen complained that he and other lay officials of the Synod really governed church affairs.

The church, however, was not immune to changes in Russia under Nicholas II. Bishops, priests, and laypersons became increasingly dissatisfied with state control over the church. Although some clergy supported the reactionary "Black Hundreds," Father Gapon was just one of many priests who sympathized with liberal or even radical political ideas in 1905.

After the 1905 revolt subsided, the government tried to suppress dissenting church voices, and the Synod urged the clergy to support the forces and parties of "order." But even among Synod members and other members of the church hierarchy, there was unhappiness with the state's failure to back what they considered reasonable reforms. The reputed influence of Rasputin, the self-proclaimed holy man, over church appointments and other matters was a final insult that upset many churchmen. When in the midst of the March 1917 revolution, the Holy Synod's procurator, N. P. Raev, sought from the Synod a proclamation supporting the monarchy, it refused.

Although this era witnessed some efforts to improve overall church conditions, by 1917 little headway had been made. Most of a series of church reforms in the late 1860s ultimately did little good. Writing about the end of this era, Gregory Freeze concluded that "despite strong and continuing interest, despite dozens of committees and commissions, despite the clamor of public opinion, reform left the Church little better—if not worse—than it was in 1825."[1] Most priests remained poor and financially dependent on their parishioners; ecclesiastical education remained inadequate; many priests were poorly trained (in 1904, only about two-thirds of the priests had even received

---

[1]*The Parish Clergy in Nineteenth Century Russia: Crisis, Reform, Counter-Reform* (Princeton, 1983), p. 459.

FIGURE 27.1. The most imposing church opened while Pobedonostsev was the procurator of the Holy Synod was the massive Cathedral of Christ the Savior in Moscow, which opened in 1883 after more than four decades of construction (architect K. Ton). (*From Jim Harter,* Images of World Architecture: A Definitive Volume of 2000 Copyright-free Images. Bonanza Books, New York, 1990, p. 431, #1.)

a seminary degree); and most parishioners remained ignorant of fundamental doctrines.

Despite Pobedonostsev's efforts to increase the number of priests and parishes, by 1904 the ratio of both to Orthodox believers had lessened, especially in rapidly growing areas. Around 1900, for example, Odessa's quarter-million Orthodox believers had only five parish churches.

THE NON-ORTHODOX AND OTHER CHALLENGES TO TRADITIONAL ORTHODOXY

The government's policy toward the one-third of its people who were non-Orthodox was consistent in its goal—to buttress state security—but oscillated in its means. At times, the government concluded that repression of the non-Orthodox stirred discontentment and was counterproductive. At other times, especially during most of Pobedonostsev's years as procurator of the Holy Synod, the state tightened its restraints and increased its discrimination against the non-Orthodox. Discrimination against Lutherans, Catholics, Jews, and Moslems was often part of the larger Russification policies that coincided with Pobedonostsev's years in office.

A law of 1883 recognized the right of schismatics (Old Believers) and sectarians (except the Skoptsy) to practice their beliefs in their houses of prayer or private homes. It prohibited them, however, most types of public display allowed to the Orthodox. It also forbade them from building new churches or proselytizing among the Orthodox faithful, who were forbidden to convert to other religions. During the next few decades, Pobedonostsev worked hard to insure that schismatic and sectarian rights remained strictly limited, and sometimes he initiated new repressions.

One group that saw its rights curtailed was that of the Stundists, a Baptist-like movement that had developed rapidly in southern Russia during the late nineteenth century. Although in 1883 the Stundists obtained the same rights as most other sects, in 1894, Pobedonostsev, alarmed at their spreading influence, persuaded the government to declare them "especially dangerous." Among the rights they lost was that of meeting together for prayer.

Several years later, persecution of the Dukhobors, most of whom advocated nonviolence, reached such a level that the great writer Leo Tolstoy began a campaign to find a home for them outside the Russian Empire. By 1900, thousands of them had been allowed to emigrate to Canada.

The increase of political agitation that marked the early twentieth century and led to the 1905 revolt pressured the government into issuing several edicts promising to respect religious toleration. Especially notable was one of April 1905 that specifically called for removing restrictions on the Old Believers—these schismatics greatly outnumbered the sectarians, and Curtiss has estimated that there were more than 17 million Old Believers in the empire by 1897. That same 1905 edict allowed Orthodox believers to convert legally to other Christian faiths or even, under certain circumstances, to certain non-Christian ones. During the next two years, more than 300,000 individuals took advantage of this new right. To implement greater toleration, the Stolypin government in late 1906–early 1907 prepared more than a dozen bills. Yet, because of the temporary waning of the revolutionary threat and the opposition of Orthodox Church leaders and conservative voices in such forums as the State Council, these bills did not become law.

During the final prewar decade, the threat of increased competition from non-Orthodox faiths was only one of many challenges facing the Orthodox Church. The increasing urbanization and modernization of society placed strains upon an institution not known for its ability to adapt to new ways. Churchmen lamented a decrease in the religiosity of the masses, both in the towns and in the villages—the revolving traffic of peasants from villages to cities and then often back again made it difficult to prevent secular urban influences from affecting village life.

A different type of challenge was presented by many intellectuals who had renounced atheism and adopted a more religious, although often not traditionally Orthodox, viewpoint. In literature and other arts, in societies and journals, the new interest in the spiritual was evident. Although a few outstanding intellectuals, such as Sergei Bulgakov (1871–1927), eventually became Orthodox priests, the religious thought of the prewar decade was diverse, free-thinking, and hardly within the Orthodox mainstream. The religious ideas of the ecumenical Vladimir Soloviev, often contrary to those of Pobedonostsev, were the chief influence on intellectuals who embraced the new spiritual interests. Many of these same intellectuals were also influenced by the ideas of Tolstoy and Germany's Friedrich Nietzsche (1844–1900), both radical critics of traditional Christianity.

EDUCATION AND SCHOLARSHIP

During the Late Imperial era, educational opportunities increased significantly, especially in its final decades. By 1914, just over half the empire's children aged eight to eleven were enrolled in primary schools, with the percentage being closer to 60 percent in European Russia. By then, there were roughly eighteen times as many pupils in the empire's primary and secondary schools as there had been in 1856, and the combined university and higher institute enrollments displayed growth just as impressive.

Because Russia existed in a competitive world, this growth must be placed in a comparative perspective. On the eve of World War I, England, France, Germany, the United States, and Japan all enrolled three times or more as high a percentage of their overall population in primary and secondary schools. Most of Russia's students, residing in the countryside, never completed more than two or three years of schooling.

Educational growth was affected by elite and popular attitudes toward it. Peasants increasingly came to appreciate the possible benefits of literacy for their children. Before the 1890s, most of the initiative for obtaining literacy, either in school or outside, came from the peasants themselves. Yet they generally had little interest or incentive in seeing their children obtain more than a few years of education.

Meanwhile, the government seemed more interested in controlling education than in greatly expanding it. After a brief liberal phase during Alexander II's first decade of rule, ministers of education such as D. A. Tolstoi (1866–1880) and I. D. Delianov (1882–1897) retightened government controls. In 1871, believing that the study of Latin, Greek, and mathematics helped instill discipline, while posing less danger than most other subjects, Tolstoi increased the class time devoted to them in the classical gymnasiums. He did not believe, however, such gymnasiums were for everyone: He encouraged ambitious students from the lower estates to attend the more vocational and technical gymnasiums (the *realschulen*). After becoming minister of interior in 1882, Tolstoi worked with Delianov to bring about the University Statute of 1884, which ended the university autonomy granted in 1863. The government took the occasion to remind professors that their teaching must be patriotic and serve state interests.

Harboring a great mistrust of secular teachers and professors, Pobedonostsev took additional steps to strengthen government control over education. Thanks largely to his efforts, a statute of 1884 authorized the establishment of a new system of parish schools under the jurisdiction of the Holy Synod. During the next two decades, these primary schools multiplied swiftly, jumping from 5,517 in 1884 to 44,421 in 1903. Their purpose, as stated in 1884, was "to strengthen the Orthodox faith and Christian morality among the people and to impart useful elementary knowledge."[2] Given Pobedonostsev's view of the church's role in buttressing state power, there is little doubt that he intended the parish schools to foster loyalty to the regime.

By the 1890s, elites, both within and outside the government, realized that widespread education was important for Russia's development. In the twenty-five years before 1914, zemstvo and central-government spending for education increased sharply. By 1907–1908, the Ministry of Education was introducing bills before the Duma calling for the gradual establishment of universal primary education.

Yet educational development after 1890 continued to be hampered by government fears. Frequent student strikes, beginning in 1899, exacerbated its distrust of the universities. Although the 1905 revolution forced some govern-

[2]As quoted in Robert F. Byrnes, *Pobedonostsev, His Life and Thought* (Bloomingson, 1968), p. 278.

FIGURE 27.2. A Siberian church school from circa 1900, with an icon in the corner and a portrait of Nicholas II in the front, at the outdoor Museum of Wooden Architecture near Irkutsk.

ment concessions, soon afterwards, under Stolypin, the state increased its efforts to insure university loyalty.

Its new measures heightened tensions, leading to new strikes, the expulsion of thousands of students, and the resignation of some professors. In 1912, Nicholas refused to establish any new universities—not counting Helsinki University and one private Moscow university, there were only ten universities in the empire (two more were approved in 1916). The government's fears of university radicalism was one reason that it continued to establish more higher technical institutes than universities. One scholar has concluded that by 1914 "relations between the Russian government and the professoriate were worse than at any time since the reign of Nicholas I."[3]

The students at a majority of the universities had their choice of four departments: history and philology, law, medicine, and natural sciences and mathematics. Law and medicine were generally the most popular choices, and history and philology was chosen least.

By the turn of the century, most university students came from the middle strata of Russian life, with many of their fathers being employed in urban occupations and government service. Few of them came from peasant or blue-collar families. Yet most students were dependent on student aid, work, or both to make their way through the universities. Subsidized dining halls helped, but few dormitories were available, and students generally lived in poor rented quarters. They were often harassed by university inspectors, who attempted to insure students' political reliability and compliance with the many rules of student conduct, which included properly wearing student uniforms.

Until the beginning of World War I, women were not allowed to enroll as regular students in the universities and even then only in small numbers. In 1876, the government permitted the establishment of separate "women's higher courses" in St. Petersburg, Moscow, Kiev, and Kazan, but at the end of the reactionary 1880s, the latter three were closed. Before 1905, only Moscow was allowed (in 1900) to reestablish such women's courses. After the 1905 revolution, other university towns were permitted to establish them, and women were also allowed to audit courses in the regular universities.

Concurrently, new advanced technical schools for women, such as the St. Petersburg Women's Technical Institute, were opened. Before 1905, some women had attended medical schools abroad or been trained at home (a women's medical school had first appeared in St. Petersburg during the 1870s), and by 1911 there were some 1500 women doctors. After 1905, opportunities to pursue advanced studies in preparation for other professions such as architecture, engineering, and law began opening up to women. Between 1900–1901 and 1913–1914, the number of women enrolled in higher educational institutions of all types increased about fifteenfold to almost 40,000.

At other educational levels, female opportunities also increased. Whereas in 1850 only about one-tenth of all primary school students were girls, by 1911

---

[3]Samuel D. Kassow, *Students, Professors, and the State in Tsarist Russia* (Berkeley, 1989), p. 40.

the percentage had reached one-third. By then, women already composed more than 60 percent of all village teachers and a much higher percentage of St. Petersburg and Moscow primary school teachers.

Both within and outside the higher educational institutions, scientists, engineers, and scholars made important contributions. In chemistry, Dmitri Mendeleev (1834–1907) presented his groundbreaking Periodic Table. In physics, P. N. Lebedev (1863–1912) measured the pressure of light, and A. S. Popov (1859–1905) demonstrated—before Marconi's patent application—that messages could be transmitted by electromagnetic waves. N. E. Zhukovsky (1847–1921) and K. E. Tsiolkovsky (1857–1935) made pioneering discoveries in aviation, with Tsiolkovsky's early contributions to rocketry being especially significant. The physiologist I. P. Pavlov (1849–1936) was awarded a Nobel Prize in 1904 for his work on digestion, and he later gained world fame for his experiments with dogs, which demonstrated the workings of conditioned reflexes.

Several important scholars did much of their work abroad. Sophia Kovalevskaia (1850–1891) studied in Germany and later became a professor of mathematics at the University of Stockholm. Her work on motion won her recognition from the Academy of Paris in 1888. Two years later, the biologist and bacteriologist I. I. Mechnikov (1845–1916) joined Paris's Pasteur Institute and in 1895 became its director. In 1908, he was a co-recipient of the Nobel Prize for Physiology and Medicine.

The Late Imperial era also provided a rich harvest in the social sciences (especially history) and philosophy. From 1851 to 1879, despite his teaching and administrative duties at Moscow University, Sergei Soloviev (1820–1879) completed each year a new volume of his *History of Russia from Ancient Times*. His pupil Vasili Kliuchevsky (1841–1911) became renowned for his graceful style, both in lecturing and writing, and his five-volume *Course in Russian History* made an indelible impression on many future historians of Russia, both within and outside the country's borders. Other historians of note included S. F. Platonov (1860–1933), who did valuable work on the Time of Troubles; Paul Miliukov, the Kadet leader; and several Ukrainian historians, especially M. I. Kostomarov (1817–1885) and M. S. Hrushevsky (1866–1934).

The empire's most important philosopher was Vladimir Soloviev (1853–1900), the son of the historian. He studied and wrote on Western philosophy and developed his own original philosophic ideas. His *The Justification of the Good* (1895) was Russia's most important work in ethical philosophy and also offered an impressive philosophy of law.

LITERATURE

The Late Imperial age was Russia's greatest literary era. First came the Golden Age of the Russian novel, which basically coincided with the reign of Alexander II. Then a little later, during the reign of Nicholas II, literature shared a Silver Age with the other arts. Bridging the two ages was Russia's great short-story writer and dramatist Anton Chekhov.

Turgenev, Dostoevsky, and Tolstoy

The three greatest novelists of the Golden Age were Ivan Turgenev (1818–1883), Fedor Dostoevsky (1821–1881), and Leo Tolstoy (1828–1910). Turgenev and Tolstoy were from wealthy noble landowning families; Dostoevsky grew up in more modest surroundings in Moscow. Although their literary styles differed in many ways, all three writers were primarily realists in an age of literary realism.

Turgenev first received wide acclaim for his *Sportsman's Sketches*. The sketches began appearing in 1847 and were published in book form in 1852. By depicting serfs sympathetically, the sketches contributed to the growing dissatisfaction with the evils of serfdom.

Turgenev's most famous novel, which created a storm in Russia when it first appeared in 1862, was *Fathers and Sons*. Literary critics and others debated the meaning and significance of its central character, the nihilist Bazarov, and whether Turgenev had depicted him too harshly or sympathetically. Other Turgenev novels include *Rudin, A Nest of the Gentry, On the Eve, Smoke,* and *Virgin Soil.*

In his novels, he often dealt with contemporary social issues. He was a liberal westernizer, spent much time in Western Europe, and was the first Russian writer to gain a widespread European following, even receiving an honorary degree from Oxford University in 1879. His characters sometimes reflect his own views, but he prided himself on his objectivity and claimed that above all he was trying to portray life realistically.

Turgenev was also the author of several plays and many pieces of short fiction. His best play was *A Month in the Country,* written in 1850 but first produced in 1872. Compared to his novels, Turgenev's many shorter works tend to be more personal, poetic, and romantic, some even dealing with fantastic, otherworldly types of occurrences. His strong lyrical gift is more evident in his shorter fiction, as are his personal feelings: He looked back nostalgically at young love (he never married), lamented his own aging, and expressed a great fear of death.

Whether writing novels or stories, Turgenev's prose was characterized by brevity and clarity. All six of his novels together fall far short of the length of Tolstoy's *War and Peace*. In contrast to Dostoevsky and Tolstoy, Turgenev did not generally tell the reader a great deal about the inner life of his characters but revealed their feelings primarily through their words and actions.

Dostoevsky's life and works were both filled with more turbulence than Turgenev's. Although he received early acclaim for his first novel, *Poor Folk,* published in 1846, his involvement in the Petrashevsky Circle led to his arrest in 1849, followed by a decade of imprisonment and exile. While in a Siberian prison, he experienced a strong religious reawakening and became convinced that Russian intellectuals like himself must be spiritually reunited with the common people and their Orthodox religious beliefs.

In 1866, Dostoevsky published *Crime and Punishment,* the first of his four major novels—the other three being *The Idiot* (1868), *The Possessed* (1872), and *The Brothers Karamazov* (1880). In *Crime and Punishment,* he attempted to demonstrate the bankruptcy of nihilism and radical thinking, which he blamed primarily on Western influences. In *The Possessed*, which reflected his alarm at the behavior of nihilists such as Sergei Nechaev, Dostoevsky suggested that westernized liberals such as Turgenev helped create a climate conducive to the growth of radicalism.

His criticism of Western influences and his Russian nationalism were sometimes accompanied by ugly prejudices, including antisemitism. At other times, as in his "Pushkin Speech" of 1880 or in *The Brothers Karamazov*, Dostoevsky spoke or wrote of universal reconciliation, establishing the Kingdom of God on earth, and displaying brotherly love toward Western Europe.

Religious themes were important to him. He believed that free will often led to sin and suffering, but that such freedom was priceless and that from suffering, both humility and redemption could flow. He intended Prince Myshkin, the hero of *The Idiot*, to be a Christ-like figure, possessing great humility. In *The Brothers Karamazov*, Alyosha Karamazov and the monk Zosima reflect some of Dostoevsky's own religious thinking.

Although Dostoevsky's reputation rests primarily on his four great novels, he also authored many other works, including other novels, short stories, sketches, and journalistic essays. *The Adolescent* is sometimes included in the ranks of his major novels. *Winter Notes on Summer Impressions* contains reflections on his 1862 trip to Western Europe. *The House of the Dead* is a novel based on his own Siberian prison experiences. *Notes from the Underground* and its Underground Man defend "irrational" behavior in the name of freedom. *The Gambler* reflects Dostoevsky's own gambling addiction during the 1860s.

Dostoevsky's style is more dramatic and frenzied than Turgenev's. The clashes of his characters often flow from their differing ideas—he was a master of the novel of ideas. His realism, which at times is mixed with gothic romantic touches, is primarily a psychological realism, and he was especially insightful when delving into the depths of abnormal behavior. Many of his characters, such as Raskolnikov of *Crime and Punishment*, were split personalities. Raskolnikov's behavior is partly explained by his residence in St. Petersburg, and much more than Turgenev and Tolstoy, Dostoevsky's prose captures the heartbeat of the new urban environments emerging in Russia.

As with Turgenev and Dostoevsky, Tolstoy first made his literary mark while still in his twenties. His trilogy *Childhood, Boyhood,* and *Youth* and his *Sevastopol Sketches,* all based largely on his own experiences, won him early acclaim for his realism. Among other works, he wrote two masterpieces, *War and Peace* during the 1860s and *Anna Karenina* during the 1870s.

While writing *Anna Karenina*, Tolstoy began experiencing a spiritual crisis—a "middle-age crisis" it might be termed today. The acute realization that "the dragon of death" awaited everyone temporarily sapped life's enjoyments and led him to despair. Like Dostoevsky in prison two decades earlier, Tolstoy was "reborn" by the example of common Orthodox believers, only not convicts, but the peasants around him. And like Dostoevsky, Tolstoy retained a faith in the common people and their essential goodness until the end of his life.

In his last three decades, Tolstoy continued writing fiction as well as many nonfictional, often religious or didactic works. He also wrote several plays, the most famous being *The Power of Darkness*. During this period, he developed his own religious-political philosophy, one that attracted Tolstoyan followers and got him into trouble with both the Orthodox Church and the government (see Chapter 23). His religious beliefs infused much of his late fiction, but despite his frequent didacticism, he still wrote many excellent works. Stories such as *Master and Man* and *Hadji Murad* are among his finest, and even the novel *Resurrection*, which the critic Prince Mirsky thought an example of Tolstoy "at his worst," has its strong defenders.

Although the fictional characters of Turgenev and Dostoevsky often reflected the political-ideological struggles of their day, Tolstoy's characters were more concerned with eternal questions such as individual and family happiness and the meaning of life and death. At times, as in *War and Peace*, Tolstoy interrupts his narrative to discourse on topics such as war and history.

Tolstoy was a master at depicting and analyzing his characters. Although some of them reflect his own inner turmoil and search for life's meanings, others exist more in their own mental worlds. Anna Karenina, Natasha (in *War and Peace*), and the Moslem warrior Hadji Murad are just a few notable examples. Although his writings before his "crisis" are full of realistic detail, his latter works are more concise and sparse.

Chekhov, Gorky, and Other Writers

Besides Turgenev, Dostoevsky, and Tolstoy, Russia's Golden Age produced other fine novelists, including Ivan Goncharov, Nikolai Leskov, Alexei Pisemsky, and Mikhail Saltykov-Shchedrin. Although both Turgenev and Tolstoy wrote a few plays, the chief playwright of their day was Alexander Ostrovsky (1823–1886), who wrote close to fifty plays. Ostrovsky's plays reflected the literary realism of the era; were usually full of drama; and often displayed the vices of merchants, patriarchal fathers, and others.

The leading poets of this generation were Nikolai Nekrasov (1821–1877) and Afanasi Fet (1820–1892). The two men presented quite a contrast. Nekrasov, the radical editor and friend of Chernyshevsky and Dobroliubov, wrote realistic poetry reflecting his social concerns. The conservative Fet, who was known to register his disapproval at the liberalism of Moscow University by spitting out his carriage window when passing it, was a proponent of "art for art's sake" and wrote melodic love and nature poems. The leading poet of the succeeding generation was Vladimir Soloviev, the philosopher, religious thinker, and mystic, who died in 1900.

From the early 1880s until his death, Anton Chekhov (1860–1904) wrote the hundreds of stories and numerous plays that have gained him a worldwide reputation. Among his plays, *The Sea Gull, Uncle Vania, The Three Sisters*, and *The Cherry Orchard* are his most famous.

Chekhov gained early success writing humorous, often satirical, short stories, which have always been more appreciated in Russia than abroad. They made it unnecessary for him to earn a living as he had been trained to do, practicing medicine. A sadder atmosphere envelopes many of Chekhov's later works, partly because of his suspicion and eventual awareness that he had tuberculosis, but also because of the social conditions of Russia.

Chekhov considered himself a realistic writer, a chronicler of his times; and being a humane and decent man, he was saddened by the life around him. His works reflect the poor state of the peasants, the backwardness of provincial life, the inhumane treatment of convicts (as depicted in his book *Sakhalin Island*), the decline of the nobility, and the ineffectualness of intellectuals.

Chekhov's characters are often bored, unable to connect with others, and more willing to talk than act. Even Chekhov's dramas are short on dramatic action. His style depends more on creating an atmosphere, a mood, a "slice of life"—often sad but lyrical. In this respect and in the conciseness of his language and frequent use of symbols, Chekhov's plays and latter stories display a strong poetic sensibility.

Another writer of short stories and plays was Alexei Peshkov (1868–1936), who adopted the pen-name Maxim Gorky. He grew up in harsh conditions, and before he reached his teens he began earning his own living—these experiences were later described in some of his best writing, an autobiographical trilogy (*Childhood, In the World, My Universities*). His short stories earned him fame in the mid-1890s, and other stories, novels, and plays soon added to his reputation. His play *The Lower Depths* (1902), like Chekhov's greatest plays, was staged by the new Moscow Art Theater, under the direction of K. S. Stanislavsky, one of the pioneer directors of modern theater. In this play and in works such as the novel *Mother* (1907), Gorky's radical sympathies are clear—although frequently supporting Lenin, Gorky also had his differences with him. In 1905, he spent more than a month in the Sts. Peter and Paul Fortress for penning a protest against Bloody Sunday. About a year after public pressure helped free him, he left Russia and lived abroad until 1913, including part of 1906 in the United States.

Literature in the Silver Age

The Silver Age was characterized by experimentation and a wide variety of writings and literary camps, but also by a new cultural spirit. It veered away from realism toward neoromanticism and philosophical idealism. In literature, this change was most evident in the new poetry of "decadence" and "symbolism."

The Silver Age was a great age for poetry. So many talented poets began writing in this period that only a small number can be mentioned here. Constantine Balmont and Valeri Briusov were two pioneering poets of the time, and Alexander Blok and Andrei Bely, both born in 1880, were two of the Symbolist movement's greatest practitioners. Viacheslav Ivanov was another leading Symbolist. A slightly younger group of poets (all born between 1886 and 1893) who published at least some of their poetry before 1917 include Nikolai Gumilev, Anna Akhmatova, Boris Pasternak (who later wrote *Doctor Zhivago*), Osip Mandelshtam, Marina Tsvetaeva, and Vladimir Maiakovsky.

A central influence on many of the poets was Vladimir Soloviev's mystical poetry, but they were also influenced by foreign works such as those of the

French Symbolist poets and Nietzsche. The experimentation and diversity that marked the poetry of the Silver Age emanated from the era's restless intellectual searching. Writers and other intellectuals sought fulfillment in religious and mystical truths and sensual delights or by helping "transform humanity," but they also feared apocalyptic catastrophe.

Although it was not a great age for the novel, Bely's *Petersburg* (1913) and Fedor Sologub's *The Petty Demon* (1907) were noteworthy. Like Bely, both Sologub and Ivan Bunin (1870–1953), another fine prose writer, were also poets of note. Bunin's short story, "The Gentleman from San Francisco" (1915), is perhaps his best-known piece of fiction. Some of Bunin's work was published by the Knowledge Publishing House, which resisted the dominant trend of the time by supporting realistic literature. Among some of the other first-rate short stories and longer fiction it published were works by Gorky, Leonid Andreev, and Alexander Kuprin.

ART AND ARCHITECTURE

Developments in painting paralleled those in literature: first an age of realism and later a reaction against it and an explosion of artistic experimentation. In 1863, fourteen art students at the St. Petersburg Academy of Arts protested its choice of a competition subject—the Feast of the Gods in Valhalla. They believed it irrelevant to their interests and those of society. Their aesthetic ideas owed a debt both to earlier pioneers of artistic realism, such as A. Venetsianov, and to new aesthetic theories, such as those of Chernyshevsky. Under the leadership of Ivan Kramskoi (1837–1887), they formed an "Association of Free Painters." In 1870, Kramskoi and others, including some who had not been among the original fourteen rebels, formed a new organization, The Society of Traveling Exhibitions. Its members, often called the "Wanderers," not only stressed artistic realism, but also the importance of taking art to the people. Some of them also hoped their paintings would contribute to social reforms.

Perhaps the most famous painting of the 1870s was "The Volga Boathaulers" (1870–1873). Its creator was Ilia Repin (1844–1930), the son of a state peasant, who joined the Wanderers later in the decade. It fit in well with the populist mood of of the 1870s, especially the going-to-the-people movement of 1874 (see Chapter 22). Like the writings of the Populist Lavrov or the poetry of Nekrasov (himself the subject of a sympathetic portrait by Kramskoi), Repin's canvas helped stimulate sympathy for the masses. Dostoevsky noted that it would awaken in those who saw it a realization of their debt to the people.

Beginning in the 1880s, many of the Wanderers were caught up in a wave of cultural nationalism, which was reflected in a new enthusiasm for Russian historical subjects. Repin painted such works as "Ivan the Terrible and His Son Ivan" and "The Zaporozhe Cossacks Writing a Letter to the Turkish Sultan." An even more prolific painter of historical canvases was Vasili I. Surikov. In 1881, he painted "The Morning of the Streltsy Execution" and in the next few decades followed it up with numerous other historical paintings, including

"Boyarynia Morozova" and "Stenka Razin." Both Repin and Surikov, like many other artists, benefited from the support of the Moscow merchant Savva Mamontov and his wife Elizabeth, who encouraged and supported the nationalist revival in the arts.

By the 1890s, new winds were blowing through the Russian art world. Mikhail Vrubel and his friend Valentin Serov, two more artists patronized by the Mamontovs, were transitional figures between the realistic art of the Wanderers and the new artists that emerged around the turn of the century. As compared to the Wanderers, the new artists were more open to foreign artistic influences and shared the Symbolist poets' reaction against realism. They were more concerned with a spiritual world that existed beyond earthly phenomena; with their own inner world; or with technical challenges relating to shapes, space, and color.

New journals such as *The World of Art* (1898–1904) helped stimulate the creation of Russia's new art. So too did the rich collections of Impressionist, Post-Impressionist, Matisse, and Picasso paintings gathered by some of Russia's Moscow merchant collectors. Still another stimulus was artists' travel and study abroad and, at home, the rediscovery of the beauty of old icons, just then being restored to their original brilliance.

Just as in poetry, so too in art, one movement after another appeared. Symbolism, Neo-Primitivism, Cubo-Futurism, Rayonism, Suprematism, and Constructivism were among the most prominent. Prolific painters such as Mikhail

FIGURE 27.3. The house of Stepan Riabushinsky, Moscow, 1900–1902, architect F. Shekhtel.

Larinov, Natalia Goncharova, and Kasimir Malevich often passed from one phase to another. Two of the most gifted younger artists at the close of this era were Vladimir Tatlin and Natalia Popova. Of the many Russian painters of the prewar period, probably the two best-known in the West are Vasili Kandinsky, one of the founders of modern abstract art, and Marc Chagall, whose modernist paintings often reflected Jewish life as well as his own rich imagination.

Although architecture displayed less creative dynamism than painting, the profession expanded rapidly, especially to meet new urban needs. Much of the new building was eclectic, but two styles are worth noting: the national-revival style and the "style moderne," which combined a decorative aestheticism with a rational-functionalist approach to new materials and technology. Late-nineteenth century examples of the national-revival style include St. Petersburg's Church of the Resurrection of the Savior on the Blood (see Figure 22.3), Moscow's History Museum, and its City Duma (later the Central Lenin Museum). The turn-of-the-century "style moderne" received support from Moscow merchant families such as the Riabushinskys. They commissioned Fedor Shekhtel, the era's most renowned architect, to design both houses and commercial buildings for them in this new style.

MUSIC

Thanks to composers such as Anton Rubinstein, Modest Musorgsky, Peter Tchaikovsky, Alexander Scriabin, and Igor Stravinsky, musical life was as vibrant as that of literature and painting. In St. Petersburg, Anton Rubinstein, a great pianist as well as a composer, founded the Russian Musical Society in 1859. In 1862, he became director of a recently opened school of music that was renamed the St. Petersburg Conservatory. His brother Nikolai followed his example in Moscow, establishing there both a branch of the Musical Society and a conservatory. Other branches and conservatories soon followed in other cities. For almost four decades, Anton Rubinstein remained the head of the St. Petersburg Conservatory, which trained many future composers, including Tchaikovsky, who later taught at the Moscow Conservatory.

Some composers found Rubinstein's musical approach too conservative and Western. The chief rebels were a group named "The Five" or "Mighty Bunch," which originated in the late 1850s–early 1860s. Their leader, and the only one who trained for a musical career, was Mili Balakirev. Alexander Borodin was a scientist, and the other three—Musorgsky, Nikolai Rimsky-Korsakov, and Caeser Cui—were all trained for military careers. Influenced by the music of Glinka and Alexander Dargomyzhsky as well as the intellectual currents of their own era, The Five espoused nationalism and realism in music.

Of The Five, Musorgsky was the most gifted. With great passion, he set out to depict Russian life, especially that of the common people. They are the true heroes of his two great operas set in Muscovite Russia, *Boris Godunov* and *Khovanshchina*.

If Musorgsky's passion for Russia's people and history, including their music and folklore, was unmatched, his interest in them was more common.

This can be seen in such operas as Borodin's *Prince Igor* and Rimsky-Korsakov's *Sadko, The Tsar's Bride,* and *The Golden Cockerel.*

The music of Tchaikovsky, both in technique and content, stands somewhere between that of Anton Rubinstein and The Five. Compositions such as his *Sixth Symphony,* his ballets *Swan Lake* and *Sleeping Beauty,* and his opera *Evgeni Onegin* are just a few of the many works that earned him international fame before his death in 1893.

During the Silver Age, the music of Alexander Scriabin reflected the strong mystical influences of Vladimir Soloviev. And Scriabin's compositions along with those of Igor Stravinsky displayed the Silver Age's passion for artistic experimentation. When Stravinsky's ballet *The Rite of Spring* premiered in Paris in 1913, its daring dissonance created an uproar that threatened to drown out the music.

DIAGILEV AND ARTISTIC CROSS-FERTILIZATION

Stravinsky's ballet was put on by Serge Diagilev and his Ballet Russes company, who a few years earlier had staged the composer's *The Firebird* and *Petrushka.* The efforts of Diagilev perhaps best exemplify an important tendency of the era—the intertwining and cross-fertilization of the arts.

Such intertwining was not new. To take one of many examples, Musorgsky was inspired by Repin's "The Volga Boathaulers" and wrote to the artist that he also wished to portray "the people" in his work. Realistic, populist, and nationalist tendencies swept through various art forms during the reigns of Alexander II and Alexander III.

But Diagilev's organizing energy on behalf of artistic interaction was unprecedented. This aim was one of the reasons why in 1898 he launched his new magazine, *The World of Art.* Its pages dealt with Russian and Western art, poetry, music, and religious ideas. Before taking his ballet company abroad, Diagilev had introduced Paris to the world of Russian painters and treated them to the music of Musorgsky, Borodin, Scriabin, Rimsky-Korsakov, and Rachmaninov. The last two composers accompanied him to Paris, where Rimsky-Korsakov conducted and Rachmaninov played the piano.

The Diagilev ballets featured not only great music, but also showcased the talents of leading choreographers and dancers, such as the famed Vaslav Nijinsky. And Diagilev employed leading artists such as Leon Bakst, Mikhail Larinov, and Natalia Goncharova to help design his sets and costumes.

POPULAR CULTURE

As urbanization, education, and literacy developed, so too did the diffusion of the fruits of high culture. Books, journals, newspapers, museums, learned societies, public lectures, performances, concerts, exhibitions, and films proliferated. The lines between elite and popular culture became increasingly blurry. For example, many of Chekhov's short stories appeared in popular humor magazines and in newspapers, and Tolstoy's short novel *The Kreutzer Sonata* (completed in 1889) appeared on the popular stage in 1911 and as a film in 1914.

The popularity of *The Kreutzer Sonata* in various forms and with various audiences was partly due to its treatment of sexuality. After the turn of the century, especially after 1905 and the reduction of censorship, popular culture (as well as high culture) increasingly dealt with sexual themes. The works of artists, poets, dancers, dramatists, filmmakers, philosophers, and especially fiction writers reflected this concern. Andreev's short stories "In the Fog" and "The Abyss" (both 1902), Mikhail Artsybashev's novel *Sanine* (1907), Kuprin's novel *Yama* (1909–1915), and Anastasiia Verbitskaia's six-volume novel *The Keys to Happiness* (1910–1913) were some of the more popular works dealing with sex. Verbitskaia's novel, which also had a feminist following, was made into a film in 1913 and became Russia's most popular pre-1917 film.

Film houses began appearing around the turn of the century, and by 1913 there were almost 1500 of them throughout the country. Other forms of urban entertainment included opera, ballet, theater, the circus, the variety stage, cabarets, concerts, dance halls, fairs, and taverns. Amusement parks, which like films appealed to people of various classes, also sprung up in increasing numbers during this era and often offered many types of entertainment. In St. Petersburg's Arcadia (opened in 1881), for example, entertainments included opera, drama, comedy, vaudeville, band music, Gypsy ensembles, clowns, a tightrope walker, wild beasts, fireworks, balloon fights, reenactments of army and naval battles, and a roller coaster. Of course, how much urban entertainment was available varied greatly, especially depending on the size of any given city.

Organized sports, including spectator sports such as horse racing, cycling, and soccer, developed during this period and sometimes drew crowds into the tens of thousands in places like the Moscow Hippodrome. By 1914, forty-eight soccer teams competed in the two major city leagues of Moscow and St. Petersburg. Besides these athletes, other individuals organized teams or clubs for ice hockey, fencing, gymnastics, lawn tennis, skating, skiing, swimming, yachting, rowing, and other sports. Boxers, weightlifters, and wrestlers participated in circuses and at fairs and organized clubs for such "heavy athletics."

As can be imagined, most working-class people had little time or money to join sports clubs (even if permitted to) or to see spectator sports. After the 1905 revolt, however, some government officials and factory owners concluded that organized sports might channel workers' energies into more constructive pursuits than revolutionary activities. Thus, the number of workers' soccer teams increased, and in 1914 such teams were permitted for the first time to play against teams made up of middle-class or upper-class men. (Future Communist party head Nikita Khrushchev once claimed that he had been on a soccer team of the foreign-owned company he worked for in pre-1917 Yuzovka.)

Overall, organized sports in Russia reflected the country's social and political makeup. Workers participated much less and the government exercised more control over sports than in more democratic countries. In 1912, an office

A Best-Selling Novel of 1907

The following selection is from Michael Artzibashef [Mikhail Artsybashev], *Sanine*, trans. Percy Pinkerton (New York, 1914), pp. 99–100, 176–177. It reflected not only the prewar decade's fascination with sexual themes, even hinting at incest, but also stressed individual (whether male or female) freedom from traditional moral constraints, another popular theme of the decade. Some critics have charged it with being both a vulgarization of Dostoevsky's *Notes from the Underground* and Nietzschean ideas. The first passage expresses Sanine's philosophy, and the second the thoughts of his sister Lida after she has allowed herself to be seduced by a young cavalry officer. Ellipses, except the final ones, are mine.

"One thing I know," replied Sanine, "and that is, that I don't want my life to be a miserable one. Thus, before all things, one must satisfy one's natural desires. Desire is everything. When a man's desires cease, his life ceases, too, and if he kills his desires, then he kills himself."

A series of books which she had read had served to give her greater freedom of thought. As she believed, her conduct was not only natural but almost worthy of praise. She had brought harm to no one thereby, only providing herself and another with sensual enjoyment. Without such enjoyment there would be no youth, and life itself would be barren and desolate as a leafless tree in autumn.

The thought that her union with a man had not been sanctioned by the church seemed to her ridiculous. By the free mind of a man such claims had long been swept aside. She ought really to find joy in this new life, just as a flower on some bright morning rejoices at the touch of the pollen borne to it on the breeze. Yet she felt unutterably degraded, and baser than the basest. . . .

. . . She had had an intrigue. Very good. It was at her own wish. People would despise and humiliate her; what did it matter? Before her lay life, and sunshine, and the wide world; and, as for men, there were plenty to be had. Her mother would grieve. Well, that was her own affair. Lida had never known what her mother's youth had been, and after her death there would be no further supervision. They had met by chance on life's road, and had gone part of the way together. Was that any reason why they should mutually oppose each other?

Lida saw plainly that she would never have the same freedom which her brother possessed. That she had ever thought so was due to the influence of this calm, strong man whom she affectionately admired. Strange thoughts came to her, thoughts of an illicit nature.

"If he were not my brother, but a stranger! . . ." she said to herself, as she hastily strove to suppress the shameful and yet alluring suggestion.

headed by a general was established to supervise sporting activity in the Russian Empire.

The government also was involved in other aspects of popular culture. Well before the turn of the century, concern with lower-class drunkenness and other vices had energized government officials and private organizations to sponsor public readings and provide "People's Houses," where respectable and morally uplifting dramas were presented. By 1913, almost 150 such "houses" had been established throughout Russia. They also usually contained tea and reading rooms. Neither in number nor in popularity, however, could they come close to competing with the taverns, which remained the favorite haunt of the lower classes.

Some entertainments and pastimes were seasonal, such as sledding, ice-skating, sleighing parties, swimming, fishing, picnics, and mushroom-picking. The church calendar also continued to affect leisure activities. Baedeker's 1914 guidebook noted that the theater season lasted from "the end of August to the beginning of May" but also pointed out that theaters "closed on the eves of the chief church festivals, and also for several weeks in Lent." Just before Lent was carnival time, when special amusements were provided.

By the early twentieth century, reading material varied from that provided by "thick journals" and serious literature to that provided by the boulevard or penny press. Major national newspapers such as *Novoe Vremia* fell somewhere in the middle. The boulevard press was inexpensive and depended on adver-tising and large sales. To make money, boulevard newspapers such as the *Moskovskii Listok* (*The Moscow Sheet*) appealed to people's interest in crime, dis-asters, human interest stories, and exposés. To the degree possible under cen-sorship, they sometimes defended the interests of the common people (most of their readers) against those who victimized them, such as dishonest merchants or officials.

Fiction produced by the boulevard press, like the new film industry that made use of it, was often melodramatic, with crime and sex being popular themes. The owner of *Moskovskii Listok*, Nikolai Pastukhov, was the author of the popular novel *The Bandit Churkin*, which his paper serialized and which served as the basis for a film and popular song. Some foreign works, including Sherlock Holmes stories and the science fiction of Jules Verne, were also pop-ular.

As Jeffrey Brooks has noted, the overall impact of popular fiction was to nudge its readers closer to modern secular and cosmopolitan attitudes and to a greater desire for social mobility and individual freedom. Thus, popular fic-tion, as so many other modern trends, tended to undermine the old tsarist, reli-gious, and patriarchal order.

A variety of songs as well as stories appealed to the expanding urban audi-ence. The songs came from many sources, including professional songwriters, and often appeared in penny songbooks, on sheet music, and on phonograph records; they were sung in cafes, restaurants, and on stage. Some singers, male and female, became very popular, toured the country, and appeared in films. "Gypsy songs"—often neither composed nor sung by gypsies and laced with bittersweet longings—were among the most popular.

Foreign characters and settings frequently appeared in popular literature and films. Foreign imports such as the tango also left their mark on Russian urban popular culture—although hardly to the extent suggested by the title of the Russian film *Everyone Tangos in Russia*. World War I reduced foreign influ-ences, and, especially in the early stages of the war, Russian popular culture mirrored wartime patriotism. Germany's Kaiser Wilhelm II, for example, was vilified in the press, on postcards, in cartoons, on the stage, and in films.

There was no absolute division between urban and rural popular cultures. Many urban workers were not long removed from village life and often returned to their native villages for varying periods of time. After leaving their villages, many workers continued to participate in customs such as collective fistfights and religious processions once they became urban laborers. When they visited their villages, they helped introduce villagers to aspects of more modern urban popular culture.

Yet village culture, like village life in general, continued to reflect much more of traditional Russia than did the rapidly expanding urban areas. The seasons and the church calendar largely determined village leisure patterns, just as they did village work life. Songs, dances, and games were major leisure pastimes, especially for young people. During the late fall and winter, they often gathered for evening parties, sometimes combining work with talk, stories, or other entertainment. Young women might gather together in a hut to spin or knit, and in some villages young men would be allowed to come by and join in the socializing.

Youth parties were part of village courting rituals. A church wedding provided a major occasion for celebration, as did a baptism. Thus, religious beliefs, sometimes intermingling pagan elements, intertwined with seasonal patterns and the family life cycle to provide much of the context for rural popular culture.

Yet by the early twentieth century, it also contained new elements, some of which Russia's elites found disturbing. Although peasants continued to dance traditional circle dances and sing traditional songs, they also began to dance newer dances, such as the polka, and sing newer songs. Many of these new songs expressed individualistic desires, hostility to the upper classes, disrespect for elders or Russian traditions, or desires for new ways or products. Peasant popular culture, like peasant life in general, was not as static as observers once thought. In the early twentieth century, the pace of change in peasant culture, as in the country as a whole, was quickening.

SUGGESTED SOURCES*

ALSTON, PATRICK L. *Education and the State in Tsarist Russia.* Stanford, 1969.

BENET, SULA, ed. *The Village of Viriatino: An Ethnographic Study of a Russian Village from Before the Revolution to the Present.* Garden City, N.Y., 1970.

BOWLT, JOHN E. *The Silver Age, Russian Art of the Early Twentieth Century and the "World of Art" Group.* Newtonville, Mass., 1979.

BROOKS, JEFFREY. *When Russia Learned to Read: Literacy and Popular Literature, 1861–1914.* Princeton, 1985.

BRUMFIELD, WILLIAM CRAFT. *A History of Russian Architecture.* Cambridge, England, 1993. Chs. 13–14.

CLOWES, EDITH, SAMUEL KASSOW, and JAMES L. WEST, eds. *Between Tsar and People: Educated Society and the Quest for Public Identity in Late Imperial Russia.* Princeton, 1991.

*See also books cited in footnotes. Many of the literary works mentioned in the text are available in English translations.

CRISP, OLGA, and LINDA EDMONDSON, eds. *Civil Rights in Imperial Russia.* New York, 1989.

CURTISS, JOHN S. *Church and State in Russia; the Last Years of the Empire, 1900–1917.* New York, 1940.

DUDGEON, RUTH. "The Forgotten Minority: Women Students in Imperial Russia, 1872–1917," *RH* 9 (1982): 1–26.

EKLOF, BEN. *Russian Peasant Schools: Officialdom, Village Culture, and Popular Pedagogy, 1861–1914.* Berkeley, 1986.

ENGELSTEIN, LAURA. *The Keys to Happiness: Sex and the Search for Modernity in Fin-de-Siècle Russia.* Ithaca, N.Y., 1992.

FRANK, JOSEPH. *Dostoevsky.* 4 vols. to date. Princeton, 1980–1995.

FRANK, STEPHEN P. "Simple Folk, Savage Customs? Youth, Sociability, and the Dynamics of Culture in Rural Russia, 1856–1914," *JSH* 25 (Summer 1992), 711–736.

FRANK, STEPHEN P., and MARK D. STEINBERG, eds. *Cultures in Flux: Lower-Class Values, Practices, and Resistance in Late Imperial Russia.* Princeton, 1994.

FRIERSON, CATHY A. *Peasant Icons: Representations of Rural People in Late Nineteenth Century Russia.* New York, 1993.

GILMAN, RICHARD. *Chekhov's Plays: An Opening into Eternity.* New Haven, 1995.

GRAY CAMILLA. *The Russian Experiment in Art: 1863–1922.* New York, 1962.

HARE, RICHARD. *Portraits of Russian Personalities between Reform and Revolution.* London, 1959.

HINGLEY, RONALD. *Russian Writers and Society, 1825–1904.* New York, 1967.

JAHN, HUBERTUS F. *Patriotic Culture in Russia during World War I.* Ithaca, N.Y., 1995.

JOHANSON, CHRISTINE. *Women's Struggle for Higher Education in Russia, 1855–1900.* Montreal, 1987.

KOBLITZ, ANN HIBNER. *A Convergence of Lives: Sofia Kovalevskaia, Scientist, Writer, Revolutionary.* New Brunswick, N.J., 1993.

McREYNOLDS, LOUISE. *The News under Russia's Old Regime: The Development of a Mass-Circulation Press.* Princeton, 1991.

MIRSKY, D. S. *A History of Russian Literature from Its Beginnings to 1900.* New York, 1958. Chs. 6–10.

MOSER, CHARLES A., ed. *The Cambridge History of Russian Literature.* Cambridge, England, 1989. Chs. 6–8.

PROFFER, CARL, and ELLENDEA PROFFER, eds. *The Silver Age of Russian Culture: An Anthology.* Ann Arbor, 1975.

READ, CHRISTOPHER. *Religion, Revolution and the Russian Intelligentsia, 1900–1912: The Vekhi Debate and Its Intellectual Background.* London, 1979.

RIORDAN, JAMES. *Sport in Soviet Society: Development of Sport and Physical Education in Russia and the USSR.* Cambridge, England, 1977.

ROSENTHAL, BERNICE GLATZER, and MARTHA BOHACHEVSKY-CHOMIAK, eds. *A Revolution of the Spirit: Crisis of Value in Russia, 1890–1924.* 2nd ed. New York, 1990.

RSH 31 (Winter 1992–1993). The whole issue is devoted to "Nightlife at the Turn of the Century."

RUANE, CHRISTINE. *Gender, Class, and the Professionalization of Russian City Teachers, 1860–1914.* Pittsburgh, 1994.

RUUD, CHARLES A. *Fighting Words: Imperial Censorship and the Russian Press, 1804–1906.* Toronto, 1982.

SCHAPIRO, LEONARD. *Turgenev, His Life and Times.* New York, 1978.

SEREGNY, SCOTT J. *Russian Teachers and Peasant Revolution: The Politics of Education in 1905.* Bloomington, 1989.

SIMMONS, ERNEST J. *Chekhov: A Biography.* Boston, 1962.

———. *Leo Tolstoy.* Boston, 1946.

SINEL, ALLEN. *The Classroom and the Chancellery: State Educational Reform in Russia under Count Dmitry Tolstoy.* Cambridge, Mass., 1973.

SLONIM, MARC. *From Chekhov to the Revolution: Russian Literature, 1900–1917.* New York, 1962.

SPENCER, CHARLES. *The World of Serge Diaghilev.* Chicago, 1974.

STITES, RICHARD. *Russian Popular Culture: Entertainment and Society since 1900.* Cambridge, England, 1992. Ch. 1.

VALKENIER, ELIZABETH. *Ilya Repin and the World of Russian Art.* New York, 1990.

———. *Russian Realist Art: The State and Society: The Peredvizhniki and Their Tradition.* Ann Arbor, 1977.

WEISS, PEG. *Kandinsky and Old Russia: The Artist as Ethnographer and Shaman.* New Haven, 1995.

YARMOLINSKY, AVRAHM. *Turgenev, the Man, His Art and His Age.* New York, 1959.

Appendix A
Chronology*

LATE 9TH C. TO 1240   KIEVAN RUS PERIOD

862	Legendary establishment of Riurikid Dynasty in Novgorod.
882	Capital transferred to Kiev.
907	Oleg attacks Constantinople; treaty signed.
911	Second treaty between Oleg and Byzantium.
912–945	Reign of Prince Igor in Kiev.
941 & 944	Igor wars against Constantinople.
945	Derevlian Rebellion and Igor's death.
945–972	Rule of Olga and then Sviatoslav.
966–967	Sviatoslav defeats the Volga Bulgars and Khazars.
967	First Balkan campaign of Sviatoslav against Bulgars.
968	Pechenegs assault Kiev.
980–1015	Reign of Vladimir.
985	Vladimir wars against Volga Bulgars.
988	Vladimir's conversion to Christianity.
1015	Murder of Boris and Gleb.
1015–1019	Vladimir's sons vie for control.
1019–1054	Yaroslav's reign in Kiev.
1031	Yaroslav attacks Poland.
1036	Pechenegs attack Kiev.
1037?	Groundbreaking for St. Sophia, Kiev.
1045–1050	Construction of St. Sophia, Novgorod.
c. 1050	Ilarion's "Sermon On Law and Grace."
1054	Schism between Eastern and Western Christians.
1054–1113	Period of frequent princely conflict.
1068–1069	Rebellion in Kiev.

*Note: Some dates, especially in the early Kievan period, are not completely verifiable but are accepted as at least close approximations.

1097	Grandsons of Yaroslav meet at Liubech Conference and attempt to settle territorial and succession claims.
1113	Rebellion in Kiev.
1113–1125	Reign of Vladimir Monomakh in Kiev.
1147	First chronicle mention of Moscow.
1157	Death of Yuri Dolgoruki, Prince of Suzdalia.
1169	Forces of Prince Andrei Bogoliubsky of Suzdalia sack Kiev.
1173–1205	Rule of Prince Roman in Volhynia and (later) Galicia.
1185	Failed campaign of Prince Igor of Novgorod-Seversk against Polovtsians. Basis of *Tale of Igor's Campaign*.
1203	Kiev sacked by forces from Smolensk and Chernigov.
1212	Death of Vsevolod III of Suzdalia.
1223?	Mongols defeat Rus forces on the Kalka River.
1227	Genghis Khan dies.
1237–1241	Batu Khan's conquest of Rus.

1240–1533   *THE MONGOLS AND THE RISE OF MOSCOW*

1240	Alexander Nevsky defeats Swedes on the Neva River.
1242	Alexander Nevsky defeats Germanic Knights at Lake Chud.
1252–1263	Reign of Alexander Nevsky as Grand Prince of Vladimir.
1263–1304	Brothers and sons of Nevsky rule as Grand Princes of Vladimir.
1317	Moscow's Prince Yuri (grandson of Nevsky) made grand prince of Vladimir by Mongol khan.
1325	Metropolitan Peter moves to Moscow.
1331?–1341	Moscow's Prince Ivan Kalita (the moneybag) serves as grand prince of Vladimir.
1340s	St. Sergius establishes the Holy Trinity Monastery.
1352–1353	Black Death devastates Russia.
1359–1389	Reign of Dmitri Donskoi.
1377	Death of Olgerd of Lithuania; by then Lithuania controlled about half the lands of old Kievan Rus.
1380	Dmitri Donskoi's victory over Khan Mamai at Kulikovo.
1382	Mocow ravaged by Mongol troops.
1385	Treaty of Krewo pledges Poland and Lithuania to a dynastic union.
1389–1425	Reign of Vasili I.
1425–1462	Reign of Vasili II, the Blind.
1427–1466	Division of Golden Horde; formation of Khanates of Crimea, Kazan, and Astrakhan.
1437–1439	Attempt to reunite Eastern and Western Churches at Council of Ferrara-Florence.
1441	Metropolitan Isidore deposed for accepting Council of Ferrara-Florence.
1453	Fall of Constantinople to the Ottoman Turks.

1462–1505	Reign of Ivan III, the Great.
1471	Moscow attacks Novgorod and defeats it.
1475–1508	Major Kremlin churches built.
1478	Moscow annexes Novgorod.
1480	Muscovite troops face down Mongol troops at Ugra River.
1485	Moscow annexes principality of Tver.
1494	Treaty with Lithuania recognizes Muscovite territorial claims.
1497	*Sudebnik* (Law Code) issued, restricts peasants' mobility.
1500	Ivan III launches military campaign against Lithuania.
1503	Muscovite–Lithuanian truce.
1505–1533	Reign of Vasili III.
1510	Moscow annexes Pskov.
1514	Muscovite forces capture Smolensk in war with Lithuania.
1517 & 1526	Herberstein in Russia on diplomatic missions.
1525	Maxim the Greek found guilty of heresy.

1533–1689   MUSCOVY AND ITS EXPANSION

1533–1584	Reign of Ivan IV, the Terrible.
1547	Ivan IV becomes first ruler to be crowned tsar.
1550	Ivan IV issues *Sudebnik* (law code) and creates *streltsy*.
1551	Church Council of the Hundred Chapters.
1552	Moscow captures Kazan.
1555	St. Basil's Cathedral on Red Square begun.
1556	Moscow's conquest of Astrakhan; Ivan IV decrees specific military obligations for all noble landowners; ordeal by battle prohibited.
1558–1583	Livonian War.
1560	Ivan IV's wife Anastasia dies.
1565	Ivan IV creates the *oprichnina*, which lasts until 1572.
1568–1571	Famine and plague.
1569	Union of Lublin creates a Polish–Lithuanian Commonwealth.
1570	Ivan IV's *oprichnina* attacks Novgorod.
1571	Crimean Tatars burn Moscow.
1581	Ermak invades western Siberia.
1584–1598	Reign of Tsar Fedor I.
1589	First Russian patriarch ordained.
1590–1595	Russo-Swedish War.
1591	Death of Prince Dmitri of Uglich; Crimean Tatar force attacking Moscow defeated.
1596	Union of Brest creates Uniate (or Greek Catholic) Church in Poland–Lithuania.
1598	Riurikid Dynasty ends.
1598–1613	Time of Troubles.
1598–1605	Reign of Tsar Boris Godunov.
1601–1604	Famine and plague.

1605–1606	Reign of the First Pseudo Dmitri, after brief reign of Godunov's son, Fedor II.
1606–1610	Rule of Vasili Shuisky.
1606–1607	Revolt of Bolotnikov.
1607–1610	Pseudo Dmitri II challenges Shuisky government.
1610–1612	Moscow occupied by Poles.
1611–1612	Russian uprising against the Poles.
1611–1617	Novgorod occupied by the Swedes.
1613	*Zemskii sobor* chooses Mikhail Romanov as tsar.
1613–1645	Reign of Tsar Mikhail Romanov.
1617	Treaty of Stolbovo with Sweden.
1618	Armistice of Deulino with Poland.
1619	Filaret, father of Tsar Mikhail, ordained as patriarch.
1632	Beginning of Kievan Academy.
1632–1634	Smolensk War with Poland.
1633	Death of Patriarch Filaret.
1634	Adam Olearius visits Moscow for the first time; Tsar Mikhail proclaims the death penalty for anyone buying or selling tobacco.
1645–1676	Reign of Tsar Alexei.
1648	Ukrainian Cossacks rebel against Poland; uprising in Moscow; Tsar Alexei outlaws *skomorokhi.*
1648–1649	Meeting of a *zemskii sobor.*
1649	Alexei's *Ulozhenie* (Law Code) finalizes serfdom and stipulates many new laws.
1650	Rebellions in Novgorod and Pskov.
1650–1652	Famine, followed by plague from 1654 to 1657.
1652	Tsar Alexei requires foreigners in Moscow to reside in the Foreign Suburb.
1652–1666	Nikon is patriarch of Moscow.
1653	Last real *zemskii sobor* meets.
1654	By Treaty of Pereiaslavl, Ukrainians pledge loyalty to Russian tsar.
1654–1667	Thirteen Years' War between Russia and Poland; by Peace of Andrusovo (1667) Poland loses Left Bank Ukraine, Kiev, and Smolensk to Russia.
1656–1661	Russo-Swedish War.
1662	Moscow "Copper Riot."
1662–1664	Bashkir Rebellion.
1667	Church Council condemns Old Believers; New Trade Regulation restricts foreign traders and increases foreign duties.
1668–1676	Solovetskii Monastery rebels against Orthodox Church reforms.
1669–1671	Rebellion of Stenka Razin.
1676–1682	Reign of Tsar Fedor III.
1676–1681	Russo-Turkish War.
1682	*Streltsy* rebellion; Archpriest Avvakum executed; end of *mestnichestvo.*

1682–1689	Regency of Sophia, with Peter I and Ivan V as co-tsars.
1685	Establishment of a Helleno-Greek Academy, later Slavonic-Greek-Latin Academy, in Moscow.
1686	Russo-Polish "eternal peace" signed.
1687	First campaign against Crimean Tatars.
1689	Second campaign against Crimean Tatars. Peter I overthrows Sophia; Russia and China sign Treaty of Nerchinsk.

1689–1855   EARLY IMPERIAL RUSSIA

1689–1725	Reign of Peter I, the Great (rules alone after the death of Ivan V in 1696).
1696	Russian capture of Azov during a war with Turks.
1697–1698	Peter I visits Western Europe.
1698	*Streltsy* revolt fails; Peter I executes leading rebels.
1700–1721	Great Northern War with Sweden. By the Treaty of Nystadt (1721), Russia gains Baltic coastlands.
1703	St. Petersburg founded; first Russian newspaper published.
1705–1711	Peter I's policies spark rebellions in Astrakhan, the Don area, and Bashkiria.
1709	Russia defeats Charles XII and Hetman Mazepa at Poltava.
1710–1711	War with Turkey.
1711	Senate established.
1716–1717	Peter I's second trip to Western Europe.
1718	Death of imprisoned Tsarevich Alexei; creation of administrative "colleges"; institution of poll (soul) tax.
1721	Peter I adopts the title of Emperor; Holy Synod founded.
1722	Peter I establishes Table of Ranks.
1722–1723	Russia gains Caspian territories in war against Persia.
1725	Peter I dies.
1725–1727	Rule of Catherine I.
1727–1730	Rule of Peter II (grandson of Peter I).
1730	Attempt of Supreme Privy Council to end autocracy.
1730–1740	Rule of Anna (daughter of Ivan V).
1733–1735	Russia participates in War of Polish Succession.
1735	Russia returns final Caspian areas gained by Peter I.
1735–1741	Russia campaign against the Bashkirs.
1736–1739	War with Turkey in which Russia reclaims Azov.
1736	Noble's military service lowered to twenty-five years.
1740–1741	Reign of the infant Ivan VI.
1741–1761	Rule of Elizabeth (Peter I's daughter).
1741	Bering Expedition discovers Alaska.
1741–1743	War with Sweden ending with Treaty of Abo, by which Russia receives a small portion of Finnish territory.
1750	Cyril Razumovsky becomes Ukrainian hetman.
1753	Abolition of death penalty.

1755	University of Moscow founded.
1756	European diplomatic revolution occurs and the Seven Years' War begins.
1761–1762	Rule of Peter III.
1762	Peter III ends mandatory state service for nobles.
1762–1796	Rule of Catherine II, the Great.
1764	Catherine II completes the secularization of church lands begun by Peter III.
1767	Legislative Commission convened.
1768–1774	Russo-Turkish War; by the Treaty of Kuchuk–Kainarji, Russia gains territory bordering the Black Sea.
1771	Plague kills about one-fifth of Moscow's population.
1772	First partition of Poland.
1773–1774	Pugachev's rebellion.
1775	Statute for the Administration of the Provinces.
1782	Premiere of Fonvizin's play *The Minor*; Falconet's statue of Peter the Great (the "Bronze Horseman") unveiled.
1783	Annexation of the Crimea.
1785	Charter of the Nobility; Charter of the Towns.
1786	Catherine II mandates expansion of Russian education.
1787–1792	War with Turkey; by the Treaty of Jassy, Turkey recognizes additional Russian gains north of the Black Sea.
1789	Moslem Ecclesiastical Council established.
1790	Radishchev's *A Journey from St. Petersburg to Moscow* slips past the censors and he is arrested.
1792	N. Novikov arrested.
1793	Second partition of Poland.
1795	Third partition of Poland.
1796–1801	Rule of Paul
1797	Paul mandates strict male tsarist succession.
1798	Russia enters war against France as part of Second Coalition.
1799	General Suvorov's legendary campaign against France in Italy and Switzerland; Russian-American Company formed.
1800	Russia allies with Napoleonic France against England.
1801–1825	Rule of Alexander I.
1801	Russia proclaims annexation of Georgia.
1802	Ministries established to replace administrative colleges.
1803–1804	Major educational reforms introduced.
1804–1813	War with Persia.
1805–1807	Russia participates in Third Coalition against Napoleon until Alexander signs the Treaty of Tilsit.
1806–1812	War with Turkey leads to Russian gain of Bessarabia.
1807–1812	Alliance of France and Russia.
1808–1809	Russo-Swedish war ends with Russian annexation of Finland.
1809	Speransky puts forth government reform plan.

1810	Council of State founded; Military Settlements begun, greatly expanded after 1816.
1812	Napoleon invades Russia.
1813–1814	Russia's European offensive.
1814	Russian troops enter Paris.
1814–1815	Congress of Vienna.
1815	Holy Alliance signed; Quadruple Alliance (Russia, Austria, Prussia, and Great Britain) renewed.
1819	M. Magnitsky begins purge of the University of Kazan.
1822	Masonic lodges dissolved.
1825	Decembrist revolt.
1825–1855	Rule of Nicholas I.
1826–1828	Russo-Persian War leads to Russian gains in Armenia.
1828–1829	Russo-Turkish War leads to Russian gains in the Caucasus and at the mouth of the Danube.
1830–1831	Polish revolt.
1833	The *Complete Collection of the Laws of the Russian Empire* published; Treaty of Unkiar-Skelessi between Russia and Turkey.
1835	Imperial School of Jurisprudence founded.
1836	First staging or publication of Glinka's *A Life for the Tsar,* Pushkin's *A Captain's Daughter,* Gogol's *Inspector General,* and Chaadaev's first "Philosophical Letter"; Briullov's painting "The Last Day of Pompeii" first exhibited in Russia.
1841	Straits Convention signed by major European Powers.
1842	Publication of Gogol's *Dead Souls.*
1847	Herzen leaves Russia forever; Belinsky writes his "Letter to Gogol"; arrest of Ukrainian nationalists in the Brotherhood of Saints Cyril and Methodius.
1848–1849	Revolutions in Europe; famine and cholera epidemic overlap in Russia.
1849	Members of Petrashevsky Circle, including Dostoevsky, arrested; Bakunin arrested in Germany and later extradited to Austria and then Russia; Russia helps Austria suppress rebellious Hungarians.
1851	Opening of the St. Petersburg–Moscow railway line; Sergei Soloviev publishes the first of his 29 volumes of Russian history.
1853–1856	Crimean War.

1855–1917   LATE IMPERIAL RUSSIA

1855–1881	Reign of Alexander II; Golden Age of the Russian Novel.
1856	Treaty of Paris ends Crimean War.
1857–1867	Herzen publishes *The Bell* (*Kolokol*).
1858	Russia and China sign treaties of Aigun and Tientsin.

1859	Russia defeats Chechens.
1860	China recognizes Russian expansion in Treaty of Peking.
1861	Emancipation of serfs; unrest among peasants and students; establishment of St. Petersburg Conservatory.
1862	Publication of Turgenev's *Fathers and Sons*.
1863–1884	Rebellion in Poland, Lithuania, and Belorussia.
1863	University Statute increases faculty rights; government changes liquor laws.
1864	Zemstvo (local government) Reform; Judicial Reform; Russia completes conquest of Caucasus.
1864–1865	Russia conquers much of Central Asia.
1866	Karakozov's attempted assassination of Alexander II; P. Shuvalov becomes head of Third Section until 1874; Dostoevsky's *Crime and Punishment* published.
1867	Sale of Alaska and Aluetian Islands to the United States.
1869	Nechaev murder of student Ivanov.
1870	Birth of Vladimir Ulianov (Lenin); formation of the Wanderers (group of painters).
1871	London Convention agrees to abolition of the Black Sea clauses of the Treaty of Paris.
1873	Formation of Three Emperors' League.
1874	Universal Military Service Statute becomes law; thousands of radicals "go to the people."
1875	Japan recognizes Sakhalin as Russian possession in Treaty of St. Petersburg.
1876	Foundation of Land and Liberty party.
1877	Tolstoy's *Anna Karenina* completed.
1877–1878	Russo-Turkish War.
1878	Treaty of San Stefano; Congress of Berlin.
1879	Land and Liberty divides into People's Will and Black Repartition.
1879–1880	Unsuccessful attempts on life of Alexander II.
1880	Death of Empress Maria and remarriage of Alexander II; Dostoevsky's *Brothers Karamazov* completed.
1880–1881	General Loris-Melikov oversees dealing with terrorists.
1880–1905	Pobedonostsev serves as procurator of Holy Synod.
1881	Members of the People's Will assassinate Alexander II.
1881–1894	Reign of Alexander III
1881	Government decrees "temporary regulations"; anti-Jewish pogroms in Ukraine; Three Emperors' Alliance signed; renewed for three years in 1884.
1882	Law prohibits factories from hiring children under twelve or from employing those aged twelve to fifteen more than eight hours a day.
1883	Death of Karl Marx; establishment of first Russian Marxist organization, the Emancipation of Labor, in Geneva.
1884	University Statutes curtail university autonomy.

1885	Russia and Britain agree on Russo-Afghan frontier; Nobles' Land Bank established.
1887	"Reinsurance Treaty" between Russia and Germany; Alexander Ulianov (brother of Lenin) hanged.
1889	Land captains established.
1890	Decree on zemstvos strengthens government's power over them.
1891	Construction of Trans-Siberian Railway begins.
1891–1892	Famine in European Russia.
1892–1903	S. Witte serves as finance minister.
1894	Final ratification of Franco-Russian Alliance (1893 O.S.).
1894–1917	Reign of Nicholas II; Silver Age of Russian culture.
1896	Coronation ceremonies of Nicholas II in Moscow.
1897	First All-Russian Census.
1898	First Congress of the Russian Social Democratic Labor party (RSDLP).
1899–1904	Russification in Finland.
1901	Party of Socialist Revolutionaries (SRs) founded.
1903	Second Congress of RSDLP in Brussels and London; Union of Liberation formed; anti-Jewish pogrom in Kishinev.
1904–1905	Russo-Japanese War.
1905	
Jan. 9	Bloody Sunday.
Feb.	All-Russian Union for Women's Equality founded.
Apr.	Government edict permits Orthodox believers to convert to other faiths.
May	Japan defeats Russia in battle of Tsushima Straits.
June	Revolt on the Battleship Potemkin.
Aug.	Publication of draft law for a consultative Duma.
Sept.	Peace of Portsmouth ends Russo-Japanese War.
Oct.	All-Russian general strike; formation of a Soviet of Workers' Deputies in St. Petersburg; Constitutional Democratic party (Kadets) formed.
Oct. 17	October Manifesto of Nicholas II promises formation of an elected legislative Duma.
Oct.–Dec.	Pogroms in Odessa and other cities; soviets established in other Russian towns.
1905–1907	Peasant disturbances.
1906	
Mar.	Government grants unions the right to gain legal status.
Apr.	Publication of Fundamental Laws; convening of First Duma.
July	Nicholas II dissolves First Duma; appointment of P. Stolypin as prime minister; Vyborg Manifesto.
1906–1911	Stolypin land reform.
1907	
Feb.–June	Second Duma in existence.
June	New electoral law promulgated.

Aug.	Anglo-Russian Entente relating to Persia.
Nov.	Third ("Masters' ") Duma convenes, lasts until 1912.
1909	Publication of *Vekhi* essays.
1911	Assassination of Stolypin.
1912	Troops fire on Workers at Lena gold-fields; Fourth Duma convenes, lasts until 1917.
1913	Stravinsky's *The Rite of Spring* creates an uproar in Paris.
1914–1918	First World War.
1914	Germany declares war on Russia; prohibition decreed.
1915	Formation of War Industries Committee and of Duma's Progressive Bloc; Nicholas goes to Mogilev to command troops personally.
1916	Murder of Rasputin.
1917	Collapse of the Romanov Dynasty.

Appendix B
Rus/Russian Rulers*

TABLE 1. Kievan Rus to 1132

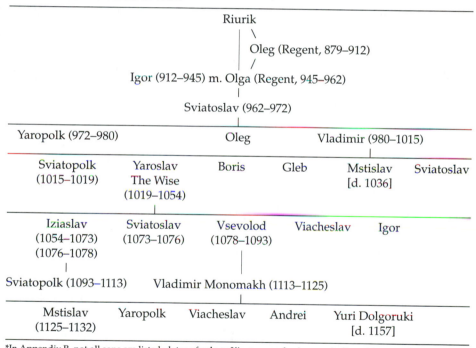

		Riurik			
		\			
		Oleg (Regent, 879–912)			
		/			
	Igor (912–945) m. Olga (Regent, 945–962)				
		Sviatoslav (962–972)			

Yaropolk (972–980)		Oleg		Vladimir (980–1015)	

Sviatopolk (1015–1019)	Yaroslav The Wise (1019–1054)	Boris	Gleb	Mstislav [d. 1036]	Sviatoslav

Iziaslav (1054–1073) (1076–1078)	Sviatoslav (1073–1076)	Vsevolod (1078–1093)	Viacheslav	Igor

Sviatopolk (1093–1113)	Vladimir Monomakh (1113–1125)

Mstislav (1125–1132)	Yaropolk	Viacheslav	Andrei	Yuri Dolgoruki [d. 1157]

*In Appendix B, not all sons are listed; dates of rule as Kievan grand prince are indicated in parenthesis.

TABLE 2. Major Rulers in Northeast Rus/Russia and Moscovy to 1613

Yuri Dolgoruki (d. 1157*)

Andrei Bogoliubsky (1157–1174)*   Vsevolod III (1176–1212)*

Yuri [d. 1238]*   Yaroslav (1238–1246)†   Sviatoslav (1247–1248)†

| Alexander Nevsky (1252–1263)† | Andrei (1248–1252) | Yaroslav [d. 1271]† | Vasili [d. 1277]† |

| Dmitri [d. 1294]† | Andrei [d. 1304]† | Daniel [d. 1303]† | Mikhail of Tver [d. 1318]† |

| Yuri [d. 1325]†,‡ | Ivan I, Kalita [d. 1341]†,‡ | Dmitri [d. 1326]† | Alexander [d. 1331]† |

Simeon [d. 1353]†,‡   Ivan II [d. 1359]†,‡

Dmitri Donskoi (1359–1389)†,‡

Vasili I (1389–1425)‡   Yuri of Galich [d. 1434]

Vasili II, the Blind (1425–1462)‡   Vasili   Dmitri Shemiaka

Ivan III, the Great (1462–1505)‡

Vasili III m. Elena Glinskaia, Regent 1533–1538 (1505–1533)‡

Ivan IV, the Terrible m. Anastasia Romanova (1st wife) (1533–1584)‡

m. Maria Nagaia (7th wife)

| Dmitri [d. 1553] | Ivan [d. 1581] | Fedor m. Irena Godunova (1584–1598)† | Dmitri (Uglich) [d. 1591] |

Boris Godunov (brother of Irena) (1598–1605)‡   Pseudo Dmitri I (1605–1606)‡

Pseudo Dmitri II (Thief of Tushino) [d. 1610]

Vasili Shuisky (1606–1610)‡   Fedor II (1605)‡

*Major rulers in Suzdalia up to 1238.
†Grand Princes of Vladimir under the Mongols up to 1389.
‡Princes/tsars of Moscow/Muscovy.

TABLE 3. The Romanov Dynasty

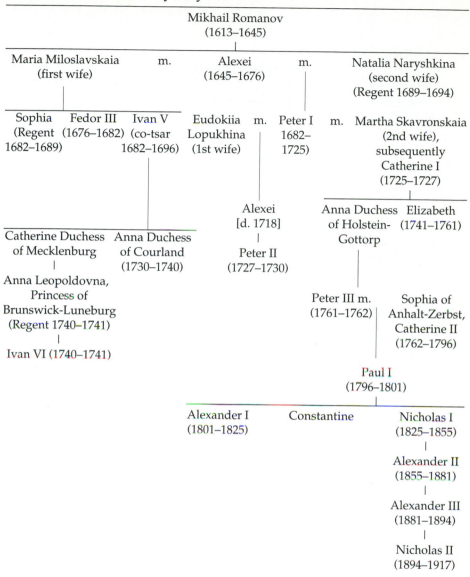

Appendix C
Glossary

Article 87 of the Fundamental Laws of 1906 by this article the tsar between Duma sessions could decree emergency laws that could continue in force for up to sixty days after a new session convened.

ataman see *hetman*.

barshchina a serf's labor service.

Black Hundreds early twentieth-century extreme right-wing organizations, especially their more activist, violent followers; often characterized by strong antisemitism.

"black" lands the lands lived on by "black" peasants, that is by peasants with no private landowner over them.

Black Sea (or Turkish) Straits two straits, the Bosphorus (or Bosporus) and Dardanelles, necessary for ships to pass through to get from the Black Sea to the Mediterranean Sea.

Bolsheviks a Marxist group led by Lenin that emerged in 1903 during the second congress of the Russian Social Democratic Labor party (RSDLP). This faction eventually became a separate party.

boyar a high-ranking noble.

Boyar Council an advisory body to a prince or tsar at various periods in Rus/Russian history. For most of the seventeenth century, it was the highest advisory body to the tsar, helping him direct his ever-increasing *prikazy* (bureaus) and sometimes acting as a court of appeal.

civil society a social sphere standing between the government and the family or individual, in which people can freely interact and create their own independent organizations.

collateral succession a system existing in Kievan Rus whereby a throne was inherited by one's oldest surviving brother and then cousins before moving on to the next generation.

colleges created by Peter I to replace many *prikazy*; colleges were replaced in the early nineteenth century by ministries.

Cossack originally a free frontiersman. The two largest concentrations of Cossacks were in the lower Dnieper and Don river regions.

Council of State (also Imperial State Council) an advisory body created by Alexander I in 1810; in 1906, it was transformed into the upper house of the new Russian legislature.

druzhina   the retinue or bodyguard of a Kievan Rus prince; his elite fighting force.

duma   a council.

Duma   lower house of legislature, which met from 1906 to early 1917.

dvoeverie   double-faith. A term sometimes used to characterize Rus and Russian folk religion, which some scholars maintain remained mainly pagan underneath its Christian surface.

dvorianin   a nobleman.

Golden Horde   the portion of the Mongol empire that ruled over Russia as well as some other areas after the Mongol conquest of Kievan Rus.

gost **(pl. *gosti*)**   a high-ranking merchant in Muscovy.

Guards regiments   elite military units, the first two of which were created by Peter I. These regiments sometimes assisted a ruler, for example, Catherine II, to come to power.

guberniia   region or province in Imperial Russia; abolished in 1923.

hesychasm   a mystical movement that came to Russia from the Balkans in the fourteenth and fifteenth centuries. It aimed at enabling an individual to attain oneness with God, the Divine Light.

hetman (or ataman)   a Cossack leader.

Holy Synod   chief administrative body of the Russian Orthodox Church in Imperial Russia, created by Peter I in 1721 and in 1722 placed under the supervision of a procurator.

icon   an Orthodox religious painting venerated by believers.

iconostasis   a screen of icons that divides the sanctuary of an Orthodox Church from the rest of its interior.

Imperial State Council   see *Council of State.*

intelligentsia   intellectuals; in Late Imperial Russia, often used more narrowly for those thinking people who maintained that Russia's sociopolitical order was unjust, especially to the lower classes.

Kadet (or Constitutional Democratic) party   a liberal party founded in 1905 and later suppressed by the Communists.

kokoshniki   arches used in church architecture that resembled a woman's arched headdress.

kormlenie   a Muscovite system whereby local administrators were to provide for themselves by obtaining supplies and payments from the people over whom they administered.

kreml (kremlin)   citadel or fortress.

Left Bank Ukraine   Eastern Ukrainian territory (east of the Dnieper River) once under the control of the Ukrainian hetman; excludes Sloboda Ukraine and southern Ukrainian territories later added to the Russian Empire (see Map 15.1).

manufactories   manufacturing plants.

Mensheviks   a Marxist group that emerged in 1903 during the second congress of the Russian Social Democratic Labor party (RSDLP). This faction was critical of Lenin's authoritarian plans for the party. The Mensheviks eventually became a separate party and were suppressed during the early Soviet period.

mestnichestvo   a Muscovite genealogical order of precedence for aristocrats. The tsar was expected to abide by it when making appointments to high government and military offices. Abolished in 1682.

metropolitan   a high-ranking bishop in the Orthodox Church; the chief Orthodox religious leader in Kievan Rus and later Russia until Russia received its first patriarch in 1589.

mir   the peasant commune; the Russian word also means universe and peace.

narod—nation, people, especially the common people.

narodnik   see *populist*.

nihilist   a radical of the 1860s who was critical of traditional authorities and thought that nothing (*nihil*), including family, society, or religion, should be accepted that was not based on reason.

obrok   a serf's payment in kind or money to his master in exchange for farming rights.

obshchestvo   society, often used to designate educated society, as contrasted to the *narod* (common people).

obshchina   peasant commune.

Octobrists   members of the "Union of October 17," a moderate liberal political party active in the 1905–1917 period; they wished to implement the promises of Nicholas II's October Manifesto of 1905.

Old Believers (Old Ritualists)   a name applied to those who refused to go along with Patriarch Nikon's changes in the Russian Orthodox Church. They were excommunicated in 1667 and formed their own religious communities, some of which continue to the present day.

oprichnik (pl. *oprichniki*)   a member of the *oprichnina*.

oprichnina   a terrorist system and administration employed by Ivan the Terrible from 1565 to 1572 to crush "traitors" and strengthen autocratic rule.

patriarch   the title of the heads of the chief Orthodox Churches. Until 1589, when the Russian Orthodox Church received its own patriarch, this church was under the jurisdiction of the patriarch of Constantinople.

patrimonial regime   a regime that fails to distinguish between political rule over a territory and private ownership of one's lands. A term used by some scholars, such as R. Pipes, to describe the Muscovite monarchy.

pomestie   land granted by rulers to nobles in exchange for service.

populist (*narodnik*)   a socialist of the 1870s–1890s period who emphasized the welfare of the common people, especially the peasants.

posad   a suburb inhabited by tradesmen, craftsmen, and other urban taxpayers. By the late seventeenth century, the *posad* was no longer so much the urban area outside the city fortress or kremlin, but a legal unit responsible for a city's *tiaglo* (burden).

posadnik   a mayorlike official in medieval Novgorod.

prikaz (pl. *prikazy*)   a Muscovite bureau or department, each of which, such as that of Foreign Affairs, dealt with a single area of government concern.

raznochintsy—a term applied to those who had abandoned the sociolegal estate (*soslovie*) of their parents but had not officially joined another estate.

ruble   a basic Russian monetary unit; worth about one-half of a U.S. dollar before World War I.

Russkaia Pravda of Yaroslav the Wise   Rus's first written law code.

Secret Chancellery (or Chancellery for Secret Investigations)   political police agency created by Peter I. It was temporarily ended in 1729 but restored in 1731. Although abolished by Peter III in 1762, Catherine II soon established a new security force, the Secret Expedition, which was expanded under Tsar Paul. It was abolished by Alexander I, although many of its functions continued to be performed by other bodies. See *Third Section*.

Senate   an administrative and judicial body of Imperial Russia, created by Peter I in 1711 and in 1722 placed under the supervision of a procurator general.

serf   a peasant bound to a master's estate (unless permitted to work elsewhere in exchange for compensation).

skomorokhi   minstrels; medieval Russian entertainers, outlawed in 1648.

soslovie   sociolegal estate in Imperial Russia, for example, that of the nobility.

soul tax   a tax from 1724 to 1887 paid by most men, including serfs; the nobility and certain other privileged groups were exempt.

soviet   council; in 1905, many soviets, primarily of workers' deputies, sprang up during the turbulence of that year; during 1917, they again sprang up, and eventually the term became associated with the new Communist government.

strelets (pl. *streltsy*)   a musketeer serving the government; *streltsy* regiments were first formed in the mid-sixteenth century.

Strigolniki   heretics of late fourteenth–early fifteenth centuries; critical of simony and accused of preaching against priestly authority.

Supreme Privy Council   an administrative and advisory body placed above the Senate by Catherine I in 1726 but abolished by Empress Anne in 1730.

Table of Ranks   fourteen parallel ranks for officers and officials in each branch of state service: the military, civil service, and at court; established by Peter I and continued, with a few minor modifications, until 1917.

terem   separate quarters where noblewomen lived in Muscovy.

Third Section   political police agency from 1826 to 1880.

tiaglo   burden; all of an urban or rural community's tax-paying and labor obligations.

Uniate (or Greek Catholic) Church   created by Union of Brest (1596). It allowed converted Orthodox to maintain their Orthodox rites and customs in exchange for recognizing the supremacy of the pope.

veche   a town council in Rus/early Russian history.

voevoda (pl. voevody)   at different times, a military commander, military governor, or other governing official.

volost   township, canton, or district.

votchina   hereditary property, as contrasted with *pomestie*.

yarlyk   a charter granted by a Mongol khan, often granting the right to rule over a certain area.

yasak   tribute, in Siberia usually in the form of furs.

zemskii sobor (pl. *sobory*)   a Muscovite "land council," which met irregularly to advise the tsar and in 1613 to elect one.

zemstvo   a local government body at the district and provincial levels; the first zemstvos were established in 1864.

General Bibliography for Russia to 1917*

1. JOURNALS AND ANTHOLOGIES CITED IN SUGGESTED SOURCES: A LIST OF ABBREVIATIONS

AHR	=	*American Historical Review*
CASS	=	*Canadian-American Slavic Studies*
CH	=	*Church History*
CMR	=	*Cahiers du Monde Russe*
DOP	=	*Dumbarton Oaks Papers*
EER	=	Raleigh, Donald J., ed., and A. A. Iskenderov, comp. *The Emperors and Empresses of Russia: Rediscovering the Romanovs.* Armonk, N.Y., 1996.
FOG	=	*Forschungen zu Osteuropäischen Geschichte*
HUS	=	*Harvard Ukrainian Studies*
JMH	=	*Journal of Modern History*
JSH	=	*Journal of Social History*
MERSH	=	Wieczynski, Joseph L., ed. *The Modern Encyclopedia of Russian and Soviet History.* 58 vols. Gulf Breeze, Fla., 1976–1994. A source of great value.
MRECT	=	Zenkovsky, Serge A., ed. *Medieval Russia's Epics, Chronicles, and Tales.* Rev. ed. New York, 1974.
RH	=	*Russian History*
RR	=	*Russian Review*
RRH	=	Kaiser, Daniel H., and Gary Marker, eds. *Reinterpreting Russian History: Readings, 860–1860s.* New York, 1994.
RSH	=	*Russian Studies in History*
SEEJ	=	*Slavic and East European Journal*
SEER	=	*Slavonic and East European Review*
SSH	=	*Soviet Studies in History*
SR	=	*Slavic Review*

*See Suggested Sources at the end of each chapter for more specific works. Listings of works dealing with Russia after 1917 can be found in Volume II of this text.

2. BIBLIOGRAPHICAL WORKS

American Bibliography of Slavic and East European Studies. (Also available electronically by subscription from University of Illinois at Urbana-Champaign.) Published annually since 1957 at varied locations. Originally published as the *American Bibliography of Russian and East European Studies.*

Clendenning, Philip, and Roger Bartlett. *Eighteenth Century Russia: A Select Bibliography of Works Published since 1955.* Newtonville, Mass., 1981.

Croucher, Murlin. *Slavic Studies: A Guide to Bibliographies, Encyclopedias, and Handbooks.* Wilmington, Del., 1993.

Crowther, Peter A. *A Bibliography of Works in English on Early Russian History to 1800.* Oxford, 1969.

Egan, David R., and Melinda A. Egan. *Russian Autocrats from Ivan the Great to the Fall of the Romanov Dynasty: An Annotated Bibliography of English Language Sources to 1985.* Metuchen, N.J., 1987. Especially good for journal and anthology articles.

European Bibliography of Soviet, East European, and Slavonic Studies. Birmingham, England. Annually since 1975.

Horak, Stephan M. *Junior Slavica: A Selected Annotated Bibliography of Books in English on Russia and Eastern Europe.* Rochester, N.Y., 1968.

————. *Russia, the USSR, and Eastern Europe: A Bibliographic Guide to English Language Publications, 1964–1974.* Littleton, Colo., 1982.

————. *Russia, the USSR, and Eastern Europe: A Bibliographic Guide to English Language Publications, 1975–1980.* Littleton, Colo., 1982.

————. *Russia, the USSR, and Eastern Europe: A Bibliographic Guide to English Language Publications, 1981–1985.* Littleton, Colo., 1987.

Horecky, Paul L., ed. *Basic Russian Publications: An Annotated Bibliography on Russia and the Soviet Union.* Chicago, 1962.

————, ed. *Russia and the Soviet Union: A Bibliographic Guide to Western-Language Publications.* Chicago, 1965.

Nerhood, Harry W., comp. *To Russia and Return: An Annotated Bibliography of Travelers' English-Language Accounts of Russia from the Ninth Century to the Present.* Columbus, Ohio, 1968.

Pearson, Raymond. *Russia and Eastern Europe, 1789–1985: A Bibliographic Guide.* Manchester, England, 1989.

Proffer, Carl R., and Ronald Meyer. *Nineteenth-Century Russian Literature in English: A Bibliography of Criticism and Translations.* Ann Arbor, 1990.

Ruthchild, Rochelle Goldberg. *Women in Russia and the Soviet Union: An Annotated Bibliography.* New York, 1993.

Schaffner, Bradley L. *Bibliography of the Soviet Union: Its Predecessors and Successors.* Metuchen, N.J., 1995. Over 3,000 references, including other bibliographies.

Schultheiss, Thomas, ed. *Russian Studies, 1941–1958: A Cumulation of the Annual Bibliographies from the Russian Review.* Ann Arbor, 1972.

Shapiro, David M. *A Select Bibliography of Works in English on Russian History, 1801–1917.* Oxford, 1962.

Sullivan, Helen F., and Robert H. Burger. *Russia and the Former Soviet Union: A Bibliographic Guide to English Language Publications, 1986–1991.* Englewood, Colo., 1994. An annotated list of over 1400 entries.

Thompson, Anthony. *Russia/U.S.S.R.: A Selective Annotated Bibliography of Books in English.* Santa Barbara, Calif., 1979.

3. DICTIONARIES, ENCYCLOPEDIAS, HANDBOOKS, AND STATISTICS

Bezer, Constance A., ed. *Russian and Soviet Studies: A Handbook.* Columbus, Ohio, 1973.

Brown, Archie, et al., eds. *The Cambridge Encyclopedia of Russia and the Former Soviet Union.* 2d ed. Cambridge, England, 1994.

Conte, Francis, ed. *Great Dates in Russian and Soviet History.* New York, 1994.

Florinsky, Michael T., ed. *McGraw-Hill Encyclopedia of Russia and the Soviet Union.* New York, 1961.

Great Soviet Encyclopedia. 3d ed. 32 vols. New York, 1973–1983.

Ho, Allan, and Dmitry Feofanov, eds. *Biographical Dictionary of Russian/Soviet Composers.* New York, 1989.

Jones, David R., ed. *The Military Encyclopedia of Russia and Eurasia.* 6 vols. up through 1995. Gulf Breeze, Fla., 1994–.

Kubiiovych, Volodymyr, and Danylo Husar Struk, eds. *Encyclopedia of Ukraine.* 5 vols. Toronto, 1984.

MERSH. See Section 1.

Mihailovich, Vasa D., comp. *Modern Slavic Literatures.* Vol. 1, *Russian Literature.* New York, 1972.

Mitchell, B. R. *International Historical Statistics: Africa, Asia, and Oceania, 1750–1988.* 2d rev. ed. New York, 1995.

———. *International Historical Statistics: Europe 1750–1988.* 3d ed. New York, 1992.

Olson, James Stuart, Lee Brigance Pappas, and Nicholas Charles Pappas, eds. *An Ethnohistorical Dictionary of the Russian and Soviet Empires.* Westport, Conn., 1994.

Paxton, John. *Encyclopedia of Russian History: From the Christianization of Kiev to the Break-Up of the U.S.S.R.* Santa Barbara, Calif., 1993.

Pushkarev, Sergei G., comp. *Dictionary of Russian Historical Terms from the Eleventh Century to 1917.* New Haven, 1970.

Rhyne, George N., ed. *The Supplement to the Modern Encyclopedia of Russian, Soviet, and Eurasian History.* Gulf Breeze, Fla., 1995–.

Rollberg, Peter, ed. *The Modern Encyclopedia of East Slavic, Baltic and Central Asian Literatures* (formerly *The Modern Encyclopedia of Russian and Soviet Literatures*). 10 vols. to date. Gulf Breeze, Fla., 1977–.

Steeves, Paul D., ed. *The Modern Encyclopedia of Religions in Russia and the Soviet Union.* 6 vols. to date. Gulf Breeze, Fla., 1988–.

Terras, Victor, ed. *Handbook of Russian Literature.* New Haven, 1985. A comprehensive and useful work.

Utechin, S. V. *Everyman's Concise Encyclopaedia of Russia.* New York, 1961.

Zickel, Raymond E., ed. *Soviet Union: A Country Study.* Washington, D.C., 1991.

4. NATIONALITIES AND PEOPLES*
(See also appropriate books mentioned in Section 3 and Davies in Section 7.)

Adshead, Samuel Adrian M. *Central Asia in World History.* New York, 1993.

Alapuro, Risto. *State and Revolution in Finland.* Berkeley, 1988.

*Includes nationalities and peoples who at least for some period were part of the Russian Empire or USSR.

Allworth, Edward. *The Modern Uzbeks: From the Fourteenth Century to the Present, A Cultural History*. Stanford, 1990.

————, ed. *Central Asia, 120 Years of Russian Rule*. Durham, 1989.

Altstadt, Audrey L. *The Azerbaijani Turks: Power and Identity under Russian Rule*. Stanford, 1992.

Basilov, Vladimir N., ed. *Nomads of Eurasia*. Seattle, 1989.

Crowe, David M. *A History of the Gypsies of Eastern Europe and Russia*. Bloomington, 1995.

Curtis, Glenn E., ed. *Armenia, Azerbaijan, and Georgia: Country Studies*. Washington, D.C., 1995.

Dmytryshyn, Basil E., E. A. P. Crownhart-Vaughan, Thomas Vaughan, eds. *The Russian American Colonies: A Documentary Record, 1798–1867*. Portland, Or., 1989.

Fisher, Alan W. *The Crimean Tatars*. Stanford, 1978.

Gerutis, Albertas, ed. *Lithuania 700 Years*. 6th ed. New York, 1984.

Gitelman, Zvi Y. *A Century of Ambivalence: The Jews of Russia and the Soviet Union, 1881 to the Present*. New York, 1988.

Hovannisian, Richard G., ed. *The Armenian People: From Ancient to Modern Times*. 2 vols. New York, 1996.

Khodarkovsky, Michael. *Where Two Worlds Met: The Russian State and the Kalmyk Nomads, 1600–1771*. Ithaca, N.Y., 1992.

Kirby, D. G., ed. *Finland and Russia, 1808–1920: From Autonomy to Independence: A Selection of Documents*. London, 1975.

Kolarz, Walter. *Russia and Her Colonies*. London, 1952.

Krawchenko, Bohdan, ed. *Ukrainian Past, Ukrainian Present: Selected Papers from the Fourth World Congress for Soviet and East European Studies, Harrogate, 1990*. New York, 1993.

Lang, David M. *A Modern History of Georgia*. London, 1962.

Lewis, Robert A., Richard H. Rowland, and Ralph S. Clem. *Nationality and Population Change in Russia and the USSR: An Evaluation of Census Data, 1897–1970*. New York, 1976.

Longworth, Philip. *The Cossacks*. London, 1969.

Lowe, Heinz-Dietrich. *The Tsar and the Jews: Reform, Reaction, and Anti-Semitism in Imperial Russia, 1772–1917*. New York, 1992.

Magocsi, Paul Robert. *The Shaping of a National Identity: Subcarpathian Rus', 1848–1948*. Cambridge, Mass., 1978.

————. *Ukraine: A Historical Atlas*. Toronto, 1985.

Meurs, Wim P. Van. *The Bessarabian Question in Communist Historiography: Nationalist and Communist Politics and History-Writing*. New York, 1994.

Olcott, Martha B. *The Kazakhs*. Stanford, 1987.

Plakans, Andrevs. *The Latvians*. Stanford, 1995.

Raun, Toivo U. *Estonia and the Estonians*. Stanford, 1991.

Rorlich, Azade-Ayse. *The Volga Tatars: A Profile in National Resilience*. Stanford, 1986.

Rubel, Paula G. *The Kalmyk Mongols: A Study in Continuity and Change*. Bloomington, 1967.

Subtelny, Orest. *Ukraine: A History*. 2d ed. Toronto, 1994.

Suny, Ronald. *Looking toward Ararat: Armenia in Modern History*. Bloomington, 1994.

————. *The Making of the Georgian Nation*. 2d ed. Bloomington, 1994.

Swietochowski, Tadeusz. *Russia and Azerbaijan: A Borderland in Transition*. New York, 1995.

Vakar, Nicholas P. *Belorussia: The Making of a Nation, a Case Study*. Cambridge, Mass., 1956.

Zaprudnik, Ia. *Belarus: At a Crossroads in History*. Boulder, 1993.

5. READINGS, COLLECTIONS, ANTHOLOGIES, AND DOCUMENTS
(See also EER, MRECT, and RRH in Section 1.)

Atkinson, Dorothy, Alexander Dallin, and Gail Warshofsky Lapidus, eds. *Women in Russia.* Stanford, 1977.

Black, Cyril E., ed. *The Transformation of Russian Society: Aspects of Social Change since 1861.* Cambridge, Mass., 1960.

Cracraft, James, ed. *Major Problems in the History of Imperial Russia.* Lexington, Mass., 1994.

Crummey, Robert O., ed. *Reform in Russia and the U.S.S.R.: Past and Prospects.* Urbana, 1989.

Dmytryshyn, Basil, ed. *Imperial Russia: A Source Book, 1700–1917.* 3d ed. Fort Worth, 1990.

———, ed. *Medieval Russia: A Source Book, 850–1700.* 3d ed. Fort Worth, 1991.

Edmonson, Linda, ed. *Women and Society in Russia and the Soviet Union.* Cambridge, England, 1992.

Freeze, Gregory L. *From Supplication to Revolution: A Documentary Social History of Imperial Russia.* New York, 1988.

Hamburg, Gary M., ed. *Imperial Russian History I, 1700–1861.* New York, 1992.

———, ed. *Imperial Russian History II, 1861–1917.* New York, 1992.

Harcave, Sidney, ed. *Readings in Russian History.* 2 vols. New York, 1962.

Hughes, Lindsey, ed. *New Perspectives on Muscovite History: Selected Papers from the Fourth World Congress for Soviet and East European Studies, Harrogate, 1990.* New York, 1993.

Kohn, Hans, ed. *The Mind of Modern Russia: Historical and Political Thought of Russia's Great Age.* New York, 1962.

Kollmann, Nancy Shields, ed. *Major Problems in Early Modern Russian History.* New York, 1992.

Mendelsohn, Ezra, and Marshall S. Shatz, eds. *Imperial Russia, 1700–1917: State, Society, Opposition, Essays in Honor of Marc Raeff.* DeKalb, Ill., 1988.

Oliva, L. Jay., ed. *Russia and the West from Peter to Khrushchev.* Boston, 1965.

Orlovsky, Daniel T., ed. *Social and Economic History of Prerevolutionary Russia.* New York, 1992.

Pipes, Richard, ed. *The Russian Intelligentsia.* New York, 1961.

Pintner, Walter M., and Don K. Rowney, eds. *Russian Officialdom: The Bureaucratization of Russian Society from the Seventeenth to the Twentieth Century.* London, 1980.

Pushkarev, S. G. *A Source Book for Russian History from Early Times to 1917.* 3 vols. New Haven, 1972.

Raeff, Marc, ed. *Russian Intellectual History: An Anthology.* New York, 1966.

Riha, Thomas, ed. *Readings in Russian Civilization.* Vols. 1 & 2. Chicago, 1964.

Riasanovsky, Alexander V., and William E. Watson. *Readings in Russian History.* Vols. 1 & 2. Dubuque, 1991, 1992.

Senn, Alfred Erich, ed. *Readings in Russian Political and Diplomatic History.* Vol. 1. Homewood, Ill., 1966.

Shanin, Teodor. *Peasants and Peasant Societies: Selected Readings.* Oxford, 1987.

Simmons, Ernest J., ed. *Continuity and Change in Russian and Soviet Thought.* Cambridge, Mass., 1955.

Taranovski, Theodore, ed. *Reform in Modern Russian History: Progress or Cycle?* Cambridge, England, 1995.

Walsh, Warren B., ed. *Readings in Russian History: From Ancient Times to the Post-Stalin Era.* Syracuse, N.Y., 1963.

Waugh, Daniel Clarke, ed. *Essays in Honor of A. A. Zimin.* Columbus, Ohio, 1985.

6. GENERAL WORKS, HISTORIES, AND HISTORIOGRAPHY

Acton, Edward. *Russia: The Tsarist and Soviet Legacy.* 2d ed. London, 1995.

Auty, Robert, and Dimitri Obolensky, eds. *An Introduction to Russian History.* Cambridge, England, 1976.

Balzer, Harley, ed. *Russia's Missing Middle Class: The Professions in Russian History.* Armonk, N.Y., 1995.

Barchatova, Y., et al. *A Portrait of Tsarist Russia: Unknown Photographs from the Soviet Archives.* New York, 1989.

Baron, Samuel H. *Explorations in Muscovite History.* Brookfield, Vt., 1991.

Berdyaev, Nicholas. *The Russian Idea.* Boston, 1962.

Berman, Harold J. *Justice in the U.S.S.R.: An Interpretation of Soviet Law.* Rev. ed. New York, 1963. Part 2 deals with pre-Soviet law.

Black, Cyril E., ed. *Rewriting Russian History: Soviet Interpretations of Russian's Past.* New York, 1962.

Black, J. L. *Nicholas Karamzin and Russian Society in the Nineteenth Century: A Study in Russian Political and Historical Thought.* Toronto, 1975.

Byrnes, Robert F. *V. O. Kliuchevskii, Historian of Russia.* Bloomington, 1995.

Carmichael, Joel. *A History of Russia.* New York, 1990.

Carter, Stephen. *Russian Nationalism: Yesterday, Today, Tomorrow.* New York, 1990.

Crankshaw, Edward. *The Shadow of the Winter Palace: Russia's Drift to Revolution, 1825–1917.* New York, 1976.

Daniels, Robert V. *Russia: The Roots of Confrontation.* Cambridge, Mass., 1985.

Danilov, A. A., et al. *Essays on the Motherland: A Brief History of Modern Russia.* Conway, Ark., 1994.

Dmytryshyn, Basil. *A History of Russia.* Englewood Cliffs, N.J., 1977.

Dukes, Paul. *A History of Russia: Medieval, Modern, Contemporary.* 2d ed. Durham, 1990.

Dvornik, Francis. *The Slavs in European History and Civilization.* New Brunswick, N.J., 1962.

Florinsky, Michael T. *Russia: A History and an Interpretation.* 2 vols. New York, 1947–1953.

———. *Russia: A Short History.* New York, 1969.

Fuller, William C. *Strategy and Power in Russia, 1600–1914.* New York, 1992.

Grey, Ian. *The Horizon History of Russia.* New York, 1970.

Hingley, Ronald. *Russia: A Concise History.* Rev. ed. London, 1991.

Hubbs, Joanna. *Mother Russia: The Feminine Myth in Russian Culture.* Bloomington, 1988.

Keep, John L. H. *Power and the People: Essays on Russian History.* Boulder, 1995.

Klyuchevsky, V. O. *The Course of Russian History.* 5 vols. New York, 1960.

Kochan, Lionel. *The Making of Modern Russia.* Harmondsworth, England, 1962.

Kucharzewski, Jan. *The Origins of Modern Russia.* New York, 1948.

Liashchenko, P. I. *History of the National Economy of Russia, to the 1917 Revolution.* New York, 1949.

Likhachev, Dmitrii S. *Reflections on Russia.* Boulder, 1991.

MacKenzie, David, and Michael W. Curran. *A History of Russia, the Soviet Union, and Beyond.* Belmont, Calif., 1993.

Masaryk, T. G. *The Spirit of Russia: Studies in History, Literature and Philosophy.* 3 vols. New York, 1955–1967.

Maxwell, Margaret. *Narodniki Women: Russian Women Who Sacrificed Themselves for the Dream of Freedom.* New York, 1990.

Mazour, Anatole G. *Modern Russian Historiography.* Westport, Conn., 1975.

Miliukov, Paul, et al. *History of Russia.* 3 vols. New York, 1968.

Mirsky, D. S. *Russia: A Social History.* London, 1952.

Nahirny, Vladimir C. *The Russian Intelligentsia: From Torment to Silence.* New Brunswick, N.J., 1983.

Neumann, Iver B. *Russia and the Idea of Europe: A Study in Identity and International Relations.* London, 1996.

Obolensky, Chloe. *The Russian Empire: A Portrait in Photographs.* New York, 1979.

Pallot, Judith, and Denis J. Shaw. *Landscape and Settlement in Romanov Russia, 1613–1917.* Oxford, 1990.

Pares, Bernard. *A History of Russia.* New York, 1926.

Pipes, Richard. *Russia Observed: Collected Essays on Russian and Soviet History.* Boulder, 1989.

———. *Russia under the Old Regime.* New York, 1974.

———, ed. *Karamzin's Memoir on Ancient and Modern Russia.* New York, 1966.

Platonov, S. F. *History of Russia.* Bloomington, Ind., 1964.

———. *Moscow and the West.* Hattiesburg, Miss., 1972.

Pokrovskii, M. N. *Russia in World History: Selected Essays.* Ann Arbor, 1970.

Prymak, Thomas M. *Mykola Kostomarov: A Biography.* Toronto, 1996.

Pushkarev, Sergei. *The Emergence of Modern Russia, 1801–1917.* New York, 1963.

Ragsdale, Hugh. *The Russian Tragedy: The Burden of History.* Armonk, N.Y., 1996.

Raleigh, Donald J., ed. *Soviet Historians and Perestroika: The First Phase.* Armonk, N.Y., 1989.

Rancour-Laferriere, Daniel. *The Slave Soul of Russia.* New York, 1995.

Riasanovsky, Nicholas V. *A History of Russia.* 5th ed. New York, 1993.

Seton-Watson, Hugh. *The Russian Empire, 1801–1917.* Oxford, 1967.

Shteppa, Konstantin F. *Russian Historians and the Soviet State.* New Brunswick, N.J., 1962.

Soloviev, S. M. *History of Russia from Earliest Times.* Gulf Breeze, Fla., 1976–. Although individual volumes of this multivolume work have been indicated in the Suggested Sources of appropriate chapters, many more volumes are now (1996) in preparation.

Sparks, John. *Realms of the Russian Bear: A Natural History of Russia and the Central Asian Republics.* Boston, 1992.

Szamuely, Tibor. *The Russian Tradition.* New York, 1974.

Thaden, Edward. *Russia since 1801: The Making of a New Society.* New York, 1971.

Thompson, John M. *Russia and the Soviet Union: An Historical Introduction from the Kievan State to the Present.* 3d ed. Boulder, 1994.

Timberlake, Charles E., ed. *Essays on Russian Liberalism.* Columbia, Mo., 1972.

Utechin, S. V. *Russian Political Thought: A Concise History.* New York, 1964.

Vernadsky, George. *A History of Russia.* 5th ed. New Haven, 1961.

———. *Russian Historiography: A History.* Belmont, Mass., 1978.

Weickhardt, George G. "Legal Rights of Women in Russia, 1100–1750," *SR* 55 (Spring 1996): 1–23.

Weidle, Wladimir. *Russia: Absent and Present.* New York, 1961.

Westwood, J. N. *Endurance and Endeavour: Russian History, 1812–1992.* 4th ed. Oxford, 1993.

Wirtschafter, Elise Kimerling. *Structures of Society: Imperial Russia's "People of Various Ranks."* Dekalb, Ill., 1994.

Wittram, Reinhard. *Russia and Europe.* New York, 1973.

Wren, Melvin C., and Taylor Stults. *The Course of Russian History.* 5th ed. Prospect Heights, Ill., 1994.

7. FOREIGN POLICY AND INTERNATIONAL RELATIONS

Allen, Robert V. *Russia Looks at America: The View to 1917.* Washington, 1988.

Anderson, M. S. *The Eastern Question, 1774–1923: A Study in International Relations.* London, 1966.

Baddeley, J. F. *The Russian Conquest of the Caucasus.* London, 1908.

Bergholz, Fred W. *The Partition of the Steppe: The Struggle of the Russians, Manchus, and the Zunghar Mongols for Empire in Central Asia, 1619–1758: A Study in Power Politics.* New York, 1993.

Broxup, Marie Bennigsen, ed. *The North Caucasus Barrier: The Russian Advance towards the Muslim World.* New York, 1992.

Davies, Norman. *God's Playground: A History of Poland.* 2 vols. Oxford, 1981.

Gaddis, John Lewis. *Russia, the Soviet Union, and the United States: An Interpretive History.* New York, 1990.

Jelavich, Barbara. *St. Petersburg and Moscow: Tsarist and Soviet Foreign Policy, 1814–1974.* Bloomington, 1974.

Lederer, Ivo J., ed. *Russian Foreign Policy: Essays in Historical Perspective.* New Haven, 1962.

Lobanov-Rostovsky, Andrei. *Russia and Asia.* Ann Arbor, 1951.

Lord, Robert H. *The Second Partition of Poland: A Study in Diplomatic History.* Cambridge, Mass., 1915.

Mancall, Mark. *Russia and China: Their Diplomatic Relations to 1728.* Cambridge, Mass., 1971.

Ragsdale, Hugh, ed. *Imperial Russian Foreign Policy.* Cambridge, England, 1993.

Rywkin, Michael, ed. *Russian Colonial Expansion to 1917.* London, 1988.

Saul, Norman E. *Distant Friends: The United States and Russia, 1763–1867.* Lawrence, Kan., 1991.

8. CULTURE, RELIGION, SCIENCE, AND EDUCATION

A. Literature
(See also MRECT in Section 1 and Mihailovich, Rollberg, and Terras in Section 3.)

Afanas'ev, A. N. *Russian Fairy Tales.* New York, 1945.

Andrew, Joe. *Russian Writers and Society in the Second Half of the Nineteenth Century.* London, 1982.

Baring, Maurice, and D. P. Costello, eds. *The Oxford Book of Russian Verse.* Oxford, 1958.

Bristol, Evelyn. *A History of Russian Poetry.* New York, 1991.

Erlich, Victor. *Modernism and Revolution: Russian Literature in Transition.* Cambridge, Mass., 1994.

Freeborn, Richard. *The Rise of the Russian Novel: Studies in the Russian Novel from Eugene Onegin to War and Peace.* Cambridge, England, 1973.

Gudzy, N. K. *History of Early Russian Literature.* New York, 1970.

Guerney, Bernard Guilbert, ed. *A Treasury of Russian Literature.* New York, 1943.

Hingley, Ronald. *Russian Writers and Society, 1825–1904.* New York, 1967.

Kelly, Catriona. *A History of Russian Women's Writing, 1820–1992.* Oxford, 1994.

Likhachev, D. S. *The Great Heritage: The Classical Literature of Old Rus.* Moscow, 1981.

Markov, Vladimir, and Merrill Sparks, eds. *Modern Russian Poetry: An Anthology with Verse Translations.* Indianapolis, 1967.

Mathewson, Rufus W. *The Positive Hero in Russian Literature.* Stanford, 1975.

Mirsky, D. S. *A History of Russian Literature, Comprising a History of Russian Literature and Contemporary Russian Literature.* New York, 1969.

Moser, Charles A., ed. *The Cambridge History of Russian Literature.* Cambridge, England, 1989 (2d enlarged ed., 1992).

Obolensky, Dimitri, ed. *The Heritage of Russian Verse.* Bloomington, 1976.

———, ed. *The Penguin Book of Russian Verse.* Harmondsworth, England, 1962.

Reeder, Roberta, ed. *Russian Folk Lyrics.* Bloomington, 1993.

Reeve, F. D., ed. *An Anthology of Russian Plays.* 2 vols. New York, 1961–1963.

Rzhevsky, Nicholas, ed. *An Anthology of Russian Literature from Earliest Writings to Modern Fiction: Introduction to a Culture.* Armonk, N.Y., 1996.

Slonim, Marc. *The Epic of Russian Literature from Its Origins through Tolstoy.* New York, 1964.

Terras, Victor. *A History of Russian Literature.* New Haven, 1992.

Yarmolinsky, Avrahm, ed. *A Treasury of Great Russian Short Stories, Pushkin to Gorky.* New York, 1955.

B. *Other Works*

(See also Ho and Feofanov, and Steeves in Section 3.)

Balzer, Marjorie Mandelstam, ed. *Culture Incarnate: Native Anthropology from Russia.* Armonk, N.Y., 1995.

Batalden, Stephen K., ed. *Seeking God: The Recovery of Religious Identity in Orthodox Russia, Ukraine, and Georgia.* Dekalb, Ill., 1993.

Berlin, Isaiah. *Russian Thinkers.* New York, 1978.

Billington, James H. *The Icon and the Axe: An Interpretive History of Russian Culture.* New York, 1970.

Brumfield, William Craft. *Lost Russia: Photographing the Ruins of Russian Architecture.* Durham, 1995.

———. *The Origins of Modernism in Russian Architecture.* Berkeley, 1991.

Campbell, Stuart, ed. *Russians and Russian Music, 1830–1880.* New York, 1994.

Clowes, Edith W. *The Revolution of Moral Consciousness: Nietzsche in Russian Literature, 1890–1914.* DeKalb, Ill., 1988.

Edie, James M., James P. Scanlan, and Mary-Barbara Zeldin, eds. *Russian Philosophy.* 3 vols. Chicago, 1965.

Emerson, Caryl, and Robert Oldani. *Modest Musorgsky and Boris Godunov: Myths, Realities, Reconsiderations.* Cambridge, England, 1994.

Florovsky, Georges. *Ways of Russian Theology.* 2 vols. Belmont, Mass., 1979, 1987.

Galitzine, George. *Imperial Splendour: Palaces and Monasteries of Old Russia.* London, 1991.

Gibian, George, and H. W. Tjalsma, eds. *Russian Modernism: Culture and the Avant-Garde, 1900–1930.* Ithaca, N.Y., 1976.

Goscilo, Helena, and Beth Holmgren, eds. *Russia, Women, Culture.* Bloomington, 1996.

Graham, Loren R. *Science in Russia and the Soviet Union: A Short History.* Cambridge, England, 1993.

Hamilton, George Heard. *The Art and Architecture of Russia.* Baltimore, 1975.

Hans, Nicholas A. *The Russian Tradition in Education.* London, 1963.

Hilton, Alison. *Russian Folk Art.* Bloomington, 1995.

Iablonskaia, M. *Women Artists of Russia's New Age, 1900–1935.* New York, 1990.

Ivanits, Linda J. *Russian Folk Belief.* Armonk, N.Y., 1989.

Joravsky, David. *Russian Psychology: A Critical History.* Oxford, 1989.

Kuvakin, Valery A., ed. *A History of Russian Philosophy: From the Tenth through the Twentieth Centuries.* Buffalo, 1994.

Leyda, Jay. *Kino: A History of the Russian and Soviet Film.* New York, 1960.

Lossky, Nicholas O. *History of Russian Philosophy.* London, 1951.

Meehan-Waters, Brenda. *Holy Women of Russia: The Lives of Five Orthodox Women Offer Spiritual Guidance for Today.* San Francisco, 1993.

Miliukov, Paul. *Outlines of Russian Culture.* 3 vols. New York, 1960.

Milner-Gulland, Robin, with Nikolai Dejevsky. *Cultural Atlas of Russia and the Soviet Union.* New York, 1989.

Nakhimovsky, Alexander D., and Alice Stone Nakhimovsky, eds. *The Semiotics of Russian Cultural History: Essays by Iurii M. Lotman, Lidiia Ia. Ginsburg, Boris A. Uspenskii.* Ithaca, N.Y., 1985.

Nichols, Robert L., and Theofanis George Stavrou, eds. *Russian Orthodoxy under the Old Regime.* Minneapolis, 1978.

Norman, John O., ed. *New Perspectives on Russian and Soviet Artistic Culture: Selected Papers from the Fourth World Congress for Soviet and East European Studies, 1990.* New York, 1994.

Ouspensky, Leonide. *Theology of the Icon.* Crestwood, N.Y., 1992.

Rimsky-Korsakov, Nikolay. *My Musical Life.* New York, 1942.

Sarab'ianov, Dmtrii V. *Russian Art: From Neoclassicism to the Avant Garde: Painting, Sculpture, Architecture.* London, 1990.

Schmidt, Albert J. *The Architecture and Planning of Classical Moscow: A Cultural History.* Philadelphia, 1989.

Seaman, Gerald R. *History of Russian Music.* New York, 1967.

Sokolov, Yu. M. *Russian Folklore.* Hatboro, Penn., 1966.

Stavrou, Theofanis George, ed. *Art and Culture in Nineteenth-Century Russia.* Bloomington, 1983.

Talbot Rice, David. *Russian Icons.* London, 1947.

Talbot Rice, Tamara. *A Concise History of Russian Art.* New York, 1963.

Volkov, Solomon. *St. Petersburg: A Cultural History.* New York, 1995.

Vucinich, Alexander. *Science in Russian Culture.* 2 vols. Stanford, 1963, 1970.

Walicki, Andrzej. *A History of Russian Thought from the Enlightenment to Marxism.* Stanford, 1979.

Ware, Timothy. *The Orthodox Church.* New ed. London, 1993.

Zenkovsky, V. V. *A History of Russian Philosophy.* 2 vols. London, 1953.

9. *ELECTRONIC SOURCES*

In recent years, the electronic sources and aids that have become available for the study of Russian history and area studies have multiplied rapidly, and many of them are without cost. Articles in journals such as the *Slavic Review* and *The Russian Review* are indexed in the electronic periodical indexes available in many libraries. Students with access to a computer and modem can download numerous other materials, for example, articles from the *Slavic Review* and the latest news and analysis regarding Russia and other parts of the former Soviet Union, furnished by such groups as the Open Media Research Institute (http://www.omri.cz) and by English-language papers such as *The St. Petersburg Press* and *Vladivostok News.* (Additional information about electronic sources regarding contemporary Russia can be found in the General Bibliography at the end of Volume II of this text.)

Students can also participate in electronic discussion groups about various Russian historical topics, check publishers' electronic lists of publications, and communicate with various sources inside Russia itself. Better equipped computers can make use of an Interactive Russian–English Dictionary and download examples of Russian music and art as well as Russian language materials.

The most comprehensive Internet access to information regarding Russian and East European Areas Studies can be found at the REES Web site of the University of Pittsburgh (http://www.pitt.edu./~cjp/rees.html). The number of "doors" opened by this gateway is almost countless. Casey Palowitch provides background information on this source in "Russian and East European Information via the WWW: the REES Home Pages," *Database* 18 (Feb/Mar 1995): 46–53.

Several convenient general indexes for Web pages are available, for example, at http://altavista.digital.com and at http:///www.hotbot.com. Using such indexes, students can rapidly find information (of varying worth) on many Russian subjects. A convenient gateway to general history and humanities information is http://humanities.ucsb.edu.shuttle/history/html. The 'NetNews column (begun in Sept. 1995) of *NewsNet: The Newsletter of the AAASS* (American Association for the Advancement of Slavic Studies) provides the latest information on electronic resources of concern to AAASS members.

Electronic information availability and processing will continue to change rapidly. But Slavic librarians at major universities have given every indication that they are equal to the challenge of continuing to provide professors, students, and other librarians with up-to-date knowledge about such changes.

Index

Yaguzhinsky, P., Procurator General, 252
Yaik Cossacks, 274–275
Yaitsk, 274
Yakuts, 182
Yakutsk, 184, 261
Yam, and Kievan Rus, 28
Yanov, Alexander, 146, 149
Yanovsky, Feodosi, 239
Yaroslav Osmomysl (Prince of Galicia), 63
Yaroslav the Wise (Prince of Kiev), 20–21
    domestic policy of, 23, 25, 42
    foreign policy of, 28, 30, 32
    testament of, 23
Yaroslavl, 93, 161, 190, 291
Yavorsky, Metropolitan Stefan, 239
Ypsilanti, Alexander, 341

Yugra, 28, 97
Yuri (Prince of Galich), 104
Yuri (Prince of Moscow), 83–84
Yuri (Prince of Vladimir-Suzdal), 73
Yuri (uncle of Vasili II), 91–92
Yuri I Dolgoruki (Prince of Suzdal), 29, 58–59, 83
Yuri II (Prince of Suzdal), 28–29, 61
Yuriev, 28
Yusupov, Prince Felix, 503
Yuzovka, 513

Zadonshchina, 122
Zakharova, Larisa, 419
Zaporozhian Host, 155, 172–173, 175

Catherine the Great and, 285, 287
Zarudnyi, Sergei, 392
Zarutsky, Ivan, 160–161, 166
Zasulich, Vera, 431, 449
Zealots of Piety, 208–209
Zemshchina, 143
Zemskii sobor, 131, 135–136, 143, 147, 153
    and national revival (1613), 160, 161, 163
    Romanovs' rule and, 165, 166, 169, 174, 177, 178–179, 181
Zemstvos, 423–424, 429, 431–432, 439–440, 445, 447, 453–455, 479, 493–494
Zguta, Russell, 212
Zhukovsky, N. E., 542
Zhukovsky, Vasili, 405
Zubov, Platon, 273, 284, 287, 330